Margaret Moor

Christmas 2001

The SCHUBERT Thematic Catalogue

OTTO ERICH DEUTSCH

in collaboration with
DONALD R. WAKELING

DOVER PUBLICATIONS, INC.
NEW YORK

Copyright

Copyright © 1995 by Dover Publications, Inc.
All rights reserved under Pan American and International Copyright Conventions.

Bibliographical Note

This Dover edition, first published in 1995, is an unabridged, corrected republication of *Schubert: Thematic Catalogue of All His Works in Chronological Order* by Otto Erich Deutsch in collaboration with Donald R. Wakeling, originally published by W. W. Norton & Company Inc., New York, n.d. [*ca.* 1951?].

The Dover edition deletes the list of "Corrections" printed on p. 566 of the original edition, incorporating these changes in the text. An "N. B." note at the bottom of that page reads: "Recent identifications by Mr. Maurice J. E. Brown have made it necessary to add notes to nos. 3, 29, and 32, combining these numbers, but without its being possible to join them together."

Library of Congress Cataloging-in-Publication Data

Deutsch, Otto Erich, 1883–1967.
    [Schubert, thematic catalogue of all his works in chronological order]
    The Schubert thematic catalogue / Otto Erich Deutsch ; in collaboration with Donald R. Wakeling.
    p.   cm.
    Reprint (corrected). Originally published: New York : W. W. Norton, 1951.
    Includes indexes.
    ISBN 0-486-28685-1 (pbk.)
    1. Schubert, Franz, 1797–1828—Thematic catalogs.
I. Wakeling, Donald R. II. Title.
ML134.S38A17 1995
780'.92—dc20
                                                95-14500
                                                      CIP
                                                        MN

Manufactured in the United States of America
Dover Publications, Inc., 31 East 2nd Street, Mineola, N.Y. 11501

TO
THE SOCIETY FOR THE PROTECTION OF SCIENCE
AND LEARNING (CAMBRIDGE, ENGLAND)
AS A TOKEN OF GRATITUDE

CONTENTS

	PAGE
Preface	ix
General Literature	xxi
Abbreviations	xxiii

THEMATIC CATALOGUE:
    Dated Works (Nos. 1–965) 1
    Undated Works (Nos. 966–92) 478
    Addenda (Nos. 993–8) 489

APPENDICES:
    I. Spurious and Doubtful Works 491
    II. Copies of Works of Other Composers . . . 492
    III. Concordance Tables:
        1. Opus Numbers 494
        2. Posthumous Songs 496
        3. Works without Numbers in Nottebohm's Catalogue (1874) . 497
        4. Collected Edition (1884–97) 498
    IV. Other Collations:
        A. Song Collections published between 1828 and 1874 . 510
        B. Publications other than those listed by Nottebohm or first printed in the Collected Edition 510
    V. Unpublished Works:
        1. Works lost 512
        2. Works not printed 512

INDICES:
    General Index 515
    Index of Authors 530
    Index of Schubert's Works:
        1. Instrumental Music 533
        2. Vocal Music 538
            A. Titles 538
            B. First Lines 550

PREFACE

'THEMATIC CATALOGUES' of music were published first by Breitkopf between 1762 and 1787. These, however, were confined to instrumental works by various composers, on sale at Leipzig in manuscript. Lists of works, devoted to single composers and supplied with 'themes,' or rather *incipits* (the opening bars), were not published, nor the term used, before the nineteenth century,[1] although Mozart kept such a catalogue from 1784 onwards, and of Haydn's works three such catalogues were compiled during his lifetime (from about 1765 till 1805). Mozart's catalogue, a diary of work, is in chronological order and written, except for the canons, in a two-stave system; Haydn's catalogues are in classified order, and mostly written in a one-stave system. To give the 'themes' of each work and, if possible, of each section of the work, in a kind of pianoforte score, on two staves, became the rule for thematic catalogues of single composers, the first of which were: Beethoven by Gustav Nottebohm (1851), Mozart by Ludwig Köchel (1862), Weber by Friedrich Wilhelm Jähns (1871), and Schubert by Nottebohm (1874). Köchel's Mozart catalogue was the first to be arranged in chronological order.[2]

Köchel's and Jähns's catalogues were very extensive, including valuations of single works. Köchel and Jähns, in common with Nottebohm, include later editions and arrangements of the original works.[3] Nottebohm, in his Schubert catalogue (pp. iii, 257–9, and 263), speaks even of *Vergriffene Ausgaben* (i.e. editions out of print) of some dance collections, while most of Schubert's works were by then available only in later issues or reprints. The reason for these excursions was apparently that the early thematic catalogues were partly destined for music dealers whose reference books were still insufficient. The information given for libraries and collectors was not very reliable. The Weber catalogue, of

---

[1] It seems the term was first used in 1802, when Ignace Pleyel (Paris) published his first edition of Haydn's string quartets in parts.
[2] Wilhelm Altmann dealt with the subject (*Über Thematische Kataloge*) in the Proceedings of the Beethoven-Zentenarfeier, Vienna, 1927, pp. 283–9, and is opposed to a chronological arrangement, except in a supplement of such a catalogue.
[3] Nottebohm's Schubert catalogue, for example, devotes nearly nine pages to a record of other editions and arrangements of the twenty songs of the cycle *Die schöne Müllerin*.

minor importance, but of major bulk, as well as the Schubert catalogue, did not run to another edition. The anonymously published Beethoven catalogue, sounder than Nottebohm's Schubert, came in its proper shape in 1864 when the compiler gave it his name, and has remained unaltered since 1868. Köchel's famous Mozart catalogue was relieved of the lists of arrangements in 1905, when Paul Graf Waldersee published the second edition, and of its aesthetic excursions in 1937 when Alfred Einstein edited his authoritative version, with considerable improvements even in bibliographical matters. Of all the thematic catalogues the Köchel alone remains venerable: when it was first compiled the publication of Mozart's Collected Edition (1876–1907) had not even started. Of course Nottebohm's Beethoven catalogue also was finally arranged before the Collected Edition (1862–88) was finished, but it lacked the relative completeness of that edition.

The first list of Schubert's works was published by his main publishers, Anton Diabelli & Co., Vienna, on 16th May 1827, on pp. 2–3 of his Op. 73, the song 'Die Rose.' The engraved pages include Schubert's works published by other firms, and ends with his Op. 74. A second issue of Op. 73 shows Diabelli's list extended up to Op. 87, published on 6th August 1827; a later issue, printed in 1831, contains a list of four pages with works up to Op. 131 and books 1 to 12 of the Posthumous Songs (*Nachgelassene musikalische Dichtungen*, etc.). On 13th August 1828 Thaddäus Weigl, another Viennese music publisher, inserted in his publication of Schubert's Op. 95, *Vier Refrain-Lieder*, two engraved pages after the title-page, giving the titles of all opus numbers printed up to that time. After Schubert's death, in the beginning of 1829, a third Viennese publisher, Josef Czerny, added to the three songs, Op. 111, two engraved pages of Schubert's works published by his house; in 1830 he augmented the list, first up to Op. 120, and then to 126.

Schubert's friend, Eduard von Bauernfeld, published on 13th June 1829 a short chronological list of Schubert's major works, as an appendix to his memorial article in the *Wiener Zeitschrift für Kunst*, etc. A more extensive survey of Schubert's works, also in chronological order, forms part of his brother Ferdinand's biographical essay, written for Robert Schumann's Leipzig magazine, *Neue Zeitschrift für Musik*, 3rd May 1839, including notes on the autographs then in Ferdinand's and Diabelli's hands. About 1843 Louis Rocca, of Leipzig, published a list of

PREFACE

Schubert's printed works: *Vollständiges Verzeichniss im Druck erschienener Kompositionen*, etc. (8 pp., quarto, a copy in the archives of the Gesellschaft der Musikfreunde, Vienna).

About 1845 Aloys Fuchs, of Vienna, compiled in manuscript *Materialen zur Verfassung eines Thematischen Catalogs über Werke von Franz Schubert* (Collected Material for Compiling a Thematic Catalogue of Works by Franz Schubert), with some additional notes by the hand of Ferdinand Schubert; the manuscript, 13 pp., folio, is now in the Schubert collection of Konsul Otto Taussig, Malmö (Sweden). A little later, about 1850, Josef Wilhelm Witteczek added to his manuscript copies of most of Schubert's works (not including symphonies, masses, and operas) a chronological list of the songs, incorporating Karl Pinterics's lost catalogue, which, in 1830, listed 505 Schubert songs. Witteczek's collection is now in the archives of the Gesellschaft der Musikfreunde, Vienna.

In 1851 A. Diabelli et Comp. published the first thematic catalogue, entitled *Thematisches Verzeichniss im Druck erschienener Compositionen von Franz Schubert* (publisher's no. 8932). On forty-nine engraved pages in quarto it comprises Opp. 1–160 (the last published in 1850), the song cycle *Schwanengesang* (published in 1829), and all the fifty books (*Lieferungen*) of the Posthumous Songs. The 'themes' are given in single staves. Current prices and publisher's numbers are added, except for works published by other Viennese firms.[1] The order of opus numbers and of *Lieferungen* has no relation to the times of composition of the works. The opus numbers up to about 100 tell us nothing more than that Schubert could not have written one of these works after it was published.[2] The Posthumous Songs were not all Schubert had left, far from it, and their order, as well as that of other posthumous publications, with or without opus numbers, was arbitrary and accidental. The grouping of songs arranged by Schubert himself is of artistic interest, and those groups are to be found in the *Schubert Documents*, pp. 938–43 (cf. no. 291).

In March 1857 Anton Schindler published in the *Niederrheinische Musikzeitung*, Cologne, another list of Schubert's works, partly based on a lost manuscript which Ferdinand Schubert had sent

---
[1] Diabelli omitted publications in Germany, e.g. that of the great Symphony in C, but even some Austrian publications are missing.
[2] In general there is no sense in calling the greater part of Schubert's works posthumous. Not even a third of them was printed during his lifetime, and few major works among them.

to him in 1841. In November of the same year, 1857, Schubert's friend, Leopold von Sonnleithner, wrote to Ferdinand Luib, who was at that time planning the first biography of Schubert (never written): 'Zur Schilderung von Schuberts künstlerischer Entwicklung ist vor allem die Herstellung eines chronologisch geordneten Verzeichnisses seiner Werke notwendig' ('Before you can describe Schubert's artistic development you have to compile a chronological list of his works').

E. W. Fritzsch, of Leipzig, published in 1870 a list of Schubert's works published in Germany (16 pp., quarto) as a supplement to the *Musikalische Wochenblatt*. At about the same time Bartholf Senff, Leipzig, printed a list of Schubert's songs.

In 1874 Diabelli's second successor, Friedrich Schreiber (*vormals* C. A. Spina), published in Vienna Gustav Nottebohm's *Thematisches Verzeichniss der im Druck erschienenen Werke von Franz Schubert* (viii, 288 pp., octavo). It comprises all works with opus numbers, i.e. Opp. 1–173; the fifty books of Posthumous Songs published by Diabelli between 1830 and 1850; other works without opus numbers in seven classified groups; a supplement in six sections: (*a*) spurious and dubious works (three); (*b*) collections of works published by various houses, all—except Schreiber—in Germany; (*c*) unpublished works (six pages, without 'themes'); (*d*) literature; (*e*) portraits; (*f*) additions and corrections; finally four indices of printed works: lists of instrumental and of vocal music in systematic order, alphabetical index of instrumental music, of song titles, and of first lines (no general index). The 'themes' are given on two staves. Although Nottebohm's catalogue was out of print for a long time it seemed superfluous to reprint it after the publication of the Collected Edition of Schubert's works.

In 1876 Konstant von Wurzbach, in his *Biographisches Lexikon des Kaisertums Österreich* (Vienna, vol. xxxii, pp. 49–98), tried to improve Nottebohm's lists.

In 1883 Sir George Grove added lists of Schubert's works to his excellent article on Schubert in his *Dictionary of Music and Musicians* (vol. iii, pp. 371–81); the lists are in classified and in chronological orders, including titles of songs and partsongs.

In 1887 Max Friedlaender, in his dissertation, *Beiträge zur Biographie Franz Schuberts* (Berlin, pp. 51–5), published several additions and corrections to Nottebohm's catalogue.

PREFACE   xvii

elsewhere), 5; arrangements of works by other composers, 2; copies of works by other composers, 9. Total 1,515.[1]

Since this book was compiled in wartime austerity seemed compulsory. It may be that those circumstances helped to create a new and useful type of thematic catalogue. There is, first, the single-stave system used for nearly all the 2,000 and more 'themes.' This system, if not so expressive as the usual extracts on two staves, is sufficient to identify the 'themes' and, therefore, the works in question. A complete entry in this catalogue may include all or some of the following information:

(a) The catalogue number.

(b) Date and (if not Vienna) place of composition.

(c) Title of work, which, in addition to the proper or generic title, may include key, voice, or instrument, author of words, translator, opus number, and finally the corresponding number in the Collected Edition (if the work is contained therein).

(d) Manuscript: the autograph or autographs and their whereabouts (if known).

(e) First performance: date and place with particulars.

(f) First edition: date, publisher, publisher's number, place of publication, and essential particulars for identification.[2]

(g) Notes: any important information concerning the composition, its history, etc.

(h) Literature: books, articles, etc., written on the particular work.

It may have been interesting to some readers to find in this book the succession of owners of autographs, and to collectors and librarians to find the details of later issues or editions of the first publications. Only rarely are such facts mentioned, namely, if they are essential to the history or the musical text of a work. In consequence the size of this book has been kept to about half of what could be expected of a thematic catalogue in the old style.

[1] Friedlaender's summary in his sketch of Schubert's life and work (Leipzig, 1928, p. 36) was as follows: 8 symphonies, 11 overtures, 2 octets, 30 works for chamber music, 451 larger and smaller piano pieces, 7 masses and 24 other works for church music, 17 works for the stage, 82 partsongs, and 604 songs (1,236 numbers in all).

[2] The dates of publication are not always correct in Nottebohm's catalogue, and the 265 first editions used in the Collected Edition are not all of those which should have been available to the editors.

PREFACE

It is, moreover, the first thematic catalogue of the works of a great master to be published in English; this, too, is due to political events.

In the chronological order of the works a special arrangement was necessary for works undated, or not exactly dated with a certain day or month. Undated works for which no time of composition could be suggested are listed at the end (nos. 966–92). The description of other undated works shows the supposed date, but with a question mark, or the word *circa* (*c.*) prefixed. The order chosen here is the following: approximate year, doubtful year, certain year; the same order for seasons, months, and days. For instance: *c.* 1817, (?) 1817, 1817; *c.* January 1817, (?) January 1817, January 1817; 1st January 1817, spring 1817, 1st April 1817, etc.[1]

Most of Schubert's autographs are preserved in the Stadtbibliothek, Vienna. Nikolaus Dumba left his great collection to the city of Vienna, except the Symphonies nos. 1, 2, 3, 4, and 6, and the Unfinished: these went to the Gesellschaft der Musikfreunde, Vienna, which already had a considerable number, among them the great Symphony in C, and which also inherited Brahms's Schubert autographs. Ferdinand Schubert, about 1844, sold a number of autographs to Prof. Ludwig Landsberg, Rome, and nearly all of these went to the Königliche Bibliothek, later the Preussische Staatsbibliothek, and now called Öffentliche Wissenschaftliche Bibliothek, Berlin, where the Symphony no. 5 is also preserved. Ferdinand gave the sketch of the Symphony in E, 1821, to Mendelssohn; it is now in the possession of the Royal College of Music, London. Most of Ferdinand's other autographs were inherited by his nephew, Dr. Eduard Schneider, who sold them to Dumba. Anton Diabelli's, the publisher's, autographs went in succession to Spina and to Cranz. Charles Malherbe's collection went to the Conservatoire, Paris. The rest of Max Friedlaender's collection, formerly in Berlin, went to the United States, and some of these autographs are now in public libraries. Jerome Stoneborough's Vienna collection, with one exception (no. 24, unpublished), went to the Library of Congress, Washington. The only private collection of importance is a comparatively new one, that of Konsul Otto Taussig, Malmö (Sweden). It should be

---

[1] Some categories, e.g. sonatas, cannot appear in the correct order whether the doubtfully dated ones are placed at the beginning, in the middle, or at the end of the period to which they belong. In consequence such categories are not numbered either in the description or in the index.

PREFACE

noted here that the families of Krasser and Siegmund are descendants of Schubert's sister Therese and of his stepbrother Andreas respectively; the family of Meangya are descendants of Therese Grob's brother, and the family of Caesar descendants of the painter, Wilhelm August Rieder.

Other sources of Schubert's works, quoted frequently in this catalogue, are the manuscript copies collected by Albert Stadler between 1815 and 1817 (Otto Taussig, Malmö), by Josef Wilhelm Witteczek after Schubert's death (Gesellschaft der Musikfreunde, Vienna), and by other of Schubert's friends. These copies are quoted under the heading Manuscript, but in brackets, as are the photostats of autographs preserved in the Photogramm-Archiv, Widmung Anthony van Hoboken, in the Musiksammlung of the Nationalbibliothek, Vienna.

The 'themes' of the songs show more than a hundred German terms introduced by Schubert as indications of tempo and expression. Although Zumsteeg tried to use such terms before Schubert, nowhere else is such a variety of them to be found as in Schubert's songs. The author would like to insert here a note on the poets of these songs and on Schubert's selection of poems. In H. G. Fiedler's *Oxforder Buch Deutscher Dichtkunst* (1911 and 1927) is a list of composers associated with the poems. It shows that Schubert set more of the poems estimated as the best of German poetry than any other composer, namely fifty. (Fiedler overlooked Schubert's setting of Schiller's ballad ' Der Taucher.') Although Schubert was, of course, the most prolific of German song-writers, one fact stresses the quality of his selection: the choice of the best German poems was larger in the times of Schumann, Brahms, and Wolf than for Schubert's day; it included, especially, the works of Eduard Mörike.

The author's sincere thanks are due first to Mr. D. R. Wakeling, formerly of University Library, Cambridge, and now resident in Sydney. It was he who extracted the 'themes' in single staves and helped the author in the lay-out of the text, the grammar of which was essentially improved by Mr. Wakeling. After 1946 some additional 'themes' were arranged by Dr. Edith Schnapper, Cambridge, who also helped the author in the proof-reading of the music. Help of various kinds was afforded, near the end of this work, by Mr. Maurice J. E. Brown, of Marlborough, an ardent Schubertian.

PREFACE

Other librarians to whom the author owes special acknowledgments are Mr. C. L. Cudworth (University Music School, Cambridge), Mr. Richard S. Hill (Library of Congress, Washington), Dr. Hedwig Kraus (Gesellschaft der Musikfreunde, Vienna), Professor Dr. Leopold Nowak (Musiksammlung der Nationalbibliothek, Vienna), and, for much assistance, Dr. Fritz Racek (Stadtbibliothek, Vienna).

Among the collectors who kindly helped in the preparation of the catalogue are Mr. Paul Hirsch, Cambridge; President William Kux, Chur (Switzerland); especially Konsul Otto Taussig, Malmö (Sweden); and Herr Ignaz Weinmann (Vienna).[1]

Of the numerous dealers who gave the author valuable assistance he would like to mention Mr. Otto Haas, London; Herr Heinrich Hinterberger, Vienna; and Mr. Walter Schatzki, New York.

In matters of Schubert's poets, hitherto unidentified, Mr. Odd Udbye, Oslo, advised the author most usefully.

In memory of his late friends, Dr. Eusebius Mandyczewski, Vienna, and Dr. Ludwig Scheibler, Godesberg, near Bonn, the author would like to record that both of them encouraged him from 1905 onwards.

Furthermore, the author would like to record here that his daughter, Mrs. Gitta Arnold, not only compiled the General Index to this catalogue, but also to the Schubert Documents.

Finally he wishes to thank the publishers for accepting his scheme, for preparing the set-up, and for producing this book in a manner worthy of its hero.

O. E. D.

Cambridge (England), December 1950.

---

[1] The largest European collections of first editions of Schubert's works are to be found in the Stadtbibliothek, Gesellschaft der Musikfreunde, and at Herr Weinmann's, Vienna; Herr Anthony van Hoboken, Lausanne; and in the British Museum, London (Paul Hirsch Library). In the United States there are considerable collections in the Library of Congress, Washington, the New York Public Library, and in the Boston Public Library (Allen A. Brown Collection of Music).

GENERAL LITERATURE
ON SCHUBERT'S WORKS

Orchestral Music (in general):
Mosco Carner, 'Orchestral Music,' in *Schubert, a Symposium*, edited by Gerald Abraham, London, 1946, New York, 1947, pp. 17–87.

Symphonies:
Sir George Grove, Appendix in Heinrich Kreissle von Hellborn, *Life of Franz Schubert*, translated by Arthur Duke Coleridge, London, 1869, vol. ii, pp. 297–324. Richard Wickenhauser, *Die Symphonien Franz Schuberts*, Leipzig [1928]. Ernst Laaff, *Franz Schuberts Sinfonien*, Wiesbaden, 1933.

Chamber Music (in general):
Willi Kahl, 'Schubert,' in W. W. Cobbett's *Cyclopaedic Survey of Chamber Music*, London, 1930, vol. ii, pp. 352–66 (with additional notes by the editor). J. A. Westrup, 'The Chamber Music,' in *Schubert, a Symposium*, etc., pp. 88–110.

String Quartets:
Otto Erich Deutsch, 'The Chronology of Schubert's String Quartets.' *Music & Letters*, London, January 1943, pp. 25–30.

Piano Music (in general):
Kathleen Dale, 'The Piano Music,' in *Schubert, a Symposium*, etc., pp. 111–48.

Piano Sonatas:
Hans Költzsch, *Franz Schubert in seinen Klaviersonaten,* Leipzig 1927. Erwin Ratz, 'Chronologie der Schubert-Sonaten,' *Stimmen*, Berlin, 1948, pp. 333–8; *Schweizerische Musikzeitung*, Zürich, 1st January 1949.

Piano Pieces:
Willi Kahl, 'Das lyrische Klavierstück Schuberts und seiner Vorgänger seit 1810,' *Archiv für Musikwissenschaft*, Bückeburg, January and April 1921, pp. 54–82, 99–122.

Masses:
Otto Wissig, *Franz Schuberts Messen*, Leipzig, 1909.

Operas:
A. Hyatt King, 'Music for the Stage,' in *Schubert, a Symposium*, etc., pp. 198-216.

Male Quartets:
Hans Georg Schmidt, *Das Männerchorlied Franz Schuberts*, Hildburghausen, 1929.

Songs:
Moritz Bauer, *Die Lieder Franz Schuberts*, Erster Band, Leipzig, 1915. Richard Capell, *Schubert's Songs*, London, 1928. Paul Mies, *Schubert, der Meister des Liedes*, Berlin, 1928.

ABBREVIATIONS

Collection of hitherto unpublished Schubert works: *Bisher unbekannte und unveröffentlichte Compositionen von Franz Schubert, herausgegeben von Heinrich von Bocklet.* Heft 1, 2. Wien, Josef Weinberger & Hofbauer (nos. 21 and 30), 1887.
Cond.: *Conductor.*
Documents: see Schubert Documents.
Ebner: *Collection of Schubert's songs copied by Johann Leopold Ebner, before September 1817* (von Wettstein family, Vienna).
Eight Duets: *Duette für zwei Singstimmen und Pianofortebegleitung. Herausgegeben von Max Friedlaender.* · Leipzig, C. A. Peters (no. 6886), [1885].
1st Ed.: *First edition.*
1st Pf.: *First performance.*
Forty Songs: *Neueste Folge nachgelassener Lieder und Gesänge von Franz Schubert, Original-Ausgabe.* Wien, J. P. Gotthard (nos. 325–61), [1872].
G.A., or Gesamtausgabe: *Franz Schuberts Werke. Kritisch durchgesehene Gesammtausgabe.* Leipzig, 1884–97.
I.1.: *Gesamtausgabe, Series I, Number 1.*
Kreissle: *Heinrich Kreissle von Hellborn, Franz Schubert,* Wien, 1865.
MS.: *Manuscript (Autograph).*
Musikverein: *Gesellschaft der Musikfreunde, and their old hall (Tuchlauben),* Wien.
Musikvereinssaal: *their new hall (Karlsplatz),* 1870 ff.
Nachlass, book 1–50: *Franz Schubert's Nachgelassene musikalische Dichtungen für Gesang und Pianoforte,* Wien [1830–50]. Lieferung 1–50.
no. (following a publisher's name): *Publisher's number.*
Nottebohm: *Gustav Nottebohm, Thematisches Verzeichniss der im Druck erschienenen Werke von Franz Schubert,* Wien, 1874.
Ph.: *Photastat in the Archiv für Photogramme musikalischer Meisterhandschriften, Widmung Anthony van Hoboken,* in the Musiksammlung of the Nationalbibliothek, Vienna.
Revisionsbericht: *sc. der Gesamtausgabe,* Leipzig, 1897.
Schubert Album, book 7: *Schubert-Album. Sammlung der*

xxiv ABBREVIATIONS

Lieder für eine Singstimme mit Pianofortebegleitung. Herausgegeben von Max Friedlaender. Band vii. Leipzig, C. F. Peters (no. 6896), Edition Peters no. 2270, [1887].
Schubert Documents: *Schubert. A Documentary Biography.* London, 1947; *The Schubert Reader.* New York, 1947.
Six Nachgelassene Lieder: *Sechs nachgelassene, zum Teil bisher ungedruckte Lieder. für Pianoforte zu 4 Händen herausgegeben von J. P. Gotthard.* Wien, V. Kratochwill (no. 253), [1876].
Six Songs: *Sechs bisher ungedruckte Lieder. Nach der in der Königl. Bibliothek zu Berlin vorhandenen Original-Handschrift herausgegeben [von Franz Espagne].* Berlin, Wilhelm Müller (no. 13), [1868].
Song: *Song with pianoforte accompaniment.*
Stadler: *Collection of Schubert's songs copied by Albert Stadler, 1815–17* (Konsul Otto Taussig, Malmö, Sweden).
Twelve Nachgelassene Lieder: *Zwölf nachgelassene, zum Theil bisher ungedruckte Lieder, für Pianoforte zu 2 Händen herausgegeben von J. P. Gotthard.* Wien, V. Kratochwill (no. 252), 1876.
Twenty Nachgelassene Lieder: *Nachgelassene (bisher ungedruckte) Lieder für eine Singstimme mit Pianofortebegleitung. Revidiert und herausgegeben von Max Friedlaender.* Heft 1, 2. Leipzig, C. F. Peters (nos. 6895, 6896), [1885].
Witteczek: *Collection of Schubert's works copied, before 1860, for Josef Wilhelm Witteczek* (Gesellschaft der Musikfreunde, Vienna).

THEMATIC CATALOGUE

1. **Fantasia in G for Pianoforte Duet** (IX 30), erroneously called 'Leichenphantasie.' 8th April–1st May 1810.

MS. Fragment of the beginning of the first version—Frau Anna Siegmund, Znaim-Znojmo (Czechoslovakia); remainder (pp. 9–24), ending with the first cancelled page of the Finale—Dr. Alwin Cranz, Vienna; final version of the Finale—Dr. Alwin Cranz, Vienna.

IST ED. 1888, Gesamtausgabe.

With indications for orchestral instruments. Frau Siegmund's father, Andreas Schubert, divided the first eight pages of the MS. of the first version into several pieces to be given to friends (one piece was given to the Schubert biographer, Richard Heuberger, Vienna); cf. 531. The MS. copy used for the first edition is not to be found any more in the archives of the Gesellschaft der Musikfreunde, Vienna; but another copy, written by Ferdinand Schubert in 1838, is in the archives of the Wiener Männergesangverein, Vienna. For the spurious title, 'Leichenphantasie,' cf. 7.

Literature. Fritz Racek, *Österreichische Musikzeitschrift*, Vienna January–February 1947.

2. **String Quartet in G.** Fragment. Not printed. (?) c. 1810.

I

MS. Fräulein Emma Schaup, Vienna, and Frau Emilie Meyer, Vienna.

On the back of the trios for male voices, ' Erinnerungen ' and ' Widerhall ' (424 and 428) is the Introduction (*Adagio*) and a fragment of the first movement (*Allegro moderato*) of a string quartet, probably written much earlier. This score, written in ink, is cancelled. On the back of the trio ' Andenken ' (423), and partly written on a second leaf (incomplete), are sketches of another string quartet written in pencil, also cancelled, and probably written at a later date.

3. Movements for String Quartet. Unpublished. *c.* 1811.

MS. (together with 4)—Otto Taussig, Malmö.
IST PF. *c.* 1811, at Schubert's home.

The first Andante, which Schubert used as the basis of 29, is incomplete; for the other two movements, see 32.

4. Overture to the Comedy with vocal numbers, ' Der Teufel als Hydraulicus,' for Orchestra (II 1). *c.* 1811.

MS. Score (together with 3)—Otto Taussig, Malmö.
IST PF. *c.* 1811, at Schubert's home?
IST ED. 1886, Gesamtausgabe.

This Overture, with trumpets and kettledrums, was probably written for a private performance of J. F. E. Albrecht's play, *Der Teufel ein Hydraulikus* (*c.* 1790), founded on Paul Weidmann's play, *Der Bettelstudent* (Vienna, 1776); both have been set to music by various composers.

5 ' **Hagar's Klage** ' (Schücking), Song (XX 1).   30th March 1811.

MS. Dr. Otto Kallir, New York.
1ST ED. 1894, Gesamtausgabe.

The poem was published in the *Göttinger Musenalmanach* for 1781 with the signature ' Schg.' ' a contraction of Schücking. The model of this first song of Schubert's, Zumsteeg's song ' Hagar's Klage in der Wüste Berseba,' published in 1797 (the year of Schubert's birth) by Breitkopf & Härtel, Leipzig, was reprinted in the supplement, pp. 1-5, to the first issue of vol. iii of Series XX of the G.A. (1895, Breitkopf & Härtel, Leipzig, no. 20,865; it was printed again as no. 540 of the series ' Deutscher Liederverlag ' by the same publishers). According to Josef von Spaun, Schubert intended to modernize Zumsteeg's setting, which greatly appealed to him. Schubert's first preserved song, like many of his following songs, was written at the Vienna Stadtkonvikt, where he remained until the autumn of 1813. Cf. note to 8.

Literature. Hans Bosch, *Die Entwicklung des Romantischen in Schuberts Liedern*, Borna-Leipzig, 1930, pp. 14 ff. Edith Schnapper, *Die Gesänge des jungen Schubert*, Berne, 1937, *passim.*

6. ' **Des Mädchens Klage** ' (from Schiller's play ' Die Piccolomini,' III vii), Song, First Version (XX 2). After 30th March 1811, or 1812.

MS. Preussische Staatsbibliothek, Berlin (together with 241).
1ST ED. 1894, Gesamtausgabe.

At the end of the MS. is the rough draft of the song ' Alles um Liebe, 241. For the other settings of Schiller's poem (written for the actress Karoline Jagemann), see 191 and 389.

7. ' **Eine Leichenphantasie** ' (Schiller), Song (XX 3). After 30th March 1811?

MS. Stadtbibliothek, Vienna.
1ST ED. 1894, Gesamtausgabe.

8. **Overture for String Quintet in C minor.** Unpublished. 29th June–12th July 1811.

MS. First and final versions—Dr. Otto Kallir, New York (Ph.).
1ST PF. 1811, at Schubert's home; first public performance—13th December 1948, Town Hall, New York (Little Orchestra Society).

Dedicated to Ferdinand Schubert. The MS. consists of a score and two incomplete sets of the parts which practically form the whole work. The themes are quoted here from August Reissmann, *Schubert*, Berlin, 1873, pp. 28–30. The first movement starts like the pf. introduction of 5.

9. **Fantasia in G minor for Pianoforte Duet** (IX 31). 20th September 1811.

1812　　　　　　　11　　　　　　　5

MS. Preussische Staatsbibliothek, Berlin.
1ST ED. 1899, Gesamtausgabe.

Bars 67–71 of *Tempo di Marcia* in their original form are given in the *Revisionsbericht*. The last leaf of the MS., with the final bars of the pf. primo part, is missing.

10. 'Der Vatermörder' (Pfeffel), Song (XX 4). 26th December 1811.

MS. Stadtbibliothek, Vienna.
1ST ED. 1894, Gesamtausgabe.

11. 'Der Spiegelritter,' Operetta in three Acts by Kotzebue, First Act only, incomplete (XXI 1 and XV 12). *c.* 1812?

No. 4.
ARIA & TERZET (Ten., Sopr., and Bass)
Andantino

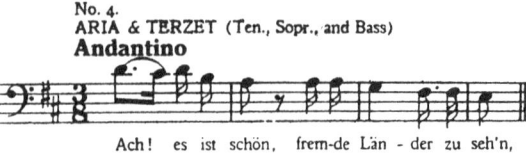

Ach! es ist schön, frem-de Län - der zu seh'n,

Allegro

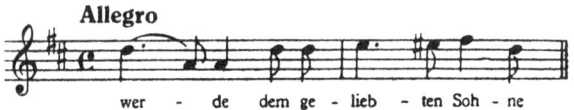

wer - de dem ge - lieb - ten Soh - ne

No. 5.
ENSEMBLE (5 Sopr., 2 Ten., 3 Basses and Mixed Chorus)
Allegro

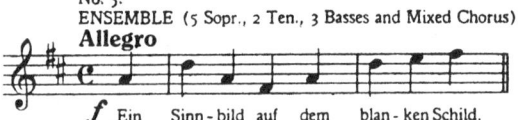

f Ein Sinn-bild auf dem blan-ken Schild,

No. 6.
ARIA (Ten.)

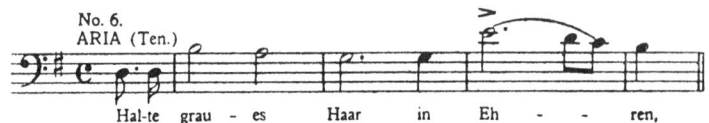

Hal-te grau - es Haar in Eh - - ren,

No. 7.
ENSEMBLE *(partly in Pf. score and unfinished)*
Allegro moderato

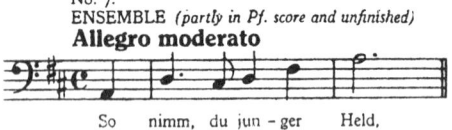

So nimm, du jun - ger Held,

MS. Overture—Conservatoire, Paris (Ph.); remainder (including the last bars of the Overture)—Stadtbibliothek, Vienna.
1ST PF. 11th December 1949, Radio Beromünster (Switzerland).
1ST ED. Operetta, without Overture—1893, Gesamtausgabe; Overture only—1897, Gesamtausgabe.

The libretto, set to music earlier by Ignaz Walter and by Vincenz Maschek, was printed at Vienna in 1802. The last of the seven numbers of the score is written in the form of a pf. sketch.

Literature. Alfred Orel, *Zeitschrift für Musikwissenschaft*, Leipzig, 1923, vol. v, pp. 214 f. (refers only to the Overture).

12. Overture in D for Orchestra (XXI 2). *c.* 1812.

Adagio

V.1. ff pp
V.2. ff pp
mf

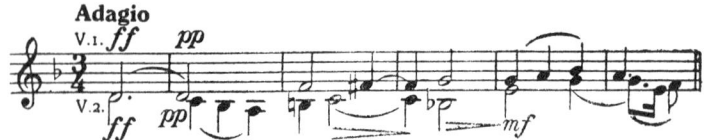

Allegro spiritoso

MS. Conservatoire, Paris (Ph.).
1ST ED. 1897, Gesamtausgabe.

13. Fugue in D minor (for Pianoforte?). Not printed. *c.* 1812.
MS. Dr. Franz Roehn, Los Angeles (together with the first sketch of the song ' Der Geistertanz,' 15).
This fugue is said to have been written in 1811 or 1813.

14. Overture for Pianoforte. Lost. *c.* 1812.
According to a letter written by Maximilian Weisse on 13th December 1857, to Ferdinand Luib, Schubert wrote this overture for him while they were at school together, but took it back some years later in order to orchestrate it (cf. 12 and 996). The MS. was never returned, and it seems to have been lost.

15. ' Der Geistertanz ' (Matthisson), **Song,** two fragmentary sketches (XX 590). *c.* 1812.

Die bret - ter-ne Kam-mer · der To - ten er - bebt,

Die bret- ter-ne Kam-mer der To - ten er - bebt,

MS. The first sketch (together with 13)—Dr. Franz Roehn, Los Angeles; second sketch—ditto.
1ST ED. 1895, Gesamtausgabe.

The second sketch bears some descriptive notes: ' Mitternacht,' ' Heulen der Winde,' ' Feierliche Stille,' and ' Tanz.' Schubert set this poem for solo voice (116) and again for male quartet (494).
Literature. Hans Holländer, *Zeitschrift für Musik*, Leipzig, May–June 1929.

— Franz de Paula Roser's Song ' Die Teilung der Erde ' (Schiller), copied by Schubert. *c.* 1812. See Appendix II, no. 1.

16. Exercises in Imitation. *c.* 1812.

MS. Stadtbibliothek, Vienna.
1ST ED. 1940, Adolf Robitschek, Vienna (in Alfred Orel's *Der junge Schubert*).

On the back of the folio leaf is the beginning of a four-part mixed chorus, starting in the soprano part.

17. ' Quell' innocente figlio ' (from Metastasio's ' Isacco,' Part I, Aria of the Angel) for various Voices. *c.* 1812.

MS. Stadtbibliothek, Vienna.
1ST PF. 31st January 1938, Gemeindehaus, Wieden, Vienna.
1ST ED. 1940, Adolf Robitschek, Vienna (in Alfred Orel's *Der junge Schubert*).

The words are set for one, two, and repeatedly for three and four voices. There are some corrections by Salieri. This and the other Metastasio settings of 1812 were written as exercises when Schubert studied with Salieri (cf. 33, 34, 35, 42, 70, 76, and 78).

18. String Quartet in mixed keys (V 1). 1812.

MS. Parts—Stadtbibliothek, Vienna.
1ST PF. 1812, at Schubert's home.
1ST ED. 1890, Gesamtausgabe.

19 and 19A. String Quartets in mixed keys. Lost. 1811, 1812.
MS. Unknown; former owner—probably Anton Diabelli, Vienna.
1ST PF. 1811, 1812, at Schubert's home.
Cf. 998.

20. Overture for String Quartet in B flat. Lost. 1812.

MS. Unknown; former owner—Ferdinand Schubert, Vienna.

1ST PF. 1812, at Schubert's home.

Written for Ferdinand Schubert.

21. Six Variations in E flat for Pianoforte. Lost. 1812.

MS. Unknown; former owner—Ferdinand Schubert.

This work is recorded by Ferdinand Schubert (cf. 24); also by Eduard von Bauernfeld and Anton Schindler, both of whose lists were based on Ferdinand's notes. Kreissle, p. 611, gives it the title Andante and Variations.

22. Twelve Minuets with Trios for Pianoforte. Lost. 1812.

MS. Unknown; former owner—Ferdinand Schubert.

According to Josef von Spaun these minuets were of special beauty, and greatly impressed Mozart's friend, Dr. Anton Schmidt, an amateur violinist. Cf. 41.

23. 'Klaglied' (Rochlitz), Song (Op. posth. 131, no. 3; XX 6). 1812.

MS. Stadtbibliothek, Vienna (rough draft).

1ST ED. 9th November 1830, Josef Czerny, Vienna (no. 342), as no. 3 of three songs, in later issues called Op. 131.

The fair copy seems to have been lost. In a copy of some Schubert songs, written by Karl Freiherr von Schönstein (on sale at Hugo Heller's, Vienna, in 1913), the song is entitled ' Klagelied. Schuberts erstes Lied anno 1812 in seinem 15t Jahre.' Schubert's first song was, in fact, ' Hagar's Klage ' (5). On the back of the MS. of the rough draft are to be found some exercises in counterpoint (cf. 25).

24. Seven (five) Variations in F major for Pianoforte. Unpublished. 1812 or 1813.

MS. Unknown, former owner—Dr. Jerome Stoneborough, Vienna (entitled ' Variationen VII,' only nos. 1–2, nos. 3 and 6 incomplete, and no. 7 preserved; nos. 4 and 5, two pages, lost).

Ferdinand Schubert states that this was the first of Schubert's compositions to be played by the composer to his father; in his list, however, Ferdinand only records Variations in E flat major, written in 1812 (21).

1812   28   11

25. **Exercises in Counterpoint.** Not printed. Started 18th June 1812.

MS. Dr. Franz Roehn, Los Angeles.

The MS. consists of three leaves, the first of which is inscribed 'Den 18. Juny 1812 den Contrapunkt angefangen. 1. Gattung.' It comprises four Cantus firmi by Johann Josef Fux, the bass written by Antonio Salieri as an exercise for his pupils, Schubert and others. Cf. 23, and Appendix II, no. 5.

26. **Overture in D for Orchestra** (II 2). Finished 26th June 1812.

MS. Stadtbibliothek, Vienna.

IST PF. Probably 1812, Stadtkonvikt, Vienna; first public performance—18th March 1838, Musikvereinssaal, Vienna (cond. Ferdinand Schubert).

IST ED. 1886, Gesamtausgabe.

The second version only is preserved; it was written some time after the date indicated above, which refers to the first version.

27. **Salve Regina in F for Soprano solo, Orchestra, and Organ.** 28th June 1812.

MS. Lost.

IST ED. 1928, Ed. Strache, Vienna (no. 21); ed. by Franz Kosch.

The incomplete copies of the parts, entitled *Motetto* and preserved in the Knabenseminar, Hollabrunn (Lower Austria), were written in 1812 by 'J. G.' Ferdinand Schubert listed this work, erroneously as printed before 1840, together with the Kyrie in D minor (31).

28. **Trio in B flat, called Sonata, in one movement, for Pianoforte, Violin, and Cello.** 27th July–28th August 1812.

MS. Score and parts—Stadtbibliothek, Vienna.
IST ED. 1923, Wiener Philharmonischer Verlag, Vienna (no. 402); ed. by Alfred Orel.

A fragment of an unidentified Pianoforte Trio is in the possession of Mrs. George R. Siedenburg, New York.

Literature. A. Orel, *Zeitschrift für Musikwissenschaft*, Leipzig, January-February 1923.

29. Andante in C for Pianoforte (XI 9).   9th September 1812.

MS. Stadtbibliothek, Vienna.
IST ED. 1888, Gesamtausgabe.
Cp. note to 3.

30. ' Der Jüngling am Bache ' (Schiller), **Song,** first version (XX 5).   24th September 1812.

MS. Stadtbibliothek, Vienna.
IST ED. 1894, Gesamtausgabe.

For the later versions, see 192 and 638.

31. Kyrie to a Mass in D minor for Chorus, Orchestra, and Organ. (XIV 14).   25th September 1812.

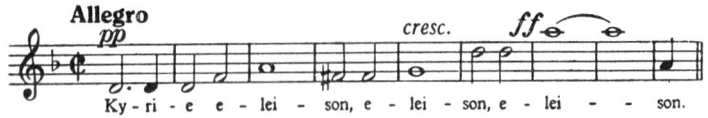

MS. Stadtbibliothek, Vienna (together with 32).
IST ED. 1888, Gesamtausgabe.

The MS. is entitled ' Missa,' but instead of completing the mass Schubert, on p. 32, commenced to write the following string quartet (32).   Ferdinand Schubert listed this Kyrie, together with the Salve Regina (27), of the same year, erroneously as already printed before 1840.

32. String Quartet in C (V 2). Fragment. End of September 1812.

MS. First movement—Stadtbibliothek, Vienna (together with 31); remainder of the MS.—Gesellschaft der **Musikfreunde,** Vienna.

1ST PF. 1812, at Schubert's home.
1ST ED. 1890, Gesamtausgabe.

The movements are: (1) Presto (finished 30th September); (2) Minuet and Trio; (3) Andante, see 3; (4) Allegro, first part, see 3; the rest printed in the *Revisionsbericht.*

33. ' **Entra l'uomo allor che nasce** ' (from Metastasio's ' Isacco,' Part II, Aria of Abramo) **for various Voices.** September–October 1812.

En - tra l'uo - mo al-lor che na - sce

MS. Stadtbibliothek, Vienna.

1ST ED. 1940, Adolf Robitschek, Vienna (in A. Orel's *Der junge Schubert*).

The words are set as an aria, as a duet for soprano and contralto, as a trio for soprano, contralto, and tenor, and repeatedly as a quartet for mixed voices. Arrangements of three versions for male voices, with German words, were printed in 1937 by the same publisher.

34. ' **Te solo adoro** ' (from Metastasio's ' La Betulia liberata,' Part II, Aria of Achior, Prince of the Ammonites) **for four mixed Voices.** Finished 5th November 1812.

Te so - lo ad - o - ro

MS. Stadtbibliothek, Vienna.

1ST ED. 1940, Adolf Robitschek, Vienna (in A. Orel's *Der junge Schubert*).

The MS. is corrected (by Salieri) and the corrected version of the first eight bars rewritten on the back. An arrangement of this aria for male voices, with German words, was printed in 1937 by the same publisher.

35. ' **Serbate, o Dei custodi** ' (from Metastasio's ' La Clemenza di Tito,' Chorus, Act I, scene v) **for various Voices.** Finished 10th December 1812.

Ser - ba - te, o Dei cu - sto - di

Ser - ba - te, o Dei cu - sto - di

MS. Stadtbibliothek, Vienna (see note).

1ST ED. 1940, Adolf Robitschek, Vienna (in A. Orel's *Der junge Schubert*).

Among other settings there is one as an aria for tenor with basso continuo (two copies, one of which was dated October 1812; both destroyed in 1945), and two arias for four mixed voices, with many corrections by Salieri. The instrumental interludes are also sketched.

36. String Quartet in B flat (V 3). 19th November 1812–21st February 1813.

MS. Score—Gesellschaft der Musikfreunde, Vienna; Parts (autograph?, dated 5th April 1813)—Stadtbibliothek, Vienna.
1ST PF. 1813, at Schubert's home.
1ST ED. 1890, Gesamtausgabe.

The minuet, written on three separate leaves of the score, was added later. The differences between the score and the parts indicate the existence of a lost second score.

37. 'Die Advokaten' (Baron Engelhart), **Comic Trio, T.T.B.,** with Pianoforte Accompaniment by Anton Fischer, altered by Schubert and published as his Op. 74 (XIX 1). 25th–27th December 1812.

MS. 1st Score (dated 25th–27th December 1812)—Otto Taussig, Malmö; 2nd Score (printer's MS.): the first 30 bars (dated 1812) —Otto Taussig, Malmö; bars 31–175—Stadtbibliothek, Vienna; title-page (dated 12th May 1827 by the censor) and the last 26 bars—Fitzwilliam Museum, Cambridge.

1ST ED. 16th May 1827, A. Diabelli & Co., Vienna (no. 2452), under Schubert's name only.

The history of this work may be compared with the Guitar Trio by Matiegka, arranged as a quartet by Schubert in 1814, but never published by him (96). The author of the poem was named as Rustenfeld in Schubert's setting. Neither Baron Engelhart nor Herr Rustenfeld (cf. Bauernfeld's pseudonym Rusticocampius) is identified. That Schubert should have chosen to publish in 1827 this insignificant arrangement, out of the vast number of his unpublished works, remains a mystery. Perhaps it was taken to the publisher by a friend of Schubert's (Franz Lachner?) without his knowledge. Fischer's original was published by Josef Eder at Vienna in about 1805, only a MS. copy of which is known.

Literature. O. E. D., *Zeitschrift für Musikwissenschaft*, Leipzig, November 1928.

38. ' Totengräberlied ' (Hölty), **Trio, T.T.B.** (XIX 20). (?) 1813.

MS. Lost.
1ST ED. 1892, Gesamtausgabe.
Schubert also set this poem as a solo song (44).

39. ' **Ich sass an einer Tempelhalle am Musenhain** ' (author unknown), **Sketch of Song.** Not printed. (?) 1813.
MS. Conservatoire, Paris (Ph.).
The first line of the poem is given here; the title is unknown.

— **Johann Josef Fux's 'Singfundament,'** eight duets arranged, copied by Schubert. *c.* 1813. See Appendix II, no. 5.

40. String Quartet in E flat. Lost. 1813.
  1ST PF. 1813, at Schubert's home.
  Perhaps identical with 87.

— **Fugue in Four Parts for Pianoforte.** 1813. Lost. See note to 967.

41. 30 (20) Minuets with Trios for Pianoforte in an easy style (XII 30, only 20 minuets). (10 minuets lost.) 1813.

No. 7.

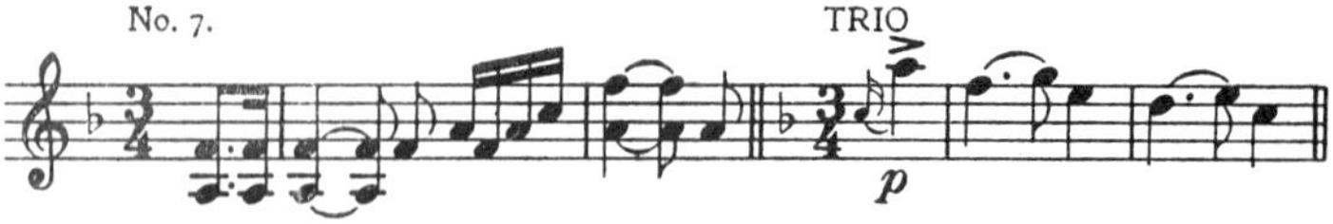

No. 8.

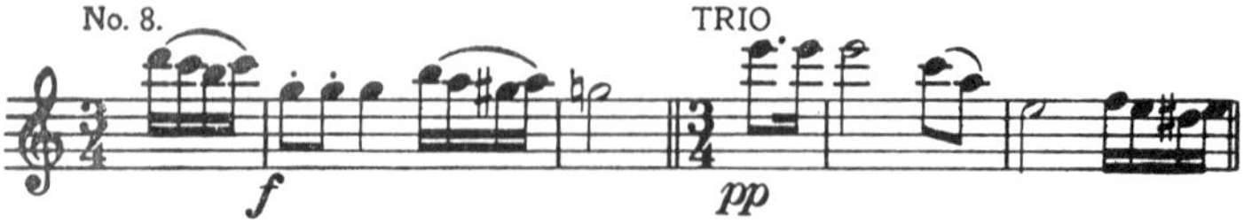

No. 9.

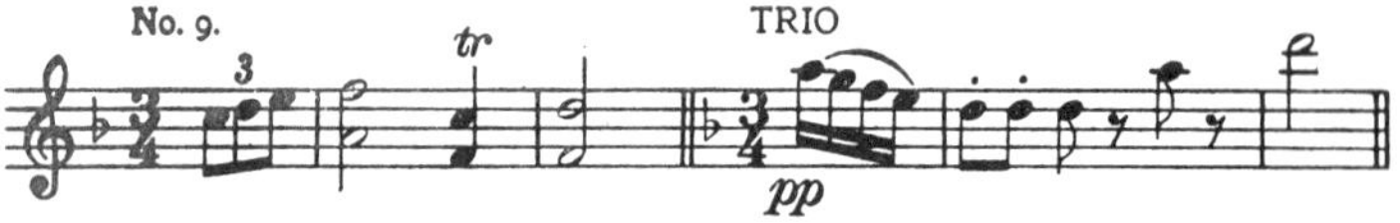

No. 10.

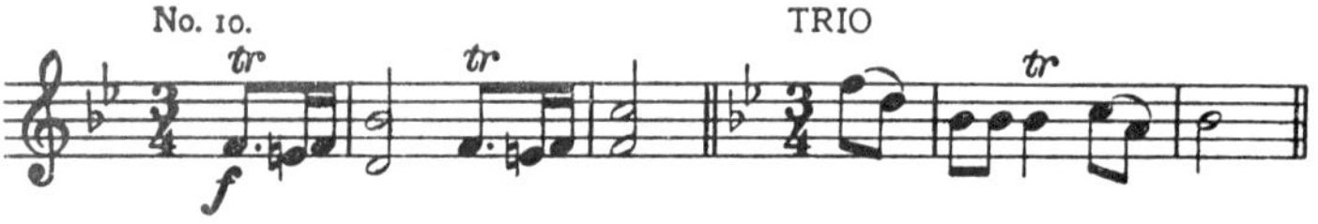

No. 11.

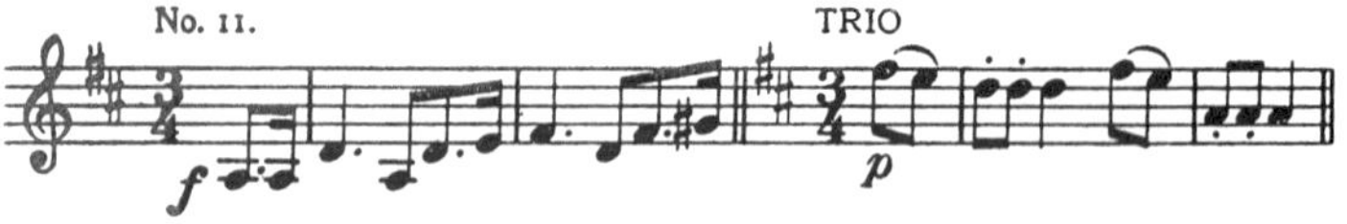

No. 12.

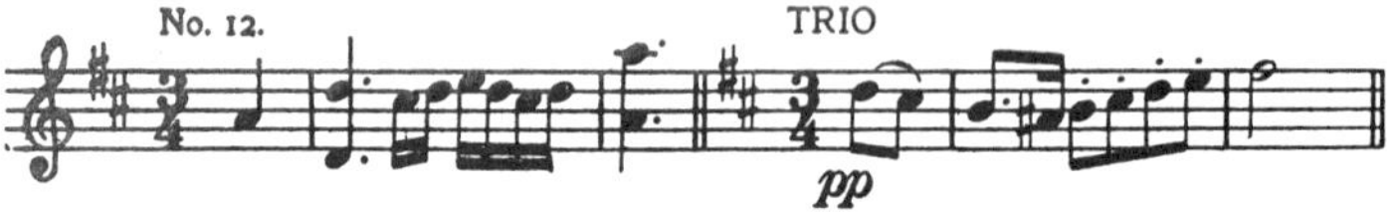

No. 13.

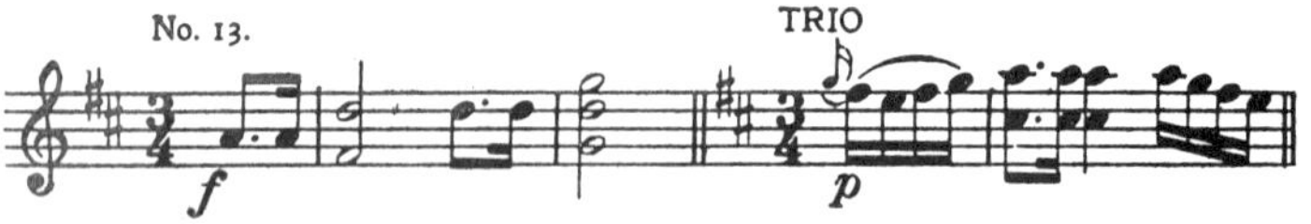

No. 14.

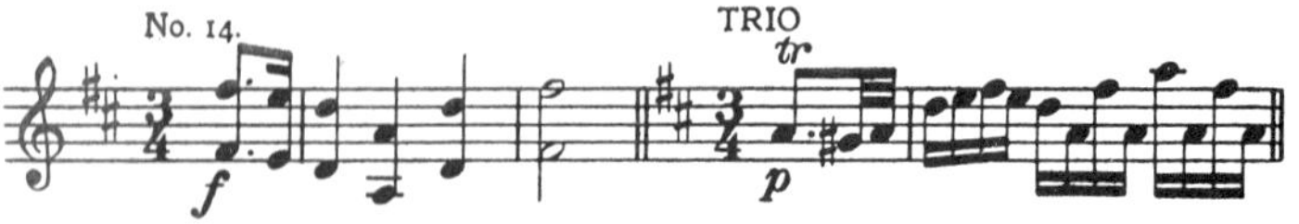

No. 15.

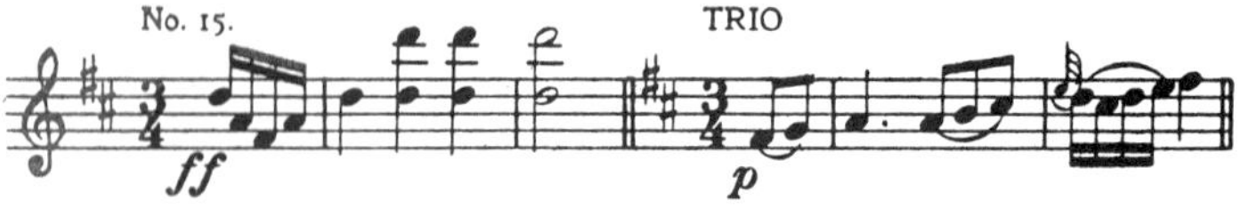

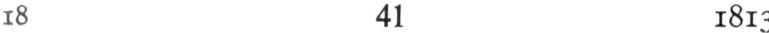

No. 16. TRIO

No. 17. TRIO

No. 18. TRIO

No. 19. TRIO

No. 20. TRIO

MS. Stadtbibliothek, Vienna.
1ST ED. 1889, Gesamtausgabe.
Written for Schubert's brother Ignaz. The MS. is numbered from 1 to 23, but the original nos. 10, 11, and 19 are missing; so are nos. 24–30. Cf. 22, 348, and 349.

42. ' Misero pargoletto ' (Timante's aria from Metastasio's ' Demofoonte,' Act III, scene v), Song (XX 570). 1813.

Andante con moto

Mi - se- ro   par - go - let - - to,

MS. Score and voice part—Stefan Zweig Collection, London (Ph.).
1ST ED. 1895, Gesamtausgabe.
The MS. contains three settings of the poem. The first setting is complete; the second with the voice-part only; the third consists only of the accompaniment.

43. ' Dreifach ist der Schritt der Zeit . . . ' (from Schiller's ' Sprüche des Confucius '), Trio, T.T.B. (XXI 43). 1813.

Adagio

Drei - fach ist der Schritt der Zeit:

MS. Parts (copy?)—Gesellschaft der Musikfreunde, Vienna.
1ST ED. 1897, Gesamtausgabe.
Cf. the settings dated 8th July 1813 (68).

44. ' Totengräberlied ' (Hölty), Song (XX 7).   19th January 1813.

Ad libitum

Gra - be, Spa - ten, gra - be!

MS. (without title, together with 50)—Otto Taussig, Malmö.
1ST ED. 1894, Gesamtausgabe.
Schubert also set this poem for male voice trio, probably in the same year (38).
— String Quartet in B flat (V 3). See 36.   21st February 1813.

45. Kyrie in B flat for Mixed Chorus (XIV 21).   1st March 1813.

Andante con espressione

Ky - ri - e   e - lei - son, e - lei - son,

MS. Stadtbibliothek, Vienna.
1ST PF. 25th December 1846, Anna-Kirche, Vienna, as part of Ferdinand Schubert's Mass in B flat major.
1ST ED. 1888, Gesamtausgabe.

Ferdinand Schubert used this Kyrie, with an added accompaniment, in his ' Pastoral Mass,' Op. 13 (MS. dated 20th October 1833—Gesellschaft der Musikfreunde, Vienna), published *c.* 1850 by Karl Haslinger, Vienna. When this Mass was performed (see above), the *Wiener Allgemeine Musikzeitung*, unconscious of the truth, called it ' an heritage of Schubertian sentiment (*Gemütlichkeit*) not to be mistaken.'

46. String Quartet in C (V 4)   3rd–7th (16th) March 1813.

Adagio   *Allegro con moto*

Andante con moto

[musical notation]

MENUETTO
Allegro

[musical notation]

TRIO

[musical notation]
decresc.

Allegro

[musical notation]

MS. Score—Stadtbibliothek, Vienna; Parts (dated 16th March 1813)—unknown; former owner—W. M. Hertz, Bradford.
IST PF. 1813, at Schubert's home.
IST ED. 1890, Gesamtausgabe.

The third movement was finished in score on the 6th, the whole quartet on the 7th March 1813. The *Andante con moto* appears as the third movement in the score, but as the second in the parts, which seem to have been written on 16th March. They indicate the existence of a lost second score.

— **Mozart's Jupiter Symphony** (in C major), the first seven bars from the minuet, copied by Schubert. See Appendix II, no. 2. *c.* 29th March 1813.

47. ' **Dithyrambe** ' (Schiller), called ' **Der Besuch,** ' **Mixed Chorus with Tenor Soli and Pianoforte Accompaniment.** Unpublished. 29th March 1813.

Allegro molto

[musical notation]

Nim - mer, das glaubt mir, er - schei - nen die Göt - ter

MS. First stanza, for tenor solo and mixed chorus—Stadtbibliothek, Vienna (dated); second and third stanzas, for chorus and soli (with Appendix II, no. 2)—Dr. Otto Kallir, New York.

For the poem and for the setting as a solo song, see **801**.

— **Zumsteeg's ' Chor der Derwische,'** for S.T.B., copied by Schubert. See Appendix II, no. 3. Spring 1813.

48. Fantasia in C minor for **Pianoforte Duet,** called '**Grande Sonate,**' two versions (IX 32). April–10th June 1813.

[musical incipits: Adagio; Allegro agitato; Andante amoroso; Allegro 1; Adagio; FUGA Allegro maestoso]

MS. First version, without the fugue (dated, by Albert Stadler, 1814)—the Gertrude Clarke Whittall Foundation Collection in the Library of Congress, Washington; second version—Stadtbibliothek, Vienna.

1ST PF. First version—8th March 1871, Musikverein, Vienna.

1ST ED. First version—1871, J. P. Gotthard, Vienna (no. 130), as ' Grosse Sonate '; second version—1888, Gesamtausgabe.

Kreissle (p. 613) lists the ' Sonate,' according to Albert Stadler, the former owner of the first version, as of 1814; Nottebohm (pp. 253 f.) places this version among the spurious works. It was reprinted by the Peters Edition and (in vol iv of Schubert's works for Piano Duet) by the Universal Edition, Vienna. The fourth movement, Allegro, is in *alla breve* time in the first version, which Stadler entitled *Grande Sonnate* (*sic*).

49. Kyrie to a Mass in D minor for Chorus and Orchestra (XIV 15).
Fragment. From the beginning of to 15th April 1813.

Allegro
Ky - ri - e   e - lei - son.

MS. Stadtbibliothek, Vienna.
1ST ED. 1888, Gesamtausgabe.

The MS. bears the title ' Missa,' but it contains only the Kyrie.

— String Quartet in B flat (V 3). See 36. 5th April 1813.

50. ' Die Schatten ' (Matthisson), Song (XX 8). 12th April 1813.

Andantino con moto
Freun - de, de - ren Grüf - te sich schon — be - moo-sten!

MS. (together with 44)—Otto Taussig, Malmö.
1ST ED. 1894, Gesamtausgabe.

The poem was written on the occasion of the death of Matthisson's friend, the Swiss scientist, Charles Bonnet.

51. ' Unendliche Freude ' (from Schiller's ' Elysium '), Trio, T.T.B. (XXI 37). 15th April 1813.

Allegretto
pp Un - end - li-che Freu-de durch - wal - let das Herz,

MS. Parts (copy?)—Gesellschaft der Musikfreunde, Vienna.
1ST ED. 1897, Gesamtausgabe.

Cf. the settings dated April and May 1813 (53, 54, 57, 58, and 60), and the setting of the whole poem as a solo song, September 1817 (584);

52. ' Sehnsucht ' (' Ach! aus dieses Tales Gründen,' Schiller), Song, first version (XX 9). 15–17th April 1813.

Allegretto
Ach,   aus die - ses T - les Grün - den,

MS. Preussische Staatsbibliothek, Berlin.

1ST ED. 1868, Wilhelm Müller, Berlin (no. 13), as no. 1 of six songs (ed. by Franz Espagne).

For the second version, see 636.

53. '**Vorüber die stöhnende Klage**' (from Schiller's 'Elysium'), **Trio**, T.T.B. (XIX 9). 18th April 1813.

Vor - ü - ber, vor - ü - ber die stöh - nen - de Kla - ge!

MS. Score—unknown; former owner—Rudolf Weis-Ostborn, Graz; Parts—Gesellschaft der Musikfreunde, Vienna.

1ST ED. 1892, Gesamtausgabe.

The MS. score is written in *alla breve* time, the tempo indication ' Adagio, con espressione.' This and the other partsongs of 1812–13 (Metastasio, see 17) and 1813 (Schiller: 43, 51, 53, 54, 55, 57, 58, 60–5, 67, 69, 70, 71) were probably written as exercises by Schubert for his teacher, Salieri. For the setting of the complete Schiller poem as a solo song, September 1817, and for the others, set as trios, April and May 1813, see 51.

54. '**Unendliche Freude**' (from Schiller's 'Elysium'), **Canon for three Basses, or two T. and B.** (XIX 22). 19th April 1813.

Andante con moto

Un - end - li - che Freu - de durch - wal - let das Herz.

MS. Stadtbibliothek, Vienna: (*a*) as full score, and (*b*) as canon on one stave; another MS. (*c*) unknown; former owner—Rudolf Weis-Ostborn, Graz.

1ST ED. 1873, J. Guttentag, Berlin, in Reissmann's *Schubert*, Appendix no. 2 (p. 3).

The MS. (*b*) bears the title ' Canon a tre Bassi,' but is written in the treble clef; at the end of this MS. Schubert notes that if the canon is to be sung once only it may be sung by one bass and two tenors, but in that case the bass must commence. The printed version in the G.A. is a canon *infinitus*, with two sketches of a coda (printed in the *Revisionsbericht*). Another MS. (*c*), undated, shows the same set as a canon *finitus*, and commencing with the third voice (bass). The latter MS. is on the first of three oblong sheets, containing a copy of Zumsteeg's ' Chor der Derwische ' (see item after 47) and the trio ' Dessen Fahne Donnerstürme wallte ' (58). Schubert had already set the stanza ' Unendliche Freude ' as a trio (XXI 37), 15th April 1813 (51).

55. ' **Selig durch die Liebe** ' (from Schiller's hymn ' Der Triumph der Liebe '), **Trio T.T.B.** (XIX 12). 21st April 1813.

MS. Score—Stadtbibliothek, Vienna.
1ST ED. 1892, Gesamtausgabe.

56. Sanctus, Canon for three Voices, with Coda (XIX 29). 21st April 1813.

MS. Stadtbibliothek, Vienna (in full score and as canon).
1ST ED. 1892, Gesamtausgabe.

57. ' **Hier strecket der wallende Pilger** ' (from Schiller's ' Elysium '), **Trio, T.T.B.** (XXI 38). 29th April 1813.

MS. Parts (copy?)—Gesellschaft der Musikfreunde, Vienna.
1ST ED. 1897, Gesamtausgabe.

58. ' **Dessen Fahne Donnerstürme wallte** ' (from Schiller's ' Elysium '), **Trio, T.T.B.** (XIX 10). Beginning of May 1813.

MS. Score—unknown; former owner—Rudolf Weis-Ostborn, Graz; Parts—Conservatoire, Paris (Ph.).
1ST ED. 1892, Gesamtausgabe.
The score is written on the third of a MS. of three oblong sheets (see 54).

59. ' **Verklärung** ' (' The Dying Christian to his Soul,' Pope, translated by Herder), **Song** (XX 10). 4th May 1813.

Le - bens-fun-ke vom Him-mel ent - glüht,

MS. Lost (copy in the Witteczek Collection).
1ST ED. 5th May 1832, A. Diabelli & Co., Vienna (no. 4017), as no. 4 of *Nachlass*, book 17.

60. ' **Hier umarmen sich getreue Gatten** ' (from Schiller's ' Elysium '), Trio, T.T.B. (XIX 11). 8th May 1813.

Hier um - ar - men sich ge - treu - e Gat- ten,

MS. Score—Stadtbibliothek, Vienna; Parts—Gesellschaft der Musikfreunde, Vienna.
1ST ED. 1892, Gesamtausgabe.

A different date, 3rd October 1813, has been written on the MS. score in another hand (Josef Hüttenbrenner?).

61. ' **Ein jugendlicher Maienschwung** ' (from Schiller's hymn ' Der Triumph der Liebe '), for three Voices (XXI 39). 8th May 1813.

Ein ju - gend-lich-er Mai - en-schwung

MS. Parts (copy?)—Gesellschaft der Musikfreunde, Vienna.
1ST ED. 1897, Gesamtausgabe.

62. ' **Thronend auf erhabnem Sitz** ' (from Schiller's hymn ' Der Triumph der Liebe '), Trio, T.T.B. (XXI 40). Fragment. 9th May 1813.

Thro - nend auf er - hab - nem Sitz

MS. Score—Stadtbibliothek, Vienna; Parts (copy?)—Gesellschaft der Musikfreunde, Vienna.
1ST ED. 1897, Gesamtausgabe.

63. **'Wer die steile Sternenbahn'** (from Schiller's hymn 'Der Triumph der Liebe'), **Trio, T.T.B.** (XIX 13). 10th May 1813.

Allegro, quasi Recitativo

Wer die stei - le Ster - nen - bahn

MS. Stadtbibliothek, Vienna (together with 65).
1ST ED. 1892, Gesamtausgabe.

64. **'Majestät'sche Sonnenrosse'** (from Schiller's hymn 'Der Triumph der Liebe'), **Trio, T.T.B.** (XXI 41). 10th May 1813.

Allegro maestoso

Ma - je - stät' - sche Son - nen - ros - se

MS. Parts (copy?)—Gesellschaft der Musikfreunde, Vienna.
1ST ED. 1897, Gesamtausgabe.

65. **'Schmerz verzerret ihr Gesicht'** (from Schiller's 'Gruppe aus dem Tartarus'), **Canon, T.T.B.** (XIX 35). Sketch. 11th May 1813.

Allegro

Schmerz ver - zer - ret ihr Ge - sicht,

MS. Stadtbibliothek, Vienna (together with 63).
1ST ED. 1892, Gesamtausgabe.
For the setting of the whole poem as a solo song, see 396 and 583.

66. **Kyrie in F for Chorus, Orchestra, and Organ** (XIV 16). 12th May 1813.

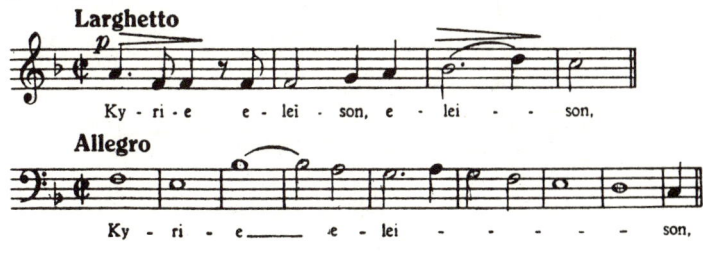

Larghetto

Ky - ri - e e - lei - son, e - lei - - son,

Allegro

Ky - ri - e —— e - lei - - - - - son,

MS. Stadtbibliothek, Vienna.
1ST ED. 1888, Gesamtausgabe.

67. ' **Frisch atmet des Morgens lebendiger Hauch** ' (from Schiller's ' Der Flüchtling,' **Trio, T.T.B.** (XXI 42). 15th May 1813.

MS. Score—Benedictine Monastery, Kremsmünster (Upper Austria); Parts—Gesellschaft der Musikfreunde, Vienna.

1ST ED. 1897, Gesamtausgabe.

Cf. the setting as a solo song (402). The poem is also known as ' Morgenfantasie.'

68. **String Quartet in B flat** (V 5). Fragment. 8th–16th June and 18th August 1813.

MS. Score—unknown; former owner—W. M. Hertz, Bradford; Parts—unknown; former owner—Ferdinand Schubert.

1ST PF. 1813, at Schubert's home.

1ST ED. 1890, Gesamtausgabe.

Two Allegro movements only; the other movements probably lost. In the Stadtbibliothek, Vienna, is an autograph variant of bars 113 to 152, in the development section of the first Allegro, written apparently later than the printed version, on the back of a MS. copy of Zumsteeg's song, ' Ritter Toggenburg' (cf. note to 397). Dr. Fritz Racek identified the variant.

69. ' **Dreifach ist der Schritt der Zeit** ' (from Schiller's ' Sprüche des Confucius '), **Canon for three Voices** (XIX 23). 8 July 1813.

MS. Joseph Muller, Closter (N.J.), U.S.A.

1ST. ED. 1892, Gesamtausgabe.

On the back of the MS. is written **70.** Schubert also set the whole stanza as a trio for male voices (43).

70. **' Ewig still steht die Vergangenheit '** (from Schiller's 'Sprüche des Confucius '), **Canon for three Voices.** 8th July 1813.

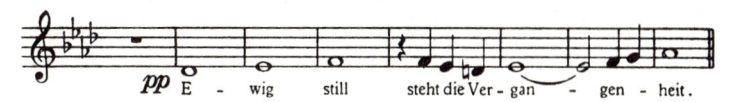

pp E - wig still steht die Ver - gan - gen - heit.

MS. Joseph Muller, Closter (N.J.), U.S.A.
1ST ED. Facsimile in *The Musical Quarterly*, New York, October 1928, opposite p. 515.

This canon, indicated by Schubert as ' Imitatio ad Haydn consuetudinem,' is written on the back of the MS. of 69. It is one of the exercises written in 1812 and 1813 for Salieri (see 53).

71. **' Die zwei Tugendwege '** (Schiller), **Trio, T.T.B.** (XIX 14). 15th July 1813.

Adagio con espressione
f Zwei sind der We - ge,

MS. Score—Stadtbibliothek, Vienna; Parts—Gesellschaft der Musikfreunde, Vienna.
1ST ED. 1892, Gesamtausgabe.

72. **Minuet and Finale in F of an Octet for Wind Instruments** (2 oboes, 2 clarinets, 2 horns, 2 bassoons; III 2). Finished 18th August 1813.

MENUETTO
Allegretto
Ob. *f*

I. TRIO
Ob.
p

II. TRIO
Corn.
p

FINALE
Allegro

MS. Stadtbibliothek, Vienna.
1ST ED. 1889, Gesamtausgabe.
 Only the minuet and finale are complete; a fragment of the first movement is preserved and printed in the *Revisionsbericht*. Schubert added a humorous postscript, printed in the English edition of the *Schubert Documents* (no. 51).
 Literature. Gerald Abraham (ed.), *Schubert*, London, 1946, p. 268; New York, 1947, p. 264.

— **String Quartet in B flat** (V 5). See 68. 18th August 1813.

73. '**Thekla. Eine Geisterstimme**' (Schiller), **Song**, first version (XX 11). 22nd–23rd August 1813.

MS. Rough draft—Preussische Staatsbibliothek, Berlin; fair copy (partly written by Albert Stadler?)—Kapten Rudolf Nydahl, Stockholm.
1ST ED. 1868, Wilhelm Müller, Berlin (no. 13) as no. 2 of six songs (ed. by Franz Espagne).
 For the two other versions, see 595.

74. **String Quartet in D** (V 6). 22nd August–September 1813.

Allegro ma non troppo

Andante

MENUETTO
Allegro

1813   76   31

TRIO

Allegro

MS. Score—Gesellschaft der Musikfreunde, Vienna; Parts—unknown; former owner—Ferdinand Schubert; first violin part—Frau Emma von Spaun, Vienna.

1ST PF. 4th October 1813, at Schubert's home, on the nameday of his father.

1ST ED. 1890, Gesamtausgabe.

The first movement was finished on 3rd September. The dedication and the occasion of the composition is indicated on the first violin part: 'Trois Quatuors . . . composés (sic) par François Schubert, écolier de Msr. de Salieri . . . Zur Nahmensfeyer meines Vaters. Franz, Sohn.' The other two quartets he mentions, however, were never written.

75. ' Trinklied ' ('Freunde, sammelt euch im Kreise,' author unknown) for **Bass Solo with Male Voice Chorus and Pianoforte Accompaniment** (XVI 16). 29th August 1813.

Allegro

Freun - de, sam - melt Euch im Krei - se,

MS. Dr. Alwin Cranz, Vienna.
1ST PF. (?) 4th May 1927, Musikvereinssaal, Vienna.
1ST ED. *c.* 1848, A. Diabelli & Co., Vienna (no. 8822), as no. 2 of *Nachlass*, book 45.

76. ' **Pensa, che questo istante** ' (Fronimo's Aria from Metastasio's ' Alcide al Bivio,' scene i), **Song** (XX 571). 13th September 1813.

Andante maestoso

Pen - sa che que - sto i - stan - te

MS. Stadtbibliothek, Vienna.

1ST ED. 1871, J. P. Gotthard, Vienna (no. 129), as no. 5 of '5 Canti' (see 688).

Albert Stadler claimed this as the earliest Schubert song preserved, and called it an exercise for Salieri. Schubert wrote several settings of this poem on the same MS.

77. '**Der Taucher**' (Schiller), **Song**, first version (XX 12a). 17th September 1813–5th April 1814.

[musical notation: Allegro — RECIT. "Wer wegt. es, Ritters-mann o-der Knapp', zu tau-chen in die-sen Schlund?"]

MS. Rough draft—Mrs. Frank La Forge, New York.
1ST ED. 1894, Gesamtausgabe.

See the second version, 111.

78. '**Son fra l'onde**' (Venus's Aria from Metastasio's 'Gli orti esperidi,' Part I), **Song** (XX 572). 18th September 1813.

[musical notation: Allegro — "Son fra l'on-de in mez-zo al ma-re,"]

MS. Stadtbibliothek, Vienna.
1ST ED. 1895, Gesamtausgabe.

This poem was also set in various ways by Schubert as an exercise in the use of the Italian language.

79. '**Eine kleine Trauermusik**' for Wind Instruments (2 clarinets, 2 bassoons, double bassoon, 2 horns, 2 trombones; III 3). 19th September 1813.

[musical notation: Grave con espressione, fz — p — fz]

MS. Stadtbibliothek, Vienna.
1ST ED. 1889, Gesamtausgabe.

There is no evidence that this work was written, as sometimes stated, in memory of Schubert's mother, who died on 28th May 1812. It may be that this work, which was not intended for the orchestra of the Stadtkonvikt, was written in some connection with the poet's, Theodor Körner's, death on 26th August 1813 (' Battle of Gladebach '). The MS. is inscribed, for no obvious reason, by another hand, ' Franz Schubert's Begräbnis-Feier.'

80. ' **Kantate zur Namensfeier des** [Schubert's] **Vaters** ' (' Ertöne Leier zur Festesfeier,' by Schubert himself) **for T.T.B. with Guitar Accompaniment** (XIX 4). Finished 27th September 1813.

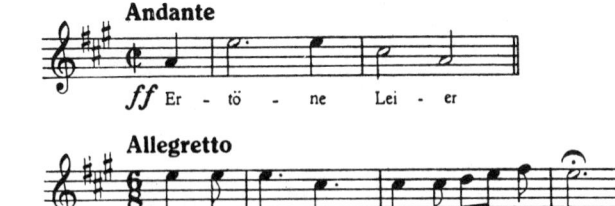

Andante

ff Er - tö - ne Lei - er

Allegretto

ff Lan - ge le - be un - ser Va - ter Franz!

MS. Score—Stadtbibliothek, Vienna; second tenor part— V. A. Heck, Vienna (1928).
1ST PF. 4th October 1813, at Schubert's home.
1ST ED. 1892, Gesamtausgabe.

This is the only work in which Schubert used the guitar as an accompaniment. It was probably performed by him (his voice had just broken) and his three brothers. The nameday of Franz (senior and junior) was the 4th October. Cf. the dedication mentioned in the note to 74, and 294.

81. ' **Auf den Sieg der Deutschen** ' (author unknown), **Song with Accompaniment for two Violins and a Violoncello** (XX 583). Autumn 1813.

Andante

Ver - schwun-den sind die Schmer - zen,

MS. Parts (together with the poem, copied separately by Schubert)—Otto Taussig, Malmö.
1ST ED. 1895, Gesamtausgabe.

The poem was said to have been written by Schubert himself, but there is no evidence to prove this assertion. The Battle of Leipzig forms the subject of the poem (cf. 104). For the setting of the same words as a canon, see 88.

82. **Symphony in D (I 1).** Finished 28th October 1813.

MS. Gesellschaft der Musikfreunde, Vienna.

1ST PF. Autumn 1813, Stadtkonvikt; first public performance of the first movement only: 30th January 1880, Crystal Palace, London (conductor August Manns); of the complete work: 5th February 1881, ditto.

1ST ED. 1884, Gesamtausgabe.

The bars 166–98 (G.A., p. 10, line 1, bar 3, to p. 11, line 1, bar 9) are cancelled in the MS. There are eleven wind instruments with kettledrums. Josef Hüttenbrenner arranged the work for piano duet in 1819 (MS.).

Literature. Walter Vetter, *Schubert*, Potsdam, 1934, pp. 30 f.

83. ' **Zur Namensfeier des Herrn Andreas Siller** ' (author unknown) **Song with Accompaniment for Violin and Harp** (XX 582). 28th October–4th November 1813.

Nicht zu geschwind

Des Phö - bus Strah-len sind· dem Aug'. ent - schwun - den,

MS. Stadtbibliothek, Vienna.
IST PF. 10th November 1813, at Andreas Siller's home, Vienna.
IST ED. 1895, Gesamtausgabe.

The MS., dated 4th November, also contains the first version in B flat, dated 28th October, transposed into G (probably for the unknown singer), and the *Allegro moderato* is altered to *Nicht zu geschwind* (*Allegro ma non troppo*). The nameday of Andreas is the 10th November. Nothing is known of Herr Siller and his relations with Schubert, or of his family. The poem, probably written by an amateur, seems to have consisted originally of more than one stanza.

84. **' Des Teufels Lustschloss,' Opera** in three acts by Kotzebue (XV 1). 30th October 1813–22nd October 1814.

OVERTURE
Allegro con fuoco

No. 1.
INTRODUCTION
Hül - fe! Hülf'! hier ist Hül - fe! Hül - fe! hier ist

No. 2.
LIED (Bass)
Andantino

Was küm-mert mich ein sump-fig Land, was

No. 3.
DUET (Sopr. and Ten.)
Andante

Ja mor - gen, wenn die Son - ne sinkt,

No. 4.
ARIA (Sopr.)
Allegretto

Wo - hin zwei Lie - ben - de sich ret - ten,

No. 5.
QUARTET (Sop., Ten. and 2 Basses)
Allegro moderato

Kaum hun - dert Schritt' von die - ser Schän - ke

No. 6.
TERZET (Sopr., Ten. and Bass)
Allegro vivace

Fort will ich, fort! den Be - trug ent - lar - ven,

No. 7.
ARIA (Sopr.)
Allegro moderato

ad libit. *tempo*

Wel-cher Fre - vel! So sind die Men-schen! Sie su - chen früh und

No. 8.
ARIA (Ten.)
Allegretto

Ge - sund - heit ist' mit Mut ver - schwi - stert,

No. 9.
DUET (Ten. and Bass)
Allegro

Herr Rit-ter, zu - Hül-fe, Herr Rit - ter, die Gei - ster, die

No. 10.
FUNERAL MUSIC
Grave *sempre pp*

Clar.
pp

No. 11.
FINALE (Sop., Ten., Bass and Male Quartet)
Allegro agitato
(schreit)

Ach, nun ist der Teu-fel los!

No. 12a.
RECITATIVE (Bass)

Ich le-be noch und glaub'es kaum, was hier ge-schah,

No. 12b.
RECITATIVE & DUET (Sopr. and Bass)

Ver - ge - bens schweif' ich durch die ö - den Hal - len!

No. 13.
ARIA (Ten.)
Andante con moto

Nie beb - te vor dem na - hen To - de

No. 14a.
MELODRAMA
Andante con moto
Ob.

pp

No. 14b.
MARCH
Marcia

f

No. 15a.
FEMALE CHORUS
Allegretto

p Hast du ver-ges - sen, kannst du er - mes - sen

No. 15b.
ENSEMBLE (Sopr., Ten. and Female Chorus)
Recit. Andante

Noch ein-mal hat das Zau-ber-spiel der Hoff-nung

No. 16a.
FUNERAL MARCH
V.I. *pp*

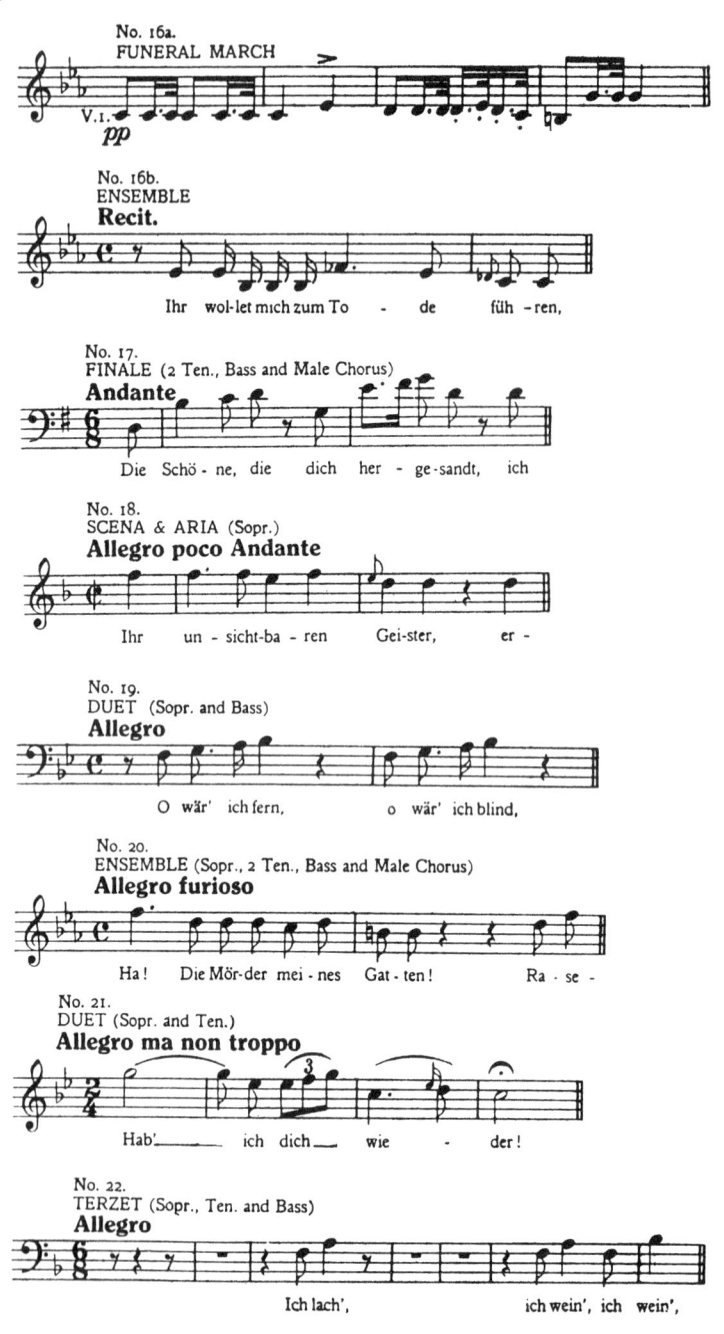

No. 16b.
ENSEMBLE
Recit.

Ihr wol-let mich zum To - de füh - ren,

No. 17.
FINALE (2 Ten., Bass and Male Chorus)
Andante

Die Schö - ne, die dich her - ge-sandt, ich

No. 18.
SCENA & ARIA (Sopr.)
Allegro poco Andante

Ihr un - sicht-ba - ren Gei-ster, er -

No. 19.
DUET (Sopr. and Bass)
Allegro

O wär' ich fern, o wär' ich blind,

No. 20.
ENSEMBLE (Sopr., 2 Ten., Bass and Male Chorus)
Allegro furioso

Ha! Die Mör-der mei - nes Gat - ten! Ra - se -

No. 21.
DUET (Sopr. and Ten.)
Allegro ma non troppo

Hab'___ ich dich___ wie - der!

No. 22.
TERZET (Sopr., Ten. and Bass)
Allegro

Ich lach', ich wein', ich wein',

MS. Parts (together with 89)—Stadtbibliothek, Vienna.
1ST PF. Probably 1813, at Schubert's home.
1ST ED. 1886, Gesamtausgabe.

Each part indicated as belonging to vol. ii, the first is lost. In 1839 Ferdinand Schubert listed six Deutsche Tänze with trios for string quartet and two horns, written in 1814, as being in his possession.

91. **Two Minuets and four Trios for Pianoforte.** Unpublished. 22nd November 1813.

MS. Preussische Staatsbibliothek, Berlin.
According to Schubert's inscription on the MS. there were ' IV Menuetti,' two minuets may, therefore, be lost.

92. ' **Lass immer in der Jugend Glanz** ' (author unknown), **Canon for two Voices.** Lost. (?) *c.* 1814.

93. ' **Don Gayseros** ' (from Fouqué's novel ' Der Zauberring '), three Songs (XX 13–15): I. ' Don Gayseros, Don Gayseros,' II. ' Nächtens klang die süsse Laute,' III. ' An dem jungen Morgenhimmel.' (?) 1814.

MS. Preussische Staatsbibliothek, Berlin.
1ST ED. 1894, Gesamtausgabe.
The authenticity of these songs is doubted; for instance by Walter Vetter. The MS., thought to be the first sketch, has no title, and the poems are not in Fouqué's order. They are to be found in the novel, vol. i, chapter 20, when, according to the story, they are sung, as sections of a ballad, with zither acc., by Don Hernandez. Nottebohm (p. 261) lists the second song under the title ' Der Mohrenkönig ' (or ' Mohrenkrieg '?) as a fragment. Cf. Kreissle, p. 605.

94. **String Quartet in D** (V 7). 1814.

MS. Score and Parts (undated)—Stadtbibliothek, Vienna.
1ST PF. 1814, at Schubert's home (cp. 112).
1ST ED. End of 1871, C. F. Peters, Leipzig (no. 5376, Edition nos. 796 and 798, score and parts).
— **Two Opera Fragments.** See note to 982. 1814.

95. ' **Adelaide** ' (Matthisson), **Song** (XX 25). 1814.

MS. Lost (Ebner's, Stadler's, and Witteczek's copies).
IST ED. *c.* 1848, A. Diabelli & Co., Vienna (no. 8819) as no. 5 of *Nachlass*, book 42.
It seems that there were two MSS., one of 1814, and another of 1815.

96. Wenzel Matiegka's Notturno for flute, viola, and guitar, Op. 21, arranged by Schubert as a **Quartet for Flute, Viola, Guitar, and Violoncello** (called Schubert's **Guitar Quartet**). 26th February 1814.

MS. William Matheson, Olten (Switzerland).
IST PF. 6th June 1925, Schloss Brühl near Cologne.
IST ED. 1926, Drei Masken Verlag, Munich (ed. by Georg Kinsky).

Matiegka's trio, dedicated to Johann Karl, Graf Esterházy, Schubert's later patron, was published by Artaria & Co., Vienna (no. 1926), in the summer of 1807; the only known copy of this work is in the possession of Th. Rischel, Copenhagen. The theme of the variations, sometimes attributed to Haydn, is a ' Ständchen ' by Friedrich Fleischmann. Trio ii of the minuet (p. 15 of the printed score) is entirely the work of Schubert; as for the rest of the work he merely added a violoncello part to Matiegka's trio for flute, viola, and guitar.

Literature. O. E. D., *Zeitschrift für Musikwissenschaft*, Leipzig, October 1928; Georg Kinsky, ditto, August 1932.

97. ' **Trost. An Elisa** ' (Matthisson), **Song** (XX 19). (? April) 1814.

MS. Lost (Stadler's and Witteczek's copies).
IST ED. 1894, Gesamtausgabe.

April is given as the month on the copy in the Witteczek Collection, but is not indicated in its index. The song is, in fact, a recitativo without arioso.

98. '**Erinnerungen**' ('Am Seegestad',' Matthisson), **Song** (XX 24). (?) April 1814.

1814

Andante

Am See - ge-stad', in lau - en Voll-monds-näch - ten.

MS. Stadtbibliothek, Vienna (rough draft, incomplete, together with 102).
IST ED. 1894, Gesamtausgabe.
The first part of the song as written in the MS. is reproduced in the *Revisionsbericht*. Schubert also set the poem as a trio, in May 1816 (424).

99. ' Andenken ' (Matthisson), Song (XX 16). April 1814.

Allegretto

Ich den - ke dein—, wenn durch den Hain

MS. Meangya family, Mödling, near Vienna (Ph.).
IST ED. 1894, Gesamtausgabe.
The autograph is marked ' Etwas geschwind.' Schubert also set the poem as a trio, in May 1816 (423).

100. ' Geisternähe ' (Matthisson), Song (XX 17). April 1814.

Adagio molto

Der Dämm'-rung Schein durch - blinkt — den Hain ;

MS. Lost (Witteczek's copy).
IST ED. 1894, Gesamtausgabe.

101. ' **Erinnerung** ' (' Kein Rosenschimmer leuchtet,' called ' Totenopfer,' Matthisson), Song (XX 18). April 1814.

Andante

Kein Ro - sen - schim - mer

MS. Lost (Witteczek's copy).
IST ED. 1894, Gesamtausgabe.

102. ' **Die Betende** ' (Matthisson), Song (XX 20). April 1814.

Adagio

Lau - ra be - tet!

MS. Sketch—Stadtbibliothek, Vienna (together with 'Erinnerungen,' 98); final version—lost (Stadler's copy).

IST ED. *c.* 1840, A. Diabelli & Co., Vienna (no. 6940) as no. 1 of *Nachlass,* book 31.

The *Revisionsbericht* corrects: p. 156, bar 13, and p. 158, bar 8, right hand—E sharp instead of E.

— 'Der Taucher,' first version (XX 12a). See 77. 5th April 1814.

103. Grave (Introduction) **and Allegro in C minor for String Quartet.** Begun 23rd April 1814.

MS. (incomplete, partly in pencil)—Gesellschaft der Musikfreunde, Vienna.

IST PF. 1814, at Schubert's home; public performance—9th February 1938, Vienna (Graf-Kurz Quartet).

IST ED. (edited and completed by Alfred Orel) Score—1939, Universal Edition, Vienna; parts—1941, Adolf Robitschek, Vienna.

It is likely that A. Diabelli, Vienna, was at one time in possession of the complete MS., the other movements of which seem to be lost. Cf. 703.

104. 'Die Befreier Europa's in Paris' (author unknown), **Song** (XX 584). 16th May 1814.

MS. Stadtbibliothek, Vienna (including a sketch of the song).
IST ED. 1895, Gesamtausgabe.

The Emperor of Austria, Franz I, together with his allies, entered Paris on 15th April 1814. The poem probably consisted of more stanzas than those preserved in the MS.

105. Mass in F for Quartet, S.A.T.B., Mixed Chorus, Orchestra, and Organ (XIII 1).   17th May–22nd July 1814.

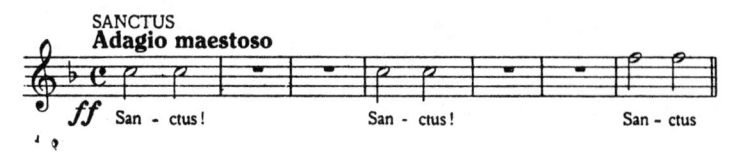

KYRIE Larghetto
pp Ky - ri - e e - lei - son,

GLORIA Allegro vivace
f Glo - ri - a, glo - ri - a

Andante con moto
Gra - - ti - as a - gi - mus ti - bi

Adagio
Do - mi - ne De - us, A - gnus De - i,

Allegro
f Quo - ni - am tu so - lus san - - ctus,

Allegro vivace
f Cum san - cto Spi - ri - tu in glo - ri - a De - i,

CREDO Andantino
p Cre - do in u - num De - um,

SANCTUS Adagio maestoso
ff San - ctus! San - ctus! San - ctus

BENEDICTUS
Andante con moto

Be - ne - di - ctus qui ve - nit in no - mi - ne Do - mi - ni,

AGNUS DEI
Adagio molto

A - gnus De - i qui tol - lis pec - ca - ta mun - di,

Andante

Do - na no - bis pa - cem,

MS. Score—Stadtbibliothek, Vienna; Violino I part—Sotheby, London (14th November 1929); Violino II part—Mrs. Mary Louise Zimbalist, Philadelphia; all the orchestral parts— unknown, former owner—Max Friedlaender, Berlin.

1ST PF. 16th October 1814, Liechtentaler Kirche, Vienna (conductor, Schubert).

1ST ED. (in parts) December 1857, F. Glöggl & Sohn, Vienna (no. 811), dedicated by Ferdinand Schubert to Cardinal Johann Baptist Scitovszky de Nagy-Kér, Primate of Hungary, Archbishop of Gran (Esztergom).

The Kyrie was finished on 18th May, the Gloria begun on 21st May, the first section of which was finished on 22nd May, the Gratias begun on 25th May; the whole of the Gloria—including the vocal parts—was finished on 31st May; the Credo was written between 30th May and 22nd June, the Sanctus between 2nd and 3rd July, the Benedictus finished on 3rd July, the Agnus Dei begun on 7th July, the Dona nobis sketched on 12th (13th?) July, and written between 15th and 22nd July. The mass was composed for the festival of the hundredth anniversary of the foundation of Liechtental church. It was performed by a relatively large orchestra, including oboes, clarinets, bassoons, and two horns. The orchestral parts included three copies each of the first and the second violins, two copies each of viola, violoncello, and bass. (At a later date Ferdinand Schubert supplied an organ acc., *ad libitum*, and, for most of the mass, a trombone part.) In the Stadtbibliothek, Vienna, there is also a sketch of the vocal parts of the Benedictus, dated 29th May 1814. The Dona nobis was replaced by another composition on 25th April 1815 (185). In the text of all his masses Schubert omitted the words: *Credo in unam sanctam ecclesiam catholicam et apostolicam.*

1814

106. **Salve Regina in B flat for Tenor Solo, Orchestra, and Organ** (XIV 9). 28th June–1st July 1814.

Andante

Sal - ve Re - gi - na, ma - ter mi - se - ri - cor - di - ae,

MS. Stadtbibliothek, Vienna.
1ST ED. 1888, Gesamtausgabe.

The dates, June to July 1814, are given on the title (a copy of which, made by Ferdinand Schubert, is in the Fitzwilliam Museum, Cambridge— see 588). The first page of the autograph MS. is dated 28th June 1814, and the last page 1st July 1814.

107. '**Lied aus der Ferne**' (Matthisson), Song (XX 21). (?) July 1814.

Allegretto

Wenn in des A -bends letz - tem Schei -ne

MS. (undated) Meangya family, Mödling, near Vienna (Ph.).
1ST ED. 1894, Gesamtausgabe.

The MS. is in D, 'Etwas geschwind.' The date is given in the Witteczek Collection, first as 4th April, and later as July 1814.

108. '**Der Abend**' (Matthisson), Song (XX 22). July 1814.

Andante con moto

Pur - pur malt die Tan - nen - hü - gel

MS. Lost (Witteczek's copy).
1ST ED. 1894, Gesamtausgabe.

109. '**Lied der Liebe**' (Matthisson), Song (XX 23). July 1814.

Allegretto

Durch Fich-ten am Hü- gel, durch Er - len am Bach,

MS. Lost (Witteczek's copy).
1ST ED. 1894, Gesamtausgabe.

110. ' Wer ist gross? ' (author unknown), **Cantata for Bass Solo and Chorus, T.T.B.B.**, with accompaniment for Orchestra (XVI 43). 24th–25th July 1814.

[musical notation: Allegretto — Wer ist wohl gross? Der ei-ne Welt im Kop-fe trägt,]

MS. Stadtbibliothek, Vienna.
1ST PF. (?) 22nd December 1927, Musikvereinssaal, Vienna.
1ST ED. 1891, Gesamtausgabe.

The score indicates that Schubert originally intended to write this cantata for mixed chorus. The poem seems to have consisted of seven stanzas, only the first of which is copied in the MS.; a different version, however, is given for the refrain of the last stanza. Another poem with the same title, also in seven stanzas, written by L. Haupt, was set to music by A. Methfessel.

111. ' **Der Taucher** ' (Schiller), **Song**, second version (XX 12*b*). Finished August 1814.

[musical notation: Allegro — Wer wagt es, Rit-ters-mann o-der Knapp', zu tau-chen in die-sen Schlund?]

MS. Fair copy (the appendix with variants lost)—Dr. Alwin Cranz, Vienna.
1ST ED. 16th June 1831, A. Diabelli & Co., Vienna (no. 3709) as *Nachlass*, book 12 (altered by Diabelli).

The MS. bears the dates ' Angefangen im September 1813. Geendigt im August 1814,' the earlier date apparently referring to the first version (77). There was also a third version, the voice part written in the treble clef, a copy of which—by Leopold Ebner—is preserved in the von Wettstein family, Vienna. Five bars of this song are written on the MS. of the 2nd symphony (125), and are printed in the *Revisionsbericht* (Series I, p. 5). These five bars indicate that even a fourth version of this lengthy song existed. Ferdinand Schubert arranged the song with an accompaniment for orchestra (produced in 1836 at Vienna).

112. String Quartet in B flat (Op. posth. 168; V 8). 5th–13th September 1814.

Allegro ma non troppo

Andante sostenuto

MENUETTO
Allegro

TRIO
pp dolce

Presto
V.1. *pp*
V.2. *pp*

MS. Albert Cranz, New York (Ph.).
1ST PF. 1814, at Schubert's home; first public performance 23rd February 1862, Musikverein, Vienna (Josef Hellmesberger's Quartet) with the Trio from the String Quartet in D (94).
1ST ED. May 1863, C. A. Spina, Vienna (no. 17,707); the publisher intended to dedicate the work to J. Hellmesberger.

Originally planned as a string trio (ten lines are written in this form). The first movement was written on 5th September in 4½ hours; the second 6th–10th September, and the third was finished on 11th September.

113. '**An Emma**' (Schiller), **Song**, three versions (Op. 58, no. 2; XX 26 (*a*), (*b*), (*c*)). 17th September 1814.

a
Andante

Weit in ne-bel-grau--er Fer--ne

[Musical notation: Etwas langsam — "Weit in ne-bel-grau-er Fer-ne"]

[Musical notation: Mässig — "Weit in ne-bel-grau-er Fer-ne"]

MS. Version (*a*): Sketch—Stadtbibliothek, Vienna; fair copy—unknown; former owner—A. Lacom, Vienna; versions (*b*) and (*c*) lost.

1ST ED. (*a*) Gesamtausgabe, 1894; (*b*) 30th June 1821, as supplement to the *Wiener Zeitschrift für Kunst, Literatur, Theater und Mode*, Vienna (also printed separately); (*c*) 6th April 1826, Thaddäus Weigl, Vienna (no. 2492), under the title 'Emma,' as no. 2 of Op. 56, later corrected to Op. 58.

According to Weigl's advertisement, Schubert avoided all difficulties in the pianoforte accompaniment of the six songs, Opp. 57 and 58.

114. '**Das Fräulein im Turme. Romanze**' (Matthisson), Song, two versions (XX 27). Finished 29th September 1814.

[Musical notation: FIRST VERSION — Ziemlich langsam — "Ein Fräu-lein klagt im fin-stern Thurm."]

[Musical notation: SECOND VERSION — Etwas langsam — "Ein Fräu-lein klagt im fin-stern Thurm."]

MS. First version: Sketch (together with 585 and 586)—Dr. Franz Roehn, Los Angeles; fair copy—Nationalbibliothek, Vienna (dated September 1814, without the day of month); second version: Preussische Staatsbibliothek, Berlin (dated 29th September 1814).

1ST ED. Second version—1868, Wilhelm Müller, Berlin (no. 13) as no. 5 of six songs (ed. by Franz Espagne).

Part of the sketch is printed in the *Revisionsbericht*; the Vienna copy is published in *Die Musik*, Berlin, 1st May 1902 (ed. by Josef Mantuani). The name of Matthisson's heroine is Rosalia von Montanver. Schubert's title for the song was 'Romanze.'

115. ' An Laura, als sie Klopstock's Auferstehungslied sang '
(Matthisson), **Song** (XX 28). 2nd–7th October 1814.

[Sehr langsam — musical incipit: "Her-zen, die gen Him-mel sich er-he-ben,"]

MS. Stadtbibliothek, Vienna.
IST ED. *c.* 1840, A. Diabelli & Co., Vienna (no. 6940) as no. 3 of *Nachlass*, book 31.

The beginning of the MS., used for the first edition, bears the date October 1814, with the ' 2 ' inserted later, and at the end it is dated 7th October 1814. The poet alludes to Graun's famous setting of Klopstock's ' Die Auferstehung ' (1758), the first of several settings.

116. ' Der Geistertanz ' (Matthisson), **Song** (XX 29). 14th October 1814.

[Etwas geschwind — musical incipit: "Die bret-ter-ne Kam-mer der To-ten er-bebt,"]

MS. Boston Public Library, Boston (Massachusetts)— incomplete (Ph.).
IST ED. *c.* 1840, A. Diabelli & Co., Vienna (no. 6940), as no. 2 of *Nachlass*, book 31.

Schubert had used the same poem for a solo song, *c.* 1812 (15), and later he set it as a quartet, T.T.B.B. (494).

117. ' Das Mädchen aus der Fremde ' (Schiller), **Song,** first version (XX 30). 16th October 1814.

[Mässig langsam — musical incipit: "In ei-nem Tal bei ar-men Hir-ten"]

MS. Charles L. Morley, New York.
IST ED. 1894, Gesamtausgabe.

Schubert wrote this song on the day of the first performance of his first mass (105). He again set the poem on 12th August 1815 (252).

118. ' Gretchen am Spinnrade ' (from Goethe's ' Faust '), **Song** (Op. 2, XX 31). 19th October 1814.

Nicht zu geschwind

[musical notation: Meine Ruh' ist hin, mein Herz ist schwer,]

MS. Fair copy—Stadtbibliothek, Vienna; fair copy, made for Goethe (the first sixteen bars only)—Preussische Staatsbibliothek, Berlin (Ph.).

1ST PF. 20th February 1823, Musikverein, Vienna.

1ST ED. 30th April 1821, Cappi & Diabelli, Vienna (no publisher's number), published for Schubert and dedicated by him to Moritz Reichsgraf Fries.

The Vienna MS. was reproduced in facsimile in *Franz Schubert's fünf erste Lieder*, Universal Edition, Vienna, 1922 (ed. by O. E. D.). The tempo was originally 'Etwas schnell.' Heuberger called this the first modern German song (*Schubert*, Berlin, 1902, p. 20). It was Schubert's first Goethe song, written three days after the first performance of his Mass in F (105), in which Therese Grob sang the soprano part. Cf. 126, 367, 440, and 564.

Literature. Max Friedlaender, Supplement to the *Schubert Album*, C. F. Peters, Leipzig (no. 2173, published in 1884), pp. 48 f.

—— '**Des Teufels Lustschloss**' (XV 1). See 84. 22nd October 1814.

119. '**Nachtgesang**' ('O gib vom weichen Pfühle,' Goethe), **Song** (XX 32). 30th November 1814.

[musical notation: Langsam — O gib vom weichen Pfühle,]

MS. Rough draft, in A flat, first line only (together with 'Trost in Thränen' of the same date, 120)—Graf Pallavicini, Vienna; fair copy made for Goethe—Conservatoire, Paris (Ph.), together with 'Der Gott und die Bajadere,' 'Sehnsucht,' and 'Mignon' of 1815 (254, 310 (*b*), and 321).

1ST ED. *c.* 1848, A. Diabelli & Co., Vienna (no. 8836) as no. 4 of *Nachlass*, book 47 (with a spurious pf. introduction).

120. '**Trost in Thränen**' (Goethe), **Song** (XX 33). 30th November 1814.

[musical notation: Etwas geschwind — Wie kommt's, dass du so traurig bist,]

MS. Graf Pallavicini, Vienna (together with 119); fair copy made for Goethe—Stadtbibliothek, Vienna.

IST ED. 9th October 1835, A. Diabelli & Co., Vienna (no. 5029), as no. 3 of *Nachlass*, book 25 (with a spurious introductory bar).

121. ' **Schäfer's Klagelied** ' (Goethe), **Song**, two versions (Op. 3, no. 1; XX 34 (*b*) and (*a*)). 30th November 1814.

FIRST VERSION
Mässig (♪ = 120)

Da dro - ben auf je - nem Ber - ge,

SECOND VERSION
Mässig

Da dro - ben auf je - nem Ber - ge,

MS. (*b*) First version in C minor, dated—Nationalbibliothek, Vienna; fair copy made for Goethe—Preussische Staatsbibliothek, Berlin (Ph.); (*a*) second version in E minor (transposed for the singer Jager?)—Stadtbibliothek, Vienna.

IST PF. (*a*) 28th February 1819, Gasthof 'Zum Römischen Kaiser,' Vienna (Franz Jäger).

IST ED. (*b*) 1894, Gesamtausgabe; (*a*) 21st May 1821, Cappi & Diabelli, Vienna (no. 768, without plate-mark) as no. 1 of Op. 3, published for Schubert and dedicated by him to Ignaz von Mosel.

This was the first Schubert song performed in public. Goethe's poem is a paraphrase of a folksong, also beginning ' Da droben auf jenem Berge.' Schubert altered the third line of Goethe's poem: *hingebogen* instead of the original *gebogen*.

Literature. Robert Haas, *Schubert-Gabe der Oesterreichischen Gitarre-Zeitschrift*, Vienna, 1928, pp. 44–6; Alfred Orel, *Jahrbuch der Grillparzer-Gesellschaft*, Vienna, 1929, vol. xxix, p. 58.

122. ' **Ammenlied** ' (Michael Lubi), **Song** (XX 38). Beginning of December 1814.

Mässig

Am ho - hen, ho - hen Turm,

MS. Lost (Witteczek's copy).

1ST ED. 1872, J. P. Gotthard, Vienna (no. 336), as no. 12 of forty songs.

According to a MS. list of Schubert's songs, by Anton Diabelli (on sale in Vienna, c. 1922), this song seems to have been written at the beginning of the month, before ' Sehnsucht ' (123).

123. ' Sehnsucht ' (' Was zieht mir das Herz so? ' Goethe), Song (XX 35). 7th December 1814.

MS. Rough draft: the first thirteen bars—Graf Pallavicini, Vienna; the rest (together with ' Am See,' 124)—Stadtbibliothek, Vienna; fair copy made for Goethe—ditto.

1ST ED. c. 1842, A. Diabelli & Co., Vienna (no. 7415) as no. 2 of *Nachlass*, book 37 (transposed).

The first MS., with a different ending, is printed in the *Revisionsbericht* which, in the *Nachtrag*, p. 3, gives the following correction: p. 208, bar 8 of the voice part—the natural to be placed in front of the grace-note E. The song was republished, in its original key, in 1887, by Weinberger & Hofbauer, Vienna (no. 30) as no. 1 of three songs (book 2 of a collection of hitherto unpublished works by Schubert, ed. by Heinrich von Bocklet).

124. ' Am See ' (' Sitz' ich im Gras,' Mayrhofer), Song (XX 36). 7th December 1814.

MS. Rough draft (incomplete)—Stadtbibliothek, Vienna (together with ' Sehnsucht,' 123).

1ST ED. 1885, C. F. Peters, Leipzig, as no. 19 of twenty *Nachgelassene Lieder* (ed. by Max Friedlaender), the first twenty bars only, with alterations to the poem, by Max Kalbeck (second stanza added).

The *Revisionsbericht, Nachtrag*, p. 3, gives the following correction: p. 210, bar 8, right hand, add a quaver rest after the first chord. This song started the friendship between Schubert and Mayrhofer. The poem deals with the heroic end of Leopold, Duke of Brunswick-Luneburg, who met his death in an attempt to save his people at the inundation of Brunswick, an act immortalized earlier in verse by Goethe and Herder.

125. **Symphony in B flat** (I 2). 10th December 1814–24th March 1815.

MS. Score—Gesellschaft der Musikfreunde, Vienna; Parts, copied by another hand, June–July 1816—ditto, given to this Society by Josef Doppler in (December?) 1828.

IST PF. Probably 1815, Stadtkonvikt; first public performance 20th October 1877, Crystal Palace, London (conductor August Manns).

IST ED. 1884, Gesamtausgabe.

As indicated on the cover of the parts, the work was dedicated to Dr. Innocenz Lang, the director of the Vienna Stadtkonvikt, where Schubert lived from 1808 to 1813. Two other dates are to be found in the autograph: 26th December 1814 at the end of the first movement and 25th February 1815 at the beginning of the fourth movement.

126. '**Szene aus Goethe's "Faust"**' ('Wie anders, Gretchen, war dir's'), **Song**, two versions (XX 37 (*a*) and (*b*)). Finished 12th December 1814.

a **Sehr langsam** RECIT. BÖSER GEIST

Wie an-ders, Gret-chen, war dir's,

b **Sehr langsam** RECIT. BÖSER GEIST

Wie an-ders, Gret-chen, war dir's,

MS. (*a*) First sketch—Preussische Staatsbibliothek, Berlin; second sketch, dated December 1814—Conservatoire, Paris (Ph.); (*b*) Final version, dated 12th December 1814—lost (Witteczek's copy).

1ST ED. First sketch—1873, J. Guttentag, Berlin, in Reissmann's *Schubert*, Appendix no. 4, pp. 5–11. Final version— 22nd December 1832, A. Diabelli & Co., Vienna (no. 4268) as no. 2 of *Nachlass*, book 20.

In both versions Schubert omitted the last words of the poem. Version (*a*) is sketched for two voices, chorus, and pf. acc., but there the song was intended to be accompanied by an orchestra. Cf. 118, 367, 440, and 564.

127. '**Selig alle, die im Herrn entschlafen**' (from Hölty's 'Elegie. Bei dem Grabe meines Vaters'), **Canon for two Voices**. Lost. *c*. 1815 (?).

Schubert used the first stanza of the poem.

128. Twelve '**Wiener Deutsche**' for Pianoforte (XXI 23). *c*. 1815.

INTRODUZIONE
f

No 1.
p

No. 2.
p   *dolce*

MS. Stadtbibliothek, Vienna.
1ST ED. 1897, Gesamtausgabe.

Ferdinand Schubert is said to have been in possession of twelve German dances with a Coda written in 1815; they are apparently not identical with this work.

129. 'Mailied' ('Grüner wird die Au,' Hölty), Trio, T.T.B. (XIX 16). *c.* 1815.

Grü - ner wird die Au,

MS. Lost.
1ST ED. 1892, Gesamtausgabe.

Schubert also set this poem for two voices with acc. for two horns, 24th May 1815 (199), and as a solo song, November 1816 (503).

130. ' **Der Schnee zerrinnt** ' (from Hölty's ' Mailied '), **Canon for three Voices** (XIX 25). *c.* 1815.

Der Schnee zer - rinnt, der Mai be - ginnt und Vo - gel - schall tönt ü - ber - all.

MS. Lost.
1ST ED. 1892, Gesamtausgabe.

A copy of this canon is to be found in Albert Stadler's MS. copies of Schubert's songs, vol. i, dated 1816 (cf. 131). See the version dated 26th May 1815 (202).

131. ' **Lacrimoso son io** ' (author unknown), **two Canons for three Voices** (XIX 28 (*a*) and (*b*)). *c.* 1815.

FIRST VERSION
La - cri - mo - so, La - cri - mo - so son i - o, son i -

SECOND VERSION
La - cri - mo - so, La - cri - mo - so son i - o, son i -

MS. One part of the first canon—William Reeves, London.
1ST ED. 1892, Gesamtausgabe.

The MS. of the first canon is written on the same leaf as 242, 243, 244, and the sketch of the trio for male voices, ' Das Leben,' dated August 1815 (see note to 269). This canon, perhaps also written in August 1815, was copied by Albert Stadler in 1816, and is to be found in vol. i of his collection of Schubert's songs (Collection Otto Taussig, Malmö). Of the second canon only one part is copied in the Witteczek Collection.

132. ' Lied beim Rundetanz,' called ' Zum Rundetanz ' (Salis), Trio, T.T.B. Lost. *c.* 1815.

Fröhlich

Auf, es dun - kelt, sil - bern fun - kelt dort der Mond ob Tan - nen-höh'n

A MS. copy of the second tenor part (written by Anton Holzapfel?) is in the possession of the Krasser family, Vienna; see the same poem set for quartet, T.T.B.B. (983, no. 2).
Literature. O. E. D., ' Drei unbekannte Salis-Terzette von Schubert,' *Wiener Zeitung*, Vienna, 6th January 1938.

133. ' Lied im Freien ' (Salis), Trio, T.T.B. Lost. *c.* 1815.

Leicht

Wie schön, ist's im Frei - en bei grü - nen-dem Mai - en

A copy of the second tenor part (written by Anton Holzapfel?) is in the possession of the Krasser family, Vienna; see July 1817, the same poem set for quartet, T.T.B.B. (572).
Literature. See 132.

134. ' Ballade ' (' Ein Fräulein schaut vom hohen Turm,' Kenner), Song (Op. posth. 126; XX 99). *c.* 1815.

Mässig geschwind

Ein Fräu - lein schaut vom ho - hen Thurm,

MS. Lost.

1ST ED. 5th January 1830, Josef Czerny, Vienna (no. 2664) as Op. 126.

A MS. of the poem, dated June 1814, was in the possession of the Spaun family at Görz. Kreissle dated the song 1814; Nottebohm's date, 1825, is probably an error.

135. Trio for Pianoforte to the Waltz, Op. 127 (XII 8), no. 3. (?) 1815.

MS. Conservatoire, Paris (Ph.).
1ST ED. 1930, Ed. Strache, Vienna (no. 23) in *Deutsche Tänze*, etc. (ed. by O. E. D. and A. Orel), p. 13.

The MS. contains also the waltz to which this trio belongs. The waltz is identical with Op. 127 (146), no. 3, which has, however, a different trio. See 139. That this was not the first of Schubert's waltzes for pianoforte is proved by a letter written by Georg Gegenbauer to Ferdinand Luib on 6th April 1858 (Stadtbibliothek, Vienna); he sent some waltzes and a march, composed between 1808 and 1813, to Luib, which pieces, however, seem to be lost.

136. ' **Erstes Offertorium** ' (' Totus in corde ') **in C for Soprano or Tenor, Clarinet or Violin Concertante, Orchestra, and Organ** (Op. 46; XIV 1). (?) 1815.

MS. Conservatoire, Paris (Ph.).
1ST PF. 8th September 1825, Maria Trost-Kirche, Vienna.
1ST ED. (in parts). Autumn of 1825, A. Diabelli & Co., Vienna (no. 1900), dedicated by Schubert to Ludwig Tietze.

Page 1 of the MS. bears the inscription ' Allegretto. Aria mit Clarinett-Solo ... für Hr [Josef] Doppler.' Ferdinand Schubert listed an offertory, apparently this work, under the year 1815; the G.A. dated it *c.* 1816. Ferdinand's copy, made in 1855 (Gesellschaft der Musikfreunde, Vienna), gives no date of composition.

137. ' **Adrast,**' **Opera** by Johann Mayrhofer (XV 14). Fragment —thirteen numbers only. (?) 1815.

No. 2. RECIT. & ARIA (Bar.)
Andante molto

War ei - ner je der Ster - blich-en be - glückt,

No. 3. CHORUS & ENSEMBLE (Bar. and Male Chorus)
Maestoso

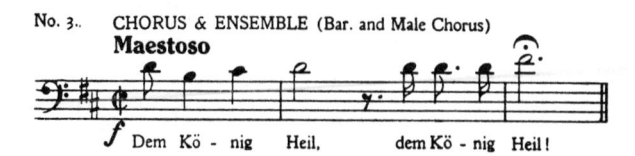

Dem Kö - nig Heil, dem Kö - nig Heil!

No. 4. FUNERAL MARCH (Orch.)

pp

No. 5. RECIT. & ARIA (Bar. and Ten.)
RECIT.

Wie liegst du starr und bleich, mein Sohn,

Andante

Wenn an - de - re mit heit' - rem Blick

No. 6. ARIA (Ten.)
Moderato

Mei - ne See - le, die dich liebt,

No. 7. RECIT & ARIA (Ten.)
Andante

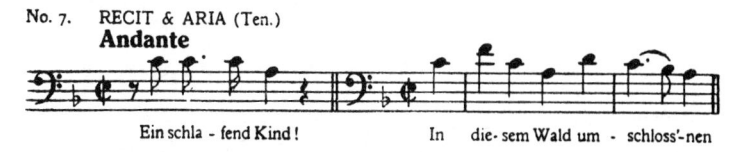

Ein schla - fend Kind! In die - sem Wald um - schloss'-nen

No. 8. (INTRODUCTION)
Moderato

p

66   138   1815

No. 9 DUET (Sopr. and Bass)
Allegretto

Er-heit' - re dich, der Lenz - ent-brei-tet

MS. Introduction and duet (nos. 8, 9, unpublished)—Nationalbibliothek, Vienna; remaining nos.—Stadtbibliothek, Vienna.

1ST PF. Introduction and duet (nos. 8, 9)—13th December 1868, Redoutensaal, Vienna (conductor, Johann Herbeck); aria (no. 6) with string acc., arranged by Herbeck—14th November 1875, Musikvereinssaal, Vienna.

1ST ED. 1893, Gesamtausgabe (without nos 8, 9 and four numbers of the main MS.).

This work is supposed by some to be of a later date (1818 or 1819 ?). Brahms advised the publishers on 7th March 1885 not to print this fragment. The libretto was lost sometime after 1843. The order of the numbers is uncertain.

138. '**Rastlose Liebe**' (Goethe), **Song** (Op. 5, no. 1; XX 177). (?) 1815.

Schnell, mit Leidenschaft ($\quarter = 152$)

Dem Schnee, dem Re-gen, dem Wind ent-ge-gen,

MS. Rough draft—lost; fair copy made for Goethe—Preussiche Staatsbibliothek, Berlin (Ph.); copy transposed for Karl Freiherr von Schönstein, May 1821—Conservatoire, Paris (Ph.).

1ST PF. 12th January 1826, Musikverein, Vienna.

1ST ED. 9th July 1821, Cappi & Diabelli, Vienna (no. 789), as no. 1 of Op. 5, published for Schubert and dedicated by him to Antonio Salieri.

On the back of the transposition (p. 6) are to be found the waltzes 145, nos. 5 and 8, written for Karoline, Komtesse Esterházy.

139. **Walzer in C sharp** (with Trio in A) **for Pianoforte.** 1815.

MS. Conservatoire, Paris (Ph.).
1ST ED. 1930, Ed. Strache, Vienna (no. 23) in *Deutsche Tänze*, etc. (ed. by O. E. D. and A. Orel), pp. 14–15.

The MS. also contains nos. 1, 3 (with a trio in E) and 4–11 of Op. 127 (146). See 135.

140. '**Klage um Ali Bey**' (Claudius) **for Trio**, S.S.A., with (?) Pianoforte accompaniment (XVIII 6). 1815.

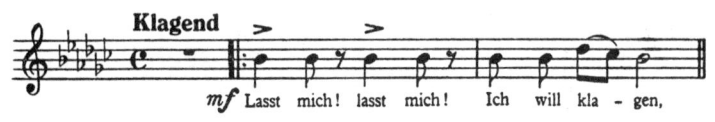

Klagend
mf Lasst mich! lasst mich! Ich will kla - gen,

MS. Lost.
1ST ED. *c.* 1848, A. Diabelli & Co., Vienna (no. 8822), as no. 3 of *Nachlass*, book 45.

The pf. acc., given in the first edition, seems to be spurious.

141. '**Der Mondabend**' (Ermin, i.e. J. G. Kumpf), **Song** (Op. posth. 131, no. 1; XX 43). 1815.

Lieblich, etwas geschwind
Rein und freund - lich lacht der Him - mel.

MS. Lost (Ebner's and Stadler's copies).
1ST ED. 9th November 1830, Josef Czerny, Vienna (no. 342), as no. 1 of Op. 131.

142. '**Geistes-Gruss**' (Goethe), **Song**, five versions (Op. 92, no. 3; XX 174 (*a*)–(*d*)). 1815.

a
RECIT.
Hoch auf dem al - ten Tur-me steht des Hel - den ed - ler Geist,

b
RECIT.
Hoch auf dem al - ten Tur-me steht des Hel - den ed - ler Geist,

B RECIT.

ƒ Hoch auf dem al - ten Tur-me steht des Hel - den ed - ler Geist,

c **Kraftvoll**
RECIT.

Hoch auf dem al - ten Tur-me steht des Hel - den ed - ler Geist,

d **Nicht zu langsam**

Hoch auf dem al - ten Tur - me

MS. (*a*) Lost (Stadler's copy); (*b* I) Karl Ernst Henrici, Berlin (12th January 1929); (*b* II) fair copy made for Goethe—Preussische Staatsbibliothek, Berlin (Ph.); (B) (score and voice-part)—Herzogin von Ratibor, Schloss Grafenegg (Lower Austria); (*c*) Fitzwilliam Museum, Cambridge (on the back of 'An Mignon,' 161 (*b*)); (*d*) Lost.

1ST ED. (*a*) and (*c*) 1895, Gesamtausgabe; (*b*) 1885, C. F. Peters, Leipzig, as no. 4 of twenty *Nachgelassene Lieder* (ed. by Max Friedlaender); (*d*) 11th July 1828, M. J. Leidesdorf, Vienna (no. 1014), as no. 3 of Op. 92 (erroneously called 87, but corrected on the title-page), dedicated by Schubert to Frau Josefine von Franck; (B) not printed.

The versions (*a*), (*b*), and (*c*) are in the key of E flat; version (B), probably written after (*b* I) and before (*c*), is written in D (in 1818?) for a bass voice (probably Johann Karl, Graf Esterházy); version (*d*) is in E. None of the preserved MSS. is dated, but Witteczek gives the date March 1816 for (*b* II), which is the fair copy of the second version. The MS. (*b* I) was formerly in the possession of Karl, Freiherr von Schönstein, and MS. (B) at one time belonged to Marie, Komtesse Breunner, *née* Esterházy (the count's elder daughter). Reissmann (*Schubert*, Berlin, 1873, p. 319) states that (*b*) was published in 1868 by W. Müller, Berlin; this, however, seems to be a mistake.

143. ' Genügsamkeit ' (Schober), **Song** (Op. posth. 109, no. 2; XX 181). 1815.

Etwas geschwind

Dort ra - get ein Berg aus den Wol - ken hehr,

1815

MS. Lost.
1ST ED. 10th July 1829, A. Diabelli & Co., Vienna (no. 3317), as no. 2 of Op. 109.
The pf. introduction is probably spurious.

— Johann Friedrich Reichardt's ' Monolog aus Goethe's Iphigenia,' copied by Schubert. See Appendix II, no. 4. 1815.

144. ' Romanze ' (' In der Väter Hallen ruhte,' Stolberg), Sketch of Song (XX, *Revisionsbericht*, p. 46). 1815 or 1816.

Ruhig, langsam

In der Vä - ter Hal - len ruh - te

MS. Erwin von Spaun, Vienna (together with 186, 188, and 411).
1ST ED. 1895, Gesamtausgabe.

145. Twelve Walzer, seventeen Ländler, and nine Écossaises for Pianoforte (Op. 18; XII 2). 1815–July 1821.

WALTZES
No. 1. (Atzenbrugger Deutsche No. 1.) No. 2. (Atzenbrugger Deutsche No. 4.)

No. 3. (Atzenbrugger Deutsche No. 2) No. 4.

No. 5. No. 6.

No. 7. No. 8.

No. 9.
No. 10.
pp
No. 11.
p
No. 12.
f
fz
fz
LÄNDLER
No. 1.
p
No. 2.
p
No. 3.
p
No. 4.
p
No. 5.
dolce
No. 6.
No. 7.
fp
fp
No. 8.
f
No. 9.
No. 10.
p
No. 11.
p
No. 12.
p
No. 13.
No. 14.
p
No. 15.
p
No. 16.
p
ÉCOSSAISES
No. 17.
f
No. 1.
p

MS. See the following entry; 299; entries before 679 and 697; entries 2 and 4 before 729; entry before 769; last two entries before 969; and 977; the autographs of the other dances—lost.

1ST ED. 5th February 1823, Cappi & Diabelli, Vienna (nos. 1216 and 1217, in two books).

—— **Nine Walzer for Pianoforte** (Op. 18; XII 2; Walzer 4-12). 1815-21.

MS. Nos. 5, 8, 9—Conservatoire, Paris (Ph.).

1ST ED. See 145.

The MS. of waltzes nos. 5 (in E flat minor) and 8 is entitled 'Deutsche für Comtesse Caroline' (i.e. Esterházy), but Schubert cancelled this dedication, crossing the name through, apparently in a very bad humour. These two dances are written on the back of the MS. 'Rastlose Liebe' (138), as transposed for Karl, Freiherr von Schönstein, May 1821. No. 9 is identical with the trio of no. 11 of twelve Deutsche Tänze (Op. 127), the MS. of which is in Paris (see 146).

146. Twenty Walzer for Pianoforte, called '**Letzte Walzer**' (Op. posth, 127, XII 8). 1815-24.

No. 1.

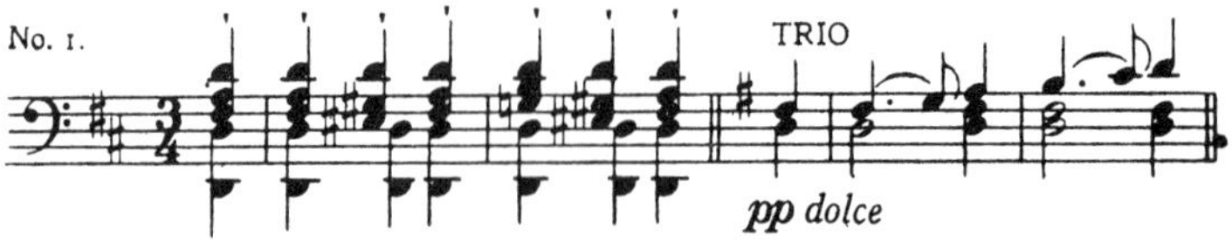

No. 2.

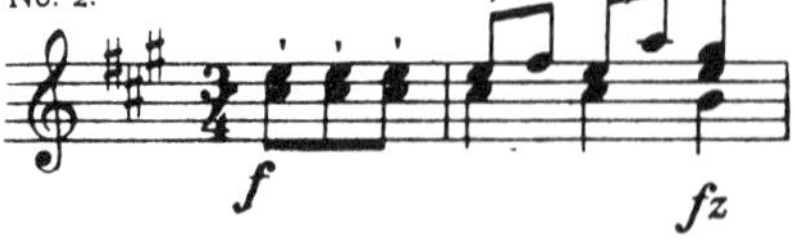

No. 3.

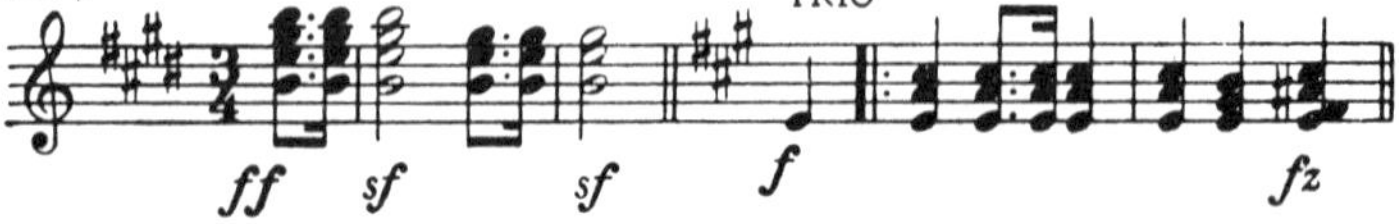

No. 4.

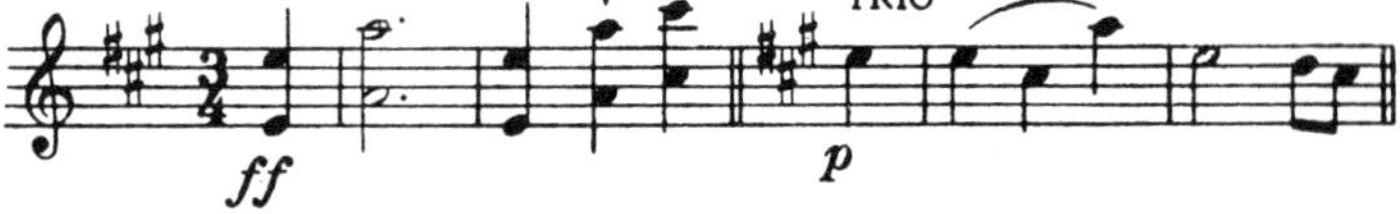

No. 5.

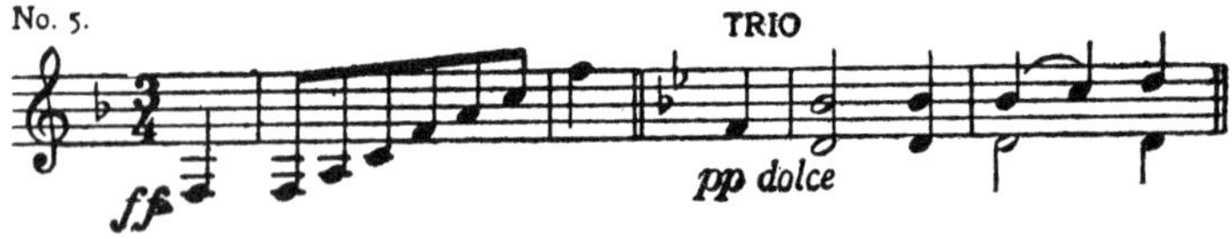

No. 6.

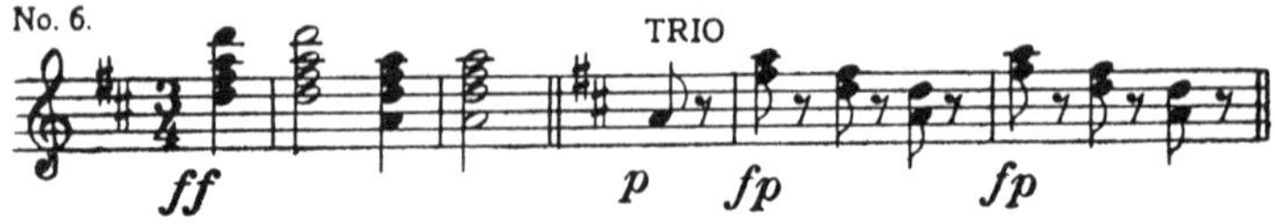

No. 7.

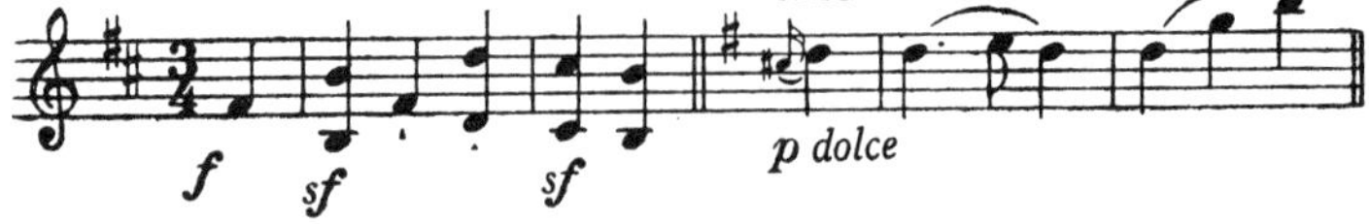

No. 8.

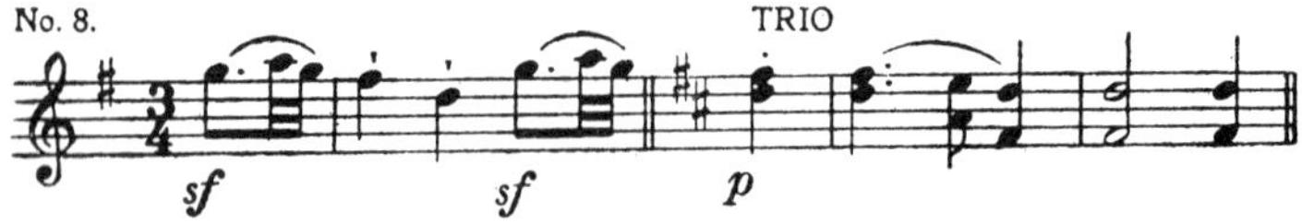

No. 9.

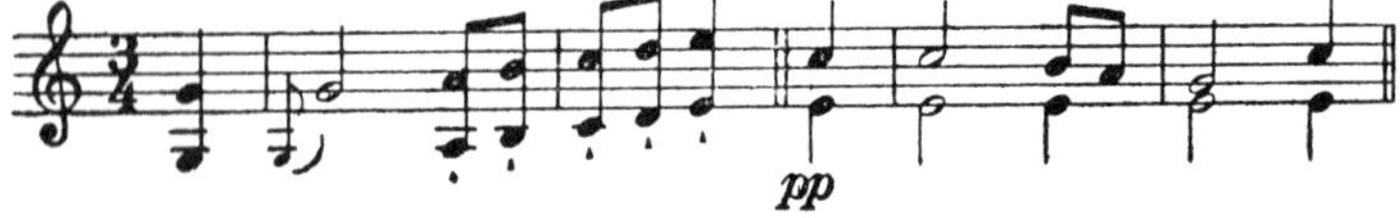

No. 10.
ff
TRIO
pp
No. 11.
f
TRIO
p
No. 12.
f
No. 13.
ff
fz
No. 14.
p
No. 15.
pp
No. 16.
f
No. 17.
pp
No. 18.
pp
No. 19.
8
p

No. 20.

Variant to No. 8.

MS. Seventeen of the twenty walzer, dated February 1823—Stadtbibliothek, Vienna; nos. 1, 3–11, with trios, dated 1815, together with two dances published in 1930 (135 and 139)—Conservatoire, Paris (Ph.); no. 2, dated 1824, entitled ' Deutsch ' (i.e. Deutscher Tanz), numbered in this MS. as no. 1 of four Deutsche Tänze (no. 2 being XII 18—769—no. 1; the nos. 3 and 4 being identical with Op. 33—783—nos. 1 and 2)—Heinrich Hinterberger, Vienna (1937); no. 8 (one of four) and no. 15 (one of six Deutsche Tänze), slightly different—Gesellschaft der Musikfreunde, Vienna (see 366 and 975).

1ST ED. 1830, A. Diabelli & Co., Vienna (no. 3579), under the title ' Franz Schubert's Letzte Walzer '; the op. no. was added only in later issues. For no. 2, see note.

No. 2 was published on 21st February 1824, as no. 5 in book 2 of the collection *Halt's enk zsamm* (Sauer & Leidesdorf, Vienna, no. 495). Variants to nos. 2 (very slight) and 13 are printed in the G.A., Series XII, supplement, pp. 158 and 160. Another trio (in E) to no. 3 was published, from the Paris MS., in 1930; see 135.

Literature. Ludwig Scheibler, *Zeitschrift der Internationalen Musikgesellschaft*, Leipzig 1907, vol. viii, p. 487.

147. ' **Bardengesang** ' (from Ossian's ' Comola,' translated by Harold), **Trio, T.T.B., with Pianoforte** accompaniment (XIX 15). 20th January 1815.

Ziemlich geschwind

Rol - le, du strö - mig - ter Ca - run

MS. Stadtbibliothek, Vienna.
1ST ED. 1892, Gesamtausgabe.

Eduard Baron de Harold's translation of Ossian was published in 1775 (2 vols.) and in 1782 (3 vols.). His MS., dedicated to Queen Charlotte, is in the National Library of Scotland, Edinburgh.

148. ' **Trinklied** ' (' Brüder, unser Erdenwallen,' Castelli) **for T.T.B.** (Solo and Chorus) **with Pianoforte accompaniment** (Op. posth. 131, no. 2; XIX 8). February 1815.

Mässig, fröhlich

Brü - der, un - ser Er - den - wal - len

MS. Lost.
1ST ED. 9th November 1830, Josef Czerny, Vienna (no. 342), as no. 2 of three songs, in later issues called Op. 131.

149. ' **Der Sänger** ' (Goethe), **Song**, two versions (Op. posth. 117; XX 45 (*a*) and (*b*)). February 1815.

a Heiter, mässig geschwind
RECIT.
Was hör' ich draus-sen vor dem Tor, was auf der Brü-cke schal-len?

b Mässig, heiter
RECIT.
Was hör ich draus-sen vor dem Tor, was auf der Brü-cke schal-len?

MS. (*a*) Rough draft—lost; (*b*) fair copy made for Goethe (together with ' Der Rattenfänger,' 255, and ' An den Mond,' 259)—Conservatoire, Paris (Ph.).
1ST ED. (*a*) 19th June 1829, Josef Czerny, Vienna (no. 340) as Op. 117, with list of Schubert's works on p. 2 (plate no. 335, from Op. 111); (*b*) 1894, Gesamtausgabe.

Goethe inserted this ballad in his novel, *Wilhelm Meister*.

150. ' **Loda's Gespenst** ' (' Spirit of Loda,' from Ossian's ' Carric-Thura,' translated by Harold), **Song** (XX 44). February 1815–17th January 1816.

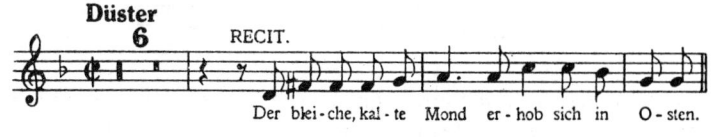

Düster
RECIT.
Der blei-che, kal - te Mond er - hob sich in O - sten.

MS. Rough draft—lost; another MS. (dated 17th January 1816)—Conservatoire, Paris (Ph.).

IST ED. 10th July 1830, A. Diabelli & Co., Vienna (no. 3633) as *Nachlass*, book 3 (Ossian Songs, book 3).

There seem to have been three MSS. in existence, one dated 29th August 1815. The first edition was corrupted by the addition of four spurious bars, and forty-two bars taken from the trio, T.T.B., ' Punschlied ' (277), arranged and supplied with new words by Leopold von Sonnleithner.

Literature. L. v. Sonnleithner, *Allgemeine musikalische Zeitung*, Leipzig, 30th January 1867.

151. ' **Auf einen Kirchhof** ' (Schlechta), **Song** (XX 39). 2nd February 1815.

Sei— ge - grüsst, ge - weih - te   Stil - le,

MS. Stadtbibliothek, Vienna.

IST ED. *c.* 1850, A. Diabelli & Co., Vienna (no. 8999), as no. 2 of *Nachlass*, book 49.

Schlechta later gave his poem the title ' Im Kirchhof.'

152. ' **Minona** ' (Bertrand), **Song** (XX 40).   8th February 1815.

Wie trei - ben die Wol- ken so fin - ster und

MS. Rough draft—Gesellschaft der Musikfreunde, Vienna; fair copy—Stadtbibliothek, Vienna.

IST ED. 1894, Gesamtausgabe.

The poet is perhaps Friedrich Anton Franz Bertrand.

153. ' **Als ich sie erröten sah** ' (Ehrlich), **Song** (XX 41).   10th February 1815.

All'____   mein   Wir - ken.

MS. Imperfect (without the last fourteen bars)—unknown; former owner—E. Kanitz, Vienna.

IST ED. *c.* 1842, A. Diabelli & Co., Vienna (no. 7417), as no. 1 of *Nachlass*, book 39.

In the Witteczek Collection the song is entitled ' **Die entfernte Geliebte, als ich sie erröten sah.**' The poet is perhaps Bernhard Ambros Ehrlich.

154. **Allegro in E for Pianoforte** (XXI 8). 11th February 1815.

MS. Stadtbibliothek, Vienna.
1ST ED. 1897, Gesamtausgabe.
This is the first movement of a sonata, i.e. one of several sketches (preserved in the MS.) for the Allegro of the Sonata in E, begun 18th February 1815 (157).

155. ' **Das Bild** ' (author unknown), **Song** (Op. posth. 165, no. 3; XX 42). 11th February 1815.

MS. Lost (Witteczek's copy).
1ST ED. *c.* 1864, C. A. Spina, Vienna (no. 9109 of his predecessors, A. Diabelli & Co., engraved *c.* 1852), as no. 3 of Op. 165.
The first edition is in the key of E flat.

156. **Ten Variations in F for Pianoforte** (XI 6). Finished 15th February 1815.

MS. Conservatoire, Paris (Ph.); a fragment—Theme, indicated ' Andante molto,' and second variation—Wittgenstein family, Vienna (together with the song ' Lambertine,' 301).
1ST ED. 1887, Weinberger & Hofbauer, Vienna (no. 21, ed. by Heinrich von Bocklet), as book 1 of a collection of hitherto unpublished Schubert works.

157. Sonata in E for Pianoforte (X 1).   Begun 18th February 1815.

Allegro ma non troppo

Andante

MENUETTO
Allegro vivace

TRIO
sempre stacc.

MS. Stadtbibliothek, Vienna.
IST ED. 1888, Gesamtausgabe.

The last movement is missing. The first movement, finished on 21st February, exists in an earlier version dated 11th February 1815 (154).

158. Écossaise in F for Pianoforte (XII 29).   21st February 1815.

MS. Unknown; former owner—J. A. Schulz, Leipzig (8th June 1889, sale catalogue, no. 187).
IST ED. 1889, Gesamtausgabe.

159. ' Die Erwartung ' (Schiller), **Song** (Op. posth. 116; XX 46). 27th February 1815 (May 1816).

Langsam RECIT.

Hör' ich das Pfört-chen nicht ge - hen?

MS. Rough draft—lost; another MS. dated May 1816—Martin Bodmer, Zürich; fair copy—lost.

IST ED. 13th April 1829, M. J. Leidesdorf, Vienna (no. 1153), as Op. 116, dedicated (by Schubert?) to Josef Hüttenbrenner.

The MS. preserved does not correspond exactly with the first edition. Leidesdorf possibly purchased this work from Schubert himself. There is no evidence concerning the dedication. Zumsteeg's song, the model on which Schubert based this song, published September 1800 in the second volume of Zumsteeg's *Kleine Balladen und Lieder*, Breitkopf & Härtel, Leipzig, is reprinted in the G.A. supplement to the first issue of vol. iii of Schubert's songs, pp. 6–10 (Breitkopf & Härtel, no. 20, 865, published 1895).

Literature. Georg Kinsky, Katalog des Wilhelm Heyer-Museums (Cologne), vol. iv, Leipzig 1916, pp. 195–7.

160. ' **Am Flusse** ' (Goethe), Song, first version (XX 47). 27th February 1815.

Wehmütig

Ver - flie - sset, viel - ge - lieb - te Lie-der,

MS. Preussische Staatsbibliothek, Berlin (together with ' An Mignon ' and ' Nähe des Geliebten,' 161 and 162).

IST ED. 1894, Gesamtausgabe.

Schubert set this poem again in December 1822 (766).

161. ' **An Mignon** ' (' Ueber Tal und Fluss getragen,' from Goethe's ' Wilhelm Meister '), Song, two versions (Op. 19, no. 2; XX 48 (*a*) and (*b*)). 27th February 1815.

a
Klagend, mässig

Ü - ber Tal und Fluss ge - tra - gen,

b
Etwas geschwind

Ü - ber Tal und Fluss ge - tra - gen,

MS. (*a*) Rough draft (together with 160 and 162) and fair copy made for Goethe (without the last four bars)—Preussische Staatsbibliothek, Berlin (Ph.); (*b*) without date—Fitzwilliam

Museum, Canbridge (on the back of the song 'Geistes-Gruss,' 142 (c)).

1ST ED. (a) 1894, Gesamtausgabe; (b) 6th June 1825, A. Diabelli & Co., Vienna (no. 1800), as no. 2 of Op. 19, dedicated by Schubert to Goethe.

162. 'Nähe des Geliebten' (Goethe), **Song,** two versions (Op. 5, no. 2; XX 49 (a) and (b)). 27th February 1815.

[Musical notation: (a) Sehr langsam, feierlich mit Anmut — "Ich den-ke dein, wenn mir der Son-ne Schim-mer"]

[Musical notation: (b) Langsam, feierlich mit Anmut (♩.= 50) — "Ich den-ke dein, wenn mir der Son-ne Schim-mer"]

MS. (a) First and only MS. (together with 160 and 161)—Preussische Staatsbibliothek, Berlin; (b) rough draft—Dr. Arthur Dacy, New York (together with 163); fair copy made for Goethe—Preussische Staatsbibliothek, Berlin (Ph.).

1ST ED. (a) 1894, Gesamtausgabe; (b) 9th July 1821, Cappi & Diabelli, Vienna (no. 789, without plate-mark), published for Schubert, and dedicated by him to Antonio Salieri.

Both versions were written on the same day; only the fair copy (for Goethe) is undated.

163. 'Sänger's Morgenlied' (Körner), **Song,** first version (XX 50). 27th February 1815.

Lieblich, etwas geschwind

Sü - sses Licht! Aus go! - de-nen Pfor - ten

MS. Dr. Arthur Dacy, New York (together with 162 (b)).
IST ED. 1894, Gesamtausgabe.
For the second version, see 165.

164. ' **Liebesrausch** ' (Körner), **Song**, first version. Fragment. March 1815.

Glanz des Gu-ten und des Schö-nen strahlt mir dein ho - hes Bild.

MS. (the last bars only, together with 174)—The Heineman Foundation, New York.
IST ED. January 1928, *Musik aus aller Welt*, Vienna, vol. i, no. 1, p. 7 (ed. by O. E. D.).
The beginning of the MS. is lost, only six bars of the music, together with the second and third stanzas of the words, are preserved. This version was cancelled by Schubert. It was first dealt with in *Das Ende vom Lied* by O. E. D., in the MS. ' Festschrift zum 70. Geburtstag Eusebius Mandyczewski's,' Vienna 1927. For the second version, see 179.

165. ' **Sängers Morgenlied** ' (Körner), **Song**, second version (XX 51). 1st March 1815.

Langsam

Sü - sses Licht! Aus gold' - - - nen

MS. Preussische Staatsbibliothek, Berlin.
IST ED. 1872, J. P. Gotthard, Vienna (no. 359), as no. 35 of forty songs.
For the first version, see 163.

166. ' **Amphiaraos** ' (Körner), **Song** (XX 52). 1st March 1815.

Etwas langsam, mit Kraft
RECIT.

Vor The-bens sie-ben-fach gäh - nen-den Tor - en

MS. Stadtbibliothek, Vienna.
1ST ED. 1894, Gesamtausgabe.
The MS. bears the indication ' In 5 Stunden ' (written within five hours).

167. Mass in G for Trio, S.T.B., Mixed Chorus, Strings (two violins, viola, contrabass), **and Organ in G** (XIII 2). 2nd–7th March 1815.

MS. Score—Gesellschaft der Musikfreunde, Vienna; Violino I part—Otto Taussig, Malmö; other parts (including the first additional parts by Ferdinand Schubert)—unknown, formerly Augustinian Abbey, Klosterneuburg, near Vienna.
1ST PF. Probably in the spring of 1815, Liechtentaler Kirche, Vienna.
1ST ED. (in parts) 1846, Marco Berra, Prague (no. 1140), under the name of Robert Führer (a plagiarism).

Ferdinand Schubert supplied parts for trumpets and kettledrums during Schubert's lifetime, and on 25th July 1847 he added parts for oboes and bassoons. Berra's successor, Josef Hoffmann's Widow, later reprinted the work under Schubert's name (nos. 2954 and 3254).
Literature. Ferdinand Schubert, *Wiener Allgemeine Musikzeitung*, 14th December 1847 (on Führer's plagiarism).

168. ' Begräbnislied ' (Klopstock), **Quartet, S.A.T.B., with Pianoforte accompaniment** (XVII 16). 9th March, 1815.

Langsam, ernst

pp Be - grabt den Leib in sei - ner Gruft

MS. Gilhofer & Ranschburg, Vienna (see 172).
1ST ED. 1872, J. P. Gotthard, Vienna (no. 323), as no. 8 of nine part-songs.

The text is a variant of the hymn, ' Nun lasset uns den Leib begraben.'

169. ' Trinklied vor der Schlacht ' (Körner), **Unison Song** (XX 53). 12th March 1815.

Schnell und feurig
2. CHORUS   1. CHORUS

ff Schlacht, du brichst an!   Schlacht, du brichst an!

MS. Gilhofer & Ranschburg, Vienna (see 172).
1ST ED. 1894, Gesamtausgabe.

The date is ascertained by the fact that this song is written on a MS. between two other songs of the same date. Josef von Gahy, in his arrangement for pf. duet made in 1863 (Stadtbibliothek, Vienna), indicates this song as written for quartet, T.T.B.B. The G.A., however, describes it as written for two unison choruses, with pf. acc., and gives cues for first and second chorus.

170. ' Schwertlied ' (Körner), **Song with Chorus** (XX 54). 12th March 1815.

Kräftig und stark

Du Schwert an mei-ner Lin-ken,

MS. Gilhofer & Ranschburg, Vienna (see 172).
1ST ED. 1873, J. Guttentag, Berlin, in Reissmann's *Schubert*, Appendix no. 1, pp. 1–2.

The poem, consisting of sixteen stanzas, was written a few hours before Körner's death, on 26th August 1813; Weber, too, set it in the same year as Schubert. Josef von Gahy, in his arrangement for pf. duet made in 1863 (Stadtbibliothek, Vienna), indicates Schubert's song as written for quartet, T.T.B.B. Cf. 363.

171. '**Gebet während der Schlacht**' (Körner), **Song** (XX 55). 12th March 1815.

Etwas langsam

Va-ter, ich ru-fe dich!

MS. Gilhofer & Ranschburg, Vienna (see 172).
1ST ED. 21st April 1831, A. Diabelli & Co., Vienna (no. 3707), as no. 7 of *Nachlass*, book 10.
The MS. is in B flat, the printed versions, however, are in G.

172. '**Der Morgenstern**' (Körner), **Song**. Fragment. Not printed. 12th March 1815.

MS. Gilhofer & Ranschburg, Vienna (1933, Collection of Josef Dessauer).

The MS. contains, besides the one line of this unfinished song, three other Körner songs (169–171); it contains also the mixed quartet (168). The poem, shortly afterwards, was set by Schubert as a duet (203).

— **Symphony in B flat** (I 2). See 125. 24th March 1815.

173. **String Quartet in G minor** (V 9). 25th March–1st April 1815

Allegro con brio

Andantino

MENUETTO
Allegro vivace

TRIO

Allegro

MS. Score—Gesellschaft der Musikfreunde, Vienna; Parts—unknown; former owner—Friedrich Schreiber, Vienna (Diabelli's and Spina's successor).
1ST PF. 1815, at Schubert's home; first public performance—29th November 1863, Musikverein, Vienna (Josef Hellmesberger's Quartet).
1ST ED. End of 1871, C. F. Peters, Leipzig (no. 5376, edition nos. 796–7, score and parts).

174. 'Das war ich' (Körner), **Song**, two versions (XX 56). 26th March 1815 (June 1816).

Erzählend

Jüngst träum-te mir, ich sah auf lich - -ten

SECOND VERSION

MS. (together with **164**)—The Heineman Foundation, New York.
1ST ED. c. 1842, A. Diabelli & Co., Vienna (no. 7417), as no. 2 of *Nachlass*, book 39.

On the back of the ' Fragment aus dem Aeschylus ' (**450**, Conservatoire, Paris), Schubert sketched another version of ' Das war ich ' in June 1816, printed in the *Revisionsbericht*.

175. Stabat Mater in G minor for Chorus, Orchestra, and Organ (XIV 12). 4th–6th April 1815.

Andante con moto

Sta - bat ma - ter do - lo - ro - sa

MS. Stadtbibliothek, Vienna.
1ST ED. 1888, Gesamtausgabe.

176. 'Die Sterne' ('Was funkelt ihr so mild,' Fellinger), Song (XX 57). 6th April 1815.

Lieblich, ziemlich langsam

Was fun - kelt ihr so mild mich an?

MS. Lost (Stadler's and Witteczek's copies).
1ST ED. 1872, J. P. Gotthard, Vienna (no. 344), as no. 30 of forty songs.

177. 'Vergebliche Liebe' (Josef Karl Bernard), Song (Op. posth. 173, no 3; XX 58). 6th April 1815.

Nicht zu geschwind

Ja, ich weiss es,

MS. Unknown; former owner—E. Rudorff, Berlin.
1ST ED. 1867, C. A. Spina, Vienna (no. 19,176), as no. 3 of Op. 173.

178. **Adagio in G for Pianoforte,** two versions (XXI 22). 8th April 1815.

FIRST VERSION

SECOND VERSION

MS. Stadtbibliothek, Vienna.
1ST ED. 1897, Gesamtausgabe.

There are two versions; only the first is dated, the second is incomplete (at least in the MS.).

179. ' **Liebesrausch** ' (Körner), **Song**, second version (XX 59). 8th April 1815.

Langsam

Dir, Mäd - chen, schlägt mit lei - sem Be - ben

MS. Schubertbund, Vienna (together with 180).
IST ED. 1872, J. P. Gotthard, Vienna (no. 343), as no. 29 of forty songs (this song dedicated by the publisher to Julius Stockhausen).

For the first version, see 164.

180. ' **Sehnsucht der Liebe** ' (Körner), **Song**, two versions (XX 60). 8th April (July) 1815.

FIRST VERSION

Wie die Nacht mit heil' - gem Be - ben

SECOND VERSION
Ruhig, langsam

Wie die Nacht mit heil' - gem Be - ben

MS. First version, fragment only—Schubertbund, Vienna (together with 179); second version—lost.
IST ED. 1894, Gesamtausgabe (second version).

Schubert's MS., the first few bars of which are given in the *Revisionsbericht*, consists only of the first eight bars, and these differ from the MS. copy of the song in the Witteczek Collection and from Stadler's copy. The G.A. used the copies. It seems that these copies were made from another MS., of July 1815, a second version of the song.

181. Offertory (' Tres sunt ') **in A minor, for Chorus, Orchestra, and Organ** (XIV 4). 10th–11th April 1815.

Allegro moderato maestoso

f Tres sunt, qui te - sti - mo - ni -um dant in coe - lo;

MS. Conservatoire, Paris (Ph.).
1ST ED. 1888, Gesamtausgabe.

182. ' **Die erste Liebe** ' (Fellinger), **Song** (XX 61).   12th April 1815.

Mässig, mit Ausdruck

Die er - ste Lie - be

MS. Lost (Witteczek's copy).
1ST ED. *c.* 1842, A. Diabelli & Co., Vienna (no. 7413), as no. 1 of *Nachlass*, book 35 (transposed into the key of B flat major).

183. ' **Trinklied** ' ('Ihr Freunde und du, gold'ner Wein,' also called ' **Freundschaft und Wein,**' Alois Zettler), **Song** (XX 62). 12th April 1815.

Mässig, lustig

Ihr Freun - de und du gold' ner Wein

MS. Lost (Witteczek's copy).
1ST ED. 1887, C. F. Peters, Leipzig, as no. 30 of *Schubert Album*, book 7 (ed. by Max Friedlaender).

Witteczek described this work as a ' song with chorus.'

184. **Gradual** ('Benedictus es, Domine') **in C for Chorus, Orchestra, and Organ** (Op. posth. 150; XIV 5).   15th April 1815.

Adagio maestoso

f Be - ne - di - ctus es, Do-mi-ne, qui in - tu - e - ris a - bys - sos et

Allegro

f Al - le - lu - ja, al' - le - lu - -

MS. Wiener Männergesangverein, Vienna.
1ST ED. *c.* 1843, A. Diabelli & Co., Vienna (no. 7973).

Ferdinand Schubert added to the MS. a German translation of the words, and entitled the work ' Hymne.'

185. Second Dona Nobis for the Mass in F, Quartet, S.A.T.B., with Mixed Chorus, Orchestra, and Organ (XIII 1 (*a*)). 25th April 1815.

Allegro moderato

f Do - na no - bis pa - cem,

MS. Stadtbibliothek, Vienna.
1ST ED. 1887, Gesamtausgabe.

This second Dona nobis may have been written for an intended revival of the Mass in F (105).

186. '**Die Sterbende**' (Matthisson), **Song** (XX 65). (?) May 1815.

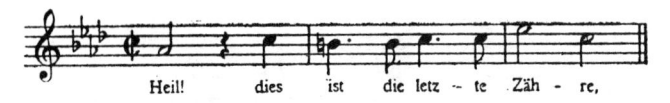

Heil! dies ist die letz - te Zäh - re,

MS. Erwin von Spaun, Vienna (together with 144, 188, and 411).
1ST ED. 1894, Gesamtausgabe.

This song is written on the same MS. as three other songs: ' Naturgenuss,' May 1815; 'Daphne am Bach,' April 1816; and the sketch for Stolberg's ' Romanze,' 1815 or 1816. It is thought that the song was written at the same time as ' Naturgenuss ' (188). Since the music was not suitable for the two other stanzas of the poem Schubert cancelled it altogether.

187. '**Stimme der Liebe**' ('Abendgewölke schweben hell,' Matthisson), **Song**, first version (XX 63). May 1815.

Lieblich

A - bend - ge - wöl - ke schwe - ben hell

MS. Stadtbibliothek, Vienna (together with no. 188).
1ST ED. 1894, Gesamtausgabe.

Schubert set this poem again as a song on 29th April 1816 (418). He wrote many love songs in May 1815, probably as a result of his passion for Therese Grob.

188. '**Naturgenuss**' (Matthisson), **Song** (XX 64). May 1815.

Ruhig

Im A - bend - schim - mer wallt der Quell

MS. Stadtbibliothek, Vienna (together with no. 187); another MS.—Erwin von Spaun, Vienna (together with 144, 186, and 411).
1ST ED. 1887, C. F. Peters, Leipzig, as no. 36 of *Schubert Album*, book 7 (ed. by Max Friedlaender).

The last bar is missing in the MS., but is to be found, together with the two other stanzas, on the MS. of 186. Schubert set the poem as a male voice quartet, T.T.B.B., in May 1816 (422). It was also used later by editors as the text of a song combining the famous ' Trauerwalzer ' (Op. 9, no. 2), and the waltz, Op. 9, no. 14 (see entry before 350, and 365), called— like the quartet—Op. 16.

189. ' **An die Freude** ' (Schiller), **Song** (Op. posth. III, no. 1; XX 66). May 1815.

Lebhaft

Freu - de, schö - ner Göt - ter - fun - ken,

MS. Lost.
1ST ED. 5th February 1829, Josef Czerny, Vienna (no. 335), as no. 1 of Op. 111.

Beethoven was occupied even earlier with this poem, which he finally used in his Ninth Symphony.

190. ' **Der vierjährige Posten**,' Singspiel in one Act by Theodor Körner (XV 2). 8th–19th May 1815.

OVERTURE
Larghetto

No. 1. INTRODUCTION (Mixed Chorus, Sopr., Ten. and Bass)
Allegretto con moto
mezza voce

Hei - ter strahlt der neu - e Mor - gen, Luft und

No. 2. DUET (Sopr. and Ten.)
Allegro vivace
a piacere

Du gut - er Hein - rich! Du süs - ses Kind!

No. 3. TERZET (Sopr., Ten. and Bass)
       Adagio con moto
       mezza voce

Mag dich die Hoff - nung nicht be - trü - gen! An

No. 4. QUARTET (Sopr., 2 Ten. and Bass)
       Allegro
       RECIT.

Freund, ei - let euch zu ret - ten! Das zwei - te Re - gi -

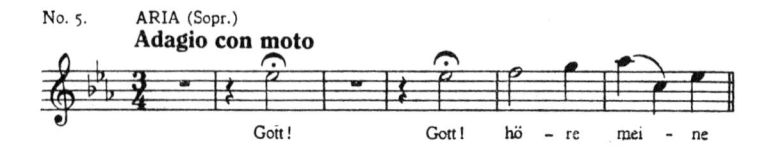

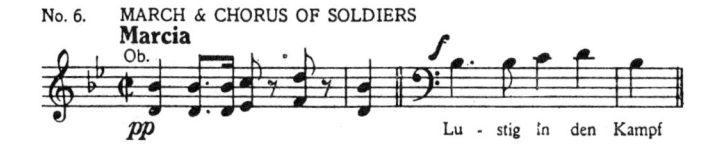

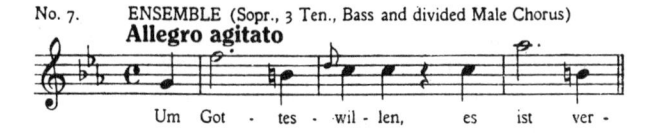

No. 5. ARIA (Sopr.)
       Adagio con moto

Gott! Gott! hö - re mei - ne

No. 6. MARCH & CHORUS OF SOLDIERS
       Marcia

pp Lu - stig in den Kampf

No. 7. ENSEMBLE (Sopr., 3 Ten., Bass and divided Male Chorus)
       Allegro agitato

Um Got - tes - wil - len, es ist ver -

No. 8. FINALE (Sopr., Contralto, Ten., Bass and Mixed Chorus)
       Allegro con brio

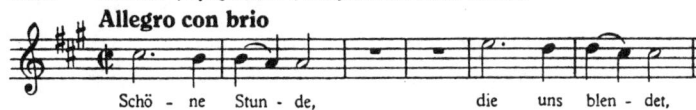

Schö - ne Stun - de, die uns blen - det,

MS. Overture only—Stadtbibliothek, Vienna; remainder—Gesellschaft der Musikfreunde, Vienna; vocal score of no. 5—Otto Taussig, Malmö.

1ST PF. The chorus, T.T.B.B., ' Lustig in den Kampf ' (no. 6)—8th December 1860, Redoutensaal, Vienna (conductor Johann Herbeck); stage performance—23rd September 1896, Dresden (arranged by Robert Hirschfeld).

1ST ED. 1888, Gesamtausgabe.

The libretto, originally entitled ' Die Vedette,' was written in Vienna

(1812), and published there in 1813, in which year Karl Steinacker's setting of it was performed at the Theater an der Wien.

—— ' **Der Morgenstern** ' (Körner), **Song**. Sketch—see 203. 12th May 1815.

191. ' **Des Mädchens Klage** ' (from Schiller's play ' Die Piccolomini '), **Song**, second version, in two (three) variants (Op. 58, no. 3; XX 67 (*a*) and (*b*)). 15th May 1815.

a Langsam
Der Eich-wald braust, die Wol - ken zieh'n,

b Sehr langsam
Der Eich-wald braust, die Wol - ken ziehn,

MS. (*a*) Stadtbibliothek, Vienna (together with 192–4); (*b*) lost.
1ST ED. (*a*) 1894, Gesamtausgabe; (*b*) 6th April 1826, Thaddäus Weigl, Vienna (no. 2493), as no. 3 of Op. 56, later corrected to Op. 58.

The MS. shows the variant (*a*), but the last seven bars are cancelled, and replaced by two other bars. These two bars are altered again in the variant (*b*), which differs only slightly in the voice part; an introduction and a postlude, however, are added to the latter. The MS. is reproduced in facsimile in Heuberger's *Schubert*, Berlin, 1902, facing pp. 32 f. Schubert set the poem in 1811 (6) and again in March 1816 (389). Cf. the note to 113.

192. ' **Der Jüngling am Bache** ' (Schiller), **Song**, second version (XX 68). 15th May 1815.

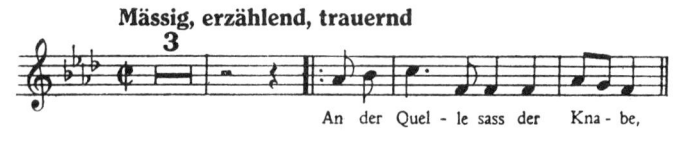

Mässig, erzählend, trauernd
An der Quel - le sass der Kna - be,

MS. Stadtbibliothek, Vienna (together with **191**, **193–4**).
1ST ED. 1887, C. F. Peters, Leipzig, as no. 40 of *Schubert Album*, book 7 (ed. by Max Friedlaender).

For the first and third versions, see 24th September 1812 (30), and *c.* 1819 (638).

193. ' **An den Mond** ' (' Geuss, lieber Mond,' Hölty), **Song** (Op. 57, no. 3; XX 69). 17th May 1815.

Langsam, wehmütig

Geuss, lie - - ber Mond,

MS. Stadtbibliothek, Vienna (together with 191, 192, and 194).
1ST ED. 6th April 1826, Thaddäus Weigl, Vienna (no. 240), as no. 3 of Op. 57 (no. 6 of the combined Opp. 56—*recte* 58- -and 57), with a spurious introduction.

The poem was written in 1774. Another MS. of the song was to be found in the collection of Ludwig Landsberg, Rome, *c.* 1850. Cf. the note to 113.

194. ' **Die Mainacht** ' (Hölty), **Song** (XX 70). 17th May 1815.

Ziemlich geschwind

Wann der sil - ber - ne Mond

MS. Stadtbibliothek, Vienna (together with 191-3).
1ST ED. 1894, Gesamtausgabe.

195. ' **Amalia** ' (from Schiller's play ' Die Räuber '), **Song** (Op. posth. 173, no. 1; XX 71). 19th May 1815.

Mässig, lieblich

Schön wie En - gel voll Wal- hal - la's Won - ne,

MS. Unknown; former owner—Gustav Petter, Vienna (Stadler's and Witteczek's copies).
1ST PF. 13th June 1816, at Frau von Jenny's home, Vienna (sung by Schubert).
1ST ED. 1867, C. A. Spina, Vienna (no. 19,174), as no. 1 of Op. 173.

196. ' **An die Nachtigall** ' (' Geuss nicht so laut,' Hölty), **Song** (Op. posth. 172, no. 3; XX 72). 22nd May 1815.

*Unruhig, klagend
Im Zeitmasse wachsend bis zur Haltung*

Geuss nicht so laut - der lieb - ent- flamm- ten Lie - der

MS. Lost (Stadler's and Witteczek's copies).
1ST ED. 1866, C. A. Spina, Vienna (no. 16,784, plate no. 16,751), as no. 3 of Op. 172.

197. ' **An die Apfelbäume, wo ich Julien erblickte** ' (Hölty), **Song** (XX 73). 22nd May 1815.

Langsam, feierlich

Ein hei - lig Säu - seln, und ein Ge - san - ges - ton

MS. Fragment—Conservatoire, Paris, together with 198.
1ST ED. *c.* 1850, A. Diabelli & Co., Vienna (no. 9000), as no. 1 of *Nachlass*, book 50.

The poem was originally entitled ' An die Apfelbäume, als ich Laura erblickte.' The MS. contains only the last thirteen bars, the other fifteen are missing.

198. ' **Seufzer** ' (Hölty), **Song** (XX 74). 22nd May 1815.

Ziemlich geschwind

Die Nach - ti - gall singt ü - ber - all

MS. Conservatoire, Paris (Ph.), together with the fragment of 197.
1ST ED. 1894, Gesamtausgabe.

Hölty's poem is entitled ' Die Nachtigall.'

199. ' **Mailied** ' (' Grüner wird die Au,' called ' Frühlingslied,' Hölty) **for two Voices or two Horns** (XIX 30). 24th May 1815.

Freudig

Grü - ner wird die Au, und der Him - mel blau!

MS. Unknown; former owner—F. G. Arendt, Hildesheim (together with 201).
1ST ED. 1885, C. F. Peters, Leipzig, as no. 7 of eight duets (ed. by Max Friedlaender).

The date is taken from a copy of the work by Ferdinand Schubert, which is preserved in the Krasser family, Vienna, together with a copy of 201. The third stanza, which is included in the MS., is missing in the G.A. This duet and four others, dated 26th May 1815 (202–5), were probably written for the Vienna Waisenhaus (Orphanage). For the other settings of the same poem, see the trio 129 and the unpublished song of November 1816 (503).

200. Symphony in D (I 3).   24th May–19th July 1815.

[Adagio maestoso — musical incipit]

[Allegro con brio — musical incipit]

[Allegretto — musical incipit]

[Menuetto Vivace — musical incipit]

[Trio — musical incipit]

[Presto. Vivace — musical incipit]

MS. Gesellschaft der Musikfreunde, Vienna.
1ST PF. Probably 1815, at a private music society meeting in Vienna; first public performance, last movement only, 2nd December 1860—Redoutensaal, Vienna (conductor Johann Herbeck); complete work—19th February 1881, Crystal Palace, London (conductor August Manns).
1ST ED. 1884, Gesamtausgabe.

Three other dates are to be found in the autograph: at bar 64 of the first movement—11th July; at the end of this movement—12th July; and at the beginning of the second movement—15th July. The symphony was written for twelve wind instruments and kettledrums.

201. ' Auf den Tod einer Nachtigall ' (Hölty), **Sketch of Song.** Fragment. Not printed. 25th May 1815.

MS. Unknown; former owner—F. G. Arendt, Hildesheim (together with 199).

A copy of the MS., made by Ferdinand Schubert on 8th March 1855, was in the possession of the Krasser family, Vienna. This sketch is in A, *alla breve*; although the voice part is nearly complete, the accompaniment is only written for the first half of the song. For the other setting, see 13th March 1816 (399).

202. ' Mailied ' (' Der Schnee zerrinnt,' Hölty), **for two Voices or two Horns** (XIX 31). 26th May 1815.

Fröhlich

Der Schnee zer-rinnt, der Mai be-ginnt,

MS. Lost.

1ST ED. 1885, C. F. Peters, Leipzig, as no. 8 of eight duets (ed. by Max Friedlaender).

Probably written for the Vienna Waisenhaus. For the other setting, as a canon for three voices, see 130.

203. ' Der Morgenstern ' (Körner), **for two Voices or two Horns** (XIX 32). 26th May 1815.

Lieblich

Stern der Lie - be, Glanz - ge - bil - de,

MS. Wittgenstein family, Vienna (together with 205 and 206).

1ST ED. 1892, Gesamtausgabe.

Schubert first attempted to set this poem as a solo song on 12th March 1815 (172). The duet was probably written for the Vienna Waisenhaus.

204. ' Jägerlied ' (from Körner's collection ' Leyer und Schwert ') **for two Voices or two Horns** (XIX 33). 26th May 1815.

Muthig, freudig

Frisch auf, ihr Jä - ger, frei und flink!

MS. Score (one half-leaf oblong folio, with the text of the first stanza; on the back of the leaf sixteen lines of a poem by Hölty, copied by Schubert)—Mrs. Mary Louise Zimbalist, Philadelphia.
IST ED. 1892, Gesamtausgabe.
Probably written for the Vienna Waisenhaus.

205. ' Lützow's wilde Jagd ' (from Körner's collection ' Leyer und Schwert '), for two Voices or two Horns (XIX 34). 26th May 1815.

Feurig, geschwind

Was glänzt dort vom Wal-de im Son - nen-schein?

MS. Wittgenstein family, Vienna (together with 203 and 206).
IST ED. 1892, Gesamtausgabe.
Probably written for the Vienna Waisenhaus.

206. ' Liebeständelei ' (Körner), Song (XX 75). 26th May 1815.

Etwas geschwind

Sü - sses Lieb - chen! Komm zu mir!

MS. Wittgenstein family, Vienna (together with 203 and 205).
IST ED. 1872, J. P. Gotthard, Vienna (no. 335), as no. 11 of forty songs; this song dedicated by the publisher to Gustav Walter.

207. ' Der Liebende ' (Hölty), Song (XX 76). 29th May 1815.

Mit drängender Eile

Be - glückt, be - glückt, wer dich er - blickt,

MS. Gesellschaft der Musikfreunde, Vienna (together with 210).
IST ED. 1894, Gesamtausgabe.
Kreissle (p. 605) calls this song, by mistake, ' Die Schiffende.' The original title of the poem was ' Lied eines Liebenden.'

208. ' Die Nonne ' (Hölty), Song, first version (XX 77, *Revisionsbericht*). 29th May 1815.

MS. First part (two-thirds)—Stadtbibliothek, Vienna; second part (last third, incomplete)—Nationalbibliothek, Vienna (together with 492).

1ST ED. 1894, Gesamtausgabe (*Revisionsbericht*, pp. 20–3: Introduction and middle section only).

For the second version, see 212.

209. ' **Der Liedler** ' (Kenner), **Song** (Op. 38; XX 98). June–12th December 1815.

MS. Xaver Mayerhofer von Grünbühel, Völkermarkt (Kärnten).
1ST ED. 9th May 1825, Cappi & Co., Vienna (no. 110), as Op. 38, dedicated by Schubert to the poet, Josef Kenner.

The *Revisionsbericht* shows the differences between the MS. and the first edition. A MS. of the poem is dated 1813. There exist some unfinished sketches by Moritz von Schwind, illustrating the poem (reproduced in O. E. D.'s *Franz Schubert, sein Leben in Bildern*, Munich, 1913, plates 195–201).

210. ' **Klärchen's Lied,**' called ' **Die Liebe** ' (from Goethe's play ' Egmont '), **Song** (XX 78). 3rd June 1815.

MS. Gesellschaft der Musikfreunde, Vienna (together with 207).
1ST ED. 1838, A. Diabelli & Co., Vienna (no. 5034), as no. 2 of *Nachlass*, book 30.

The title ' Die Liebe ' was taken by Schubert from Reichardt's collection of Goethe songs.

211. ' **Adelwold und Emma** ' (Bertrand), **Song** (XX 79). 5th–14th June 1815.

Mässig, ernst

Hoch, und eh - ern schier von Dau - er,

MS. Stadtbibliothek, Vienna.
IST ED. 1894, Gesamtausgabe.
The poet was perhaps Friedrich Anton Franz Bertrand.

212. 'Die Nonne' (Hölty), Song, second version (XX 77). 16th June 1815.

Mässig, erzählend

Es liebt' in Welsch-land ir - gend-wo ein

MS. Stadtbibliothek, Vienna.
IST ED. 1894, Gesamtausgabe.
For the first version, see 208.

213. 'Der Traum' (Hölty), Song (Op. posth. 172, no. 1; XX 80). 17th June 1815.

Tändelnd. Sehr leise

Mir träumt', ich war ein Vö - gel-ein,

MS. Lost (Stadler's and Witteczek's copies).
IST ED. 1866, C. A. Spina, Vienna (no. 16,784, plate no. 16,749), as no. 1 of Op. 172.
Hölty's poem was entitled 'Ballade.'

214. 'Die Laube' (Hölty), Song (Op. posth. 172, no. 2; XX 81). 17th June 1815.

Mit Wehmut, langsam

Nim - mer werd' ich, nim - mer dein ver - ges - sen,

MS. Lost (Witteczek's copy).
IST ED. 1866, C. A. Spina, Vienna (no. 16,784, plate no. 16,750), as no. 2 of Op. 172.

215. 'Jägers Abendlied' (Goethe), **Song,** first version. 20th June 1815.

Sehr langsam

Im Fel - de schleich' ich still und wild,

MS. (together with 216)—Frau Anna Siegmund, Znaim-Znojmo (Czechoslovakia).
1ST ED. 'Die Musik,' Berlin, 15th January 1907, vol. vi, no. 7, supplement, pp. 2–3 (ed. by Eusebius Mandyczewski).

For the second setting of this poem, see 368.

216. 'Meeres Stille' (Goethe), **Song** (Op. 3, no. 2; XX 82). 20th–21st June 1815.

Sehr langsam, ängstlich (♩ = 72)

Tie - fe Stil - le herrscht im Was - ser,

MS. First sketch, dated 20th June 1815 (together with 215)—Frau Anna Siegmund, Znaim-Znojmo (Czechoslovakia); rough copy (together with 217)—Gesellschaft der Musikfreunde, Vienna; a cancelled version of the last five bars on a MS. of 'Cronnan,' 5th September 1815 (282)—Moritz von Caesar, Baden, near Vienna; fair copy made for Goethe—Preussische Staatsbibliothek, Berlin (Ph.).
1ST ED. 22nd May 1821, Cappi & Diabelli, Vienna (no. 768), as no. 2 of Op. 3, published for Schubert and dedicated by him to Ignaz von Mosel.

The metronomic indication 27 in the *Gesamtausgabe* is a misprint for 72. Schubert did not set to music the companion poem, 'Glückliche Fahrt' (cf. Beethoven's Op. 112, composed in 1815 and published in 1823).

217. 'Colma's Klage' (from Ossian's 'The Songs of Selma,' translated by (?) Franz von Hummelauer), **Song** (XX 83). 22nd June 1815.

Ziemlich langsam

Rund um mich Nacht, ich irr' al - lein,

MS. Rough copy (without the first of the three parts, indicated
'Ziemlich langsam,' *alla breve*)—Moritz von Caesar, Baden, near
Vienna; final version (incomplete, together with 216)—Gesellschaft der Musikfreunde, Vienna.

1ST ED. 10th July 1830, A. Diabelli & Co., Vienna (no. 3632),
as no. 2 of *Nachlass*, book 2 (Ossian Songs, book 2).

The first MS. (parts 2 and 3) has three instead of two stanzas to each
part. The second MS. is entitled 'Lieder nach Ossian. Kolma's Klage I.'
Unlike the other Ossian songs set by Schubert the German version of this
poem is not by Harold. It resembles somewhat Goethe's translation of the
same poem as inserted in his novel *Werther's Leiden*. Anton Schindler says
that Hummelauer revised the German version of Ossian's songs for Schubert. Schubert since his schooldays knew Zumsteeg's setting of this poem,
published in 1793. Reichardt used Harold's translation and published his
song in 1798.

218. '**Grablied**' (Kenner), **Song** (XX 84). 24th June 1815.

Langsam

Er fiel den Tod fürs Va - ter-land.

MS. Unknown; former owner—Heyer Museum, Cologne (together
with 219).

1ST ED. *c.* 1848, A. Diabelli & Co., Vienna (no. 8819), as no. 4
of *Nachlass*, book 42.

A MS. of the poem, dated 18th July 1813, was formerly in the possession
of the von Spaun family at Görz.

219. '**Das Finden**' (Kosegarten), **Song** (XX 85). 25th June 1815.

Etwas langsam, unschuldig

Ich hab' ein Mäd-chen fun - den,

MS. Rough copy—unknown; former owner—Heyer Museum,
Cologne (together with 218); fair copy—Albert Cranz, New
York.

1ST ED. *c.* 1848, A. Diabelli & Co., Vienna (no. 8819), as no. 2
of *Nachlass*, book 42.

220. '**Fernando**,' **Singspiel** in one Act by Albert Stadler (XV 3).
27th June–9th July 1815.

No. 1. INTRODUCTION
Largo

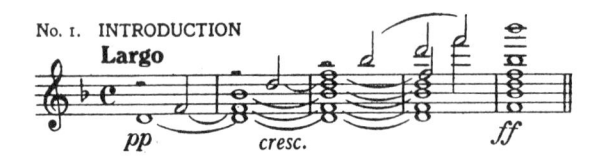

pp — *cresc.* — *ff*

RECIT. (Sopr.)

Mut - ter! Mut - ter! Wo bist du?

No. 2. ARIA (Ten.)
Allegro moderato

Lässt mich mein Ver - bre - chen nicht schla - fen?

No. 3. ROMANCE (Sopr.)
Andantino quasi Allegretto

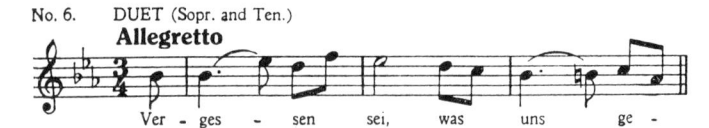

Als einst schon hin - ter blau - er Ber - ge Rü - cken im

No. 4. DUET (Sopr. and Ten.)
Andante

Wärst du mir auf im - mer nicht ent - ris - sen,

No. 5. ARIA (Sopr.)
Allegro maestoso

Nicht der Er - de Schät - ze loh - nen, was hier

No. 6. DUET (Sopr. and Ten.)
Allegretto

Ver - ges - sen sei, was uns ge -

No. 7. FINALE (2 Sopr., Ten. and Basses)

Auf dich träuf - le Thau - es - re - gen,

MS. Stadtbibliothek, Vienna.
IST PF. The final chorus—21st March 1830, Landhaussaal, Vienna (conductor Ferdinand Schubert); concert performance —13th April 1907, Vienna (Wiener Schubertbund); stage

performance—18th August 1918, Magdeburg (music revised by B. Engelke).

1ST ED. 1888, Gesamtausgabe.

The name of the author is indicated on the MS. only by his initials. The time signature of no. 6 is indicated in the G.A. erroneously as 4/4. In Stadler's autograph text, dated 28th April 1815, below the list of dramatis personae, there is the following note by Schubert: 'Die Musik ist von Franz Schubert, Schüler des H[errn] Salieri.' (Collection Otto Taussig, Malmö.)

—'Sehnsucht der Liebe' (XX 60). See note to 180. July 1815.

221. 'Der Abend' ('Der Abend blüht, Temora glüht,' Kosegarten), Song (Op. posth. 118, no. 2; XX 95). July 1815.

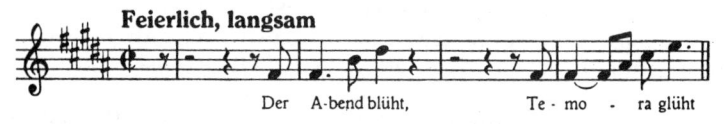

MS. Fair copy—Albert Cranz, New York.

1ST ED. 19th June 1829, Josef Czerny, Vienna (no. 341), as no. 2 of Op. 118.

Kosegarten's first version of the poem reads 'Der Abend blüht, Arkona glüht,' Arkona being a promontory of the isle of Rügen. Temora is probably the residence of Ossian's kings of Ireland. Leopold Ebner, in a letter written 1858 to Ferdinand Luib (Stadtbibliothek, Vienna), called Schubert's song, copied by Ebner before 1818, 'Temora.'

222. 'Lieb Minna' (Albert Stadler), Song (XX 86). 2nd July 1815.

MS. Stadtbibliothek, Vienna.

1ST ED. 1885, C. F. Peters, Leipzig, as no. 14 of twenty *Nachgelassene Lieder* (ed. by Max Friedlaender).

In Stadler's copy of the song it is indicated that the second and the third stanzas are to be sung without the pause (⌒) between the stanzas.

223. 'Zweites Offertorium' ('Salve Regina') in F for Soprano, Orchestra, and Organ (Op. 47; XIV 2). 5th July 1815, and 28th January 1823.

Andante con moto

Sal - ve Re - gi - na, sal - ve Re - gi - na

MS. First version—Preussische Staatsbibliothek, Berlin; the additional wind-instrument parts (see note)—Otto Taussig, Malmö.
IST PF. 8th September 1825, Maria Trost-Kirche, Vienna.
IST ED. (in parts) 4th August 1825, A. Diabelli & Co., Vienna (no. 1901)—second version.
The first version was written for Therese Grob's soprano voice with acc. for two violins and organ; the second for soprano with orchestral acc. Ferdinand Schubert made a copy of the first version, to which Schubert added the parts for wind instruments on 28th January 1823; Ferdinand made a separate score for the wind instruments on 29th January 1823 (Hans Laufer, London). The wind parts are indicated *ad libitum*.

224. '**Wandrers Nachtlied**' (I, 'Der du von dem Himmel bist,' Goethe), **Song**, (Op. 4, No. 3; XX 87). 5th July 1815.

Langsam, mit Ausdruck (♩ = 50)

Der du von dem Him - mel bist,

MS. Rough copy (together with 225)—British Museum, London; fair copy made for Goethe—Preussische Staatsbibliothek, Berlin (Ph.).
IST ED. 29th May 1821, Cappi & Diabelli, Vienna (no. 773), as no. 3 of Op. 4, published for Schubert and dedicated by him to Johann Ladislaus Pyrker von Felsö-Eör.

225. '**Der Fischer**' (Goethe), **Song** (Op. 5, no. 3; XX 88). 5th July 1815.

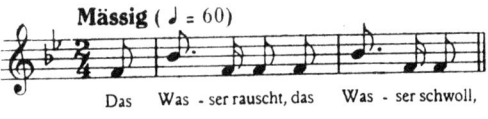

Mässig (♩ = 60)

Das Was - ser rauscht, das Was - ser schwoll,

MS. Rough copy (together with 224)—British Museum, London; fair copy made for Goethe—Preussische Staatsbibliothek, Berlin (Ph.).
IST ED. 9th July 1821, Cappi & Diabelli, Vienna (no. 789), as no. 3 of Op. 5, published for Schubert and dedicated by him to Antonio Salieri.

226. '**Erster Verlust**' (Goethe), **Song** (Op. 5, no. 4; XX 89). 5th July 1815.

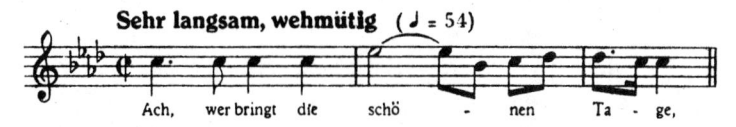

[musical incipit: Sehr langsam, wehmütig (♩ = 54) — Ach, wer bringt die schö - nen Ta - ge,]

MS. Rough copy—unknown; former owner—Gustav Petter, Vienna; fair copy made for Goethe—Preussische Staatsbibliothek, Berlin (Ph.).

1ST ED. 9th July 1821, Cappi & Diabelli, Vienna (no. 789), as no. 4 of Op. 5, published for Schubert and dedicated by him to Antonio Salieri.

The MS. bears the time signature ¢ (*alla breve*) and the first edition C (4/4).

227. '**Idens Nachtgesang**,' called '**Ida's Nachtgesang**' (Kosegarten), **Song** (XX 90). 7th July 1815.

[musical incipit: Zart, langsam — Ver - nimm es, Nacht, was I - da dir ver-trau - et,]

MS. British Museum, London (Ph.); another MS.—Albert Cranz, New York.

1ST ED. 1885, C. F. Peters, Leipzig, as no. 8 of twenty *Nachgelassene Lieder* (ed. by Max Friedlaender).

The first MS. is reproduced in Herbert Antcliffe's *Schubert*, London, 1910, after p. 60. The second MS. may be a fair copy.

228. '**Von Ida**' (Kosegarten), **Song** (XX 91). 7th July 1815.

[musical incipit: Klagend — Der Mor - gen blüht; der O - sten glüht;]

MS. Rough copy—Walter Schatzki, New York; fair copy—Albert Cranz, New York.

1ST ED. 1894, Gesamtausgabe.

In later editions of Kosegarten's works the poem is entitled 'Agnes.'

229. '**Die Erscheinung**,' called '**Erinnerung**' ('Ich lag auf grünen Matten,' Kosegarten), **Song** (Op. 108, no. 3; XX 92). 7th July 1815.

MS. Rough copy—Walter Schatzki, New York; fair copy—Albert Cranz, New York.
1ST ED. 11th December 1824, Sauer & Leidesdorf, Vienna (no. 590), in *Album musicale*, vol. ii; reprinted 9th December 1825, ditto, in the collection *Guirlandes*, book 3; again, 28th January 1829, M. J. Leidesdorf, Vienna (no. 1102), as no. 3 of Op. 93 (later corrected to Op. 108), under the title 'Erinnerung.' This Op. '93' was advertised as early as Easter 1828.

230. '**Die Täuschung**' ('Im Erlenbusch, im Tannenhain,' Kosegarten), **Song** (Op. posth. 165, no. 4; XX 93). 7th July 1815.

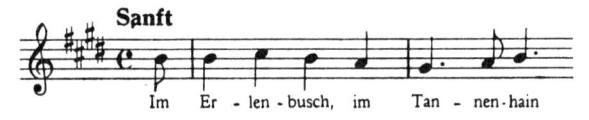

MS. First copy (together with 231)—Dr. Alwin Cranz, Vienna; fair copy (together with 231)—Stadtbibliothek, Vienna (Ph.).
1ST ED. 11th May 1855, as a supplement to *Zellner's Blätter für Musik, Theater und Kunst*, C. A. Spina, Vienna, vol. i, no. 29; reprinted *c.* 1864, C. A. Spina, Vienna (no. 16,553, engraved *c.* 1858) as no. 4 of Op. 165.

231. '**Das Sehnen**' (Kosegarten), **Song** (Op. posth. 172, no. 4; XX 94). 8th July 1815.

MS. First copy (together with 230)—Dr. Alwin Cranz, Vienna; fair copy (together with 230)—Stadtbibliothek, Vienna (Ph.).
1ST ED. 1866, C. A. Spina, Vienna (no. 16,784, plate no. 16,758), as no. 4 of Op. 172.

232. '**Hymne an den Unendlichen**' (Schiller), **Quartet, S.A.T.B.,** with **Pianoforte accompaniment** (Op. posth. 112, no. 3; XVII 8). 11th July 1815.

Mit Majestät. Sehr langsam

f Zwi - schen Him - mel und Erd' hoch

MS. (first draft, without the acc. to the last seven bars)—Stadtbibliothek, Vienna.
1ST PF. 28th February 1836, Redoutensaal, Vienna.
1ST ED. 11th March 1829, Josef Czerny, Vienna (no. 338 on the plates, no. 339 on the title-page), as no. 3 of three quartets, Op. 112, and separately.

For alterations in the MS. see *Revisionsbericht*. The copy made by Albert Stadler in 1816 practically corresponds with the first edition. The word 'Blitz,' instead of 'Blick,' is a misprint in both editions.

—— **Symphony in D** (I 3). See 200. 11th–19th July 1815.

233. '**Geist der Liebe**' ('Wer bist du,' Kosegarten), **Song** (Op. posth. 118, no. 1; XX 96). 15th July 1815.

Mit Kraft

Wer bist du, Geist der Lie - be,

MS. Albert Cranz, New York.
1ST ED. 19th June 1829, Josef Czerny, Vienna (no. 341), as no. 1 of Op. 118.

234. '**Tischlied**' (Goethe), **Song** (Op. posth. 118, no. 3; XX 97). 15th July 1815.

Guter Laune

Mich er - greift, ich weiss nicht wie,

MS. Fair copy made for Goethe—Stadtbibliothek, Vienna.
1ST ED. 19th June 1829, Josef Czerny, Vienna (no. 341), as no. 3 of Op. 118.

Goethe's poem ('Mich ergreift, ich weiss nicht wie') is a paraphrase of the student song 'Mihi est propositum in taberna mori.'

235. '**Abends unter der Linde**' (Kosegarten), **Song**, first version (XX 100). 24th July 1815.

[musical notation: Wo-her, o— na-men-lo-ses Seh-nen,]

MS. Preussische Staatsbibliothek, Berlin (together with 240).
1ST ED. 1894, Gesamtausgabe.
For the second version, see 237.

236. ' **Das Abendrot** ' ('Der Abend blüht, der Westen glüht,' Kosegarten), **for three Voices with Pianoforte accompaniment** (XIX 6). 25th July 1815.

[musical notation: *mf* Der A-bend blüht, der We-sten glüht!]

MS. (together with 237 and 238)—Dr. Alwin Cranz, Vienna.
1ST ED. 1892, Gesamtausgabe.
The date, 20th July 1815, as given by Nottebohm and in the G.A., is wrong. According to Witteczek, the acc. is *ad libitum*.

237. ' **Abends unter der Linde** ' (Kosegarten), **Song**, second version (XX 101). 25th July 1815.

[musical notation: Langsam — Wo-her, o na-men-lo-ses Seh-nen,]

MS. Rough copy—Albert Cranz, New York; fair copy (together with 236 and 238)—Dr. Alwin Cranz, Vienna.
1ST ED. 1872, J. P. Gotthard, Vienna (no. 334), as no. 10 of forty songs, this song dedicated by the publisher to Gustav Walter.
For the first version, see 235.

238. ' **Die Mondnacht** ' (Kosegarten), **Song** (XX 102). 25th July 1815.

[musical notation: Mässig — Sie-he, wie die Mon-des-strah-len]

MS. First copy, dated and signed (together with 236 and 237)—Dr. Alwin Cranz, Vienna; fair copy, without date or signature —Fitzwilliam Museum, Cambridge.
1ST ED. 1894, Gesamtausgabe.

239. '**Claudine von Villa Bella**,' **Singspiel** in three Acts by Goethe (XV 11). Incomplete. Begun 26th July 1815.

OVERTURE
Adagio

No. 1. INTRODUCTION (Sopr., Ten., Bass)
Allegro moderato

Das hast du wohl be - rei - tet,

No. 2. ENSEMBLE (Sopr., Ten., Bass and Mixed Chorus)
Allegretto

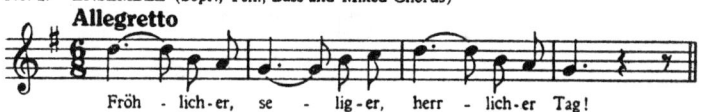

Fröh - lich-er, se - lig-er, herr - lich-er Tag!

No. 3. ARIETTA (Sopr.)
Allegretto

Hin und wie - - der flie-gen die Pfei - le,

No. 4. ARIA (Sopr.)
Andantino

Al - le Freu - den, al - le Ga - ben,

No. 5. ARIA (Ten.)
Maestoso

Es er - hebt sich ei - ne Stim - me,

No. 6. ARIETTA (Sopr.)
Andantino quasi Allegretto

Lie - be schwärmt auf al - len We - gen;

No. 7. SONG OF VAGABONDS (Ten. and Male Chorus)
Andantino

Mit Mäd - chen sich ver - tra - gen,

No. 8. FINALE OF ACT I. (Ten., Bass and Male Chorus)
Allegro ma non troppo

Dei-nem Wil - len nach - zu - ge - ben,

No. 9. ARIETTA (Ten.)
Andante con moto

Lieb - li-ches Kind, kannst du mir sa-gen,

No. 10. DUET (Sopr. and Bass)
Andante

Mich um-fängt ein ban - ger Schau-er

MS. Voice parts of two ariettas (' Liebliches Kind,' from Act II, and ' Liebe schwärmt auf allen Wegen,' from Act I), and of the duet ' Mich umfängt ein banger Schauer,' from Act III—Dr. Franz Roehn, Los Angeles; full score of the overture and Act I—Gesellschaft der Musikfreunde, Vienna.

1ST PF. A performance of the overture, intended to be given at the Landhaussaal, Vienna, on 1st October 1818, was cancelled; Act I (with pf. acc. by Adolf Kirchl)—26th April 1913, Gemeindehaus Wieden, Vienna (Wiener Schubertbund).

1ST ED. Claudine's arietta ' Liebe schwärmt auf allen Wegen ' and Lucinde's arietta ' Hin und wieder fliegen die Pfeile ' (with pf. acc.)—1885, C. F. Peters, Leipzig (no. 6895), as nos. 5 and 6 of twenty *Nachgelassene Lieder* (ed. by Max Friedlaender); score of the overture and Act I—1893, Gesamtausgabe.

The first act was finished on 5th August 1815. The second and the third acts of the MS. were accidentally burned at Josef Hüttenbrenner's lodgings in Vienna in 1848. Rugantino's arietta from Act II and Claudine's and Pedro's duet from Act III, preserved without acc., have not been published. Josef Hüttenbrenner started to make an arrangement for piano duet, but it was never finished. The MS. of this fragment of Hüttenbrenner's arrangement was in the possession of Rudolf Weis-Ostborn, Graz.

240. ' **Huldigung** ' (Kosegarten), **Song** (XX 103). 27th July 1815.

Etwas geschwind

Ganz— ver - lo - ren, ganz— ver - sun - ken

MS. Rough draft (together with 235)—Preussische Staatsbibliothek, Berlin; first copy—Albert Cranz, New York; fair copy (together with 241)—Dr. Alwin Cranz, Vienna.

1ST ED. 1894, Gesamtausgabe.

The first version of bar 12 is given in the *Revisionsbericht*. The poem, consisting of nine stanzas, was entitled ' Minnesang ' in later editions of Kosegarten's works.

241. ' **Alles um Liebe** ' (Kosegarten), **Song** (XX 104). 27th July 1815.

Mässig, herzlich

Was ist es, das die See - le füllt?

MS. Rough draft (together with 6)—Preussische Staatsbibliothek, Berlin; first copy—Albert Cranz, New York; fair copy (together with 240)—Dr. Alwin Cranz, Vienna.

1ST ED. 1894, Gesamtausgabe.

The poem consists of ten stanzas.

242. ' **Trinklied im Winter** ' (Hölty), **Trio, T.T.B.** (XIX 18). (?) August 1815.

Feurig

Das Glas ge - füllt! der Nord - wind brüllt;

MS. William Reeves, London.

1ST ED. 1892, Gesamtausgabe.

The MS. is written on the same leaf as 131, 243, 244, and the sketch of the trio for male voices, ' Das Leben,' dated August 1815 (see note to 269).

243. '**Frühlingslied**' ('Die Luft ist blau,' author unknown), **Trio, T.T.B.** (XIX 19). (?) August 1815.

Die Luft ist blau, das Tal ist grün,

MS. William Reeves, London.
1ST ED. 1892, Gesamtausgabe.

The MS. is written on the same leaf as 131, 242, 243, and the sketch of the trio for male voices, 'Das Leben,' dated August 1815 (see note to 269). Schubert also set the poem as a solo song on 13th March 1816 (398). It was wrongly attributed to Hölty.

244. '**Willkommen, lieber schöner Mai**' (from Hölty's 'Mailied'), **two Canons for three Voices**, two versions (XIX 27 (*a*) and (*b*)). (?) August 1815.

a
Will-kom-men, lie-ber schö-ner Mai,

b
Will-kom-men, lie-ber schö-ner Mai,

MS. William Reeves, London.
1ST ED. 1892, Gesamtausgabe.

Both versions are written on the same leaf as 131, 242, 243, and the sketch of the trio for male voices, 'Das Leben,' dated August 1815 (see note to 269).

—— '**Das Leben**' (Wannovius), **Sketch of a Trio, T.T.B.** See 269. August 1815.

—— '**Lacrimoso son io**,' **Canon** (XIX 28*a*). See 131. August 1815.

245. '**An den Frühling**' (Schiller), **Song**, first version, in **B flat** (XX 107 (*a*)). August 1815.

Will-kom-men, schö-ner Jüng-ling!

MS. (dated)—Dr. Alwin Cranz, Vienna.
1ST ED. 1885, C. F. Peters, Leipzig, as no. 15 of twenty *Nachgelassene Lieder* (ed. by Max Friedlaender).

For the second version, see 283; for the version in the key of A, see 587; for the setting as quartet, T.T.B.B., see 338.

246. ' **Die Bürgschaft** ' (Schiller), **Song** (XX 109). August 1815.

MS. Lost.
1ST ED. 26th October 1830, A. Diabelli & Co., Vienna (no. 3705), as *Nachlass*, book 8.

Schubert in 1816 used a libretto, based on the same legend, for an unfinished opera (435).

247. ' **Die Spinnerin** ' (Goethe), **Song** (Op. posth. 118, no. 6; XX 119). August 1815.

MS. Rough draft—lost; fair copy made for Goethe—Preussische Staatsbibliothek, Berlin (Ph.).
1ST ED. 19th June 1829, Josef Czerny, Vienna (no. 341), as no. 6 of Op. 118.

248. ' **Lob des Tokayers** ' (Gabriele von Baumberg), **Song** (Op. posth. 118, no. 4; XX 135). August 1815.

MS. Lost.
1ST ED. 19th June 1829, Josef Czerny, Vienna (no. 341), as no. 4 of Op. 118.

249. ' **Die Schlacht** ' (Schiller). First sketch of a **Cantata.** Not printed. 1st August 1815.

MS. Rudolf Ibach, Vienna.
See the second sketch, March 1816 (387).

—— '**Wer kauft Liebesgötter?**' **Song.** See note to **261.** 4th August 1815.

250. '**Das Geheimnis**' ('Sie konnte mir kein Wörtchen sagen,' Schiller), **Song,** first version (XX 105). 7th August 1815.

Sehr langsam

Sie konn - te mir kein Wört - chen sa - gen.

MS. Dr. Alwin Cranz, Vienna (together with 251).
1ST ED. 1872, J. P. Gotthard, Vienna (no. 352), as no. 28 of forty songs; this song dedicated by the publisher to Julius Stockhausen.

According to Kreissle, p. 603, there were two versions, one of 1815 and the other of 1816, the MSS. of which at one time were in the possession of Karoline, Komtesse Esterházy. If this is correct, then the second version is lost. For the later version, see May 1823 (793).

251. '**Hoffnung**' ('Es reden und träumen die Menschen,' Schiller), **Song,** first version (XX 106). 7th August 1815.

Etwas geschwind

Es re - den und träu - men· die Men - schen viel

MS. Sketch—unknown; former owner—Ludwig Landsberg, Rome; final version—Dr. Alwin Cranz, Vienna (together with 250).
1ST ED. 1872, J. P. Gotthard, Vienna (no. 347), as no. 23 of forty songs; this song dedicated by the publisher to Nikolaus Dumba.

For the second version, see 637.

252. '**Das Mädchen aus der Fremde**' (Schiller), **Song,** second version (XX 108). 12th August 1815.

Langsam, lieblich

In ei - nem Tal bei ar - men Hir - ten

MS. Lost (see Note).

IST ED. 1887, C. F. Peters, Leipzig, as no. 41 of *Schubert Album*, book 7 (ed. by Max Friedlaender).

In the Witteczek Collection there is a copy of the MS. made by Ferdinand Schubert. For the first version, see 117.

253. ' Punschlied. Im Norden zu singen ' ('Auf der Berge freien Höhen,' Schiller), Song (XX 110). 18th August 1815.

Auf der Ber - ge frei - en Hö - hen,

MS. Dr. Alwin Cranz, Vienna (together with 254).
IST ED. 1887, C. F. Peters, Leipzig, as no. 42 of *Schubert Album*, book 6 (ed. by Max Friedlaender).

Schubert set another ' Punschlied ' by Schiller for trio, T.T.B., with pf. acc., 29th August 1815 (277).

254. ' Der Gott und die Bajadere. Indische Legende ' (Goethe), Song (XX 111). 18th August 1815.

Ma - ha - döh, der Herr— der — Er - de,

MS. Rough draft (together with 253)—Dr. Alwin Cranz, Vienna; fair copy for Goethe—Conservatoire, Paris (Ph.), together with ' Nachtgesang ' (119), ' Sehnsucht ' (310 (*b*)), and ' Mignon ' (321).

IST ED. 1887, Weinberger & Hofbauer, Vienna (no. 30), as no. 2 of three songs, in book 2 of a collection of hitherto unpublished Schubert works (ed. by Heinrich von Bocklet).

Max Friedlaender published this song in the same year (1st October 1887) as no. 48 of *Schubert Album*, book 7, with C. F. Peters, Leipzig. The Vienna publishers owned the MS. in 1887.

255. ' Der Rattenfänger ' (Goethe), Song (XX 112). 19th August 1815.

Ich bin der wohl - be - kann - te Sän - ger,

MS. Rough draft (together with 256 and 257)—Musikbibliothek Peters, Leipzig; fair copy made for Goethe (together with ' Der Sänger (149) and ' An den Mond ' (259))—Conservatoire, Paris (Ph.).
1ST ED. c. 1848, A. Diabelli & Co., Vienna (no. 8836), as no. 3 of *Nachlass*, book 47 (with a spurious pf. introduction).

The three MSS. owned by the Peters Library were reproduced in facsimile at Röder in Leipzig, 1929.

256. ' **Der Schatzgräber** ' (Goethe), **Song** (XX 113). 19th August 1815.

Mässig

Arm am Beu - tel, krank am Herz - en.

MS. Musikbibliothek Peters, Leipzig (together with 255 and 257).
1ST ED. 1887, C. F. Peters, Leipzig, as no. 47 of *Schubert Album*, book 7 (ed. by Max Friedlaender).

257. ' **Heidenröslein** ' (Goethe), **Song** (Op. 3, no. 3; XX 114). 19th August 1815.

Lieblich (♩ = 69)

Sah ein Knab' ein Rös - lein stehn.

MS. Rough draft—Musikbibliothek Peters, Leipzig (together with 255 and 256; fair copy made for Goethe—Preussische Staatsbibliothek, Berlin (Ph.).
1ST ED. 22nd May 1821, Cappi & Diabelli, Vienna (no. 768, without plate no.), as no. 3 of Op. 3, published for Schubert and dedicated by him to Ignaz von Mosel.

Literature. Max Friedlaender, Supplement to the *Schubert Album*, C. F. Peters, Leipzig (no. 2173), (1884), pp. 49 f.

258. ' **Bundeslied** ' (Goethe), **Song** (XX 115). 19th August 1815.

Mässig

In al - len gu - ten Stun - den,

MS. Rough draft (together with 259)—Dr. Alwin Cranz, Vienna; fair copy made for Goethe—Stadtbibliothek, Vienna.

1ST ED. 1887, Weinberger & Hofbauer, Vienna (no. 30), as no. 3 of three songs, in book 2 of a collection of hitherto unpublished Schubert works (ed. by Heinrich von Bocklet).

The last bar, which is different in the rough draft, is printed in the *Revisionsbericht*.

259. '**An den Mond**' ('Füllest wieder Busch und Tal,' Goethe), **Song**, first version (XX 116). 19th August 1815.

Ziemlich langsam

Fül - lest wie - der Busch und Tal

MS. Rough draft (together with 258)—Dr. Alwin Cranz, Vienna; fair copy, made for Goethe (together with 149 and 255)—Conservatoire, Paris (Ph.).

1ST ED. *c.* 1848, A. Diabelli & Co., Vienna (no. 8836), as no. 5 of *Nachlass*, book 47 (with a spurious pf. introduction).

The stanza printed in brackets was apparently not intended to be sung. For the second version, see **296**.

260. '**Wonne der Wehmut**' (Goethe), **Song** (Op. posth. 115, no. 2; XX 117). 20th August 1815.

Etwas geschwind

Trock - net nicht, trock - net nicht,

MS. Rough draft (together with 261)—Gesellschaft der Musikfreunde, Vienna; fair copy made for Goethe—Preussische Staatsbibliothek, Berlin (Ph.).

1ST ED. 16th June 1829, M. J. Leidesdorf, Vienna (no. 1152), as no. 2 of Op. 115.

Eduard von Bauernfeld included the poem in his libretto, *Der Graf von Gleichen*, which he wrote for Schubert (918), as an aria for Ottilie, Act II, scene i.

261. '**Wer kauft Liebesgötter?**' (Goethe), **Song** (XX 118). 21st August 1815.

Mässig, lieblich

Von al-len schö-nen Wa-ren,

MS. Rough draft (together with 260)—Gesellschaft der Musikfreunde, Vienna; fair copy made for Goethe—Stadtbibliothek, Vienna.

1ST ED. *c.* 1848, A. Diabelli & Co., Vienna (no. 8836), as no. 2 of *Nachlass*, book 47 (transposed into the key of A major).

The poem is to be found in Goethe's continuation of *Die Zauberflöte* as a duet between Papageno and Papagena. Goethe's original title of the poem, which he published separately in 1796, was ' Die Liebesgötter auf dem Markte.' Witteczek's copy of Schubert's song is in A flat major, and dated 4th August 1815.

262. ' **Die Fröhlichkeit** ' (Martin Josef Prandstetter), **Song** (XX 134). (?) 22nd August 1815.

Lebhaft

Wess' A-dern leicht-es Blut durch-springt,

MS. Fair copy, undated—Karl Ernst Henrici, Berlin (sale, 9th October 1920), together with 264.

1ST ED. 1895, Gesamtausgabe.

263. ' **Cora an die Sonne** ' (Gabriele von Baumberg), **Song** (XX 123). 22nd August 1815.

Langsam, mit Ausdruck

Nach so vie-len trü-ben Ta-gen send'

MS. Library of Congress, Washington (together with 265).

1ST ED. *c.* 1848, A. Diabelli & Co., Vienna (no. 8819), as no. 3 of *Nachlass*, book 42.

264. ' **Der Morgenkuss nach einem Ball** ' (Gabriele von Baumberg), **Song** (XX 124). 22nd August 1815.

Langsam

Durch ei-ne gan-ze Nacht sich nah__ zu sein,

MS. Fair copy (dated, together with 262)—Karl Ernst Henrici, Berlin (sale, 9th October 1920).
1ST ED. c. 1848, A. Diabelli & Co., Vienna (no. 8822), as no. 4 of *Nachlass*, book 45 (corrupt).

There is a facsimile of the MS. reproduced in the catalogue of the sale quoted above. Schubert entitled the song simply 'Der Morgenkuss.' The song was republished, but in the original key and time, in 1872, by J. P. Gotthard, Vienna (no. 357) as no. 33 of forty songs.

265. 'Abendständchen. An Lina' (after an unidentified French poem, Gabriele von Baumberg), **Song (XX 125)**. 23rd August 1815.

MS. Library of Congress, Washington (together with 263).
1ST ED. 1895, Gesamtausgabe.

The *Revisionsbericht* corrects p. 52, bar 12, voice part: the first note C instead of B flat.

266. 'Morgenlied' ('Willkommen, rotes Morgenlicht,' Stolberg), **Song (XX 126)**. 24th August 1815.

MS. (together with 276)—Dr. Alwin Cranz, Vienna.
1ST ED. 1895, Gesamtausgabe.

267. 'Trinklied' ('Auf! jeder sei nun froh,' author unknown), **Quartet, T.T.B.B., with Pianoforte accompaniment (XVI 17)**. 25th August 1815.

MS. Albert Cranz, New York.
1ST PF. (?) 4th May 1927, Musikvereinssaal, Vienna.
1ST ED. 1872, J. P. Gotthard, Vienna (no. 317), as no. 2 of nine part-songs (corrupt).

268. '**Bergknappenlied**' (author unknown), **Quartet, T.T.B.B.**, with Pianoforte accompaniment (XVI 18).   25th August 1815.

[musical notation: Mässig — Hin-ab, ihr Brü-der, in den Schacht!]

MS. Stadtbibliothek, Vienna (together with 271).
1ST ED. 1872, J. P. Gotthard, Vienna (no. 319), as no. 4 of nine part-songs (corrupt).

269. '**Das Leben**' (J. C. Wannovius), **Trio, S.S.A.**, with Pianoforte accompaniment (XVIII 5).   25th August 1815.

[musical notation: Ruhig — Das Le-ben ist ein Traum, man merkt, man fühlt ihn kaum;]

MS. (autograph?)—Albert Cranz, New York; sketch of another version, see note.
1ST ED. *c.* 1848, A. Diabelli & Co., Vienna (no. 8821), as no. 4 of *Nachlass*, book 44.

The pf. acc. seems to be spurious. There exists the sketch of a setting for trio, T.T.B., without acc., dated August 1815; on the same leaf as this sketch may be found the trios nos. 131, 242–4 (William Reeves, London).

270. '**An die Sonne**' ('Sinke, liebe Sonne,' Gabriele von Baumberg), **Song** (Op. posth. 118, no. 5; XX 127).   25th August 1815.

[musical notation: Sehr langsam — Sin-ke, lie-be Son-ne, sin-ke;]

MS. Lost.
1ST ED. 19th June 1829, Josef Czerny, Vienna (no. 341), as no. 5 of Op. 118.

The title of this poem in Baumberg's *Gedichte*, Vienna 1800, is 'Als ich einen Freund des nächsten Morgens auf dem Lande zum Besuche erwartete.' Cf. 272.

271. '**Der Weiberfreund**' (Abraham Cowley, translated by J. F. von Ratschky), **Song** (XX 128).   25th August 1815.

Scherzhaft

Noch fand von E - vens Töch - ter-scha - ren ich kei - ne,

MS. Stadtbibliothek, Vienna (together with 268).
1ST ED. 1895, Gesamtausgabe.

The names of the poet and the translator were discovered by Odd Udbye, Oslo. The verse is the first four lines of ' The Inconstant ' in *The Mistresse*.

272. ' **An die Sonne** ' (' Königliche Morgensonne,' C. A. Tiedge), **Song** (XX 129). 25th August 1815.

Mit Majestät

Kö - nig - li - che Mor - gen - son - ne,

MS. (together with 273–5)—Albert Cranz, New York.
1ST ED. 1872, J. P. Gotthard, Vienna (no. 333), as no. 9 of forty songs, this song dedicated by the publisher to Gustav Walter.

The name of the poet was discovered by Odd Udbye, Oslo. Cf. 270.

273. ' **Lilla an die Morgenröte** ' (author unknown), **Song** (XX 130). 25th August 1815.

Etwas geschwind, mit Anmut

Wie schön bist du, du güld - ne Mor - gen - rö — te,

MS. (together with 272, 274, 275)—Albert Cranz, New York.
1ST ED. 1895, Gesamtausgabe.

274. ' **Tischlerlied** ' (author unknown), **Song** (XX 131). 25th August 1815.

Etwas langsam

Mein Hand-werk geht durch al - le Welt und

MS. (together with 272, 273, 275)—Albert Cranz, New York.
1ST ED. *c.* 1848, A. Diabelli & Co., Vienna (no. 8837), as no. 7 of *Nachlass*, book 48 (with a spurious pf. introduction).

The poem may have been written by the same author as that of 273.

275. ' **Totenkranz für ein Kind** ' (Matthisson), **Song** (XX 132). 25th August 1815.

Etwas geschwind

Sanft wehn, im Hauch der— A - bend-luft,

MS. (together with 272–4)—Albert Cranz, New York.
1ST ED. 1895, Gesamtausgabe.

276. ' **Abendlied** ' (' Gross und rotentflammet,' Stolberg), **Song** (XX 133). 28th August 1815.

Ruhig, mässig

Gross und rot - ent - flam - met schwe-bet

MS. (together with 266)—Dr. Alwin Cranz, Vienna.
1ST ED. 1895, Gesamtausgabe.

277. ' **Punschlied** ' (' Vier Elemente, innig gesellt,' Schiller), **Trio, T.T.B., with Pianoforte accompaniment** (XIX 7). 29th August 1815.

Feurig

Vier E - le - men - te, in - nig ge-sellt,

MS. Unknown; former owner—A. Cranz, Leipzig.
1ST ED. 1892, Gesamtausgabe.

An arrangement of this trio, for solo voice with pf. acc., by Leopold von Sonnleithner, who also supplied new words, was adapted as a second part of the song ' Loda's Gespenst ' (150) in *Nachlass*, book 3. Schubert set another ' Punschlied ' by Schiller as a solo song (253).

278. ' **Ossian's " Lied nach dem Falle Nathos " ** ' (from ' Darthula,' translated by Harold), **Song,** two versions (*Revisionsbericht* and XX 147). (?) September 1815.

FIRST VERSION
Ruhig

Beugt euch aus eu - ren Wol - ken nie - der, ihr

Gei - ster mei - ner Vä - ter!

FINAL VERSION
Ruhig

Beugt euch aus eu - ren Wol - ken nie - der, ihr Gei - ster mei - ner Vä - ter!

MS. First version (incomplete)—Stadtbibliothek, Vienna; final version (undated, together with 281)—Moritz Caesar, Baden, near Vienna.

1ST ED. 10th July 1830, A. Diabelli, Vienna (no. 3634), as no. 2 of *Nachlass*, book 4 (Ossian Songs, book 4), with a spurious first bar.

The first version, entitled 'Ossian's Lied nach dem Tode Nathos,' is printed in the *Revisionsbericht* to Series XX, pp. 34–6.

279. Sonata for Pianoforte in C (X 2). Unfinished. September 1815.

Allegro moderato

Andante

MENUETTO
Allegro vivace

TRIO

MS. Stadtbibliothek, Vienna; the minuet only, with a different Trio—Fräulein Marie Schubert, Vienna.

1ST ED. 1888, Gesamtausgabe.

The MS. is marked 'Sonate I.' The third movement, with another trio, was written earlier as a single minuet, undated; published by O. E. D. in *Moderne Welt*, Vienna, December 1925, music supplement, pp. 3–4. Walter Rehberg completed the sonata in 1927, using the undated Allegretto in C (346) as a fourth movement (Steingräber-Verlag, Leipzig, 1928, no. 2381, edition no. 2577).

280. '**Das Rosenband**,' called '**Cidli**' (Klopstock), Song (XX 139). September 1815.

Mässig, lieblich

Im Früh-lings-gar-ten fand ich sie,

MS. Lost (Witteczek's copy).

1ST ED. 25th April 1837, A. Diabelli & Co., Vienna (no. 5032), as no. 3 of *Nachlass*, book 28.

Cf. 285.

281. '**Das Mädchen von Inistore**' (from Ossian's 'Fingal,' translated by Harold), Song (XX 148). September 1815.

Nicht zu langsam, klagend

Mäd-chen I - ni - sto - res,

MS. Moritz Caesar, Baden, near Vienna (without the last five bars, undated, together with 278). (Ebner's and Stadler's copies.)

1ST ED. 10th July 1830, A. Diabelli & Co., Vienna (no. 3634), as no. 3 of *Nachlass*, book 4 (Ossian Songs, book 4).

Inis-tore is the Gaelic name of the Orkney Islands.

282. '**Cronnan**' (from Ossian's 'Carric-Thura,' translated by Harold, revised by (?) Franz von Hummelauer), Song (XX 188). 5th September 1815.

Langsam, schauerlich

SHILRIC

Ich sitz' bei der moo-sig-ten Quel-le,

MS. Rough draft—Moritz von Caesar, Baden, near Vienna (the

last seventeen bars missing, dated (together with 216); the last seventeen bars (together with the Claudius song called ' Lied ' of 1816, 362)—Stadtbibliothek, Vienna.

1ST ED. 10th July 1830, A. Diabelli & Co., Vienna (no. 3632), as no. 1 of *Nachlass*, book 2 (Ossian Songs, book 2).

This poem, Harold's version of which is printed in the *Gesamtausgabe*, is a continuation of ' Shilric und Vinvela,' which Schubert set on 20th September 1815 (293).

283. ' **An den Frühling** ' (Schiller), **Song**, second version (Op. posth. 172, no. 5; XX 136). 6th September 1815.

Mässig, heiter

Will - kom - men, schö - ner Jüng - ling!

MS. Unknown; former owner—A. Cranz, Leipzig.

1ST ED. 1866, C. A. Spina, Vienna (no. 16,784, plate no. 16,761), as no. 5 of Op. 172.

For the first version, in B flat and A, see 245 and 587; for the setting as a quartet, T.T.B.B., see 338. The autographs of 283 and 284, originally in one MS., have been separated at some time since 1895.

284. ' **Lied** ' (' Es ist so angenehm,' Schiller), **Song** (XX 137). 6th September 1815.

Zart

Es ist so an - ge - nehm, so süss, um

MS. Dr. Alwin Cranz, Vienna.

1ST ED. 1895, Gesamtausgabe.

The poem was first published, after Schiller's death, in the *Taschenbuch für Damen auf das Jahr 1809* (Tübingen), p. 250. Karl Goedeke, who does not doubt Schiller's authorship, says the poem may have been written for an operetta planned in 1786. There is no foundation for the statement given by Johann Lorenz Greiner in his edition of Schiller's poems (Graz, 1824, vol. iii, p. 155) that it was extemporized for a *Singspiel* in 1787. Cf. 283.

285. ' **Furcht der Geliebten**,' called ' **An Cidli** ' (Klopstock), **Song**, two versions (XX 138 (*a*) and (*b*)). 12th September 1815.

a [musical notation]
pp Cid - li, du wei - nest, und ich schlum-m're si - cher,

b **Sanft** [musical notation]
p Cid - li, du wei - nest, und ich schlum - m're si - cher,

MS. (*a*) Sketch—Moritz Caesar, Baden, near Vienna; complete MS., dated—Conservatoire, Paris (Ph.); (*b*) Lost.

IST ED. (*a*) 1895, Gesamtausgabe; (*b*) 1885, C. F. Peters, Leipzig (no. 6896), as no. 10 of twenty *Nachgelassene Lieder* (ed. by Max Friedlaender).

Schubert used both titles. Cidli was the nickname of Meta (Margarethe) Moller, later the wife of the poet (cf. 280). Witteczek dates (*b*) July 1817 in the index of his collection, but this must be incorrect as Albert Stadler had already made a copy of this version in 1816. The second version may have been written shortly after the first.

286. '**Selma und Selmar**' (Klopstock), **Song**, two versions (XX 140 (*a*) and (*b*)). 14th September 1815.

a **Etwas langsam, innig** [musical notation]
Wei - ne du nicht o, die ich in - nig lie - be,

b **Etwas geschwind** [musical notation]
Wei - ne du nicht o, die ich in - nig lie - be,

MS. (*a*) Lost (Stadler's and Witteczek's copies); (*b*), together with 287–9—Dr. Alwin Cranz, Vienna.

IST ED. (*a*) 1895, Gesamtausgabe; (*b*) 25th April 1837, A. Diabelli & Co., Vienna (no. 5032), as no. 2 of *Nachlass*, book 28 (with a spurious pf. introduction).

287. '**Vaterlandslied**' (Klopstock), **Song**, two versions (XX 141 (*a*) and (*b*)). 14th September 1815.

a **Mässig** [musical notation]
Ich bin ein deut - sches Mäd - chen!

b Etwas geschwind, mit Feuer

Ich bin ein deut-sches Mäd-chen!

MS. (*a*) together with nos. 286, 288, 289—Dr. Alwin Cranz, Vienna; (*b*) Lost.

1ST ED. 1895, Gesamtausgabe.

Klopstock wrote the poem for Johanna Elisabeth von Winthem. There is a setting by Gluck.

288. 'An Sie' (Klopstock), Song (XX 142). 14th September 1815.

fp Zeit. Ver-kün-.. di-ge-rin der be-sten Freu-den,

MS. Dr. Alwin Cranz, Vienna (together with 286, 288, 289).
1ST ED. 1895, Gesamtausgabe.

289. 'Die Sommernacht' (Klopstock), Song, two versions (XX 143 (*a*) and (*b*)). 14th September 1815.

a Nicht zu langsam RECIT.

Wenn der Schim-mer von dem Mon-de

b Langsam, feierlich RECIT.

Wenn der Schim-mer von dem Mon-de

MS. (*a*) together with 286–8—Dr. Alwin Cranz, Vienna; (*b*) Lost (Ebner's, Stadler's, and Witteczek's copies).
1ST ED. 1895, Gesamtausgabe.

290. 'Die frühen Gräber' (Klopstock), Song (XX 144). 14th September 1815.

Etwas geschwind

Will-kom-men, o sil-ber-ner Mond.

MS. Rough draft—Gesellschaft der Musikfreunde (together with 291 and 293); fair copy—lost.
1ST ED. 25th April 1837, A. Diabelli & Co., Vienna (no. 5032),

as no. 5 of *Nachlass*, book 28 (in G minor), with a spurious pf. introduction).

The MS. gives ' Mässig ' (originally ' Ruhig,' which is crossed through) as the tempo; line 3, bars 1 and 2 of the acc., as counted in the G.A., are given in the *Revisionsbericht* according to the version in the MS.

291. ' Dem Unendlichen ' (Klopstock), **Song,** three versions (XX 145 (*a*), (*b*), and (*c*)). 15th September 1815.

[musical notation: Sehr langsam — Wie er-hebt sich das Herz, wenn es dich, Un-end-lich-er, denkt!]

[musical notation: Sehr langsam]

[musical notation: Sehr langsam, RECIT.]

MS. (*a*) First draft, together with 290 and 293—Gesellschaft der Musikfreunde, Vienna; (*b*) fair copy (together with 322)—Albert Cranz, New York; (*c*) fair copy—Preussische Staatsbibliothek, Berlin (see note).

1ST ED. (*a*) 1895, Gesamtausgabe; (*b*) 21st April 1831, A. Diabelli & Co., Vienna (no. 3707), as no. 1 of *Nachlass*, book 10; (*c*) 1895, Gesamtausgabe.

The MS. of the third version, formerly including 295, 296, and 495, is entitled ' Vier deutsche Gedichte . . .'

292. ' Klage ' (' Trauer umfliesst mein Leben,' author unknown), **Song,** first version (XX 185 (*a*)). (?) 20th September 1815.

[musical notation: Langsam — Trau-er um-fliesst mein Le-ben,]

MS. Stadtbibliothek, Vienna (undated, together with 293).
1ST ED. 1895, Gesamtausgabe.

This is a sketch only. For the second version, see January 1816 (371). The poem was wrongly attributed to Hölty.

293. '**Shilric und Vinvela**' (from Ossian's 'Carric-Thura,' translated by Harold, revised by (?) Franz von Hummelauer), **Song** (XX 146). 20th September 1815.

MS. The first seven pages of the rough draft (together with 290 and 291)—Gesellschaft der Musikfreunde, Vienna; remainder of the rough draft (together with 292)—Stadtbibliothek, Vienna; fair copy—lost.

1ST ED. 10th July 1830, A. Diabelli & Co., Vienna (no. 3634), as no. 1 of *Nachlass*, book 4 (Ossian Songs, book 4).

The text differs in the rough draft and the first edition. See 'Cronnan (282).

294. '**Namensfeier**,' für Franz Michael Vierthaler, called '**Gratulations-Kantate**,' or—erroneously—'**Namensfeier für Schubert's Vater**' (author unknown), for Soli, Chorus, S.T.B., and Orchestra (XVII 4). 27th September 1815.

MS. Preussische Staatsbibliothek, Berlin.
1ST PF. 29th September (Michaelmas Day) 1815, Waisenhaus, Vienna (conductor, Ferdinand Schubert).
1ST ED. 1892, Gesamtausgabe.

This composition is mentioned in Ferdinand Schubert's list of Schubert's works among the pieces written for the former, under the title *Gratulations-Kantate*. In the Museums-Bibliothek, Salzburg, there exists a MS. piano score by Ferdinand Schubert, without Schubert's name, dedicated to Vierthaler, the director of the Vienna Orphanage. Cf. 80.

Literature. O. E. D., *Zeitschrift für Musikwissenschaft*, Leipzig, November 1928.

295. '**Hoffnung**' ('Schaff', das Tagwerk meiner Hände,' Goethe), **Song**, two versions (XX 175 (*a*) and (*b*)). (?) Autumn 1815 and (?) 1817.

130   296   1815

MS. (*a*) Preussische Staatsbibliothek, Berlin (together with 296); (*b*) fair copy—Mrs. Whittall Collection, Library of Congress, Washington (together with ' Thekla,' November 1817, 595 (*b*)).

1ST ED. (*a*) 1872, J. P. Gotthard, Vienna (no. 338), as no. 14 of forty songs, this song dedicated by the publisher to Gustav Walter; (*b*) 1895, Gesamtausgabe.

See 291.

296. ' **An den Mond** ' (' Füllest wieder Busch und Tal,' Goethe), **Song,** second version (XX 176). (?) Autumn 1815.

MS. Preussische Staatsbibliothek, Berlin (together with 295).
1ST ED. 1868, Wilhelm Müller, Berlin (no. 13), as no. 3 of six songs (ed. by Franz Espagne).

For the first version, see 259.

297. ' **Augenlied** ' (Mayrhofer), **Song** (XX 171). (?) October 1815.

MS. Lost (Witteczek's copy).
1ST ED. *c*. 1850, A. Diabelli & Co., Vienna (no. 9000), as no. 3 of *Nachlass*, book 50.

An early nineteenth-century copy of the MS., bearing **Schubert's** signature, is preserved in the monastery of Kremsmünster, Upper Austria. The recorded date is dubious, since Josef von Spaun tells us that the song was not finished until after Johann Michael Vogl met Schubert for the first time in the spring of 1817.

298. ' Liane ' (Mayrhofer), Song (XX 170). October 1815.

Sehr langsam, zart

"Hast du Li - a - nen nicht ge - se - hen?"

MS. Artaria & Co., Vienna (sale, 22nd March 1934).
1ST ED. 1895, Gesamtausgabe.

299. Twelve Écossaises for Pianoforte (XXI 29, nos. 1–8). Begun 3rd October 1815.

No. 1.

No. 2.

No. 3.

No. 4.

No. 5.

No. 6.

MS. Nos. 1–8 only, dated—Gesellschaft der Musikfreunde.
1ST ED. No. 1: see 145; nos. 2–8: 1897, Gesamtausgabe, 1897;
nos. 9–12: *Die Musik*, Berlin, 1st September 1912 (ed. by
O. E. D.).

No. 1 of the MS. is almost identical with no. 1 of the nine écossaises in Op. 18 (145), variants to be found in bar 3 and the last two bars of the first part. Another MS. existed, written in 1816, for Fräulein Marie von Spaun (cf. 420 and 421), which contained twelve écossaises dedicated to her, i.e. the first eight dances of 1815, published in 1821 and 1897 respectively, and the four dances (probably of 1816), published in 1912. Two copies of the second MS. are preserved: one in the family of von Wettstein, Vienna, was formerly in the possession of Leopold Ebner (copied before September 1817); the other (now with the compiler) was formerly in the possession of Fräulein Josefine von Koller (dated—

erroneously?—1818). Variants in the first MS. (eight écossaises) and the copies of the second MS. (twelve écossaises) may be found as follows: no. 4, second bar of the second part; no. 8, fifth bar of the second part. The copies indicate that the dances with odd numbers should be repeated after playing the even numbers. These twelve écossaises have never been printed as a complete set.

300. '**Der Jüngling an der Quelle**' (Salis), **Song** (XX 398). 12th October 1815 (?).

[musical notation: Etwas langsam — "Lei - se, rie - seln der Quell,"]

MS. Lost (Witteczek's copy).
IST ED. *c.* 1842, A. Diabelli & Co., Vienna (no. 7414), as no. 1 of *Nachlass*, book 36.

In the Witteczek Collection it is dated 1821; it was, however, probably written not later than 1817. According to Reissmann the song was written on 12th October 1815.

301. '**Lambertine**' (J. L. Stoll), **Song** (XX 149). 12th October 1815.

[musical notation: Langsam, mit Ausdruck — "O Lie - be, die mein Herz er - fü - llet,"]

MS. Wittgenstein family, Vienna (together with a fragment of 156).
IST ED. *c.* 1842, A. Diabelli & Co., Vienna (no. 7414), as no. 2 of *Nachlass*, book 36.

302. '**Labetrank der Liebe** (Stoll), **Song** (XX 150). 15th October 1815.

[musical notation: Zart — "Wenn im Spie - le lei - ser Tö - ne"]

MS. Rough draft (together with 303-8)—Albert Cranz, New York; fair copy—New York Public Library, New York.
IST ED. 1895, Gesamtausgabe.

303. '**An die Geliebte**' (Stoll), **Song** (XX 151). 15th October 1815.

Mässig

O, dass ich dir vom stil - len Au - ge,

MS. (together with 302, 304–8)—Albert Cranz, New York.
1ST ED. 1887, C. F. Peters, Leipzig, as no. 49 of *Schubert Album*, book 7 (ed. by Max Friedlaender).

304. '**Wiegenlied**' ('Schlumm're sanft,' Körner), **Song** (XX 152). 15th October 1815.

Langsam, ruhig

Schlum - m're sanft! Noch an dem Mu - tter - her - zen

MS. (together with 302–3, 305–8)—Albert Cranz, New York.
1ST ED. 1895, Gesamtausgabe.

305. '**Mein Gruss an den Mai**' (Ermin, i.e. J. G. Kumpf), **Song** (XX 153). 15th October 1815.

Fröhlich

Sei mir ge-grüsst, o Mai,

MS. (together with 302–4, 306–8)—Albert Cranz, New York.
1ST ED. 1895, Gesamtausgabe.

Schubert noted in the MS. 'Dazu 8 Strophen' (eight stanzas to be added). The poem is unknown apart from the song, thus the eight additional stanzas have not been traced. Kumpf was the editor of Fellinger's poems (see 307).

306. '**Skolie**' ('Lasst im Morgenstrahl des Mai'n,' Deinhardstein), **Song** (XX 154). 15th October 1815.

Lustig

Lasst im Mor - gen - strahl des Mai'n

MS. (together with 302–5, 307, 308)—Albert Cranz, New York.
1ST ED. 1895, Gesamtausgabe.

307. ' **Die Sternenwelten** ' (Fellinger), Song (XX 155).   15th October 1815.

Langsam, feierlich

O - ben dre - hen sich die gro - ssen

MS. (together with 302–6 and 308)—Albert Cranz, New York.
1ST ED. 1895, Gesamtausgabe.

Schubert noted in the MS. ' Dazu 2 Strophen ' (two stanzas to be added), but the poem is not included in Kumpf's edition of Fellinger's works (Klagenfurt 1819 and 1821, two vols.) and the additional stanzas are unknown.

308. ' **Die Macht der Liebe** ' (Kalchberg), Song (XX 156).   15th October 1815.

Mässig

Ü - ber - all, wo - hin mein Au - ge bli - cket.

MS. (together with 302–7)—Albert Cranz, New York.
1ST ED. 1895, Gesamtausgabe.

Schubert noted in the MS. ' Dazu eine Strophe ' (one stanza to be added), but Kalchberg's collected works contain only a sonnet with this title, the second stanza of which was used in the G.A. Kalchberg, like Fellinger (see 307), was a Styrian; Kumpf was the editor of Fellinger's works (see 305). It is possible that Schubert obtained these poems from his new friend, Anselm Hüttenbrenner, another Styrian.

309. ' **Das gestörte Glück** (Körner), Song (XX 157).   15th October 1815.

Lustig

Ich hab' ein hei - sses jun - ges Blut,

MS. Rough draft (together with 313)—William Kux, Chur (Switzerland); fair copy—unknown, former owner—Herr Bauernschmied, Ried (Lower Austria).
1ST ED. 1872, J. P. Gotthard, Vienna (no. 332), as no. 8 of forty songs.

—— **Rondo in C major for Pianoforte**, 2/4, beginning only. Not printed.   See note to 310.   16th October 1815.

310. ' **Sehnsucht** ' (' Nur wer die Sehnsucht kennt,' from Goethe's ' Wilhelm Meister '), **Song**, two versions (XX 158 (*a*) and (*b*)). 18th October 1815.

a Sehr langsam, mit Ausdruck
Nur wer die Sehn - sucht kennt,

b Sehr langsam, mit höchstem Affekt
Nur wer die Sehn - sucht kennt,

MS. (*a*) Heinrich Rosenthal, Lucerne; (*b*) rough draft (together with 320 and 321)—Dr. Alwin Cranz, Vienna; fair copy made for Goethe (together with 119, 254, and 321)—Conservatoire, Paris (Ph.).

1ST ED. 1895, Gesamtausgabe.

At the top of p. 1 of (*b*) is the cancelled beginning of a Rondo in C major for pianoforte, 2/4, dated 16th October 1815. On p. 3 of the fair copy Schubert commenced writing, by mistake, a fair copy of ' Der Zufriedene ' (320). For other settings of this poem see the note to 481.

311. ' **An den Mond** ' (author unknown), **Song**. Fragment. Not printed. (?) 19th October 1815.

Lieblich

MS. Stadtbibliothek, Vienna (together with 318 and 319).

This sketch contains only the first twelve bars of the melody, without text and without pf. acc.

312. ' **Hektor's Abschied** ' (Schiller), **Song**, two versions (Op. 58, no. 1; XX 159 (*a*) and (*b*)). 19th October 1815.

a Langsam ANDROMACHE
Will sich Hek - tor e - wig von mir wen - den,

b Langsam ANDROMACHE
Will sich Hek - tor e - wig von mir wen - den,

MS. (*a*) Conservatoire, Paris (Ph.); (*b*) Lost.
1ST ED. (*a*) 1895, Gesamtausgabe; (*b*) 6th April 1826, Thaddäus Weigl, Vienna (no. 2491), as no. 1 of Op. 56, later corrected to Op. 58.

The *Revisionsbericht* gives part of the first version which Schubert altered in MS. (*a*). Cf. note to 312.

313. '**Die Sterne**' ('Wie wohl ist mir im Dunkeln,' Kosegarten), **Song** (XX 160). 19th October 1815.

Langsam, lieblich

Wie wohl ist mir im Dun - keln!

MS. Rough draft (together with 309)—William Kux, Chur (Switzerland); final version (together with 314)—unknown, former owner—Max Friedlaender, Berlin.
1ST ED. 1895, Gesamtausgabe.

314. '**Nachtgesang**' ('Tiefe Feier schauert um die Welt,' Kosegarten), **Song** (XX 161). 19th October 1815.

Sehr langsam

Tie - fe Fei - er schau - ert um die Welt.

MS. Rough draft (together with 315–19)—Albert Cranz, New York; final version (together with 313)—unknown; former owner—Max Friedlaender, Berlin.
1ST ED. 1887, C. F. Peters, Leipzig, as no. 38 of *Schubert Album*, book 7 (ed. by Max Friedlaender).

315. '**An Rosa I**' ('Warum bist du nicht hier,' Kosegarten), **Song** (XX 162). 19th October 1815.

Mässig, lieblich

Wa - rum bist du nicht hier,

MS. Rough draft (together with 314, 316–19) and final version (together with 316 and 317)—Albert Cranz, New York.
1ST ED. 1895, Gesamtausgabe.

This is the second of four poems, 'An Rosa,' by Kosegarten, two of which Schubert set as songs (cf. 316).

316. '**An Rosa II**' ('Rosa, denkst du an mich,' Kosegarten), **Song**, two versions (XX 163 (*a*) and (*b*)). 19th October 1815.

Ex. 316.

a **Langsam**

Ro - sa, denkst du an mich?

b **Langsam**

Ro - sa, denkst du an mich?

MS. First version (together with 314, 315, 317–19) and second version (together with 315 and 317)—Albert Cranz, New York.

1ST ED. 1895, Gesamtausgabe.

This is the third of four poems, 'An Rosa,' by Kosegarten, two of which Schubert set as songs (cf. 315).

317. '**Idens Schwanenlied**' (Kosegarten), **Song** (XX 164) 19th October 1815.

Traurig

Wie schaust du aus dem Ne - bel - flor,

MS. Rough draft (together with 314–16, 318, 319) and final version (together with 315 and 316)—Albert Cranz, New York.

1ST ED. 1895, Gesamtausgabe.

There is no indication as to how many of the seventeen stanzas of the poem should be sung.

318. '**Schwangesang**' ('Endlich steh'n die Pforten offen,' Kosegarten), **Song** (XX 165). 19th October 1815.

Langsam

End - lich steh'n die Pfor - ten of - fen,

MS. Rough draft (together with 311 and 319)—Stadtbibliothek, Vienna; final version (together with 314–17 and 319)—Albert Cranz, New York.

1ST ED. 1895, Gesamtausgabe.

The rough draft bears Schubert's note: '6 Strophen' (six stanzas to be added).

319. '**Louisens Antwort**' (Kosegarten), **Song** (XX 166). 19th October 1815.

[musical notation: Klagend — "Wohl wei-nen Got-tes En-gel,"]

MS. Rough draft (together with 311 and 319)—Stadtbibliothek, Vienna; final version (together with 314–18)—Albert Cranz, New York.

1ST ED. 1895, Gesamtausgabe.

There is no indication as to how many of the nineteen stanzas of the poem should be sung.

320. '**Der Zufriedene**' (Reissig), **Song** (XX 167). 23rd October 1815.

[musical notation: Mässig — "Zwar schuf das Glück hie-nie-den"]

MS. Dr. Alwin Cranz, Vienna (together with 310 and 321).

1ST ED. 1895, Gesamtausgabe.

For a MS. containing the beginning of a fair copy, see note to 310.

321. '**Mignon**' ('Kennst du das Land,' from Goethe's '*Wilhelm Meister*'), **Song** (XX 168). 23rd October 1815.

[musical notation: Mässig — "Kennst du das Land, wo die Zi-tro-nen blühn,"]

MS. Rough draft (together with 310 and 320)—Dr. Alwin Cranz, Vienna; fair copy made for Goethe (together with 119, 254, and 310)—Conservatoire, Paris (Ph.).

1ST ED. 22nd December 1832, A. Diabelli & Co., Vienna (no. 4268), as no. 3 of *Nachlass*, book 20.

The date, May 1816, written by another hand on the fair copy, merely indicates the time when Schubert copied several of his Goethe songs to be sent to the poet at Weimar.

322. '**Hermann und Thusnelda**' (Klopstock), **Song** (XX 169). 27th October 1815.

Froh, doch mit Majestät

[musical notation: RECIT. "Ha, dort kömmt er, mit Schweiss, mit Rö-mer-blut."]

MS. Rough draft—Stadtbibliothek, Vienna; fair copy (together with 291)—Albert Cranz, New York.

1ST ED. 25th April 1837, A. Diabelli & Co., Vienna (no. 5032), as no. 1 of *Nachlass*, book 28.

323. ' **Klage der Ceres** ' (Schiller), **Song** (XX 172).   9th November 1815–June 1816.

Etwas geschwind

[musical notation: RECIT. "Ist der hol-de Lenz er-schie-nen?"]

MS. Stadtbibliothek, Vienna.
1ST ED. 1895, Gesamtausgabe.

The second part of the MS., written in June 1816, with repetition of the section, p. 5, line 5, bar 7, to p. 8, line 1, bar 3, is headed ' Fortsetzung zur Klage der Ceres ' (continuation of the song).   There are two versions of the song, the second being incomplete.   Some differences between the old version and the (partly revised) new version are given in the *Revisionsbericht*.

324. **Mass in B flat for Quartet, S.A.T.B., mixed Chorus, Orchestra, and Organ** (Op. posth. 141, XIII 3).   Begun 11th November 1815.

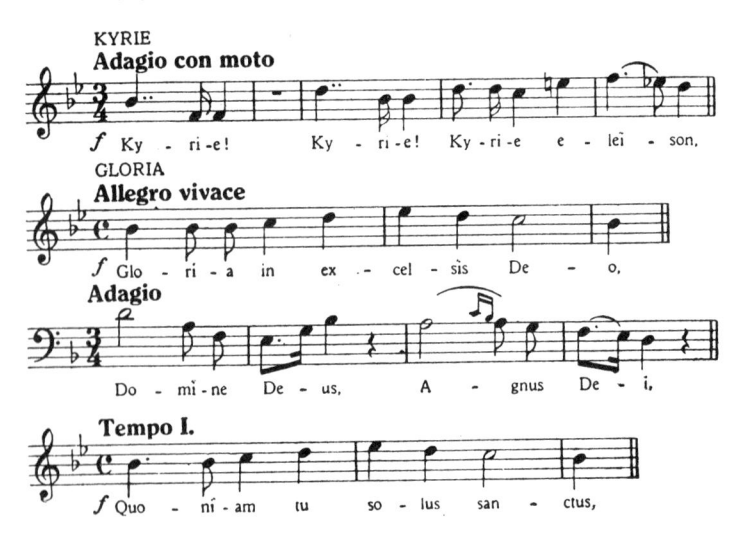

KYRIE
Adagio con moto

[musical notation: "Ky-ri-e! Ky-ri-e! Ky-ri-e e-lei-son."]

GLORIA
Allegro vivace

[musical notation: "Glo-ri-a in ex-cel-sis De-o,"]

Adagio

[musical notation: "Do-mi-ne De-us, A-gnus De-i,"]

Tempo I.

[musical notation: "Quo-ni-am tu so-lus san-ctus,"]

CREDO
Allegro vivace

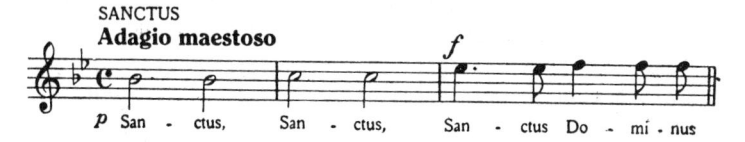

f Cre - do in u - num De - um

Adagio

Et in - car - na - tus est de Spi - ri - tu san - cto

Tempo I.

f Et re - sur - re - xit ter - ti - a di - e,

SANCTUS
Adagio maestoso

p San - ctus, San - ctus, San - ctus Do - mi - nus

BENEDICTUS
Andante con moto

Be - ne - di - ctus, qui

AGNUS DEI
Andante molto

A - gnus De - i, qui

Allegro moderato

Do - na no - bis pa - cem,

MS. Score—British Museum, London; chorus parts—Stadtbibliothek, Vienna.

1ST PF. Probably end of 1815, Liechtentaler Kirche, Vienna.

1ST ED. (in parts) 1838, Tobias Haslinger, Vienna (no. 7330), dedicated by Ferdinand Schubert to Josef Spendou, published by subscription.

Another performance during Schubert's lifetime is recorded by his brother Ferdinand as given in the parish church of Hainburg, Lower Austria, in September 1824 (*Schubert Documents*, pp. 377 f.). Ferdinand, who attended the performance, did not supply the MS. copy which was used on this occasion. A small orchestra was engaged for the first performance. Horn and trombone parts were probably supplied later by Ferdinand, as was also the organ acc. for the first edition. The printed appeal for subscriptions is dated Vienna, July 1837. (A copy of this was on sale at Henrici's sale, Berlin, 22nd January 1929.)

325. '**Harfenspieler**' ('Wer sich der Einsamkeit ergibt,' from Goethe's 'Wilhelm Meister'), Song (XX 173). 13th November 1815.

Klagend
Wer sich der Ein - sam - keit er - gibt,

MS. Destroyed in 1945; former owner—Stadtbibliothek, Vienna.
1ST ED. 1895, Gesamtausgabe.

There were some gaps in the acc., owing to damage of the MS., which have been filled in in the G.A. by Mandyczewski. For other settings of the same poem, see September 1816 (478).

326. '**Die Freunde von Salamanka,**' Singspiel in two acts by Johann Mayrhofer (XV 4). 18th November–31st December 1815.

OVERTURE
Allegro vivace
ff fz

No. 1. INTRODUCTION (2 Ten. and Bass)
Moderato
Die Son - ne zieht in gold'- nen, Strah -

No. 2. ARIA (Bass)
Andantino quasi Allegretto
Man ist so glück - lich und so frei von

No. 3. QUARTET (3 Ten. and Bass)
Allegro
Mor - gen, wenn des Hah - nes Ruf er - schallt,

No. 4. ARIA (Sopr.)
Adagio con moto

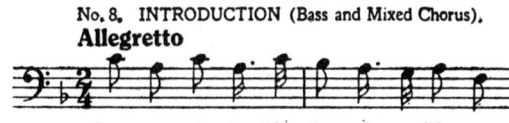

Ein - sam schleich' ich durch die Zim - mer,

No. 5. TERZET (3 Sopr.)
Andantino

Le - bens-mut und fri - sche Küh - lung weht mir

No. 6. TERZET (2 Ten. and Bass)
Allegro molto moderato

Freund, wie wird die Sa - che en - den, ban - ge.

No. 7. FINALE (2 Sopr., 2 Ten., 2 Basses and Mixed Chorus)
Larghetto

Mild senkt sich der A - bend nie - der,

No. 8. INTRODUCTION (Bass and Mixed Chorus).
Allegretto

Lasst nur al - les leicht-fer - ti - ge We - sen,

No. 9. SONG OF GUERRILLAS (2 Basses)
Allegro giusto

Guer - ril - la, zieht durch Feld und Wald in

No. 10. ARIA (Ten.)
Andantino

Aus Blu - men deu - ten die Da - men gern ge -

No. 11. DUET (Ten. and Bass)
Allegro moderato

Ein wack-res Tier. das müsst Ihr sa - gen,

No. 12. DUET (Sopr. and Ten.)
Andantino

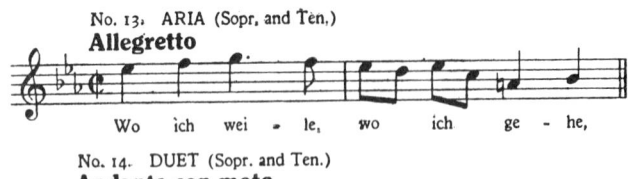

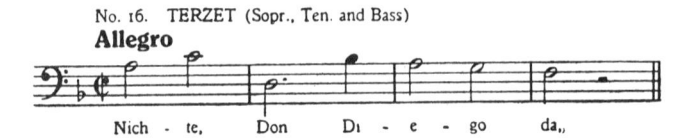

Ge - la - gert un - term hel - len Dach der Baü - me

No. 13. ARIA (Sopr. and Ten.)
Allegretto

Wo ich wei - le, wo ich ge - he,

No. 14. DUET (Sopr. and Ten.)
Andante con moto

Von tau - send Schlan - gen - bis - sen der

No. 15. ROMANCE (Ten.)
Allegretto

Es mur - meln die Quel - len, es

No. 16. TERZET (Sopr., Ten. and Bass)
Allegro

Nich - te, Don Di - e - go da,,

No. 17. ARIA (Sopr.)
Andante molto

Trau - rig geht der Ge - lieb - te von dan - nen,

No. 18. FINALE (3 Sopr., 3 Ten. and 2 Basses)
Andante con moto

Gnäd' - ge Frau, ich hab' die Eh - re— wenn er

MS. Stadtbibliothek, Vienna.
1ST PF. Extracts (nos. 4, 9, 12, and 8)—19th December 1875, Musikvereinssaal, Vienna (conductor, Johann Herbeck); stage performance: 6th May 1928, Halle (dialogue supplied by G. Ziegler).
1ST ED. 1888, Gesamtausgabe.

Josef Hüttenbrenner arranged at least three numbers in piano score (MS.—Krasser family, Vienna). The libretto is lost, only the lyrics being preserved. Three other attempts were made to supply a suitable dialogue and to enrich the opera, but it was never successful.

327. 'Lorma' (from Ossian's 'Battle of Lora,' translated by Harold), Song, first version. Fragment. 28th November 1815.

[musical excerpt: Langsam, RECIT. "Lor-ma sass in der Hal-le von Al-do."]

MS. William Kux, Chur (Switzerland).
1ST ED. Facsimile—1928, Walter Schulz, Stuttgart (privately printed).

This version commences in A minor, 3/4, and continues, after the *recitativo*, in G minor, *alla breve*. For the second version, see 376.

328. 'Erlkönig' (Goethe), Song, four versions (Op. 1; XX 178 (*a*)-(*d*)). Late autumn 1815.

[musical excerpt: Schnell. a (for versions b–d see note) "Wer rei-tet so spät durch Nacht und Wind?"]

MS. (*a*) Lost (see note); (*b*) The Heineman Foundation, New York; (*c*) fair copy made (in 1816) for Goethe—Preussische Staatsbibliothek, Berlin (Ph.); (*d*) Lost.
1ST PF. 25th January 1821, Musikverein, Vienna.
1ST ED. (*a*) and (*b*) 1895, Gesamtausgabe; (*c*) see note; (*d*) 2nd April 1821, Cappi & Diabelli, Vienna (without publisher's or plate no., and without metronome indication), published for Schubert and dedicated by him to Moritz Graf Dietrichstein.

Some variants in (*b*), (*c*), and (*d*) are as follows: (*b*)-(*d*) Introduction consists of fourteen bars; (*c*) Acc. for right hand written without triplets; (*d*) Metronome indication (♩=152) added. Only Stadler's and Ebner's copies of the first version (*a*) are preserved; the second version (*b*) was given to Benedikt Randhartinger after it was offered for publication, without success, in 1817 to Breitkopf & Härtel; of the third version (*c*), a facsimile was published by W. Müller, Berlin, in 1868, ed. by Franz Espagne; the fourth version (*d*) shows some alterations, probably made for Johann Michael Vogl's performance in 1821, and mentioned in the *Revisionsbericht*. Three hundred copies of the first edition were sold within one and a half years (before 18th October 1822). Ferdinand Schubert, on 26th January

1830, arranged the song for solo voice, mixed chorus, and full orchestra (first performed on 21st March 1830, Vienna), with the following alternative: a flute—instead of the chorus—as narrator, a clarinet in C as the child, a horn in B flat as the Erlking, and a bass trombone as the father.

329. 'Die drei Sänger' (author unknown), **Song** (XX 591). Fragment. 23rd December 1815.

MS. Stadtbibliothek, Vienna.
1ST ED. 1895, Gesamtausgabe.

It seems that Schubert finished the song, but the second sheet of the MS. is lost.

— **'Der Liedler'** (XX 98). See 209. 12th December 1815.

330. 'Das Grab' (Salis), **Song**, first version (XX 182). 28th December 1815.

MS. Otto Taussig, Malmö (Witteczek's copy).
1ST ED. 1895, Gesamtausgabe.

This song may have been conceived by Schubert as a chorus, as indicated in the MS., for male or for mixed voices. On the back of the MS. is, in fact, the cancelled beginning of an earlier setting for mixed chorus, in canon form, without accompaniment (undated):

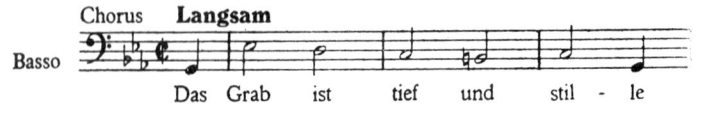

For the second and third versions, see 11th February 1816 (**377**) and June 1817 (**569**).

— 'Die Freunde von Salamanca' (XV 4). See 326. 31st December 1815.

331. 'Der Entfernten' (Salis), Quartet, T.T.B.B. (XVI 38). (?) *c.* 1816.

pp Wohl denk' ich all - ent - hal - ben,

MS. Lost.

1ST PF. 15th March 1863, Redoutensaal, Vienna (conductor, Johann Herbeck).

1ST ED. 1867, C. A. Spina, Vienna (no. 18,404), in the key of C instead of the original C sharp.

Schubert used only the first two of the five stanzas of Salis's poem, and, according to the two preserved copies of the score, altered the words 'falben' to 'fallen' and 'Schleifen' to 'Streifen.' Kreissle possessed the MS. of a second tenor part of another setting (332), on the back of which is the second tenor part of another part-song, beginning 'Lass dein Vertrauen nicht schwinden' (333). Schubert set Salis's poem also as a solo song (350).

332. 'Der Entfernten' (Salis), Trio, T.T.B. Lost. (?) *c.* 1816.

A copy of the second tenor part is in the possession of the Kreissle family, Vienna; see 331.

Literature. See 132.

333. 'Lass dein Vertrauen nicht schwinden' (title and author unknown), (?) Trio, T.T.B. Lost. (?) *c.* 1816.

A copy of the second tenor part is in the possession of the Kreissle family, Vienna; see 331.

334. Minuet in A with Trio for Pianoforte (XXI 24). *c.* 1816.

MS. Stadtbibliothek, Vienna.
1ST ED. 1897, Gesamtausgabe.

Alfred Einstein (*Schubert*, New York and London, 1951) suggests that this Minuet belonged originally to the Sonata in A minor of March 1817 (537).

335. **Minuet in E with two Trios for Pianoforte** (XXI 25).   *c.* 1816.

MS. Stadtbibliothek, Vienna.
1ST ED. 1897, Gesamtausgabe.

336. **Minuet in D with Trio for Pianoforte** (XXI 26).   *c.* 1816.

MS. Stadtbibliothek, Vienna.
1ST ED. 1897, Gesamtausgabe.

337. '**Die Einsiedelei**,' called '**Lob der Einsamkeit**' (Salis), **Quartet, T.T.B.B.** (XVI 39).   *c.* 1816.

MS. Parts—Stadtbibliothek, Vienna (together with 338).
1ST PF. 7th October 1858, in front of Schubert's birthplace, Vienna.
1ST ED. c. 1860, C. A. Spina, Vienna (no. 16,606, later corrected to 18,427).

Schubert omitted the third, fourth, and even the sixth, stanzas; but the main point of the poem is lost by the omission of the last, the sixth, stanza. For settings of the same poem as solo songs, see 393 and 563.

338. ' An den Frühling ' (Schiller), **Quartet, T.T.B.B.** (XVI 40). c. 1816.

MS. Parts—Stadtbibliothek, Vienna (together with 337).
1ST ED. 1891, Gesamtausgabe.

Schubert also set the poem for solo voice with pf. acc., in August 1815 (245), on 6th September 1815 (283), and again in October 1817 (587).

339. ' Amor's Macht,' called ' Amor's Zauber ' (Matthisson), **Trio, T.T.B.** Lost. c. 1816.

A copy of the second tenor part (written by Anton Holzapfel ?) is in the possession of the Krasser family, Vienna; see 425.

340. ' Badelied ' (Matthisson), **Trio, T.T.B.** Lost. c. 1816.

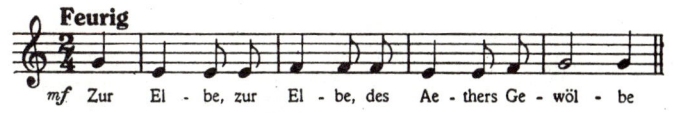

A copy of the second tenor part (written by Anton Holzapfel (?)) is in the possession of the Krasser family, Vienna; see 425.

341. ' Sylphen,' called ' **Die Elfenkönigin** ' (Matthisson), **Trio, T.T.B.** Lost. c. 1816.

Leicht, mässig

Was un-term Mon-de gleicht uns Syl-phen, flink und leicht

A copy of the second tenor part (written by Anton Holzapfel (?)) is in the possession of the Krasser family, Vienna; see 425.

342. ' Seraphine an ihr Klavier,' called 'An mein Klavier,' and sometimes ' **Schubert an sein Klavier** ' (Schubart), **Song** (XX 238). *c.* 1816.

Etwas geschwind

Sanf - tes Cla - vier, sanf - tes Cla - vier!

MS. Lost (Stadler's copy).
1ST ED. 1876, V. Kratochwill, Vienna (no. 253), as no. 4 of six *Nachgelassene Lieder*, arranged for pf. duet and ed. (with words) by J. P. Gotthard.

In 1872 there was either an autograph or a copy with Father Robert Weissenhofer, of the monastery of Seitenstetten (Lower Austria), entitled ' Seraphine an ihr Klavier ' (this is the correct title of the poem), in the key of A, with four stanzas. Max Friedlaender republished the song as no. 9 of twenty *Nachgelassene Lieder*, C. F. Peters, Leipzig, 1885. Albert Stadler's copy, which was used by the editor of the G.A., Series XX, lacks the third and fifth stanzas.

343. ' **Am Tage Aller Seelen**,' called ' **Litanei auf das Fest Aller Seelen** ' (Jacobi), **Song** (XX 342). *c.* 1816.

Langsam, andächtig

Ruh'n in Frie - den al - le See - len,

MS. Fair copy—Meangya family, Mödling, near Vienna (Ph.).
1ST ED. 21st April 1831, A. Diabelli & Co., Vienna (no. 3707), as no. 5 of *Nachlass*, book 10.

The MS. is entitled ' Am Tage aller Seelen.' It has no pf. introduction, and differs slightly from the printed version. In Therese Grob's album, in which the MS. is to be found, there are no Schubert songs dated after 1816. The name of the poet also suggests 1816; therefore the date August 1818, given in the Witteczek Collection, seems to be incorrect.

344. **'Am ersten Maimorgen'** (Claudius), **Song.** Unpublished. c. 1816.

Etwas geschwind, freudig

Heu-te will ich fröh-lich, fröh-lich sein

MS. Meangya family, Mödling, near Vienna (Ph.).

345. **Concerto**, called '**Konzertstück**,' in D for Violin and Orchestra (XXI 3). (?) 1816.

Adagio

Allegro

MS. (in parts)—Otto Taussig, Malmö.
IST ED. 1897, Gesamtausgabe.

The work, entitled 'Konzertstück' in the G.A., but 'Concerto pour Violino' in a copy preserved with the Schubert family, was written for his brother Ferdinand who listed it under the year 1816.

346. **Allegretto in C for Pianoforte** (XXI 17). Fragment. (?) 1816.

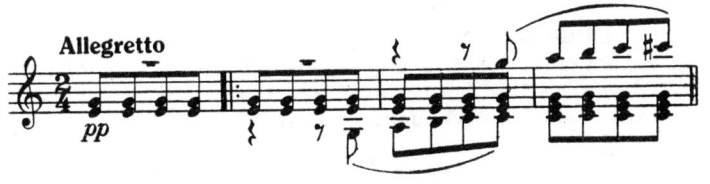

Allegretto

MS. Stadtbibliothek, Vienna.
IST ED. 1897, Gesamtausgabe.
There is no title on the MS. Cf. 279.

347. **Allegro moderato in C for Pianoforte** (XXI 18). Fragment. (?) 1816.

Allegro moderato

MS. Stadtbibliothek, Vienna.
1ST ED. 1897, Gesamtausgabe.
There is no title on the MS. It consists of three pages, the following five pages containing the fugue 967.

348. **Andantino in C for Pianoforte** (XXI 19). Fragment. (?) 1816.

MS. Stadtbibliothek, Vienna.
1ST ED. 1897, Gesamtausgabe.
There is no title on the MS. This Andantino is written on the back of two sheets with nos. 20 and 19 of thirty (twenty) minuets; the end of the Andantino may have been lost, together with the ten missing minuets (see 41).

349. **Adagio in C for Pianoforte** (XXI 21). Fragment. (?) 1816.

MS. Stadtbibliothek, Vienna.
1ST ED. 1897, Gesamtausgabe.
There is no title on the MS. Most of this Adagio is written between the last movement of the Sonata in E (459), and the sketch of the song ' Sehnsucht ' (Mayrhofer, 516); but part of it is written on the back of one of the pages of the thirty (twenty) minuets (see 41).

— **Five Deutsche Tänze for Pianoforte** (Op. 9, XII 1, nos. 1-4 and 15), among them (no. 2) the ' **Trauerwalzer**.' (?) 1816.
MS. All the five dances—Leo Liepmannssohn, Berlin (Catalogue 56, no. 213, November 1929), entitled *Ländler*, with 365, no. 16, as no. 6 of the set; no. 2 only, rewritten for Anselm Hüttenbrenner, 14th March 1818—Wittgenstein family, Vienna; the same number rewritten for Ignaz Assmayr, March 1818—Stefan Zweig Collection, London (together with 607); no. 3 only (with an Écossaise in E flat)—Karl Ernst Henrici, Berlin (23rd August 1924).
1ST ED. See 365 (the title ' Trauerwalzer ' appears inside).

Nos. 1-4 were written not later than 1816, since their themes are given on the MS. of 'La Pastorella' (528), dated January 1817. The 'Trauerwalzer' became famous during Schubert's lifetime: it was frequently arranged for various instruments, varied, and even supplied with words. It was also attributed to Beethoven during the lifetime of both composers. The so-called 'Sehnsuchts-Walzer,' published by B. Schott's Söhne at Mainz in August 1826, and attributed to Beethoven, is a composite of Schubert's 'Trauerwalzer' and Fr. H. Himmel's 'Favorite-Walzer.' The original dance, entitled by Schubert simply 'Deutscher,' is said to have been written in 1816; but it is assumed that all five waltzes were written in that year. The 'Trauerwalzer' was also published by A. Diabelli & Co., Vienna, this time arranged for guitar, as no. 4 in book 5 of the guitar collection *Apollo an der Damen-Toilette*, 19th July 1826. Cf. 188.

350. 'Der Entfernten' (Salis), Song (XX 203). (?) 1816.

Wohl denk' ich all - ent - hal - ben,

MS. Unknown; former owner—A. Cranz, Leipzig (together with 351).
1ST ED. 1876, V. Kratochwill, Vienna (no. 252), as no. 1 of twelve *Nachgelassene Lieder*, arranged for pf. solo and ed. (with words) by J. P. Gotthard).

The song was republished by Max Friedlaender as no. 18 of twenty *Nachgelassene Lieder*, C. F. Peters, Leipzig, in 1885. Schubert set the same poem as a quartet, T.T.B.B. (331), and as a trio, T.T.B. (332).

351. 'Fischerlied' (Salis), Song, first version (XX 204). (?) 1816.

Das Fi - scher- ge - wer - be gibt rü - sti - gen Mut!

MS. Unknown; former owner—A. Cranz, Leipzig (together with 350).
1ST ED. 1895, Gesamtausgabe.

Schubert set the same poem again as a song in May 1817 (562), and as a quartet, T.T.B.B., *c.* 1816/7 (364).

352. 'Licht und Liebe,' called '**Nachtgesang**' (Matthäus von Collin), Song (XX 286). (?) 1816.

[Langsam, Tenor: "Lie-be ist ein süsses Licht,"]

MS. Lost.

1ST ED. *c.* 1849, A. Diabelli & Co., Vienna (no. 8818), as no. 1 of *Nachlass*, book 41, second issue.

The first issue of *Nachlass*, book 41, contained, as no. 1, in error, ' Lied eines Kriegers ' (822), which had been published earlier as no. 2 of *Nachlass*, book 35, and was therefore cancelled. The first edition of ' Licht und Liebe ' has a spurious pf. introduction.

353. **String Quartet in E** (Op. posth. 125, no. 2; V 11). 1816.

[Allegro con fuoco]

[Andante]

[MENUETTO Allegro vivace]

[TRIO, pp legato]

[RONDO Allegro vivace, pp]

MS. Unknown; former owner—A. Diabelli, Vienna.

1ST PF. Probably 1816, at a private music society meeting, Vienna.

1ST ED. Early 1830, Josef Czerny (no. 2663).

Nottebohm's Thematic Catalogue (p. 257) mentions a string quartet in F, unpublished in 1872, which might have been this one in E if there was a mistake in the indication of the key.

354. **Four 'Komische Ländler' in D** (for Pianoforte?). 1816.

MS. Stadtbibliothek, Vienna (together with 355 and 370).
1ST ED. No. 4—May 1928, *Festblätter für das 10. Deutsche Sängerbundesfest, Wien 1928*, Vienna, no. 9, p. 217 (ed. by O. E. D.); nos. 1–3 (together with no. 4)—1930, Ed. Strache, Vienna (no. 23) in *Deutsche Tänze*, etc. (ed. by O. E. D. and A. Orel), pp. 16–17.

As these dances are written for treble only it is likely that they were intended as duos for other instruments (violins?).

355. **Eight Ländler in F sharp minor for Pianoforte.** 1816.

MS. Stadtbibliothek, Vienna (together with 354 and 370).

1ST ED. May 1928, *Festblätter für das 10. Deutsche Sängerbundesfest, Wien 1928*, Vienna, no. 9, pp. 215–18 (ed. by O. E. D.).

The first edition was based on an old copy in the editor's possession (formerly belonging to Brahms), which also contains 354.

356. 'Trinklied' ('Funkelnd im Becher,' author unknown), **Quartet, T.T.B.B.**, with (lost) **Pianoforte accompaniment.** 1816.

MS. Score (without acc.)—Stadtbibliothek, Vienna.

1ST ED. 1st June 1844, *Allgemeine Wiener Musikzeitung*, as Supplement no. 4 (vol. iv, no. 66), Pietro Mechetti, Vienna (no. 3946).

Not included in the G.A. The pf. acc. of the first edition is by Karl Czerny (his MS. is attached to Schubert's autograph).

357. 'Gold'ner Schein' (from Matthisson's 'Abendlandschaft'), **Canon for three Voices** (XIX 24). 1816.

MS. Sketch, dated 1st May 1816 (together with 419 and 442)—Dr. Alwin Cranz, Vienna; final version—lost.
1ST PF. (?) 4th May 1927, Musikvereinssaal, Vienna.
1ST ED. 1892, Gesamtausgabe.

358. ' Die Nacht ' (Uz), Song (XX 235). 1816.

[Musical notation: Langsam — "Du ver-störst uns nicht, o Nacht!"]

MS. Fragment only (together with 363)—Otto Taussig, Malmö.
1ST ED. c. 1848, A. Diabelli & Co., Vienna (no. 8821), as no. 2 of *Nachlass*, book 44.

The first five bars of the voice part and the right-hand part of the acc. are missing in the MS.; the first chord, however, of the pf. introduction is genuine.

359. ' Lied der Mignon ' (' Nur wer die Sehnsucht kennt,' from Goethe's ' Wilhelm Meister '), Song (XX 260). 1816.

[Musical notation: Mässig — "Nur wer die Sehn-sucht kennt, weiss, was ich lei-de!"]

MS. Lost (Witteczek's copy).
1ST ED. 1872, J. P. Gotthard, Vienna (no. 337), as no. 13 of forty songs, this song dedicated by the publisher to Fräulein Helene Magnus.

For other settings of this poem, see the note to 481.

360. ' Lied eines Schiffers an die Dioskuren ' (Mayrhofer), Song (Op. 65, no. 1; XX 268). 1816.

[Musical notation: Langsam — "Di-os-ku-ren, Zwil-lings-ster-ne,"]

MS. Lost.
1ST ED. 24th November 1826, Cappi & Czerny, Vienna (no. 221) as no. 1 of Op. 65.

Mayrhofer called this poem ' Schiffers Nachtlied.'

361. 'Am Bach im Frühling' (Schober), **Song** (Op. posth. 109, no. 1; XX 272). 1816.

Nicht zu langsam

Du brachst sie nun, die kal - te Rin - de,

MS. Lost.
1ST ED. 10th July 1829, A. Diabelli & Co., Vienna (no. 3317), as no. 1 of Op. 109.
The pf. introduction of the first edition is probably spurious.

362. '**Lied**' ('Ich bin vergnügt,' Claudius), **Song**, first version (XX 280). 1816.

Ich bin ver - gnügt, im Sie - ges - ton

MS. Stadtbibliothek, Vienna (together with 'Cronnan,' 282).
1ST ED. 1895, Gesamtausgabe.

For the second version, see 501.

363. '**An Chloen**' (I) ('Die Munterkeit ...', Uz), **Song**. Fragment. Not printed. 1816.

MS. (together with 358)—Otto Taussig, Malmö.
The first five bars of the voice-part and of the right-hand part of the acc. are missing. Only this fragment is preserved. This song, together with 170 and 358, was mentioned in a letter by Schubert's nephew, Eduard Schneider, to Anton Diabelli about 1850. Cf. 462.

364. '**Fischerlied**' (Salis), **Quartet, T.T.B.B.** (XXI 35). *c.* 1816–1817 (?).

Etwas langsam

p Das Fi - scher-ge - wer - be gibt rü - sti - gen Mut!

MS. Unknown; former owner—A. Cranz, Leipzig.

1816

IST PF. (?) 18th April 1925, Musikvereinssaal, Vienna.
IST ED. 1897, Gesamtausgabe.
Schubert also set this poem for solo voice with pf. acc. See 351 and 562.

365. Thirty-six Originaltänze (later called **Erste Walzer**) for **Pianoforte** (Op. 9, XII 1). 1816–July 1821.

No. 12.

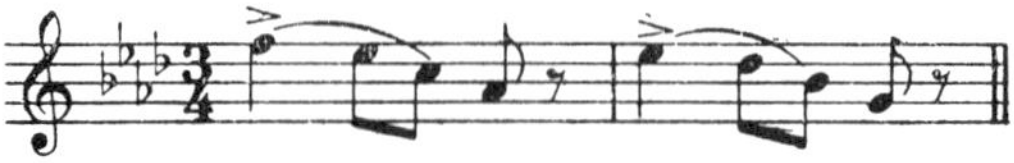

No. 13.

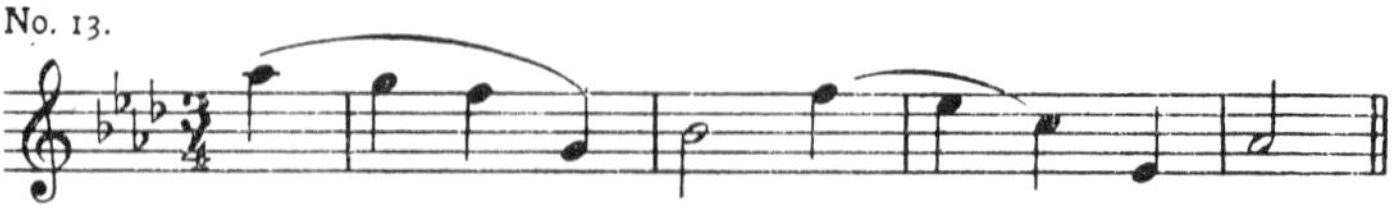

No. 14.

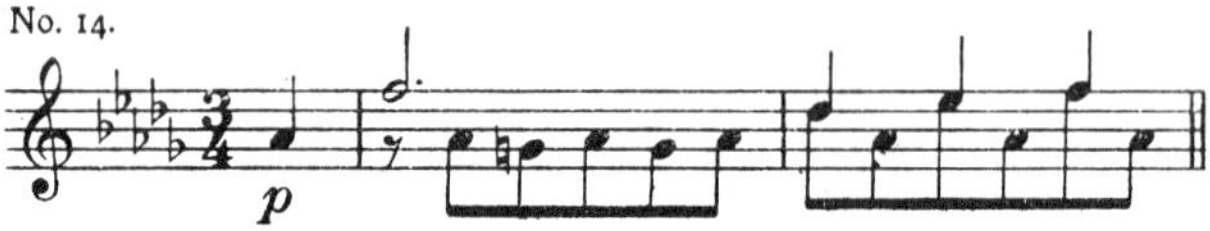

No. 15.

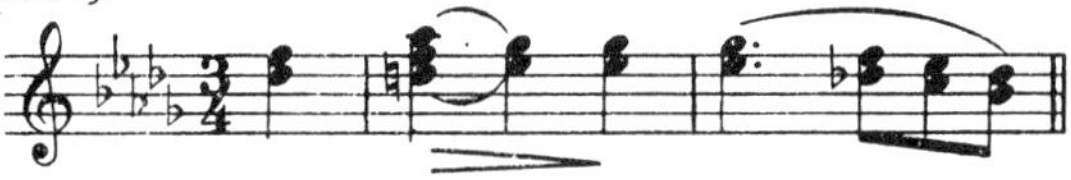

No. 16.

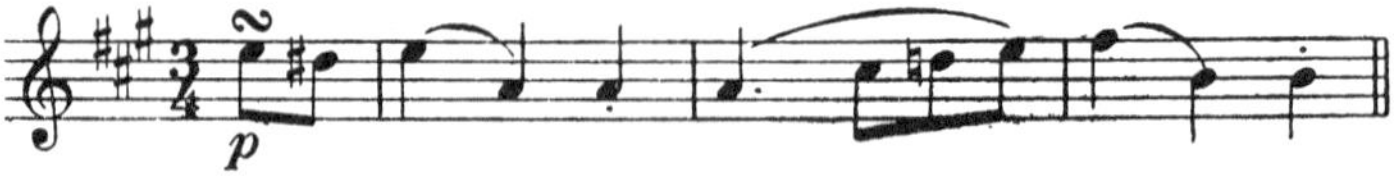

No. 17.

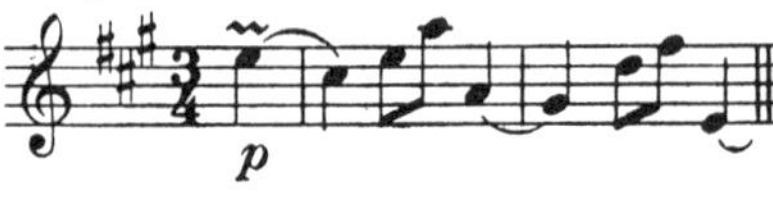

No. 18.

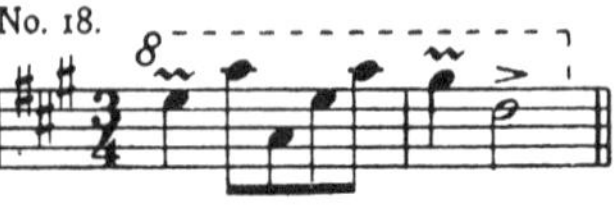

No. 19.

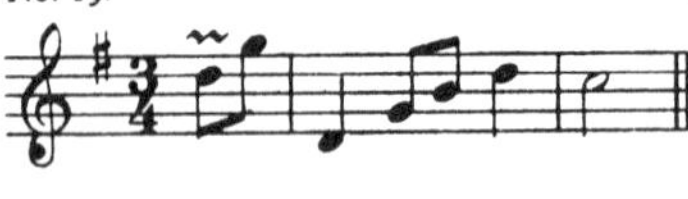

No. 20.

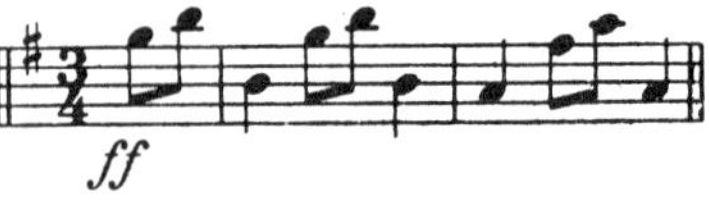

No. 21.

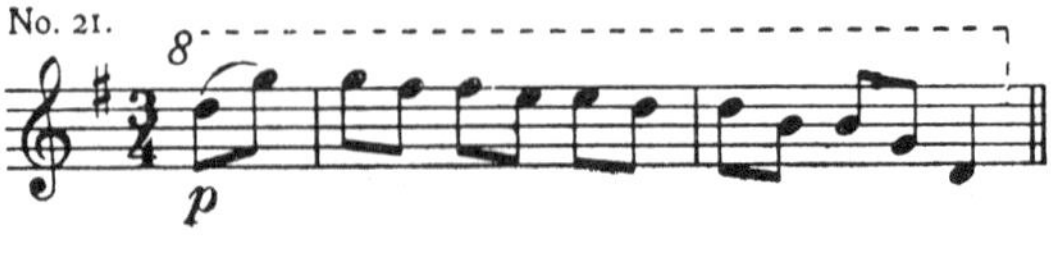

No. 22.

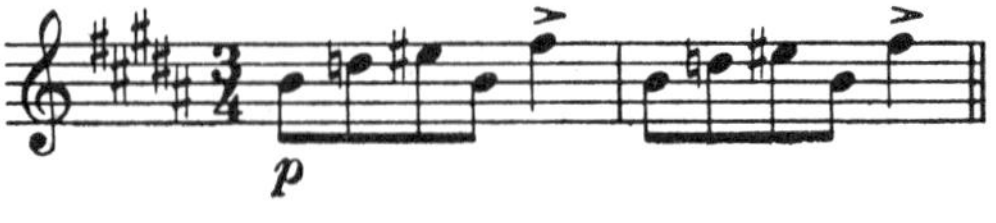

No. 23.

No. 24.

No. 25.

No. 26.

No. 27.

No. 28.

No. 29. *(Atzenbrugger Deutsche No. 3)*

No. 30. *(Atzenbrugger Deutsche No. 5.)*

No. 31. *(Atzenbrugger Deutsche No. 6.)*

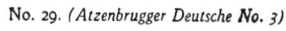

No. 32.

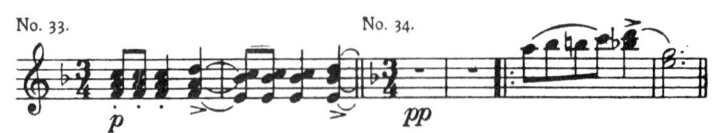

No. 33.   No. 34.

No. 35.   No. 36.

MS. See the entry before 350, the following entry, 640, the entries before 679 and 722, the third and fourth entries before 729; the autographs of nos. 14, 16, 19–24, 26, and 27 lost.

1ST ED. 29th November 1821, Cappi & Diabelli, Vienna (nos. 873 and 874, in two books).

An arrangement for flute, violin, or guitar was published by A. Diabelli & Co., Vienna (no. 979) in 1822.

—— **Ten Deutsche Tänze for Pianoforte** (Op. 9, XII 1, nos. 14, 16, 19–24, 26, and 27). 1816–21.

MS. Lost.

1ST ED. See 365.

Since the other dances of Op. 9 were composed between 1816 and 1821 it is supposed that these ten dances, the MSS. of which are lost, were written during the same period (probably about 1819).

366. Seventeen Deutsche Tänze (called **Ländler**) **for Pianoforte** (XII 10). 1816–November 1824.

No. 1.   No. 2.

No. 3.   No. 4.

No. 5.

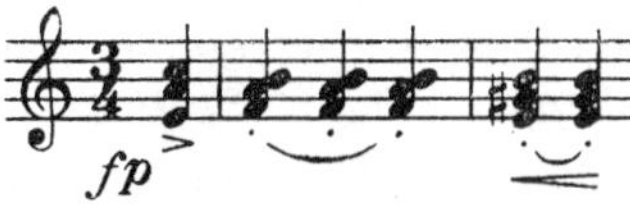

No. 6.

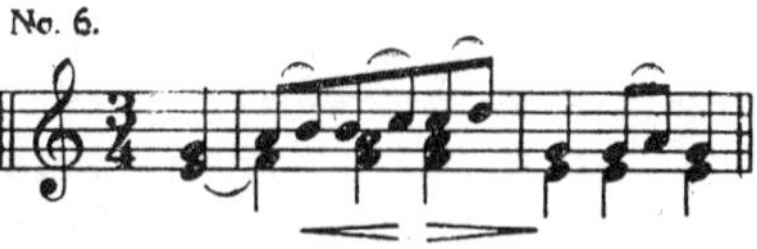

No. 7.

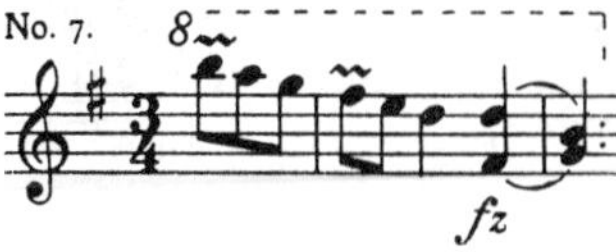

No. 8.

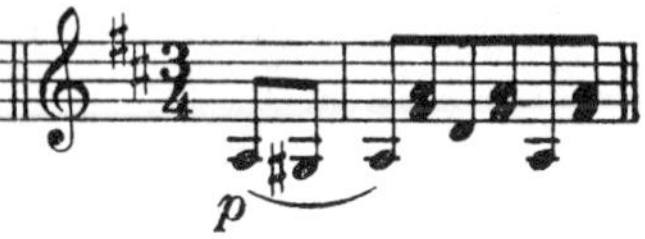

No. 9.

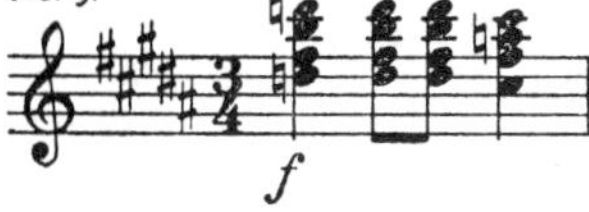

No. 10.

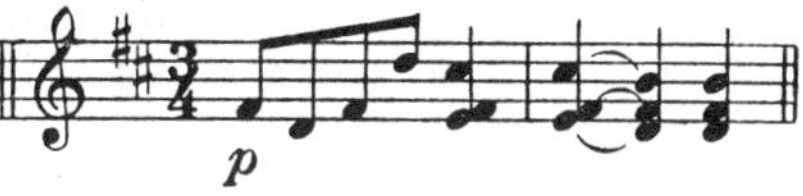

No. 11.

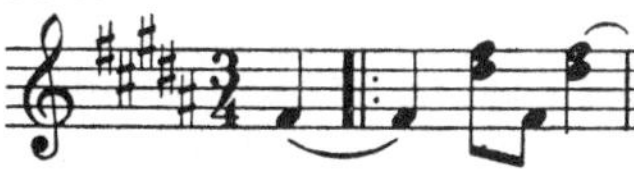

No. 12.

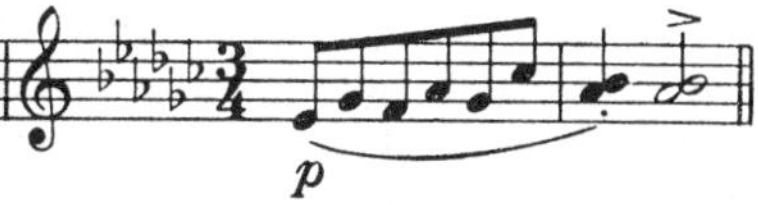

No. 13.

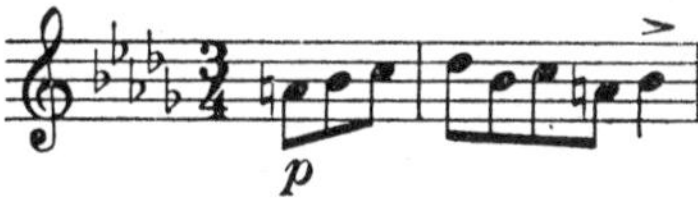

No. 14.

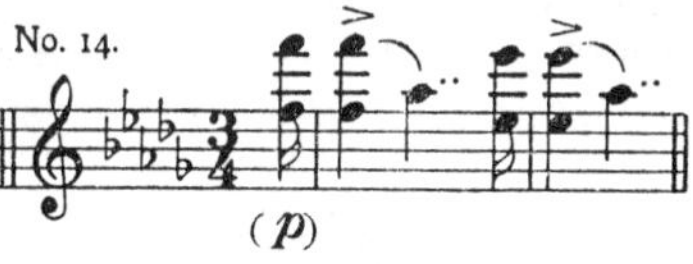

No. 15.

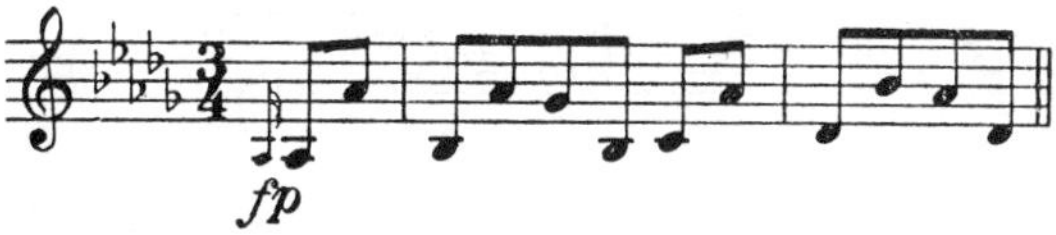

No. 16.

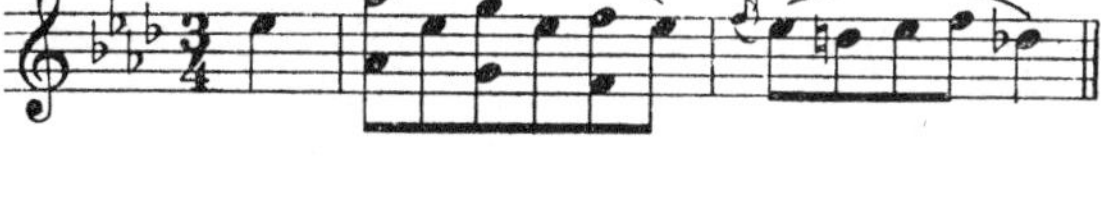

No. 17.

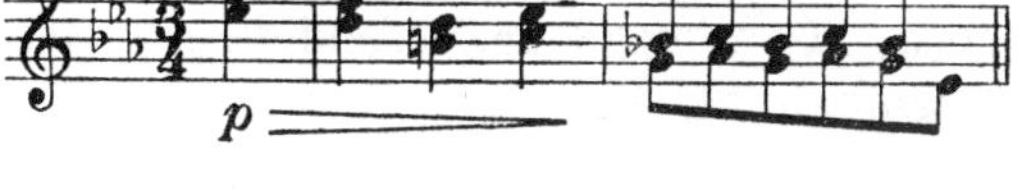

MS. Nos. 1, 4, 6, 7, 9, 10, 13, 14, and 15 (some called *Ländler*, others *Deutsche Tänze*)—Gesellschaft der Musikfreunde, Vienna (see second and last entries before 969; 974 and 975); nos. 2, 3, 5, 8, 12—Fräulein Helene Hauptmann, Leipzig (all, except no. 8, dated July 1824, Zseliz); the trio of no. 7 for piano duet—Stadtbibliothek, Vienna; no. 17, for piano duet (together with Op. 33 (783), no. 8, entitled ' Allemandes,' and dated November 1824)—Frau Marie Floersheim, Wildegg in Aargau (Switzerland).

1ST ED. Nos. 6 and 17—see Note; nos. 1–16—1869, J. P. Gotthard, Vienna (no. 12), in *Zwanzig Ländler* (ed. anonymously by Johannes Brahms), the last four (including no. 17) arranged by the publisher for pf. solo (see 814).

No. 1 is identical with no. 2 of Op. posth. 171, May 1823 (790). The second part of no. 10 is identical, apart from the key, with the second part of no. 8 of the same posthumous Op. No. 6 was first published in the collection *Halt's enk zsamm*, book 2, no. 1 (Sauer & Leidesdorf, Vienna, no. 495) on 21st February 1824. The trio of no. 7 is identical with the first trio of the Deutsche Tänze with two trios and coda for pf. duet, summer 1818 (618). The theme of no. 16 is given on the MS. of the song ' La Pastorella ' (528), dated January 1817. No. 17, originally written for pf. duet in July 1824 (814, no. 1) and arranged by Schubert for pf. solo in November 1824, was first published as a ' waltz ' on 22nd December 1824, as no. 29 of the collection *Musikalisches Angebinde zum neuen Jahre*, Vienna (ed. by K. F. Müller).

367. ' **Der König in Thule** ' (Goethe), **Song** (Op. 5, no. 5; XX 261). Beginning of 1816.

Etwas langsam ($\boldsymbol{\downarrow}$ = 66)

Es war ein Kö - nig in Thu - le,

MS. Fair copy made for Goethe—Preussische Staatsbibliothek, Berlin (Ph.).

1ST ED. 9th July 1821, Cappi & Diabelli, Vienna (no. 789), as no. 5 of Op. 5, published for Schubert and dedicated by him to Antonio Salieri.

The ballad is sung by Gretchen (Margarete) in Goethe's *Faust*. Cf. 118, 126, 440, and 564.

368. ' **Jägers Abendlied** ' (Goethe), **Song**, second version (Op. 3, no. 4; XX 262). Beginning of 1816.

Sehr langsam, leise ($\flat$ = 63)

Im Fel - de schleich' ich still und wild,

MS. Fair copy made for Goethe—Preussische Staatsbibliothek, Berlin (Ph.).
1ST ED. 29th May 1821, Cappi & Diabelli, Vienna (no. 768), as no. 4 of Op. 3, published for Schubert and dedicated by him to Ignaz von Mosel.

According to the copies of Ebner and Stadler, Schubert did not omit the third stanza, as was the case in the printed editions. For the first version, see 215.

369. ' **An Schwager Kronos** ' (Goethe), Song (Op. 19, no. 1; XX 263). Beginning of 1816.

Nicht zu schnell

Spu - 'te dich, Kro - nos!

MS. Lost.
1ST PF. 11th January 1827, Musikverein, Vienna.
1ST ED. 6th June 1825, A. Diabelli & Co., Vienna (no. 1800), as no. 1 of Op. 19, dedicated by Schubert to the poet.

— ' **Die gefangenen Sänger** ' (XX 389). See 712. January (?) 1816.

370. **Eight Ländler in D for Pianoforte.** January 1816.

1.

2.

3.

MS. Stadtbibliothek, Vienna (together with 354 and 355), melody only.

1ST ED. 1930, Ed. Strache, Vienna (no. 23), in *Deutsche Tänze*, etc. (ed. by O. E. D. and A. Orel), pp. 6–8 (arranged by Orel).

The MS. contains, in fact, nine Ländler, the original no. 7, in D, however, being identical with no. 6 of eight Ländler in B flat for pf., 13th February 1816 (378). The eight Ländler in F sharp minor (355) and the four *Komische Ländler* (354) are included also in this MS.

371. ' Klage ' (' Trauer umfliesst mein Leben,' author unknown), Song, second version (XX 185 (*b*)). January 1816.

MS. Dr. Alwin Cranz, Vienna (together with 431–3).

1ST ED. 1872, J. P. Gotthard, Vienna (no. 345), as no. 21 of forty songs.

For the poem and the first setting, see 292. Schubert's nephew, Eduard Schneider, Vienna, possessed six songs, five of which, dated May 1816 came into the Cranz collection; among them this song, written in the MS. between 'Blumenlied' and 'Der Leidende' (431, 432). The autographs of 429 and 430 have been separated from those three songs at some time since 1895.

372. **'An die Natur'** (Stolberg), **Song** (XX 183).   15th January 1816.

Mässig

Sü - sse, hei - li - ge Na - tur,

MS. Stadtbibliothek, Vienna (together with 373); another MS.
—Meangya family, Mödling, near Vienna (Ph.).
IST ED. 1895, Gesamtausgabe.

The Mödling MS. is written in the key of A. Johann Michael Vogl set this famous poem in 1812 for Antonie Adamberger, for inclusion in Kotzebue's play *Die Erbschaft*, performed at the Burgtheater in Vienna.

373. **'Lied'** ('Mutter geht durch ihre Kammern,' from Fouqué's 'Undine'), **Song** (XX 184).   15th January 1816.

Mut - ter geht durch' ih - re Kam-mern,

MS. Stadtbibliothek, Vienna (together with 372).
IST ED. 1895, Gesamtausgabe.

—— **'Loda's Gespenst'** (XX 44).   See 150.   17th January 1816.

374. **Six Ländler in B flat for (?) Violin Solo.**   February 1816.

No. 4.

No. 6.

No. 8.

No. 9.

No. 10.

No. 11.

MS. Unknown; former owner—Frau Marie Radler-Warhanek, Graz (without date, together with 377).

1ST ED. *Festblätter zum 6. Deutschen Sängerbundesfest in Graz 1902*, no. 9, pp. 346–51, 27th July 1902 (ed. by Wilhelm Kienzl).

The MS. contains eleven Ländler, inscribed 'Violino,' five of which were printed earlier. Nos. 1–3 are identical with 378, nos. 1–3; no. 5 with no. 7; and no. 7 with no. 4. The indication, given by Kienzl, that these eleven dances were written at Wildbach in Styria is without foundation. The MS. was, in fact, given by Schubert's heirs to the Gesangsverein of Iglau (now Jihlava, in Czechoslovakia) and it passed at a later date to Frau Radler; furthermore, Schubert visited Wildbach on one occasion only—in 1827.

375. '**Der Tod Oskar's**' (anonymous, translated by Harold, revised by (?) Franz Hummelauer), **Song** (XX 187). February 1816.

Mässig, in schmerzlicher Erinnerung

Wa - rum öff - nest du wie - der, Er - zeug-ter von Al- pin,

MS. Lost.

1ST ED. 10th July 1830, A. Diabelli & Co., Vienna (no. 3635), as *Nachlass*, book 5 (Ossian Songs, book 5).

The poem was published by Macpherson in his notes to Ossian's 'Temora,' but he does not attribute it to Ossian. In the Schubert song, however, it is attributed to Ossian. The G.A. replaced the version of the first edition by Harold's translation; but it is quite possible that Schubert used the text as given in the first edition. Cf. 221.

376. '**Lorma**' (from Ossian's 'Battle of Lora,' translated by Harold), **Song**, second version (XX 592). Fragment. 10th February 1816.

[musical notation: Traurig, langsam, RECIT. — "Lor-ma sass in der Hal-le von Al-do."]

MS. Stadtbibliothek, Vienna.
1ST ED. 1895, Gesamtausgabe.
The remainder of the MS. seems to have been lost. For the first version, see 327.

377. '**Das Grab**,' called '**Das stille Land**' (Salis), **Song**, second version (XX 186). 11th February 1816.

[musical notation: CHORUS, Langsam — "Das Grab ist tief und stil-le"]

MS. Sketch and fair copy (without date)—unknown; former owner—Frau Marie Radler-Warhanek, Graz (together with 374).
1ST ED. 1872, J. P. Gotthard, Vienna (no. 320), as no. 5 of nine part-songs.

This song, intended to be published in 1829 by Tobias Haslinger, Vienna, may have been conceived by Schubert as a chorus, as indicated in the G.A., for male or for mixed voices. For the first and third versions, see 330 and 569.

378. **Eight Ländler in B flat for Pianoforte** (XII 12). 13th February 1816.

[musical notation: No. 1.]

[musical notation: No. 2.]

No. 3.

No. 4.

No. 5.

No. 6.

No. 7.

No. 8.

MS. Stadtbibliothek, Vienna.
1ST ED. 1889, Gesamtausgabe.

For nos. 1–3, see 378.   No. 2 is similar to the trio of Op. 127 (146), no. 10. No. 6 is identical with no. 7 (in D) of nine Ländler dated January 1816 (370).

379. Salve Regina, called 'Deutsches Salve Regina,' or 'Hymne an die heilige Mutter Gottes' (translator unknown), in F for Mixed Chorus, S.A.T.B., and Organ (XIV 17).   21st February 1816.

p Sei, Mut - ter der Barm - her - zig - keit,

MS. Alfred Wiede, Weissenborn, near Zwickau, Saxony.

1ST ED. (score and parts) 1859, Karl Haslinger, Vienna (no. 12265), dedicated by Ferdinand Schubert to a Viennese society of artists, called 'Hesperus,' in acknowledgment of their patronage of Schubert's works.

Ferdinand Schubert added an orchestral acc. in 1832 (MS.—Wiener Männergesangverein, Vienna). This may have been the reason why the whole work was sometimes ascribed to Ferdinand. There is a copy of the soprano part by Ferdinand in the Gesellschaft der Musikfreunde, Vienna.

380. Two Minuets with a Trio to each, for Pianoforte (XXI 28). 22nd February 1816.

MS. Stadtbibliothek, Vienna.
1ST ED. 1897, Gesamtausgabe.
The MS. also contains an unfinished minuet.

381. 'Morgenlied' ('Die frohe neubelebte Flur,' author unknown), **Song** (XX 189). 24th February 1816.

MS. (together with 382)—Frau Marie Floersheim, Wildegg in Aargau (Switzerland).
1ST ED. 1895, Gesamtausgabe.

382. '**Abendlied**' ('Sanft glänzt die Abendsonne,' author unknown), **Song** (XX 190). 24th February 1816.

Sanft glänzt die A - bend - son - ne

MS. (together with 381)—Frau Marie Floersheim, Wildegg in Aargau (Switzerland).
1ST ED. 1895, Gesamtausgabe.
381 and 382 may have been written by the same author.

383. **Stabat Mater** (German words by Klopstock) **in F for Soli, Chorus (S.A.T.B.), and Orchestra** (XIV 13). 28th February 1816.

No. 1. CHORUS
Largo
p Je - sus Chri - stus   schwebt   am Kreu - ze!

No. 2. ARIA (Sopr.)
Andantino
Bei des Mitt - lers Kreu - ze   stan - den

No. 3. CHORUS
Andante
Lie - bend nei - get   er   sein   Ant - litz!

No. 4. DUET (Sopr. and Ten.)
Allegretto
p En - gel   freu - ten   sich   der   Won - ne,

No. 5. CHORUS
Larghetto

p Wer wird Zäh - ren sanf - ten Mit - leids

No. 6. ARIA (Ten.)
Adagio

Ach, was hät - ten wir em - pfun - den,

No. 7. CHORUS
Allegro maestoso

f Er - ben sol - len. sie am Thro - ne,

No. 8. ARIA Bass)
Andantino

Sohn des Va - ters, a - ber lei - den,

No. 9. CHORUS
Maestoso O O du
du, herr - li - cher, du

f O du herr - li - cher, du herr - li - cher, du

No. 10. TERZET (Sopr., Ten., and Bass)
Allegro moderato

Er - den - freu - den und ihr E - lend,

No. 11. TERZET with CHORUS (Sopr., Ten., and Bass)
Andante sostenuto

Dass der - einst wir, wenn im To - de wir ent - schla - fen,

No. 12. CHORUS

f A - men, a - men, a - - - - - - - - - men.

MS. Sketches for the end of section 5 and for section 6—E. H. W. Meyerstein, London; full score—Stadtbibliothek, Vienna (together with 386).

1ST PF. 24th March 1833, Vienna.
1ST ED. 1888, Gesamtausgabe.

—— **Several Goethe Songs.** Fair copies. *c.* March 1816.
MS. Preussische Staatsbibliothek, Berlin (Ph.).

See 142 and 321. These songs were sent to Goethe, together with Josef von Spaun's letter to the poet, on 17th April 1816, asking him to accept the dedication. No favourable answer was received, but the songs were returned. Cf. entry before 435.

Literature. O. E. D., *Die Musik*, Berlin, October 1928. *Lieder von Goethe komponiert von Franz Schubert*, ed. by Georg Schünemann, Berlin, 1943 (with facsimiles of all the sixteen extant songs of the first volume, sent to Goethe).

384. Sonatina in D for Pianoforte and Violin (Op. posth. 137, no. 1; VIII 2). March 1816.

MS. Score (except end of last movement)—Dr. Alwin Cranz, Vienna; end of last movement—Otto Taussig, Malmö; the last six bars (slightly different)—Newberry Library, Chicago (see 396); pf. part of the first movement—Dr. Alwin Cranz, Vienna.

1ST ED. 1836, A. Diabelli & Co., Vienna (no. 5848), as no. 1 of Op. 137.

Schubert entitled the work ' Sonate fürs Pianoforte mit Begleitung der Violine.' Cf. 385 and 408.

Literature. W. Daly, *The Musical Educator*, London, 1910, vol. iv, pp. 37–50.

385. Sonatina in A minor for Pianoforte and Violin (Op. posth. 137, no. 2; VIII 3). March 1816.

MS. Score of the first three movements—Library of Congress, Washington (Ph.).

IST ED. 1836, A. Diabelli & Co., Vienna (no. 5849), as no. 2 of Op. 137.

The work is entitled, probably by another hand, 'Sonate II pour le Pianoforte et Violon.' Cf. 384 and 408.

386. **Salve Regina in B flat for Mixed Chorus** (XIV 20).   March 1816.

MS. Stadtbibliothek, Vienna (sketch, together with 383).
IST ED. 1888, Gesamtausgabe.

387. '**Die Schlacht**' (Schiller), second sketch of a **Cantata with Pianoforte accompaniment** (XXI 44).   March 1816.

INTRODUCTION
Marcia

Schwer und dum-pfig, ei-ne Wet - - ter-wol-ke

MS. Stadtbibliothek, Vienna.
1ST ED. 1897, Gesamtausgabe.

Schubert used the pf. introduction for the first of his three 'Marches héroiques,' pf. duet, Op. 27 (602). See also the earlier sketch, 249.

388. '**Laura am Klavier**' (Schiller), **Song**, two versions (XX 193 (*a*) and (*b*)). March 1816.

a **Mässig**
RECIT.
Wenn dein Fın-ger durch die Sai ten mei-stert.

b **Mässig**
Wenn dein Fin-ger durch die Sai - ten mei-stert.

MS. (*a*) Only the last three bars (together with the fragments of 389 and 402)—unknown; former owner—Johann von Päumann, Vienna; (*b*) lost.
1ST ED. 1895, Gesamtausgabe.

Besides the Witteczek copy of (*a*), and the copies of (*b*) by Ebner and Stadler, there is also a copy of (*b*) by Ferdinand Schubert, preserved by the Krasser family, Vienna.

389. '**Des Mädchens Klage**' (from Schiller's '*Die Piccolomini*'), **Song**, third version (XX 194). March 1816.

Langsam
Der Eich - wald braust,

MS. Title and date only—unknown; former owner—Johann von Päumann, Vienna (together with 388 and 402).
1ST ED. 1873, J. Guttentag, Berlin, in August Reissmann's *Schubert*, Appendix no. 5, pp. 12–14.
There are fragments of three songs on the MS., which contains only the titie and the date of this song. For the first and second versions, see 6 and 191.

390. ' Die Entzückung an Laura ' (Schiller), Song, first version (XX 195). March 1816.

In sanfter Bewegung

Lau - ra, ü - ber die - se Welt

MS. Leo Liepmannssohn, Berlin (1929, sale 56).
1ST ED. 1895, Gesamtausgabe.
For the other version, see 577.

391. ' Die vier Weltalter ' (Schiller), Song (Op. posth. 111, no. 3; XX 196). March 1816.

Behaglich

Wohl per - let im Gla - se der pur - pur - ne Wein.

MS. Lost.
1ST ED. 5th February 1829, Josef Czerny, Vienna (no. 335), as no. 3 of Op. 111.
The poem consists of twelve stanzas.

392. ' Pflügerlied ' (Salis), Song (XX 197). March 1816.

Ruhig

Ar - beit - sam und wa - cker,

MS. Rough draft (together with 393)—Albert Cranz, New York; fair copy—Meangya family, Mödling, near Vienna (Ph.).
1ST ED. 1895, Gesamtausgabe.

393. ' Die Einsiedelei ' (Salis), Song, first version (XX 198). March 1816.

[musical notation: "Es ric - selt, klar und we - hend"]

MS. Rough draft, incomplete (together with 392)—Albert Cranz, New York.
1ST ED. *c.* 1842, A. Diabelli & Co., Vienna (no. 7416), as no. 1 of *Nachlass*, book 38.

For the second version see 563, and for the setting of the same poem as a quartet (T.T.B.B.) see 337.

394. '**Gesang an die Harmonie,**' called '**An die Harmonie,**' or '**An die Harmonien**' (Salis), **Song** (XX 199). March 1816.

[musical notation: Mässig — "Schöp - fe - rin be - seel - ter Tö - ne!"]

MS. Lost (Witteczek's copy).
1ST ED. 1895, Gesamtausgabe.

395. '**Lebensmelodien**' (August Wilhelm von Schlegel), **Song** (Op. posth. III, no. 2; XX 205). March 1816.

[musical notation: Mässig, ruhig — "Auf den Was - sern wohnt mein stil - les Le - ben,"]

MS. Lost.
1ST ED. 5th February 1829, Josef Czerny, Vienna (no. 335), as no. 2 of Op. III (with only one stanza).

396. '**Gruppe aus dem Tartarus**' (Schiller), **Song**, first version. Fragment. Not printed. March 1816.
MS. (together with the last six bars of 384)—Newberry Library, Chicago.

The MS. contains only the first fourteen bars, in C minor, 4/4, 'Mässig.' For the second version, see 583, and for the setting as a canon for trio, T.T.B., see 65.

397. '**Ritter Toggenburg**' (Schiller), **Song** (XX 191). 13th March 1816.

Ruhig

"Rit - ter, treu - e Schwe - ster • lie - be

MS. Sketch and fair copy—Karl Ernst Henrici, Berlin (June 1922).
1ST ED. 29th October 1832, A. Diabelli & Co., Vienna (no. 4267), as no. 2 of *Nachlass*, book 19 (corrupt).

Schubert's model for this song, Zumsteeg's setting, was published in February 1800, in the first vol. of his *Kleine Balladen und Lieder*, Breitkopf & Härtel, Leipzig, and reprinted in the G.A., supplement to the first issue of vol. iii of Schubert's songs, pp. 11–13, Breitkopf & Härtel (no. 20865), 1895. There exists a MS. copy, by another hand, of the beginning of Zumsteeg's setting (Stadtbibliothek, Vienna), on the back of which Schubert wrote a variant of a section of the string Quartet in B flat (68).

398. '**Frühlingslied**' ('Die Luft ist blau,' author unknown), **Song** (XX 217). 13th March 1816.

Heiter

Die Luft ist blau, das Tal ist grün,

MS. (together with 399–401)—Library of Congress, Washington.
1ST ED. 1887, C. F. Peters, Leipzig, as no. 39 of *Schubert Album*, book 7 (ed. by Max Friedlaender).

The date in the G.A., 13th May 1816, is an error. Schubert also set the poem as a trio, T.T.B. (243). The poem was wrongly attributed to Hölty.

399. '**Auf den Tod einer Nachtigall**' (Hölty), **Song** (XX 218). 13th March 1816

Traurig. Sehr langsam

Sie ist da - hin,

MS. (together with 398, 400, 401)—Library of Congress, Washington.
1ST ED. 1895, Gesamtausgabe.

The date in the G.A., 13th May 1816, is an error. For the sketch, see 201.

400. 'Die Knabenzeit' (Hölty), **Song** (XX 219). 13th March 1816.

Wie glück-lich, wem das Kna-ben-kleid

MS. (together with 398, 399, 401)—Library of Congress, Washington.
1ST ED. 1895, Gesamtausgabe.

The date in the G.A., 13th May 1816, is an error. A sketch for a second version, consisting of only four bars of the melody, is to be found in the *Revisionsbericht*.

401. 'Winterlied' (Hölty), **Song** (XX 220). 13th March 1816.

Kei-ne Blu-men blühn;

MS. (together with 398–400)—Library of Congress, Washington.
1ST ED. 1895, Gesamtausgabe.

The date in the G.A., 13th May 1816, is an error.

402. 'Der Flüchtling' (Schiller), **Song** (XX 192). 18th March 1816.

Ziemlich langsam

Frisch at-met des Mor-gens le-ben-di-ger Hauch;

MS. Fragment—unknown; former owner—Johann von Päumann, Vienna (together with the fragments of 388 and 389).
1ST ED. 1872, J. P. Gotthard, Vienna (no. 360), as no. 36 of forty songs, this song dedicated by the publisher to Gustav Walter.

The MS. was reproduced in facsimile in the *Illustrierte Zeitung*, Leipzig, 8th May 1880. Apparently there was, in 1887, a complete MS. in the possession of Herr E. Kanitz, Vienna, with the tempo indication ' Feierlich ' instead of ' Ziemlich langsam.' For another setting of the poem, as a trio, T.T.B., see 67.

403. 'Lied' ('In's stille Land,' Salis), **Song,** two versions (XX 201 (*a*) and (*b*)). 27th March–April 1816, August 1823.

a Mässig

In's stil - le Land!

b Mässig, mit Sehnsucht

In's stil - le Land!

MS. (*a*) In G minor, dated 27th March 1816—Preussische Staatsbibliothek, Berlin (together with 405); (*b*) in A minor, dated March 1816, with pf. introduction—Meangya family, Mödling, near Vienna (Ph.); another MS., dated April 1816, without pf. introduction—Stadtbibliothek, Vienna (together with 404); and yet another MS. of the song, probably an album leaf, dated August 1823, with another pf. introduction—Sotheby, London (3rd April 1950).
1ST ED. (*a*) *c*. 1842, A. Diabelli & Co., Vienna (no. 7417), as no. 3 of *Nachlass*, book 39 (with a spurious pf. introduction, (?) added by Diabelli); (*b*) 1895, Gesamtausgabe.

404. '**Wehmut**' ('Mit leisen Harfentönen,' Salis), called '**Die Herbstnacht**,' Song (XX 200). End of March–April 1816.

Langsam

Mit lei - sen Har - fen - tö - nen sei,

MS. Rough draft, dated March 1816 (together with 406)—Mrs. Mary Louise Zimbalist, Philadelphia; final version, dated April 1816 (together with 403)—Stadtbibliothek, Vienna (Witteczek's copy).
1ST ED. (after the rough draft) *c*. 1860, C. A. Spina, Vienna (no. 16760), together with 406.

Schubert misnamed the song 'Die Herbstnacht' in the rough draft, this being the title of another Salis poem. The first edition is not mentioned in Nottebohm's catalogue, which probably accounts for Max Friedlaender including this song as no. 4 of twenty *Nachgelassene Lieder* published by C. F. Peters, Leipzig, 1885.

405. '**Der Herbstabend**' (Salis), **Song** (XX 202). End of March–April 1816.

[Musical notation: Langsam]

A - bend - glo - cken - hal - le__ zit__ tern

MS. Sketch—Preussische Staatsbibliothek, Berlin (together with 403); complete MS., with pf. introduction—Meangya family, Mödling, near Vienna (Ph.); fair copy, dated April 1816 (together with 406)—Stadtbibliothek, Vienna.

1ST ED. 1895, Gesamtausgabe.

The poem has a sub-title: ' An Sie.'

406. ' **Abschied von der Harfe** ' (Salis), **Song** (XX 208). End of March–April 1816.

[Musical notation: Etwas bewegt]

Noch ein - mal tön', o Har - fe,

MS. Rough draft (together with 404)—Mrs. Mary Louise Zimbalist, Philadelphia; fair copy, dated April 1816 (together with 405)—Stadtbibliothek, Vienna.

1ST ED. (after the rough draft) c. 1860, C. A. Spina, Vienna (no. 16,760), together with 404.

The first edition is neither mentioned in Nottebohm's catalogue nor in the *Revisionsbericht*. On account of this, no doubt, Max Friedlaender included the song as a first edition in the *Schubert Album*, book 7, no. 34, published by C. F. Peters, Leipzig, in 1887. The rough draft gives the tempo as ' Etwas geschwind,' and the fair copy as ' Etwas langsam.'

407. ' **Beitrag zur fünfzigjährigen Jubelfeier des Herrn Salieri** ' ('Gütigster, Bester, Weisester,' Schubert), **Cantata for Quartet, T.T.B.B., Tenor Solo with Pianoforte accompaniment, and Canon for three voices,** first version (XVI 44). Spring 1816.

[Musical notation: QUARTET, Adagio molto]

Gü - tig - ster, Be - ster! Wei - se - ster, Gröss - ter!

[Musical notation: Andantino]

So Güt' als Weis- heit strö - men mild,

CANON A TRE
Moderato

Un-ser al-ler Gross-pa-pa, blei-be noch recht lan-ge da.

MS. Conservatoire, Paris (Ph.).
1ST ED. 1891, Gesamtausgabe (incomplete).
The Paris MS. seems to be the first, and only complete, version of the cantata; for the setting as a trio with pf. acc., see 441.

408. Sonatina in G minor for Pianoforte and Violin (Op. posth. 137, no. 3; VIII 4). April 1816.

Allegro giusto

f

Andante

p dolce

Menuetto
tr

f

TRIO

p dolce

Allegro moderato

p

MS. Score, first movement—Dr. Alwin Cranz, Vienna; remainder—Otto Taussig, Malmö.
1ST ED. 1836, A. Diabelli & Co., Vienna (no. 5850), as no. 3 of Op. 137 (cf. 384 and 385).
Schubert describes the MS. as 'Sonate III.'

409. 'Die verfehlte Stunde' (August Wilhelm von Schlegel), **Song**, two versions (the first XX 206, the second not printed). April (September) 1816.

Unruhig

Quä-lend un-ge-still-tes Seh-nen

MS. First version—Preussische Staatsbibliothek, Berlin; second version—Leo Liepmannssohn, Berlin (March 1929).
1ST ED. 1872, J. P. Gotthard, Vienna (no. 350), as no. 26 of forty songs, this song dedicated by the publisher to Frau Louise Dustmann.

The Witteczek Collection contains a copy of the second version, dated September 1816.

410. '**Sprache der Liebe**' (August Wilhelm von Schlegel), **Song** (Op. posth. 115, no. 3; XX 207). April 1816.

Zart, lieblich

Lass dich mit ge-lin- - den Schlä-gen rüh-ren,

MS. In a private collection in Germany (1912).
1ST ED. 16th June 1829, M. J. Leidesdorf, Vienna (no. 1152), as no. 3 of Op. 115.

The pf. introduction, thought to be spurious, is proved to be genuine by the facsimile of the MS. in Dahms' *Schubert*, first edition, supplement, p. 34. The motto of the poem, reprinted in the G.A., is by Ludwig Tieck.

411. '**Daphne am Bach**' (Stolberg), **Song** (XX 209). April 1816.

Ich hab' ein Bäch-lein fun-den

MS. Erwin von Spaun, Vienna (together with 144, 186, 188).
1ST ED. 1887, C. F. Peters, Leipzig, as no. 37 of *Schubert Album*, book 7 (ed. by Max Friedlaender).

412. '**Stimme der Liebe**' ('Meine Selinde,' Stolberg), **Song**, (XX 210). April 1816.

Langsam

Mei-ne Se-lin-de!

MS. Fräulein Marie Schubert, Vienna (in the key of E).
IST ED. June 1838, A. Diabelli, Vienna (no. 5033), as no. 1 of *Nachlass*, book 29.

413. ' Entzückung ' (Matthisson), **Song** (XX 211). April 1816.

Nicht zu geschwind

Tag voll— Him - mel!

MS. Dr. Alwin Cranz, Vienna (together with 414 and 415).
IST ED. 1895, Gesamtausgabe.

414. ' **Geist der Liebe** ' (' Der Abend schleiert Flur und Hain,' Matthisson), **Song** (XX 212). April 1816.

Ruhig, zart

Der A - bend schlei - ert Flur und Hain

MS. Dr. Alwin Cranz, Vienna (together with 413 and 415).
IST ED. 1895, Gesamtausgabe.
Schubert set the same poem for quartet, T.T.B.B., in January 1822 (747).

415. ' **Klage** ' (' Die Sonne steigt,' Matthisson), **Song** (XX 213). April 1816.

Ruhig

Die Son - ne steigt, die Son - ne sinkt,

MS. Dr. Alwin Cranz, Vienna (together with 413 and 414).
IST ED. 1895, Gesamtausgabe.
Schubert has converted the first four stanzas of the poem into two verses of his song; it is uncertain whether the fifth stanza should be omitted, or sung to one-half of the melody.

416. ' **Lied in der Abwesenheit** ' (Stolberg), **Song**. April 1816.

Langsam

Ach, mir ist das Herz so schwer, trau - rig irr' ich hin und her,

MS. Fräulein Marie Schubert, Vienna.

1ST PF. 14th December 1925, Musikvereinssaal, Vienna.
1ST ED. December 1925, *Moderne Welt*, Vienna, Supplement, pp. 1–2 (ed. by O. E. D.).

The last five bars are missing in the MS., and were supplied by E. Mandyczewski for the first edition.

417. Symphony in C minor, called ' **The Tragic** ' (I 4). Finished 27th April 1816.

MS. Sketch of the last movement (on the back of which is part of a vocal composition)—Sotheby, London (3rd April 1935, not identified in the catalogue); Score—Gesellschaft der Musikfreunde, Vienna.

1ST PF. Probably 1816, at a meeting of a private music society in Vienna; first public performance: 19th November 1849, Buchhändlerbörse, Leipzig (conductor, A. F. Riccius).

1ST ED. 1884, Gesamtausgabe (see note).

The word 'Tragische' was added on the title of the symphony by Schubert himself, but at a later date. The second movement (Andante) was published in score by Peters (no. 5404) at the beginning of 1871. The third movement, *Allegro vivace*, is entitled 'Minuetto' in Schubert's MS.; this designation is missing in the Gesamtausgabe score. An arrangement for piano duet of the complete work was published shortly after 1870 by Hugo Ulrich (no. 766 of the Peters edition).

418. 'Stimme der Liebe' ('Abendgewölke schweben hell,' Matthisson), Song, second version (XX 214). 29th April 1816.

Mässig
A - bend - ge - wöl - ke schwe - ben hell

MS. N. Simrock, Berlin.
1ST ED. 1895, Gesamtausgabe.
For the first version, see 187.

419. 'Julius an Theone' (Matthisson), Song (XX 215). 30th April 1816.

Geschwind
Nim - mer, nim - mer darf ich dir ge - ste - hen,

MS. Dr. Alwin Cranz, Vienna (together with 357 and 442).
1ST ED. 1895, Gesamtausgabe.

Schubert slightly altered the text of the third stanza (see *Revisionsbericht*).

420. **Twelve Deutsche Tänze for Pianoforte** (XII 11 (*a*)). (?) May 1816.

No. 1.
p

No. 2.
(*p*)

MS. Lost.

1ST ED. 1871, J. P. Gotthard, Vienna (no. 132), together with five of eight écossaises dated February 1817 (529).

On the title of the first edition the date 1817 is given for both groups of dances. A copy of the MS., which includes a coda, was formerly in the possession of the von Spaun family at Görz, dated by Josef von Spaun 1816. These dances may have been written for Spaun's sister Marie (cf. 299 and 421).

421. Six Écossaises for Pianoforte (XII 27, nos. 1-6). May 1816.

MS. Gesellschaft der Musikfreunde, Vienna.
1ST ED. 1889, Gesamtausgabe.

The MS. shows dance no. 1 written in A flat instead of B, as in Op. 18, XII 2, Écossaise no. 5 (145). These dances are said to have been written at the house of Professor Heinrich Josef Watteroth (see 451), Erdberggasse, in the Vienna suburb Landstrasse, where Schubert stayed as the ' prisoner ' of Josef von Spaun. It is a fact that Schubert stayed in Watteroth's house in May 1816, together with Spaun and Josef Wilhelm Witteczek. At the end of the MS. is the note: ' Gott sey Lob und Dank.' This note has been variously quoted, which may indicate that the MS. was at one time more extensive than it is to-day. Kreissle quoted it, in a letter to Schober, 5th August 1861, as follows: ' In meiner Behausung in Erdberg als Gefangener componirt. Gott sei Dank! ' and in his *Schubert* (Vienna, 1865, p. 97), in the following form: ' Als Arrestant in meinem Zimmer in Erdberg componirt. Mai. [At the end of the MS.:] Gott sei Dank! ' On p. 612 of his book, Kreissle quotes the note in yet another form: ' als Arrestant des Herrn Witteczek in Erdberg,' and states that the dances were dedicated to Fräulein Marie von Spaun, Josef's sister, a statement which seems to be incorrect (cf. 299 and 420).

422. ' **Naturgenuss** ' (Matthisson), **Quartet, T.T.B.B.** (Op. 16, no. 2; XVI 8). May 1816 and February 1822.

MS. Stadtbibliothek, Vienna (without acc.).
1ST PF. 18th May 1851, Vienna.
1ST ED. 9th October 1823, Cappi & Diabelli, Vienna (no. 1175), as no. 2 of Op. 16.

The pf. acc. was added in February 1822; the guitar acc. is spurious. For the setting of this poem for solo voice see 188.

423. ' **Andenken** ' (' Ich denke dein,' Matthisson), **Trio, T.T.B.** May 1816.

[Musical notation: Ruhig, 6/8 — "Ich den-ke dein, wenn durch den Hain"]

MS. Fräulein Emilie Schaup, Vienna (together with 424; see also 428).

1ST ED. Facsimile of Albert Stadler's copy—November 1927, *Festblätter für das 10. Deutsche Sängerbundesfest, Wien 1928*, no. 3, p. 59 (ed. by O. E. D.).

The autograph was found after the publication of the facsimile. (See note to 2.) For the setting as a solo song, see 99.

424. '**Erinnerungen**' ('Am Seegestad',' Matthisson), **Trio, T.T.B.** May 1816.

[Musical notation: Langsam, 6/8 — "Am See-ge-stad' in lau-en Voll-monds-näch-ten"]

MS. Fräulein Emilie Schaup, Vienna (together with 2 and 423; see also 428).

1ST ED. Facsimile of Albert Stadler's copy—November 1927: *Festblätter für das 10. Deutsche Sängerbundefest, Wien 1928*, no. 3, p. 58 (ed. by O. E. D.).

The autograph was found after the publication of the facsimile. For the setting as a solo song, see 98.

425. '**Lebenslied**' (Matthisson), **Trio, T.T.B.** Lost. May 1816.

[Musical notation: Bewegt — "f Kom-men und schei-den, p su-chen und mei-den"]

MS. Unknown; former owner (1858)—Albert Stadler (see 428).

A copy of the second tenor part (written by Anton Holzapfel (?)) is in the possession of the Krasser family, Vienna (together with 339–41). Stadler, in a letter to Ferdinand Luib, 1858 (Stadtbibliothek, Vienna) erroneously called this trio 'Lebensbilder.' For the setting of the same poem as a solo song, see 508.

426. '**Trinklied**' ('Herr Bacchus ist ein braver Mann,' author unknown), **Trio, T.T.B.** Lost. May 1816.

MS. Unknown; former owner (1858)—Albert Stadler (see 428).

The poem, commonly attributed to Matthisson, is not by him; it resembles the words of an aria in Mozart's *Die Entführung aus dem Serail*: 'Vivat Bacchus, vivat Bacchus, Bacchus war ein braver Mann' (libretto by Christoph Friedrich Bretzner, arranged by Gottlieb Stephanie the younger).

427. '**Trinklied im Mai**' (Hölty), **Trio, T.T.B.** (XIX 17). May 1816.

Lebhaft

Be - krän - zet die Ton - nen und - za - pfet mir Wein;

MS. Unknown; former owner—Eduard Schneider, Vienna (together with 434).

1ST ED. 1892, Gesamtausgabe.

There is a copy of the second tenor part (written by Anton Holzapfel (?)), dated 1817, in the possession of the Krasser family, Vienna.

428. '**Widerhall**' ('Auf ewig dein,' Matthisson), **Trio, T.T.B.** May 1816.

Langsam

p Auf e - wig dein, wenn Berg und Mee - re tren - nen

MS. (together with 2)—unknown; former owner—Frau Emilie Meyer, Vienna (1913).

1ST ED. Facsimile of Albert Stadler's copy—November 1927: *Festblätter für das 10. Deutsche Sängerbundesfest, Wien 1928*, no. 3, p. 57 (ed. by O. E. D.).

Schubert used the first stanza of the poem only. On the back of the MS. is part of a cancelled sketch of a string quartet in G (2), the beginning of which is written on the back of 424 and continued on the same page as, and on the back of, 423. Stadler divided the MS. which in 1853 contained the two other trios and, perhaps, on the bottom half of the second leaf, the lost trios 425 and 426.

429. '**Minnelied**' ('Holder klingt der Vogelsang,' Hölty), **Song** (XX 221). May 1816.

Hol - der klingt der Vo - gel - sang,

MS. Dr. Otto Kallir, New York (together with 430).
1ST ED. 1885, C. F. Peters, Leipzig, as no. 3 of twenty *Nachgelassene Lieder* (ed. by Max Friedlaender).

After writing the three original words of the poem in bar 13, Schubert altered the text (see *Revisionsbericht*). Nottebohm dstes 429-33, erroneously, 12th May 1816.

430. '**Die frühe Liebe**' (Hölty), **Song** (XX 222). May 1816.

[musical notation: Schon im bun-ten Kna-ben-klei-de]

MS. Dr. Otto Kallir, New York (together with 429).
1ST ED. 1895, Gesamtausgabe.

It seems that Schubert omitted the fifth stanza intentionally.

431. '**Blumenlied**' (Hölty), **Song** (XX 223). May 1816.

[musical notation: Es ist ein hal-bes Him-mel-reich,]

MS. Dr. Alwin Cranz, Vienna (together with nos. 371, 432, and 433).
1ST ED. 1887, C. F. Peters, Leipzig, as no. 46 of *Schubert Album*, book 7 (ed. by Max Friedlaender).

432. '**Der Leidende**,' called '**Klage**' ('Nimmer trag' ich,' author unknown), **Song**, two versions (XX 224 (*a*) and (*b*)). May 1816.

a Unruhig
[musical notation: Nim-mer trag' ich län-ger die-ser Lei-den Last;]

b Unruhig
[musical notation: Nim-mer trag' ich län-ger die-ser Lei-den Last;]

MS. (*a*) and (*b*) Dr. Alwin Cranz, Vienna (together with nos. 371, 431, and 433).

IST ED. (*a*) *c*. 1850, A. Diabelli & Co., Vienna (no. 9000), as no. 2 of *Nachlass*, book 50; (*b*) 1895, Gesamtausgabe.

The MS., entitled 'Der Leidende,' shows both versions; the second, apparently made at a later date for another voice, is written in red pencil. There is also a third setting of this poem, which was wrongly attributed to Hölty, made about 1817, but it remains unpublished (512).

433. 'Seligkeit,' called '**Minnelied**' ('Freuden sonder Zahl,' Hölty), **Song** (XX 225). May 1816.

MS. Dr. Alwin Cranz, Vienna (together with 371, 431, and 432).
IST ED. 1895, Gesamtausgabe.

The MS. was at one time in the possession of Schubert's nephew, Eduard Schneider, in Vienna. The order of the songs in this MS., recently divided, was as follows: 431, 371, 432, 433, 429, 430.

434. '**Erntelied**' (Hölty), **Song** (XX 226). May 1816.

MS. Unknown; former owner—Eduard Schneider, Vienna (together with no. 427) (Witteczek's copy).
IST ED. *c*. 1848, A. Diabelli & Co., Vienna (no. 8837), as no. 2 of *Nachlass*, book 48 (with a spurious pf. introduction).

The poem consists of five stanzas, the fourth of which was omitted by Schubert. It is, however, added in the G.A.

—— '**Die Erwartung**' (XX 46). See 159. May 1816.

—— **Several Goethe Songs**. Fair copies. May 1816.

MS. Conservatoire, Paris (seven songs), and Stadtbibliothek, Vienna (five songs) (Ph.).

Cf. entry before 384. These are some of the Goethe songs intended to form part of a second MS. book to be sent to Goethe in the event of Josef von Spaun's letter of 17th April 1816, addressed to the poet, receiving a favourable reply. No such reply, however, was received.

Literature. O. E. D., *Die Musik*, Berlin, October 1928.

—— '**Gold'ner Schein.**' See 357. 1st May 1816.

435. 'Die Bürgschaft,' Opera, in three Acts, by an unknown author (XV 13). Unfinished. Begun 2nd May 1816.

No. 1. CHORUS (Mixed Chorus)
Allegro moderato

Hil - fe! Ret - tung! Hil - fe!

No. 2. ARIA (Bar.)
Allegro agitato

Muss ich füh - len in tie - fer Brust

No. 3. CHORUS (Mixed Chorus)
Allegro moderato

Wie dür - stet der Ät - na, der hei - sse Ko - loss,

No. 4. CHORUS (Mixed Chorus)
Vivace

Es le - be, es le - be der meut' - ri - sche Tor,

No. 5. ARIA (Bar.)
Moderato

Die - se Gna - de dank' ich dir, werd' sie stets dir den - ken,

No. 6. ARIA (Bass)
Allegro
RECIT.

Ob er wohl wie - der-kehrt?

No. 7. ROMANCE (Sopr.)
Andantino

Die Mut - ter sucht ihr lie - bes Kind,

No. 8. DUET (2 Sopr.)
Andantino

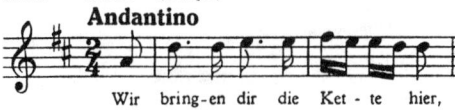

Wir bring-en dir die Ket - te hier,

No. 9. FINALE (3 Sopr., Bar., Male Chorus)
Allegro

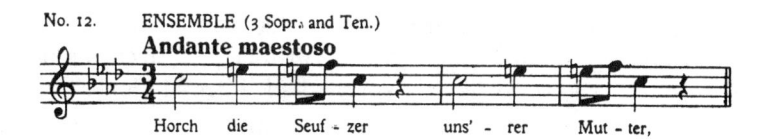

Du gehst in Ker - ker, du?

No. 10. ENTR'ACTE & ARIA (Bar.)
Moderato

O Göt - ter! O Dank euch!

No. 11. ARIA (Sopr.)
Andante

Wel - che Nacht hab' ich er - lebt!

No. 12. ENSEMBLE (3 Sopr. and Ten.)
Andante maestoso

Horch die Seuf - zer uns' - rer Mut - ter,

No. 13. QUARTET (Male Quartet unaccomp.)

pp Hin - ter Bü - schen, hin - term Laub,

No. 14. SCENA & ARIA (Bar.)
ad lib.

O— gött - li - che Ru - he!

No. 15. ENTR'ACTE
Andante

No. 16. ENSEMBLE (Bar. and Male Chorus) *(unfinished)*
Moderato

Der A - bend rückt her - an,

MS. Stadtbibliothek, Vienna.
1ST PF. (in concert form)—7th March 1908, Vienna (Wiener Schubertbund).
1ST ED. 1893, Gesamtausgabe.

The first and the second acts are complete, the third contains only the second *entr'acte* and an unfinished *ensemble*. The MS. includes autograph parts of the quartet ' Räuberlied ' (no. 13). Schubert set Schiller's poem, based on the same legend, as a solo song in August 1815 (246).

—· **Duet for Violins** (Sketch). See note to 450. 8th May 1816.

436. ' **Klage an den Mond** ' (' Dein Silber schien,' Hölty), **Song**, first version (XX 216). 12th May 1816.

Mässig

Dein Sil - ber schien durch Ei - chen - grün,

MS. Lost (Ebner's, Stadler's, and Witteczek's copies).
1ST ED. *c.* 1848, A. Diabelli & Co., Vienna (no. 8837), as no. 3 of *Nachlass*, book 48 (with a spurious pf. introduction).

The poem, written in 1773, was originally entitled ' An den Mond,' later it was called ' Klage.' Schubert set it a second time as a song (437).

437. ' **Klage an den Mond** ' (Hölty), **Song**, second version. Unpublished. After May 1816.
MS. Meangya family, Mödling, near Vienna (Ph.).

The MS. is entitled ' Klage '; the month, November, is crossed out in the title. The interlude after the first stanza is repeated here after the second stanza. For the first setting, see 436.

438. **Rondo in A for Violin Solo and String Orchestra** (XXI 4). June 1816.

Adagio

Allegro giusto

MS. (score)—Dr. Alwin Cranz, Vienna (Ph.).
1ST ED. 1897, Gesamtausgabe.
The Gesamtausgabe gives the accompaniment as string quartet.

439. 'An die Sonne' (Uz), **Quartet, S.A.T.B., with Pianoforte accompaniment** (XVII 12). June 1816.

Adagio molto

O Son - ne, Kö - ni - gin der Welt,

MS. Unknown; former owner—Emil Sulzbach, Frankfurt am Main.
1ST ED. 1872, J. P. Gotthard, Vienna (no. 321), as no. 6 of nine part-songs.

440. '**Chor der Engel**' (from Goethe's 'Faust'), **Mixed Chorus, S.A.T.B.** (XVII 18). June 1816.

Langsam

Christ ist er - stan - den! Christ ist er - stan - den!

MS. Lost.
1ST ED. 18th June 1839, A. R. Friese, Leipzig, in *Neue Zeitschrift für Musik*, Supplement (ed. by Robert Schumann).
Cf. 118, 126, 367, and 564.

441. '**Beitrag zur fünfzigjährigen Jubelfeier des Herrn Salieri**' ('Gütigster, Bester, Weisester,' Schubert), **for two Tenors and Bass** (the second tenor also as solo voice) **with Pianoforte accompaniment**, second version (XIX 5). June 1816.

Sostenuto

Gü - tig - ster,   Be - ster,   Wei - se - ster,

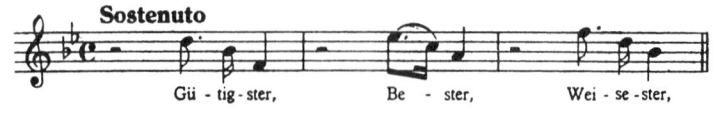

MS. Stadtbibliothek, Vienna (together with 449).
1ST PF. 16th June, 1816, at Salieri's home, Vienna.
1ST ED. 1892, Gesamtausgabe.

This version, containing the two stanzas without the chorus (canon), seems to have been intended as the final setting. See the version for quartet, T.T.B.B., etc. (407). The solo with pf. acc. is identical in both versions, and the canon for three voices was probably sung also with this version of the cantata.

—— ' **Klage der Ceres** ' (XX 172). See 323. June 1816.

442. ' **Das grosse Halleluja** ' (Klopstock), **Song** (XX 227). June 1816.

Feierlich

mf Eh - re sei dem Hoch - er - hab' - nen,

MS. First sketch—Dr. Alwin Cranz, Vienna (together with 357 and 419); fair copy—lost.
1ST ED. *c*. 1847, A. Diabelli & Co., Vienna (no. 8818), as no. 2 of *Nachlass*, book 41 (as a chorus for three female voices with pf. acc.).

Schubert omitted the penultimate stanza of the poem. It is possible that Schubert intended this work as a trio with pf. acc., but no indication is to be found on the MS. or in the copy of the Witteczek Collection.

443. ' **Schlachtgesang**,' called ' **Schlachtlied** ' (Klopstock), **Song** (XX 228). June 1816.

Feurig, geschwind

Mit un - serm Arm ist nichts ge - than,

MS. Preussische Staatsbibliothek, Berlin (together with 444).
1ST ED. 1895, Gesamtausgabe.

Schubert also set the poem, the original title of which was ' Schlachtlied,' as a quartet, T.T.B.B., 28th February 1827 (912).

444. ' **Die Gestirne** ' (Klopstock), **Song** (XX 229). June 1816.

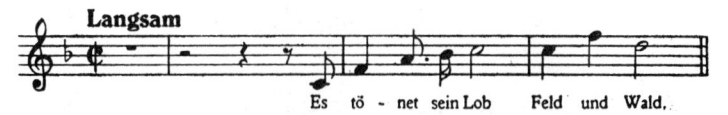

Langsam

Es tö - net sein Lob Feld und Wald.

MS. Preussische Staatsbibliothek, Berlin (together with 443).
1ST ED. 21st April 1831, A. Diabelli & Co., Vienna (no. 3707), as no. 2 of *Nachlass*, book 10.

It is assumed that the pf. introduction is to be played only before the first stanza, and that the choice of stanzas—fifteen in all—is left to the singer.

445. ' Edone ' (Klopstock), Song (XX 230). June 1816.

Mässig, zart

Dein sü - sses Bild. E - do - ne.

MS. Gesellschaft der Musikfreunde, Vienna; another MS.—Meangya family, Mödling, near Vienna (Ph.).
1ST ED. 25th April 1837, A. Diabelli & Co., Vienna (no. 5032), as no. 4 of *Nachlass*, book 28.

According to a note in the Witteczek Collection Schubert later transposed the song into the key of D, but made no further alteration.

446. ' Die Liebesgötter ' (Uz), Song (XX 231). June 1816.

Zart

Cy - pris, mei - ner Phyl - lis gleich.

MS. Lost (Witteczek's copy).
1ST ED. 1887, C. F. Peters, Leipzig, as no. 45 of *Schubert Album*, book 7 (ed. by Max Friedlaender).

447. ' An den Schlaf ' (Uz (?)), Song (XX 232). June 1816.

Ruhig

Komm, und sen - ke die um - flor- ten Schwin - gen,

MS. Lost (Witteczek's copy).
1ST ED. 1895, Gesamtausgabe.

The poem seems to have more than one stanza, as indicated by the repeat signs.

448. ' **Gott im Frühlinge** ' (Uz), Song (XX 233). June 1816.

Mässig

In sei - nem schim - mern-den Ge - wand

MS. N. Simrock, Berlin; another MS. (without the pf. postlude) —Meangya family, Mödling, near Vienna (Ph.).
1ST ED. 1887, C. F. Peters, Leipzig, as no. 43 of *Schubert Album*, book 7 (ed. by Max Friedlaender).

The Mödling MS. is marked ' Langsam, mit Gefühl.' Schubert used only the first three stanzas of the poem for this song.

449. ' **Der gute Hirte** ' (Uz), Song (XX 234). June 1816.

Vertrauensvoll

Was sor - gest du?

MS. Rough draft (without pf. introduction and postlude)—Stadtbibliothek, Vienna (together with 441); fair copy—lost.
1ST ED. 1872, J. P. Gotthard, Vienna (no. 331), as no. 7 of forty songs.

Schubert omitted the fifth and sixth stanzas of the poem. The pf. introduction and postlude are dubious.

450. ' **Fragment aus dem Aeschylus** ' (from a Chorus of the ' Eumenides,' translated by Mayrhofer), **Song,** two versions (XX 236 (*a*) and (*b*)). June 1816.

a *Mässig*

So wird der Mann, der son-der Zwang ge - recht ist,

b *Mässig, geschwind*
RECIT.

So wird der Mann, der son-der Zwang ge - recht ist,

MS. (*a*) Dr. Franz Roehn, Los Angeles; (*b*) (together with 174, second version)—Conservatoire, Paris (Ph.).
1ST PF. 26th March 1828, Musikverein, Vienna (Schubert's concert).

1ST ED. (*a*) 1895, Gesamtausgabe; (*b*) 4th January 1832, A. Diabelli & Co., Vienna (no. 4014), as no. 2 of *Nachlass*, book 14.

This translation is not included in the two editions of Mayrhofer's poems. The MS. of (*a*) is entitled ' Aus dem Aeschylus.' On p. 3 of this MS. is a Duet in D, *alla breve*, for violins, beginning in the form of a canon, dated 8th May 1816; probably written for a pupil. This duet is cancelled, no doubt to enable Schubert to finish the song on the same piece of paper.

— ' Das war ich ' (XX 56). See 174. June 1816.

— ' Klage der Ceres ' (XX 172). See 323. June 1816.

451. Cantata ' Prometheus ' (Philipp Dräxler von Carin), **for the Nameday of Heinrich Josef Watteroth.** Lost. 17th June 1816.

DUET (GAJA–PROMETHEUS)
Gaja
Bist du be - reit, das tief - ste Gra - men

FIRST CHORUS (key uncertain)
Ihr Nym - phen her - bei und Na - ja - den.

1ST PF. 24th July 1816 (originally planned for the 12th, but postponed), in the garden of Watteroth's house, Erdberggasse, Vienna (conductor, Schubert).

The work consisted of an overture (E minor, 4/4), soli, a duet, some recitatives, and three choruses. Cf. 421.

Literature. Leopold von Sonnleithner, *Blätter für Theater, Musik und bildende Kunst*, Vienna, 5th March 1867 (with themes). O. E. D., *Der Merker*, Vienna, July 1919.

452. Mass in C, for Quartet, S.A.T.B., Mixed Chorus, Small Orchestra, and Organ (Op. 48, XIII 4). June–July 1816.

KYRIE **Andante con moto**
p Ky - ri - e e - lei - son, e - lei - son,

GLORIA **Allegro vivace**
f Glo - ri - a, Glo - ri - a,

CREDO

Allegro

f Cre - do in u - num De - um,

Adagio molto

p Et in - car - na - tus est de Spi - ri - tu,

Tempo I.

f Et re - sur - re - xit

SANCTUS

Adagio

p San - ctus, San - ctus, San - ctus Do - mi - nus Sa - ba - oth

BENEDICTUS

Andante

Be - ne - di - ctus, qui ve - nit,

AGNUS DEI

Adagio

A - gnus De - i, a - gnus De - i, qui

Allegro vivace

p Do - na no - bis pa - cem,

MS. Wittgenstein family, Vienna.

1ST PF. Probably summer 1816, Liechtentaler Kirche, Vienna; otherwise 8th September 1825, Maria Trost-Kirche, Vienna.

1ST ED. (in parts) 3rd September 1825, A. Diabelli & Co., Vienna (no. 1902), as Op. 48, dedicated by Schubert to Michael Holzer, choir-master of the church in the Vienna suburb of Liechtental.

A copy of the score, made by Ferdinand Schubert, with autograph dedication and the Op. no. 42 (!) written by Franz, confirms the date, and the fact that the parts for oboi, clarini, and tympani were written *ad libitum* (on sale in Vienna, Dorotheum, 25th October 1928). The second Benedictus was substituted in October 1828 (961). The MS. of the title-page of the mass, dedicated to Holzer and dated, it was said, June 1810 (instead of 1816), together with the beginning of the Kyrie, was exhibited in Vienna in 1897 (Schubert-Ausstellung), and sold there by auction in 1899. The MS. of the mass, however, is now complete. Schubert omitted the words *ex Maria virgine* (between *et incarnatus est de Spirito sancto*, and *et homo factus est*) in the Credo. Cf. 460 and 461.

453. Requiem in E flat. Fragment. Not printed. (? July) 1816.

lu - ce - at e - - - is, lu - ce - at e - - is.

MS. (former owner, Johannes Brahms) Gesellschaft der Musikfreunde, Vienna (undated).

The MS. score, the first pages of which are missing, consists of five leaves in oblong folio, containing 64 bars; it ends with the second bar of the second Kyrie. Schindler dated the fragment 1816, Kreissle (p. 618) July 1816.

454. 'Grablied auf einen Soldaten' (Schubart), **Song** (XX 239). July 1816.

Zieh hin, du bra - ver Krie - ger du!

MS. (together with 455)—Sibley Music Library, University of Rochester (New York).

1ST ED. 1872, J. P. Gotthard, Vienna (no. 330), as no. 6 of forty songs (with the name of Jacobi as the poet).

The MS. was disfigured by a former owner who used it as a writing-pad and tested a stave-pen on the paper. Schubart's title of the poem was 'Totenmarsch,' and it consisted of two parts, the second of which is reprinted in the *Revisionsbericht*.

455. 'Freude der Kinderjahre' (F. von Köpken), **Song** (XX 240). July 1816.

Freu - de, die im frü - hen Len - ze

MS. (together with 454)—Sibley Music Library, University of Rochester (New York).

1ST ED. 1887, C. F. Peters, Leipzig, as no. 35 of *Schubert Album*, book 7 (ed. by Max Friedlaender).

Max Kalbeck added a second stanza to this poem (*Musik für alle*, Berlin, November 1908, vol. v, no. 2, p. 39).

456. ' **Das Heimweh** ' (' Oft in einsam stillen Stunden,' Th. Hell), **Song** (XX 241). July 1816.

MS. (together with 458)—Conservatoire, Paris (Ph.).

1ST ED. 1887, C. F. Peters, Leipzig, as no. 28 of *Schubert Album*, book 7 (ed. by Max Friedlaender).

The first edition has a second and third stanza added by Max Kalbeck.

457. ' **An die untergehende Sonne** ' (Kosegarten), **Song** (Op. 44, XX 237). July 1816 (May 1817).

MS. First sketch, incomplete (seventeen or eighteen bars only), dated July 1816 (together with 467) (Ph.)—Otto Haas, London (1936, Catalogue 1, no. 244); final version, dated May 1817 (together with the song without text, 555)—Sotheby, London (21st April 1943).

1ST ED. 5th January 1827, A. Diabelli & Co., Vienna (no. 2252), as Op. 44.

Schubert omitted the third and fourth stanzas of the poem. In the final version, bar 54 is corrected as follows:

458. ' **Aus Diego Manazares** ' (Schlechta), **Song** (XX 242). 30th July 1816.

MS. (together with 456)—Conservatoire, Paris (Ph.).
1ST ED. 1872, J. P. Gotthard, Vienna (no. 349), as no. 25 of forty songs, this song dedicated by the publisher to Louise Dustmann, entitled erroneously ' Aus Diego Manzanares.'
The title in the MS. is ' Aus Diego Manazares. Ilmerine,' i.e. a soprano.

459. **Sonata in E,** called ' **Fünf Klavierstücke** ' (XI 14). August 1816.

MS. Fragment (entitled 'Sonate' and dated, containing the first movement and the beginning of the second movement)—1947 on sale in New York (Ph.); another fragment (the end of the last movement)—Stadtbibliothek, Vienna.

1ST ED. October 1843, C. A. Klemm, Leipzig (nos. 451–5), as 'Fünf Klavierstücke' (so called also in the G.A.).

The second fragment is printed, but not identified, in the *Revisionsbericht* (XXI 21). One of the *Scherzi* was apparently to be omitted. Cf. 349.

460. **Tantum ergo in C, for Chorus, Orchestra, and Organ** (XIV 7). August 1816.

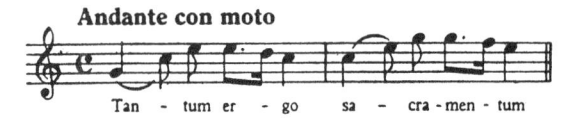

[musical notation: Andante con moto — Tan - tum er - go sa - cra - men - tum]

MS. Wittgenstein family, Vienna (with figured organ-part).
1ST ED. 1888, Gesamtausgabe.

According to the MS. this composition was dedicated by Schubert to Michael Holzer, as was the Mass in C (452), for which this Tantum ergo was apparently used as an introduction. There is another Tantum ergo in C written the same month (461).

461. **Tantum ergo in C, for Soli, Chorus, S.A.T.B., and Orchestra.** August 1816.

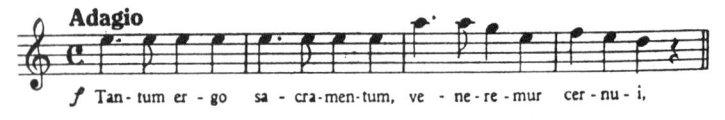

[musical notation: Adagio — f Tan - tum er - go sa - cra - men - tum, ve - ne - re - mur cer - nu - i,]

MS. William Kux, Chur, Switzerland.
1ST PF. In German—18th January 1924, Aula der Universität, Berlin (conductor, Max Friedlaender); in the original form—30th September 1924, Grosser Konzerthaussaal, Vienna.
1ST ED. 18th January 1924, Berlin, privately printed (ed. by Max Friedlaender,) with words by W. H. Helling, entitled 'An das Vaterland,' lithographed (together with a similar arrangement of the Tantum ergo in B flat, of 16th August 1821, 730); the original form—1935, Universal Edition, Vienna (no. 10,735, ed. by Karl Geiringer).

Parts, copied by another hand, preserved in the Peters-Kirche, Vienna. The work was written as an alternative to the Tantum ergo in C (460) for the Mass in C (452).

462. 'An Chloen' (II) ('Bei der Liebe reinsten Flammen,' Jacobi), Song (XX 244). August 1816.

Etwas geschwind

Bei der Lie - be rein - sten Flam - men

MS. Lost (Witteczek's copy).
1ST ED. 1895, Gesamtausgabe.
Cf. 363.

463. 'Hochzeitslied' (Jacobi), Song (XX 245). August 1816.

Lebhaft, herzlich

Will sin - gen euch im al - ten Ton

MS. Lost (Witteczek's copy).
1ST ED. 1895, Gesamtausgabe.

464. 'In der Mitternacht' (Jacobi), Song (XX 246). August 1816.

Sehr langsam

To - des - stil - le deckt das Tal

MS. Unknown; former owner—R. Fellinger, Vienna.
1ST ED. 1895, Gesamtausgabe.

This MS., or perhaps another of the same song, originally formed part of the complete MS. to which the songs 465 and 466 belong.

465. 'Trauer der Liebe' (Jacobi), Song (XX 247). August 1816.

Mässig

Wo die Taub' in stil - len Bu - chen

MS. Rough copy (together with 466)—Conservatoire, Paris (Ph.); fair copy (with a different postlude of four bars)—Meangya family, Mödling, near Vienna (Ph.).

IST ED. 1876, V. Kratochwill, Vienna (no. 253), as no. 5 of six *Nachgelassene Lieder*, arranged for pf. duet and ed. (with words) by J. P. Gotthard.

Max Friedlaender republished this song, in its original form, as no. 11 of twenty *Nachgelassene Lieder*, C. F. Peters, Leipzig, in 1885.

466. ' **Die Perle** ' (Jacobi), **Song** (XX 248).   August 1816.

Schreitend

Es ging ein Mann zur Früh - lings - zeit

MS. (together with 465)—Conservatoire, Paris (Ph.).
IST ED. 1872, J. P. Gotthard, Vienna (no. 355), as no. 31 of forty songs, this song dedicated to Nikolaus Dumba.

The pf. introduction is probably intended to be played only before the first stanza.

467. ' **Pflicht und Liebe** ' (Gotter), **Song** (XX 593).   Fragment. August 1816.

Langsam

Du, der e - wig um mich trau - ert,

MS. (together with 457)—Otto Haas, London (1936, catalogue I, no. 244) (Ph.).
IST ED. 1885, C. F. Peters, Leipzig, as no. 17 of twenty *Nachgelassene Lieder* (ed. and arranged by Max Friedlaender).

The MS. is complete except for the last bar.

468. ' **An den Mond** ' (' Was schauest du so hell . . . ?', Hölty), **Song** (XX 243).   7th August 1816.

Mässig

Was schau - est du so hell und klar

MS. Stadtbibliothek, Vienna.
IST ED. 1895, Gesamtausgabe.

The poem was written in 1775.

469. ' **Mignon** ' (II, ' So lasst mich scheinen,' from Goethe's

' Wilhelm Meister '), **Song**, first and second versions, incomplete (*Revisionsbericht* to XX 395). September 1816.

[musical notation: Langsam — So lasst mich schei-nen, bis ich wer-de,]

MS. Beginning of the first and end of the second version—Stadtbibliothek, Vienna (together with 480 (2)).

1ST ED. 1895, Gesamtausgabe, *Revisionsbericht*, Series XX, pp. 86–7.

The first version is entitled ' Mignon, 1. Weise.' For later settings, see 727 and 877, no. 3.

470. Overture in B flat for Orchestra (without Clarinets and Trombones) (II 3). September 1816.

[musical notation: Adagio maestoso]

[musical notation: Allegro]

MS. Score—Stadtbibliothek, Vienna; Parts (ten written by Schubert, four by his brother Ferdinand, fourteen by another hand)—William Kux, Chur, Switzerland.

1ST PF. 1816, or 22nd January 1817; revived September 1818 and 16th August 1829—Waisenhaus, Vienna (conductor, Ferdinand Schubert); first public performance—21st March 1830, Landhaussaal, Vienna (conductor, Ferdinand Schubert).

1ST ED. 1886, Gesamtausgabe.

This overture probably belongs to the cantata in honour of Josef Spendou (472), which begins in the same key.

471. String Trio in B flat, in one movement (VI). September 1816.

[musical notation: Allegro]

Andante sostenuto

p

MS. Stadtbibliothek, Vienna.
1ST ED. 1890, Gesamtausgabe.

The beginning of a second movement, *Andante sostenuto*, is printed in the *Revisionsbericht*.

472. Kantate zu Ehren Josef Spendou's (Johann Hoheisel) for Solo Voices, Chorus, S.A.T.B., and Orchestra (Op. posth. 128, XVII 2). September 1816.

Grave
RECIT. (Bass)

pp Da liegt er, starr, vom To - de hin - ge - streckt,

SOLO & CHORUS (Widow and Children)
Andante

Weh euch Kin-dern, weh euch Ar - men!

RECIT. (Bass)

Got - tes Bild ist Fürst und Staat,

DUET (Widow and Orphan)
Allegro moderato

Will - kom - men, du Trö - ster im Lei - - de!

RECIT. (Bass)
Andante molto

Ein Punkt nur ist der Mensch in die - sem Welt - ge - bäu - de;

CHORUS (Widows)
Allegro maestoso

Spen - dou! so hall's in un - se - rem Ver - ein,

RECIT. (Bass)
Adagio con moto

Die Son - ne sticht.

QUARTET (Widow, Orphan, Ten. and Bass)
a tempo

Va - ter un - ter Se - raphs - reih'n

MS. Stadtbibliothek, Vienna.
1ST PF. (?) 1816, (?) Waisenhaus, Vienna; first public performance—21st March 1830, Landhaussaal, Vienna (conductor, Ferdinand Schubert). 1ST ED. Pf. score by Ferdinand Schubert—6th July 1830, A. Diabelli, Vienna (no. 3611), under the title ' Cantate. Empfindungsäusserungen des Witwen-Institutes der Schullehrer Wiens für den Stifter und Vorsteher desselben '; score—1892, Gesamtausgabe.

Spendou was a patron of the Schubert family. The poem was printed in 1816 (copy in the archives of the Gesellschaft der Musikfreunde, Vienna). The first performance may not have been given until 22nd January 1817, the twentieth anniversary of the foundation of the Society of the Widows of Viennese Schoolmasters. When Ferdinand Schubert performed the work again, in 1830, a hundred copies of his pf. score were already available. Neither the printed score nor the MS. contains the overture, which was revived at the Vienna Orphanage in September 1818 (conductor, Ferdinand Schubert). Anton Schindler mentions it in his list of Schubert's works in 1857. This overture is probably identical with 470.

—— ' **Die verfehlte Stunde** ' (XX 206). See 409. September 1816.

473. ' **Liedesend** ' (Mayrhofer), **Song**, two versions (XX 249 (*a*) and (*b*)). September 1816.

a **Majestätisch**

Auf sei - nem gold' - nen Thro - ne

b **Majestätisch, nicht zu langsam**

Auf sei - nen gold' - nen Thro - ne

MS. (*a*) Rough draft, and (*b*) fair copy (together with 474)—Stadtbibliothek, Vienna.

1ST ED. (*a*) 1895, Gesamtausgabe; (*b*) 27th July 1833, A. Diabelli & Co., Vienna (no. 4271), as no. 2 of *Nachlass*, book 23.

474. ' Lied des Orpheus, als er in die Hölle ging,' called ' **Orpheus** ' (Jacobi), **Song**, two versions (XX 250 (*a*) and (*b*)). September 1816.

Mässig, mit Kraft

Wäl - ze dich hin - weg, du wil - des Feu - er!

MS. (*a*) Incomplete—Stadtbibliothek, Vienna (together with 473 (*b*)); (*b*) date uncertain—lost (Witteczek's copy).

1ST ED. (*a*) 1895, Gesamtausgabe; (*b*) 29th October 1832, A. Diabelli & Co., Vienna (no. 4267), as no. 1 of *Nachlass*, book 19.

The second version, in *alla breve* time, differs from the first version, in 4/4, mainly after the first third of the song.

475. ' **Abschied (nach einer Wallfahrtsarie)** ' ('Ueber die Berge zieht ihr fort,' Mayrhofer), **Song** (XX 251). September 1816.

Langsam, wehmütig

Ü - ber die Ber - ge zieht ihr fort,

MS. Lost (Witteczek's copy).

1ST ED. 1876, V. Kratochwill, Vienna (no. 252), as no. 12 of twelve *Nachgelassene Lieder*, arranged for pf. solo and ed. (with words) by J. P. Gotthard.

The song was republished by Max Friedlaender as no. 7 of twenty *Nachgelassene Lieder*, C. F. Peters, Leipzig, in 1885. The poem is entitled ' Lunz.' Lunz is a small village in the Vienna woods, on the Erlafsee (see 586), not far from Maria-Zell, a place of pilgrimage in Styria. The pilgrim's air, mentioned in the title of the song, has not been identified.

476. ' **Rückweg** ' (Mayrhofer), **Song** (XX 252). September 1816.

Etwas geschwind

Zum Do - nau-strom, zur Kai - ser -stadt

MS. Stadtbibliothek, Vienna (together with 479 (*a*), 480, and 484).
1ST ED. 1872, J. P. Gotthard, Vienna (no. 339), as no. 15 of forty songs.

477. ' Alte Liebe rostet nie ' (Mayrhofer), **Song** (XX 253). September 1816.

Mässig

Al - te Lie - be ro - stet nie,

MS. Dr. Alwin Cranz, Vienna (together with 478 (*a*) and 479 (*a*)).
1ST ED. 1895, Gesamtausgabe.

478. ' **Harfenspieler I** ' (' Wer sich der Einsamkeit ergibt,' from Goethe's ' Wilhelm Meister '), **Song**, two versions (Op. 12, no. 1; XX 254 (*a*) and (*b*)). September, 1816.

a **Langsam**

Wer sich der Ein - sam - keit er - gibt,

b **Sehr langsam**

Wer sich der Ein - sam - keit er - gibt,

MS. (*a*) Dr. Alwin Cranz, Vienna (together with 477 and 479 (*a*)); (*b*) lost.

1ST ED. (*a*) 1895, Gesamtausgabe; (*b*) 13th December 1822, A. Diabelli & Co., Vienna (no. 1161), as no. 1 of Op. 12 (' Gesänge des Harfners aus Wilhelm Meister '), published for Schubert and dedicated by him to Johann Nepomuk von Dankesreither.

In Goethe's novel this poem is no. 2 (see 479). For the earlier version of the song, see 325.

479. ' **Harfenspieler II** ' (' An die Türen will ich schleichen,' from Goethe's ' Wilhelm Meister '), **Song**, two versions (Op. 12, no. 3; XX 255 (*a*) and (*b*)). September 1816.

a **Mässig**

An die Tü - ren will ich schlei - chen,

b   **Mässig, in gehender Bewegung**

An die Tü-ren will ich schlei-chen,

MS. (*a*) The first forty bars—Dr. Alwin Cranz, Vienna (together with 477 and 478 (*a*)); the last twelve bars—Stadtbibliothek, Vienna (together with 476, 480, and 484); (*b*) lost.

1ST ED. (*a*) 1895, Gesamtausgabe; (*b*) 13th December 1822, A. Diabelli & Co., Vienna (no. 1161), as no. 3 of Op. 12, published for Schubert and dedicated by him to Johann Nepomuk von Dankesreither.

Schubert altered Goethe's order of the three poems (see 478 and 480). This one, Goethe's third, is stated fictitiously in his novel to be the last stanza of a longer poem.

480. '**Harfenspieler III**' ('Wer nie sein Brot mit Thränen ass,' from Goethe's '*Wilhelm Meister*'), **Song**, three versions (Op. 12, no. 2; XX 256, 257, 258).   September 1816 (autumn 1822).

1. **Klagend**
    Wer nie sein Brot mit Thrä-nen ass,

2. **Etwas geschwind**
    Wer nie sein Brot mit Thrä-nen ass,

3. **Langsam**
    Wer nie sein Brot mit Thrä-nen ass,

MS. (1) (XX 256, including a first sketch)—Stadtbibliothek, Vienna (together with 476, 479 (*a*) and 484); (2) (XX 257)—Stadtbibliothek, Vienna (together with 469); (3) (XX 258) lost.

1ST ED. (1) and (2) 1895, Gesamtausgabe; (3) 13th December 1822, A. Diabelli & Co., Vienna (no. 1161), as no. 2 of Op. 12, published for Schubert and dedicated by him to Johann Nepomuk von Dankesreither.

The little sketch of (1) is printed in the *Revisionsbericht*. According to Schubert's letter of 7th December 1822, the third version (3) was written in 1822, shortly before the publication of the first edition. It is possible that the last versions of ' Harfenspieler ' I and II were written also in 1822. Schubert altered Goethe's order of these songs, using the poet's no. 1 as his no. 3 (see 479).

Literature. Max Kalbeck, *Neues Wiener Tagblatt,* Vienna, 12th December 1916 (on the order of the poems); Hans Bosch, *Die Entwicklung des Romantischen in Schubert's Liedern,* Borna 1930, p. 91 (on the date of the final versions).

481. ' **Lied der Mignon,**' called ' **Sehnsucht** ' (' Nur wer die Sehnsucht kennt,' from Goethe's ' Wilhelm Meister '), **Song (XX 259).** September 1816.

MS. In A minor, dated—Conservatoire, Paris (Ph.).
1ST ED. 1895, Gesamtausgabe.

The copy in the Witteczek Collection was used for the G.A. For other settings of this poem, see the solo songs 310, 359, and 877, nos. 1 and 4, and the quintet, T.T.B.B.B. (656).

482. ' **Der Sänger am Felsen** ' (Karoline Pichler), **Song (XX 264).** September 1816.

MS. (together with 483)—Sotheby, London (17th June 1947).
1ST ED. 1895, Gesamtausgabe.

483. ' **Lied** ' (' Ferne von der grossen Stadt,' from Karoline Pichler's idyllic poem ' Der Sommer-Abend '), **Song (XX 265).** September 1816.

MS. (together with 482)—Sotheby, London (17th June 1947).
1ST ED. 1895, Gesamtausgabe.

484. 'Gesang der Geister über den Wassern' (Goethe), Song (XX 594). Fragment. September 1816.

MS. Stadtbibliothek, Vienna (together with 476, 479 (a), and 480).

1ST ED. 1895, Gesamtausgabe.

The rest of the MS. seems to be lost. For other settings of this poem, see 538, 704, 705, and 714.

485. **Symphony in B flat,** called the **Symphony without Trumpets and Drums** (I 5). September–3rd October 1816.

MS. Score—Preussische Staatsbibliothek, Berlin; parts, copied by another hand (not by Ferdinand Schubert)—Gesellschaft der Musikfreunde, Vienna.

1ST PF. Autumn 1816, at the house of Otto Hatwig, Schottenhof, Vienna; first public performance—1st February 1873, Crystal Palace, London (conductor, August Manns).

1ST ED. 1885, Gesamtausgabe (see note).

Schubert himself started to make an arrangement for pf. duet, of which a fragment of the first movement is in the possession of Mr. John Bass, New York. Another arrangement, by Hugo Ulrich, for four hands, was published by C. F. Peters, Leipzig, about 1870 (no. 767 of the Peters edition).

486. Magnificat in C for Soli, Chorus, Orchestra, and Organ (XIV 11). 15th or 25th September 1816.

Allegro maestoso
Ma - gni - fi - cat a - ni - ma me - a Do - mi - num,

Andante
De - po - - - su - it po - ten - tes de se - de,

Allegro vivace
ff Glo - ri - a Pa - tri et Fi - li - o et Spi - ri - tu - i san - cto,

MS. Score—Dr. Alwin Cranz, Vienna; some of the instrumental parts (not all in autograph)—Dr. Franz Roehn, Los Angeles.

1ST ED. 1888, Gesamtausgabe.

Ferdinand Schubert listed this work, as 'Grosses Magnificat,' erroneously among the works composed in 1815.

487. Adagio and Rondo concertante in F for Pianoforte, Violin, Viola, and Violoncello, called **Klavier-Konzert (VII 2).** October 1816.

Pf. *Adagio*
ff

RONDO
Pf. *Allegro vivace*
p

MS. Score—Dr. Alwin Cranz, Vienna; string parts (the cello part incomplete)—Otto Taussig, Malmö.

1ST PF. Probably autumn 1816 in the house of the Grob family, Liechtental (a suburb of Vienna); first public performance—1st November 1861, Vienna (Ludwig Bösendorfer's Salon).

1ST ED. 1866, A. O. Witzendorf, Vienna.

Probably written for Heinrich Grob, an amateur 'cellist. No copy of the first edition was available to ascertain the publisher's number.

488. '**Auguste jam coelestium**,' **Duet in G for Soprano and Tenor with Orchestral accompaniment** (XIV 10). October 1816.

MS. Wittgenstein family, Vienna (title: ' Duett Arie ').
1ST ED. 1888, Gesamtausgabe.

489. '**Der Unglückliche**,' called '**Der Wanderer**,' also called '**Der Fremdling**' (Schmidt von Lübeck), **Song**, first version, (XX 266 (*a*)). October 1816.

MS. (former owner, Johannes Brahms). Gesellschaft der Musikfreunde, Vienna (together with 490).
1ST ED. Facsimile—*c.* 1883, Karl Simon, Berlin.

Schubert found the poem in Ludwig Deinhardstein's anthology *Dichtungen für Kunstredner*, Vienna, 1815, where it is entitled ' Der Unglückliche,' and attributed, erroneously, to ' Werner '; Schubert wrote both this title and the name of Werner on his MS. Schmidt himself entitled his poem ' Des Fremdlings Abendlied.' For the final version, see 493.

Literature. Max Friedlaender, Supplement to the *Schubert Album*, C. F. Peters, Leipzig (Peters edition, no. 2173) (1884), pp. 50–4.

490. '**Der Hirt**' (Mayrhofer), **Song** (XX 267). October 1816.

MS. (former owner, Johannes Brahms) Gesellschaft der Musikfreunde, Vienna (together with 489).
1ST ED. 1895, Gesamtausgabe.

491. 'Geheimnis. An Franz Schubert' ('Sag an, wer lehrt dich Lieder,' Mayrhofer), Song (XX 269). October 1816.

Mässig geschwind

Sag an, wer lehrt dich Lie - der,

MS. Lost (Witteczek's copy).
1ST ED. 1887, C. F. Peters, Leipzig (no. 6896), as no. 21 of *Schubert Album*, book 7 (ed. by Max Friedlaender).

492. 'Zum Punsche' (Mayrhofer), Song (XX 270). October 1816.

Feurig

Wo - get brau - send, Har - mo - nie - en,

MS. Rough draft, without the last bar—Nationalbibliothek, Vienna (together with the end of 208); final version—lost (Witteczek's copy).
1ST ED. c. 1848, A. Diabelli & Co., Vienna (no. 8821), as no. 3 of *Nachlass*, book 44.

The Vienna MS. was reproduced in facsimile in *Die Musik*, Berlin, May 1902, vol. i, nos. 15–16 (ed. by Josef Mantuani).

493. 'Der Wanderer' ('Ich komme vom Gebirge her,' Schmidt von Lübeck), Song, second version (Op. 4, no. 1; XX 266 (*b*)). After October 1816.

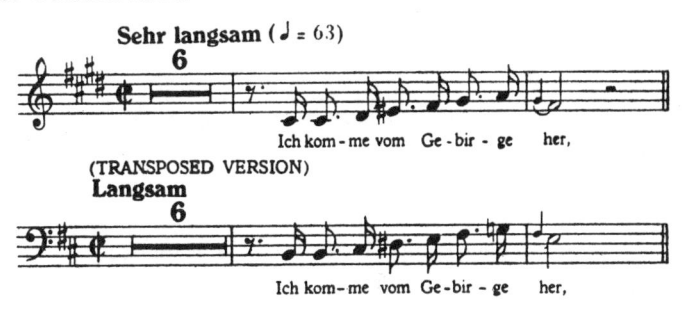

Sehr langsam ($\goodbreak \downarrow = 63$)

Ich kom - me vom Ge - bir - ge her,

(TRANSPOSED VERSION)
Langsam

Ich kom - me vom Ge - bir - ge her,

MS. Original version—lost; score and voice-part, transposed for bass (Johann Karl, Graf Esterházy) in B minor, entitled ' Der Wanderer oder: Der Fremdling oder: Der Unglückliche Gedichtet von Z. Werner ' and written in (?) 1818—Herzogin von Ratibor, Schloss Grafenegg, Lower Austria; former owner— Marie, Gräfin Breunner, *née* Esterházy).

IST PF. 18th November 1821—Gasthof ' Zum Romischen Kaiser,' Vienna.

IST ED. 29th May 1821, Cappi & Diabelli, Vienna (no. 773), as no. 1 of Op. 4, published for Schubert, and dedicated by him to Johann Ladislaus Pyrker von Felsö-Eör.

The name of the poet is given correctly in the first edition, which proves that the version for bass, which differs considerably, was written earlier (before the first edition), probably in the summer of 1818 at Zseliz. Cf. the first version (489), and the Wanderer Fantasia (760).

494. ' Der Geistertanz ' (Matthisson) for Chorus, T.T.B.B. (XVI 32). November 1816.

pp Die bret - ter - ne Kam - mer der To - ten er - bebt,

MS. Stadtbibliothek, Vienna.

IST PF. 13th December 1863, Redoutensaal, Vienna (conductor, Johann Herbeck).

IST ED. 1871, J. P. Gotthard, Vienna (no. 160).

Schubert attempted to set this poem as a song as early as *c*. 1812. See the two sketches (15). He finally set it as a song on 14th October 1814 (116).

495. ' Abendlied der Fürstin ' (Mayrhofer), Song (XX 271). November 1816.

Der A - bend rö - thet nun — das Thal,

MS. Preussische Staatsbibliothek, Berlin.

IST ED. 1868, Wilhelm Müller, Berlin (no. 13), as no. 6 of six songs (ed. by Franz Espagne).

See 291.

496. ' Bei dem Grabe meines Vaters ' (' Friede sei um diesen Grabstein her,' Claudius), Song (XX 274). November 1816.

Nicht zu langsam

Frie - de sei um die - sen Grab-stein her!

MS. Lost (see note).
1ST ED. 1885, C. F. Peters, Leipzig, as no. 12 of twenty *Nachgelassene Lieder* (ed. by Max Friedlaender).

Besides the copies in the Witteczek and Stadler Collections, there exists another copy by Josef von Spaun, which was in the possession of Hermann von Spaun, Görz, about 1900.

497. ' **An die Nachtigall** ' (' Er liegt und schläft,' Claudius), **Song** (Op. 98, no. 1; XX 276). November 1816.

Mässig

Er liegt und schläft an mei - nem Her - zen,

MS. Lost.
1ST ED. 10th July 1829, A. Diabelli & Co., Vienna (no. 3315), as no. 1 of Op. 98.

It is possible that Schubert himself allotted the opus number to this posthumously published collection of three songs, of which this is the first (see 498 and 573).

498. ' **Wiegenlied** ' (' Schlafe, schlafe, holder, süsser Knabe,' author unknown), **Song** (Op. 98, no. 2; XX 277). November 1816.

Langsam

Schla - fe, schla* - fe, hol - der, süs - ser Kna - be,

MS. Lost.
1ST ED. 10th July 1829, A. Diabelli & Co., Vienna (no. 3315), as no. 2 of Op. 98 (see 497).

Claudius is given as the poet, not only in the first edition, but also in the copies by Ebner and Stadler; Schubert was wrong in this indication, and was probably misled by other poems of Claudius, which he set to music during the same month.

499. ' **Abendlied** ' (' Der Mond ist aufgegangen,' Claudius), **Song** (XX 278). November 1816.

Ruhig

Der Mond ist auf - ge - gan - gen,

MS. Unknown; former owner (*c.* 1850)—Ludwig Landsberg, Rome (Stadler's and Witteczek's copies).

1ST ED. 1885, C. F. Peters, Leipzig, as no. 13 of twenty *Nachgelassene Lieder* (ed. by Max Friedlaender).

Friedlaender dated the song December 1816. His edition differs slightly from the G.A. Schubert omitted the last two stanzas of the poem, which are given in the *Revisionsbericht*.

500. ' Phidile ' (Claudius), Song (XX 279). November 1816.

Unschuldig

Ich war erst sechs - zehn Som - mer alt,

MS. Unknown; former owner (*c.* 1860)—Eduard Schneider, Vienna (Witteczek's copy).

1ST ED. 1895, Gesamtausgabe.

The poem, consisting of nine stanzas, has a subtitle, ' Als sie nach der Trauung allein in ihr Kämmerlein gegangen war.' It is recorded that Schubert's mother often sang the song in an older setting, perhaps that of the Austrian, Josef Anton Steffan, published in 1778.

Literature. Max Friedlaender, *Das deutsche Lied im 18. Jahrhundert*, Stuttgart, 1902, vol. ii, pp. 224, 244, 559.

501. ' **Lied**,' called ' **Zufriedenheit** ' (' Ich bin vergnügt,' Claudius), **Song**, second version (XX 281). November 1816.

Lebhaft
10

Ich bin ver - gnügt, im Sie - ges - ton

MS. (in G). Meangya family, Mödling, near Vienna (Ph.).

1ST ED. 1895, Gesamtausgabe.

For the first version, see 362. The MS. is inscribed ' Vergnügt. Zufriedenheit '; the copy by Ebner and that in the Witteczek Collection, probably made from a (lost) rough draft, are also entitled ' Zufriedenheit.'

502. 'Herbstlied' (Salis), Song (XX 282). November 1816.

MS. Lost (Witteczek's copy).
1ST ED. 1872, J. P. Gotthard, Vienna (no. 348), as no. 24 of forty songs, this song dedicated by the publisher to Fräulein Helene Magnus.

503. 'Mailied' ('Grüner wird die Au,' Hölty), Song. Unpublished. November 1816.

MS. Meangya family, Mödling, near Vienna (Ph.).
In the MS. Schubert only copied one of the four stanzas. For the setting as a duet, see 199, and as a trio see 129.

504. 'Am Grabe Anselmo's' (Claudius), Song (Op. 6, no. 3; XX 275). 4th November 1816.

MS. Rough copy—Werner Reinhart, Winterthur (Switzerland); final version—Meangya family, Mödling, near Vienna (Ph.).
1ST ED. 23rd August 1821, Cappi & Diabelli, Vienna (no. 790), as no. 3 of Op. 6, published for Schubert and dedicated by him to Johann Michael Vogl (with the title 'Am Grabe Anselmo's').
The rough copy of the MS. bears the title 'Bei dem Grabe Anselmo's,' the final version 'Bei Anselmo's Grabe.' The second MS. is indicated 'Sehr langsam,' and shows some slight alterations. The fourth issue of the first edition has a vignette by Leopold Kupelwieser on the title-page.

505. **Adagio in D flat for Pianoforte** (Op. posth. 145, no. 1; XI 5, no. 1). (?) December 1816.

Adagio

MS. Unknown; former owner—A. Diabelli & Co., Vienna (c. 1850).

1ST ED. c. 1847, A. Diabelli & Co., Vienna (no. 8719), as introduction in ' Adagio und Rondo ' in E (the Adagio transposed and shortened (?) by the publishers).

The association of 505 and 506 is spurious. The original form of the Adagio is to be found in the *Revisionsbericht*. It seems to be identical with the second movement of the 1818 Sonata, 625.

506. Rondo in E for Pianoforte (Op. posth. 145, no. 2; XI 5, no. 2). (?) December 1816.

Allegretto moto

MS. Fragment (undated, together with the dated song, 508)—Sotheby, London, 18th February 1899.

1ST ED. The same as 505.

According to the copy in the Witteczek Collection the original MS. was entitled ' Sonate.' This Allegretto is supposed to be the Finale of the 1817 Sonata, 566.

507. ' **Skolie** ' (' Mädchen entsiegelten,' Matthisson), **Song** (XX 283). December 1816.

Freudig

Mäd-chen ent - sie - gel - ten, Brü - der, die Fla-schen;

MS. (together with 509)—New York Public Library, New York.

1ST ED. 1895, Gesamtausgabe.

The MS. is dated 1816, without the month, but Ferdinand Schubert copied the two songs (507 and 509), possibly from another MS., on 12th November 1856, dating them December 1816 (Krasser family, Vienna).

508. ' **Lebenslied** ' (Matthisson), **Song** (XX 284). December 1816.

Mässig geschwind

Kom - men und Schei - den, Su - chen und Mei - den,

MS. Rough copy, without the last six bars (together with 506) —Sotheby, London, 18th February 1899; fair copy—Gesellschaft der Musikfreunde, Vienna (together with 509): both MSS. dated December 1816.

1ST ED. *c.* 1842, A. Diabelli & Co., Vienna (no. 7416), as no. 2 of *Nachlass*, book 38.

Written on the fair copy, which was probably made from memory, is the note ' In der Wohnung des H[errn] v[on] Schober ' (see 509). Some differences between the two MSS. are given in the *Revisionsbericht.* Schubert also set the poem as a partsong (see 425).

509. ' Leiden der Trennung,' called ' Sehnsucht ' ('Vom Meere trennt sich die Welle,' from Metastasio's ' Artaserse,' translated by Heinrich von Collin), Song (XX 285). December 1816.

Etwas langsam

Vom Mee - re trennt sich die Wel - le,

MS. Rough copy—New York Public Library, New York (together with 507); fair copy—Gesellschaft der Musikfreunde, Vienna (together with 508).

1ST PF. 1873, Vienna (Helene Magnus).

1ST ED. 1872, J. P. Gotthard, Vienna (no. 356), as no. 32 of forty songs, this song dedicated by the publisher to Fräulein Helene Magnus.

The rough copy of the MS. contains only the first eighteen bars, the fair copy only the first eight bars. The first is the original state and is printed in the *Revisionsbericht*; the second bears the same note as ' Lebenslied ': ' In der Wohnung des H[errn] v[on] Schober ' (see 508). The first MS. is dated simply 1816, but the second MS. and a copy by Ferdinand Schubert (see 507) give the full date: December 1816. The poem is a translation of Arbace's aria ' L'onda dal mare divisa,' from the opera *Artaserse*, III. i.

510. '**Vedi, quanto adoro**' (Didone's aria, from Metastasio's 'Didone abbandonata,' II. iv), called '**Arie**' (XX 573). December 1816.

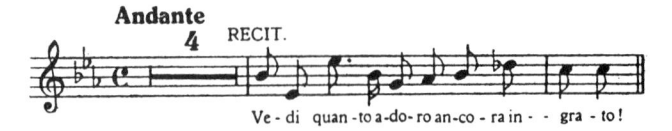

Andante

Ve - di quan - to a-do- ro an-co - ra in - - gra - to!

MS. Stadtbibliothek, Vienna.
1ST ED. 1895, Gesamtausgabe.
There are various sketches for different settings of the same poem in the MS.

511. Écossaise in E flat for Pianoforte. *c.* 1817.

MS. (together with Op. 9 (365), no. 3 (a Deutscher Tanz))— Karl Ernst Henrici, Berlin (see first edition).
1ST ED. Facsimile—23rd August 1924, Berlin, Henrici's sale catalogue 91, no. 275.

The MS. was written as an album leaf for an unknown friend of Schubert's, and has a humorous verse at the foot of each page (*Schubert Documents*, p. 77).

512. 'Der Leidende,' called **'Klage'** (author unknown), **Song,** third version. Unpublished. *c.* 1817.

Unruhig und etwas schnell

Nim-mer län - ger trag' ich die - ser Lei - den . Last;

MS. Copy—Meangya family, Mödling, near Vienna (Ph.).
Schubert altered the first line from 'Nimmer trag' ich länger.' In this version the song is in A minor, *durchkomponiert*; the poem has been further altered and is entitled 'Klage.' For Schubert's first and second versions of the song, see 432.

513. 'La Pastorella' (Goldoni), **Quartet, T.T.B.B., with Pianoforte accompaniment** (XVI 19). (?) 1817.

Andante

La pa - sto - rel - la al pra - to

MS. Stadtbibliothek, Vienna.

1ST PF. (?) 4th May 1927, Musikvereinssaal, Vienna (in German).
1ST ED. 1891, Gesamtausgabe.

The poem, also set by Schubert in January 1817 as a solo song (528), is taken from Carlo Goldoni's libretto *Il Filosofo di Campagna* (opera by Galuppi, Venice, 1754). His colleague, while Schubert was a pupil of Salieri, Karl, Freiherr von Doblhoff, set the same poem as a vocal quartet, which was printed about 1820 in Doblhoff's *Sei Divertimenti Campestri*, dedicated to Salieri.

— ' Lob der Thränen ' (XX 294). See 711. (?) 1817.

514. ' Die abgeblühte Linde ' (Széchényi), Song (Op. 7, no. 1; XX 300). (?) 1817.

MS. Lost.

1ST PF. 6th March 1823, Musikverein, Vienna.
1ST ED. 27th November 1821, Cappi & Diabelli, Vienna (no. 855), as no. 1 of Op. 7, published for Schubert and dedicated by him to the poet.

515. ' Der Flug der Zeit ' (Széchényi), Song (Op. 7, no. 2; XX 301). (?) 1817.

MS. Lost.

1ST ED. 27th November 1821, Cappi & Diabelli, Vienna (no. 855), as no. 2 of Op. 7, published for Schubert and dedicated by him to the poet.

516. ' Sehnsucht ' (' Der Lerche wolkennahe Lieder,' Mayrhofer), Song (Op. 8, no. 2; XX 386). (?) 1817.

MS. Sketch—Stadtbibliothek, Vienna (together with 349); final version—lost.

1ST ED. 9th May 1822, Cappi & Diabelli, Vienna (no. 872), as no. 2 of Op. 8, dedicated by Schubert to Johann Karl, Graf Esterházy.

The sketch is printed in the Supplement of the *Revisionsbericht* of Series XX, pp. 1–2.

517. ' Der Schäfer und der Reiter ' (Fouqué), Song (Op. 13, no. 1; XX 293). 1817.

Mässig, heiter

Ein Schä - fer sass im Grü - nen.

MS. Lost.

1ST ED. 13th December 1822, Cappi & Diabelli, Vienna (no. 1162), as no. 1 of Op. 13, published for Schubert and dedicated by him to Josef von Spaun.

The poem was entitled 'Schäfer und Reiter.'

—— ' Lob der Thränen ' (XX 294). See 711. 1817.

518. ' An den Tod,' called ' Lied an den Tod ' (Schubart), Song (XX 326). 1817.

Langsam

Tod, du Schre-cken der Na - tur,

1ST ED. 26th June 1824, Lithographisches Institut, Vienna, as a supplement to the *Allgemeine musikalische Zeitung mit besonderer Rücksicht auf den österreichischen Kaiserstaat*, no. 5 (also published separately on 2nd July 1824), lithographed.

The original poem is printed in the *Revisionsbericht* for comparison with Schubert's arrangement of the words. The song was republished on 5th May 1832 by A. Diabelli & Co., Vienna (no. 4017) as no. 3 of *Nachlass*, book 17.

519. ' Die Blumensprache ' (Eduard Platner), Song (Op. posth. 173, no. 5; XX 299). (?) January 1817.

Etwas geschwind

Es deu-ten die Blu-men des Her-zens Ge - füh - le,

MS. (together with 527)—Sibley Music Library, University of Rochester (New York).

1ST ED. 1867, C. A. Spina, Vienna (no. 19,178), as no. 5 of Op. 173.

Schubert omitted the fourth stanza of the poem, published in W. G. Becker's *Taschenbuch zum geselligen Vergnügen auf das Jahr 1805*, Leipzig, and signed ' Pl.' Another MS. was, about 1840, in the possession of Karoline, Komtesse Esterházy (together with 627 and 793).

520. ' Frohsinn ' (author unknown), Song (XX 289). January 1817.

Heiter

Ich bin von lo - cke-rem Schla - ge,

MS. Rough copy—Gesellschaft der Musikfreunde, Vienna (together with 521); fair copy—lost.

1ST ED. c. 1848, A. Diabelli & Co., Vienna (no. 8822), as no. 1 of *Nachlass*, book 45 (with a spurious pf. introduction).

The pf. introduction is also in the copy of the second MS. in the Witteczek Collection.

521. ' Jagdlied,' called ' Jagdchor ' (Zacharias Werner), Song (XX 290). January 1817.

Feurig

f Tra - rah!___ Tra - rah!___ wir keh - ren da - heim.___

MS. Rough copy—Gesellschaft der Musikfreunde, Vienna (together with 520); fair copy—lost.

1ST ED. 1895, Gesamtausgabe (see note).

The pf. introduction is missing in Stadler's copy of the second MS., where it is entitled ' Jagdchor.' The poem, written for male chorus, is taken from the end of the first act of Werner's *Wanda, Königin der Sarmaten*. The song was used by Anton Diabelli in 1830, with corrupt text, as a supplement to the song ' Die Nacht ' (534).

522. ' **Die Liebe** ' (' Wo weht der Liebe hoher Geist? ', Gottlieb Leon), Song (XX 291). January 1817.

Mässig

Wo weht der Lie - be ho - her - Geist?—

MS. Lost (Witteczek's copy).
1ST ED. 1895, Gesamtausgabe.

523. ' **Trost** ' (' Nimmer lange weil' ich hier,' author unknown), Song (XX 292). January 1817.

Langsam, mit schwärmerischer Sehnsucht

Nim - mer lan - ge weil' ich hier,

MS. Lost (Witteczek's copy).
1ST ED. 1885, C. F. Peters, Leipzig, as no. 2 of twenty *Nachgelassene Lieder* (ed. by Max Friedlaender).

524. ' **Der Alpenjäger** ' (' Auf hohem Bergesrücken,' Mayrhofer), Song, two versions (Op. 13, no. 3; XX 295 (*b*) and (*a*)). January 1817.

b (FIRST VERSION)
Froh und frei

Auf ho - hem Ber - ges - rü - cken,

a (SECOND VERSION)
Frisch, doch nicht zu schnell

Auf ho - hem Ber - ges - rü - cken,

A (SECOND VERSION, transposed)
Lebhaft

f Auf ho - hem Ber - ges - rü - cken,

MS. (*b*) in E—lost (Stadler's copy); (*a*) in F—lost; (A) score and voice part, transposed into D for bass (Johann Karl, Graf Esterházy, probably in the summer of 1818 at Zseliz)—

Herzogin von Ratibor, Schloss Grafenegg, Lower Austria (formerly in the possession of Marie, Gräfin Breunner, *née* Esterházy).

1ST ED. (*b*) 1895, Gesamtausgabe; (*a*) 13th December 1822, Cappi & Diabelli, Vienna (no. 1162), as no. 3 of Op. 13, published for Schubert and dedicated by him to Josef von Spaun.

The two versions, (*a*) and (*b*), are placed in the wrong order in the G.A.

525. ' Wie Ulfru fischt ' (Mayrhofer), Song (Op. 21, no. 3; XX 296). January 1817.

Mässig

Die An - gel zuckt, die Ru — te bebt,

MS. Lost.

1ST ED. 19th June 1823, Sauer & Leidesdorf, Vienna (no. 276), as no. 3 of Op. 21, dedicated by Schubert to the poet.

526. ' Fahrt zum Hades ' (Mayrhofer), Song (XX 297). January 1817.

Langsam

Der Na - chen dröhnt, Cy - pres - sen flü - stern,

MS. Unknown; former owner (*c.* 1865)—Herr Jünger, Vienna (Stadler's and Witteczek's copies).

1ST ED. 12th July 1832, A. Diabelli & Co., Vienna (no. 4018, on the title-page erroneously 4108), as no. 3 of *Nachlass*, book 18.

Some differences between the copies of the Witteczek Collection and of Stadler may be seen in the *Revisionsbericht*. The first edition was not used for the G.A.

527. ' Schlaflied,' called ' Schlummerlied ' or ' Abendlied ' (' Es mahnt der Wald,' Mayrhofer), Song (Op. 24, no. 2; XX 298). January 1817.

Moderato

Es mahnt der Wald,

MS. Rough copy (together with 519)—Sibley Music Library, University of Rochester (New York).
1ST ED. 27th October 1823, Sauer & Leidesdorf, Vienna (no. 429), as no. 2 of Op. 24.

The first edition has the title 'Schlummerlied' and the fair copy of the MS. 'Abendlied'; Ebner's copy gives the name of the poet, erroneously, as Claudius. Mayrhofer's *Gedichte* was used by the editor of the G.A., Series XX, for the correct version of the words.

528. '**La Pastorella al prato**,' called '**Ariette**' (from Goldoni's 'Il Filosofo di Campagna'), **Song** (XX 574). January 1817.

MS. Preussische Staatsbibliothek, Berlin (together with the themes of nine dances, among them the five mentioned in the notes before 350 and to 366).
1ST ED. 1872, J. P. Gotthard, Vienna (no. 343), as no. 19 of forty songs.

For the first setting of the poem, as a quartet, T.T.B.B., see 513.

529. **Eight Écossaises for Pianoforte** (XII 11 and XXI 30). February 1817.

No. 2. (5)

No. 3. (7)

MS. Erwin von Spaun, Vienna.
1ST ED. Nos. 1–5—1871, J. P. Gotthard, Vienna (no. 132), together with twelve Deutsche Tänze of 1816 (420); nos. 6–8—1889, Gesamtausgabe.

The order of the dances in the MS. is as follows: XII 11, Écossaises 1–5 are numbered 1, 2, 3, 6, 8; and XXI 30, Écossaises 1–3 are numbered 4, 5, 7. No. 8 of the MS. (XII 11, Écossaise 5) is indicated by Schubert 'Nach einem Volkslied.' This folk-song has not been identified.

530. 'An eine Quelle' (Claudius), Song (Op. posth. 109, no. 3; XX 273). February 1817.

Mässig

Du klei - ne grün - um-wachs'-ne Quel - le,

MS. Martin Bodmer, Zürich (Ph.).
1ST ED. 10th July 1829, A. Diabelli & Co., Vienna (no. 3317), as no. 3 of Op. 109.

The MS. is dated, and shows the censor's permit of 8th July 1829 (probably given on the same day also for the two other songs of this opus, 143 and 361). The pf. introduction of the first edition is spurious. Facsimiles of the first and fourth pages of the MS. were published in the *Neue Musikzeitung*, Stuttgart, 1928, no. 11.

531. 'Der Tod und das Mädchen' (Claudius), Song (Op. 7, no. 3; XX 302). February 1817.

Mässig (♩ = 54)   Etwas geschwinder
                      DAS MÄDCHEN

Vor - ü - ber,   ach vor - ü - ber,

MS. Eight pieces (see note)—Gesellschaft der Musikfreunde, Vienna (together with the end of 532).
1ST ED. 27th November 1821, Cappi & Diabelli, Vienna (no.

855), as no. 3 of Op. 7, published for Schubert and dedicated by him to Ludwig, Graf Széchényi von Sárvár-Felsö-Vidék.

It was Andreas Schubert, the composer's step-brother, who divided the MS. into eleven pieces, nine squares and two strips, in order to distribute the parts among friends (cf. 1). The Gesellschaft der Musikfreunde, Vienna, possesses six of the squares and the two strips. No tempo indications appear in this (dated) MS., but they were given in another MS., since lost, from which Ebner and Stadler made their copies.

532. ' Das Lied vom Reifen ' (Claudius), Song (XX 303). February 1817.

MS. The first ten bars—unknown; former owner—A. Cranz, Leipzig; bars 11–13—Gesellschaft der Musikfreunde, Vienna (together with 531).

1ST ED. 1895, Gesamtausgabe.

The last bar (14) is missing in the MS., but is supplied in the G.A. The poem consists of fifteen stanzas.

533. ' Täglich zu singen ' (Claudius), Song (XX 304). February 1817.

MS. Unknown; former owner—A. Cranz, Leipzig.

1ST ED. 1876, V. Kratochwill, Vienna (no. 252), as no. 7 of twelve *Nachgelassene Lieder*, arranged for pf. solo and ed. (with words) by J. P. Gotthard.

Schubert omitted the third, fifth, sixth, seventh, and eighth stanzas of the poem.

534. ' Die Nacht ' (anonymous, translated by Harold), Song (XX 305). February 1817.

MS. Lost.
1ST ED. 10th July 1830, A. Diabelli & Co., Vienna (no. 3631), as *Nachlass*, book 1 (Ossian Songs, book 1).

The poem was wrongly attributed to 'Ossian.' In a footnote to Ossian's *Cronnan*, Macpherson states that he discovered this poem and judges it to be the best example of songs produced at competitions of Scottish bards ' a thousand years later than Ossian.' The first edition of the song was corrupted by the addition of the ' Jagdlied,' 521 (sixty-four bars). The G.A. also includes, in smaller type, the postlude of ' Die Nacht,' which Diabelli inserted before the addition of the ' Jagdlied '; it is, however, spurious. Schubert's music ends on p. 13, line 2, bar 3 of the G.A.; a few bars of the pf. part are missing.

Literature. O. E. D., *Neue Musikzeitung*, Stuttgart 1928, vol. xlix, no. 11, pp. 355–7.

535. ' Lied ' (' Brüder, schrecklich brennt die Thräne,' author unknown), Song with accompaniment for small Orchestra (XX 585.) February 1817.

Andante

Brü - der, schreck-lich brennt die Thrä - ne,

MS. Stadtbibliothek, Vienna.
1ST ED. 1895, Gesamtausgabe.

It is supposed in the G.A. that this song was written for the Vienna Orphanage. This supposition, however, is not substantiated in the Schubert records. It seems more likely that the song was ordered by the Vienna Verein für verschämte Arme (Society for Poor Gentlefolk). As Schubert's repeat signs indicate, the poem consisted of more stanzas than those preserved in the song.

536. ' Der Schiffer ' (' Im Winde,' Mayrhofer), Song (Op. 21, no. 2; XX 318). (?) March 1817.

Geschwind und feurig

Im Win - de, im Stur - me be - fahr' ich den Fluss,

MS. Rough, hurried copy—Wiener Männergesangverein, Vienna (with only the first stanza in full); voice part (with the two first stanzas in full, the others added by Leopold von Sonnleithner)—private collection, Vienna.

1ST ED. 19th June 1823, Sauer & Leidesdorf, Vienna (no. 276), as no. 2 of Op. 21, dedicated by Schubert to the poet.

The poem was published in the *Beiträge zur Bildung für Jünglinge*, Vienna, 1818, vol. ii, p. 325. One copy of this magazine, edited by Schubert's Upper Austrian friends, is in the Nationalbibliothek, Vienna.

537. **Sonata in A minor for Pianoforte** (Op. posth. 164, X 6). March 1817.

MS. Conservatoire, Paris (Ph.).
1ST ED. *c.* 1852, C. A. Spina, Vienna (no. 9106, from the plates of his predecessors, A. Diabelli & Co.), called 'Siebente Sonate.'

This was, in fact, Schubert's fourth sonata. Cf. note to 334.

538. '**Gesang der Geister über den Wassern**' (Goethe) for **Quartet, T.T.B.B.** (XVI 33). March 1817.

MS. Lost.
1ST ED. 1891, Gesamtausgabe.

For other settings of the same poem, see **484, 704, 705,** and **714**.

539. '**Am Strome**' (Mayrhofer), **Song** (Op. 8, no. 4; XX 306). March 1817.

Mässig

Ist mir's doch, als sei mein Le-ben

MS. Fragment—Stadtbibliothek, Vienna (together with 540).
IST ED. 9th May 1822, Cappi & Diabelli, Vienna (no. 872), as no. 4 of Op. 8, dedicated by Schubert to Johann Karl, Graf Esterházy.

The fragment of the MS. contains only the end of the song, from bar 23 onwards.

540. ' Philoktet ' (Mayrhofer), Song (XX 307). March 1817.

Unruhig, schnell

Da sitz' ich oh - ne Bo-gen,

MS. Stadtbibliothek, Vienna (together with 539).
IST ED. 21st April 1831, A. Diabelli & Co., Vienna (no. 3708), as no. 3 of *Nachlass*, book 11 (first issue).

The publishers made some alterations in the second issue.

541. ' Memnon ' (Mayrhofer), Song (Op. 6, no. 1; XX 308). March 1817.

Sehr langsam, schwärmerisch ($\jmath$ = 50)

Den Tag hin-durch nur ein-mal mag ich spre-chen,

MS. Stadtbibliothek, Vienna.
IST ED. 23rd August 1821, Cappi & Diabelli, Vienna (no. 790), as no. 1 of Op. 6, published for Schubert and dedicated by him to Johann Michael Vogl.

542. ' Antigone und Oedip ' (Mayrhofer), Song (Op. 6, no. 2; XX 309). March 1817.

Langsam ($\jmath$ = 54)
ANTIGONE

Ihr ho - hen Himm-li-schen, er - hö - ret der Toch - ter

MS. Rough copy—Conservatoire, Paris (Ph.); fair copy—unknown; former owner—Karl Meinert, Dessau (Frankfurt am Main).
1ST ED. 23rd August 1821, Cappi & Diabelli, Vienna (no. 790), as no. 2 of Op. 6, published for Schubert and dedicated by him to Johann Michael Vogl.

543. ' **Auf dem See** ' (Goethe), **Song**, two versions (Op. 92, no. 2; XX 310 (*a*) and (*b*)). March 1817.

a Mässig, ruhig

b Mässig

MS. (*a*) and (*b*) lost. ((*a*) Witteczek's copy.)
1ST ED. (*a*) 1895, Gesamtausgabe; (*b*) 11th July 1828, M. J. Leidesdorf, Vienna (no. 1014), as no. 2 of Op. 92 (at first erroneously numbered 87, but corrected in later issues), dedicated by Schubert to Frau Josefine von Franck.
One of the MSS. is said to be in a private collection at Zürich.

544. ' **Ganymed** ' (Goethe), **Song** (Op. 19, no. 3; XX 311). March 1817.

Etwas langsam

MS. Stadtbibliothek, Vienna.
1ST ED. 6th June 1825, A. Diabelli & Co., Vienna (no. 1800), as no. 3 of Op. 19, dedicated by Schubert to the poet.

545. ' **Der Jüngling und der Tod** ' (Josef von Spaun), **Song**, two versions (XX 312 (*a*) and (*b*)). March 1817.

a Sehr langsam DER JÜNGLING DER TOD

[musical notation: Sehr langsam — DER JÜNGLING / DER TOD — "Die Son-ne sinkt." / "Es ruht sich kühl"]

MS. (*a*) Dr. Alwin Cranz, Vienna (together with 546 and 547); (*b*) only the last eleven bars—Miss Anahid Iskian, New York (Witteczek's copy).

1ST ED. (*a*) 1895, Gesamtausgabe; (*b*) 1872, J. P. Gotthard, Vienna (no. 342), as no. 18 of forty songs.

The song, a counterpart to 'Der Tod und das Mädchen' (531), was originally written in duet form, but in the MS. Schubert provides an alternative version for a single voice.

546. 'Trost im Liede' (Schober), Song (XX 313). March 1817.

[musical notation: Mässig — "Braust des Un-glücks Sturm em-por."]

MS. Dr. Alwin Cranz, Vienna (together with 545 and 547).

1ST ED. 23rd June 1827, as a supplement to the *Wiener Zeitschrift für Kunst*, etc., Vienna (together with 'Wandrers Nachtlied II,' 768, in type).

The MS. lacks the last three semiquavers of the pf. introduction. H. A. Probst, Leipzig, reprinted the song as no. 3 of his so-called Op. 101 (no. 431, 12th December 1828).

547. 'An die Musik' (Schober), Song, two versions (Op. 88, no. 4; XX 314 (*a*) and (*b*)). March 1817.

a [musical notation: Etwas bewegt — "Du hol-de Kunst, in wie viel grau-en Stun-den,"]

b [musical notation: Mässig — "Du hol-de Kunst, in wie viel grau-en Stun-den,"]

MS. (*a*) Rough copy—Dr. Alwin Cranz, Vienna (together with 545 and 546); (*a*1) first album leaf written for an unknown friend

—Conservatoire, Paris (Ph.); (*b*) fair copy—Stefan Zweig Collection, London; (*b1*) second album leaf (written on 24th April 1827 for Albert Sowinski)—private collection, Paris (sold in 1914).

IST ED. (*a*) 1895, Gesamtausgabe; (*b*) 12th December 1827, Thaddäus Weigl, Vienna (no. 2696), as no. 4 of Op. 88 (first issue, without the list of Schubert's works).

The poem is missing in the two editions of Schober's poems, but is included in the MS. collection (Stadtbibliothek, Vienna). The MSS. of the song, except that of Cranz, have been reproduced; Conservatoire copy—*Musical Quarterly*, New York, October 1928, opposite p. 495; Zweig copy—privately by the former owner, Siegfried Ochs, Berlin, and in Dahms's *Schubert*, Berlin, 1912, Appendix, p. 33; Sowinski copy—H. Barbedette's *Schubert*, Paris, 1866, frontispiece. The MS. of the Conservatoire is a version which varies between (*a*) and (*b*). It is probable that Schubert wrote the three later MSS. from memory.

548. ' Orest auf Tauris ' (Mayrhofer), Song (XX 382). March 1817.

Mässig langsam

Ist dies Tau - ris,

MS. Leo Liepmannssohn, Berlin (19th May 1919).

IST ED. 21st April 1831, A. Diabelli & Co., Vienna (no. 3708), as no. 1 of *Nachlass*, book 11 (corrupt).

The first half of the MS., which is dated March 1817, was not found until after the publication of the G.A. The date given in the Witteczek Collection, September 1820, is spurious. The author's title for the poem was 'Der landende Orest.'

549. 'Mahomet's Gesang' (Goethe), **Song**, first version, **for a female voice** (XX 595). Fragment. March 1817.

Mässig 5

Seht den Fel - sen-quell,

MS. Stadtbibliothek, Vienna.

IST ED. 1895, Gesamtausgabe.

Only the first sheet of the MS. is preserved. It is boldly written, without hesitation. For the later version, see 721.

1817　　　　　　　550　　　　　　　241

550. ' Die Forelle ' (Schubart), **Song,** five versions (Op. 32, XX 327 (a)–(d)). Version (e) not engraved (but see *Literature*). Spring 1817.

a **Mässig**

In ei-nem Bäch-lein hel - le, da schoss in fro - her Eil'

b **Etwas geschwind**

In ei-nem Bäch-lein hel - le, da schoss in fro - her Eil'

c **Nicht zu geschwind**

In ei-nem Bäch-lein hel - le, da schoss in fro - her Eil'

d **Etwas lebhaft**

In ei-nem Bäch-lein hel - le, da schoss in fro - her Eil'

e **Etwas lebhaft**

p In ei-nem Bäch-lein hel-le, da schoss in fro - her Eil',

MS. (*a*) Rough copy—lost (Ebner's and Stadler's copies); (*b*) Album leaf for Josef Hüttenbrenner, 21st February 1818—unknown; former owner—Nikolaus Dumba, Vienna (*c*. 1895); (*c*) Album leaf for Franz Sales Kandler, June or July 1817—Frau Marie Floersheim, Wildegg in Aargau (Switzerland); (*d*) Written in (?) 1820 for the first printing and given to Anselm Hüttenbrenner—unknown; former owner—G. R. Salvini, Porto (Italy); (*e*) October 1821, written for the first edition—Mrs. Whittall Collection, Library of Congress, Washington.

IST ED. (*a*), (*b*), (*c*) 1895, Gesamtausgabe; (*d*) 9th December 1820, as a supplement to the *Wiener Zeitschrift für Kunst*, etc., Vienna, vol. v, no. 148, in type; (*e*) *c*. 1828, A. Diabelli & Co., Vienna (no. 1703), with cover-title ' Die Forelle,' opus number

32, and the head title no. 152 of the pf. collection *Philomele* (corrupt).

Schubert omitted the last stanza of the poem. MS. (*b*), written at Anselm Hüttenbrenner's lodgings, was reproduced in facsimile by Fr. Wendling, Vienna, *c.* 1870 (published *c.* 1876 by Karl Simon, Berlin). It is dated by Anselm Hüttenbrenner. MS. (*d*) shows a dedication by the same Hüttenbrenner, and a note by an editor, probably Johann Schickh, who was the editor of the *Wiener Zeitschrift.* MSS. (*a*)–(*d*) are without pf. introduction. MS. (*e*), discovered at Vienna in 1925, contains a pf. introduction of five bars (the first in Op. 32 is spurious). The first page of this MS. was reproduced in the *Annual Report of the Library of Congress*, 1941, Washington, 1942, after p. 122. Between the publication of the first printing and the issue with opus number two earlier issues of Diabelli's separate edition appeared: the first issue, 13th January 1825, and a second issue without the title on the cover, both without opus number. N.B. The first printing in the *Wiener Zeitschrift* appears sometimes with a line, and at other times with an ornament at the end; which of these issues is the earlier has not yet been determined.

Literature. Alfred Orel, *Archiv für Musikwissenschaft*, Leipzig, 1937, vol. ii, no. 3, pp. 299–307 (on MS. (*e*)). Frank C. Campbell, *The Library of Congress Quarterly Journal of Current Acquisitions*, Washington, August 1949, vol. vi, no. 4, pp. 4–6 (also on MS. (*e*), with facsimile of both pages).

551. ' **Pax vobiscum** ' (Schober), **Song** (XX 315). April 1817.

Mit heiliger Rührung

"Der Frie - de sei mit euch!"

MS. Stadtbibliothek, Vienna.

1ST ED. 21st April 1831, A. Diabelli & Co., Vienna (no. 3707), as no. 6 of *Nachlass*, book 10 (with a spurious introductory chord).

Schubert's MS. contains only one of the three stanzas. Schober wrote a second version for Schubert's funeral, which was sung in the Josef-Kirche, in the Vienna suburb Margareten, on 21st November 1828 by a chorus with an acc. of wind instruments, arranged and conducted by Johann Baptist Gänsbacher.

552. ' **Hänflings Liebeswerbung** ' (Kind), **Song** (Op. 20, no. 3; XX 316). April 1817.

Etwas geschwind

A - hi - di, ich lie - be, A - hi - di, ich lie - be!

MS. Stadtbibliothek, Vienna.
1ST ED. 10th April 1823, Sauer & Leidesdorf, Vienna (no. 231), as no. 3 of Op. 20, dedicated by Schubert to Frau Justine von Bruchmann.

553. 'Auf der Donau' (Mayrhofer), Song (Op. 21, no. 1; XX 317). April 1817.

[musical notation: Langsam — "Auf der Wel-len Spie-gel schwimmt der Kahn,"]

MS. Lost.
1ST ED. 19th June 1823, Sauer & Leidesdorf, Vienna (no. 276), as no. 1 of Op. 21, dedicated by Schubert to the poet.

554. 'Uraniens Flucht,' called 'Urania' (Mayrhofer), Song (XX 319). April 1817.

[musical notation: Lebhaft — RECIT. "Lasst uns, ihr Himm-li-schen, ein Fest be-ge-hen!"]

MS. Conservatoire, Paris (Ph.).
1ST ED. 1895, Gesamtausgabe.

555. A Song without title or words. (?) May 1817.

[musical notation: Unruhig]

MS. (together with the final version of 457)—Sotheby, London (21st April 1943).
1ST ED. 21st September 1934, *Radio Wien*, Vienna, vol. x, no. 52, p. 13 (ed. by O. E. D.).

The autograph, from which Ferdinand Schubert made a copy before he gave it away, contains the complete melody and accompaniment of a song without title or words. Ferdinand's copy is preserved with the Krasser family, Vienna.

556. Overture in D for Orchestra (II 4). May 1817.

MS. (score)—Dr. Alwin Cranz, Vienna.

1ST PF. Probably 1817, at a meeting of a private music society, Vienna; first public performance, arranged by Ferdinand Schubert—17th April 1836, Musikverein, Vienna (conductor, Leopold Jansa).

1ST ED. 1886, Gesamtausgabe.

Instrumental parts, written by another hand, and a pf. arrangement by Ferdinand Schubert, dated 28th January 1838, are preserved with the Krasser family, Vienna.

557. Sonata in A flat for Pianoforte (X 3). May 1817.

MS. (incomplete)—unknown; former owner—Emil Sulzbach, Frankfurt am Main.

1ST ED. 1888, Gesamtausgabe.

The third, and last, movement is in E flat.

558. 'Liebhaber in allen Gestalten' (Goethe), Song (XX 120). May 1817.

Etwas lebhaft

Ich wollt', ich wär' ein Fisch.

MS. (together with 559 and 560)—Conservatoire, Paris (Ph.).
IST ED. 1887, C. F. Peters, Leipzig, as no. 44 of *Schubert Album*, book 7 (ed. by Max Friedlaender).

From the date on the MS. it is evident that this song was not written in 1815, as stated in the G.A. Schubert used only the first, second, third, and ninth stanzas of Goethe's poem, with slight alterations to the third and the ninth.

559. 'Schweizerlied' (Goethe), Song (XX 121). May 1817.

Mässig

Uf'm Berg - li bin i g'säs - se,

MS. (together with 558 and 560)—Conservatoire, Paris (Ph.).
IST ED. 1885, C. F. Peters, Leipzig, as no. 16 of twenty *Nachgelassene Lieder* (ed. by Max Friedlaender).

The G.A. also dates this song 1815 (see 558).

560. 'Der Goldschmiedsgesell' (Goethe), Song (XX 122). May 1817.

Mässig

Es ist doch mei - ne Nach - ba - rin

MS. (together with 558 and 559)—Conservatoire, Paris (Ph.).
IST ED. *c.* 1848, A. Diabelli & Co., Vienna (no. 8837), as no. 6 of *Nachlass*, book 48 (with a spurious pf. introduction).

The pf. introduction of the printed editions is spurious, the key (F), however, is correct. There is no tempo indication in the MS. The G.A. dates the song 1815; the year, and probably the month, of the undated MS. is indicated by the two other dated songs in the same autograph (see 558 and 559). Schubert omitted the second and third stanzas of Goethe's poem.

— 'An die untergehende Sonne' (XX 237). See 457. May 1817.

561. 'Nach einem Gewitter' (Mayrhofer), Song (XX 320). May 1817.

[musical notation: Mässig — Auf___ den Blu-men]

MS. Lost (Witteczek's copy).
IST ED. 1872, J. P. Gotthard, Vienna (no. 329), as no. 5 of forty songs.

The poem was originally entitled 'Nach dem Gewitter.'

562. 'Fischerlied' (Salis), Song, second version (XX 321). May 1817.

[musical notation: Mässig, ruhig — Das Fi-scher-ge-wer-be gibt rü-sti-gen Muth!]

MS. Preussische Staatsbibliothek, Berlin (together with 563).
IST ED. 1895, Gesamtausgabe.

For the first version, see 351; for the same poem set as a quartet, T.T.B.B., see 364.

563. 'Die Einsiedelei' (Salis), Song, second version (XX 322). May 1817.

[musical notation: Etwas bewegt — Es rie-selt, klar und we-hend,]

MS. Preussische Staatsbibliothek, Berlin (together with 562).
IST ED. 1887, C. F. Peters, Leipzig, as no. 31 of *Schubert Album*, book 7 (ed. by Max Friedlaender).

The G.A. dated the song, by mistake, March 1817, but corrected this in the Appendix to the *Revisionsbericht*, p. 3. For the first version, see 393, and for the setting as a quartet, T.T.B.B., 337.

564. 'Gretchen vor der Mater dolorosa,' called 'Gretchen,' or

'Gretchen's Bitte,' or 'Gretchen im Zwinger' (from Goethe's 'Faust'), Song (XX 596). Fragment. May 1817.

[Musical notation: Sehr langsam — "Ach nei-ge, du Schmer-zen-rei-che,"]

MS. Goethe-Museum, Frankfurt am Main.
1ST ED. June 1838, A. Diabelli & Co., Vienna (no. 5033), as no. 3 of *Nachlass*, book 29.

The song is incomplete. The first edition contains a spurious ending, supplied by the publishers (see Diabelli's MS. copy in the archives of the Gesellschaft der Musikfreunde, Vienna). N. C. Gatty published another version of the end in *Music & Letters* (London, October 1928), and Benjamin Britten supplied yet another ending (performed for the first time at Cambridge on 25th April 1943). Cf. 118, 126, 367, and 440.

565. 'Der Strom' (Schubert (?)), Song (XX 324). (?) June 1817.
MS. Stadtbibliothek, Vienna (together with 569).

[Musical notation: Schnell — "Mein Le-ben wälzt sich mur-rend fort."]

1ST ED. 1876, E. W. Fritzsch, Leipzig, in *Blätter für Hausmusik* (1877 re-issued separately), with a note which was suggested by Brahms.

Inscribed 'Zum Andenken für Herrn [Albert] Stadler.' Republished by Max Friedlaender as no. 29 of *Schubert Album*, book 7, C. F. Peters, Leipzig, in 1887. The G.A. atrributes the poem to Stadler.

566. Sonata in E minor for Pianoforte (first movement, X 4). June 1817.

[Musical notation: Moderato]

[Musical notation: Allegretto]

SCHERZO
Allegro vivace

TRIO

MS. Frau Hella Prieger, Bonn; another autograph of the first movement (marked 'Sonate I,' but the number cancelled by Schubert himself)—Preussische Staatsbibliothek, Berlin.

1ST PF. of the Allegretto—9th May 1907, Bonn, Beethoven-Haus (Ernst von Dohnányi); of all the three movements—12th October 1928, Munich (Josef Pembaur).

1ST ED. *Moderato*—1888, Gesamtausgabe; *Allegretto* — May 1907, Breitkopf & Härtel, Leipzig (ed. by Erich Prieger); *Scherzo*—October 1928, *Die Musik*, Berlin, vol. xxi, no. 1, supplement (ed. by Adolf Bauer).

The three movements of the Sonata, together with the Allegretto, 506, as Finale, were published in 1948 by Kathleen Dale (London, British and Continental Music Agencies, no. 60.)

567. Sonata in D flat for Pianoforte (XXI 9). Three movements only. June 1817.

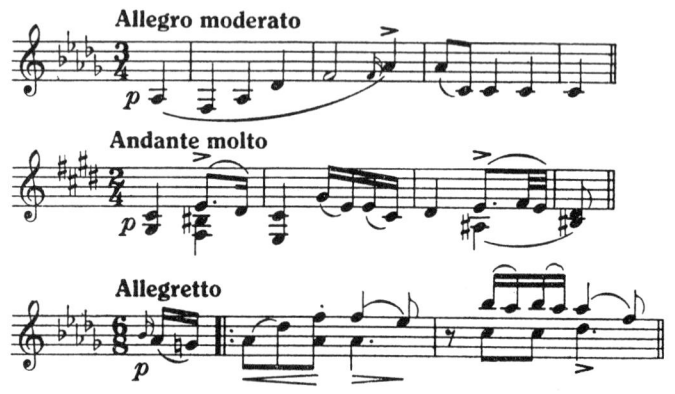

Allegro moderato

Andante molto

Allegretto

MS. First movement only (incomplete)—Krasser family, Vienna; movements 1–3 (without the last leaf)—Stadtbibliothek, Vienna.
1ST ED. 1897, Gesamtausgabe.

This is the first version of the Sonata in E flat (568). Both MSS. are entitled 'Sonate II.'

568. Sonata in E flat for Pianoforte (Op. posth. 122; X 7). June 1817.

MS. Lost.
IST ED. *c.* 1829, A. Pennauer, Vienna (no. 436) as 'Troisième grande Sonate.'

The second movement, Andante, is sketched in D minor, instead of G minor, on the back of Beethoven's song 'Ich liebe dich' (with owner's note by Brahms, Gesellschaft der Musikfreunde, Vienna; see 573A). The E flat Sonata is, however, only a later version of the D flat Sonata, 567. For the trio, see 593.

569. '**Das Grab**' (Salis), **Song**, third version (XX 323). June 1817.

MS. Stadtbibliothek, Vienna (together with 565).
IST ED. 1895, Gesamtausgabe.
The MS. is indicated 'Männerchor' (in unison), but it existed in this

form only in Schubert's imagination. For the first and second settings of this poem, see 330 and 377.

570. Scherzo in D and Fragment of Allegro in F sharp minor for Pianoforte (XXI 20). (?) July 1817.

MS. Stadtbibliothek, Vienna.
1ST ED. 1897, Gesamtausgabe.

The MS. is not dated and without title. The order of the two movements is reversed in the G.A. Ludwig Scheibler assumed, probably rightly, that these movements belonged to the Allegro in F sharp minor (571).

571. Allegro in F sharp minor for Pianoforte (XXI 10). Unfinished. July 1817.

MS. Stadtbibliothek, Vienna.
1ST ED. 1897, Gesamtausgabe.

This is the first movement of an unfinished sonata, numbered ' V.' See the two movements, 570. Walter Rehberg completed the sonata in 1927 (Steingräber-Verlag, Leipzig, 1928, no. 2384, edition no. 2580). Heinz Jolles completed the Allegro only in 1925.

572. 'Lied im Freien' (Salis) **for Chorus, T.T.B.B.** (XVI 34). July 1817.

Lebhaft, doch nicht zu geschwind

f Wie schön ist's im Frei - en.

MS. Stadtbibliothek, Vienna (score and parts).
1ST ED. 1872, J. P. Gotthard, Vienna (no. 318), as no. 3 of nine part-songs (incorrect).

Ferdinand Schubert's additions to the incomplete autograph score proved misleading to the publisher of the first edition, who gave them a wrong interpretation, as appears from the carefully written parts which were found at a later date. Schubert had set this poem *c.* 1815 as a trio (133).

573. 'Iphigenia' (Mayrhofer), Song (Op. 98, no. 3; XX 325). July 1817.

Nicht zu langsam

Blüht ___ denn hier an Tau - ris Stran-de,

MS. Lost (see note).
1ST ED. 10th July 1829, A. Diabelli & Co., Vienna (no. 3315), as no. 3 of Op. 98 (see 497).

The only preserved copy of the autograph, in the Witteczek Collection, is in G flat; the first edition, probably transposed by the publishers, is in F.

573A. **Lesson in Notation.** July 1817.
MS. Gesellschaft der Musikfreunde, Vienna (on p. 4 of the 'Three Masters' Autograph,' see note to 568).
1ST ED. Facsimile—*Die Musik*, Berlin, 15th January 1907 (vol. vi, no. 8).

The notes are written by Schubert, and the corresponding letters by one of his young pupils, some of which are corrected by Schubert. Cf. 679.
Literature. O. E. D., *Neues Beethoven-Jahrbuch*, Brunswick, 1933, vol. v, pp. 21–7.

574. **Sonata in A for Pianoforte and Violin** (Op. posth. 162; VIII 6). August 1817.

Allegro moderato

p

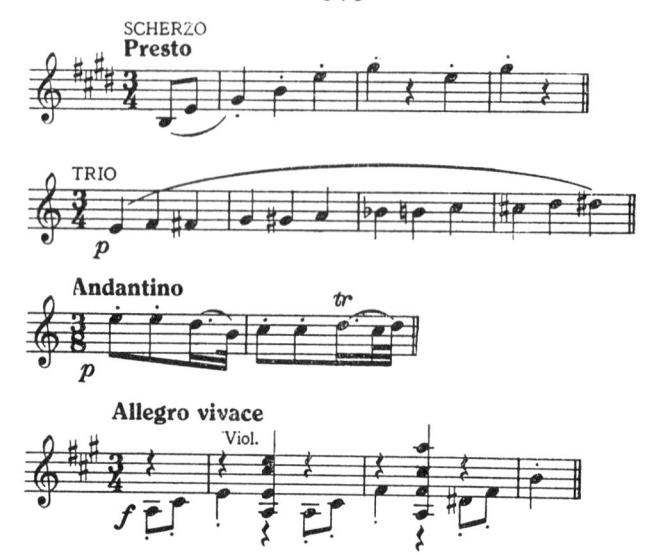

MS. Unknown; former owner—Eduard Schneider, Vienna (*c.* 1870).

1ST PF. 3rd March 1864, Musikverein, Vienna.

1ST ED. End of 1851, A. Diabelli & Co., Vienna (no. 9100), under the title ' Duo.'

575. **Sonata in B for Pianoforte** (Op. posth. 147; X 5). August 1817

MS. Sketch only—Gesellschaft der Musikfreunde, Vienna.
1ST ED. *c.* 1844, A. Diabelli & Co., Vienna (no. 7970), dedicated by the publishers to Siegmund Thalberg.

In the MS. the Scherzo forms the second and the Andante the third movement. Other differences are given in the *Revisionsbericht*.

576. **Thirteen Variations, on a Theme by Anselm Hüttenbrenner, in A minor for Pianoforte** (XI 7). August 1817.

MS. Stadtbibliothek, Vienna (without dedication).
1ST ED. 1867, C. A. Spina, Vienna (no. 19304), dedicated by (?) Schubert to his friend and schoolfellow, Anselm Hüttenbrenner.

The theme is taken from Anselm Hüttenbrenner's first String Quartet in E, Op. 3, published by S. A. Steiner & Co., Vienna, in 1816 or 1817.

577. '**Die Entzückung an Laura**' (Schiller), **Song**, second version (XX 597, I and II). Two fragments. August 1817.

MS. I—Preussische Staatsbibliothek, Berlin (together with Appendix II, no. 5); II—Stadtbibliothek, Vienna.

1ST ED. I (facsimile)—1873, J. Guttentag, Berlin, in Reissmann's *Schubert*; II—1895, Gesamtausgabe.

The autograph consists of fragments only of a song; a section of the MS. between I and II is lost, the song, however, was never finished. MS. I is written on the title-pages of the parts of Appendix II, no. 5. Schubert corrupted the title, by mistake, into: 'Entzückung eines [. . .] Lauras Abschied.' Schiller's original title was 'Die seligen Augenblicke.' For the first version, see 390.

578. 'Abschied,' called 'Abschied von einem Freunde' ('Lebe wohl,' Schubert), Song (XX 586), 24th August 1817.

MS. Conservatoire, Paris (Ph.).

1ST ED. June 1838, A. Diabelli & Co., Vienna (no. 5033), as no. 4 of *Nachlass*, book 29.

The words and music were written by Schubert as an album leaf on the occasion of Franz von Schober's intended departure for Sweden.

579. 'Der Knabe in der Wiege,' called 'Wiegenlied' ('Er schläft so süss,' Ottenwalt), Song, two versions (XX 335). September (?) and November 1817.

MS. First version—lost (Witteczek's copy; another with Albert Cranz, New York); second version (the first thirty-eight bars only)—Conservatoire, Paris (Ph.).

1ST ED. 1872, J. P. Gotthard, Vienna (no. 340), as no. 16 of forty songs, this song dedicated by the publisher to Gustav Walter.

An autograph of the poem is in the possession of Erwin von Spaun, Vienna. The music of the first version (according to a letter by the author, written before October 1817) is only suitable for the first stanza (i.e. first and second verses of the poem). Schubert sang the second version to the poet at Linz in August 1819, and on 2nd November 1821 for some unknown reason asked Josef von Spaun to return his copy of this version.

580. Polonaise in B flat for Violin and String Orchestra. September 1817.

MS. Fragment (in the album of Henriette Sontag)—William Kux, Chur, Switzerland (Ph.).

1ST PF. 29th September 1818, Waisenhaus, Vienna (without bassoons); Ferdinand Schubert as soloist.

1ST ED. 1928, Ed. Strache, Vienna (no. 17), ed. by O. E. D.

A MS., probably complete, was in the possession of Ferdinand Schubert, Vienna, in 1839. A copy of the complete work was made by J. C. Teufel in 1820.

581. String Trio in B flat (XXI 5). September 1817.

MENUETTO
Allegretto

TRIO
Va.

RONDO
Allegretto

MS. Score—Dr. Alwin Cranz, Vienna (Ph.); parts—Stadtbibliothek, Vienna; another set—Otto Taussig, Malmö.
1ST PF. 15th February 1869, St. James's Hall, London (Joachim, Blagrove, Piatti).
1ST ED. 1897, Gesamtausgabe.

582. ' **Augenblicke im Elysium** ' (Schober), **Song.** No date. Lost.

The poem is indicated in the second edition of Schober's verses (1865) as having been composed by Schubert. See 683. (This item is inserted here to fill a blank after the compilation of the catalogue.)

583. ' **Gruppe aus dem Tartarus** ' (Schiller), **Song,** second version (Op. 24, no. 1; XX 328). September 1817.

Etwas geschwind

Horch, wie Mur-meln des em - pör - ten Mee-res,

MS. Lost.
1ST PF. 8th March 1821, Musikverein, Vienna.
1ST ED. 27th October 1823, Sauer & Leidesdorf, Vienna (no. 429), as no. 1 of Op. 24.

It is assumed in the *Revisionsbericht* that the voice part was originally written in the bass clef. For the first version, see 396; for the setting as a canon for trio, T.T.B., see 65.

584. 'Elysium' (Schiller), Song (XX 329). September 1817.

Nicht zu langsam

Vor-ü-ber die stöh-nen-de Kla-ge!

MS. Fragment (without the first nineteen bars)—Stadtbibliothek, Vienna (together with 585 and 586).

1ST ED. 1830 (? summer), A. Diabelli & Co., Vienna (no. 3636), as *Nachlass*, book 6 (without the note of copyright registration).

For settings of parts of the same poem as trios, T.T.B., see 51, 53, 54, 57, 58, 60.

585. 'Atys' (Mayrhofer), Song (XX 330). September 1817.

Etwas geschwind

Der Kna-be seufzt ü-ber's grü-ne Meer,

MS. Stadtbibliothek, Vienna (together with 584 and 586); a fragment, with the end only (together with 114 and 586)—Dr. Franz Roehn, Los Angeles.

1ST ED. 4th June 1833, A. Diabelli & Co., Vienna (no. 4270), as no. 2 of *Nachlass*, book 22.

The poem is based on the same legend as Catullus' 'Attis.'

586. 'Erlafsee,' called 'Am Erlafsee' (Mayrhofer), Song (Op. 8, no. 3; XX 331). September 1817.

Ziemlich langsam

Mir ist so wohl, so weh'

MS. Rough draft—Stadtbibliothek, Vienna (together with 584 and 585); fragment of a fair copy, with words written in another hand (together with 114 and 585)—Dr. Franz Roehn, Los Angeles.

1ST ED. 6th February 1818, Anton Doll, Vienna, as a supplement to the almanac *Mahlerisches Taschenbuch für Freunde interessanter Gegenden, Natur- und Kunst-Merkwürdigkeiten der Oesterreichischen Monarchie*, edited by Franz Sartori, vol. vi, in type, under the title 'Am Erlafsee.'

This was the first work published by Schubert. The almanac also contains the poem printed separately (reprinted in the *Revisionsbericht*, but with ' dunkle ' instead of ' blaue ' in line 6), together with an engraving of the lake. The song was republished, by Cappi & Diabelli, Vienna (no. 872), on 9th May 1822, as no. 3 of Op. 8, dedicated by Schubert to Johann Karl, Graf Esterházy. This version has ' dunklen ' instead of ' glatten,' in line 8. The poem appeared again in Mayrhofer's *Gedichte*, Vienna, 1824 (with ' dunkle ' in line 6, but ' glatten ' in line 8). Schubert used only two of the six stanzas. Cf. 475.

587. ' An den Frühling ' (Schiller), Song, first version, in A (XX 107 (*b*)). October 1817.

MS. First sketch (without words)—Leo Liepmannssohn, Berlin (May 1931); final copy—Wissenschaftlicher Klub, Vienna.
IST ED. 1895, Gesamtausgabe.

The first sketch lacks title, time-signature, tempo, and words; on the back is to be found a fragment of a song, probably not by Schubert, written by another hand, the particulars of which are as follows: seven bars, in E, 2/4, '. . . an ihren Segensbrüsten liegt,' and two more stanzas, beginning ' Und wie sie jeden Säugling liebt ' and ' Dann fühl' ich hohen Busendrang.' For the first version, in B flat, of ' An den Frühling,' see 245, for the second version, see 283, and for the setting as a quartet, T.T.B.B., see 338.

588. ' Der Alpenjäger ' (' Willst du nicht das Lämmlein hüten,' Schiller), Song, two versions (Op. 37, no. 2; XX 332). October 1817.

MS. Fragment of rough draft (together with Ferdinand Schubert's title to the Salve Regina in B flat, 106)—Fitzwilliam Museum, Cambridge; final version—lost.

1ST PF. 10th April 1825, Musikverein, Vienna.

1ST ED. The fragment of the first version—*Revisionsbericht* to Series XX, pp. 66–9; the final version—28th February 1825, Cappi & Co., Vienna (no. 71), as no. 2 of Op. 37, dedicated by Schubert to his friend, L. F. Schnorr von Carolsfeld.

The *Revisionsbericht* also includes a different beginning to the last part of the song, printed from a copy in the Witteczek Collection.

589. Symphony in C, called the **Little Symphony in C** (I 6). October 1817–February 1818.

MS. Gesellschaft der Musikfreunde, Vienna (entitled 'Grosse Sinfonie')

1ST PF. 1818, at the house of Otto Hatwig, Gundelhof, Vienna;

260 590 1817

first public performance—14th December 1828, Redoutensaal, Vienna, at a concert of the Gesellschaft der Musikfreunde (conductor, Johann Baptist Schmiedel).
1ST ED. 1895, Gesamtausgabe.

590. Overture ' im italienischen Stile ' in D for Orchestra (II 5). (?) November 1817.

MS. Dr. Albert Cranz, Vienna (undated).
1ST PF. Probably 1817, at a meeting of a private music society, Vienna; first public performance—1st March 1818, Gasthof 'Zum Römischen Kaiser,' Vienna (Eduard Jaell's concert). This was the first public performance of a work by Schubert—but see note.
1ST ED. 1886, Gesamtausgabe.

The title, ' im italienischen Stile,' given in Ferdinand Schubert's list of Schubert's works to both overtures, 590 as well as 591, is doubtful in the case of this work. It is possible that the first work of Schubert's to be given a public performance was the Overture in C (591). Cf. Schubert's own arrangement for piano duet, 592.

Literature. Gerald Abraham (editor), *Schubert*, London, 1946, p. 267; New York, 1947, p. 263.

591. Overture ' im italienischen Stile ' in C for Orchestra (Op. posth. 170, II 6). November 1817.

Allegro

MS. Score (dated)—Dr. Alwin Cranz, Vienna; Parts—Frau Marie Floersheim, Wildegg in Aargau (Switzerland).

1ST PF. Probably end of 1817 in the house of Otto Hatwig, Gundelhof, Vienna; first public performance—21st March 1830, Landhaussaal, Vienna (conductor, Ferdinand Schubert)—but see note.

1ST ED. Score—1866, C. A. Spina, Vienna (no. 17979); parts —*ibidem*, as Op. 170.

This, or the Overture in D (590), was the first work of Schubert to be given a public performance (1st March 1818). Jaell played first violin at Hatwig's. Cf. Schubert's arrangement of this overture for piano duet, 597.

592. Overture ' im italienischen Stile ' in D for Piano Duet (IX 10). November 1817.

Adagio **Allegro**

MS. Unknown; former owner—Anton Diabelli, Vienna (c. 1850), and later—Rosa, Gräfin Almásy, Vienna (c. 1860).

1ST PF. Cf. Overture in C, 597.

1ST ED. 1872, J. P. Gotthard, Vienna (no. 249).

Arranged by Schubert from the Overture for Orchestra, 590.

593. Two Scherzi, in B flat and D flat, for Pianoforte (XI 15). November 1817.

No. 1. **Allegretto**

TRIO *legato*

MS. Lost.
1ST ED. 1871, J. P. Gotthard, Vienna (no. 161), dedicated by the publisher to Anton Door.

The trio of the second Scherzo was used earlier in the Sonata in E flat, 568.

594. 'Der Kampf,' called 'Freigeisterei der Leidenschaft' (Schiller), Song (Op. posth. 110, XX 333) November 1817.

MS. Unknown; former owner (*c.* 1867)—Josef Hüttenbrenner, Vienna. (Copies formerly in the possession of Josef von Spaun and of Albert Stadler.)
1ST PF. 6th December 1827, Musikverein, Vienna.
1ST ED. January 1829, Josef Czerny, Vienna (no. 334), as Op. 110.

The poem, with the subtitle, 'Als Laura vermählt war im Jahr 1782,' has twenty-two stanzas, six of which Schubert set to music (nos. 1, 2, 6–9).

595. 'Thekla' (Schiller), Song, second and third versions (Op. 88, no. 2; XX 334 (*a*) and (*b*)). November 1817.

MS. (*a*) Conservatoire, Paris (Ph.); (*b*) second half only (together with ' Hoffnung ' of 1815, 295 (*b*)—Mrs. Whittall Collection, Library of Congress, Washington.

1ST ED. (*a*) 1895, Gesamtausgabe; (*b*) 12th December 1827, Thaddäus Weigl, Vienna (no. 2696), as no. 2 of Op. 88.

In version (*a*) Schubert altered the tempo from ' Leise, von ferne ' to ' Sehr leise, von ferne,' and finally to ' Langsam und sehr leise, von ferne.' For the first version see 73.

—— ' Der Knabe in der Wiege ' (XX 335). See 579. November 1817.

596. ' Lied eines Kindes ' (author unknown), Song (XX 598). Unfinished. November 1817.

MS. Lost (Witteczek's copy).
1ST ED. 1895, Gesamtausgabe.

A few bars of the acc. only are missing at the end of the song.

597. Overture ' im italienischen Stile ' in C for Piano Duet (IX 9). (?) December 1817.

MS. Stadtbibliothek, Vienna.
1ST PF. 12th March 1818, Gasthof 'Zum Römischen Kaiser,' Vienna (eight hands on two pianos, performed by the sisters Therese and Babette Kunz, Schubert, and Anselm Hüttenbrenner).

IST ED. 1872, J. P. Gotthard, Vienna (no. 249).

Arranged by Schubert from the Overture for Orchestra, 591. The MS. of this arrangement was formerly in the possession of Karoline, Komtesse Esterházy. The date of the first performance indicated above is possibly that of 592. No arrangement for eight hands of either of these overtures is preserved, and, according to Alfred Einstein (*Schubert*, New York and London, 1951), the performance was nothing more than a doubling of the parts.

597A. Variations in A for Violin Solo. Sketches. Lost. December 1817.

MS. Unknown; former owner—Ferdinand Schubert, Vienna (*c.* 1850).

598. ' Das Dörfchen ' (Bürger), Sketch of Quartet, T.T.B.B., first version (XVI 46). December 1817.

MS. (sketch)—Wiener Schubertbund, Vienna (Ph.).
IST ED. 1891, Gesamtausgabe.

Schubert used the poem in a shortened form. For the final version, see **641**.

598A. Exercises in Thorough-Bass. Not printed. (?) *c.* 1818.

MS. Preussische Staatsbibliothek, Berlin.

The MS. shows three examples of figured bass, i.e. § 41, nos. 15 and 16, and—not elaborated—§ 43 of an unidentified text-book.

599. Four Polonaises for Piano Duet (Op. 75, IX 26). *c.* 1818.

MS. Lost.
1ST ED. 6th July 1827, A. Diabelli & Co., Vienna (no. 2650).
There are sketches to nos. 2 and 4, dated July 1818, in the Isham

Memorial Library, Harvard University, Cambridge (Mass.); see 618A.
The six Polonaises, Op. 61 (824), were published before these four Polonaises.

600. Minuet in C sharp minor for Pianoforte (XXI 27). c. 1818.

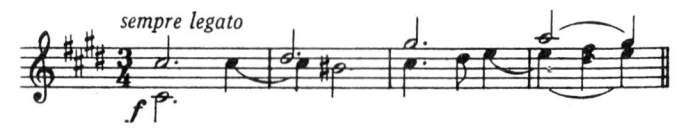

MS. Stadtbibliothek, Vienna.
1ST ED. 1897, Gesamtausgabe.
Cf. the Trio to the lost minuet, rewritten in February 1818, 610.

601. String Quartet in B flat. Fragment. Not printed. (?) 1818.

MS. (32 bars)—Stadtbibliothek, Vienna (together with 604).

602. Three Marches for Piano Duet (Op. 27, IX 1), in B minor, C, and D. (?) 1818.

No. 1. **Allegro moderato**

TRIO

No. 2. **Maestoso**

TRIO

No. 3. **Moderato**

MS. Lost.

1ST ED. 18th December 1824, Sauer & Leidesdorf, Vienna (no. 698), as *Trois Marches héroiques*, Op. 27.

The first two parts of March no. 1 were used originally as the introduction to the unfinished setting of Schiller's 'Die Schlacht,' 387.

603. **Introduction and [4] Variations on an original Theme, in B flat, for Piano Duet** (Op. posth. 82, no. 2; IX 18). (?) 1818.

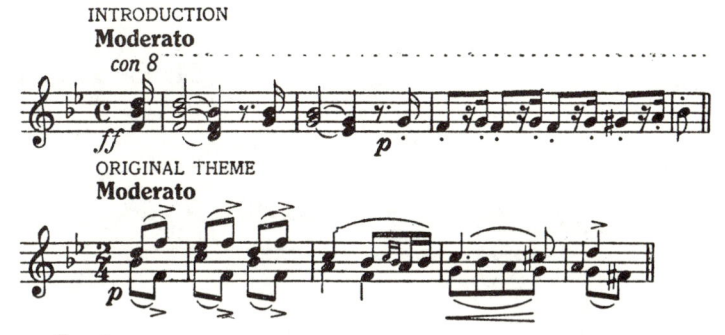

MS. Lost.

1ST ED. 1860, Julius Schuberth & Co., Hamburg (no. 2564).

Nottebohm, p. 253, places this work among three 'spurious and doubtful' compositions (48, and Appendix I).

604. **Andante in A for Pianoforte** (XI 10). (?) 1818.

MS. Stadtbibliothek, Vienna (together with 601).
1ST ED. 1888, Gesamtausgabe.

The MS. has no title. Alfred Einstein (*Schubert*, New York and London, 1951) suggests that this movement was originally written for the Sonata in D, Op. 53, of August 1825 (850).

605. **Fantasia in C for Pianoforte** (XXI 15). Fragment. (?) 1818.

MS. Stadtbibliothek, Vienna (without title).
1ST ED. 1897, Gesamtausgabe.

606. March in E for Pianoforte (XI 16). 1818.

MS. Lost.
1ST ED. *c.* 1840, Artaria & Co., Vienna (no. 3142).
The date is according to Ferdinand Schubert's list.

607. Evangelium Johannis (translated by Luther), **Chapter vi, Verses 55-8, for Soprano with Figured Bass. 1818.**

MS. p. 1—Stefan Zweig Collection, London; p. 2—Stadtbibliothek, Vienna.
1ST ED. Facsimile (first page: autograph, second page: copy)—1902, in Heuberger's *Schubert*, Berlin, Harmonie, following p. 56.

The first page of the MS. is written on the back of the 'Trauerwalzer,' rewritten March 1816 for Ignaz Assmayr, see entry before 350; only Anselm Hüttenbrenner's copy of the second page was known when Heuberger reproduced the facsimile. This is the only example of prose set to music by Schubert. The task of setting these words to music was suggested to Schubert by A. Hüttenbrenner as an experiment.

Literature. Richard Heuberger, *Schubert,* second edition, Berlin, 1908, p. 55.

608. Rondo in D for Piano Duet (Op. posth. 138; IX 14). January 1818.

MS. Sketch only—Nationalbibliothek, Vienna.

1ST ED. May 1835, A. Diabelli & Co., Vienna (no. 5419), under the spurious title ' Notre amitié est invariable,' as Op. 138 (without price on the title-page).

There is no confirmation of the supposition in Hans Költzsch's book on Schubert's pf. sonatas (p. 42) that the title alludes to Schubert's friendship with Josef von Gahy. The crossing of the players' hands, at the end of the Rondo, might, however, have had some significance in the choice of the title.

609. ' Lebenslust ' (author unknown) **for Quartet, S.A.T.B., with Pianoforte accompaniment** (XVII 13). January 1818.

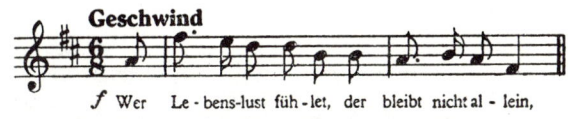

MS. Score—Conservatoire, Paris (Ph.); parts (fair copy, with all the stanzas in S. and A. parts)—Conservatoire, Paris (Ph.).

1ST ED. 1872, J. P. Gotthard, Vienna (no. 322), as no. 7 of nine partsongs.

There are four stanzas, only one of which is printed. A copy of the whole poem is to be found at the Gesellschaft der Musikfreunde, Vienna.

— **Symphony in C** (I 6). See 589. February 1818.

610. Trio to a lost Minuet for Pianoforte (XII 31). February 1818.

MS. J. A. Stargardt, Berlin (sale, 1st February 1928).
1ST ED. 1889, Gesamtausgabe.

The MS. bears the inscription ' Trio zu betrachten als verlorner Sohn eines Menuetts von Franz Schubert für seinen geliebten Herrn Bruder eigens niedergeschrieben im Feb. 1818.' The work seems to have been written before Schubert made this copy, from memory, for (?) Ferdinand. It probably belongs to the Minuet in C sharp minor, 600.

— ' Die Forelle ' (XX 327 (b)). See 550. 21st February 1818.

611. ' Auf der Riesenkoppe ' (Körner), Song (XX 336). March 1818.

Etwas geschwind RECIT.

Hoch auf dem Gi - pfel dei - ner Ge - bir - ge

MS. Kapten Rudolf Nydahl, Stockholm.
1ST ED. *c.* 1850, A. Diabelli & Co., Vienna (no. 8999), as no. 1 of *Nachlass*, book 49.

The Riesenkoppe, or Schneekoppe, in Austrian Silesia, where Körner also wrote his ' Sonnenaufgang auf der Riesenkoppe,' is near Zuckmantel, the home of Schubert's mother.

— ' **Trauerwalzer**,' rewritten for Anselm Hüttenbrenner (and again in the same month for Ignaz Assmayr) (XII 1, no. 2). See entry before 350. 14th March 1818.

Both MSS. commence with a crotchet (E flat) instead of the original three quavers. There are other variants in the early version as shown in the facsimile of the Assmayr album leaf (Heuberger, *Schubert*, Berlin, 1902, opposite p. 36). The two album leaves have humorous inscriptions (*Schubert Documents*, pp. 88 f.).

612. **Adagio in E for Pianoforte** (XI 11). April 1818.

MS. Conservatoire, Paris (Ph.).
1ST ED. 1869, J. Rieter-Biedermann, Winterthur (no. 616).

613. **Two Movements of a Sonata in C for Pianoforte** (XXI 11). Fragment. April 1818.

MS. Stadtbibliothek, Vienna.
1ST ED. 1897, Gesamtausgabe.
Probably the first and the last movements of an unfinished sonata.

614. 'An den Mond in einer Herbstnacht' (Alois Schreiber), Song (XX 337). April 1818.

Freund - lich ist dein Ant - litz,

MS. Charles L. Morley, New York.
1ST ED. 12th July 1832, A. Diabelli & Co., Vienna (no. 4018, on the title-page—by mistake—4108), as no. 2 of *Nachlass*, book 18.

A facsimile of p. 1 of the MS. is to be found in catalogue 7 of Otto Haas, London (1938). Schubert did not use the last line of the last stanza; it is to be found on page 176 of the first edition of Schreiber's poems (Heidelberg, 1812), but Schubert seems to have used the Tübingen edition (1817-18), which also contains the other poems he set to music.

615. Symphony in D. Sketches. Not printed. May 1818.

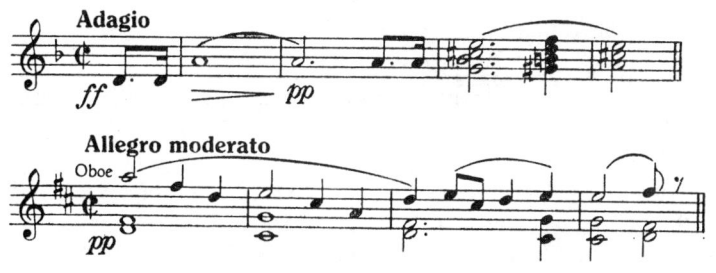

MS. Stadtbibliothek, Vienna.

IST ED. Facsimile of the first page—*Neue Musikzeitung*, Stuttgart, 1889, vol. x, no. 12.

Seven movements, in form of a piano score, are written on seventeen leaves (34 pages) oblong folio; the first page is dated.

Literature. Maurice J. E. Brown, *Music & Letters*, London, April 1950.

616. ' Grablied für die Mutter ' (author unknown), Song (XX 338). June 1818.

Trauernd

Hau - che mil - der.   A - bend-luft.

MS. Stadtbibliothek, Vienna.

IST ED. 1838, A. Diabelli & Co., Vienna (no. 5034), as no. 3 of *Nachlass*, book 30.

This song was written on the occasion of the death of Josef Ludwig von Streinsberg's mother, Anna Maria, according to the former's letter to Ferdinand Luib, 29th May 1858 (Franz Josef Böhm, Mürzzuschlag, Styria).

617. Sonata in B flat for Piano Duet (Op. 30, IX 11). (?) Summer 1818, (?) Zseliz.

Allegro moderato .... *loco*

decresc.

Andante con moto

pp

Allegretto

p

MS. Lost.

IST ED. 30th December 1823, Sauer & Leidesdorf, Vienna (no. 428), as Op. 30, under the title ' Grande Sonate,' dedicated by Schubert to Ferdinand, Graf Pálffy von Erdöd.

The date 1824 is given erroneously in the G.A. The work was advertised as 'Première grande Sonate,' the word 'Première,' however, appeared only on the title of the second edition, after Schubert had written the Sonata in C in 1824 (Op. 140, 812).

618. Deutscher Tanz with two Trios and Coda, and two other Deutsche Tänze for Piano Duet. Summer 1818 (Zseliz).

MS. Stadtbibliothek, Vienna.

1ST ED. 1909, Leipzig, *Festschrift für Hugo Riemann*, p. 484 and Supplement (ed. by Max Friedlaender).

The first trio, in G, is identical with that of no. 7 of seventeen *Ländler* (366). The second of the two other German dances is intended to be played as a trio to the first. When Brahms found the MS. at Julius Stockhausen's, Stuttgart, in May 1872, he suggested in vain its publication to the Vienna publisher, J. P. Gotthard (see *Die Musik*, vol. ii, no. 15; Berlin, 1st May 1903).

618A. Polonaises for Piano Duet. Sketches. Not printed. July 1818 (Zseliż).

MS. Isham Memorial Library, Harvard University, Cambridge (Mass.).

Schubert started this MS. of four pages oblong folio as a score for one Polonaise for Piano Duet. This Polonaise, the incipit of which is given above, is complete in the first treble part only. Apparently, the whole MS. contains nothing but treble parts. At the bottom of p. 1 Schubert noted down the tune of Queen Hortense's song (see 624), not exactly as published by her. On p. 3 is an incomplete Trio, identical with the Polonaise, Op. 75, no. 4 (599). On the lower half of p. 4 is another Polonaise which appears to be a first, and slightly longer, draft of Op. 75, no. 2 (599).

619. Vocal Exercises for two Voices (Soprano and Alto) with Figured Bass (XIX 36). July 1818 (Zseliz).

MS. Preussische Staatsbibliothek, Berlin.
1ST ED. 1892, Gesamtausgabe.

These Exercises were written for Marie (soprano), and Karoline (contralto), Komtessen Esterházy, to whom Schubert gave lessons. The MS. was formerly in the possession of Komtesse Karoline.

620. 'Einsamkeit,' called 'Der Einsame' ('Gib mir die Fülle der Einsamkeit,' Mayrhofer), **Song** (XX 339). July 1818 (Zseliz).

"Gib mir die Fül - le der Ein - sam - keit!"

MS. Fair copy, dated June 1822—Mrs. Whittall Collection, Library of Congress, Washington.
1ST ED. *c.* 1841, A. Diabelli & Co., Vienna (no. 6989), as *Nachlass*, book 32.

Schubert mentions this song as just finished in a letter from Zseliz, dated 3rd August 1818; hence the assumed date of composition.

621. Deutsche Trauermesse, called 'Deutsches Requiem' (author unknown), for four Voices with Organ accompaniment. August 1818 (Zseliz).

1. ZUM EINGANG
   Langsam

   Bei des Ent-schlaf-nen Trau-er — bah-re

2. NACH DER EPISTEL
   Etwas bewegter

   Der Tod rückt See-len vor's Ge-richt,

3. ZUM EVANGELIUM
   Mässig

   Wie tröst-lich ist, was Je-sus lehrt;

4. ZUM OFFERTORIUM
   Langsam

   Dir, Va-ter! wei-hen wir hier Ga-ben

5. ZUM SANCTUS
   Feierlich

   Dro-ben nur ist wah-res Le-ben!

6. ZUR WANDLUNG
   Mässig

   Je-su! dir leb' ich; Je-su! dir sterb' ich;

7. ZUM MEMENTO FÜR DIE ABGESTORBENEN
   Langsam

   Der From-men ab-ge-schied-ne See-len,

8. ZUM AGNUS DEI
   Sehr langsam

   Lamm Got-tes! Gna-de, Heil und Le-ben

9. ZUR KOMMUNION
Langsam

O ho - hes Glück, vor dir zu steh'n!

10. AM ENDE DER MESSE
Langsam

p Euch, die von uns ge - schie - den,

MS. Lost.

1ST PF. (?) September 1818, Waisenhaus, Vienna, as by Ferdinand Schubert.

1ST ED. End of 1825, or beginning of 1826, A. Diabelli & Co., Vienna (nos. 2068–9), as 'Deutsches Requiem,' by Ferdinand Schubert, Op. 2, dedicated to Johann Georg Fallstich, Vicedirector of the Vienna Orphanage; republished as the work of Franz Schubert (by O. E. D.), 1928, Ed. Strache, Vienna (no. 19).

This little requiem was written by Franz Schubert to help his brother in the performance of an official duty; afterwards Ferdinand submitted it, as his own work, for an examination on 23rd December 1819. Cf. 872 and Appendix II, no. 9.

622. '**Der Blumenbrief**' (Schreiber), **Song** (XX 340). August 1818 (Zseliz).

Mit Empfindung

Euch Blüm-lein will ich sen - den zur schö - nen Jung - frau dort,

MS. (in D)—Stadtbibliothek, Vienna.

1ST ED. 14th February 1833, A. Diabelli & Co., Vienna (no. 4269), as no. 1 of *Nachlass*, book 21.

The song is printed, in the first edition as well as in the G.A., in the key of B flat.

623. '**Das Marienbild**' (Schreiber), **Song** (XX 341). August 1818 (Zseliz).

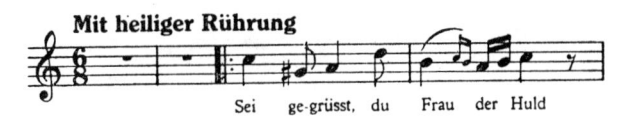

> Mit heiliger Rührung
>
> *Sei ge-grüsst, du Frau der Huld*

MS. Lost.
IST ED. 21st April 1831, A. Diabelli & Co., Vienna (no. 3707), as no. 3 of *Nachlass*, book 10.

—— ' Am Tage Aller Seelen ' (XX 342). See 343. August 1818 (Zseliz).

624. **Eight Variations on a French Song**, in E minor, for Piano Duet (Op. 10, IX 15). September 1818 (Zseliz).

> THEME
> Allegretto

MS. Fragment (theme with variation 1 and part of variation 2) —Frau Braun-Fernwald, Vienna (Ph.); another fragment (variation 5 and parts of 4 and 6)—Sibley Music Library, University of Rochester (New York).
IST ED. 19th April 1822, Cappi & Diabelli, Vienna (no. 996), dedicated by Schubert to Beethoven.

The song is ' Reposez-vous, bon chevalier,' by Queen Hortense, or rather Louis Drouet, which Schubert found in a MS. copy, or in the Paris edition (1813) of her romances at Zseliz. Cf. 618A.
Literature. O. E. D., *La Revue musicale*, Paris, 1st December 1928, pp. 23-30.

625. **Sonata in F minor for Pianoforte** (XXI 12). Incomplete. September 1818 (Zseliz).

> Allegro

> SCHERZO
> Allegretto

MS. Lost.
1ST ED. 1897, Gesamtausgabe.
This Sonata is nearly complete; there are three movements. Walter Rehberg completed the Sonata in 1927 (Steingräber-Verlag, Leipzig, 1928, no. 2388, edition no, 2584). In a MS. thematic catalogue of Schubert's pf. and chamber music, compiled by (?) Ferdinand Schubert and formerly in the Kreissles' possession, the incipits of four movements are given for this Sonata (without date), among them as no. 2 the Adagio in D flat (505).

626. ' Blondel zu Marien ' (author unknown), Song (XX 343). September 1818 (Zseliz).

MS. Sotheby, London (3rd April 1935).
1ST ED. *c.* 1842, A. Diabelli & Co., Vienna (no. 7412), as no. 2 of *Nachlass*, book 34 (corrupt).
The MS., in E flat minor, was formerly in the possession of Karoline, Komtesse Esterházy. The first edition, which ascribes the poem to Grillparzer, and the copy of the Witteczek Collection, are in C minor.

627. ' Das Abendrot ' (Schreiber), Song (Op. posth. 173, no. 6; XX 344). November 1818 (Zseliz).

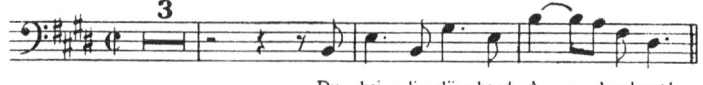

MS. Mrs. Gisella Selden-Goth, New York.
1ST ED. 1867, C. A. Spina, Vienna (no. 19179), as no. 6 of Op. 173.
Another MS., written in the bass clef, key of E, was formerly in the possession of Karoline, Komtesse Esterházy (together with 519 and 793). The song was apparently written for her father, Johann Karl, Graf Esterházy.

628. '**Sonett I**' ('Apollo, lebet noch dein hold Verlangen,' Petrarch, translated by August Wilhelm von Schlegel), **Song** (XX 345). November 1818.

A - pol - lo, le - bet noch dein hold Ver - lan-gen,

MS. (together with 629)—Leo Liepmannssohn, Berlin (sale, 29th October 1900).
1ST ED. 1895, Gesamtausgabe.
The footnote to the poem, reprinted in the G.A., is by the translator.

629. '**Sonett II**' ('Allein, nachdenklich, wie gelähmt,' Petrarch, translated by August Wilhelm von Schlegel), **Song** (XX 346). November 1818.

Al - lein, nach-denk-lich, wie gelähmt vom Kram - pfe,

MS. (together with 628)—Leo Liepmannssohn, Berlin (sale, 29th October 1900).
1ST ED. 1895, Gesamtausgabe.

630. '**Sonett III**' ('Nunmehr, da Himmel, Erde,' Petrarch, translated by J. D. Gries), **Song** (XX 347). December 1818.

Nun - mehr, da Him - mel, Er - de schweigt und Win - -de,

MS. Stadtbibliothek, Vienna.
1ST ED. 1895, Gesamtausgabe.
The G.A., misled by the index of the Witteczek Collection, attributed the poem to Dante.
Literature. Hugo Daffner, *Zeitschrift für Musikwissenschaft*, Leipzig, August 1926; and Moritz Bauer, *Zeitschrift für Musikwissenschaft*, October 1926.

631. '**Blanka**,' called '**Das Mädchen**' ('Wenn mich einsam Lüfte fächeln,' Friedrich von Schlegel), **Song** (XX 348). December 1818.

Wenn mich ein - sam Lüf - te fä - cheln,

MS. Frau Emma von Spaun, Vienna (together with 632).

1ST ED. 1876, V. Kratochwill, Vienna (no. 252), as no. 6 of six *Nachgelassene Lieder*, arranged for pf. solo and ed. (with words) by J. P. Gotthard, under the title ' Das Mädchen,' as given by the poet (cf. ' Das Mädchen,' 652).

Max Friedlaender republished the song as no. 20 of twenty *Nachgelassene Lieder* with C. F. Peters, Leipzig, in 1885.

632. 'Vom Mitleiden Mariae' (Friedrich von Schlegel), Song (XX 349). December 1818.

Langsam

Als bei dem Kreuz Ma - ri - a stand.

MS. Frau Emma von Spaun, Vienna (together with 631).

1ST ED. 21st April 1831, A. Diabelli & Co., Vienna (no. 3707), as no. 4 of *Nachlass*, book 10.

633. ' Der Schmetterling ' (from Friedrich von Schlegel's ' Abendröte '), Song (Op. 57, no. 1; XX 179). (?) *c.* 1819.

Etwas geschwind

Wie soll ich nicht tan - zen.

MS. (together with 634)—unknown; former owner—Ludwig Landsberg, Rome (*c.* 1850).

1ST ED. 6th April 1826, Thaddäus Weigl, Vienna (no. 2494), as no. 1 of Op. 57 (no. 4 of the combined Opp. 56—*recte* 58—and 57).

The Witteczek Collection dates this song 1815. ' Abendröte ' is a cycle of poems by Schlegel.

634. ' Die Berge ' (from Friedrich von Schlegel's ' Abendröte '), Song (Op. 57, no. 2; XX 180). (?) *c.* 1819.

MS. (together with 633)—unknown; former owner—Ludwig Landsberg, Rome (c. 1850).

1ST ED. 6th April 1826, Thaddäus Weigl, Vienna (no. 2495), as no. 2 of Op. 57 (no. 5 of the combined Opp. 56—*recte* 58—and 57).

The Witteczek Collection dates this song 1815. Cf. note to 312.

635. 'Ruhe' ('Leise, leise lasst uns singen,' (?) Schubert), **Quartet, T.T.B.B.** *c.* 1819.

MS. (together with 640)—Stadtbibliothek, Vienna (entitled 'Quartetto').

1ST ED. 1900, Ries & Erler, Berlin (ed. by Rudolf Weis-Ostborn, with new words by Robert Graf), under the title 'Ständchen'; facsimile of the MS., 1902, in Heuberger's *Schubert*, Berlin, Verlag Harmonie, opposite p. 40.

The title 'Ruhe' may be spurious. The work was written in honour of Fräulein Fanny Hügel (the stanza ends with the words 'Fanny erwache'), an able singer who lost her reason in 1822. It was printed again, erroneously as a first publication, but with the original words, under the title 'Ständchen' (ed. by E. Mandyczewski), in *Die Musik*, Berlin, 15th January 1907 (vol. vi, no. 7, Supplement, p. 4).

636. 'Sehnsucht' ('Ach, aus dieses Tales Gründen,' Schiller), **Song**, second version, two variants (Op. 39, XX 357 (*a*) and (*b*)). *c.* 1819.

MS. (*a*) Fair copy—Wittgenstein family, Vienna; (*b*) **Fragment** (the last two leaves only)—British Museum, London.

1ST PF. 8th February 1821, Musikverein, Vienna.

1ST ED. (*a*) 1895, Gesamtausgabe; (*b*) 8th February 1826, A. Pennauer, Vienna (no. 207), as Op. 39.

Kreissle (p. 594) dates (the (?) second version of) the song 1821. The fair copy of (*a*) bears the two following inscriptions by its former owner, the amateur bass singer, Adalbert Rotter, Vienna: ' Erhalten zum Andenken von H[errn] Fr. Schubert Wien den 24ten April 1824,' and ' Am 12. October 1824 sang " Die Sehnsucht " H[err] Vogl, pens[ionierter] k. k. Hofopernsänger.' For the first setting, see 52.

637. ' **Hoffnung** ' (' Es reden und träumen die Menschen,' Schiller), **Song**, second version (Op. 87, no. 2; XX 358). *c.* 1819.

MS. Lost.

1ST ED. 6th August 1827, A. Pennauer, Vienna (no. 330), as no. 2 of Op. 87 (numbered, in error, Op. 84), under the title ' Die Hoffnung,' with some misprints.

For the first setting, see 251.

638. ' **Der Jüngling am Bache** ' (Schiller), **Song**, third version, two variants (Op. 87, no. 3; XX 259 (*b*) and (*a*)). *c.* 1819.

MS. (*b*) in D minor, dated April 1819—Stadtbibliothek, Vienna; (*a*) in C minor—unknown.

1ST ED. (*b*) 1895, Gesamtausgabe; (*a*) 6th August 1827, A. Pennauer, Vienna (no. 330), as no. 3 of Op. 87 (numbered, in error, Op. 84).

The variant (*b*) was written before (*a*). For the first and second versions, see **30** and **192**.

639. 'Widerschein' (Schlechta), **Song**, first version. c. 1819.

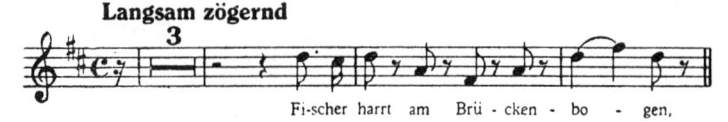

Langsam zögernd

Fi-scher harrt am Brü-cken-bo - gen.

MS. Lost.
1ST ED. 1821 (actually, autumn of 1820), G. J. Göschen, Leipzig, as a supplement to the almanac *Taschenbuch zum geselligen Vergnügen*, ed. by Friedrich Kind.

The first version of the poem (' Fischer harrt am Brückenbogen ') was published in the *Wiener Zeitschrift für Kunst*, etc., 1818, p. 804. The song was advertised and reviewed as a supplement to the almanac, but no complete copy of the almanac is known; a few copies of the supplement, however, printed on four pages in type, are preserved (Stadtbibliothek, Vienna; Paul Hirsch Library, British Museum, London; A. van Hoboken, Lausanne). For the second version, see 949.
Literature. O. E. D., *Schubert's Fünf Erste Lieder*, Universal Edition, Vienna, 1922 (with facsimile of the first and only edition).

640. **Two Ländler** ((?) for Pianoforte). Unpublished. c. 1819.

MS. Stadtbibliothek, Vienna (together with 635).

The MS. shows a treble part only. It consists of six dances, of which these are nos. 5 and 6. Nos. 1 to 4 are identical with nos. 17, 18, 25, and 28 of Op. 9 (365), except for the second half of no. 28 (a variant).

641. ' Das Dörfchen ' (Bürger), **Quartet, T.T.B.B.**, second version (Op. 11, no. 1; XVI 4). (?) 1819.

Allegretto

p Ich rüh-me mir mein Dörf-chen hier,

Andantino

p Dort krän - zen Schle - hen die brau - ne Kluft,

O Se-lig-keit, dass doch die Zeit dich nie____ zer-stö-re.

MS. Lost.

1ST PF. 7th March 1821, Kärntnertor-Theater, Vienna (unaccompanied); 8th September 1822, Redoutensaal, Graz (with pf. acc.).

1ST ED. 12th June 1822, Cappi & Diabelli, Vienna (no. 1017), as no. 1 of Op. 11, dedicated by Schubert to Josef Barth (one of the tenors who sang at the first performance in Vienna).

The first edition contains accompaniments for pf. or guitar; the former is dubious, the latter spurious. For the sketch (first version) see 598. The poem was further shortened for the second version.

642. 'Das Feuerwerk' ('Viel tausend Sterne prangen,' A. G. Eberhard), Chorus, S.A.T.B., with Pianoforte accompaniment. (?) 1819.

Viel tau-send Ster-ne pran-gen am Him-mel

MS. Stadtbibliothek, Vienna (without title).

1ST PF. 30th September 1924, Vienna, Konzerthaus.

1ST ED. 1937, Universal Edition, Vienna (no. 10,898, ed. by A. Orel, arr. for male voices by H. H. Scholtys).

The first two stanzas of the text were printed, under the title 'Das Feuerwerk' in the *Zeitung für die elegante Welt*, Leipzig, 1807, col. 1467. The poem was first set for male voice chorus by Leonhard Call (in 'Sechs Gesänge für vier Männerstimmen,' Op. 97, Leipzig, A. Kühnel, 1810). Schubert's partsong was arranged, as were many of his songs, for pf. duet, by Josef von Gahy (MS. Stadtbibliothek, Vienna).

643. Deutscher Tanz in C sharp minor and Écossaise in D flat for Pianoforte (XII 21). 1819.

DEUTSCHER TANZ

ECOSSAISE

MS. Gesellschaft der Musikfreunde, Vienna (entitled 'Teutscher für HE. [Herrn] Hüttenbrenner,' together with the Écossaise).
IST. ED. 1889, Gesamtausgabe.
The German dance was written for Josef Hüttenbrenner.

644. 'Die Zauberharfe,' Magic Play—with Music—in three Acts, by Georg von Hofmann (XV 7). 1819-20.

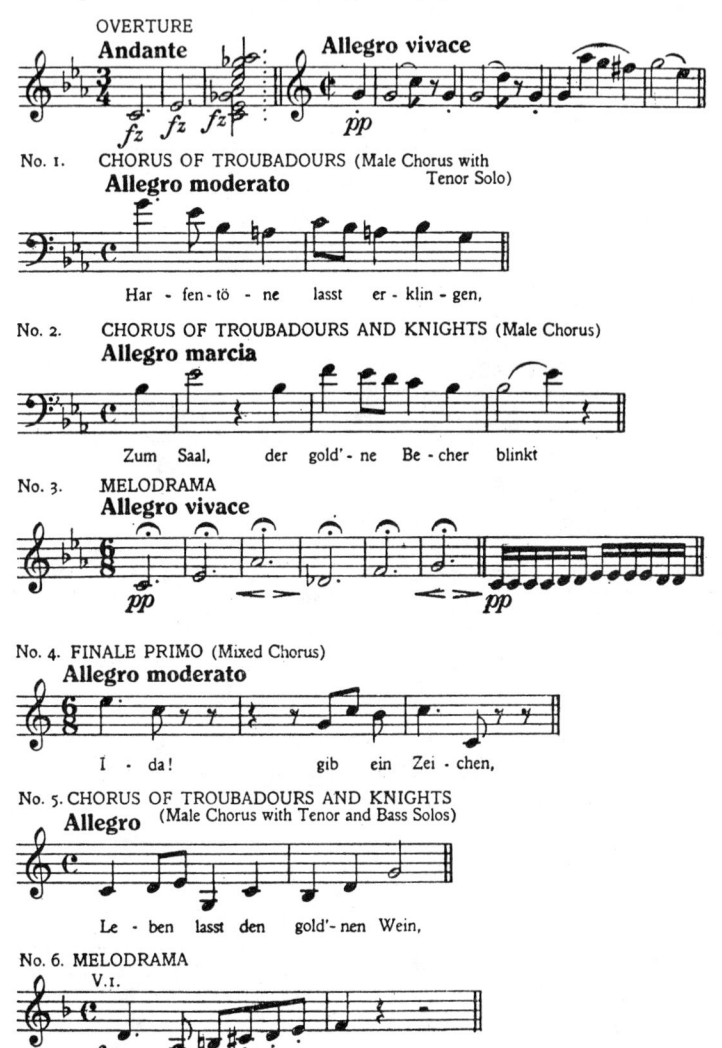

OVERTURE

No. 1. CHORUS OF TROUBADOURS (Male Chorus with Tenor Solo)

Har - fen - tö - ne lasst er - klin - gen,

No. 2. CHORUS OF TROUBADOURS AND KNIGHTS (Male Chorus)

Zum Saal, der gold'-ne Be-cher blinkt

No. 3. MELODRAMA

No. 4. FINALE PRIMO (Mixed Chorus)

I - da! gib ein Zei - chen,

No. 5. CHORUS OF TROUBADOURS AND KNIGHTS (Male Chorus with Tenor and Bass Solos)

Le - ben lasst den gold'- nen Wein,

No. 6. MELODRAMA
V.1.

No. 7. CHORUS OF KNIGHTS (Male Chorus)
Allegro moderato

Die Zau-be-rin lasst uns be - trü - gen,

No. 8. MELODRAMA
Allegro moderato

No. 8a. ROMANCE
Andantino

pp Was— be - lebt die schö - ne Welt?

No. 9. CHORUS OF GENII (Female Chorus)
Larghetto

Schla - fe, Lieb - li - che,

OVERTURE TO ACT 3
Allegro, ma non troppo

No. 10. MELODRAMA
Allegro

No. 11. MELODRAMA BEHIND THE SCENES
Andante

No. 12. MELODRAMA
Tempo I.

No. 13. FINAL SONG (Mixed Chorus)
Andantino

Durch der Tö - ne Zau - ber-macht,

MS. Overture to Act I in score (without title)—Conservatoire, Paris (Ph.); overture to Act III in score—private collection, Los Angeles; remainder (all the other music)—Stadtbibliothek, Vienna; the Chorus of the Genii (no. 9) and the Finale of Act II (the Romance in D, ' Was belebt die schöne Welt,' in its first version, unpublished)—*ibidem*.

1ST PF. 19th August 1820, Theater an der Wien, Vienna (performed there eight times in all).

1ST ED. Overture to Act I, arranged for pf. duet, and published under the title ' Ouvertüre zum Drama Rosamunde '—c. 1827, M. J. Leidesdorf, Vienna; ' Ouvertüre zur Oper Rosamunde,' in parts, 1854, C. A. Spina, Vienna; in score—January 1867, *ibidem* (no. 19,102); complete score—1891, Gesamtausgabe.

Josef Hüttenbrenner's MS. of the arrangement of the Overture to Act I (in the possession of the compiler) is entitled ' Zauberharfe,' and dated by Andreas Schubert (Franz's step-brother) as composed in 1819. (For this overture, cf. ' Rosamunde,' 797.) Schubert did not receive the honorarium of 500 florins Vienna currency, which he was promised by the theatre for the music. The autograph of the Romance in its second version, for concert performance, was at one time in the possession of Josef Hüttenbrenner; a copy of it is still in the archives of the Gesellschaft der Musikfreunde, Vienna. Josef Hüttenbrenner arranged it with pf. acc., and Max Friedlaender published it in this form, 1887, with C. F. Peters, Leipzig, as no. 32 of *Schubert Album*, book 7. The third version of the romance, purely instrumental, is to be found at the end of Act I in both MS. and printed scores (intermezzo in no. 3, with solo clarinet in place of the voice, and violoncello instead of oboe concertante). This alteration was occasioned by the inefficiency of the tenor, Ferdinand Schimon. The concert version may have been written later, in January 1823, for another tenor, Franz Jäger.

645. ' **Abend** ' (' Wie ist es denn, dass . . . ,' author unknown), **Sketch of Song.** Not printed. (?) January 1819.

MS. Karl, Baron Vietinghoff, Berlin (together with 646).

The sketch consists of the treble part of the pf. introduction and the complete voice part only.

646. ' **Die Gebüsche** ' (from Friedrich von Schlegel's ' Abendröte '), **Song** (XX 350). January 1819.

[Langsam musical incipit: "Es we-het kühl und lei-se"]

MS. Karl, Baron Vietinghoff, Berlin (together with 645).
1ST ED. 1885, C. F. Peters, Leipzig (no. 6895), as no. 1 of twenty *Nachgelassene Lieder* (ed. by Max Friedlaender).

The last lines of the poem were used by Schumann as a motto to his Fantasia for pianoforte in C, Op. 17 (1836):

> *Durch alle Töne tönet*
> *Im bunten Erdentraum*
> *Ein leiser Ton gezogen*
> *Für den, der heimlich lauscht.*

647. 'Die Zwillingsbrüder,' Singspiel, (?) after 'Les Deux Valentins,' in one Act by Georg von Hofmann (XV 5). Finished January 1819.

OVERTURE
Allegro

No. 1. INTRODUCTION (Ten. and Mixed Chorus)
Allegretto
[musical incipit: "Ver-glü-het sind die Ster-ne,"]

No. 2. DUET (Sopr. and Ten.)
Andantino
[musical incipit: "Vor dem Bu-sen"]

No. 3. ARIA (Sopr.)
Andantino
[musical incipit: "Der Va-ter mag wohl im-mer Kind mich nen-nen,"]

No. 4. ARIA (Bass)
Allegro con fuoco

Mag es stür - men, don - nern, bli - tzen,

No. 5. QUARTET (Sopr., Ten. and 2 Basses)
Andante moto

Zu rech-ter Zeit bin ich ge-kom-men,

No. 6. ARIA (Bass)
Larghetto

Lie - be teu - re Mut - ter - er - de,

No. 7. DUET (Sopr. and Ten.)
Allegretto

Nur dir _ will ich _ ge - hö - ren,

No. 8. TERZET (Sopr., Ten. and Bass)
Allegro

Wa - gen Sie, Ihr Wort zu bre - chen?

No. 9. QUINTET AND CHORUS (Sopr., Ten., 3 Basses and Male Chorus)
Allegro vivace

Packt ihn, führt ihn vor Ge - richt,

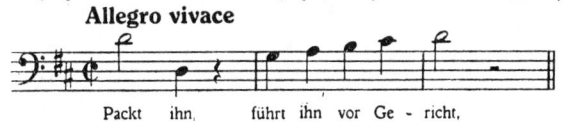

No. 10. FINAL SONG (Mixed Chorus)
Allegro

Die Brü - der ha - ben sich ge - fun - den

MS. Gesellschaft der Musikfreunde, Vienna.
1ST PF. 14th June 1820, Kärntnertor-Theater, Vienna (performed there seven times in all).
1ST ED. Piano score—1872, C. F. Peters, Leipzig (no. 5492); score—1889, Gesamtausgabe.

The overture is dated 19th January 1819. The work may have been started at the end of 1818. It was commissioned by the Kärntnertor-Theater, but the production was postponed for the performances of new operas by Rossini. MS. copies, as used at the theatre, are in the Nationalbibliothek, Vienna. A MS. piano score by Ferdinand Schubert is in the archives of the Gesellschaft der Musikfreunde, Vienna.

648. Overture in E minor for Orchestra (II 7).   February 1819.

MS. Stadtbibliothek, Vienna.
1ST PF. Probably 14th March 1819, Müller'scher Saal, Vienna.
1ST ED. 1886, Gesamtausgabe.

The work was probably revived on 2nd March 1820, in the house of Anton von Pettenkoffer, Vienna, and was again performed in the Redoutensaal, Vienna, on 18th November 1821 (conductor, Leopold Sonnleithner).

649. ' **Der Wanderer** ' ('Wie deutlich des Mondes Licht,' from Friedrich von Schlegel's ' Abendröte '), **Song** (Op. 65, no. 2; XX 351).   February 1819.

MS. Lost.
1ST ED. 24th November 1826, Cappi & Czerny, Vienna (no. 221), as no. 2 of Op. 65.

650. ' **Abendbilder** ' (Silbert), **Song** (XX 352).   February 1819.

MS. Unknown; former owner—Otto Goldschmidt, London.
1ST ED. 21st April 1831, A. Diabelli & Co., Vienna (no. 3706), as no. 3 of *Nachlass*, book 9.

651. 'Himmelsfunken' (Silbert), Song (XX 353). February 1819.

[musical notation: Langsam, 3/4]

Der O - dem Got - tes weht.

MS. Lost.

1ST ED. 21st April 1831, A. Diabelli & Co., Vienna (no. 3707), as no. 8 of *Nachlass*, book 10.

There exists an undated copy of the lost MS., by Ferdinand Schubert (Krasser family, Vienna), which shows that the first edition was correct in its version of bar 3 of the pf. introduction (in the right hand) where the five-part setting is interrupted. The G.A. assumed this to be a misprint, but the original version is reproduced in the *Revisionsbericht*. The copy, however, is in G minor.

652. 'Das Mädchen' ('Wie so innig,' from Friedrich von Schlegel's 'Abendröte'), Song (XX 354). February 1819.

[musical notation: 3/8]

Wie so in - nig, möcht' ich sa - gen,

MS. Gesellschaft der Musikfreunde, Vienna (together with 653 and 654).

1ST ED. c. 1842, A. Diabelli & Co., Vienna (no. 7418), as no. 1 of *Nachlass*, book 40.

Cf. 631.

653. 'Bertha's Lied in der Nacht' (Grillparzer), Song (XX 355). February 1819.

[musical notation: Sehr langsam]

Nacht um - hüllt mit we - hen-dem Flü - gel

MS. Gesellschaft der Musikfreunde, Vienna (together with 652 and 654).

1ST ED. c. 1842, A. Diabelli & Co., Vienna (no. 7418), as no. 2 of *Nachlass*, book 40.

The poem, slightly altered by Schubert, was written in February 1817 and published in 1818, as an additional song to the tragedy *Die Ahnfrau* (after line 291). Among other composers, W. A. Mozart the younger also set this poem to music (published in the *Wiener Zeitschrift fur Kunst*, ete., 1821, no. 112).

654. ' **An die Freunde** ' (Mayrhofer), **Song** (XX 356). March 1819.

Im Wald, im Wald, da grabt ___ mich ein,

MS. Gesellschaft der Musikfreunde, Vienna (together with 652 and 653).
1ST ED. *c.* 1842, A. Diabelli & Co., Vienna (no. 7418), as no. 3 of *Nachlass*, book 40.
The song is said to have been specially addressed to Josef Kenner.

655. **Allegro in C sharp minor for Pianoforte** (XXI 13). April 1819.

MS. Stadtbibliothek, Vienna.
1ST ED. 1897, Gesamtausgabe.
This is the sketch for the first movement of an unfinished sonata.

656. ' **Sehnsucht** ' (' Nur wer die Sehnsucht kennt,' from Goethe's ' Wilhelm Meister '), **Quintet, T.T.B.B.B.** (XVI 35). April 1819.

Langsam

pp Nur wer die Sehn-sucht kennt, weiss was ich lei - de!

MS. Karl Ernst Henrici, Berlin (1919).
1ST PF. 5th January 1868,, Vienna (conductor, Johann Herbeck).
1ST ED. 1867, C. A. Spina's Nachfolger, Vienna (no. 18,447). Engraved in 1865, ed. by Johann Herbeck.
Republished in 1886 by Max Friedlaender at N. Simrock, Berlin (on the occasion of the performance on 29th November 1886, Frankfurt am Main). For settings of the same poem as solo songs see 310, 359, 481, 877 (nos. 1 and 4).

657. ' Ruhe, schönstes Glück der Erde ' (author unknown), Quartet, T.T.B.B. (XVI 36). April 1819.

Andantino

MS. Stadtbibliothek, Vienna.
IST PF. 12th March 1871, Musikvereinssaal, Vienna.
IST ED. 1871, J. P. Gotthard, Vienna (no. 131).
—— ' Der Jüngling am Bache ' (XX 259*b*). See 638. April 1819.

658. ' Marie ' (Novalis), Song (XX 364). (?) May 1819.

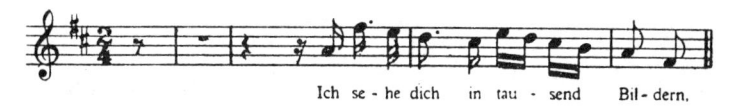

MS. (undated)—Karl & Faber, Munich.
IST ED. 1895, Gesamtausgabe.

Ludwig Tieck, as editor, inserted this song as the last of Novalis's *Geistliche Lieder*, to which Schubert's four ' Hymnen,' of the same month, belong (659–62). The title ' Marie ' was chosen by Schubert himself. Novalis's real name was Friedrich von Hardenberg.

659. ' Hymne I ' (' Wenige wissen das Geheimnis,' Novalis), Song (XX 360). May 1819.

Mit Andacht

MS. Dr. Alwin Cranz, Vienna (together with 660–2).
IST ED. 1872, J. P. Gotthard, Vienna (no. 561), together with 660–2, as nos. 37–40 of forty songs.

660. ' Hymne II ' (' Wenn ich ihn nur habe,' Novalis), Song (XX 361). May 1819.

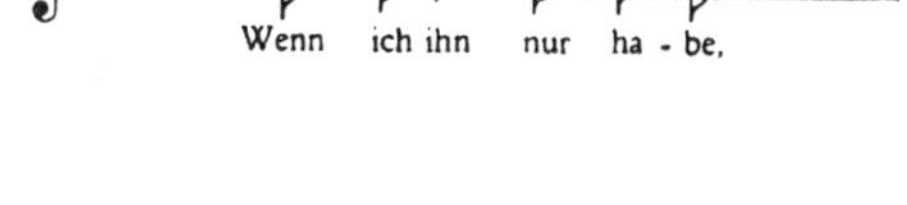

MS. Dr. Alwin Cranz, Vienna (together with 659, 661, 662).
1ST ED. See 659.

This song was first reproduced on the saucer of a chocolate cup (with Schubert's portrait on the cup), probably made for presentation to Schubert himself—now in the Schubert Museum, Vienna (see O. E. D., *Franz Schubert, Sein Leben in Bildern*, p. 54).

661. ' **Hymne III** ' ('Wenn alle untreu werden,' Novalis), **Song** (XX 362). May 1819.

[musical notation: Wenn al-le un-treu wer-den,]

MS. Dr. Alwin Cranz, Vienna (together with 659, 660, 662).
1ST ED. See 659.

662. ' **Hymne IV** ' (' Ich sag' es jedem,' Novalis), **Song** (XX 363). May 1819.

[musical notation: Ich sag' es je-dem, dass er lebt,]

MS. Dr. Alwin Cranz, Vienna (together with 659–61).
1ST ED. See 659.

663. ' **Der 13. Psalm** ' (translated by Moses Mendelssohn), **Song**. June 1819.

[musical notation: Andante — Ach, Herr, wie lan-ge willst du mein so ganz ver-ges-sen?]

MS. Fräulein Marie Schubert, Vienna.
1ST PF. 9th June 1927, Burggarten, Vienna (Julius Patzak).
1ST ED. Facsimile, August 1927, *Festblätter für das 10. Deutsche Sängerbundesfest, Wien 1928*, no 1, pp. 8–9 (ed. by O. E. D.).

The two-page MS., entitled—in error—' XII Psalm,' is without the last (six (?)) bars which were probably written on a third page.

664. **Sonata in A for Pianoforte** (Op. posth. 120, X 10). (?) July 1819 (Steyr).

Allegro moderato

Andante

Allegro

MS. Lost.
1ST ED. End of 1829, Josef Czerny, Vienna (no. 2656).
Written for Josefine von Koller, of Steyr in Upper Austria, but Schubert, on a later visit to Steyr (1823 or 1825), took the MS. away.

665. 'Im traulichen Kreise . . .' (author unknown), **Quartet, S.S.T.B.** Lost. (?) Summer 1819 (Steyr).

According to Kreissle, p. 161, the quartet was written in D, 6/8, to the following words:

> Im traulichen Kreise
> Beim herzlichen Kuss
> Beisammen zu leben,
> Ist Seelengenuss.

—— Maximilian Stadler's Sacred Aria 'Unendlicher Gott, unser Herr.' Copy. See Appendix II, no. 6. Summer 1819 (Steyr).

666. '**Kantate zum Geburtstag des Sängers Johann Michael Vogl**,' called '**Der Frühlingsmorgen**' (Albert Stadler), Trio, **S.T.B.**, with **Pianoforte** accompaniment (Op. posth. 158, XIX 3). Beginning of August 1819 (Steyr).

Moderato

Sän - ger, der von Her - zen sin - get

Allegretto

Die - se Ber - ge sah'n dich blü - hen,

MS. Stadtbibliothek, Vienna.
1ST PF. 10th August 1819, at the house of Josef von Koller, Steyr.
1ST ED. 1849, A. Diabelli & Co., Vienna (no. 8878), under the title 'Der Frühlingsmorgen,' with new words, as Op. 158.

Schubert and Vogl were at Steyr when this cantata was performed by Fräulein Josefine von Koller, Bernhard Benedict, Albert Stadler (pf.) and Schubert himself.

667. **Pianoforte Quintet in A,** called **Forellen** (Trout) Quintet (Op. posth. 114, VII 1). (?) Autumn 1819.

MS. Lost.
1ST PF. Probably at the end of 1819, in Sylvester Paumgartner's house at Steyr.
1ST ED. Spring of 1829, Josef Czerny, Vienna (no. 2625).

Written for Paumgartner, an amateur cellist. The theme of the fourth movement is the song ' Die Forelle ' (550). According to the testimony of Albert Stadler, who copied the parts for Paumgartner in Vienna, Schubert had in mind Hummel's pf. quintet as a model for this work.

668. Overture in G minor for Piano Duet (XXI 6).   October 1819.

MS. Stadtbibliothek, Vienna.
1ST ED. 1897, Gesamtausgabe.
Probably a pf. score of a lost orchestral work.

669. ' Beim Winde ' (Mayrhofer), **Song** (XX 365).   October 1819.

MS. Preussische Staatsbibliothek, Berlin (together with 670).
1ST ED. 23rd June 1829, as a Supplement to the *Wiener Zeitschrift für Kunst*, etc., Vienna (in type).

The song was republished as no. 3 of *Nachlass*, book 22, by A. Diabelli & Co., Vienna (no. 4270), on 4th June 1833.

670. ' Die Sternennächte ' (Mayrhofer), **Song** (Op. posth. 165, no. 2; XX 366).   October 1819.

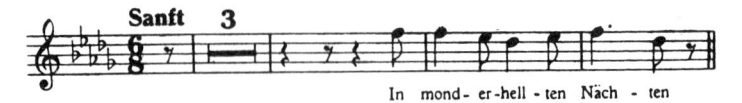

[musical incipit: Sanft, 6/8]
In mond- er-hell- ten Näch - ten

MS. In D flat: first half (together with 669)—Preussische Staatsbibliothek, Berlin; second half (together with 671)—Conservatoire, Paris (Ph.).

1ST ED. *c.* 1852, C. A. Spina, Vienna (no. 9108), as no. 2 of Op. 165.

The first edition, like the copy in the Witteczek Collection (probably made from a later copy, since lost) is in B flat.

671. ' Trost ' (Mayrhofer), **Song** (XX 367). October 1819.

[musical incipit: Mässig, 6/8]
Hör - ner-klän - ge ru - fen kla-gend

MS. (together with 670)—Conservatoire, Paris (Ph.).

1ST ED. *c.* 1848, A. Diabelli & Co., Vienna (no. 8821), as no. 1 of *Nachlass*, book 44.

The poem is not included in the two editions of Mayrhofer's works. The second stanza is not in the Paris MS., but is to be found in the first edition.

672. ' **Nachtstück** ' (Mayrhofer), **Song** (Op. 36, no. 2; XX 368). October 1819.

[musical incipit: Sehr langsam, C]
Wenn ü - ber Ber - ge sich der Ne - bel brei - tet,

MS. Gesellschaft der Musikfreunde, Vienna.

1ST ED. 11th February 1825, Cappi & Co., Vienna (no. 60), as no. 2 of Op. 35 (later corrected to 36), dedicated by Schubert to Frau Katharina von Lászny, *née* Buchwieser.

The MS. is in C sharp minor, and the first edition in C minor. The *Revisionsbericht* gives the original sketch of the last bars.

673. ' **Die Liebende schreibt** ' (Sonnet by Goethe), **Song** (Op. posth. 165, no. 1; XX 369). October 1819.

Mässig, zart

Ein Blick von dei-nen Au-gen in die mei-nen,

MS. Lost.
1ST ED. 26th June 1832, as a supplement to the *Wiener Zeitschrift für Kunst*, etc., Vienna (in type).

The song was republished, in A major, as no. 1 of Op. 165 by C. A. Spina, Vienna (no. 9107), *c.* 1852.

674. ' **Prometheus** ' (Goethe), **Song** (XX 370). October 1819.

Kräftig
RECIT.

Be-de-cke dei-nen Him-mel, Zeus, mit Wol-ken-dunst,

MS. Gesellschaft der Musikfreunde, Vienna.
1ST ED. *c.* 1848, A. Diabelli & Co., Vienna (no. 8836), as no. 1 of *Nachlass*, book 47 (the voice part in the G clef).

675. **Overture in F for Piano Duet** (Op. 34, IX 8). November 1819.

Adagio **Allegro**

con 8
cresc.

MS. Unknown; former owner—Josef Hüttenbrenner, Vienna (*c.* 1850).
1ST ED. 28th February 1825, Cappi & Co., Vienna (no. 56), as Op. 34.

Written for Josef Hüttenbrenner at his lodgings in the so-called Bürgerspital, Vienna.

676. ' **Drittes Offertorium** ' (' Salve Regina ') **in A, for Soprano and Orchestra** (Op. posth. 153, XIV 3). November 1819.

MS. Library of Congress, Washington.
1ST ED. (in parts) *c.* 1843, A. Diabelli & Co., Vienna (no. 7978), in *alla breve* time, shortened and with a spurious pf. acc. *ad lib.*, in place of the original string quartet acc.; the original version—1888, Gesamtausgabe.

Ferdinand Schubert arranged the work for tenor solo, with horn acc. (parts in MS.—Gesellschaft der Musikfreunde, Vienna).

677. '**Strophe von Schiller**,' called '**Fragment aus Schiller's Gedicht " Die Götter Griechenlands "** ' (' Schöne Welt, wo bist du? '), Song, two versions (XX 371 (*a*) and (*b*)). November 1819.

MS. Stadtbibliothek, Vienna (both versions, the first dated).
1ST ED. *c.* 1848, A. Diabelli & Co., Vienna (no. 8819), as no. 1 of *Nachlass*, book 42.

The second version was superimposed by Schubert on the MS. of the first version. The first title is Schubert's, and he used only the twelfth stanza of Schiller's poem, which contains sixteen.

Literature. Paul Mies, *Schubert der Meister des Liedes*, Berlin, 1928, p. 267. J. A. Westrup, *The Listener*, London, 8th February 1945.

678. **Mass in A flat for Quartet, S.A.T.B., Mixed Chorus, Orchestra, and Organ** (XIII 5). November 1819–September 1822.

GLORIA

Allegro maestoso e vivace

Andantino

Allegro moderato

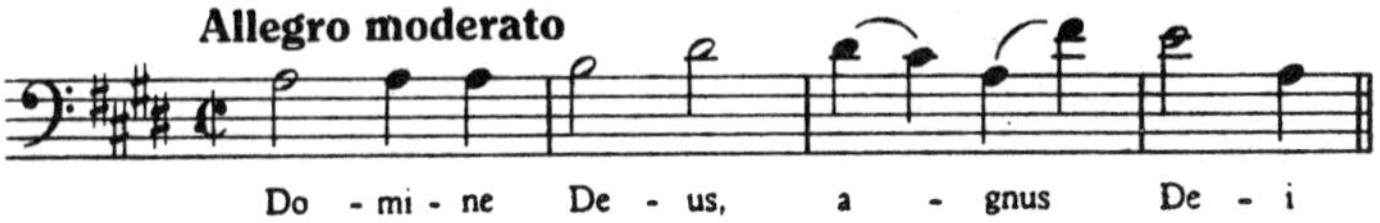

CREDO

Allegro maestoso e vivace

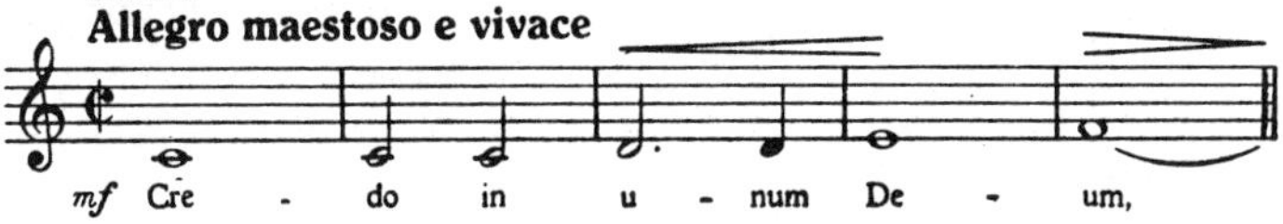

Grave

Tempo I.

SANCTUS

Andante

Allegro

BENEDICTUS
Andante con moto

p Be - ne - di - ctus qui —

AGNUS DEI
Adagio

A - gnus De - i

Allegretto

Do - na no - bis pa - cem.

CUM SANCTO SPIRITU *(2nd Version)*

Cum san - cto Spi - ri - tu in glo - ri - a De - i

OSANNA *(2nd Version)*
Allegro moderato

p O - san - na in ex-cel - sis De - o.

MS. Score—Gesellschaft der Musikfreunde, Vienna (entitled 'Missa solemnis'); a cancelled section of the first version of the Gloria—unknown; former owner—Rudolf Weis-Ostborn, Graz (with fragment of the bass part of the Gloria); organ part and score of the first version of the Osanna, and sketch to 'Confiteor' in the Credo—Stadtbibliothek, Vienna.

1ST PF. *c.* 1822, Alt-Lerchenfelder Kirche, Vienna.

1ST ED. (score) March 1875, Friedrich Schreiber, Vienna (no. 23,524), corrupt.

There exist two versions of some sections of this Mass; the variants, probably written after 1822, are given in the *Revisionsbericht*. Schubert intended to dedicate the Mass to the emperor and empress (Franz I and Karolina Augusta).

—— **Nine Deutsche Tänze for Pianoforte** (Op. 9, XII 1, nos. 5-13). 12th November 1819.

MS. Gesellschaft der Musikfreunde, Vienna (see note); another MS. of nos. 6 and 7 (together with Op. 18, XII 2, 145, Ländler nos. 5 and 8)—John Bass, New York.

1ST ED. See 365.

The Vienna MS. is written in the following order: nos. 6-9, 13, 10, 5, 11-12. No. 6, not dated, is identical with no. 16 of seventeen *Ländler* (366).

679. Two Ländler in E flat for Pianoforte. (?) *c.* 1820.

MS. Weis-Ostborn family, Graz.
1ST ED. 1st December 1925, *Moderne Welt*, Vienna, music supplement, p. 4 (ed. by O. E. D.).
The MS. is written on the back of somebody else's exercises in music writing (cf. 573A).

680. Two Ländler in D flat for Pianoforte. (?) *c.* 1820.

MS. Gesellschaft der Musikfreunde, Vienna.
1ST ED. 1930, Ed. Strache, Vienna (no. 23), in *Deutsche Tänze*, etc. (ed. by O. E. D. and A. Orel), p. 12 (arranged by Orel).
The MS. contains eight Ländler in D flat; nos. 1-4 are identical with nos. 4, 6, 7, 8, of the Ländler in Op. 18 (145). Only the treble part is written for nos. 5-8 (except in the case of no. 6, where the first four bars have the bass added). Nos. 7 and 8 are identical with nos. 9 and 12 of the Ländler in Op. 18 (145). Nos. 5 and 6 were published in the first edition, mentioned above, where the missing last four bars of no. 6 are substituted completely.

681. Twelve (Eight) Ländler for Pianoforte. (?) *c.* 1820.

MS. Conservatoire, Paris (Ph.).
1ST ED. 1930, Ed. Strache, Vienna (no. 23), in *Deutsche Tänze*,
etc. (ed. by O. E. D. and A. Orel), pp. 9–11.

The MS. contains only these eight dances, numbered 5–12; the first four are lost.

682. ' **Ueber allen Zauber Liebe,**' called ' **Lied** ' (' Sie hüpfte mit mir auf grünem Plan,' Mayrhofer), **Song** (XX 599).   Unfinished. *c.* 1820.

MS. Stadtbibliothek, Vienna.
1ST ED. 1895, Gesamtausgabe.

The song was not finished; the last line of the first stanza is missing in the MS., the second stanza has been added in the *Revisionsbericht*. The title of Mayrhofer's poem may have been taken from August Wilhelm von Schlegel's translation (published in 1803) of Calderón's play *El mayor encanto amor* (*Love the Greatest Enchantment*).

683. ' **Die Wolkenbraut** ' (Schober), **Song.** No date. Lost.

The poem is indicated in the second edition of Schober's verses (1865) as having been composed by Schubert. Cf. 582. (This item is inserted here to fill a blank after the compilation of the catalogue.)

684. ' **Die Sterne** ' (' Du staunest, o Mensch,' from Friedrich von Schlegel's ' Abendröte '), **Song** (XX 378). 1820.

MS. Lost (Witteczek's copy).
1ST ED. *c.* 1848, A. Diabelli & Co., Vienna (no. 8837), as no. 1 of *Nachlass*, book 48.

685. ' **Morgenlied** ' (' Eh' die Sonne früh aufersteht,' from Zacharias Werner's ' Die Söhne des Tales '), **Song** (Op. 4, no. 2; XX 379). 1820.

MS. (former owner, J. Brahms) Gesellschaft der Musikfreunde, Vienna.

1ST ED. 29th May 1821, Cappi & Diabelli, Vienna (no. 773), as no. 2 of Op. 4, published for Schubert and dedicated by him to Johann Ladislaus Pyrker von Felsö-Eör.

The MS. bears the inscription ' NB. Der Sängerin P. und dem Clavierspieler St. empfehl' ich dieses Lied ganz besonders ! ! ! 1820.' ' P.' stands for Pepi, i.e. Josefine, von Koller, and ' St.' for Albert Stadler (see ' Namenstagslied,' 695).

686. ' **Frühlingsglaube** ' (Uhland), **Song,** two versions (Op. 20, no. 2; XX 380 (*a*) and (*b*)). 1820 (November 1822).

a Mässig

Die lin - den Lüf - te sind er - wacht.

b Ziemlich langsam

Die lin - den Lüf - te sind er - wacht.

MS. (*a*) Preussische Staatsbibliothek, Berlin, dated by Ferdinand Schubert. (*b*) Étienne Charavay, Paris (1881). See note.

1ST ED. (*a*) 1895, Gesamtausgabe (see note); (*b*) 10th April 1823, Sauer & Leidesdorf, Vienna (no. 231), as no. 2 of Op. 20, dedicated by Schubert to Frau Justine von Bruchmann.

Schubert withdrew one version on 31st October 1822, and handed over to the publishers the last version in November 1822. Max Friedlaender used MS. (*a*) for his edition of the song in vol. i of Peters's *Schubert Album*; see the supplement to this album, 1884, pp. 55–6. Another version of (*a*), probably later but dated, by Schubert himself, 1820, was found in the Bayerische Staatsbibliothek, Munich; the prelude, with different barring, occupies only three and a half bars.

687. '**Nachthymne**' (Novalis), **Song** (XX 372).   January 1820.

Hir - ü - ber wall' ich.

MS. Gesellschaft der Musikfreunde, Vienna.

1ST ED. 1872, J. P. Gotthard, Vienna (no. 328), as no 4 of forty songs, this song dedicated by the publisher to Julius Stockhausen.

688. '**Vier Canzonen**' (Vittorelli and Metastasio), **Songs** (XX 575–8).   January 1820.

Andante moto

Non t'ac - cos - tar all' — ur - na.

2. Andante

Guar - da, che bian - ca lu - na.

3. **Allegretto**

Da quel sem-bian-te ap-pre-si

4. **Andantino**

Mio ben ri-cor-da-ti.

MS. Wiener Schubertbund, Vienna.
1ST PF. Nos. 1 and 2—8th March 1871, Vienna.
1ST ED. 1871, J. P. Gotthard, Vienna (no. 129), as nos. 1-4 of
' 5 Canti ' (for no. 5, see 76).

These vocal exercises are said to have been written for Fräulein Franziska von Roner, later Josef von Spaun's wife, who formerly possessed the MS. It is probable, however, that Schubert did not give her the MS. until the beginning of 1828. The author of nos. 1 and 2 was identified by Odd Udbye, of Oslo, and they are acknowledged as the best of Vittorelli's poems. The text of no. 3 is Lisinga's aria from *L'Eroe Cinese* (I. iii), and no. 4 Gandarte's aria from *Alessandro nell' Indie* (III. vii).

689. ' **Lazarus, oder Die Feier der Auferstehung** ' (A. H. Niemeyer), **Easter Cantata** (Religious Drama) **in three Acts, for Solo Voices, Chorus, S.A.T.B., and Orchestra** (XVII 1). Fragment. February 1820.

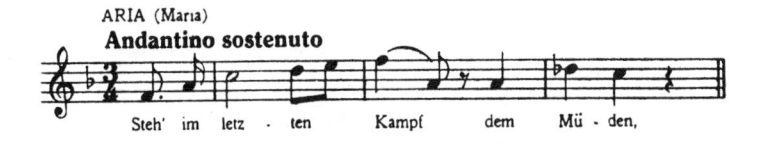

FIRST ACT
Andante
(Lazarus)

Hier lasst mich ruh'n die letz-te Stun-de.

ARIA (Maria)
Andantino sostenuto

Steh' im letz-ten Kampf dem Mü-den,

ARIA (Nathanael)
Allegro moderato

Wenn ich ihm nach-ge-run-gen ha-be,

[ARIA] (Maria)
Andantino

Got - - - tes Lie - be

ARIA (Jemina)
Andante

So schlum-mert auf Ro - sen

CHORUS OF LAZARUS' FRIENDS (Mixed Chorus)
Andante

p All - gnä - di-ger, hei - le— du

SECOND ACT
RECITATIVE (Simon)
Largo

Wo bin ich? wo bin ich?

ARIA (Simon)
Allegro moderato

O könnt' ich, All - ge - wal - ti - ger, im

RECITATIVE (Nathanael)

Wess ist der Kla-ge Stim-me

CHORUS OF LAZARUS' FRIENDS (Male and Female Choruses)
Andante sostenuto

p Sanft und still schläft un - ser Freund.

RECITATIVE (Nathanael)

So legt ihn in die Blu - men,

ARIA (Martha) [Fragment]

Hebt mich der Stür - me Flü - gel

MS. First act—Nationalbibliothek, Vienna; second act (incomplete)—Stadtbibliothek, Vienna; third act—missing.

1ST PF. Acts I and II only—11th April 1830 (Easter Sunday evening), Anna-Kirche, Vienna (conductor, (?) Ferdinand Schubert).

1ST ED. Piano score (arranged by Johann Herbeck)—January 1866, C. A. Spina, Vienna (no. 18544); score—1892, Gesamtausgabe.

It seems that the work was never finished, because even in 1830, when Ferdinand Schubert sold the first act to A. Diabelli & Co., only two acts had been performed. In his list of Schubert's works, 1839, Ferdinand mentions only the first (completed) act. The next performance was on 27th March 1863, Redoutensaal, Vienna (conductor, Herbeck), when practically the whole work preserved was given with the exception of the fragment of the last recitative, which is also missing in Herbeck's pf. score. There was a stage performance, on 19th November 1928, Konzerthaus, Vienna. The text was first published in Niemeyer's *Gedichte*, Leipzig, 1778, with vignettes by Chodowiecki; it was also printed in a separate edition of the Cantata. Schubert only slightly altered the words, some of the alterations having been made by Niemeyer himself in 1814, after the poem had been set to music by J. H. Rolle.

690. '**Abendröte**' (Friedrich von Schlegel), **Song** (XX 376). Beginning of March 1820.

Langsam

Tie - fer sin - ket schon— die Son - ne.

MS. Kapten Rudolf Nydahl, Stockholm.

1ST ED. 26th October 1830, A. Diabelli & Co., Vienna (no. 3704), as no. 3 of *Nachlass*, book 7.

Schubert used the title of Schlegel's whole cycle of poems, published in 1809, to the first part of which this poem (without an individual title) forms the introduction. Schubert called it 'Abendröte. Erster Teil.' The cycle was read on 15th February 1828 at the home of Schubert's friend, Franz von Schober (probably in Schubert's presence). The *Revisionsbericht* suggests a mistake in p. 2, line 2, bar 3 of the G.A.; according to the MS., found in the meantime, the version in the G.A., however, is correct.

691. 'Die Vögel' (from Friedrich von Schlegel's 'Abendröte'), Song (Op. posth. 172, no. 6; XX 373). March 1820.

MS. Leo Liepmannssohn, Berlin (sale, 29th October 1900).
1ST ED. 1866, C. A. Spina, Vienna (no. 16764, on the title-page 16784), as no. 6 of Op. 172.

692. 'Der Knabe' (from Friedrich von Schlegel's 'Abendröte'), Song (XX 374). March 1820.

MS. Fair copy (fragment only, consisting of the beginning to p. 3, line 5, bar 5 inclusive, of the G.A.)—Albert Cranz, New York.
1ST ED. 1872, J. P. Gotthard, Vienna (no. 346), as no. 22 of forty songs, this song dedicated by the publisher to Nikolaus Dumba.

693. 'Der Fluss' (from Friedrich von Schlegel's 'Abendröte'), Song (XX 375). March 1820.

MS. Unknown; former owner—Max Friedlaender, Berlin (fragment only, consisting of the last twenty-four bars and stanzas 2 and 3).
1ST ED. 1872, J. P. Gotthard, Vienna (no. 351), as no. 27 of forty songs.

694. 'Der Schiffer' ('Friedlich lieg' ich hingegossen,' Friedrich von Schlegel), Song (XX 377). March 1820.

Ziemlich langsam

Fried - lich lieg' ich hin - ge - gos - sen.

MS. Score—unknown; former owner—Max Friedlaender, Berlin; voice-part only—William Kux, Chur, Switzerland.

1ST ED. *c.* 1842, A. Diabelli & Co., Vienna (no. 7411), as no. 1 of *Nachlass*, book 33.

The Kux MS. gives the four stanzas in the following order: 2, 1, 3, 4, and the words are written by another hand (? Leopold von Sonnleithner). This, one of the few poems by Friedrich von Schlegel which Schubert did not take from the cycle 'Abendröte,' is one of Schlegel's earliest 'Spring Poems' ('Frühlingsgedichte').

695. 'Namenstagslied' (Albert Stadler), **Song** (XX 587). March 1820.

Moderato

Va - ter, schenk' mir die - se Stun - de.

MS. E. H. W. Meyerstein, London.

1ST PF. See note.

1ST ED. 1895, Gesamtausgabe.

The song was written for Pepi, i.e. Josefine, von Koller, and Albert Stadler, to be performed at Steyr (Upper Austria) on 19th March 1820, the name-day of Josefine's father, Josef von Koller. (Cf. 685.) At the end of the MS. is a note written by Schubert: ' Stadler schreibt die Singstimme ab und setzt dieses [die 2. und 3. Strophe] zur Wiederholung darunter' (Stadler is to copy out the voice part and to add this [the 2nd and 3rd stanza] for the repetition of the song).

696. Six Antiphons for the Consecration of Palms on Palm Sunday, for Mixed Chorus (Op. posth. 113, XIV 18). April 1820.

No. 1.
Allegro molto moderato

f Ho - san - na fi - li - o Da - vid,

No. 2.
Adagio

pp In mon - te O - li - ve - ti

No. 3. **Adagio**

p San - ctus, san - ctus, *f* san - ctus

No. 4. **Moderato**

p Pu - e - ri He - brae - o - rum

No. 5.

Cum an - ge - lis et pu - e - ris

No. 6. **Andante**

In - gre - di - en - te Do - mi - no

MS. (pencil, on rough paper)—Stadtbibliothek, Vienna.

1ST PF. 28th March, Palm Sunday, 1820, Alt-Lerchenfelder Kirche, Vienna.

1ST ED. (in parts) 21st March 1829, A. Diabelli & Co., Vienna (no. 3261).

Written at the request of Ferdinand Schubert, then still a teacher at the Orphanage in Vienna, and newly appointed choirmaster of the above-named church. Schubert wrote it offhand at the Orphanage, in half an hour.

—— **Écossaise for Pianoforte** (Op. 18, XII 2, Écoss. no. 6). May 1820.

MS. Gesellschaft der Musikfreunde, Vienna (together with **697**).
1ST ED. See **145**.

697. Five Écossaises for Pianoforte (XII 28). May 1820.

No. 1.

fp

No. 2.

p

No. 3.

No. 4. No. 5.

MS. Gesellschaft der Musikfreunde, Vienna (together with the preceding entry).
1ST ED. 1889, Gesamtausgabe.

698. 'Des Fräuleins Liebeslauschen,' called 'Liebeslauschen,' or 'Romanze' (Schlechta), Song (XX 381). September 1820.

Andantino

Hier un-ten steht ein Rit-ter im hel-len Mon-den-strahl.

MS. Stadtbibliothek, Vienna.
1ST ED. 4th January 1832, A. Diabelli & Co., Vienna (no. 4015), as no. 2 of *Nachlass*, book 15.
It is said that Franz von Schlechta wrote two poems, 'Des Ritters Liebeslauschen' and 'Des Fräuleins Liebeslauschen': the first on the subject of a painting ('Des ritterlichen Jägers Liebeslauschen'), exhibited in April 1820, and the second of a lithograph, published in 1821, by Ludwig Ferdinand Schnorr von Carolsfeld. The second poem, the text of this song, was printed, together with the lithograph, in the Vienna *Conversationsblatt*, vol. iii, no. 1, p. 7. It is probable, however, that the lithograph was made as an illustration to the poem. Louis von Hardtmuth, in 1824, published a musical setting of this poem, at Sauer & Leidesdorf's, Vienna, as his Op. 7, dedicated to the sister of the author, Fräulein Therese von Schlechta, later Hardtmuth's wife. A MS. copy of Schubert's song, transposed from A to G, is to be found in the album of Franziska Tremier (Stadtbibliothek, Vienna). The words of the first edition differ greatly from those of the first version, used by Schubert; but they were, nevertheless, provided by the author himself.
Literature. Alfred Orel, *Festschrift. Johannes Biehle zum 60. Geburtstag überreicht*, Leipzig, 1930, pp. 71–81.

699. 'Der entsühnte Orest' (Mayrhofer), Song (XX 383). September 1820.

[Musical notation: Sehr langsam, mit Kraft — "Zu mei-nen Fü-ssen brichst du dich,"]

MS. Lost.

1ST ED. 21st April 1831, A. Diabelli & Co., Vienna (no. 3708), as no. 2 of *Nachlass*, book 11.

The poem is given in a different version in the second edition of Mayrhofer's works, ed. by Ernst von Feuchtersleben (Vienna, 1843).

700. '**Freiwilliges Versenken**' (Mayrhofer), **Song** (XX 384). September 1820.

[Musical notation: Sehr langsam — "Wo-hin? O He-li-os!"]

MS. Lost.

1ST ED. 21st April 1831, A. Diabelli & Co., Vienna (no. 3708), as no. 4 of *Nachlass*, book 11.

The first edition was published in two issues, the first of which commences with the notes F sharp, G, as in the Gesamtausgabe; in the second issue this is changed to A, B flat. The words were altered by Schubert.

701. '**Sakuntala.**' **Opera in three Acts** (after Kalidasa's Indian Play), by Johann Philipp Neumann. **Sketches** of two Acts only (one chorus published). October 1820.

[Musical notation: INTRODUCTION. No. 1 (Chorus and Orchestra) Andante con moto — "Das hol-de Licht des Ta-ges"]

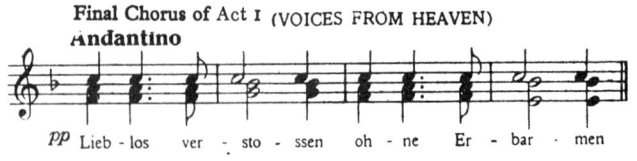

[Musical notation: Final Chorus of Act 1 (VOICES FROM HEAVEN) Andantino — "pp Lieb-los ver-sto-ssen oh-ne Er-bar-men"]

MS. Stadtbibliothek, Vienna.

1ST PF. Bass aria—25th January 1882, Hofoper, Vienna ('Romanze,' arranged by Johann Nepomuk Fuchs, sung by Ernst Scaria as Spiess in *Die Zwillingsbrüder*, **647**).

IST ED. Final chorus of Act I—1929, Steingräber-Verlag, Leipzig, as supplement in no. 2 of *Neue Zeitschrift für Musik* (ed. by Edmund Richter).

The Indian play was translated, from Sir William Jones's English version (1789), in prose by G. Forster (Mainz, 1791, Frankfurt a. M., 1803, Heidelberg, 1820), in metre by W. Gerhard (Leipzig, 1820). There are six nos. of Act I and five nos. of Act II in sketch-form, mostly confined to the voice part and bass, with some indications of instruments. Only the final chorus of Act I, with the acc. for wind instruments, is completed. Schubert's nephew, Eduard Schneider, started to write, but never finished, a pf. score (Krasser family, Vienna). Brahms advised the publishers of the G.A., on 7th March 1885, not to print these sketches. The beginning of the introductory chorus, quoted here, resembles no. 1 of the *Deutsche Messe* (872), the words of which are by the same author as those of this opera.

Literature. Kreissle, *Schubert*, pp. 186–96. Edmund Richter, *Neue Zeitschrift für Musik*, Leipzig, 1929, vol. xcvi, pp. 90 ff., with the supplement mentioned above.

702. '**Der Jüngling auf dem Hügel** ' (Heinrich Hüttenbrenner), **Song** (Op. 8, no. 1; XX 385). November 1820.

MS. Gesellschaft der Musikfreunde, Vienna.

IST PF. (?) 2nd December 1821, Gasthof 'Zum Römischen Kaiser,' Vienna.

IST ED. 9th May 1822, Cappi & Diabelli, Vienna (no. 872), as no. 1 of Op. 8, dedicated by Schubert to Johann Karl, Graf Esterházy.

703. Allegro in C minor for String Quartet, called ' **Quartett-Satz**' (V 12). December 1820.

MS. (former owner, J. Brahms) Gesellschaft der Musikfreunde, Vienna.

IST PF. Probably 1821, at a meeting of a private music society, Vienna; first public performance—1st March 1867, Musikverein, Vienna (Josef Hellmesberger's Quartet).

IST ED. December 1870, B. Senff, Leipzig (no. 939), score and parts.

Cf. 103. The first movement is followed by forty-one bars only of an Andante in A flat (*Revisionsbericht*, pp. 78–82):

704. '**Gesang der Geister über den Wassern**' (Goethe), **for Male Voice Octet with String accompaniment** (two violas, two violoncellos), first, unfinished sketch (XVI 45). December 1820.

MS. Preussische Staatsbibliothek, Berlin.
1ST PF. 27th December 1857, Vienna.
1ST ED. 1891, Gesamtausgabe.

For the final version, see **714**; for other settings of the same poem, see **484, 538, 705**.

705. '**Gesang der Geister über den Wassern**' (Goethe), **for Male Voice Chorus, T.T.B.B., with Pianoforte accompaniment**, second sketch (XXI 34). December 1820.

MS. Unknown; former owner—Julius Epstein, Vienna (*c.* 1900).
1ST ED. 1897, Gesamtausgabe.

Published again as the first edition, by mistake, in *Die Musik*, Berlin, October 1928 (ed. by Hannes Bauer). For the final version, see **714**. Cf. **704**.

706. '**Der 23. Psalm** (translated by Moses Mendelssohn), **for Chorus, S.S.A.A., with Pianoforte accompaniment** (Op. posth. 132, XVIII 2). December 1820.

MS. Sketch of the beginning, and score—Stadtbibliothek, Vienna.
1ST PF. 30th August 1821, Gundelhof, Vienna (conductor, Anna Fröhlich).
1ST ED. 1831, A. Diabelli & Co., Vienna (no. 3182), as Op. 132.
The work was written for the pupils of Fräulein Anna Fröhlich at the Vienna Conservatoire (cf. 757). It was advertised as early as the end of 1828 by Tobias Haslinger and engraved in 1829 by Diabelli. The arrangement for male voice quartet is by Ferdinand Schubert; that for male voice trio is spurious.

707. 'Der zürnenden Diana,' called 'Die zürnende Diana' (Mayrhofer), Song, two versions (Op. 36, no. 1; XX 387 (*a*) and (*b*)). December 1820.

a **Entschlossen**
Ja, span-ne nur den Bo-gen mich zu tö - ten,

b **Feurig**
Ja, span-ne nur den Bo-gen mich zu tö - ten,

MS. (*a*) Rough draft (former owner, J. Brahms)—Gesellschaft der Musikfreunde, Vienna; (*b*) fair copy—Stadtbibliothek, Vienna.
1ST PF. 24th February 1825, Musikverein, Vienna.
1ST ED. (*a*) 1895, Gesamtausgabe; (*b*) 11th February 1825, Cappi & Co., Vienna (no. 60), as no. 1 of Op. 36, dedicated by Schubert to Frau Katharine Lászny, *née* Buchwieser.

MS. (*a*) shows some pencilled alterations which indicate that Schubert anticipated another version; these alterations are printed in the *Revisionsbericht*, and suggest a version intermediate between (*a*) and (*b*). The MSS. and the first edition are entitled 'Die zürnende Diana.'

708. 'Im Walde,' called 'Waldesnacht' ('Windesrauschen, Gottesflügel,' Friedrich von Schlegel), Song (XX 388). December 1820.

Geschwind
Win-des Rau - schen,

MS. Gesellschaft der Musikfreunde, Vienna.
1ST ED. 12th March 1832, A. Diabelli & Co., Vienna (no. 4016), as *Nachlass*, book 16, under the title ' Waldesnacht.'

709. ' Frühlingsgesang,' called ' Frühlingslied ' (Schober), **Quartet, T.T.B.B.**, first version (XVI 31). (?) *c.* 1821.

Etwas lebhaft

Schmü-cket die Lo-cken mit duf-ti-gen Krän-zen

MS. Score—Otto Taussig, Malmö; parts (see note)—Dr. Franz Roehn, Los Angeles.
1ST ED. 1891, Gesamtausgabe.

In the MS. of the parts only the second halves of the first tenor, second tenor, and first bass parts are in Schubert's handwriting. For the second version, see **740**.

—— Beethoven's Song ' Abendlied unterm gestirnten Himmel ' (Heinrich Goebel). Copy, transposed from E to D. See Appendix II, no. 7. *c.* 1821.

710. ' **Im Gegenwärtigen Vergangenes** ' (from Goethe's ' West-östlicher Divan '), for **Male Quartet, T.T.B.B., with Pianoforte** accompaniment (XVI 15). (?) 1821.

Andante moto

Ros' und Li-lie mor-gen-tau-lich

Allegretto

Und da duf-tet's wie vor Al- - ters,

Allegro moderato

p Nun die Wäl-der e-wig spros-sen,

Andantino quasi Allegretto

Und mit die-sem Lied und Wen-dung

MS. Stadtbibliothek, Vienna.

1ST PF. 12th December 1869, Vienna.
1ST ED. *c.* 1848, A. Diabelli & Co., Vienna (no. 8820), as *Nachlass*, book 43.

It is remarkable that on the title of the first edition Marianne von Willemer is indicated (by her initials) as the real author, which she was, in fact, not of this poem, but of three other poems in Goethe's cycle, among them the two ' Suleika ' songs (717 and 720), to the authorship of which Frau von Willemer did not confess before 1850.

711. ' Lob der Thränen ' (August Wilhelm von Schlegel), **Song** (Op. 13, no. 2; XX 294). (?) 1821.

Ziemlich langsam

Lau - e   Lüf - te,   Blu - men - düf - te,

MS. Rough draft, probably 1817—unknown; former owner—Karl Meinert, Dessau (*c.* 1895, later Frankfurt am Main).
1ST ED. 13th December 1822, Cappi & Diabelli, Vienna (no. 1162), as no. 2 of Op. 13, published for Schubert and dedicated by him to Josef von Spaun.

712. ' Die gefangenen Sänger ' (August Wilhelm von Schlegel), **Song** (XX 389). January 1821.

Lieblich, klagend

Hörst du von den Nach - ti - gal - len

die Ge - bü - sche wi - der - hal - len?

MS. (together with 721)—Alfred Cortot, Lausanne (Witteczek's copy).
1ST ED. *c.* 1842, A. Diabelli & Co., Vienna (no. 7411), as no. 2 of *Nachlass*, book 33.

According to the index of the Witteczek Collection, this poem was twice set by Schubert, in January 1816 and in January 1821; the 1816 version, however, is unknown.

713. ' Der Unglückliche ' (' Die Nacht bricht an,' Karoline Pichler), **Song**, two versions (Op. 87, no. 1; XX 390 (*a*) and (*b*)). January 1821.

a [musical notation: Langsam 12/8] Die Nacht bricht an,— mit lei-sen Lüf-ten sin-ket sie.

b [musical notation: Langsam 6/8] Die Nacht bricht an,— mit lei-sen Lüf-ten sin-ket sie

MS. Sketch (incomplete)—Stadtbibliothek, Vienna; (*a*) Gilhofer & Ranschburg, Vienna (sale, 21st October 1901); (*b*) lost.

1ST ED. (*a*) 1895, Gesamtausgabe; (*b*) 6th August 1827, A. Pennauer, Vienna (no. 330), as no. 1 of Op. 84 (later corrected to 87).

The sketch, without corrections, and minus the last leaf, is printed in the *Revisionsbericht*, pp. 81–5.

714. '**Gesang der Geister über den Wassern**' (Goethe), **for Octet, four Tenors and four Basses, with accompaniment for String Instruments** (two violas, two violoncellos, and contrabass) (Op. posth. 167, XVI 3).   February 1821.

[musical notation: Adagio molto] *pp* Des Men-schen See-le gleicht dem Was-ser,

MS. Dr. Alwin Cranz, Vienna.

1ST PF. 7th March 1821, Kärntnertor-Theater, Vienna (concert).

1ST ED. March 1858, C. A. Spina, Vienna (nos. 16373–4), dedicated by the publisher to Schubert's friend, Leopold von Sonnleithner, with acc. for pf. duet added by Johann Herbeck.

Heuberger (*Schubert*, Berlin, 1902, p. 48) called this Octet the *Faust* among Schubert's works for male voice chorus. This version was written for the above-mentioned concert. Ferdinand Schubert wrote also a pf. acc. to this work, 3rd to 6th May 1836 (MS.—Gesellschaft der Musikfreunde, Vienna).   For other settings of the poem see **484, 538, 704,** and **705.**

715. '**Versunken**' (from Goethe's 'West-östlicher Divan'), **Song** (XX 391).   February 1821.

[musical notation: Geschwind 2/4] Voll Lo-cken kraus ein Haupt so— rund,

1821

MS. Nationalbibliothek, Vienna (together with **719** and **720**); transposed for a low voice (July 1825)—Stadtbibliothek, Vienna.

IST ED. c. 1842, A. Diabelli & Co., Vienna (no. 7416), as no. 3 of *Nachlass*, book 38.

Schubert omitted two verses of the poem (cf. the *Revisionsbericht*).

716. ' **Grenzen der Menschheit** ' (Goethe), **Song** (XX 393). February–March 1821.

Nicht ganz langsam
16

Wenn der ur - al - te hei - li - ge Va - ter

MS. Version for bass (February 1821)—Dr. Franz Roehn, Los Angeles; version for contralto—lost.

IST ED. 4th January 1832, A. Diabelli & Co., Vienna (no. 4014), as no. 1 of *Nachlass*, book 14.

The clef of the first MS. was altered by Diabelli from bass to treble. The version for contralto is said to have been written in March 1821. Schubert wrote ' kindliche Schauer tief in der Brust ' instead of Goethe's ' . . . treu in der Brust ' (line 10 of the poem).

717. ' **Suleika II** ' ('Ach, um deine feuchten Schwingen,' Marianne von Willemer, in Goethe's ' West-östlicher Divan '), called ' Westwind,' Song (Op. 31, XX 397). (?) March 1821.

Mässige Bewegung
8

Ach, um dei - ne feuch - ten Schwin-gen.

MS. Rough draft—lost; fair copy (beginning of 1825)—lost.

IST PF. 9th June 1825, Jagor'scher Saal, Berlin (Anna Milder).

IST ED. 12th August 1825, A. Pennauer, Vienna (no. 133), as Op. 31, dedicated by Schubert to Frau Milder.

The poem was written in 1815 by Frau von Willemer and included by Goethe in his book in 1819. Cf. **720** and note to **710**. The song is said to have been composed for Frau Milder. The first issue of the first edition has the misprints ' aus dem öst-westlichen Divan ' and ' no. 130 ' on the title-page.

718. Variation in C minor, on a Waltz by Anton Diabelli, for Pianoforte (XI 8). March 1821.

MS. Nationalbibliothek, Vienna.

1ST ED. 9th June 1824, A. Diabelli & Co., Vienna (C. & D. 1381), as no. 38 of the fifty Variations on a Waltz, set by fifty Austrian composers, under the title *Vaterländischer Künstlerverein*, second part (p. 61).

Beethoven had used the same theme in his Op. 120 (later called *Vaterländischer Künstlerverein*, first part), published by Cappi & Diabelli, who also prepared the second part of the collection for publication.

Literature. Heinrich Rietsch, *Beethoven-Jahrbuch*, Munich, 1908, vol. i, pp. 31, 36, and 40.

719. ' Geheimes ' (from Goethe's ' West-östlicher Divan '), **Song** (Op. 14, no. 2; XX 392). March 1821.

MS. First draft—Nationalbibliothek, Vienna (together with 715 and 720).

1ST ED. 13th December 1822, Cappi & Diabelli, Vienna (no. 1163), as no. 2 of Op. 14, dedicated by Schubert to Franz von Schober.

Schubert copied the poem on a separate sheet (Karl Ernst Henrici, Berlin, sale, 14–15th May 1925). The first edition was to have been ornamented with a vignette by Schwind, portraying Fräulein Anna Hönig, but the vignette was not engraved, and its design is lost.

720. ' **Suleika I** ' (' Was bedeutet die Bewegung,' Marianne von Willemer, in Goethe's ' West-östlicher Divan '), called ' **Ostwind,**' or ' **Glückliches Geheimnis,**' Song (Op. 14, no. 1; XX 396). March 1821.

MS. Rough draft—Nationalbibliothek, Vienna (together with 715 and 719).

1ST ED. 13th December 1822, Cappi & Diabelli, Vienna (no. 1163), as no. 1 of Op. 14, dedicated by Schubert to Franz von Schober.

The poem was written in 1815, and included by Goethe in his book in 1819 (cf. 717 and note to 710). For the vignette intended for this songbook, cf. note to 719.

721. ' Mahomet's Gesang ' (Goethe), **Song, second version, for a male voice** (XX 600). Fragment. March 1821.

Mässig geschwind

Seht den Fel-sen-quell, freu-de-hell,

MS. (together with 712)—Alfred Cortot, Lausanne (Witteczek's copy).

1ST ED. 1895, Gesamtausgabe.

This version was not finished. For the first version, which was probably completed, see 549.

—— **Five Deutsche Tänze in F sharp for Pianoforte** (Op. 9, XII 1, nos. 32–6). 8th March 1821.

MS. Preussische Staatsbibliothek, Berlin (a MS. of seven dances, dated as above, and numbered as 1–4 and 6; for the other two see 722 and first note on p. 326).

1ST ED. See 365.

In the MS. these five dances are written in the key of F sharp, and not F, as printed in the first edition and in the G.A.

722. **Deutscher Tanz in G flat for Pianoforte** (XII 19). 8th March 1821.

MS. No. 5 of the MS. in the Preussische Staatsbibliothek, Berlin (see the preceding note).

1ST ED. 1889, Gesamtausgabe.

723. **Aria and Duet inserted in Hérold's Opera ' Das Zauberglöckchen,' or ' La Clochette '** (libretto by E. G. M. Théaulon de Lambert) (XV 15). Spring 1821.

No. 1. ARIA (Ten.)
Allegro

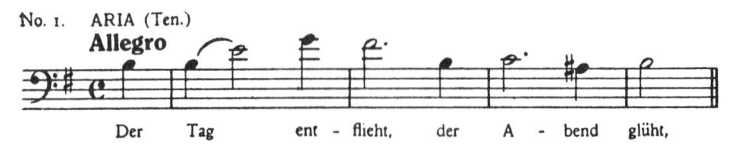

Der Tag ent - flieht, der A - bend glüht,

No. 2. DUET (Ten. and Bass)
Allegro moderato

Nein, nein, nein, nein, das ist zu viel.

MS. Aria of Azolin (beginning of Act I)—Gesellschaft der Musikfreunde, Vienna; Duet for Bedur and Zedir—lost.

1ST PF. 20th June 1821, Kärntnertor-Theater, Vienna (performed there eight times in all).

1ST ED. 1893, Gesamtausgabe.

A copy of the duet (Act II) is preserved in the Kärntnertor-Theater score (Nationalbibliothek, Vienna). Ferdinand Schubert arranged both pieces with pf. acc. (Gesellschaft der Musikfreunde, Vienna). The words may have been written by Friedrich Treitschke, the translator of the French libretto.

724. ' Die Nachtigall ' (Unger), **Quartet, T.T.B.B.** (Op. 11, no. 2; XVI 5). April 1821.

Allegretto

p Be - schei - den ver - bor - gen im busch - ich - ten Gang

Allegro

So, Freun-de, ver-hall - te manch' himm-li - sches Lied,

MS. Lost.

1ST PF. 22nd April 1821, Kärntnertor-Theater, Vienna (unaccompanied); 15th September 1822, Redoutensaal, Linz (with pf. acc.).

1ST ED. 12th June 1822, Cappi & Diabelli, Vienna (no. 1018), as no. 2 of Op. 11, dedicated by Schubert to Josef Barth.

Of the accompaniments, to be found in the first edition as well as in the G.A., the pf. acc. is dubious, the guitar acc. spurious.

725. ' Linde Lüfte wehen ' (author unknown), **Duet for Mezzo-soprano and Tenor with Pianoforte accompaniment.** Fragment. April 1821.

MS. Unknown; former owner—Schubertbund, Vienna.
IST ED. 1929, Martin Breslauer, Berlin, in *Festschrift für Johannes Wolf*, p. 36 (ed. by Max Friedlaender).

726. ' Mignon ' (I. ' Heiss' mich nicht reden,' from Goethe's ' Wilhelm Meister '), **Song,** first version (XX 394). April 1821.

MS. Stadtbibliothek, Vienna (together with 727).
IST ED. 1870, J. P. Gotthard, Vienna (no. 59).
For the other setting of this poem, see **877,** no. 2.

727. ' Mignon ' (II. ' So lasst mich scheinen,' from Goethe's ' Wilhelm Meister '), **Song,** third version (XX 395). April 1821.

MS. Stadtbibliothek, Vienna (together with **726**).
IST ED. *c.* 1848, A. Diabelli & Co., Vienna (no. 8837), as no. 5 of *Nachlass*, book 48.

On p. 193 of the G.A. read ' fühlt ' instead of ' fühl'.' Schubert sketched the first and second versions in September 1816 (469), and completed a fourth version in January 1826 (877, no. 3).

728. ' Johanna Sebus ' (Goethe), **Song** (XX 601). Fragment. April 1821.

MS. Stadtbibliothek, Vienna.
1ST ED. 1895, Gesamtausgabe.

—— '**Rastlose Liebe**' (XX 177). See 138. May 1821.

—— **Three Walzer for Pianoforte** (Op. 18, XII 2, Walzer, nos. 1–3. 20th May–July (Atzenbrugg) 1821.
MS. No. 2 only—Preussische Staatsbibliothek, Berlin; complete—Gesellschaft der Musikfreunde, Vienna.
1ST ED. See 145.

These three dances are nos. 1, 2, and 4 of the six *Atzenbrugger Deutsche sc. Tänze*), dated July 1821, nos. 3, 5, and 6 having been used for Op. 9, 65 (nos. 29–31, see the note to the next entry). No. 2 was first written on oth May 1821; it is no. 7 of the Berlin MS. (see entry before 722, and 722), .he first six dances of which are dated 8th March 1821.

—— **Three Deutsche Tänze for Pianoforte** (Op. 9, XII 1, nos. 29–31). July 1821 (Atzenbrugg).
MS. Gesellschaft der Musikfreunde, Vienna.
1ST ED. See 365.

These three dances are nos. 3, 5, and 6 of the six *Atzenbrugger Deutsche* (*Tänze*), nos. 1, 2, and 4 belong to Op. 18, 145 (Walzer, nos. 1–3)—see the preceding note.

—— **Four Deutsche Tänze for Pianoforte** (from Opp. 9 and 18, see note). August 1821.
MS. Gesellschaft der Musikfreunde, Vienna (former owner, Johannes Brahms).

The dances are: Op. 9, XII 1, 365, nos. 32 and 33 (each in a different key), and Op. 18, XII 2, 145, Ländler nos. 2 and 5 (the latter in a different key).

729. Symphony in E. Sketch only. Not printed. Beginning of August 1821.

(SECOND SUBJECT) [musical notation] Clar. I.

Andante [musical notation]

SCHERZO **Allegro** [musical notation]

(TRIO) [musical notation] Va.

(FINALE) **Allegro giusto** [musical notation]

MS. Royal College of Music, London (Ph.).
1ST PF. See note.
1ST ED. See note.

The MS. comprises 20 pp. full score (Adagio and seventy-eight bars of Allegro), followed by an instrumental sketch, mostly confined to violin and bass; and at the end is the word 'Fine.' Mendelssohn, Sullivan, and Brahms are said to have contemplated finishing the sketch. It was completed first by J. F. Barnett, and his version was performed at the Crystal Palace, London, 5th May 1883. A piano score of Barnett's version was published by Breitkopf & Härtel, Leipzig, about 1884. Another attempt to complete the work was made by Felix Weingartner, performed at Vienna, Musikvereinssaal, 9th December 1934, and published in score by the Universal Edition, Vienna, 1934 (preface by Karl Geiringer).

730. Tantum ergo in B flat for Soli, Chorus, S.A.T.B., and Orchestra. 16th August 1821.

[musical notation] Andante (♩ = 66) *p* Tan - tum er - go sa - cra - men - tum

MS. Stadtbibliothek, Vienna (the first five bars of the score only); for copies of score and parts, see 1ST ED.

1ST PF. In German—18th January 1924, Aula der Universität, Berlin (conductor, Max Friedlaender), with other words (see first edition); the original—30th September 1924, Grosser Konzerthaussaal, Vienna.

1ST ED. Vocal score—January 1924, Universitäts-Chor, Berlin, with other words, by A. von Troschke, entitled ' Die deutsche Eiche,' lithographed (ed. by Max Friedlaender, after the old incomplete copy of the parts in the possession of Dr. L. Wieck, Lohnsburg, Upper Austria), together with a similar arrangement of the second Tantum ergo in C, of August 1816 (461), privately printed; original version, piano score—1926, Anton Böhm & Sohn, Augsburg (no. 6573, ed. by Alfred Schnerich, with the spurious organ-part, printed after the old copy of the complete score in the Peters-Kirche, Vienna, together with two other Tantum ergos composed by Schubert).

Written for Josef Mayssen of Hernals, near Vienna. The indication on the MS. copy of the organ part, that it was composed for the headmaster, Franz Wieck, is not plausible; he did not receive the copy of the parts until 1876.

731. 'Der Blumen Schmerz' (Mayláth), Song (Op. posth. 173, no. 4; XX 399). September 1821.

MS. Frau Marie Floersheim, Wildegg in Aargau (Switzerland), in the album of Alois Fuchs, a collection of autographs started in 1830.

1ST PF. 3rd February 1825, Musikverein, Vienna.

1ST ED. 8th December 1821, as a supplement to the *Wiener Zeitschrift für Kunst*, etc., Vienna (in type).

The song was reprinted as no. 4 of Op. 173, by C. A. Spina, Vienna (no. 19177), in 1867.

732. '**Alfonso und Estrella**,' **Opera in three Acts** by Franz von Schober (XV 9, the Overture in XV 8). 20th September 1821–27th February 1822.

OVERTURE
Andante

Allegro

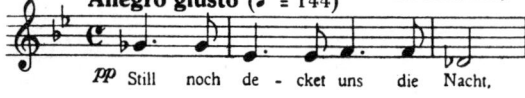

No. 1. INTRODUCTION (Mixed Chorus with Contralto and Tenor Soli)
Allegro giusto (♩ = 144)

pp Still noch de - cket uns die Nacht,

No. 2.   ARIA (Bar.)
Andante molto (♩ = 76)

Sei mir ge - grüsst, o Son - ne,

No. 3. CHORUS & ENSEMBLE (Mixed Chorus, Bar., Sopr. and Ten. Soli)
Allegro (♩. = 72)

Ver - sam - melt euch, Brü - der, singt fröh - li - che Lie - der,

No. 4. DUET (Ten. and Bar.)
Andante (♩ = 58)

Ge - schmückt von Glanz und Sie - gen

No. 5. RECITATIVE & ARIA (Ten.)
Allegro ma non troppo (♩ = 126)
Recit.

Es ist dein streng Ge - bot, dass ich aus die - sem

Larghetto
Aria

Schon, wenn es be - ginnt zu ta - gen,

No. 6. RECITATIVE & DUET (Ten. and Bar.)
Moderato
Recit.

Du rührst mich, Teu - rer, sehr,

Allegro moderato (♩ = 100)
Duet

Schon schlei - chen mei - ne Spä - her

No. 7. CHORUS & ARIA (Sopr. and Female Chorus)
Allegro (♩ = 120)

Zur Jagd, zur Jagd! Die luf - ti - gen Räu - me,

Allegro moderato (♩ = 120)

Es schmückt die wei - ten Sä - le

No. 8. RECIT. & ARIA (Bass)
Allegro (♩ = 106)

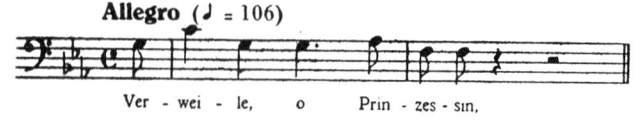

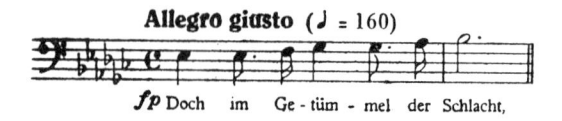

Ver - wei - le, o Prin - zes - sin,

Allegro giusto (♩ = 160)

fp Doch im Ge - tüm - mel der Schlacht,

No. 9. DUET (Sopr. and Bass)
Andantino (♩ = 88)

Ja gib, ver - nimm mein Fle - hen, gib dei - ne Lie - be mir.

No. 10. FINALE (Sopr., Bar., Bass, Male and Female Choruses)
Tempo di Marcia (♩ = 132)

Glän - zen - de Waf - fe den Krie - ger er-freut,

No. 11. RECIT. & ARIA (Bar.)
Andante con moto (♩ = 66)

O sing' mir, Va - ter, noch ein-mal das schö - ne Lied

No. 12. RECIT. & DUET (Sopr. and Ten.)
Recit.

Wie rüh - ret mich dein herr - li - cher Ge - sang

Andantino (♩ = 116)
Duet

Von Fels und Wald um - run - gen,

No. 13. RECIT. & ARIA (Ten.)
Un poco più moto

Wer bist du, hol - des We - sen,

Andante

Wenn ich dich, Hol - de, se - he, so

No. 14. DUET (Sopr. and Ten.)
Allegro moderato ($\quarternote = 108$)

Freund - lich bist du mir er - schie - nen,

No. 15. ARIA (Sopr.)
Andantino ($\quarternote = 120$)

Könnt' ich e - wig hier ver - wei - len

No. 16. DUET (Sopr. and Ten.)
Allegro moderato ($\quarternote = 138$)

Lass dir als Er - inn - rungs - zei - chen

No. 17. CHORUS & ENSEMBLE (Bass and Male Chorus)
Allegro agitato ($\quarternote = 144$)

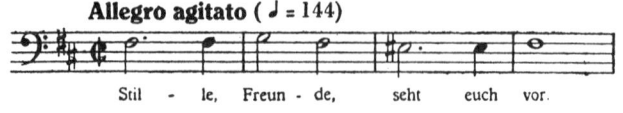

Stil - le, Freun - de, seht euch vor.

No. 18. CHORUS & ARIA (Bar. and Male Chorus)
Allegro ($\quarternote = 160$)

Wo ist sie, was kommt ihr zu kün - den?

No. 19. ENSEMBLE (Bar. and Male Chorus)
Allegro molto ($\quarternote = 112$)

Die Prin - zes - sin ist er - schie - nen!

No. 20. DUET & CHORUS (Sopr. Bar. and Male Chorus)
Un poco piu lento ($\quarternote = 160$)

Darf dich dein Kind um - ar - men?

1821

No. 21. ARIA (Sopr.)
Andantino (♩ = 80)
Herr-lich auf des Ber-ges Hö-hen

No. 22. FINALE (Sopr., Bar., Female and Male Choruses)
Allegro (♩ = 88)
Recit.
Sag', wo ist er hin-ge-kom-men,

No. 23. INTRODUCTION
Allegro (♩ = 160)
p — p fp fp fp

No. 24. DUET (Sopr., Ten. and Female Chorus)
Tempo I.
Hörst du ru-fen, hörst du lär-men?

No. 25. DUET (Sopr. and Bass)
Allegro assai (♩. = 84)
Du wirst mir nicht ent-rin-nen!

No. 26. TERZET & CHORUS (Sopr., Ten., Bass and Male Chorus)
Allegro molto (o = 84)
Hül-fe! Wel-che Stum-me!

No. 27. DUET (Sopr. and Ten.)
Andante moto (♩ = 84)
Doch nun wer-de dei-nem Ret-ter

No. 28. RECIT. & DUET (Sopr. and Ten.)
Allegro
Ja ich, ich bin ge-ret-tet,

No. 29. DUET with CHORUS (Sopr., Ten. and Male Chorus)
Allegro assai (♩ = 138)

We he, we he, mei - nes Va - ters Scha - ren

No. 30. ENSEMBLE (Ten. and Male Chorus)
Allegro (♩. = 104)

Sie ha-ben das Ru-fen ver-nom - men,

No. 31. RECIT. & ENSEMBLE (Sopr., Ten., Bar. and Male Chorus)
Allegro
Recit.

Was geht hier vor, was wol-let ihr be - gin-nen?

No. 32. ARIA (Bar.)
Allegro agitato (♩ = 104)

Wo find' ich nur den Ort

No. 33. DUET (2 Bar.)
Andante (♩ = 100)

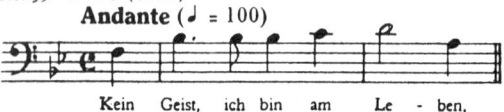

Kein Geist, ich bin am Le - ben,

No. 34. TERZET (Sopr. and 2 Bar.)
Recit.

Em - pfan - ge nun aus mei - ner Hand

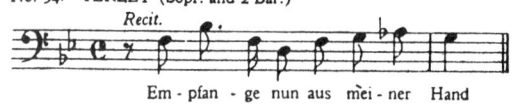

FINALE (Sopr., Ten., 2 Bar., Bass, Female and Male Choruses)
A tempo (♩ = 120)

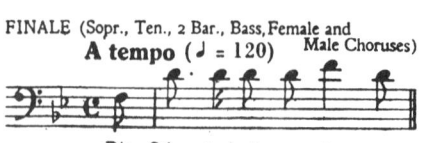

Die Schwer-ter hoch ge -schwun-gen,

MS. Overture—Dr. Alwin Cranz, Vienna; the remainder—Gesellschaft der Musikfreunde, Vienna (with metronome indications); two arias (nos. 8 and 13), arranged with pf. acc.—Preussische Staatsbibliothek, Berlin.

1ST PF. Overture—20th December 1823, Theater an der Wien (*Rosamunde*); cut version of the opera—24th June 1854, Weimar (conductor, Franz Liszt), with Anton Rubinstein's Festival Overture (' God save the King ').

1ST ED. For Schubert's arrangement of the overture for pf. duet, see 773. Overture in parts—1866, in score—January 1867, C. A. Spina, Vienna; aria for bass (no. 8) and cavatina for tenor (no. 13)—*c.* 1832, A. Diabelli & Co., Vienna (nos. 4453 and 4454), with authentic pf. acc.; vocal score of the opera—1882, A. M. Schlesinger, Berlin (no. 7442, arranged by J. N. Fuchs); score—1892, Gesamtausgabe.

The first act was finished on 16th October at St. Pölten, the second begun there on 18th October and finished at Vienna on 2nd November 1821; the third finale was finished on 27th February 1822. An old MS. copy of the score, with clarini, tympani, and tromboni to the first finale, supplied by Ferdinand Schubert, is in the Nationalbibliothek, Vienna (Opern-Archiv, no. 236). A pf. score of the overture, not printed, written by Schubert in November 1822, is in the collection of Mr. Carl Hein, New York. After the opera was finished Schubert thought the overture too noisy, and intended to write another. The ' noisy ' one was performed in December 1823 for *Rosamunde* (797). The part of Troila is said to have been written for Johann Michael Vogl.

Literature. Liszt, *Neue Zeitschrift für Musik*, Leipzig, 1st September 1854.

—— ' Die Forelle ' (XX 327 (*e*)). See 550. October 1821.

733. Three Marches militaires for Piano Duet (Op. 51, IX 3).
c. 1822.

No. 2.
Allegro molto moderato

TRIO

No. 3.
Allegro moderato

TRIO

MS. Lost.
1ST ED. 7th August 1826, A. Diabelli & Co., Vienna (no. 2236).

734. Sixteen Ländler and two Écossaises for Pianoforte, called
' Wiener Damen-Ländler ' (Op. 67, XII 5). *c.* 1822.

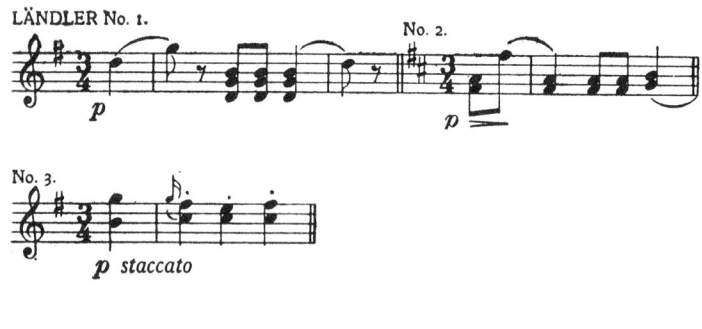

LÄNDLER No. 1.   No. 2.

No. 3.
p staccato

No. 4.   No. 5.

MS. Lost.
1ST ED. 12th February 1827, A. Diabelli & Co., Vienna (no. 2442), under the title 'Hommage aux belles Viennoises. Wiener Damen-Ländler.'

The title was not approved by Schubert. The date of publication is given according to the advertisement in the official *Wiener Zeitung*; the music, however, was printed before 17th December 1826 (according to Franz von Hartmann's diary).

735. Galop and Eight Écossaises (Op. 49, XII 23). *c.* 1822.

MS. Lost.

1ST PF. 6th January 1826, Saal zu den 7 Churfürsten, Pest (arranged for orchestra).

1ST ED. 21st November 1825, A. Diabelli & Co., Vienna (no. 2072), under the title 'Galoppe [*sic*] et Ecossaises'; the second issue (printed for Karl Lichtl in Pest) is entitled 'Galoppe und Ecossaisen . . . Aufgeführt in den Gesellschafts-Bällen im Saale zu den 7 Churfürsten in Pesth, im Carneval 1826.'

Karl Theodor Müller, Pest, reprinted the Galop, but his edition was confiscated; only one copy of it is preserved (City Archives, Budapest). Karl Gustav Förster, Breslau, also reprinted the Galop, as an addition to Herrmann's 'Favoritgalopp.' Both reprints were made in 1826.

Literature. K. Isoz in *Zenei Szemle*, Budapest, 1929, no 1.

736. 'Ihr Grab' (Richard Roos, i.e. Karl August Engelhardt), **Song** (XX 402). (?) 1822.

Sehr langsam

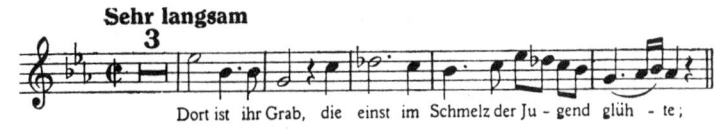

Dort ist ihr Grab, die einst im Schmelz der Ju-gend glüh-te;

MS. Frau Emma von Spaun, Vienna (the date has been cut off the MS.).

1ST ED. *c.* 1842, A. Diabelli & Co., Vienna (no. 7414), as no. 3 of *Nachlass*, book 36.

The poem was published at the end of 1821 in the *Taschenbuch zum geselligen Vergnügen auf das Jahr 1822* at Leipzig by Johann Friedrich Gleditsch. Sophie Müller mentions, in her diary, this song among other ' new ' songs brought to her by Schubert on 7th March 1825; but they were —except perhaps ' Der Einsame ' (800)—new only to her.

737. ' **An die Leier** ' (after Anacreon, by Bruchmann), **Song** (Op. 56, no. 2; XX 414). (?) 1822.

Geschwind

RECIT.

Ich will von A-treus Söh-nen,

MS. Lost.

1ST ED. Spring of 1826, A. Pennauer, Vienna (no. 259), as no. 2 of Op. 56 (book 2), dedicated by Schubert to Karl Pinterics. (Italian words were added to the second issue.)

The Italian text, possibly provided by Jakob Nikolaus Craigher de Jachelutta, was advertised in the title of the first edition of Op. 56, but the Italian words were omitted in the first issue—at least in book 2.

738. ' **Im Haine** ' (Bruchmann), **Song** (Op. 56, no. 3; XX 415). (?) 1822.

Mässig

Son-nen-strah-len durch die Tan-nen,

MS. Lost.

1ST ED. Spring of 1826, A. Pennauer, Vienna (no. 259), as no. 3 of Op. 56 (book 2), dedicated by Schubert to Karl Pinterics. (Italian words were added to the second issue.)

For the Italian text see note to 737.

739. Tantum ergo in C for Chorus, Orchestra, and Organ (Op. 45, XIV 6). 1822.

Adagio maestoso

Tan - tum er - go   sa - cra - men - tum   ve - ne - re - mur cer - nu - i

MS. Lost.
1ST PF. 8th September 1825, Maria-Trost-Kirche, Vienna.
1ST ED. (in parts) Beginning of September 1825, A. Diabelli & Co., Vienna (no. 1899), as Op. 45.

A copy of the parts, written by Ferdinand Schubert, which differs slightly from the printed version, is preserved in the archives of the Gesellschaft der Musikfreunde, Vienna. For information concerning an arrangement of this work by Ferdinand Schubert, see *Wiener Allgemeine Musik-Zeitung*, Vienna, 14th December 1847, p. 518.

740. ' **Frühlingsgesang**,' called ' **Frühlingslied** ' (Schober), **Quartet, T.T.B.B., with Pianoforte accompaniment**, second version (Op. 16, no. 1; XVI 7). 1822.

Etwas geschwind

Schmü - cket die Lo - cken mit   duf - ti - gen Krän - zen

Heiter, doch nicht zu schnell

Drum schmü-cke die Lo-cken mit   bräut-li-chen Krän - zen

MS. Conservatoire, Paris (Ph.).
1ST PF. 7th April 1822, Kärntnertor-Theater, Vienna (unaccompanied).
1ST ED. 9th October 1823, Cappi & Diabelli, Vienna (no. 1175), as no. 1 of Op. 16, with pf. or guitar acc. *ad libitum*.

The guitar acc. is spurious. For the first version, without acc., see **709**.

741. ' **Sei mir gegrüsst!** ' (Rückert), **Song** (Op. 20, no. 1; XX 400). 1822.

Langsam

O du Ent - riss'- ne mir   und mei-nem Kus - se!

MS. Lost.

IST ED. 10th April 1823, Sauer & Leidesdorf, Vienna (no. 231), as no. 1 of Op. 20, dedicated by Schubert to Frau Justine von Bruchmann.

The date 1821, given by Nottebohm according to the Witteczek Collection, is doubtful. Schubert's other Rückert songs were written in 1823 (775–8), and Rückert's cycle, *Oestliche Rosen*, which contains these five poems, was published with the date 1822 (probably issued at the end of 1821). Since Schubert apparently refers to the songs, later published as Op. 20, in his letter to Josef Hüttenbrenner dated 31st October 1822, it seems feasible that this song was written before the other four Rückert songs. The G.A. dates it at the end of 1821. The poem has no title; it was reprinted in Rückert's *Gesammelte Gedichte*, 1837, as a ghazal.

742. '**Der Wachtelschlag**' ('Il canto della Quaglia,' Samuel Friedrich Sauter), **Song** (Op. 68, XX 401). 1822.

MS. Lost.

IST ED. 30th July 1822, as a supplement to the *Wiener Zeitschrift für Kunst*, etc., Vienna (in type).

The first edition was reprinted at Stuttgart as early as 1826. The song was republished as Op. 68, by A. Diabelli & Co., Vienna (no. 2451), on 16th May 1827, with German and Italian words, the latter possibly provided by Jakob Nikolaus Craigher de Jachelutta. It is said erroneously that the poem, set by Beethoven much earlier, was translated from Metastasio. Sauter, in fact, based his poem on the anonymous 'Wachtelschlag' (or Wachtelwacht') from the collection *Des Knaben Wunderhorn* (two versions on p. 159 of vol. i, 1806). Sauter's poem is dated 23rd June 1796, and was published in K. Lang's *Taschenbuch für häusliche Freuden*, Heilbronn, 1799, p. 250.

743. '**Selige Welt**' (Senn), **Song** (Op. 23, no. 2; XX 406). 1822.

MS. Fair copy, undated—Preussische Staatsbibliothek, Berlin (together with 744 and 754).

IST ED. 4th August 1823, Sauer & Leidesdorf, Vienna (no. 367), as no. 2 of Op. 23.

The poem is not to be found in Senn's collected poems (Innsbruck, 1838).

744. '**Schwanengesang**' ('Wie klag' ich's aus,' Senn), **Song** (Op. 23, no. 3; XX 407). 1822.

MS. Fair copy—Preussische Staatsbibliothek, Berlin (together with 743 and 754).

IST ED. 4th August 1823, Sauer & Leidesdorf, Vienna (no. 367), as no. 3 of Op. 23 (corrupt).

The poem is printed in Senn's *Gedichte*, Innsbruck, 1838, p. 15, with the note 'In Musik gesetzt von Fr. Schubert.'

745. '**Die Rose**' (from Friedrich von Schlegel's 'Abendröte'), **Song**, two versions (Op. 73, XX 408 (*a*) and (*b*)). 1822.

MS. (*a*) Lost; (*b*) Frau Emma von Spaun, Vienna; another MS. —Stadtbibliothek, Vienna.

IST ED. (*a*) 7th May 1822, as a supplement to the *Wiener Zeitschrift für Kunst*, etc., Vienna (in type); (*b*) 1895, Gesamtausgabe.

The first version was republished as Op. 73 by A. Diabelli, Vienna (no. 2490), with a list of Schubert's works, including Op. 74. In the other MS. of the second version (Stadtbibliothek) the words are written by another hand.

746. '**Am See**' ('In des Sees Wogenspiele,' Bruchmann), **Song** (XX 422). 1822–3.

[Musical notation: Mässig 6/8, with lyrics "In des Se-es Wo-gen-spie-le"]

MS. Hugo Neuburger, Los Angeles.

1ST ED. 21st April 1831, A. Diabelli & Co., Vienna (no. 3706), as no. 2 of *Nachlass*, book 9.

Nottebohm states that this song is 'said to have been written March 1817 (?).' There is no evidence for this statement, which was not suggested by Witteczek.

747. **'Geist der Liebe'** ('Der Abend schleiert Flur und Hain,' Matthisson), **Quartet, T.T.B.B.** (Op. 11, no. 3; XVI 6). January 1822.

[Musical notation: Etwas bewegt 6/8, with lyrics "p Der A-bend schlei-ert Flur und Hain in-"]

[Musical notation: Etwas geschwind 3/4, with lyrics "O Geist der Lie-be, füh-re du dem Jüng-ling die Er-kor-ne zu,"]

MS. (without acc.)—Gesellschaft der Musikfreunde, Vienna.

1ST PF. 3rd March 1822, Redoutensaal, Vienna, without acc.; 2nd pf.—26th May 1822, Kärntnertor-Theater, Vienna, with pf. acc.; 3rd pf.—(?) 27th August 1822, Theater an der Wien, Vienna, with guitar acc. (the Quartet is not named on the theatre bill).

1ST ED. 12th June 1822, Cappi & Diabelli, Vienna (no. 1019), as no. 3 of Op. 11, dedicated by Schubert to Josef Barth.

The pf. acc. is dubious, the guitar acc. spurious. For the setting of this poem as a solo song, see 414.

748. **'Am Geburtstage des Kaisers'** (Deinhardstein), **for S.A.T.B.** **(Soli and Chorus) and Orchestra** (Op. posth. 157, XVII 3). January 1822.

[Musical notation: Moderato, with lyrics "Steig em-por, um-blüht von Se-gen,"]

MS. Gesellschaft der Musikfreunde, Vienna.
IST PF. 11th February 1822, Theresianum, Vienna (conductor, Leopold Sonnleithner).
IST ED. Early in 1822, privately printed.

Only the proofs of the first edition are preserved (Anthony van Hoboken, Lausanne). They consist of a folio sheet of three lithographed pages in full score, with pf. score by Josef Hüttenbrenner, who also corrected the proofs. They were entitled, erroneously, 'Am Namensfeste [instead of Geburtsfeste] Se. Majestät des Kaisers' (Franz I). The text differs slightly in Schubert's version, beginning 'Hoch entzückt, im reichen Segen, Den du spendest jeden Tag.' Deinhardstein's original title was 'Volkslied'; his model was Lorenz Leopold Haschka's text for Haydn's Austrian 'Volkshymne.' The work was printed again, in 1848, by A. Diabelli & Co., Vienna (no. 8873), as Op. 157, under the title 'Constitutionslied.' For this publication the author completely rewrote the first stanza and made alterations to three others, at the same time adapting the poem for the reign of Emperor Franz Josef I. In the MS. only the first stanza is written by Schubert.

749. '**Herrn Josef Spaun,**' called '**Epistel**' or '**Sendschreiben**' **an den Assessor Spaun in Linz** (Matthäus von Collin), **Song** (XX 588). January 1822.

MS. Walter Slezak, Hollywood.
IST ED. *c.* 1848, A. Diabelli & Co., Vienna (no. 8823), as *Nachlass*, book 46.

Collin was a cousin of Spaun's. The music is a parody of Italian opera style.

—— '**Naturgenuss**' (XVI 8). See 422. February 1822.

—— '**Alfonso und Estrella**' (XV 9). See 732. 27th February 1822.

750. **Tantum ergo in D for Chorus, Orchestra, and Organ** (XIV 8). 20th March 1822.

MS. Conservatoire, Paris (Ph.).
IST ED. 1888, Gesamtausgabe.

There is an old MS. copy in the Peters-Kirche, Vienna.

751. 'Die Liebe hat gelogen' (Platen), **Song** (Op. 23, no. 1; XX 410). Spring 1822.

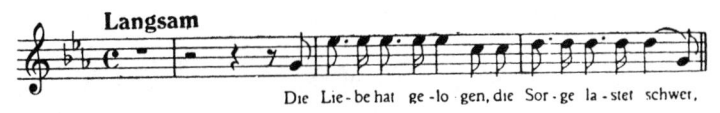

Langsam

Die Lie-be hat ge-lo-gen, die Sor-ge la-stet schwer.

MS. Unknown; former owner—August, Graf Platen von Hallermünde, Erlangen (1822).

1ST ED. 4th August 1823, Sauer & Leidesdorf, Vienna (no. 367), as no. 1 of Op. 23.

According to Franz von Bruchmann's letter to the poet, written in Vienna on 17th April 1822, and which accompanied the MS., the song was written before that date.

752. 'Nachtviolen,' called 'Nachtviolenlied' (Mayrhofer), **Song** (XX 403). April 1822.

Langsam

Nacht - vi - o - len. Nacht - vi - o - len!

MS. Rough draft, first half (together with the last bars of 755)—Frau Alberta von Hofer, Konstanz (c. 1906); second half (together with 754)—Nationalbibliothek, Vienna.

1ST ED. 1872, J. P. Gotthard, Vienna (no. 344), as no. 20 of forty songs.

The first edition does not quite correspond with the MS.

753. 'Heliopolis,' called 'Aus "Heliopolis" I' ('Im kalten rauhen Norden,' Mayrhofer), **Song** (Op. 65, no. 3; XX 404). April 1822.

Mässig

Im kal - ten, rau - hen Nor - den

MS. The last bars only, without date (together with the first half of 573)—Frau Alberta von Hofer, Konstanz (c. 1906).

1ST ED. 24th November 1826, Cappi & Czerny, Vienna (no. 221), as no. 3 of Op. 65.

754. 'Im Hochgebirge,' called ' Aus " Heliopolis " II ' (' Fels auf Felsen hingewälzet,' Mayrhofer), **Song** (XX 405).   April 1822.

Geschwind und kräftig

Fels   auf   Fel - sen   hin . ge - wäl - zet.

MS. Rough draft (together with the end of 752)—Nationalbibliothek, Vienna; fair copy (together with 743 and 744)—Preussische Staatsbibliothek, Berlin.

1ST ED. *c.* 1842, A. Diabelli & Co., Vienna (no. 7415), as no. 1 of *Nachlass,* book 37.

Both MSS. are entitled ' Heliopolis Nr. 12, 'which cannot be explained. The title applies only to the other poem (753), where the reference to the ' City of the Sun ' (' Sonnenstadt ') occurs. In his collected poems, 1824, the author called the poem ' Im Hochgebirge,' and in the second edition of these poems, ed. by Ernst von Feuchtersleben in 1843, it is, together with two other poems, entitled ' An Franz,' which may refer to Schubert, or, more likely, to Franz von Schober. In the autograph collection of Mayrhofer's poems (Stadtbibliothek, Vienna, formerly in Schober's possession) the poem is dated September–October 1821. As mentioned in the *Revisionsbericht,* Schubert's rough draft corresponds exactly with the fair copy.

755. Mass in A minor.   Fragment.   Not printed.   May 1822.

Andante (Chorus and Orchestra)

Ky - ri - e   e - lei - - son,

MS. (41 bars) Stadtbibliothek, Vienna.

The sketch, indicated as composed ' Für meinen Bruder Ferdinand,' is written only as far as the beginning of ' Christe eleison ' in the Kyrie.

—— **' Einsamkeit '** (XX 339).   See 620.   June 1822.

756. ' **Du liebst mich nicht** ' (Platen), **Song,** two versions (Op. 59, no. 1; XX 409 (*a*) and (*b*)).   July 1822.

a   *Mässig*

Mein   Herz   ist   zer - ris - sen.

Mässig

Mein Herz ist zer - ris sen.

MS. (*a*) Benedictine Abbey, Kremsmünster, Upper Austria; (*b*) lost.

IST ED. (*a*) 1895, Gesamtausgabe; (*b*) 21st September 1826, Sauer & Leidesdorf, Vienna (no. 932), as no. 1 of Op. 59 (the opus number inserted by hand).

The MS. (*a*) is entitled ' Du liebst mich nicht. Ghasele . . . July 1822.

757. ' **Gott in der Natur** ' (Ewald Christian von Kleist) **for two Sopranos and two Altos with Pianoforte accompaniment** (Op. 133, XVIII 3). August 1822.

Maestoso, Adagio molto

Gross ist der Herr. gross ist der Herr!

Allegro giusto

f Lobt den Ge - wal - ti - gen. den gro - ssen Herrn.

MS. Stadtbibliothek, Vienna.
IST PF. 8th March 1827, Musikverein, Vienna.
IST ED. *c*. 1838, A. Diabelli & Co., Vienna (no. 6264), as Op. 133.

In Schubert's MS., in the first edition, and even in the G.A., the poem is attributed to Gleim. In fact, it is the ' Hymne ' from Kleist's *Oden*, containing seventeen stanzas, of which Schubert, after making some alterations, used only four. The work was written for the pupils of Fräulein Anna Fröhlich (cf. 706).

—— **Mass in A flat** (XIII 5). See 678. September 1822.

758. ' **Todesmusik** ' (Schober), **Song** (Op. 108, no. 2; XX 411). September 1822.

Langsam, feierlich

In des To - des Fei - er - stun - de.

MS. Wiener Schubertbund, Vienna (in G flat).
1ST ED. 28th January 1829, M. J. Leidesdorf, Vienna (no. 1102), as no. 2 of Op. 93, later corrected to Op. 108.

The first edition is in G; the MS. and a copy with autograph title (song book of Frau Franziska Tremier—Stadtbibliothek, Vienna) are in G flat. The title-page of the first edition bears the misprint ' Todeskuss,' but on the first page of the music the song is entitled ' Todes Musick.' The song was advertised at Easter 1828 (as Op. 93), but was not published until after Schubert's death.

—— ' **Harfenspieler III** ' (XX 258). See 480. Autumn 1822.

759. Symphony in B minor, called **The Unfinished** (I 8). Full score begun 30th October 1822.

MS. Score and sketches—Gesellschaft der Musikfreunde, Vienna (fascimile published by Drei-Masken-Verlag, Munich, 1924).
1ST PF. 17th December 1865, Musikvereinssaal, Vienna (conductor, Johann Herbeck).
1ST ED. December 1866, C. A. Spina, Vienna (no. 19138—score, 19165—parts).

The score contains nine bars of a Scherzo. The sketches for all three movements, in the form of a pianoforte score, are printed in the *Revisionsbericht*; they were not sent by Schubert to Graz, as was the score, in 1823, but both were brought together again by Nikolaus Dumba, who left the

MS. to the present owners. The version of the G.A. was revised (by Heinrich Schenker and O. E. D.) for the 1927 issue of the pocket score, published by Wiener Philharmonischer Verlag (reprinted by Boosey & Hawkes, London, 1941). Anselm Hüttenbrenner arranged the work in 1853 for pf. duet (MS). August Ludwig was the first to write two supplementary movements; Frank Merrick also composed two additional movements in 1928.

Literature. O. E. D., ' The Riddle of Schubert's Unfinished Symphony,' the *Music Review*, Cambridge, February 1940; Hans Gal, ' The Riddle of Schubert's Unfinished Symphony,' the *Music Review*, February 1941; and T. C. L. Pritchard, ' The Unfinished Symphony,' the *Music Review*, February 1942.

760. Fantasia in C, called **Wanderer Fantasia, for Pianoforte** (Op. 15, XI 1). November 1822.

MS. (with the dedication in French)—Frank Black, New York.
1ST PF. (?) 1832, Musikverein, Vienna (Karl Maria von Bocklet).
1ST ED. 24th February 1823, Cappi & Diabelli, Vienna (no. 1174), as Op. 15, dedicated by Schubert to Emanuel, Edler von Liebenberg de Zsittin.

The second movement, Adagio, is based on the song ' Der Wanderer ' (493). The first of the so-called misprints of the first edition, noted in the *Revisionsbericht*, is not a mistake of the engraver; the bar in question corresponds with Schubert's MS.

Literature. D. F. Tovey, *Essays in Musical Analysis*, London, 1936, vol. iv, pp. 70–3.

— **Overture to ' Alfonso und Estrella.' Arranged for Pianoforte Solo.** Not printed. See 732. November 1822.

— **' Frühlingsglaube '** (XX 380 (*b*)). See 685. November 1822.

761. ' Schatzgräbers Begehr ' (Schober), **Song,** two versions (Op. 23, no. 4; XX 412 (*a*) and (*b*)). November 1822.

a Gehend

In tief-ster Er-de— ruht ein alt Ge-setz

b In mässiger Bewegung

In tief-ster Er-de— ruht ein alt Ge-setz.

MS. (*a*) Lost; (*b*) fair copy (formerly in the album of Johann Vesque von Püttlingen, whose pseudonym as a composer was J. Hoven)—William Kux, Chur, Switzerland.

1ST ED. (*a*) 4th August 1823, Sauer & Leidesdorf, Vienna (no. 367), as no. 4 of Op. 23; (*b*) 1895, Gesamtausgabe (Series XX, vol. vii, Supplement, pp. 187–9).

The MS. (*b*) was inserted in the album by its original owner.

762. ' Schwestergruss ' (Bruchmann), **Song** (XX 413). November 1822.

Langsam

Im Mon-den-schein' wall' ich auf und ab.

MS. Stadtbibliothek, Vienna.
1ST ED. 27th July 1833, A. Diabelli & Co., Vienna (no. 4271), as no. 1 of *Nachlass*, book 23.

The poem was written on the occasion of the death of Sybilla von Bruchmann, sister of the author, 18th July 1820.

763. ' Geburtstagshymne,' or **' Hymne zur Genesung des Herrn Ritter,** called **'Des Tages Weihe'** ('Schicksalslenker, blicke nieder,' author unknown), **Quartet, S.A.T.B.,** with **Pianoforte accompaniment** (Op. posth. 146, XVII 11). 22nd November 1822.

Larghetto

p Schick - sals - len - ker.

MS. Lost.

1ST PF. (in public) 1st February 1861, Weimar ('Des Tages Weihe').

1ST ED. *c.* 1841, A. Diabelli & Co., Vienna (no. 7140), as Op. 146 under the title 'Des Tages Weihe. Hymne zur Namens-oder Geburtsfeier . . . Kindliches Dankopfer No. 6,' with new words and additional parts for violin and violoncello acc.

This Quartet (not a trio, as suggested by Kreissle, p. 608) was ordered by Fräulein Anna Fröhlich on behalf of Barbara, Freiin von Geymüller, who paid Schubert fifty gulden Viennese currency. Nothing is known about Herr Ritter.

764. '**Der Musensohn**' (Goethe), **Song,** two versions (Op. 92, no. 1; XX 416 (*a*) and (*b*)). Beginning of December 1822.

a **Ziemlich lebhaft**

Durch Feld und Wald zu schwei-fen.

b **Ziemlich lebhaft**

Durch Feld und Wald zu schwei-fen.

MS. (*a*) Preussische Staatsbibliothek, Berlin (together with 765–7); (*b*) lost.

1ST ED. (*a*) 1895, Gesamtausgabe; (*b*) 11th July 1828, M. J. Leidesdorf, Vienna (no. 1014), as no. 1 of Op. 92 (Op. 87 in the heading), dedicated by Schubert to Frau Josefine von Franck.

MS. (*a*) was written at the beginning of the month, since it is dated December 1822, and already mentioned, with 765–7, in Schubert's letter of 7th December 1822.

765. '**An die Entfernte**' (Goethe), **Song** (XX 417). Beginning of December 1822.

[Musical incipit: Langsam — "So hab' ich wirk-lich dich ver-lo-ren?"]

MS. Preussische Staatsbibliothek, Berlin (together with 764, 766, and 767).

1ST ED. 1868, Wilhelm Müller, Berlin (no. 13), as no. 4 of six songs (ed. by Franz Espagne).

766. 'Am Flusse' (Goethe), Song, second version (XX 418). Beginning of December 1822.

[Musical incipit: Mässig 4/4 — "Ver-flie-sset, viel-ge-lieb-te Lie-der,"]

MS. Preussische Staatsbibliothek, Berlin (together with 764, 765, and 767).

1ST ED. 1872, J. P. Gotthard, Vienna (no. 326), as no. 3 of forty songs, this song dedicated by the publisher to Julius Stockhausen.

For the first version, see 160.

767. 'Willkommen und Abschied' (Goethe), Song, two versions (Op. 56, no. 1; XX 419 (*a*) and (*b*)). Beginning of December 1822.

[Musical incipit *a*: Geschwind — "Es schlug mein Herz, ge-schwind zu Pfer-de!"]

[Musical incipit *b*: Geschwind — "Es schlug mein Herz, ge-schwind zu Pfer-de!"]

MS. (*a*) Preussische Staatsbibliothek, Berlin (together with nos. 764–6); (*b*) lost.

1ST ED. (*a*) 1895, Gesamtausgabe; (*b*) spring of 1826, A. Pennauer, Vienna (no. 258), as no. 1 (book 1) of Op. 56, dedicated by Schubert to Karl Pinterics (with Italian words added, possibly supplied by Jakob Nikolaus Craigher de Jachelutta).

768. ' **Wandrers Nachtlied** ' (II. ' Ueber allen Gipfeln,' Goethe), Song (Op. 96, no. 3; XX 420). *c.* 1823.

Langsam

Ü - ber al - len Gip - feln ist Ruh',

MS. Lost.
1ST ED. 23rd June 1827, as a supplement to the *Wiener Zeitschrift für Kunst*, etc., Vienna (together with 546, in type).
The song was republished as no. 3 of Op. 96 (Lithographisches Institut, Vienna, whose manager was then Franz von Schober) in the summer of 1828, dedicated by Schubert to Karoline, Fürstin von Kinsky, *née* Freiin von Kerpen (signed and the opus number added by Schubert). The dedication is printed in brown ink. H. A. Probst, Leipzig (no. 431), published on 12th December 1828 an unauthorized reprint as no. 4 of a spurious Op. 101 (the opus number inserted by hand), containing four songs which were published earlier in the *Wiener Zeitschrift*.

— **Écossaise** for Pianoforte (Op. 18, XII 2, Écossaise no. 8), transposed from B minor to G sharp minor with note values doubled, as an album leaf for Fräulein Seraphine Schellmann, Steyr, *c.* 1823.
MS. Dr. Marx, Bethlen, near Bielefeld, Germany.
1ST ED. See 145.
Reproduced in facsimile in *Franz Schubert, Sein Leben in Bildern*, p. 46 (ed. by O. E. D.).

769. Two **Deutsche Tänze** for Pianoforte (XII 18). (?) 1823.

No. 1.

pp Mit der Verschiebung

No. 2.

p

MS. No. 1 (together with Op. 33, 783, nos. 1 and 2, and Op. 127, 146, no. 2, dated 1824)—Heinrich Hinterberger, Vienna (1937); nos. 1 and 2, dated January 1824—unknown; former owner—Alfred Rothberger, Vienna.
1ST ED. No. 1—1889, Gesamtausgabe; no. 2—in vol. i of the almanac *Album musical*, p. 25, as waltz, Sauer & Leidesdorf, Vienna (no. 490), 19th December 1823; reprinted in the collection *Guirlandes*, book 3, 9th December 1825, by the same publishers.

770. 'Drang in die Ferne' (Leitner), Song (Op. 71, XX 424). (?) 1823.

Etwas geschwind (♩ = 76)

Va - ter, du glaubst es nicht.

MS. Lost.

1ST ED. 25th March 1823, as a supplement to the *Wiener Zeitschrift für Kunst*, etc., Vienna (in type).

The poem, sent by Leitner to the *Wiener Zeitschrift*, was set to music by Schubert on the suggestion of the editor, Johann Schickh, who published both together. The words differ considerably from the version in Leitner's collected poems (first and second editions). The song was republished as Op. 71 by A. Diabelli & Co., Vienna (no. 2486), on 2nd March 1827 (corrupt). Schubert's friend, Albert Stadler, published his setting of the same poem as Op. 2 with Friedrich Eurich in Linz.

771. 'Der Zwerg' (Matthäus von Collin), Song (Op. 22, no. 1; XX 425). (?) 1823.

Nicht zu geschwind

Im trü - ben Licht ver-schwin-den schon die Ber - ge.

MS. Lost.

1ST PF. 21st December 1826, Musikvereinssaal, Vienna.

1ST ED. 27th May 1823, Sauer & Leidesdorf, Vienna (no. 357, plate no. 337 in the first issue), as no. 1 of Op. 22, dedicated by Schubert to the author.

The first issue has no marks of expression; these were supplied and the plate number corrected to 357 in later issues. The title was engraved by Herr Fischer. Kreissle thought the poem to be a fragment of another, entitled 'Treubruch,' and ascribed it, erroneously, to Matthäus's famous brother, Heinrich von Collin. Josef von Spaun mentions this song among those written between 1820 and 1822.

772. 'Wehmut' ('Wenn ich durch Wald und Fluren geh,' Matthäus von Collin), Song (Op. 22, no. 2; XX 426). (?) 1823.

Langsam

Wenn ich durch Wald und Flu - ren geh'.

MS. Lost.

1ST ED. 27th May 1823, Sauer & Leidesdorf, Vienna (no. 357), as no. 2 of Op. 22, dedicated by Schubert to the author.

For the errors in the first issue, see 771.

773. **Overture to 'Alfonso und Estrella,'** arranged for **Piano Duet** (Op. 69). 1823.

MS. Étienne Charavay, Paris (sale, 5th May 1890).

1ST ED. 20th February 1826, Sauer & Leidesdorf, Vienna (no. 860), as Op. 52 (later corrected to Op. 69), dedicated by Schubert to Fräulein Anna Hönig.

The later issue, published by A. Diabelli & Co., Vienna (no. 3542), c. 1830, has the correct opus number 69. This arrangement was omitted in error from the G.A. For the original version and the arrangement for pf. solo, see 732.

774. **'Auf dem Wasser zu singen'** (Stolberg), **Song** (Op. 72, XX 428). 1823.

MS. Lost.

1ST ED. 30th December 1823, as a supplement to the *Wiener Zeitschrift für Kunst*, etc., Vienna (in type).

This song was republished as Op. 72 by A. Diabelli & Co., Vienna (no. 2487), on 2nd March 1827 (corrupt). The poem was originally entitled 'Lied auf dem Wasser zu singen, für meine Agnes.'

775. **'Dass sie hier gewesen'** (Rückert), **Song** (Op. 59, no. 2; XX 453). 1823.

[musical incipit: Sehr langsam, 2/4 — "Dass der Ost-wind Düf-te"]

MS. Lost.

1ST ED. 21st September 1826, Sauer & Leidesdorf, Vienna (no. 932), as no. 2 of Op. 59 (the opus number inserted by hand).

The poem had no title when it was published by the author in his book, *Oestliche Rosen*, 1821 (written 1819–20). It was not reprinted in his *Gesammelte Gedichte*, 1834 onwards.

776. '**Du bist die Ruh**,' called '**Kehr ein bei mir**' (Rückert), **Song** (Op. 59, no. 3; XX 454). 1823.

[musical incipit: Langsam, 3/8 — "Du bist die Ruh, der Frie-de mild."]

MS. Lost.

1ST ED. 21st September 1826, Sauer & Leidesdorf, Vienna (no. 932), as no. 3 of Op. 59 (the opus number inserted by hand).

The poem, originally without title (cf. 775), was later called 'Kehr ein bei mir' when the author included this and other poems from his book *Oestliche Rosen* in his *Gesammelte Gedichte*, vol. i, 1834 onwards.

777. '**Lachen und Weinen**,' called '**Lachens und Weinens Grund**' (Rückert), **Song** (Op. 59, no. 4; XX 455). 1823.

[musical incipit: Etwas geschwind, 2/4 — "La-chen und Wei-nen zu jeg-li-cher Stun-de"]

MS. Lost.

1ST ED. 21st September 1826, Sauer & Leidesdorf, Vienna (no. 932), as no. 4 of Op. 59 (the opus number inserted by hand).

The poem, originally without title (cf. 775), was later called 'Lachens und Weinens Grund' when the author included this and other poems from his book *Oestliche Rosen* in his *Gesammelte Gedichte*, vol. i, 1834 onwards.

778. '**Greisengesang**,' called '**Vom künftigen Alter**' (Rückert), **Song** (Op. 60, no. 1; XX 456). 1823.

Mässig, langsam

Der Frost hat mir be-rei-fet des Hau-ses Dach;

MS. Fair copy—Stadtbibliothek, Vienna.
1ST ED. 10th June 1826, Cappi & Czerny, Vienna (no. 192), as no. 1 of Op. 60.

The poem, originally without title (cf. 775), was later called 'Vom künftigen Alter' when the author included this poem from his book *Oestliche Rosen* in his *Gesammelte Gedichte*, 1837, as a ghazal, with four verses added (see *Revisionsbericht*). Josef von Spaun mentions this song among those written between 1820 and 1822. The first edition commences 'Der Ernst' instead of 'Der Frost,' and in the first issue there are no tempo indications.

779. **Thirty-four Valses sentimentales for Pianoforte** (Op. 50, XII 4). 1823 (?–1824).

No. 1.
No. 2.
No. 3.
No. 4.
No. 5.
No. 6.
No. 7.
No. 8.
No. 9.
No. 10.

No. 11.
f
No. 12.
p
No. 13.
Zart
p
No. 14.
p
3
No. 15.
p
No. 16
ff
fz
No. 17.
p
No. 18.
p
No. 19.
p
No. 20
p
No. 21.
p
No. 22.
p
No. 23.
p
No. 24.
p
No. 25.
No. 26.
p
No. 27.
p
No. 28.
mf

No. 29.

No. 30.

No. 31.

No. 32.

No. 33.

No. 34.

No. 1. (Variant)

No. 2. (Variant)

No. 4. (Variant)

No. 8. (Variant)

No. 9. (Variant)

No. 12. (Variant)

No. 33. (Variant)

MS. Nos. 1–4, 33, and 34—Stadtbibliothek, Vienna (together with XII 16, 973).

1ST ED. 21st November 1825, A. Diabelli & Co., Vienna (nos. 2073 and 2074, in two books).

The title was probably given by the publishers, who seem to have acquired the work (at least the first half of it) before April 1823. In the undated MS. nos. 34 and 33 are numbered as nos. 7 and 8. Variants to nos. 1, 2, 4, 8, 9, 12, 14 (very slight), and 33 are printed in the G.A., Series XII, Supplement, pp. 158–61. The G.A. dates no. 8 from February 1823; the autograph of this valse, however, seems to be lost.

780. Six Moments musicaux for Pianoforte (Op. 94, XI 4). 1823 (?–1828).

BOOK 1.
No. 1. **Moderato**

No. 2. **Andantino**

No. 3. **Allegro moderato**

BOOK 2.
No. 4. **Moderato**

No. 5. **Allegro vivace**

No. 6. **Allegretto**

MS. Lost.
1ST ED. Spring 1828, M. J. Leidesdorf, Vienna (nos. 1043 and 1044, in two books), under the title *Moments musicals*.

No. 3 was published as 'Air russe' in the almanac *Album musical*, vol. i, Sauer & Leidesdorf, Vienna (no. 490), 19th December 1823; no. 6 as 'Plaintes d'un Troubadour,' in *Album musical*, vol. ii (no. 590), 11th December 1824, and reprinted in *Guirlandes*, first book, Sauer & Leidesdorf, 9th December 1825. The title *Moments musicals* was probably also an invention of the publishers.

—— **Two Écossaises for Pianoforte** (Op. 33, XII 3, Écossaises nos. 1–2). See 783. *c.* January 1823.

MS. No. 2 (together with eleven other Écossaises, dated January 1823, see 781)—Gesellschaft der Musikfreunde, Vienna.
1ST ED. See 783.

781. Twelve (Eleven) Écossaises for Pianoforte (XII 25). January 1823.

No. 1. No. 2.

No. 3. No. 4.

No. 5. No. 6.

MS. (eleven Écossaises and Op. 33, no. 2, see preceding entry)—Gesellschaft der Musikfreunde, Vienna.

1ST ED. Nos. 3 and 6—21st February 1824, Sauer & Leidesdorf, Vienna (no. 602), in the collection *Nouvelles Galoppes favorites et Écossaises* by Schubert and M. J. Leidesdorf (in this collection no. 3 (E flat minor) is given the no. 7 (E minor), and no. 6 (G flat), the no. 9 (G)); nos. 1, 2, 4, 5, 7–11—1889, Gesamtausgabe.

Another Écossaise, printed as no. 8 in the above-mentioned collection, was republished in 1912 (782).

782. Écossaise in D for Pianoforte. January 1823.

MS. Lost.
1ST ED. 21st February 1824, as no. 8 of the Écossaises in *Nouvelles Galoppes favorites et Écossaises*, by Schubert and M. J. Leidesdorf, Sauer & Leidesdorf, Vienna (no. 602).

Reprinted in *Die Musik*, Berlin, 1st September 1912, vol. xi, no. 23, Supplement, p. 3 (ed. by O. E. D.); cf. no. 781.

783. Sixteen Deutsche Tänze and two Écossaises for Pianoforte (Op. 33, XII 3). January 1823–November 1824.

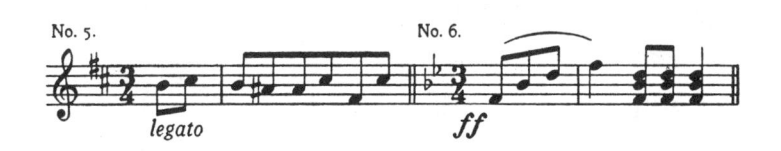

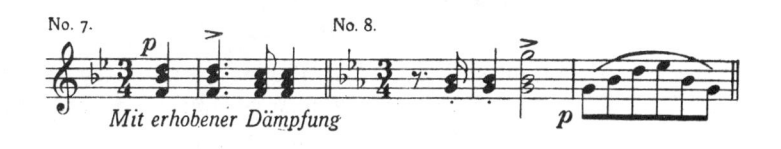

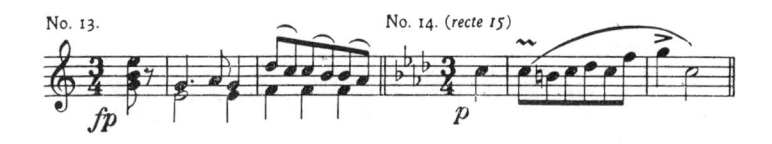

DEUTSCHE TÄNZE

No. 15. (recte 14)

No 16.

No. 6. (Variant)

ÉCOSSAISES
No. 1.　　　　　　　　No. 2.

MS. See 366, 769, entry before 781; 790, 814, first entry before 821, and 975; the MSS. of the *Deutsche Tänze* nos. 3-5, 7, 10-11, 13-15, and of the Écossaise no. 1—lost.

1ST ED. 8th January 1825, Cappi & Co., Vienna (no. 45), as Op. 33.

There is also a variant to no. 10 of the *Deutsche Tänze*; see 790.

—— '**Zweites Offertorium**' ('Salve Regina') in **F** (XIV 2). See 223. 28th January 1823.

784. Sonata in A minor for Pianoforte (Op. posth. 143, X 8). February 1823.

Allegro giusto

Andante

Allegro vivace

MS. Otto Taussig, Malmö.
1ST ED. 1839, A. Diabelli & Co., Vienna (no. 6566), dedicated by the publishers to Felix Mendelssohn-Bartholdy.

—— **Valse,** Op. 50, no. 8 (XII 4). See 779. February 1823.

—— **Walzer,** Op. 127, no. 17 (XII 8). See 146. February 1823.

785. ' **Der zürnende Barde** ' (Bruchmann), **Song** (XX 421). February 1823.

Geschwind, kraftvoll

Wer wagt's, wer wagt's, wer wagt's.

MS. William Kux, Chur, Switzerland.
1ST ED. 21st April 1831, A. Diabelli & Co., Vienna (no. 3706), as no. 1 of *Nachlass*, book 9.

786. ' **Viola** ' (Schober), **Song** (Op. posth. 123, XX 423). March 1823.

Mässig

Schnee-glöck-lein, o Schnee-glöck-lein.

MS. Rough draft—lost; fair copy (the third, and last, part written by another hand)—Dr. Franz Roehn, Los Angeles (Ph.).
1ST ED. 26th November 1830, A. Pennauer, Vienna (no. 484), as Op. 123.

This poem and ' Vergissmeinnicht,' which Schubert set to music in May 1823 (792), were both entitled ' Blumenballade ' by the author.
Literature. D. F. Tovey, *Chamber Music,* London, 1944, pp. 137–41.

787. ' **Die Verschworenen,**' later called ' **Der häusliche Krieg,**' **Singspiel**—after Aristophanes' comedies, ' Ecclesiazusae ' and ' Lysistrata '—**in one Act** by I. F. Castelli (XV 6). (? March–) April 1823.

No. 1a. DUET (Sopr. and Ten.)
Allegro
Sie ist's! Er ist's!

No. 1b. DUET (2 Sopr.)
Allegro
Sie ist's! Er ist's!

No. 2. ROMANCE (Sopr.)
Ich schlei-che bang' und still her-um,

No. 3. ENSEMBLE (3 Sopr. and Female Chorus)
Allegro moderato
Ihr habt auf Eu-re Burg ent-bo-ten die

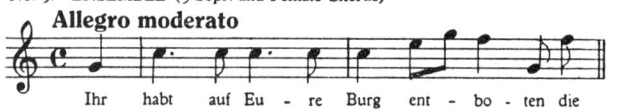

No. 4. CONSPIRACY CHORUS (Sopr. and Female Chorus)
Allegro
Ja, wir schwö-ren,

No. 5. MARCH & CHORUS (Male Chorus)
Allegro moderato
Vor-ü-ber ist die Zeit,

No. 6. ENSEMBLE (Sopr., Bass and Male Chorus)
Allegro moderato
Ver-rä-te-rei hab ich ent-deckt,

No. 7. CHORUS OF KNIGHTS AND LADIES
Andantino
Will-kom-men, schön will-kom-men,

No. 8. DUET (Sopr. and Ten.)
Andantino

Ich muss sie fin- den

No. 9. ARIETTA (Bass)
Allegro moderato

Ich ha - be ge - wagt und ha - be ge - strit - ten,

No. 10. ARIETTA (Sopr.)
Allegro

Ge - setzt, ihr habt wirk - lich ge - wagt und ge - strit - ten,

No. 11. FINALE (Sopr., Bass, Female and Male Choruses)
Allegro giusto

Wie, darf ich mei - nen Au - gen trau'n?

ENSEMBLE (Sopr., Female and Male Choruses)
Andante

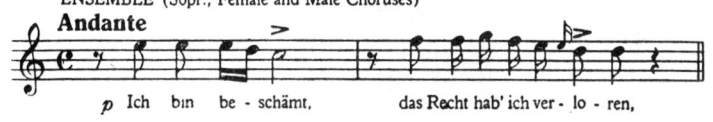

p Ich bin be - schämt, das Recht hab' ich ver - lo - ren,

MS. No. 1 (Duet Isella-Udolin, in A)—Gesellschaft der Musikfreunde, Vienna; complete *Singspiel*—British Museum, London.
1ST PF. Concert form (with the overture to *Des Teufels Lustschloss*)—1st March 1861, Musikvereinssaal, Vienna (conductor, Johann Herbeck); stage performance—29th August 1861, Frankfurt am Main (conductor, Georg Gottermann).
1ST ED. Piano score (by Schubert's nephew, Eduard Schneider) —1862, C. A. Spina, Vienna (no. 17331-41); score—1889, Gesamtausgabe.

The libretto, written in 1820, was published in no. 8 of Castelli's *Dramatisches Sträusschen auf das Jahr 1823*, J. B. Wallishausser, Vienna, in February 1823. The duet no. 1 is written with an alternative part so that Udolin, the page, may be sung by either a tenor or a soprano;

otherwise his part in the *Singspiel* is for soprano. There was a private performance of this work at the house of Giannatasio del Rio in Vienna, probably after Schubert's death, about 1830.

788. '**Lied,**' called '**Die Mutter Erde**' ('Des Lebens Tag ist schwer,' Stolberg), **Song** (XX 427). April 1823.

MS. (without the last four bars)—Stadtbibliothek, Vienna; voice part (with pf. introduction and interlude, in A flat)—Stadtarchiv, Altona, near Hamburg (Ph.).
1ST ED. June 1838, A. Diabelli & Co., Vienna (no. 5033), as no. 2 of *Nachlass*, book 29, under the title 'Die Mutter Erde.'

Nottebohm, quoting Witteczek, says that the song, the original version of which was written in A minor, dates from August 1815.

789. '**Pilgerweise**' (Schober), **Song** (XX 429). April 1823.

MS. Stadtbibliothek, Vienna.
1ST ED. 12th July 1832, A. Diabelli & Co., Vienna (no. 4018, misprinted on the title-page as 4108), as no. 1 of *Nachlass*, book 18.

790. Twelve Deutsche Tänze, called **Ländler, for Pianoforte** (Op. posth. 171, XII 9). May 1823.

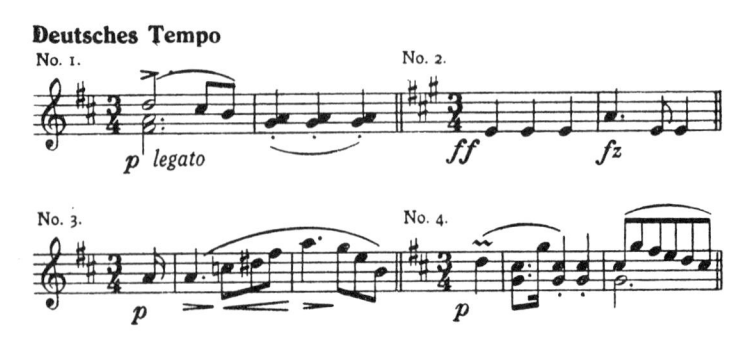

[Musical examples No. 5 – No. 12]

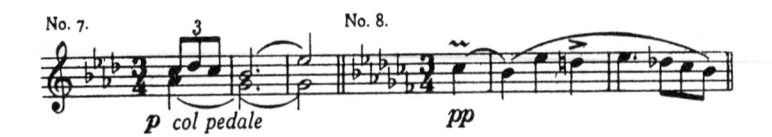

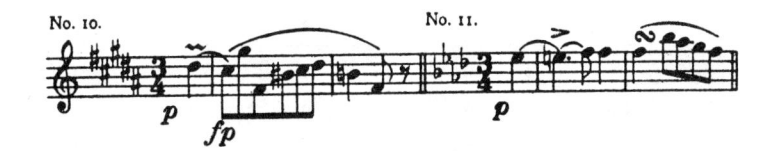

MS. (headed *Deutsches Tempo*)—Gesellschaft der Musikfreunde, Vienna.

1ST ED. 1864, C. A. Spina, Vienna (no. 18180), under the title ' Zwölf Ländler ' (ed. anonymously by Johannes Brahms).

Deutsches Tempo indicates the time signature of *Deutsche Tänze* (3/4). No. 2 is identical with Op. 33, no. 1; the second part of no. 8, apart from the key, is identical with the second part of Op. 33, no. 10. Cf. 783.

791. **Sketches for an Opera (' Rüdiger ')** (author unknown). Not printed. May 1823.

[Musical example: INTRODUCTION. No. 1 (Male Chorus, Tenor Solo and Orchestra), Allegro molto moderato — "Durch der Ost-see wil-de Wo-gen,"]

MS. Stadtbibliothek, Vienna.

1ST PF. Tenor solo with male voice chorus and orchestra, under the apocryphal title 'Rüdiger's Heimkehr,' arranged by Johann Herbeck, with the text altered and augmented—5th January 1868, Redoutensaal, Vienna (conductor Herbeck).

1ST ED. Tenor solo (in Herbeck's arrangement)—*c.* 1868, C. A. Spina, Vienna (no. 18429, later 19473).

The sketches contain the original aria sung by Rüdiger with a chorus of knights and horsemen; also a duet for Rüdiger and Balderon (2 tenors). Schubert's proposed title for the opera is unknown.

792. '**Vergissmeinnicht**' (Schober), **Song** (XX 430). May 1823.

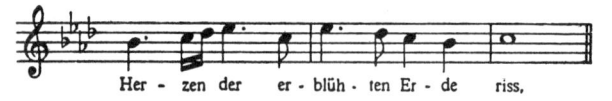

MS. The Heineman Foundation, New York.

1ST ED. 14th February 1833, A. Diabelli & Co., Vienna (no. 4269), as no. 2 of *Nachlass*, book 21.

Schober possessed a MS. copy, now in the Sächsische Landesbibliothek, Dresden. This poem and 'Viola' (786) were both entitled 'Blumenballade' by the author.

793. '**Das Geheimnis**' ('Sie konnte mir kein Wörtchen sagen,' Schiller), **Song**, second version (Op. posth. 173, no. 2; XX 431). May 1823.

MS. Dr. Alwin Cranz, Vienna (together with **794**).

1ST ED. 1867, C. A. Spina, Vienna (no. 19175), as no. 2 of Op. 173.

The Supplement to the *Revisionsbericht* of Series XX corrects p. 128, bar 7, right hand, as follows: last chord C E C instead of C E A. Another MS. (together with 519 and 627) was formerly in the possession of Karoline, Komtesse Esterházy. For the first version, see **250**.

794. '**Der Pilgrim**' (Schiller), **Song** (Op. 37, no. 1; XX 432). May 1823.

[music: Mässig — "Noch in mei-nes Le-bens Len-ze"]

MS. Rough draft (in E, incomplete)—Dr. Alwin Cranz, Vienna (together with 793).
1ST ED. 28th February 1825, Cappi & Co., Vienna (no. 71), as no. 1 of Op. 37, dedicated by Schubert to Ludwig Ferdinand Schnorr von Carolsfeld.

The final version, also in E, was published by Richard Heuberger (see *Literature*) after a MS. copy by Ferdinand Schubert in the former's possession (Vienna). The song, first printed in D, was probably transposed at the request of the publishers.

Literature. Richard Heuberger, *Der Merker*, Vienna, 10th November 1909, vol. i, no. 3, p. 92, and Supplement, pp. 1–4.

795. '**Die schöne Müllerin**,' called '**Müllerlieder**' (Wilhelm Müller), **Cycle of twenty Songs** (Op. 25, XX 433–52). May–November 1823.

BOOK I.
1. DAS WANDERN

[music: Mässig geschwind — "Das Wan-dern ist des Mül-lers Lust,"]

2. WOHIN?

[music: Mässig — "Ich hört' ein Bäch-lein rau-schen"]

3. HALT!
Nicht zu geschwind

[music: "Ei-ne Müh-le seh' ich blin-ken"]

4. DANKSAGUNG AN DEN BACH
Etwas langsam

[music: "War es al-so ge-meint, mein rau-schen-der Freund,"]

BOOK II.
5. AM FEIERABEND
Ziemlich geschwind

Hätt' ich tau-send Ar-me zu rüh-ren,

6. DER NEUGIERIGE
Langsam

Ich fra-ge kei-ne Blu-me,

7. UNGEDULD
Etwas geschwind

Ich schnitt' es gern in al-le Rin-den ein,

8. MORGENGRUSS
Mässig

Gu-ten Mor-gen, schö-ne Mül-le-rin!

9. DES MÜLLERS BLUMEN
Mässig

Am Bach viel klei-ne Blu-men steh'n,

BOOK III.
10. THRÄNENREGEN
Ziemlich langsam

Wir sas-sen so trau-lich bei-sam-men

11. MEIN!
Mässig geschwind

Bäch-lein, lass dein Rau-schen sein,

12. PAUSE
Ziemlich geschwind

Mei-ne Lau-te hab' ich ge-hängt an die Wand,

BOOK IV.
13. MIT DEM GRÜNEN LAUTENBANDE
Mässig

"Schad' um das schö - ne grü - ne Band,

14. DER JÄGER
Geschwind

Was sucht denn der Jä - ger am Mühl-bach hier?

15. EIFERSUCHT UND STOLZ
Geschwind

Wo - hin so schnell, so kraus und wild,

16. DIE LIEBE FARBE
Etwas langsam

In Grün will ich mich klei - den,

17. DIE BÖSE FARBE
Ziemlich geschwind

Ich möch - te zieh'n in die Welt hin-aus,

BOOK V.
18. TROCKNE BLUMEN
Ziemlich langsam

Ihr Blüm - lein al - le, die sie mir gab,

19. DER MÜLLER UND DER BACH
Mässig (Der Müller)

Wo ein treu - es Her - ze in Lie - be ver - geht,

20. DES BACHES WIEGENLIED
Mässig

Gu - te Ruh', gu - te Ruh', tu' die Au - gen zu,

MS. Original—lost; nos. 7–9, transposed into the keys of F, A, and G respectively—private collection, Vienna; no. 15—Gesellschaft der Musikfreunde, Vienna (dated October 1823, in the album of Marie, Gräfin Wimpffen, *née* Freiin Eskeles).

1ST PF. First public performance of the whole cycle—May 1856, Vienna (Julius Stockhausen).

1ST ED. 17th February, 24th March, and 12th August 1824, Sauer & Leidesdorf, Vienna (nos. 502, 503; 651; 653, 654), in five books, dedicated by Schubert to Karl, Freiherr von Schönstein.

Schubert omitted the poems 'Das Mühlenleben' (after 'Der Neugierige'), 'Erster Schmerz, letzter Schmerz' (after 'Eifersucht und Stolz'), and 'Blümlein Vergissmein' (after 'Die böse Farbe'). The complete cycle of the poems, including a prologue and an epilogue, was published in book 1 of Müller's *Gedichte aus den hinterlassenen Papieren eines reisenden Waldhornisten*, Dessau, 1821. Müller entitled the first poem 'Wanderschaft.' 'Ungeduld' resembles a passage in Edmund Spenser's 'Colin Clout's come home again' of 1591. The first edition is somewhat corrupt. Schönstein's MS. copy is in the possession of Mr. Hans Laufer, London; J. M. Vogl's MS. copy (with alterations) was formerly in the possession of Josef Standhardtner, Vienna.

Literature. Julius Rissé, *Müllerlieder*, Erfurt, 1872. Bruno Hake, *Wilhelm Müller*, dissertation, Berlin, 1908. Max Friedlaender, *Einführung* to the jubilee edition of the cycle, C. F. Peters, Leipzig, 1922 (with a facsimile of no. 15). Franz Valentin Damian, *Die schöne Müllerin*, Leipzig, 1928.

—— **Sixteen Deutsche Tänze for Pianoforte** (XII 3, nos. 1–16). May 1823–November 1824.

MS. Nos. 1 and 2 (of 1824, together with Op. 127, 146, no. 2, and 769, no. 1, numbered in the MS. 3 and 4 of four *Deutsche Tänze*) —Heinrich Hinterberger, Vienna (1937); nos. 2 and 12 (together with nos. 8 and 9, the latter in A flat, for pf. duet, dated Zseliz, July 1824)—Fräulein Helene Hauptmann, Leipzig; no. 8 (together with 366, no. 17, dated November 1824)—Frau Marie Floersheim, Wildegg in Aargau (Switzerland); the other nos. —lost.

1ST ED. See 783.

No. 1 is almost identical with Op. 171, 790, no. 2 (May 1823); a variant of no. 6 is printed in the Supplement to Series XII, p. 160. For the Hauptmann MS. see the four *Ländler*, July 1824 (814).

796. '**Fierabras**,' Opera, after the old French romance 'Fierabras' and the German legend 'Eginhard und Emma' in three Acts by Josef Kupelwieser (XV 10). 25th May–2nd October 1823.

OVERTURE
Andante

No. 1. INTRODUCTION (Sopr and Female Chorus)
Andantino

Der run - de Sil - ber - fa - den

No. 2. DUET (Sopr. and Ten.)
Andantino

O mög' auf fro - her Hoff - nung Schwin - gen

No. 3. MARCH & CHORUS (Sopr., Alto, Ten. and Bass)

Zu ho - hen Ruh - mes - pfor - ten

No. 4. ENSEMBLE
  a. RECIT. & CHORUS
Allegro ma non troppo

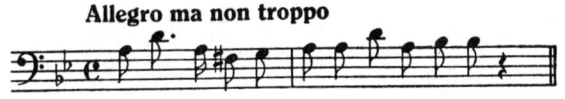

Die Beu - te lass, o Herr, die Krie-ger tei-len,

  b. ENSEMBLE (Bass and Chorus)
Allegro moderato

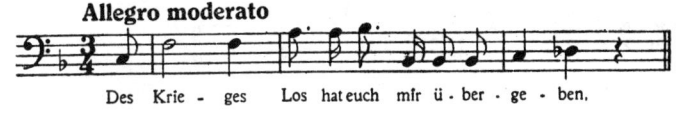

Des Krie - ges Los hat euch mir ü - ber - ge - ben,

  c. NARRATION (Bar.)
    a tempo

Am Rand der Eb' - ne,

  d. ENSEMBLE (Sopr., Bass, Female Chorus)
Andantino

Der Lan - des - töch - ter from - me Pflich - ten

e. QUARTET WITH CHORUS (Sopr., Ten., Bar., Bass and Male Chorus)
Allegretto

Dem Er-folg ver - trau - en wir des Frie-dens Glück,

No. 5. DUET (Ten. and Bar.)
Allegro maestoso con forza

Lass uns mut-voll hof - fen.

No. 6. FINALE
a. ROMANCE (Ten. and Sopr.)
Andante

Der A - bend sinkt auf stil - ler Flur,

b. RECIT. & ARIA (Ten.)
Un poco più moto

Was quälst du mich, o Miss - ge - schick!

c. ENSEMBLE (Sopr., 2 Ten. and Male Chorus)
Un poco più mosso

Doch horch! was regt sich noch in stil- ler Nacht?

d. TERZET (Sopr. and 2 Ten.)
Allegro vivace

Ha, hier wal - tet ein Ver - rat!

e. RECIT.

Nun fas - set Mut! So sehr mein Herz auch bebt,

f. RECIT. & TERZET (Sopr., Ten. and Bass)

Sopr. Bass

Ten. Ha! Wie? Em- ma hier? an des Bar-ba - ren Arm?

g. QUARTET WITH CHORUS (Sopr., 2 Ten., Bass and Male Chorus)
Allegro vivace

Dich rief ich, Eg-in-hard, den ein-zig Treu-en,

No. 7. SONG WITH CHORUS (Ten., Bar. and Male Chorus)
Andantino

Im jun-gen Mor-gen-strah-le den Blick dir zu-ge-wandt,

No. 8. RECIT., MARCH & ENSEMBLE (Ten., Bass and Male Chorus)
Allegro vivace

Be-schlo-ssen ist's, ich lö-se sei-ne Ket-ten!

DUET WITH CHORUS (Ten., Bar. and Male Chorus)
Allegro molto vivace

Was ist ihm ge-scheh'n?

No. 9. DUET (2 Sopr.)
Andante con moto

Weit ü-ber Glanz und Er-den-schim-mer

No. 10. QUINTET (2 Sopr., Ten. and 2 Basses)
Andante con moto

Ver-der-ben denn und Fluch, und Fluch der

No. 11. CHORUS (Sopr., Alto, Ten., Bass)
Allegro moderato

Lasst Frie-de in die Hal-len des Für-sten-sit-zes zi-eh'n,

No. 12. TERZET WITH CHORUS (Sopr., Bar., Bass and 2 Male Choruses)
Allegro vivace

Im To - de sollt ihr bü - ssen

No. 13. ARIA (Sopr.)
Allegro furioso

Die Brust, ge - beugt von Sor - gen,

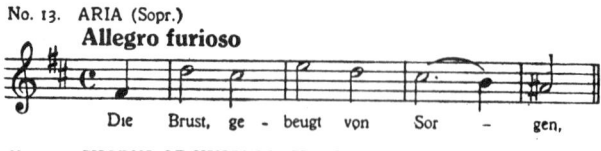

No. 14. CHORUS OF KNIGHTS (Male Chorus, without acc.)
Andante sostenuto

p O teu - res Va - ter - land!

No. 15. a. MELODRAMA, RECIT. & ENSEMBLE (Sopr., Bar. and Male Chorus)
Allegro molto

Wo ist er, wo ist er?

b. DUET WITH CHORUS (Sopr., Bar. and Male Chorus)
Allegretto

Selbst an des Gra - bes Ran - de

No. 16. CHORUS & MELODRAMA (Male Chorus)
Allegro moderato

Der Hoff - nung Strahl, den du ge - ge - ben,

fp

No. 17. SECOND FINALE
  a. TERZET & CHORUS (Sopr., Ten., Bar. and Male Chorus)
  Allegro ma non troppo

Uns führt der Vor - sicht wei - se Hand

  b. MELODRAMA

No. 18. CHORUS (Sopr. and Female Chorus)
  Allegro moderato

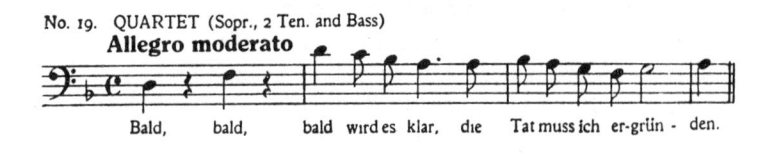

Bald tö - net der Rei - gen, die Lust

No. 19. QUARTET (Sopr., 2 Ten. and Bass)
  Allegro moderato

Bald, bald, bald wird es klar, die Tat muss ich er-grün - den.

No. 20. TERZET (Sopr., and 2 Ten.)
  Allegro moderato

Wenn hoch im Wol - ken- si - tze der Göt - ter Grimm er-wacht,

No. 21. ARIA WITH CHORUS (Sopr. and Male Chorus)
  Andante con moto

Des Jam - mers her - be Qua - len

No. 22. CHORUS & ENSEMBLE (Sopr., Bar., Bass and 2 Male Choruses)
  Tempo I. di Marcia

Der Ra - che O - pfer fal - len,

No. 23. FINALE
a. RECIT.
Allegro moderato

Er ist mein Va - ter, hal - te ein!

b. ENSEMBLE (2 Sopr., 2 Ten., Bar., 2 Basses and Chorus)

Der Sieg be - glei - tet mei - ne ta - pfern Hee - re,

c. RECIT. & CLOSING CHORUS (2 Sopr., 2 Ten., Bar., 2 Basses and Chorus)

Nun lasst des lang - er -.sehn- ten Glück's uns freu - en,

MS. Overture—Dr. Alwin Cranz, Vienna; remainder—Stadtbibliothek, Vienna (the duet no. 9 in two versions).
1ST PF. Overture—1st January 1829, Musikverein, Vienna (conductor, Ignaz Schuppanzigh); sections of the opera in concert form—7th May 1835, Theater in der Josefstadt, Vienna (conductor Konradin Kreutzer); the march with chorus, no. 3, and a soprano aria with chorus—17th April 1836, Musikverein, Vienna (conductor, Leopold Jansa); the arias 7 and 21—28th February 1858, Redoutensaal, Vienna; the choruses 14 and 22 —14th December 1862, Redoutensaal, Vienna. Stage performance—9th February 1897, Karlsruhe (conductor, Felix Mottl), text revised by O. Neitzel, music revised by F. Mottl.
1ST ED. Overture, arranged for pf. duet by Karl Czerny, 1827, A. Diabelli & Co., Vienna (no. 2523), as op. 76; overture in parts —1866, in score—January 1867, C. A. Spina, Vienna; aria for soprano with chorus (no. 21)—4th January 1842, supplement to the *Neue Zeitschrift für Musik*, Leipzig; Chor der Mauren (no. 22), with acc. for pf. duet—1872, J. P. Gotthard, Vienna (no. 316); full score—1886, Gesamtausgabe.

The name of Fierabras, originally the hero of the romance, means boaster, or swaggerer. The first Act was finished on 30th May, the second on 5th June, the third on 26th September. (Dahms suggests that the first two dates should read 30th June and 5th August.) The libretto was passed by the censor on 21st July 1823. The overture was written on 2nd October 1823. For Schubert's arrangement of the overture, as a pf. duet, see **798**.

—— 'Lied' ('In's stille Land, Salis),' Song (XX 201 *b*). See 403. August 1823.

797. 'Rosamunde, Fürstin von Cypern,' Romantic Play with Music in four Acts by Helmina von Chézy (XV 8). Autumn 1823.

No. 1. ENTR'ACTE, after the 1st ACT
Allegro molto moderato

No. 2. BALLET
Allegro moderato

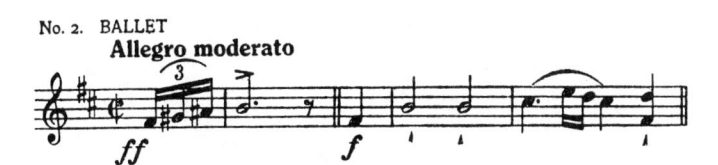

No. 3a. ENTR'ACTE, after the 2nd ACT
Andante

No. 3b. ROMANCE (Contralto)
Andante con moto

Der Voll - mond strahlt auf Ber - ges - höh'n,

No. 4. CHORUS OF SPIRITS (Male Chorus)
Adagio

In der Tie - fe wohnt das Licht,

No. 5. ENTR'ACTE, after the 3rd ACT
Andantino

No. 6. SHEPHERD'S MELODY
Andante

No. 7. CHORUS OF SHEPHERDS (Mixed Chorus)
Allegretto

p Hier auf den Flu - ren, mit ro - si - gen Wan - gen,

No. 8. CHORUS OF HUNTSMEN (Mixed Chorus)
Allegro moderato

p Wie lebt sich's so fröh-lich im Grü - nen

No. 9. BALLET
Andantino

MS. Ballet music—Stadtbibliothek, Vienna; three entr'actes—Nationalbibliothek, Vienna; 'Hirtenmelodie'—Dr. Alwin Cranz, Vienna; 'Hirtenmelodie' (another MS.)—Fräulein Marie Schubert, Vienna; three Choruses and Romance—lost.

1ST PF. 20th December 1823, Theater an der Wien, Vienna (with the overture to *Alfonso und Estrella*; two performances only).

1ST ED. Romanze (3 *b*), Jägerchor (8), Geisterchor (4), and Hirtenchor (7)—24th March ff., 1824, Sauer & Leidesdorf, Vienna (nos. 601-4, in four books), as Op. 26, with pf. acc. arranged by Schubert; Geisterchor, with the original wind acc. in parts—1828, M. J. Leidesdorf, Vienna (no. 1098); entr'actes nos. 1 and 3 in score—October 1866, C. A. Spina, Vienna (no. 18577); ballet music, nos. 1 and 2 in score—1867, C. A. Spina. Vienna (no. 19404); full score (with the overture to *Alfonso und Estrella*)—1891, Gesamtausgabe.

The play, said to be founded on a Spanish novel, is lost, only the lyrics are preserved. The old copies of the parts used at the Theater an der

Wien are now in the archives of the Gesellschaft der Musikfreunde, Vienna. For the overture used for *Rosamunde*, see *Alfonso und Estrella* (732); for the one first published as *Rosamunde* overture, see *Die Zauberharfe* (644). The G.A. complicated the matter by printing the overture to *Alfonso und Estrella* with the *Rosamunde* score. For the third entr'acte. no. 5, cf. **804** and **935**.

Literature. O. E. D., Preface to *Tagblatt-Bibliothek*, Vienna, no. 634, 1928 (Hugo Engelbrecht's (sc. Schwarz) rhymed version, for concert performance of *Rosamunde*).

—— '**Fierabras**' (XV 10). See **796**. 2nd October 1823.

798. Overture to 'Fierabras,' arranged for **Piano Duet** (XXI 7). c. 1824.

MS. Conservatoire, Paris (Ph.).
1ST ED. 1897, Gesamtausgabe.

Another arrangement for pf. duet, by Karl Czerny, was published in 1827 as Schubert's Op. 76. Cf. **796**.

799. 'Im Abendrot' (Lappe), **Song** (XX 463). (?) 1824.

MS. Fair copy, dated February 1825 (together with 'Der blinde Knabe,' **833**)—unknown; former owner—Julius Epstein, Vienna (1928 on sale).

1ST ED. 22nd December 1832, A. Diabelli & Co., Vienna (no. 4268), as no. 1 of *Nachlass*, book 20.

Witteczek and Nottebohm date this song 1824. Franz Lachner, Schubert's friend, set the poem to music about the same time, and published his version in 1826 as a supplement to the *Wiener Zeitschrift für Kunst*, etc., no. 75.

800. ' **Der Einsame** ' (Lappe), Song, two versions (Op. 41, XX 465 (*a*) and (*b*)). (?) 1824.

Mässig, ruhig

Wann mei-ne Gril-len schwir-ren, bei Nacht,

BAR 14
Version '*a*'

schwert, so leicht, so un-be-

Version '*b*'

-schwert, so leicht, so un-be-

MS. (*a*) and (*b*)—Lost.
1ST PF. 23rd November 1826, Musikverein, Vienna.
1ST ED. (*a*) 12th March 1825, as a supplement to the *Wiener Zeitschrift für Kunst*, etc., Vienna (in type); (*b*) 5th January 1827, A. Diabelli & Co., Vienna (no. 2251), as Op. 41.

According to Kreissle, pp. 316 and 594, this song was written in the Vienna General Hospital, i.e. in 1823; Spaun dates it 1824; according to Sofie Müller's diary, 7th March 1825, the song was then new, but probably only new to her. It is possible, however, that Schubert showed her the proofs of the first edition.

—— **Twenty Walzer for Pianoforte** (XII 8). See 146. 1824.

801. ' **Dithyrambe**,' called ' **Der Besuch** ' (Schiller), Song (Op. 60, no. 2; XX 457). 1824.

Geschwind und feurig

Nim-mer, das glaubt mir, er-schei-nen die Göt-ter,

MS. Unknown; former owner—Max Friedlaender, Berlin (Ph.).
1ST PF. 20th November 1828, Musikverein, Vienna (the day after Schubert's death).
1ST ED. 10th June 1826, Cappi & Czerny, Vienna (no. 192), as no. 2 of Op. 60.

The poem was published in the *Musenalmanach* for 1797 under the title Der Besuch '; this information was given on the bill advertising the first performance. The MS. is written on paper marked 'C. Hennigsches Notenpapier Nr. 2,' to be had from Halla & Comp. at Prague. The first edition is not quite authentic. For the setting of the same poem as a choral work, see 47.

802. Introduction and [7] Variations in E minor on a Theme (' Ihr Blümlein alle ') from the Song Cycle ' Die schöne Müllerin,' **for Pianoforte and Flute** (Op. posth. 160; VIII 7). January 1824.

MS. Stadtbibliothek, Vienna.

1ST ED. April 1850, A. Diabelli & Co., Vienna (no. 8889).

The theme is taken from the song ' Trockne Blumen,' Op. 25 (795), no. 18. Probably written for the flautist Ferdinand Bogner. The date, January 1824, is given according to Moritz von Schwind's letter to Franz von Schober, 13th February 1824 (*Schubert Documents*, no. 435, p. 327), and according to Nottebohm.

— **Two Deutsche Tänze for Pianoforte** (XII 18). See 769. January 1824.

803. Octet in F for String and Wind Instruments (Op. posth. 166; III 1). February–1st March 1824.

MS. Stadtbibliothek, Vienna.

1ST PF. Probably spring 1824, at the lodgings of Graf Ferdinand Troyer, Spielmann'sches Haus, Graben (now no. 13), Vienna; first public performance—16th April 1827, Musikverein, Vienna (Ignaz Schuppanzigh's concert).

1ST ED. March 1853, C. A. Spina, Vienna (no. 9141, plate mark of his predecessors, A. Diabelli & Co.), without movements 4 and 5; *c.* 1875, Friedrich Schreiber, Vienna (Spina's successor), complete.

The work was written for Troyer who played the clarinet. It is scored for two violins, viola, violoncello, double bass, clarinet, horn, and bassoon. In the first edition the second movement is headed *Andante un poco mosso*.

Literature. William Glock, 'Schubert,' in A. L. Bacharach (ed.), *Lives of the Great Composers*, London, 1936, p. 499.

804. String Quartet in A minor (Op. 29, no. 1; V 13).   February, or early March 1824.

MS. Lost.

1ST PF. 14th March 1824, Musikverein, Vienna (Ignaz Schuppanzigh's Quartet).

1ST ED. 7th September 1824, Sauer & Leidesdorf, Vienna (no. 594), dedicated by Schubert to Schuppanzigh.

The first of three quartets planned by Schubert. The theme of the Andante was taken from the third entr'acte of *Rosamunde* (797); cf. the third impromptu of Op. 142 (935).

805. '**Der Sieg**' (Mayrhofer), **Song** (XX 458). Beginning of March 1824.

Mässig langsam

O un - be-wölk - tes Le - ben!

MS. Gesellschaft der Musikfreunde, Vienna (the last bars only, together with 806).
1ST ED. 4th June 1833, A. Diabelli & Co., Vienna (no. 4270), as no. 1 of *Nachlass*, book 22.

806. '**Abendstern**' (Mayrhofer), **Song** (XX 459). Beginning of March 1824.

Ziemlich langsam

Was weilst du ein - sam an dem Him - mel,

MS. Gesellschaft der Musikfreunde, Vienna (together with 805).
1ST ED. 4th June 1833, A. Diabelli & Co., Vienna (no. 4270), as no. 4 of *Nachlass*, book 22.

807. '**Auflösung**' (Mayrhofer), **Song** (XX 460). (? Beginning of) March 1824.

Nicht zu geschwind

Ver - birg dich, Son - ne,

MS. J. A. Stargardt, Berlin (*c.* 1938).
1ST ED. *c.* 1842, A. Diabelli & Co., Vienna (no. 7412), as no. 1 of *Nachlass*, book 34.

808. '**Gondelfahrer**' (Mayrhofer), **Song** (XX 461). Beginning of March 1824.

[Musical notation: Mässig, 6/8, with text "Es tan - zen Mond und Ster - ne"]

MS. Preussische Staatsbibliothek, Berlin.
IST ED. 1872, J. P. Gotthard, Vienna (no. 326), as no. 2 of forty songs, this song dedicated by the publisher to Julius Stockhausen.

This was the last poem by Mayrhofer to be set to music by his friend. For the setting as a quartet, T.T.B.B., see 809.

809. 'Der Gondelfahrer' (Mayrhofer) for Quartet, T.T.B.B., with Pianoforte accompaniment (Op. 28, XVI 9). (? Beginning of) March 1824.

[Musical notation: Andante con moto, with text "Es tan - zen Mond und Ster - ne"]

MS. Lost.
IST PF. 17th November 1825, Musikverein, Vienna.
IST ED. 12th August 1824, Sauer & Leidesdorf, Vienna (no. 599 on the plates, 652 on the title-page), as Op. 28.

See the version set as a solo song (808), entitled, as in Mayrhofer's poems, 'Gondelfahrer.'

810. String Quartet ('Der Tod und das Mädchen') in D minor (V 14). March 1824–January 1826.

[Musical notation: Allegro, ff ... pp]

[Musical notation: Andante con moto, pp]

SCHERZO
Allegro molto

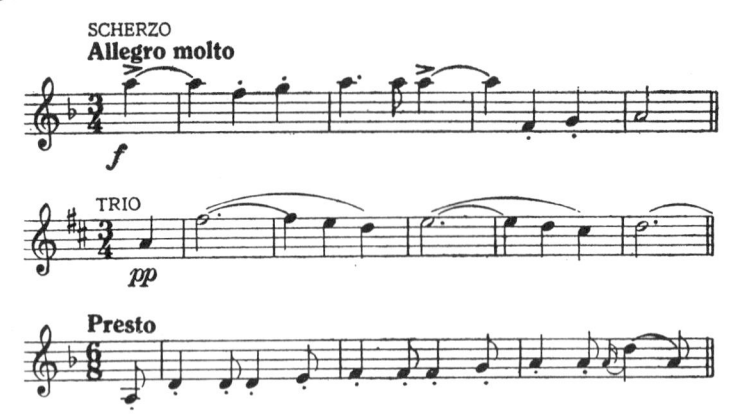

TRIO

Presto

MS. Fragment—William Kux, Chur, Switzerland.
1ST PF. 1st February 1826, at the home of Josef Barth, Vienna; first public performance—12th March 1833, Berlin (Karl Moser's concert).
1ST ED. July 1831, Josef Czerny, Vienna (no. 2686).

The second movement is based on the song ' Der Tod und das Mädchen ' (531). The autograph contains the first movement complete, and the second without the last thirty bars; the third and fourth movements are missing. The work was finished or revised in January 1826.

811. Salve Regina in C for Quartet, T.T.B.B. (Op. posth. 149; XIV 19). April 1824.

Andantino

Sal - ve Re - gi - na,   ma - ter mi - se - ri - cor - di - ae,

MS. Preussische Staatsbibliothek, Berlin.
1ST ED. (score and parts) *c.* 1843, A. Diabelli & Co., Vienna (no. 7972), corrupt.

The organ part, *ad libitum*, was added by the publisher.

812. Sonata in C for Piano Duet, called **Grand Duo** (Op. posth. 140; IX 12). June 1824 (Zseliz).

Allegro moderato

MS. Miss Margaret Deneke, Oxford.

1ST PF. 18th December 1859, Musikverein, Vienna (Karl Meyer and Eduard Pirkhert).

1ST ED. 1838, A. Diabelli & Co., Vienna (no. 6269), dedicated by the publishers to Fräulein Klara Wieck (later Schumann's wife).

On account of its orchestral character, this duo was thought to be the piano score of the lost Gmunden-Gastein Symphony (849), and therefore orchestrated by Josef Joachim in 1855 (produced 9th February 1856, concert room of the opera house, Hanover, conducted by Joachim himself, and published in 1873 by Friedrich Schreiber, Vienna).

Literature. Robert Schumann, *Neue Zeitschrift für Musik*, Leipzig, 5th June 1838.

813. **Eight Variations on an Original Theme in A flat for Piano Duet** (Op. 35, IX 16).   Summer of 1824 (Zseliz).

MS. Lost.

1ST ED. 9th February 1825, Sauer & Leidesdorf, Vienna (no. 661), as Op. 35, dedicated by Schubert to Anton, Graf Berchtold.

This work seems to have been written in June, or at the beginning of July, 1824.

814. Four Ländler for Piano Duet (IX 27). July 1824 (Zseliz).

MS. Fräulein Helene Hauptmann, Leipzig (together with Op. 33, 783, nos. 9 and 8, for piano duet, as nos. 5 and 6).

1ST ED. Arranged by the publisher, for piano solo—1869, J. P. Gotthard, Vienna (no. 12) in *Zwanzig Ländler* (edited anonymously by Johannes Brahms, see 366), as nos. 17–20; original—c. 1870, C. F. Peters, Leipzig (edition no. 155 (*d*), Supplement to the collection of Schubert's compositions for piano duet).

Schubert set no. 1 for piano solo in November 1824; see 366, no. 17. The MS. also contains other dances; the order of all the dances is as follows: 366, no. 4, 783, nos. 2 and 12, 366, no 12 for piano solo; 814, nos. 1–4, 783, nos. 9 and 8 for piano duet; 366, nos. 2, 8, 3, and 5 for piano solo. The MS. is signed and dated (' Zeléz 1824 July ') at the end, but the date seems to refer to all the dances.

815. ' Gebet ' (' Du Urquell aller Güte,' Fouqué), **Quartet, S.A.T.B., with Pianoforte accompaniment** (Op. posth. 139 (*a*); XVII 10). Beginning of September 1824 (Zseliz).

Andante

Du Ur-quell al-ler Gü-te,

Andantino

Wo-hin du mich willst ha-ben, mein Herr!

MS. Score—Stadtbibliothek, Vienna; parts—Karl Geigy-Hagenbach, Basle.

1ST PF. 3rd April 1859, Redoutensaal, Vienna (conductor, Johann Herbeck).

1ST ED. *c.* 1838, A. Diabelli & Co., Vienna (no. 6268), as Op. 139, dedicated by the publishers to Karl, Freiherr von Schönstein.

In the MSS. the first section is written in *alla breve* time. The work was composed for Johann Karl, Graf Esterházy, his wife, two daughters, and Schönstein. Haslinger numbered the quartet 'Nachtgesang im Walde' (913) also Op. 139.

816. Three Écossaises for Pianoforte. Unpublished. September 1824 (Zseliz).

No. 1.

No. 2.

No. 3.

MS. 1937, V. A. Heck, Vienna (on sale, but withdrawn by the owner).

817. Ungarische Melodie in B minor for Pianoforte. 2nd September 1824 (Zseliz).

Allegretto

MS. Martin Bodmer, Zürich (Ph.).
1ST PF. 18th July 1928, Burggarten, Vienna (Otto Schulhof).
1ST ED. 1928, Ed. Strache, Vienna (no. 20), edited by O. E. D. (together with Liszt's arrangement of Schubert's version of the same movement for piano duet).

This is the first version of the third movement (Allegretto) of the *Divertissement à la hongroise* (818) for piano duet. The original title is 'Ungerische Melodie.'

818. **Divertissement à la hongroise in G minor for Piano Duet** (Op. 54, IX 19). (?) Autumn 1824 (? Zseliz).

Andante

Marcia. Andante con moto

TRIO

Allegretto

MS. Lost.
1ST ED. 8th April 1826, Matthias Artaria, Vienna (no. 826), dedicated by Schubert to Frau Katharina von Lászny, *née* Buchwieser.

1824   819   395

For the first version of the third movement, written for pianoforte solo, see 817. Schubert received 300 florins, Viennese currency, from the publisher for this divertissement.

819. Six Grandes Marches and Trios for Piano Duet (Op. 40, IX 2). (?) October 1824 (? Zseliz).

No. 5. **Andante**

TRIO

No. 6. **Allegro con brio**

TRIO

MS. Lost.

1ST ED. 7th May and 21st September 1825 (in two books), Sauer & Leidesdorf, Vienna (nos. 803 and 846), as Op. 40, dedicated by Schubert to his doctor, J. Bernhardt.

According to Josef von Spaun this work was written in 1824. No. 5 was later called 'Trauermarsch.'

820. **Six Deutsche Tänze for Pianoforte.** October 1824 (Zseliz).

1. **Tempo giusto**

2.

MS. George A. Steinbach, New York.
1ST PF. 7th May 1931, Musikvereinssaal, Vienna.
1ST ED. May 1931, Universal Edition, Vienna (no. 2743), ed.
by Hans Wagner-Schönkirch (with a preface by O. E. D.).
The MS. was formerly in the possession of Karoline, Komtesse Esterházy.
— Deutscher Tanz for Pianoforte (XII 3, no. 8). See 366, no. 17, and 783, no. 8. November 1824.
— Walzer for Pianoforte. See 814, no. 1. November 1824.

821. Sonata for Pianoforte and Arpeggione (VIII 8). November 1824.

MS. Conservatoire, Paris (Ph.).
1ST PF. (?) December 1824, privately, at Vienna (the arpeggione played by Vincenz Schuster).
1ST ED. January 1871, J. P. Gotthard, Vienna (no. 142).

Ferdinand Schubert listed this work by mistake under 1823. Schubert himself called the guitar-violoncello an arpeggione. His MS. is written in a careless manner, which shows Schubert's lack of affection for the work (Mandyczewski). Appended to the MS. is a violin part, written by another hand. The first edition contains parts for violoncello and violin, as alternatives for the arpeggione (violin and pf. performance in Vienna—8th March 1871). Later the arpeggione part was arranged for viola or guitar.

Literature. Karl Geiringer, *Schubert-Gabe der Österreichischen Gitarre-Zeitschrift*, Vienna, 1928, pp. 27–9.

822. ' Lied eines Kriegers,' called ' Reiterlied ' (author unknown), Song for Bass with Unison Chorus (XX 464). 31st December 1824.

MS. W. Westley Mannings, London (with both titles).
1ST ED. c. 1842, A. Diabelli & Co., Vienna (no. 7413), as no. 2 of *Nachlass*, book 35.

The MS., written in the bass clef, lacks the accompaniment from bar 46 onwards, except that the right-hand part is indicated in bars 56–9. The song was again published, by mistake, but in a more reliable version, as no. 1 of the first issue of *Nachlass*, book 41, c. 1847, where it was later exchanged for ' Licht und Liebe ' (352). This version differs from the first edition, especially in the last bars, which are, however, spurious in both editions. The G.A. also is not quite authentic.

Literature. Alfred Orel, *Archiv für Musikwissenschaft*, Leipzig, 1937, vol. ii, no. 3, pp. 285–98 (with the voice-part, printed from the MS., on pp. 292 f.).

823. Divertissement (à la française) in E minor for Piano Duet (Op. 63, no. 1, and Op. 84, nos. 1 and 2; IX 20–2). c. 1825.

MS. Lost.

1ST ED. 17th June 1826, Thäddaus Weigl, Vienna (no. 2520), as Op. 63, no. 1, and 6th July 1827, Thaddäus Weigl, Vienna (no. 2677 and 2678), as Op. 84, nos. 1 and 2, under the titles ' Divertissement en forme d'une Marche brillante et raisonnée ' and ' Andantino varié et Rondeau brillant . . . sur des motifs origineaux Français.'

There is no doubt that the work was divided by the publisher without Schubert's consent. The second and third movements were apparently intended as Op. 63, nos. 2 and 3.

824. Six Polonaises for Piano Duet (Op. 61, IX 25). *c.* 1825.

824

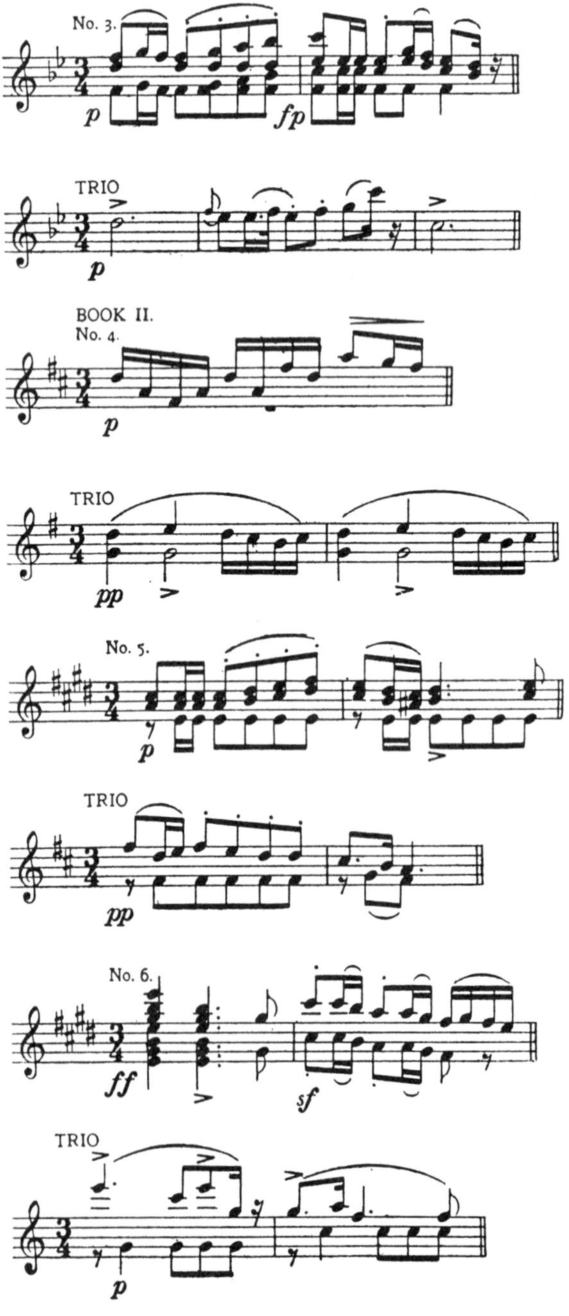

MS. Lost.
1ST ED. 8th July 1826, Cappi & Czerny, Vienna (nos. 211 and 212), in two books.
Cf. 599.

825. '**Wehmut**' (Heinrich Hüttenbrenner), '**Ewige Liebe**' (Ernst Schulze), '**Flucht**' (Karl Lappe), **Quartets, T.T.B.B.** (Op. 64, XVI 24–6). *c.* 1825.

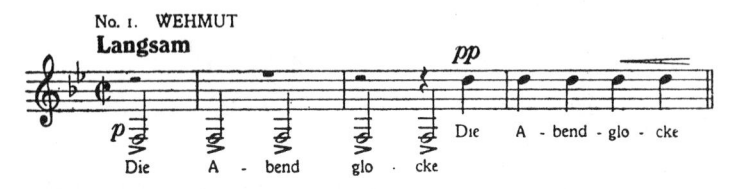

MS. Lost.
1ST PF. No. 3—20th March 1825, Landhaussaal, Vienna.
1ST ED. 6th October 1828, A. Pennauer, Vienna (no. 400), as Op. 64.

It seems that the first edition was intended to be published in the autumn of 1826. The poem of no. 2 has no title in Schulze's *Poetisches Tagebuch*, but is headed simply with the date: 'Am 27. Oktober 1814.' The date of quartet no. 3 is determined by the first performance.

826. '**Der Tanz**' (Schnitzer), **Quartet, S.A.T.B.**, with Pianoforte accompaniment (XVII 14). (?) 1825.

MS. Stadtbibliothek, Vienna.
1ST ED. 1892, Gesamtausgabe.

This humorous quartet was written to warn Fräulein Irene von Kiesewetter, for her health's sake, against the danger of dancing. The second stanza is printed in O. E. D., *Franz Schubert. Die Dokumente seines Lebens und Schaffens*, Munich, 1914, vol. ii, part 1, p. 292. The date 1823 is written on the MS. in another hand; this date is incorrect. If the work was not written in 1825 the date is more likely to be 1827. The first four lines are a parody of the corresponding lines in Schiller's *Hoffnung* (cf. 251 and 637).

827. ' **Nacht und Träume** ' (Matthäus von Collin), **Song** (Op. 43, no. 2; XX 470). (?) 1825.

Sehr langsam

[musical notation: Heil' ge Nacht, du sin-kest nie - der;]

MS. Lost.

1ST ED. 25th July 1825, A. Pennauer, Vienna (no. 136), as no. 2 of Op. 43 (the first twenty copies contain some misprints).

The name of the poet was given as Schiller in the first edition.

828. ' **Die junge Nonne** ' (Craigher), **Song** (Op. 43, no. 1; XX 469). 1825.

Mässig

[musical notation: Wie braust durch die Wip fel der heu-len-de Sturm!]

MS. Lost.

1ST PF. 28th December 1826, Musikverein, Vienna.

1ST ED. 25th July 1825, A. Pennauer, Vienna (no. 136), as no. 1 of Op. 43 (the first twenty copies contain some misprints).

The poem, written in 1823, is printed in Craigher's *Poetische Betrachtungen in freien Stunden* (issued under the pseudonym Nicolaus), Vienna, 1828, p. 58. Sofie Müller refers to the song as new in her diary on 7th March 1825; but, as in other cases, it is possible that the song was only new to her. For the misprints in the first edition, see the *Revisionsbericht*. Ferdinand Schubert arranged the song with orchestral accompaniment (performed in 1836, Vienna).

829. ' **Abschied von der Erde** ' (from Adolf von Pratobevera's play ' Der Falke '), **Melodrama** (XX 603). 1825-6.

Langsam

[musical notation: *pp* Con pedale, appassionato]

MS. Gesellschaft der Musikfreunde, Vienna.

IST PF. 17th February 1826, at the home of Karl Josef von Pratobevera, in the so-called Bürgerspital, Vienna.

IST ED. 1873, J. Guttentag, Berlin, in Reissmann's *Schubert*, Appendix no. 6, pp. 15–18.

The G.A. dates the work 1817 or 1818, and suggests that the *Melodram* was written for one of the social gatherings of Schubert's friends. A tradition in the poet's family contradicts both suggestions. This one-act play was written on the occasion of the birthday of the poet's father; Schubert, however, composed the music for the final scene only, which is sung by the character Mechtild, the wife of Ritter Robert. The poet, by the way, later became the brother-in-law of Schubert's biographer, Kreissle. The MS. of the play was last in the possession of Felix Hasslinger, Maria Enzersdorf, near Vienna, a descendant of the author.

830. '**Lied der Anne** (Annot) **Lyle**' (from Sir Walter Scott's novel 'A Legend of Montrose,' translated by Sofie May), **Song** (Op. 85, no. 1; XX 541). (?) Beginning of 1825.

Mässig

Wärst du bei mir im Le - bens - tal,

MS. Lost.

IST ED. 14th March 1828, A. Diabelli & Co., Vienna (no. 2877), as no. 1 of Op. 85.

The text was taken by Scott from Andrew MacDonald's comedy 'Love and Loyalty.' The G.A. dates Schubert's song according to Witteczek and Nottebohm, 1827. The diary of Sofie Müller suggests that it was probably completed before 1st March 1825. She speaks, however, of ' new songs [*sic*] from *The Pirate* (831), also *The Rose*' (*Montrose*, or 745 ?).

— '**Suleika II**' (XX 377). See 717. Beginning of 1825.

831. '**Gesang der Norna**' ('Norna's Song,' from Sir Walter Scott's novel ' The Pirate,' translated by Samuel Heinrich Spiker), **Song** (Op. 85, no. 2; XX 542). Beginning of 1825.

Nicht zu langsam

Mich führt mein Weg wohl mei - len-lang

MS. Lost.

IST ED. 14th March 1828, A. Diabelli & Co., Vienna (no. 2877), as no. 2 of Op. 85.

The G.A. dates this song according to Witteczek and Nottebohm, 1827. The diary of Sofie Müller, however, proves that it was completed before 1st March 1825. Cf. note to 830.

832. ' **Des Sängers Habe** ' (Schlechta), **Song** (XX 466). February 1825.

Etwas geschwind

Schlagt mein gan - zes Glück in Split - ter

MS. Rough draft, but only MS.—Conservatoire, Paris (Ph.)
1ST ED. 26th October 1830, A. Diabelli & Co., Vienna (no. 3704), as no. 1 of *Nachlass*, book 7.

—— ' **Im Abendrot** ' (XX 463). See **799**. February 1825.

833. ' **Der blinde Knabe** ' (' The Blind Boy,' Colley Cibber, translated by Craigher), **Song**, two versions (Op. posth. 101; XX 468 (*a*) and (*b*). February–April 1825.

Langsam

O sagt, ihr Lie - ben, mir ein-mal.

BAR 7
Version 'a'
nie - mals ich ge-kannt, die

Version 'b'
nie-mals ich ge-kannt, die

MS. (*a*) Rough draft (together with 842), dated February 1825—Stadtbibliothek, Vienna; (*b*) fair copy (together with the fair copy of 799), dated April 1825—unknown; former owner—Julius Epstein, Vienna (1928 on sale).
1ST ED. (*a*) 1895, Gesamtausgabe; (*b*) 25th September 1827, as a supplement to the *Wiener Zeitschrift für Kunst*, etc., Vienna (in type).

The translation, probably made for Schubert, was not included in Craigher's works. The poet's name was omitted in the various editions of this song. The poem was also translated in Vienna by Mayláth, and set to music by Sechter about the same time as this setting of Schubert's. The first edition was reprinted by H. A. Probst, Leipzig, on 12th December 1828, as no. 2 of a spurious Op. 101, which contains only reprints from the

Wiener Zeitschrift. The song, in a corrupt form, was republished by A. Diabelli & Co., Vienna (no. 3058, i.e. no. 242 of the pf. collection *Philomele*) on 16th March 1829, under the same opus number (101), which Schubert himself had reserved for the four impromptus, later called Op. 142.

834. '**Im Walde**' ('Ich wandre über Berg und Tal,' Schulze), **Song** (Op. 93, no. 1; XX 476). March 1825.

[Musical incipit: Nicht zu schnell — "Ich wan-dre ü-ber Berg und Tal"]

MS. Wiener Schubertbund, Vienna.

1ST ED. 30th May 1828, J. A. Kienreich, Graz (no publisher's number), as no. 1 of Op. 90 (later corrected to 93), lithographed by Josef Franz Kaiser, with the erroneous indication that the two songs (this and 'Auf der Bruck,' 853) were written during Schubert's sojourn at Graz (September 1827).

The poem in Schulze's *Poetisches Tagebuch* was inscribed 'Im Walde hinter Falkenhagen. Den 22sten Julius 1814.' It has no connection with the woods. Falkenhagen is a village near Göttingen. This was the only work by Schubert published in Austria outside Vienna during his lifetime. On taking over the opus, Diabelli later published a new edition, in which he made some alterations to this song, and changed the key to G minor.

835. '**Bootgesang**' (from Sir Walter Scott's poem 'The Lady of the Lake,' translated by Adam Storck), **Quartet, T.T.B.B., with Pianoforte accompaniment** (Op. 52, no. 3; XVI 10). Spring or summer 1825.

[Musical incipit: Mässig und kräftig — "Tri-umph, er naht. Heil, Heil dem Hel-den."]

MS. Lost.

1ST PF. (?) 9th April 1873, Musikvereinssaal, Vienna (conductor, Rudolf Weinwurm).

1ST ED. 5th April 1826, Matthias Artaria, Vienna (no. 813), as no. 3 of Op. 52 (book 1), dedicated by Schubert to Sofie, Gräfin Weissenwolff, *née* Komtesse Breuner.

Published with English and German words, with the first stanza under the music and the other three on a separate leaf.

836. '**Coronach**' (from Sir Walter Scott's poem 'The Lady of the Lake,' translated by Adam Storck), **Chorus, S.S.A., with Pianoforte accompaniment** (Op. 52, no. 4; XVIII 1). Spring or summer 1825.

Er ist—— uns ge-schie - den vom Berg— und vom Wal - de

MS. Lost.

1ST ED. 5th April 1826, Matthias Artaria, Vienna (no. 813), as no. 4 of Op. 52 (book 1), dedicated by Schubert to Sofie, Grafin Weissenwolff, *née* Komtesse Breuner.

The title of the first edition (published with English and German words) is 'Coronach (Totengesang der Frauen und Mädchen).'

837. '**Ellens Gesang I**' ('Raste Krieger,' from Sir Walter Scott's poem 'The Lady of the Lake,' translated by Adam Storck), **Song** (Op. 52, no. 1; XX 471). Spring or summer 1825.

Ra—— ste. Krie - ger. Krieg ist — aus.

MS. Lost.

1ST ED. 5th April 1826, Matthias Artaria, Vienna (no. 813), as no. 1 of Op. 52 (book 1), dedicated by Schubert to Sofie, Gräfin Weissenwolff, *née* Komtesse Breuner.

Published with English and German words.

838. '**Ellens Gesang II**' ('Jäger, ruhe von der Jagd,' from Sir Walter Scott's poem 'The Lady of the Lake,' translated by Adam Storck), **Song** (Op. 52, no. 2; XX 472). Spring or summer 1825.

Jä - ger. ru - he von der Jagd!

MS. Lost.

1ST ED. 5th April 1826, Matthias Artaria, Vienna (no. 813), as no. 2 of Op. 52 (book 1), dedicated by Schubert to Sofie, Gräfin Weissenwolff, *née* Komtesse Breuner.

Published with English and German words.

839. ' **Ellens Gesang III** ' (' Ave Maria,' from Sir Walter Scott's poem ' The Lady of the Lake,' translated by Adam Storck), **Song** (Op. 52, no. 6; XX 474). Spring or summer 1825.

MS. Lost.
1ST PF. 31st January 1828, Musikverein, Vienna.
1ST ED. 5th April 1826, Matthias Artaria, Vienna (no. 814), as no. 6 of Op. 52 (book 2), dedicated by Schubert to Sofie, Gräfin Weissenwolff, *née* Komtesse Breuner.

Published with English and German words. Schubert's brother Ferdinand arranged this song for use in churches, with orchestral acc., on 31st December 1842 (MS. in the Peters-Kirche, Vienna).

840. **Sonata in C,** called ' **Reliquie,**' for **Pianoforte** (XXI 14). April 1825.

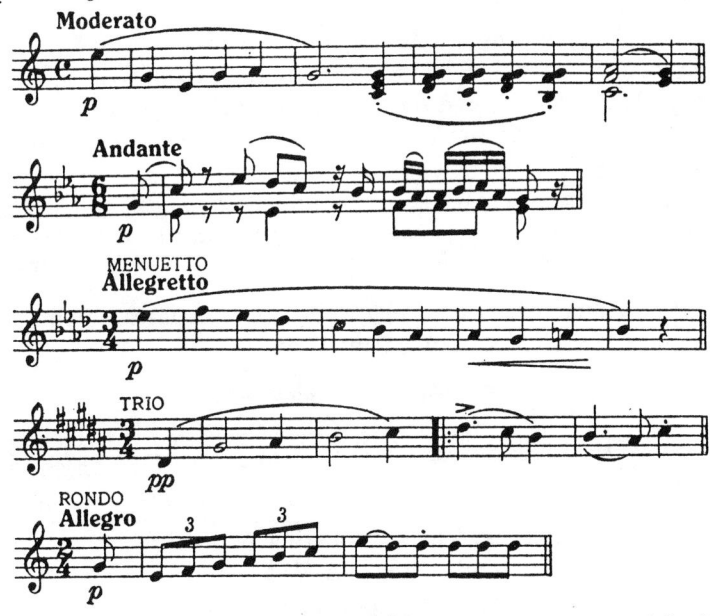

MS. *Moderato*, first leaf—Stadtbibliothek, Vienna, second leaf—Fitzwilliam Museum, Cambridge; end of *Andante* and beginning of *Menuetto*—Gerd Rosen, Berlin (sale, 3–4 April 1851); rest of *Menuetto* with *Trio*—Stadtbibliothek, Vienna.

1ST ED. Second movement—*Neue Zeitschrift für Musik*, Leipzig, 10th December 1839, supplement; complete, under the title ' Reliquie. Letzte Sonate (unvollendet) '—1861, F. Whistling, Leipzig (no. 857).

Robert Schumann originally possessed the whole MS. which was divided at a later date. The third and fourth movements only are incomplete. The sonata was completed, first by Ernst Krenek in 1921 (published by the Universal Edition, Vienna, in 1923) and in 1927 by Walter Rehberg (published by Steingräber-Verlag, Leipzig, edition no. 2589).

841. Two Deutsche Tänze for Pianoforte. April 1825.

MS. J. A. Stargardt, Berlin (1926).

1ST ED. Facsimile—September 1926, Berlin, in Catalogue 261 of J. A. Stargardt; first (engraved) edition—1930, Ed. Strache, Vienna (no. 23) in *Deutsche Tänze*, etc. (ed. by O. E. D. and A. Orel), p. 5.

A *Deutscher Tanz* was published on 7th February 1825 in a Viennese dance collection, called *Terpsichore* (no copy known); it seems, however, not to be identical with one of the two dances above, which are of later date.

842. ' Totengräbers Heimwehe,' called ' Gräbers Heimweh ' (Craigher), **Song** (XX 467). April 1825.

MS. Stadtbibliothek, Vienna (together with 833).

1ST ED. 25th September 1833, A. Diabelli & Co., Vienna (no. 4272), as no. 2 of *Nachlass*, book 24.

The poem was written in 1823 and published in Craigher's *Poetische Betrachtungen in freien Stunden* (issued under the pseudonym Nicolaus), Vienna, 1828, pp. 59 f., under the title ' Gräbers Heimweh.' The title in the first edition is ' Totengräbers Heimweh.'

843. 'Lied des gefangenen Jäger' ('Lay of the Imprisoned Huntsman,' from Sir Walter Scott's poem 'The Lady of the Lake,' translated by Adam Storck), Song (Op. 52, no. 7; XX 475). 4th April 1825.

Etwas geschwind

Mein Ross so müd' in dem Stal-le sich steht,

MS. Lost.
1ST PF. 8th February 1827, Musikverein, Vienna.
1ST ED. 5th April 1826, Matthias Artaria, Vienna (no. 814), as no. 7 of Op. 52 (book 2), dedicated by Schubert to Sofie, Gräfin Weissenwolff, *née* Komtesse Breuner.
Published with English and German words.

844. Walzer in G, called 'Albumblatt,' for Pianoforte (XXI 31). 16th April 1825.

MS. Unknown; former owner—Xaver Mayerhofer von Grünbühel, Völkermarkt (Carinthia).
1ST ED. 1897, Gesamtausgabe.

Written in the album of Fräulein Anna Hönig, later Frau Mayerhofer von Grünbühel, in which the painter Moritz von Schwind, Schubert's friend, wrote another pf. piece on 7th August 1827. Published again as a first edition, in error, by Max Friedlaender in *Funde und Forschungen* (*Eine Festgabe für Julius Wahle*), Leipzig, 1921, pp. 11 f.

845. Sonata in A minor for Pianoforte (Op. 42; X 9). (? May) 1825.

Moderato

Andante poco moto

SCHERZO
Allegro vivace

TRIO
Un poco più lento

pp Mit Verschiebung

RONDO
Allegro vivace

pp legato

MS. Lost.

1ST ED. Between September 1825 and February 1826, A. Pennauer, Vienna (no. 177) as ' Première grande Sonate,' dedicated by Schubert to the Archduke of Austria, Cardinal Rudolf. On the jacket is the title ' Bibliothèque musicale de nos contemporains. Recueil de compositions originales pour Pianoforte . . . Nr. 1.'

846. ' **Normans Gesang** ' (from Sir Walter Scott's poem *The Lady of the Lake*, translated by Adam Storck), **Song** (Op. 52, no. 5; XX 473). Summer 1825.

Geschwind

Die Nacht bricht bald her -ein.

MS. Lost.

1ST PF. 8th March 1827, Musikverein, Vienna (acc. played by Schubert himself).

1ST ED. 5th April 1826, Matthias Artaria, Vienna (no. 814), as no. 5 of Op. 52 (book 2), dedicated by Schubert to Sofie, Gräfin Weissenwolff, *née* Komtesse Breunner.

Published with the German words only. Schubert was paid 200 florins, *Konventions-Münze* (associated coinage), by the publisher for Op. 52.

847. ' **Trinklied aus dem XVI. Jahrhundert,** ' in Latin, **Quartet, T.T.B.B.** (Op. posth. 155; XVI 29). July 1825 (Gmunden).

[musical notation: Geschwind]

p E - dit Non - na, e - dit Cle - rus,

MS. Sotheby, London (21st April 1943).
1ST PF. (?) 15th July 1870, Musikvereinssaal, Vienna.
1ST ED. 1849, A. Diabelli & Co., Vienna (no. 8849), corrupt, with the note ' aus dem Werke: Historische Antiquitäten von Rittgräff.'

The title of the first edition gives the poem as of the fourteenth century, which is an error in the text of the *Historische Antiquitäten*; the right date, however, is given in the index of that book. The work appeared in two volumes, published by Karl Gerold, Vienna, in 1815, and the poem is printed in the second volume on p. 90 in Latin, and on p. 91 in German. The editor was Andreas Rittig von Flammenstein, but the author was the late Franz Gräffer; hence the pseudonym Rittgräff. The poem is inserted in the chapter ' Mancherlei Kirchen-Feierlichkeiten und Volksgebräuche,' after Enoch Wiedemann's ' Chronik der Stadt Hof,' and is introduced with the words ' Fastnacht. Beim Becherklang ertönte das gefällige Liedchen.' The German translation in the book runs ' Nonnen schmausen, Pfaffen zechen . . .', and in the music of the first edition ' Seht, der Mönch trinkt mit der Nonne . . . ,' but there is also an alternative text, ' Auf, ihr Freunde, auf und trinket. . . .' These two German versions are not in Schubert's MS., nor is the pf. acc., which was added by the publisher. The quartet was probably written for Ferdinand Traweger, Schubert's host at Gmunden, and his friends. According to K. von Wurzbach, the censorship did not permit publication of this quartet before 1848.

Literature. O. E. D., *Neue Musikzeitung*, Stuttgart, 1928, vol. xlix, no. 11, pp. 355–7.

848. ' **Nachtmusik** ' (Karl Siegmund Seckendorf), **Chorus, T.T.B.B.** (Op. posth. 156; XVI 30). July 1825 (Gmunden).

[musical notation: Mässig]

p Wir stim - men dir— mit Flö - ten-sang.

MS. Nationalbibliothek, Vienna.
1ST ED. 1848, A. Diabelli & Co., Vienna (no. 8850), with a spurious pf. acc. *ad libitum*.

The author himself set the poem as a song which was published in the *Göttinger Musenalmanach* for 1780. Schubert's serenade was possibly addressed to Fräulein Therese Clodi at Schloss Ebenzweier on the Traunsee, near Gmunden.

—— **'Versunken'** (XX 391). See 715. July 1825 (Gmunden).

849. **Symphony in ?** Lost. July–August 1825 (Gmunden-Gastein).

Literature. George Grove, *Athenaeum*, London, 19th November 1881. O. E. D., *Neue Freie Presse*, Vienna, 11th July 1925. Cf. 812.

850. **Sonata in D for Pianoforte** (Op. 53; X 11). August 1825 (Gastein).

MS. Nationalbibliothek, Vienna.

1ST ED. 8th April 1826, Matthias Artaria, Vienna (no. 825), dedicated by Schubert to the pianist K. M. von Bocklet, under the title 'Seconde grande Sonate.'

In the MS. the first movement is written in *alla breve* time. Another autograph, dated December 1825, is mentioned by Grove; no trace of this can be found. Cf. **604**.

851. **'Das Heimweh'** ('Ach, der Gebirgssohn,' Pyrker), **Song**, two versions (Op. 79, no. 1; XX 478 (*a*) and (*b*)). August 1825 (Gastein).

Ziemlich langsam

Ach, der Ge-birgs-sohn hängt mit kind-li-cher Lieb' an der Hei - mat.

BAR 26
Version 'a'
wel - ket die Blu - me, so

Version 'b'
wel - ket die Blu - me, so

MS. (*a*) and (*b*) Preussische Staatsbibliothek, Berlin.

IST ED. (*a*) 1895, Gesamtausgabe; (*b*) 16th May 1827, Tobias Haslinger, Vienna (no. 5027), as no. 1 of Op. 79, dedicated by Schubert to the poet, Johann Ladislaus Pyrker von Felsö-Eör.

Both versions (in one MS.) are in A minor, the first edition, however, was published in G minor. Here the song is dated, as in the MS., 'Gastein im August 1825.' The *Allgemeine musikalische Zeitung*, Leipzig, 23rd January 1828, suggests that this song is based on the theme of a 'Ranz des vaches,' from Emmental (Switzerland); the so-called 'Emmentaler Lied,' bears little resemblance. The poem, not printed before the first edition of the song, was apparently written for Schubert.

852. '**Die Allmacht**' (Pyrker), Song (Op. 79, no. 2; XX 479). August 1825 (Gastein).

Langsam, feierlich

Gross ist Je - ho - vah, der Herr,

MS. Lost.

IST ED. 16th May 1827, Tobias Haslinger, Vienna (no. 5027), as no. 2 of Op. 79, dedicated by Schubert to the poet.

Kreissle (pp. 595 f.) mentions another, unfinished, setting of this poem, for quartet, T.T.B.B., the MS. of which was said to have been in the possession of Johann Herbeck, Vienna (*c.* 1865). This, however, is not probable. The text is taken from Pyrker's *Perlen der heiligen Vorzeit* (*biblische Dichtungen in Hexametern*), Ofen, 1821, section 'Elisa,' 1st canto: 'Tod,' lines 93–101.

853. '**Auf der Bruck**,' called '**Auf der Brücke**' (Schulze), **Song** (Op. 93, no. 2; XX 477). August 1825.

[Musical notation: Geschwind, "Frisch tra-be son-der Ruh' und Rast."]

MS. Lost.
1ST ED. 30th May 1828, J. A. Kienreich, Graz (no publisher's number), as no. 2 of Op. 90 (later corrected to 93), lithographed by Josef Franz Kaiser, with the corrupt title 'Auf der Brücke,' and the erroneous indication that the two songs (this and 834) were written during Schubert's sojourn at Graz (September 1827).

The poem was headed in Schulze's *Poetisches Tagebuch* ' Auf der Bruck. Den 25sten Julius 1814.' The Bruck is a wooded hill near Göttingen.

854. '**Fülle der Liebe**' (Friedrich von Schlegel), **Song** (XX 480). August 1825.

[Musical notation: Nicht zu langsam, "Ein seh-nend Stre-ben teilt mir das Herz,"]

MS. Preussische Staatsbibliothek, Berlin (together with 855).
1ST ED. 9th October 1835, A. Diabelli & Co., Vienna (no. 5029), as no. 1 of *Nachlass*, book 25.

855. '**Wiedersehn**' (August Wilhelm von Schlegel), **Song** (XX 481). September 1825.

[Musical notation: Nicht zu langsam, "Der Früh-lings-son-ne hol-des Lä-cheln"]

MS. Preussische Staatsbibliothek, Berlin (together with 854); an additional MS., containing the second and third stanzas, with some alterations to the voice part—Richard Zeune, Leipzig (1870, sale 20, catalogue no. 231).
1ST ED. 1843, Tauer & Sohn, Vienna, in Andreas Schumacher's symposium, *Lebensbilder aus Oesterreich*, Supplement no. 3 (with Friedrich von Schlegel's name as the author).

The song was republished in 1872 by J. P. Gotthard, Vienna (no. 325) as no. 1 of forty songs.

856. **'Abendlied für die Entfernte'** (August Wilhelm von Schlegel), **Song** (Op. 88, no. 1; XX 482). September 1825.

In mässiger Bewegung

Hin - aus, mein Blick! hin - aus in's Tal!

MS. Lost.
1ST ED. 12th December 1827, Thaddäus Weigl, Vienna (no. 2696), as no. 1 of Op. 88.

Schubert omitted the third stanza of the poem; it is reprinted in the *Revisionsbericht*. He also altered the last line of the fourth stanza (see *Revisionsbericht*).

857. **Two Scenes from the Play 'Lacrimas'** (Wilhelm von Schütz), called **Florio** and **Delphine**, **Songs** (Op. posth. 124; XX 483 and 484). September 1825.

1. *Langsam*

Nun, da — Schat - ten nie - der - glei - ten,

2. *Mässige Bewegung*

Ach, was soll ich be - gin - nen vor Lie - be?

MS. Lost.
1ST ED. 30th October 1829, A. Pennauer, Vienna (no. 453), as no. 2 and 1 of Op. 124 (corrupt).

The first edition names August Wilhelm von Schlegel, the editor of the play (published anonymously in Berlin, 1803), as the author and reverses the order of the two songs. According to the play, Florio's song ('Nun, da Schatten niedergleiten,' Act III, scene vi, p. 92) precedes Delphine's song ('Ach, was soll ich beginnen vor Liebe,' Act IV, scene ii, p. 118). There are alterations to the text other than those indicated in the *Revisionsbericht*.

858. **March for two Pianofortes** (eight hands). Doubtful. Unpublished. November 1825.

MS. Unknown; former owner—private collection, Heidelberg (1899).

There was a pencil note on the MS., giving the names of (Anselm?) Hüttenbrenner and Schwammerl (Schubert's nickname).

Literature. Prager Tagblatt, Prague, 31st August 1899.

859. Grande Marche funèbre à l'occasion de la mort de S. M. Alexandre I, Empereur de toutes les Russies, in C minor for Piano Duet (Op. 55, IX 4).   December 1825.

MS. Lost.
1ST ED. 8th February 1826, A. Pennauer, Vienna (no. 245), as Op. 55.
Alexander I died on 1st December 1825. Cf. **885**.

860. ' An mein Herz ' (Schulze), **Song** (XX 485).   December 1825.

MS. Rough draft (together with 862)—Dr. Alwin Cranz, Vienna.
1ST ED. 4th January 1832, A. Diabelli & Co., Vienna (no. 4013), as no. 1 of *Nachlass,* book 13.
The poem was headed simply ' Am 23sten Januar 1816 ' in Schulze's *Poetisches Tagebuch;* the title ' An mein Herz ' was given by Schubert.

861. ' Der liebliche Stern ' (Schulze), **Song** (XX 486).   December 1825.

MS. The first thirty-four bars—Karl Ernst Henrici, Berlin (sale, 13th February 1923); the remainder (together with 884) —Dr. Alwin Cranz, Vienna.

1ST ED. 4th January 1832, A. Diabelli & Co., Vienna (no. 4013), as no. 2 of *Nachlass*, book 13.

The poem was headed simply ' Am 28sten April 1814 ' in Schulze's *Poetisches Tagebuch*; the title ' Der liebliche Stern ' was given by Schubert.

862. ' **Um Mitternacht** ' (Schulze), **Song** (Op. 88, no. 3; XX 499). December 1825.

Sehr mässig

Kei - ne Stim-me .hör' ich schal-len,

MS. Rough copy, dated, without the last thirteen bars—Wittgenstein family, Vienna; the remainder (together with 860)— Dr. Alwin Cranz, Vienna); final version—lost.

1ST ED. 12th December 1827, Thaddäus Weigl, Vienna (no. 2696), as no. 3 of Op. 88.

The rough copy was cancelled by Schubert in red pencil. The final version also was probably dated. The date, March 1826, given in the G.A., was taken from Nottebohm, who had copied Witteczek. This date was suggested, no doubt, by the fact that three other Schulze songs were written during that month (882-4). The poem was headed simply ' Am 5ten März 1815, Nachts um 12 Uhr ' in Schulze's *Poetisches Tagebuch*; the title ' Um Mitternacht ' was given by Schubert.

863. ' **An Gott** ' (Hohlfeld), **Song.** Lost. *c.* 1826.

The poem was published in *Lieder für Blinde und von Blinden*, ed. by Johann Wilhelm Klein, the director of the Vienna Blind Institute, in 1827, p. 9, with the note: ' Musik von Franz Schubert.'

864. ' **Das Totenhemdchen** ' (Bauernfeld), **Song.** Lost. *c.* 1826.

In the *Album österreichischer Dichter*, Vienna, 1850, where it was first published, and in the collections of Bauernfeld's verses (1852, 1856, 1873), the poem is indicated as having been set by Schubert.

865. ' **Widerspruch** ' (Seidl), **Quartet, T.T.B.B., with Pianoforte accompaniment** (Op. 105, no. 1; XVI 12). (?) 1826.

Ziemlich geschwind

Wenn ich durch Busch und Zweig brech' auf be-schränk-tem Steig,

M.S. Stadtbibliothek, Vienna.

1ST PF. 27th November 1828, Musikverein, Vienna (by male voice chorus).

1ST ED. 21st November 1828 (the day of Schubert's funeral), Josef Czerny, Vienna (no. 329, plate-mark 330), as no. 1 of Op. 105 (also separately); the parts published in folio.

The first edition, containing the pf. score and the parts, offers the alternative of a solo song with pf. acc. The alternative, although not indicated in the MS., is mentioned in the newspaper advertisement as having been arranged by Schubert.

866. **Vier Refrain-Lieder**: 'Die Unterscheidung' or 'Gretchen's Gehorsam,' 'Bei dir allein!' 'Die Männer sind méchant!' 'Irdisches Glück' (Seidl), Songs (Op. 95, XX 508–11). (?) 1826.

1. DIE UNTERSCHEIDUNG
Mässig

Die Mut-ter hat mich jüngst ge-schol-ten,

2. BEI DIR ALLEIN
Nicht zu geschwind, doch feurig

Bei dir al-lein___ em-pfind' ich,

3. DIE MÄNNER SIND MÉCHANT
Etwas langsam

Du sag-test mir es, Mut-ter:

4. IRDISCHES GLÜCK
Ziemlich geschwind

So Man-cher sieht mit fin-strer Mie-ne

MS. Lost.

1ST ED. (?) Middle of 1826, Thaddäus Weigl, Vienna (nos. 2794–7), as nos. 1–4 of Op. 95, dedicated by Schubert to the poet.

In a later printing of the poem 'Die Unterscheidung,' in the almanac *Das Veilchen*, Vienna, 1835, pp. 43 f., it is called 'Gretchens Abscheu vor der Liebe.'

867. **'Wiegenlied'** ('Wie sich der Äuglein kindlicher Himmel,' Seidl), **Song** (Op. 105, no. 2; XX 512). (?) 1826.

[musical notation: Langsam — Wie sich der Äug-lein kind-li-cher Him-mel,]

MS. Lost.

1ST ED. 21st November 1828 (the day of Schubert's funeral), Josef Czerny, Vienna (no. 329, plate-mark 331), as no. 2 of Op. 105 (also separately).

868. **'Das Echo'** (Castelli), **Song** (Op. posth. 130; XX 513). (?) 1826.

[musical notation: Mässig — Herz-lie-be, gu-te Mut-ter,]

MS. Lost.

1ST ED. 12th July 1830, Thaddäus Weigl, Vienna (no. 2935), as Op. 130.

The advertisement of this song in the *Wiener Zeitung* mentions six humorous songs which Schubert intended to write for the publisher; only this one, however, was written before Schubert died. Cf. 866.

869. **'Totengräber-Weise'** (Schlechta), **Song** (XX 496). 1826.

[musical notation: Ziemlich langsam — Nicht so dü-ster und so bleich]

MS. Mrs. Whittall Collection, Library of Congress, Washington.

1ST ED. 4th January 1832, A. Diabelli & Co., Vienna (no. 4015), as no. 3 of *Nachlass*, book 15.

A second version of the poem (not set by Schubert) was at first entitled 'Fischerlied,' and later was given the title 'An der Bahre.'

870. **'Der Wanderer an den Mond'** (Seidl), **Song** (Op. 80, no. 1; XX 506). 1826.

Etwas bewegt

Ich auf der Erd', am Him-mel du,

MS. Rough copy (together with 871)—Preussische Staatsbibliothek, Berlin; final version (together with 871 and 880)—unknown; former owner—Frau von Lanna, Prague.

1ST ED. 25th May 1827, Tobias Haslinger, Vienna (no. 5028), as no. 1 of Op. 80, dedicated by Schubert to Josef Witteczek.

The poem and the song contain the line 'Aus Westens Wieg' in Ostens Grab,' an error in Seidl's *Dichtungen*, Vienna, 1826, p. 24, corrected in a later version of the poem to 'Aus Ostens Wieg' in Westens Grab,' with some further alterations.

871. ' **Das Zügenglöcklein** ' (Seidl), **Song** (Op. 80, no. 2; XX 507). 1826.

Langsam

Kling' die Nacht durch, klin - ge

MS. Rough copy—Preussische Staatsbibliothek, Berlin (together with 870); final version (together with 870 and 880)—unknown; former owner—Frau von Lanna, Prague.

1ST ED. 25th May 1827, Tobias Haslinger, Vienna (no. 5028), as no. 2 of Op. 80, dedicated by Schubert to Josef Witteczek.

872. ' **Gesänge zur Feier des heiligen Opfers der Messe,**' called ' **Deutsche Messe,**' with an Appendix ' **Das Gebet des Herrn** ' (Johann Philipp Neumann), **for Mixed Chorus, Wind Instruments, and Organ** (XIII 7). 1826-7.

1. ZUM EINGANG
Mässig

p Wo - hin soll ich mich wen - den,

2. ZUM GLORIA
Mit Majestät

f Eh - re, Eh - re sei Gott in der Hö - he!

3. ZUM EVANGELIUM UND CREDO
Nicht zu langsam

p Noch lag die Schö-pfung form-los da,

4. ZUM OFFERTORIUM
Sehr langsam

p Du gabst, o Herr, mir Sein und Le-ben,

5. ZUM SANCTUS
Sehr langsam

pp Hei-lig, hei-lig, hei-lig,

6. NACH DER WANDLUNG
Sehr langsam

p Be-tracht-tend Dei-ne Huld und Gü-te,

7. ZUM AGNUS DEI
Mässig

p Mein Hei-land, Herr und Mei-ster,

8. SCHLUSSGESANG
Nicht zu langsam

p Herr, du hast mein Fleh'n ver-nom-men,

ANHANG. DAS GEBET DES HERRN
Mässig

f An-be-tend dei-ne Macht— und Grös-se

MS. First version (with organ acc. only, the Appendix written by another hand)—unknown; former owner—Max Friedlaender,

Berlin; final version (written for the author)—Stadtbibliothek, Vienna.

1ST PF. 8th December 1846, Anna-Kirche, Vienna (conductor Ferdinand Schubert), with acc. for two oboes and three trombones (instead of the organ).

1ST ED. Appendix ' Das Gebet des Herrn '—1845, Tobias Haslinger, Vienna (no. 9831), in *Album für Gesang . . . zum Besten der durch Ueberschwemmung verunglückten Böhmen*, ed. by Josef Dessauer, pp. 76–8; the remainder (corrupt)—1854, J. B. Wallishausser, Vienna, in Josef Ferdinand Kloss's *Allgemeine Kirchenmusik-Lehre in Vorträgen für Präparanden des pädagogischen Lehramtes*, Supplement, pp. xvii–xxv (without acc.); complete—1870, J. P. Gotthard, Vienna (score and parts, nos. 117 and 119), with a preface by the publisher.

This German mass was written to be sung as low mass in Catholic churches. The original version, first printed in the G.A. (1887), is for mixed chorus with acc. of wind instruments and organ. About 1830 Ferdinand Schubert arranged it for three boys' voices with organ acc. (published in his collection *Messgesänge und Kirchenlieder* for the use of the *K. k. Normal-Hauptschule zu St. Anna*, Vienna, A. Strauss, without date); in 1845 he set it for four mixed voices with organ acc., and in 1855 for four male voices without acc. (MS. copies—Gesellschaft der Musikfreunde, Vienna, and Wiener Schubertbund, Vienna). Ignaz von Seyfried's (?) arrangement for male voice chorus was edited anonymously by Johann Herbeck—1866, C. A. Spina, Vienna (no. 18400). The text is said to have been printed separately in 1826 as 'Geistliche Lieder für das heilige Messopfer,' with the names of the author and the composer, by Anton Benko in Vienna, but no copy of this publication is known. It was, however, published in 1827 as 'Gesänge zur Feier des heiligen Opfers der Messe. Nebst einem Anhange, Das Gebeth des Herrn,' without their names, by Anton von Haykul at Vienna. Cf. **621, 701,** and Appendix II, no. 9.

Literature. O. E. D., *Musica Divina*, Vienna, January–April 1914, and *Neues Wiener Tagblatt*, 15th January 1928.

873. **Canon a sei.** Unpublished. (?) January 1826.

MS. Preussische Staatsbibliothek, Berlin (together with 875).

874. ' **O Quell, was strömst du rasch und wild** ' (Schulze), **Sketch of Song.** Not printed. (?) January 1826.

MS. Bodleian, Oxford (together with 876).

The sketch contains four bars of pf. introduction and fourteen bars of voice part with words (the first of four stanzas) and indications for pf. acc. The poem is simply headed ' 8ten Januar 1814 ' in Schulze's *Poetisches Tagebuch*; similarly Schubert's sketch only bears the heading ' Jänner.' The poem represents a dialogue between a flower and a spring.

—— **String Quartet in D minor** (V 14). See 810. January 1826.

875. ' **Mondenschein** ' (Schober), **Quintet, T.T.B.B.B., with Pianoforte accompaniment** (Op. 102; XVI 27). January 1826.

MS. (together with 873)—Preussische Staatsbibliothek, Berlin, without the acc.; the pf. acc. only—B. Schott's Söhne, Mainz.

1ST PF. 3rd January 1828, Musikverein, Vienna (without the acc.).

1ST ED. 1829, A. Diabelli & Co., Vienna (no. 3181), with a spurious pf. acc. *ad lib.*

The poem was originally entitled ' Vollmondnacht.' The composition was first offered to Schott, who printed it, unauthorized, in 1831 or 1832 (no. 3659, no copy known), with—the original?—acc. and without it.

876. ' **Ich bin von aller Ruh' geschieden,**' called ' **Tiefes Leid** ' (Schulze), **Song** (XX 487). January 1826.

MS. Bodleian, Oxford (together with 874).

1ST ED. 1838, A. Diabelli & Co., Vienna (no. 5034), as no. 1 of *Nachlass*, book 30.

The poem was headed ' Am 17ten Januar 1817 ' in Schulze's *Poetisches Tagebuch*, but simply ' Im Jänner 1817 ' in Schubert's MS.; the title ' Tiefes Leid ' was added to the MS. by another hand, probably for the first edition. The MS. copy in the Witteczek Collection, however, bears Schulze's date and the dubious title.

877. 'Gesänge aus "Wilhelm Meister"' (Goethe): 1. 'Mignon und der Harfner' ('Nur wer die Sehnsucht kennt'); 2. 'Lied der Mignon' ('Heiss' mich nicht reden'); 3. 'Lied der Mignon' ('So lasst mich scheinen'); 4. 'Lied der Mignon' ('Nur wer die Sehnsucht kennt'), Songs (Op. 62; XX 488-91). January 1826 (?-1827).

1. MIGNON UND DER HARFNER
Langsam

Nur___ wer___ die Sehn-sucht kennt,

2. LIED DER MIGNON
Langsam

Heiss mich nicht re-den, heiss___ mich schwei-gen,

3. LIED DER MIGNON
Nicht zu langsam

So lasst mich schei-nen, bis ich wer-de;

4. LIED DER MIGNON
Langsam

Nur wer die Sehn-sucht kennt, weiss, was___ ich lei-de.

MS. Nos. 1-3—Sächsische Landesbibliothek, Dresden; voice part of nos. 1-3—Stadtbibliothek, Vienna; no. 4—unknown; former owner—Max Kalbeck, Vienna.

1ST ED. 2nd March 1827, A. Diabelli & Co., Vienna (no. 2253), as nos. 1-4 of Op. 62, dedicated by Schubert to Mathilde, Fürstin Schwarzenberg (first issue on thick paper).

It seems that no. 4 was written later, probably for the first edition, because two MSS. contain only the three first songs. The MS. score shows the publisher's directions to the engraver. The voice part, with indications for the acc. (mostly for the right hand only), is a fair copy, probably written for a particular performance. In this fair copy the interlude in no. 2 is elaborated, and it is thus printed in the *Revisionsbericht*. Other settings of these songs are listed as follows: 'Nur wer die Sehnsucht kennt,' 310, 359, and 481; 'Heiss' mich nicht reden,' 726; 'So lasst mich scheinen,' 469 and 727.

878. 'Am Fenster' (Seidl), Song (Op. 105, no. 3; XX 492). March 1826.

[musical notation: Langsam]

Ihr lie - ben Mau-ern hold und traut,

MS. Stadtbibliothek, Vienna (together with 879–81); another MS. (together with a fragment of 879)—Wittgenstein family, Vienna.
1ST ED. 21st November 1828 (the day of Schubert's funeral), Josef Czerny, Vienna (no. 329, plate no. 332), as no. 3 of Op. 105 (also separately).

879. 'Sehnsucht' ('Die Scheibe friert,' Seidl), Song (Op. 105, no. 4; XX 493). March 1826.

[musical notation: Nicht zu geschwind]

Die Schei - be friert, der Wind ist rauh,

MS. Stadtbibliothek, Vienna (together with 878, 880, and 881); a fragment (together with 878)—Wittgenstein family, Vienna.
1ST ED. 21st November 1828 (the day of Schubert's funeral), Josef Czerny, Vienna (no. 329, plate no. 333), as no. 4 of Op. 105 (also separately).

There are some alterations in the bass of the last four bars in the MS., probably made by Schubert for the first edition.

880. 'Im Freien' (Seidl), Song (Op. 80, no. 3; XX 494). March 1826.

[musical notation: Mässig, mit Innigkeit]

Drau-ssen in der— wei-ten Nacht

MS. Rough copy—Stadtbibliothek, Vienna (together with 878, 879, and 881); final version—unknown; former owner—Frau von Lanna, Prague (together with 870 and 871).
1ST PF. 6th May 1827, Festsaal der Universität, Vienna.
1ST ED. (Final version) 25th May 1827, Tobias Haslinger,

Vienna (no. 5028), as no. 3 of Op. 80, dedicated by Schubert to Josef Witteczek.

The *Revisionsbericht* shows the difference between the first MS. and the first edition.

881. '**Fischerweise**' (Schlechta), **Song**, two versions (Op. 96, no. 4; XX 495 (*a*) and (*b*)). March 1826.

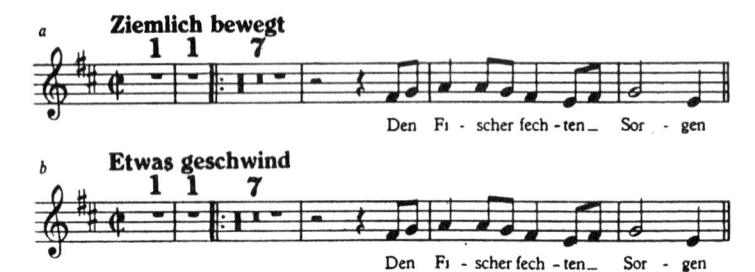

a **Ziemlich bewegt**

Den Fi - scher fech - ten _ Sor - gen

b **Etwas geschwind**

Den Fi - scher fech - ten _ Sor - gen

MS. (*a*) Stadtbibliothek, Vienna (together with 878–80); (*b*) lost.

1ST PF. (*b*) 26th March 1828, Musikverein, Vienna (Schubert's concert).

1ST ED. (*a*) 1895, Gesamtausgabe; (*b*) Summer 1828 (Lithographisches Institut, Vienna, without publisher's number), as no. 4 of four songs, without opus number (later called Op. 96), dedicated by Schubert to Karoline, Fürstin Kinsky, *née* Freiin von Kerpen (lithographed).

This is the second of three versions of the poem, altered, apparently, by the author himself (cf. his 'Widerschein,' set by Schubert in May 1828, 949).

882. '**Im Frühling**' (Schulze), **Song** (XX 497). March 1826.

Andante

Still sitz' ich an des Hü-gels Hang,

MS. Lost.

1ST ED. 16th September 1828, as a supplement to the *Wiener Zeitschrift für Kunst*, etc., Vienna (in type).

The poem was headed simply 'Am 31sten März 1815' in Schulze's *Poetisches Tagebuch*; the title 'Im Frühling' was given by Schubert. The song was reprinted on 12th December 1828, by H. A. Probst, Leipzig (no. 431), as no. 1 of a spurious Op. 101, which consists only of reprints from the *Wiener Zeitschrift*; later republished by A. Diabelli & Co., Vienna (no. 5029), as no. 2 of *Nachlass*, book 25 (9th October 1835).

883. 'Lebensmut' ('O wie dringt das junge Leben,' Schulze), Song (XX 498). March 1826.

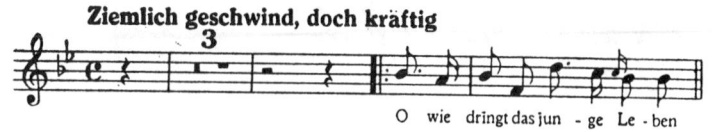

Ziemlich geschwind, doch kräftig

O wie dringt das jun - ge Le - ben

MS. Lost (Witteczek's copy).
1ST ED. 5th May 1832, A. Diabelli & Co., Vienna (no. 4017), as no. 1 of *Nachlass*, book 17.

The poem was headed simply 'Am 1sten April 1815' in Schulze's *Poetisches Tagebuch*; the title 'Lebensmut' was given by Schubert.

884. 'Ueber Wildemann' (Schulze), Song (Op. 108, no. 1; XX 500). March 1826.

Schnell

Die Win - de sau - sen am Tan - nen - hang,

MS. Rough sketch (incomplete, together with 861)—Dr. Alwin Cranz, Vienna; final version—lost.
1ST ED. 28th January 1829, M. J. Leidesdorf, Vienna (no. 108), as no. 1 of Op. 93, later corrected to 108 (advertised at Easter 1828).

The poem was entitled in Schulze's *Poetisches Tagebuch* 'Ueber Wildemann, einem Bergstädtchen am Harz. Den 28sten April 1816.' The sketch (up to 'ich wandle in Eile durch') differs slightly from the final version. An old MS. copy of the lost autograph (final version) was in the possession of Karl Liebleitner, Mödling, near Vienna.

885. **Grande Marche héroïque composée à l'occasion du Sacre de Sa Majesté Nicolas I, Empereur des toutes les Russies, in A minor for Piano Duet** (Op. 66, IX 5). (?) Spring 1826.

Maestoso

ff

Allegro giusto

Allegro giusto *(as above)*

MS. Lost.
1ST ED. 14th September 1826, A. Pennauer, Vienna (no. 274), as Op. 66.
Cf. 859.

886. **Two Marches caractéristiques in C for Piano Duet** (Op. posth. 121, IX 6). (?) Spring of 1826.

No 1.
Allegro vivace

No. 2.
Allegro vivace

MS. Lost.

1ST ED. February 1830, A. Diabelli & Co., Vienna (no. 3552), as Op. 121.

Schober, writing to Bauernfeld in June 1826, mentions that Schubert had written some new marches for pf. duet; it is likely that he refers to these. (*Schubert Documents*, no. 663, p. 532.)

887. **String Quartet in G** (Op. posth. 161, V 15). 20th–30th June 1826 (Währing, near Vienna).

MS. Score—Nationalbibliothek, Vienna; parts (written before 5th March 1827)—lost.

1ST PF. First movement only—26th March 1828, Musikverein, Vienna, at Schubert's concert (Ignaz Schuppanzigh's Quartet); complete work—8th December 1850, Musikverein, Vienna (Josef Hellmesberger's Quartet).

1ST ED. November 1851, A. Diabelli & Co., Vienna (no. 9099), as Op. 161.

The tune of the Andante is said, by Anna Fröhlich, to have been taken from a Swedish folk-song (or rather a song by Isaac Albert Berg). If there is any truth in this story, then it relates to the second movement of the pf. Trio in E flat, Op. 100 (929), written in November 1827, because Berg is said to have sung Swedish songs to Schubert during his visit to Vienna in 1827.

888. 'Trinklied' ('Bacchus, feister Fürst,' from Shakespeare's 'Antony and Cleopatra,' translated by Ferdinand Mayerhofer von Grünbühel and (?) Eduard von Bauernfeld), Song (XX 502). Beginning of July 1826 (Währing).

MS. Stadtbibliothek, Vienna (on small paper ruled in pencil, together with 889–91).
1ST ED. c. 1848, A. Diabelli & Co., Vienna (no. 8837), as no. 4 of *Nachlass*, book 48.

Währing was, at that time, a village outside Vienna, where Schubert stayed during the summer of 1826. He took the poem from the Vienna edition of Shakespeare's works (J. P. Sollinger, 1825–7). A second stanza was added in the first edition of the song; it was probably written by Friedrich Reil (cf. 889). It is possible to sing the original words to this music.

889. 'Ständchen' ('Horch, horch die Lerch,' from Shakespeare's 'Cymbeline,' translated by August Wilhelm von Schlegel), Song (XX 503). Beginning of July 1826 (Währing).

MS. Stadtbibliothek, Vienna (together with 888, 890, and 891).
1ST ED. 26th October 1830, A. Diabelli & Co., Vienna (no. 3704), as no. 4 of *Nachlass*, book 7.

Schubert spells the name of the author as 'Schakespear' at the head of this song. The second and the third stanzas in the first edition were written by Friedrich Reil. It is possible to sing the original words to this music.

890. 'Hippolit's Lied' (from Johanna Schopenhauer's novel 'Gabriele'), Song (XX 504). Beginning of July 1826 (Währing).

Etwas langsam

Lasst mich, ob ich auch still ver-glüh.

MS. Stadtbibliothek, Vienna (together with 888, 889, 891).
1ST ED. 26th October 1830, A. Diabelli & Co., Vienna (no. 3704), as no. 2 of *Nachlass*, book 7.

891. 'Gesang,' called 'An Sylvia' (from Shakespeare's 'Two Gentlemen of Verona,' translated by Eduard von Bauernfeld), Song (Op. 106, no. 4; XX 505). Beginning of July 1826 (Währing).

Mässig

Was ist Syl-via, sa-get an.

MS. Stadtbibliothek, Vienna (together with 888–90).
1ST ED. Spring 1828 (Lithographisches Institut, Vienna, without publisher's number), as no. 4 of four songs without opus number, later called Op. 106, dedicated by Schubert to Frau Marie Pachler (lithographed).

Schubert used Shakespeare's title 'Song'; the title 'An Sylvia' is spurious, and was added in the first edition. No. 4 of Op. 106 was originally reserved for 'altschottische Ballade' (923), for which this song was substituted. It is possible to sing the original words to this music.

892. 'Nachthelle' (Seidl) for Tenor Solo and Male Voice Chorus with Pianoforte accompaniment (Op. posth. 134, XVI 13). September 1826.

Andante con moto

p Die Nacht ist hei-ter und ist rein.

MS. Stadtbibliothek, Vienna.
1ST PF. 25th January 1827, Musikverein, Vienna.
1ST ED. *c.* 1838, A Diabelli & Co., Vienna (no. 6265), as Op. 134.

The MS. shows a section of the work in an earlier state; this section is printed in the *Revisionsbericht*.

893. 'Grab und Mond' (Seidl), Quartet, T.T.B.B. (XVI 41). September 1826.

[Langsam musical notation: *pp* Sil-ber-blau-er Mon-den-schein fällt her-ab.]

MS. Preussische Staatsbibliothek, Berlin.
1ST PF. (?) 2nd April 1864, Vienna.
1ST ED. 8th October 1827, Tobias Haslinger, Vienna (no. 3551), as no. 1 of the collection *Die deutschen Minnesänger* (cf. 901 and 914).

The first edition does not correspond exactly with the MS. For an error in the G.A. see the note by Johannes Wolf in *Schubertforschung*, Augsburg, 1929, p. 151.

894. Sonata, called Fantasia, in G for Pianoforte (Op. 78, X 12). October 1826.

[Molto moderato cantabile, *pp*]

[Andante, *p*]

[MENUETTO Allegro moderato, *f*]

[TRIO, *pp* decresc *ppp*]

[Allegretto, *p*]

MS. British Museum, London (Ph.).
1ST ED. 11th April 1827, Tobias Haslinger, Vienna (no. 5010), under the title ' Fantasie, Andante, Menuetto und Allegretto,'

as vol. 9 of the *Museum für Claviermusik* (*Musée musical des Clavecinistes*); dedicated by Schubert to Josef von Spaun.

The MS. is entitled 'IV Sonate,' the word 'Fantasie' being added by the publisher. The heading of the music reads 'Fantasie/ou/Sonate.' Spaun's consent to the dedication, dated 15th December 1826, was formerly attached to the MS.

Literature. Heinrich Schenker, in *Der Kunstwart*, Munich, March 1929, pp. 363–5 (on the Minuet only).

895. **Rondo in B minor for Pianoforte and Violin** (Op. 70, VIII 1). End of 1826.

MS. The Heineman Foundation, New York.

1ST PF. Beginning of 1827, at the lodgings of Domenico Artaria, Vienna (performed by Karl Maria von Bocklet and Josef Slawjk, in the presence of Schubert).

1ST ED. 19th April 1827, Artaria & Co., Vienna (no. 2929, price 1 fl. 30 kr. C.M.), as Op. 70, under the title 'Rondeau brillant.'

Possibly written for Slawjk.

896. '**Fröhliches Scheiden**' (Leitner), **Sketch of Song.** *c.* 1827.

MS. Stadtbibliothek, Vienna.

1ST ED. Facsimile—1902, Verlag Harmonie, Berlin, in Heuberger's *Schubert*, between pp. 16 and 17.

The sketch includes the complete melody and words, but only occasional indications of an acc.

897. Adagio in E flat, called 'Notturno,' for Pianoforte Trio (Op. posth. 148, VII 5). (?) 1827.

MS. Nationalbibliothek, Vienna.
1ST ED. 1845, A. Diabelli & Co., Vienna (no. 7971), as Op. 148.

The title 'Nocturne' (Notturno) in the first edition and in the G.A. is apocryphal, and the work may have been the second or third movement of an intended trio.

898. Trio in B flat for Violin, Violoncello, and Pianoforte (Op. 99, VII 3). (?) 1827.

MS. Lost.
1ST ED. 1836, A. Diabelli & Co., Vienna (no. 5847), as Op. 99.
There is no confirmation that this Trio was written in October 1827, shortly before 929, as stated in George Grove's Schubert article, in his *Dictionary of Music and Musicians*, London, 1882, vol. iii, p. 348.

899. Four Impromptus for Pianoforte (Op. 90, XI 2). (?) 1827.

MS. Sketch to no. 1 (in C minor, written in pencil)—Stadtbibliothek, Vienna; complete MS.—Paul Oppenheim, Princeton (N.J.).
1ST ED. 10th December 1827—Tobias Haslinger, Vienna (nos. 5071 and 5072); and c. 1857—Karl Haslinger, Vienna (nos. 12075 and 12076), in four books.

No. 3 was written in G flat, double *alla breve* time; the publisher altered it to G, *alla breve*; the title 'Impromptus' too, was given by the publisher. The sketch to no. 1 is reproduced in Gerhard Preitz's edition of Opp. 90, 94, and 142 (*Urtext und Bearbeitung vereinigt. Studien-Ausgabe*), Cologne, 1926. Cf. 935.

900. Allegretto in C minor for Pianoforte (XXI 16). **Fragment.** (?) 1827.

MS. Stadtbibliothek, Vienna.
1ST ED. 1897, Gesamtausgabe.

901. ' Wein und Liebe ' (Haug). Quartet, T.T.B.B. (XVI 37).
(?) 1827.

f Lieb - chen und der Saft der Re - ben

So ver - schön' ich oh - ne Kum- mer

MS. Preussische Staatsbibliothek, Berlin.
1ST PF. (?) 14th December 1862, Redoutensaal, Vienna.
1ST ED. 8th October 1827, Tobias Haslinger, Vienna (no. 3554), as no. 4 of the collection *Die deutschen Minnesänger* (cf. 893 and 914).

Possibly the quartet mentioned by Wilhelm von Chézy in his *Memoirs* (Schaffhausen, 1863, vol. i, part 2, p. 192) as the ' vertrunkene Quartett.' If this is so, then the date 1827 would appear to be correct, but the MS. rather suggests the early twenties. The MS. bears the censor's permit, dated 2nd June 1827 (cf. ' Frühlingslied,' 914).

902. ' Drei Gesänge ': ' L'incanto degli occhi (Die Macht der Augen),' ' Il traditor deluso (Der getäuschte Verräter),' ' Il modo di prender moglie (Die Art, ein Weib zu nehmen),' (nos. 1 and 2—Metastasio; no. 3—author unknown), Songs (Op. 83, XX 579–81). 1827.

1. Allegretto

Da voi, ca - ri lu - mi, di - pen - de il mio sta - to;

2. Allegro assai

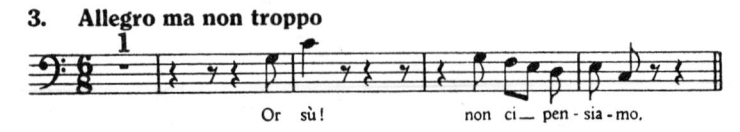

Ai - mè, io tre - mo!

3. Allegro ma non troppo

Or sù! non ci pen - sia - mo.

MS. Sketch of no. 2—Stadtbibliothek, Vienna; complete MS.—British Museum, London.

1ST ED. 12th September 1827, Tobias Haslinger, Vienna (nos. 5061-3), as nos. 1-3 of Op. 83, dedicated by Schubert to Luigi Lablache (Italian and German words).

The titles of the songs do not appear in the MS. Poem no. 1 is Licinio's aria from the opera *Attilio Regolo* (II. v); no. 2 is Atalia's aria from the oratorio *Gioas, Rè di Giuda* (Part 2), beginning ' Ahime, qual forza ignota anima quelle voci! Io tremo . . .'; no. 3 is apparently not by Metastasio, although in the first edition all three poems are attributed to him.

903. ' Zur guten Nacht ' (Rochlitz), for Baritone Solo and Male Voice Chorus with Pianoforte accompaniment (Op. 81, no. 3; XVI 11). January 1827.

Etwas langsam

Horcht auf! Es schlägt die Stun - de,

MS. (together with 904 and 905)—Gilhofer & Ranschburg, Vienna (1906, sale 21, catalogue no. 278).

1ST PF. (?) 16th May 1872, Musikvereinssaal, Vienna.

1ST ED. 28th May 1827, Tobias Haslinger, Vienna (no. 5029), as no. 3 of Op. 81, dedicated—on a separate leaf—by the publisher to the poet.

The MSS. of this opus bear the censor's permit, dated 26th February 1827. The G.A. dates the opus, erroneously, 1816, but partially corrects the date in the Supplement to the *Revisionsbericht*, Series XX, p. 1.

904. ' Alinde ' (Rochlitz), Song (Op. 81, no. 1; XX 287). January 1827.

[Musical notation: Mässig, 6/8, "Die Son-ne sinkt in's tie-fe Meer,"]

MS. (together with 903 and 905)—Gilhofer & Ranschburg, Vienna (1906).
1ST ED. 28th May 1827, Tobias Haslinger, Vienna (no. 5029), as no. 1 of Op. 81, dedicated by the publisher to the poet.
See 903.

905. ' **An die Laute** ' (Rochlitz), **Song** (Op. 81, no. 2; XX 288). January 1827.

[Musical notation: Etwas geschwind, 6/8, "Lei-ser, lei-ser, klei-ne Lau-te."]

MS. (together with 903 and 904)—Gilhofer & Ranschburg, Vienna (1906).
1ST ED. 28th May 1827, Tobias Haslinger, Vienna (no. 5029), as no. 2 of Op. 81, dedicated by the publisher to the poet.
See 903.

906. ' **Der Vater mit dem Kind** ' (Bauernfeld), **Song** (XX 514). January 1827.

[Musical notation: Langsam, "Dem Va-ter liegt das Kind im Arm."]

MS. Gesellschaft der Musikfreunde, Vienna (undated).
1ST ED. 5th May 1832, A. Diabelli & Co., Vienna (no. 4017), as no. 2 of *Nachlass*, book 17.

The Vienna MS. shows that Schubert originally intended to write this song in 6/8 time.

907. ' **Romanze des Richard Löwenherz** ' (' The Crusader's Return,' from Sir Walter Scott's novel ' Ivanhoe,' translated by (?) Karl Ludwig Methusalem Müller), **Song** (Op. 86, XX 501). Beginning of January 1827.

Mässig, doch feurig

Gro-sser Ta-ten tat der Rit-ter

MS. Lost.
IST PF. 2nd February 1828, Landhaussaal, Vienna.
IST ED. 14th March 1828, A. Diabelli & Co., Vienna (no. 2878), as Op. 86.

The date given by Witteczek, Nottebohm, and Mandyczweski is March 1826; but Franz von Hartmann, in his diary on 12th January 1827, mentions the first private performance of this ' quite new ' song.

908. Eight Variations on a theme from Hérold's opera ' Marie,' in C, for Piano Duet (Op. 82, IX 17). February 1827.

THEME
Allegretto

p legato

MS. Preussische Staatsbibliothek, Berlin.
IST ED. 3rd September 1827, Tobias Haslinger, Vienna (no. 5040), as Op. 82, dedicated by Schubert to Professor Kajetan Neuhaus, Linz.

Hérold's opera was produced at Vienna (shortly after the Paris *première*) on 18th December 1826; the theme is Lublin's (the miller's) song ' Sur la rivière comme mon père ' (Castelli's translation: ' Was einst vor Jahren '). The MS. bears the censor's permit, dated 5th July 1827. See 603.

909. ' Jägers Liebeslied ' (Schober), Song (Op. 96, no. 2; XX 515). February 1827.

Mässig geschwind

Ich schiess' den Hirsch im grü-nen Forst

MS. (Ph.) Sächsische Landesbibliothek, Dresden (together with Schober's copies of ' Vergissmeinnicht,' ' Uraniens Flucht,' ' Der Kreuzzug,' ' Einsamkeit '—the Mayrhofer song—and ' Gretchen am Spinnrade,' all formerly in Schober's possession).

1ST ED. 23rd June 1827, as a Supplement to the *Wiener Zeitschrift für Kunst*, etc., Vienna (in type).

'Vergissmeinnicht' precedes 'Jägers Liebeslied' in the MS. The poem was written in imitation of Johann Gottlieb Schulz's 'Jägerlied.' The last stanza was altered in the second edition of Schober's poems. Later, the poem was set to music, anonymously, and became a popular song in Transylvania. Schubert's song was republished in the summer of 1828 (Lithographisches Institut, Vienna, without publisher's number) as no. 2 of four songs without opus number, later called Op. 96, dedicated by Schubert to Karoline, Fürstin Kinsky, *née* Freiin von Kerpen (lithographed).

910. 'Schiffers Scheidelied' (Schober), **Song** (XX 516). February 1827.

MS. Lost (Witteczek's copy).
1ST ED. 25th September 1833, A. Diabelli & Co., Vienna (no. 4272), as no. 1 of *Nachlass*, book 24.

911. '**Winterreise**' (Wilhelm Müller), **Song Cycle** (Op. 89, XX 517–25, 526 (*a*) and (*b*), 527, 528 (*a*) and (*b*), 529–39, 540 (*a*) and (*b*)). February–October 1827.

BOOK I.
1. GUTE NACHT

2. DIE WETTERFAHNE

3. GEFROR'NE THRÄNEN

1827

4. ERSTARRUNG
Ziemlich schnell

Ich such' im Schnee ver-ge-bens

5. DER LINDENBAUM
Mässig

Am Brun-nen vor dem To-re

6 WASSERFLUT
Langsam

Man-che Thrän' aus mei-nen Au-gen

7. AUF DEM FLUSSE
Langsam

Der du so lu-stig rausch-test,

8. RÜCKBLICK
Nicht zu geschwind

Es brennt mir un-ter bei-den Soh-len,

9. IRRLICHT
Langsam

In die tief-sten Fel-sen-grün-de

10a. RAST
Mässig

Nun merk' ich erst, wie müd' ich bin,

10b. RAST
Mässig

Nun merk' ich erst, wie müd' ich bin,

11. FRÜHLINGSTRAUM
Etwas bewegt

Ich träum-te von bun-ten Blu-men.

12a. EINSAMKEIT
Langsam

Wie ei - ne trü - be Wol - ke

12b. EINSAMKEIT
Langsam

Wie ei - ne trü - be Wol - ke

BOOK II.
13. DIE POST
Etwas geschwind

Von der Stra - sse her ein Post - horn klingt.

14. DER GREISE KOPF
Etwas langsam

Der Reif hat ei - nen wei - ssen Schein

15. DIE KRÄHE
Etwas langsam

Ei - ne Krä - he war mit mir

16. LETZTE HOFFNUNG
Nicht zu geschwind

Hie und da ist an den Bäu - men

17. IM DORFE
Etwas langsam

Es bel - len die Hun - de, es ras - seln die Ket - ten

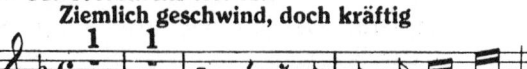

18. DER STÜRMISCHE MORGEN
Ziemlich geschwind, doch kräftig

Wie hat der Sturm zer - ris - sen

19. TÄUSCHUNG
Etwas geschwind

Ein Licht tanzt freund-lich vor mir her,

20. DER WEGWEISER
Mässig

Was ver - meid' ich denn die We - ge,

21. DAS WIRTSHAUS
Sehr langsam

Auf ei - nen To - ten - a - cker

22. MUT
Ziemlich geschwind, kräftig

Fliegt der Schnee mir in's Ge - sicht,

23. DIE NEBENSONNEN
Nicht zu langsam

Drei Son - nen sah ich am Him - mel steh'n,

24a. DER LEIERMANN
Etwas langsam

Drü - ben hin - term Dor - fe steht ein Lei - er - mann,

24b. DER LEIERMANN
Etwas langsam

Drü - ben hin - term Dor - fe steht ein Lei - er - mann,

MS. Rough copy of no. 23, incomplete—Gesellschaft der Musikfreunde, Vienna; complete MS.—Frau Marie Floersheim, Wildegg in Aargau (Switzerland).

1ST PF. No. 1—10th January 1828, Musikverein, Vienna.

1ST ED. First part—14th January 1828, Tobias Haslinger, Vienna (nos. 5101–12), with the price of this part only, p. 1 blank; second part—30th December 1828 (after Schubert's death), Tobias Haslinger, Vienna (nos. 5113–24; publisher's nos. on both parts, 5101–13), as Op. 89, nos. 1–24; nos. 10 (a), 12 (a), and 24 (a)—1895, Gesamtausgabe.

Part 1 of the complete MS. is also a rough copy, with the exception, perhaps, of nos. 1 and 8; part 2 is a fair copy. The MS. shows no. 6 written in F sharp minor, but it was altered by Schubert to E minor; no. 10 in D minor, with indications transposing it to C minor; no. 12 in D minor, altered to B minor; no. 22 in A minor (G minor), and no. 24 in B minor (A minor). The first part is dated February, the second part October 1827. Each part contains twelve songs. The cycle of Müller's poems was published as follows: the first twelve in the almanac *Urania*, Leipzig, for 1823 (together with twelve ghazals by Platen, which were greatly admired by Schubert's friends), another ten in *Deutsche Blätter für Poesie*, etc., Breslau, 14th March 1823; complete cycle in vol. ii of Muller's *Gedichte aus den hinterlassenen Papieren eines reisenden Waldhornisten*, Dessau, 1824, dedicated to Karl Maria von Weber. Schubert used the original order of part 1. The statement in the *Revisionsbericht* (Series XX), concerning alterations in the text, is corrected in the Supplement, p. 2; some of these alterations were in fact Müller's first version. The MS. of the first part had to be rewritten for the engraver, on account of many alterations in the music. This copy passed from Haslinger to Schlesinger, Berlin, and was offered for sale by Walter Hoeckner, Zwenkau, near Leipzig, in 1929 (Ph.). It is a copy by another hand with corrections by Schubert himself, dated 1827, and bears the censor's permit, dated 24th October 1827. The G.A. prints nos. 10, 12, and 24 in the transposed variants of the first edition. Further differences between the autograph MS. and the first edition, together with some alterations in the autograph, are shown in the *Revisionsbericht*, especially in nos. 2, 3, 4, 5, 7, 9, 11, 12, and 23. Not all the mistakes of the first edition, corrected in the *Revisionsbericht*, are proved by the MS. copy of part 1. The *Revisionsbericht* also shows some differences in the rough copy of no. 23. N.B.—The following correction to the text of no. 12 is to be found in the *Revisionsbericht*, Series XX,'Supplement: 'p. 40, bar 11, read " Tannen " instead of " Tanne" '.

Literature. Erwin Schaeffer, *Musical Quarterly*, New York, January 1938, pp. 39–57.

912. ' Schlachtlied,' called ' **Schlachtgesang** ' (Klopstock), **for Male Voice Double Chorus** (Op. posth. 151, XVI 28). 28th February 1827.

Nicht zu geschwind, kraftvoll

f Mit un-serm Arm ist nichts ge-tan.   steht uns der Mäch-ti-ge nicht bei.

MS. Fragment of the first sketch—Carl Hein, New York; full score—Stephan Zweig Collection, London.
1ST PF. 26th March 1828, Musikverein, Vienna (Schubert's concert), as ' Schlachtgesang.'
1ST ED. *c*. 1843, A. Diabelli & Co., Vienna (no. 7974), as Op. 151, with a spurious acc. for pianoforte or physharmonica *ad lib*.

Schubert also set the poem as a solo song (443).

913. ' Nachtgesang im Walde ' (Seidl), Quartet, T.T.B.B., with an accompaniment for four horns (Op. posth. 139 (*b*), XVI 1). April 1827.

Andante con moto
Sei uns stets ge-grüsst, ' o Nacht!

Allegro molto vivace
pp Es regt in den Lau-ben des Wal-des sich schon,

MS. Lost.
1ST PF. 22nd April 1827, Musikverein, Vienna (see note).
1ST ED. 1846, Tobias Haslinger, Vienna (no. 10011—score, 10012—parts), with a pf. acc. added as an alternative.

The poem was published in the *Allgemeine Theaterzeitung*, Vienna, on 28th August 1827. Although the Quartet was not published until 1846, Haslinger advertised it as early as the end of 1828. It was written for the horn player Josef Eduard Lewy's benefit concert, and the rehearsals were held at Dornbach, at that time a village outside Vienna. Kreissle mentions that the Quartet was performed as a chorus by twenty singers (*Taschenbuch für deutsche Sänger*, Vienna, 1864, vol. i, p. 329). See 815.

914. ' Frühlingslied ' (Aaron Pollak), Quartet, T.T.B.B. (XXI 36 (*a*)). April 1827.

Ge - öff - net sind des Win - ters Rie - gel,

MS. Stanford University, Stanford (California).
1ST PF. 9th November 1878, Musikvereinssaal, Vienna.
1ST ED. 1897, Gesamtausgabe.

Tobias Haslinger, Vienna, intended to publish this Quartet in January 1829; in fact, it had passed the censor as early as 2nd June 1827. Apparently it was to have been substituted for 'Grab und Mond' (893) as a companion to 901. For the setting of the same poem as a solo song, see 919.

— ' An die Musik ' (XX 314 (b)). See 547. 24th April 1827.

915. Allegretto in C minor for Pianoforte (XI 12). 27th April 1827.

MS. William Kux, Chur, Switzerland.
1ST ED. 1870, J. P. Gotthard, Vienna (no. 99).

Written in the album of Schubert's ' dear friend,' Ferdinand Walcher, before his departure to Venice.

916. ' Das stille Lied ' (Gottwald), **Quartet, T.T.B.B. Sketch.** Not printed. May 1827.

Schwei - ge nur, süs - ser Mund der heil-gen Lie - be,

MS. Stadtbibliothek, Vienna.

The sketch gives the first tenor part only. Gottwald is probably the pseudonym of Johann Georg Seegemund. Schubert wrote 'Gottwalt.'

917. ' Das Lied im Grünen ' (Reil), **Song** (Op. posth. 115, no. 1; XX 543). June 1827.

Ins Grü - ne, ins Grü - ne, da lockt uns der Früh-ling.

MS. Stanford University, Stanford (California).
1ST ED. 16th June 1829, M. J. Leidesdorf, Vienna (no. 1152), as no. 1 of Op. 115.

Schubert seems to have used only some of the seven stanzas of the poem, which was published on 13th October 1827 in the *Allgemeine Theaterzeitung*, Vienna. In addition to the original stanzas, reprinted in the G.A., the first edition contains three other stanzas, ' als Traueropfer dem Verklärten von dem Dichter nachgeweiht und der Melodie unterlegt ' (dedicated by the poet as a memorial to the deceased and adapted to the melody). Leidesdorf probably purchased this work from Schubert before his death. The MS. differs from the printed version in key, and shows erasures and corrections.

918. ' **Der Graf von Gleichen,** ' **Opera** in three Acts by Eduard von Bauernfeld. **Sketch** (one chorus only published). Middle of 1827–8.

INTRODUCTION (Chorus and Orchestra)
Allegro giusto

Es fun-kelt der Mor-gen, wie Per-len und Glut,

MS. (thirty-six leaves in quarto and fifty-two in octavo, partly written in pencil; the introduction dated 19th June 1827)— Stadtbibliothek, Vienna.
1ST PF. Introductory chorus (dated), under the title ' Morgengesang im Walde,' orchestrated, and the text augmented, by Johann Herbeck—15th December 1865, Redoutensaal, Vienna (conductor Herbeck); Suleika's Arietta (' Ihr Blumen, ihr Bäume') and the quintet (I. vi), both arranged by Herbeck— 10th October 1868, Redoutensaal, Vienna (conductor Herbeck).
1ST ED. The chorus (Herbeck's version)—*c*. 1868, C. A. Spina, Vienna (no. 19192).

The libretto, containing Goethe's poem ' Wonne der Wehmut ' (cf. 260) as an additional song, was not approved by the censor, October 1826. The arietta, in Herbeck's version, is preserved in the Gesellschaft der Musikfreunde, Vienna (MS.). Several other numbers of Act I and the ' Chor der Schnitter ' of Act II, also in Herbeck's arrangements, are preserved by the Herbeck family, Vienna (MSS.).

Literature. Ludwig Herbeck, *Johann Herbeck*, Vienna, 1885, pp. 179 and 206 f.; Alfred Nathansky, ' Bauernfeld und Schubert,' in the 56. *Jahresbericht des K.k. Staatsgymnasiums in Triest*, Vienna, 1906; the libretto (MS.—Stadtbibliothek, Vienna), published in vol. 57 of the same periodical, 1907.

919. ' **Frühlingslied** ' (Aaron Pollak), **Song** (XXI 36 (*b*)). (?) Summer 1827.

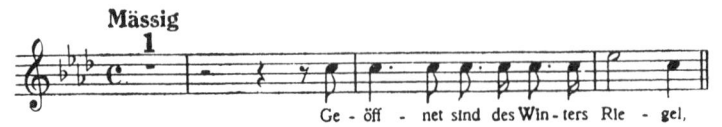

Mässig

Ge - öff - net sind des Win-ters Rie - gel,

MS. Lost.
1ST ED. 1897, Gesamtausgabe.
For the setting of the same poem as a Quartet, T.T.B.B., see 914.

920. ' **Ständchen** ' (' Zögernd leise '), called ' **Notturno** ' (Grillparzer), first version, **for Contralto Solo and Chorus, T.T.B.B., with Pianoforte accompaniment** (XVI 14). July 1827.

Andante

p Zö - gernd, lei - se

MS. Stadtbibliothek, Vienna.
1ST ED. 1891, Gesamtausgabe.
This is the first version of the famous Serenade, written shortly afterwards for contralto solo (Josefine Fröhlich) and female voice chorus (921).

921. ' **Ständchen** ' (' Zögernd leise '), called ' **Notturno** ' (Grillparzer), second version, **for Contralto Solo and Chorus, S.S.A.A., with Pianoforte accompaniment** (Op. posth. 135, XVIII 4). July 1827.

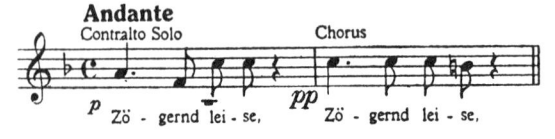

Andante
Contralto Solo | Chorus

p Zö - gernd lei - se, pp Zö - gernd lei - se,

MS. Wilhelm Dieterle, Canoga Park (California).
1ST PF. 11th August 1827, in the garden of Josef von Lang's house at Döbling, then a village outside Vienna; first public performance—24th January 1828, Musikverein, Vienna.
1ST ED. *c.* 1838, A. Diabelli & Co., Vienna (no. 6266), as Op. 135.
The poem and the music were written for the birthday of Fräulein Louise Gosmar. For the first version, see 920.

922. ' **Heimliches Lieben** ' (Karoline Louise von Klenke), **Song**, two versions (Op. 106, no. 1; XX 544 (*a*) and (*b*)). September 1827 (Graz).

[Musical notation: (a) "O du, wenn dei-ne Lip-pen mich be-rüh-ren,"]

[Musical notation: Mässig 5, (b) "O du, wenn dei-ne Lip-pen mich be-rüh-ren,"]

MS. (*a*) Albert Cranz, New York (together with 923); (*b*) unknown; former owner—Heinrich Anschütz, Vienna (died 1865).

1ST ED. 1895, Gesamtausgabe; (*b*) spring 1828 (Lithographisches Institut, Vienna, without publisher's number), as no. 1 of four songs, without opus number (later called Op. 106), dedicated by Schubert to Frau Marie Pachler (lithographed).

Julius Schneller, who altered the first line and the title (originally ' An Myrtill ') sent the poem—without the name of the author (Helmina von Chézy's mother)—to Frau Pachler at Graz, who recommended it to Schubert.

923. ' **Eine altschottische Ballade** ' (' Edward, Edward,' from Thomas Percy's ' Reliques of Ancient English Poetry,' translated by Herder), **Song**, two versions (Op. posth. 165, no. 5; XX 545 (*a*) and (*b*)). September 1827 (Graz).

[Musical notation: (a) "Dein Schwert, wie ist's von Blut so rot,"]

[Musical notation: (b) Female Voice "Dein Schwert, wie ist's von Blut so rot,"]

MS. (*a*) lost (Witteczek's copy); (*b*) Albert Cranz, New York (together with 922).

1ST ED. (*a*) 1895, Gesamtausgabe; (*b*) c. 1864, C. A. Spina, Vienna (no. 17822), as no. 5 of Op. 165.

Herder's translation was published in his *Volkslieder* (Leipzig, 1778–9). Schubert's song was intended to be published as no. 4 of Op. 106, but was finally replaced by ' An Sylvia ' (891).

924. **Twelve Grazer Walzer for Pianoforte** (Op. 91, XII 7). Autumn 1827.

MS. Lost.

IST ED. 5th January 1828, Tobias Haslinger, Vienna (no. 5151), as Op. 91, under the title 'Graetzer-Walzer' (without the advertisement added later at the end).

Schubert had visited Graz in September 1827. Cf. 925.

925. Grazer Galopp for Pianoforte (XII 24). Autumn 1827.

MS. Lost.

IST ED. 5th January 1828, Tobias Haslinger, Vienna (no. 5152), as no. 10 of the collection *Favorit Galoppe*, under the title 'Grätzer Galoppe' (*sic*).

A second issue of the first edition contains on the back of the title-page a list of Haslinger's 'Stadt-Galoppe,' another general title for his 'Favorit Galoppe'; they are entitled 'Lieblings-Galoppe' in the pf. duet arrangement. In the second issue of the first edition of 924 the 'Grazer Galopp is advertised as Op. 92; this number, however, was finally used by M. J. Leidesdorf for three songs of Schubert's (764, 543, 142).

926. 'Das Weinen' (Leitner), Song (Op. 106, no. 2; XX 546). (?) October 1827.

MS. Lost.

IST ED. Spring 1828 (Lithographisches Institut, Vienna, without publisher's number), as no. 2 of four songs without opus number (later called Op. 106), dedicated by Schubert to Frau Marie Pachler (lithographed).

927. 'Vor meiner Wiege' (Leitner), Song (Op. 106, no. 3; XX 547). (?) October 1827.

MS. Lost.

1ST ED. Spring 1828 (Lithographisches Institut, Vienna, without publisher's number), as no. 3 of four songs, without opus number (later called Op. 106), dedicated by Schubert to Frau Marie Pachler (lithographed).

—— 'Winterreise' (XX 517–40). See 911. October 1827.

928. Kindermarsch in G for Piano Duet (IX 7). 11th October 1827.

MS. Gesellschaft der Musikfreunde, Vienna (dated 12th October 1827).
1ST PF. 4th November 1827, in Karl Pachler's house, Graz.
1ST ED. 1870, J. P. Gotthard, Vienna (no. 53).

This march was written for Pachler's nameday, and was performed by his wife, Marie Leopoldine, and his son, Faust, then seven years of age.

929. Trio in E flat for Violin, Violoncello, and Pianoforte (Op. 100, VII 4 (*b*) and (*a*)). November 1827.

MS. Sketches (the first one dated)—Gesellschaft der Musikfreunde, Vienna; score—Wittgenstein family, Vienna.

1ST PF. 26th December 1827, Musikverein, Vienna (Schuppanzigh's Quartet); second performance, 26th March 1828, at the same place (Schubert's concert).

1ST ED. (*b*) Parts—October or November 1828, H. A. Probst, Leipzig (no. 414), as Op. 100; score—1886, Gesamtausgabe.

The MS. of the Pianoforte Trio in E flat was formerly in the possession of Karoline, Komtesse Esterházy. This is the only work by Schubert published outside Austria during his lifetime. The G.A. issued separately the first version, with the last movement in full, as VII, 4*b*, in 1891. It was described as the '2nd enlarged edition,' or as 'enlarged version.' In fact, Schubert, in his only MS. score, cut the last movement for the publication. Leopold von Sonnleithner wrote to Ferdinand Luib in 1857 (Gesellschaft der Musikfreunde, Vienna): 'Fortunately, the Trio was cut in recent performances—it was too long' (for instance, in London on 5th February 1853). The C minor melody of the Andante was said, by Sonnleithner, to be taken from a Swedish folk-song, or rather a lost song by Isaak Albert Berg (sung by him to Schubert during his visit to Vienna in 1827, cf. 887), which song, according to a MS. note by Nottebohm, is in D minor and begins 'Se solen sjunker' (The sun is down).

930. '**Der Hochzeitsbraten**' (Schober), **Comic Trio, S.T.B., with Pianoforte accompaniment** (Op. posth. 104, XIX 2). November 1827.

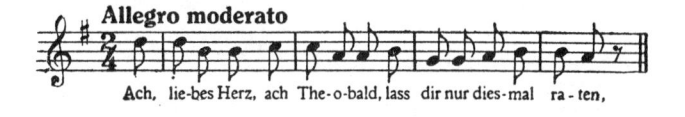

Ach! statt den Ha-sen-rü-cken muss ich den Jä-ger spi-cken

Das Herz ist frei von sei-ner Last,

MS. Dr. Otto Kallir, New York.
IST PF. *c.* 1st January 1828, Vienna, privately; in public—1829, Theater in der Josefstadt, Vienna, acted on the stage (conductor Franz Roser).
IST ED. 1829, A. Diabelli & Co., Vienna (no. 3316), as Op. 104, with a vignette by Moritz von Schwind.

Father Heinrich Hassak, of the monastery at Kremsmünster (Upper Austria), about 1830 possessed a china cup ornamented with the same vignette copied from the original engraving. The cup was inherited by Father Georg Huemer, but it is no longer at Kremsmünster.

931. '**Der Wallensteiner Lanzknecht beim Trunk**' (Leitner), **Song** (XX 548). November 1827.

He! schen-ket mir im Hel-me ein!

MS. (together with 932 and 933)—Frau Marie Floersheim, Wildegg in Aargau (Switzerland).
IST ED. 1830, Anton Strauss's selig Witwe, Vienna, as a supplement to the almanac *Gemeinnütziger und erheiternder Hauskalender für den österreichischen Kaiserstaat*.

The song was republished on 9th October 1835 by A. Diabelli & Co., Vienna (no. 5031) as no. 1 of *Nachlass*, book 27. In a later version of the poem (1847) the title is corrected into '... Landsknecht ...'

932. '**Der Kreuzzug**' (Leitner), **Song** (XX 549). November 1827.

Ein Mü-nich steht in sei-ner Zell',

MS. (together with 931 and 933)—Frau Marie Floersheim, Wildegg in Aargau (Switzerland); another MS.—Stadtbibliothek, Vienna.

1ST PF. 26th March 1828, Musikverein, Vienna (Schubert's concert).

1ST ED. 5th January 1832, as a supplement to the *Wiener Allgemeiner musikalischer Anzeiger*, Vienna.

The poem was published in the *Wiener Zeitschrift für Kunst*, etc., on 19th March 1825. The song was republished, in the key of E, on 9th October 1835 by A. Diabelli & Co., Vienna (no. 5031), as no. 2 of *Nachlass*, book 27.

933. '**Des Fischers Liebesglück**' (Leitner), **Song** (XX 550). November 1827.

MS. The first four bars only (together with 931 and 932)—Frau Marie Floersheim, Wildegg in Aargau (Switzerland); Witteczek's copy is complete.

1ST ED. 9th October 1835, A. Diabelli & Co., Vienna (no. 5031), as no. 3 of *Nachlass*, book 27 (with a list of this collection).

The contents of book 27 of the *Nachlass* were advertised at the beginning of 1829 by Tobias Haslinger who, however, never published the three songs of that book (931–3).

934. **Fantasia in C** ('Sei mir gegrüsst!'), **for Pianoforte and Violin** (Op. posth. 159, VIII 5). December 1827.

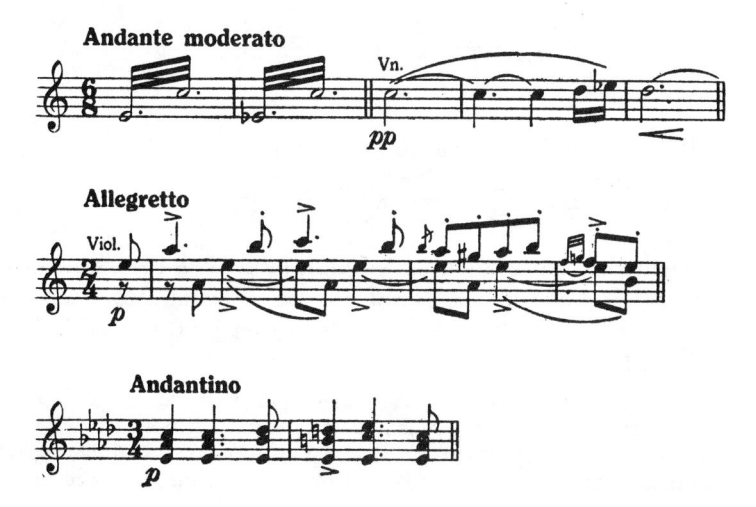

Allegro vivace

MS. Stadtbibliothek, Vienna.

1ST PF. 20th January 1828, Landhaussaal, Vienna (Karl Maria von Bocklet and Josef Slawjk, at the latter's concert).

1ST ED. 1850, A. Diabelli & Co., Vienna (no. 8888), as Op. 159.

Written for Slawjk. The MS. was at one time divided in two halves, which were brought together in 1922. The theme of the third movement is taken from the song ' Sei mir gegrüsst! ' (741).

935. Four Impromptus for Pianoforte (Op. posth. 142, XI 3). December 1827.

No. 1. **Allegro moderato**

No. 2. **Allegretto**
sempre legato

No. 3. THEME **Andante**

No. 4. **Allegro scherzando**

MS. (entitled '4 Impromptus')—Musikbibliothek Peters, Leipzig.

1ST ED. End of 1838, A. Diabelli & Co., Vienna (nos. 6526 and 6527, in two books), as Op. 142, dedicated by the publishers to Franz Liszt.

These pieces are numbered in the MS. 5-8, as a second part of Op. 90; Schubert later intended to publish them as Op. 101, nos. 1-4; Diabelli eventually published them as Op. 142, nos. 1-4. Schubert had then agreed to the title ' Impromptus ' (cf. 899). Robert Schumann, in his review of the first edition, assumed that this work was, in fact, a sonata, and Alfred Einstein (*Schubert*, New York and London, 1950) agrees with him. With reference to no. 3 cf. 797 and 804.

Literature (to no. 3). Martin Frey, in *Zeitschrift für Musik*, Leipzig, April 1925, pp. 198 and 200; Alfred Heuss, *ibidem*, p. 208.

936. '**Kantate zur Feier der Genesung des Fräulein Irene von Kiesewetter**' (in Italian, author unknown), **Sextet**, S.A.T.T.B.B., with Piano Duet accompaniment (XVII 15). 26th December 1827.

[musical notation: Allegro moderato — Al par del rus-cel-let-to chia-ro la tu-a vi-ta scor-ra, I-]

[musical notation: Più mosso — Ev-vi-va dun-que la bel-la I-re-ne,]

MS. Stadtbibliothek, Vienna.

1ST PF. (in public) 1871, Musikvereinssaal, Vienna (as 'Die Erde und der Frühling,' with German words by M. A. Grandjean).

1ST ED. 1892, Gesamtausgabe.

The poet may have been inspired by Metastasio's arias and cantatas addressed to another 'bella Irene.'

937. '**Lebensmut**' ('Fröhlicher Lebensmut,' Rellstab), **Song** (XX 602). Fragment. 1828.

[musical notation: Fröh-li-cher Le-bens-mut braust in dem ra-schen Blut;]

MS. Gesellschaft der Musikfreunde, Vienna (together with **957**, nos. 1 and 3).

1ST ED. 1872, J. P. Gotthard, Vienna (no. 341), as no. 17 of forty songs, this song dedicated by the publisher to Gustav Walter.

Schubert intended to commence his third song-cycle, later called Schwanengesang' (957), with this song; it was, however, never finished. The second and third stanzas of the poem, one of Rellstab's *Gesellschafts-Lieder*, are reprinted in the *Revisionsbericht*. Schubert finally selected love songs only from Rellstab's poems for his cycle.

938. '**Winterabend**,' called '**Der Winterabend**' (Leitner), **Song** (XX 551). January 1828.

Nicht zu langsam

Es ist so still, so heim-lich um mich,

MS. Sir Newman Flower, Blandford (Dorset).
1ST ED. 9th October 1835, A. Diabelli & Co., Vienna (no. 5030), as *Nachlass*, book 26.

The poem, published in the *Wiener Zeitschrift für Kunst*, etc., Vienna, 1825, p. 533, was slightly cut by Schubert, as shown in the *Revisionsbericht*. Although the song was advertised by Tobias Haslinger at the beginning of 1829, it was never published by him.

939. '**Die Sterne**' ('Wie blitzen die Sterne,' Leitner), **Song** (Op. 96, no. 1; XX 552). January 1828.

Etwas geschwind

Wie bli-tzen die Ster-ne so hell durch die Nacht!

MS. Graf Eugen Czernin, Neuhaus in Bohemia, Czechoslovakia (Ph.).
1ST PF. 26th March 1828, Musikverein, Vienna (Schubert's concert).
1ST ED. Summer 1828 (Lithographisches Institut, Vienna, without publisher's number), as no. 1 of four songs, without opus number (later called Op. 96), dedicated by Schubert to Karoline, Fürstin Kinsky, *née* Freiin von Kerpen (lithographed).

940. **Fantasia in F minor for Piano Duet** (Op. 103, IX 24). January–April 1828.

Allegro molto moderato

Largo

ff ben marcato

MS. Sketch—Frau Marie Floersheim, Wildegg in Aargau (Switzerland); fair copy—Nationalbibliothek, Vienna.

1ST ED. 16th March 1829, A. Diabelli & Co., Vienna (no. 3158), as Op. 103, dedicated by Schubert to Karoline, Komtesse Esterházy de Galantha.

An outline-sketch, dated January 1828, was in the possession of Josef Dessauer (sold 1933 by Gilhofer & Ranschburg, Vienna). The fair copy, dated April 1828, bears the opus number given by Schubert. He played the work with Franz Lachner to his friend Bauernfeld on 9th May 1828.

941. '**Hymnus an den heiligen Geist**' ('Komm, heil'ger Geist,' A. Schmidl), **Quartet, T.T.B.B.**, first version. Lost. March 1828.

For the second version, see **948**, and for the final version, **964**.

942. '**Mirjam's Siegesgesang**' (Grillparzer) **for Soprano Solo and Chorus, S.A.T.B., with Pianoforte accompaniment** (Op. posth. 136, XVII 9). March 1828.

Allegro moderato

ff Sturm! 's ist der Herr in sei-nem Grim-me.

Andantino

Tauchst du auf, Pha - ra - o?

Tempo I.

D'rum mit Cym-beln und mit Sai - ten

MS. Sketch—Stadtbibliothek, Vienna; score—Stefan Zweig Collection, London.

1ST PF. 30th January 1829, Musikverein, Vienna (with tenor instead of soprano solo).

1ST ED. Sketch—facsimile 1902, Harmonie-Verlag, Berlin, in Heuberger's *Schubert*, opposite p. 88; final version—1839, A. Diabelli & Co., Vienna (no. 6267), as Op. 136, dedicated by the publishers to Josef Witteczek.

Grillparzer wrote the poem especially for Schubert, and Schubert composed the solo part for Josefine Fröhlich. It is stated that Schubert intended to orchestrate the work himself. Franz Lachner's arrangement with orchestral acc. was performed on 28th March 1830, Redoutensaal, Vienna, and published in 1873 by B. Senff, Leipzig (MS.—Gesellschaft der Musikfreunde, Vienna).

Literature. Leopold von Sonnleithner, *Monatsberichte der Gesellschaft der Musikfreunde des österreichischen Kaiserstaates*, Vienna, March 1829, vol. i, no. 3, pp. 41–6, with the first printing of the poem.

943. '**Auf dem Strom(e)**' (Rellstab), **Song with accompaniment for Pianoforte and Horn or Violoncello** (Op. posth. 119, XX 568). March 1828.

Mässig

Nimm die letz-ten Ab - schieds-küs - se,

MS. Professor George B. Weston, Cambridge (Mass.).

1ST PF. 26th March 1828, Musikverein, Vienna (Schubert's concert).

1ST ED. 27th October 1829, M. J. Leidesdorf, Vienna (no. 1161), as Op. 119.

The song was written for Josef Rudolf Lewy who played the horn part at the first performance, with Schubert at the piano. Both played the accompaniment again on 20th April 1828 in the Kleiner Redoutensaal, Vienna. The alternative violoncello part was played for the first time, in Vienna, on 30th January 1829 by Josef Linke. Leidesdorf probably purchased the work from Schubert some time before his death.

944. **Symphony in C,** called the **Great Symphony in C** (I 7). Begun March 1828.

MS. Gesellschaft der Musikfreunde, Vienna (together with the instrumental parts, copied by another hand, the string parts of which were checked by Ferdinand Schubert in November 1839).
1ST PF. (in a shortened version) 21st March 1839, Gewandhaus, Leipzig (conductor Felix Mendelssohn).
1ST ED. Parts 1840, Breitkopf & Härtel, Leipzig (no. 6203); Score 1849, Breitkopf & Härtel (no. 7954).

A complete performance in Vienna was frustrated on two occasions (14th December 1828 and 15th December 1839) by the musicians, who objected to the length of the work and to the technical difficulties for the violins in the fourth movement; even Ferdinand Schubert's attempt to perform the last movement only failed for the same reasons (17th April 1836, Redoutensaal, conductor Leopold Jansa); similar opposition was met later in Paris (1842), and in London (1844).

Literature. Robert Schumann, *Neue Zeitschrift für Musik*, Leipzig, 10th March 1840.

944A. Deutscher Tanz for Pianoforte. Lost. 1st March 1828.

Composed on given notes. See *Schubert Documents*, p. 746, no. 1053.

—— **Fantasia in F minor for Piano Duet** (IX 24). See 941. April 1828.

945. 'Herbst' (Rellstab), **Song** (XX 589). April 1828.

MS. Rough copy—lost; fair copy—Branner's Bibliofile Antikvariat, Copenhagen (1950).
1ST ED. 1895, Gesamtausgabe.

This song, which may have been intended for the so-called 'Schwanengesang' cycle (957), was rewritten in the album of Heinrich Panofka on the date mentioned above. The date of 28th April 1828, given by Nottebohm and the G.A., is not on the MS.

946. Three Impromptus, called 'Drei Klavierstücke,' for Pianoforte (XI 13). *c.* May 1828.

MS. Stadtbibliothek, Vienna (without a title).
1ST ED. 1868, J. Rieter-Biedermann, Winterthur (no. 564 (*a*)–(*c*)), ed. anonymously by Johannes Brahms, under the title ' Drei Clavierstücke.'

The third impromptu is said to have been written before the first, which is dated on the first page, May 1828. The Andantino in no. 1, cancelled by Schubert in the MS., was not included in the text of the G.A., but is reprinted in the *Revisionsbericht*. Schubert intended to write four numbers, as in Opp. 90 and 142 (899 and 935).

947. **Allegro in A minor**, called ' Lebensstürme,' for **Piano Duet** (Op. posth. 144, IX 23). May 1828.

MS. Lost.
1ST ED. *c.* 1840, A. Diabelli & Co., Vienna (no. 6704), as Op. 144, under the spurious title ' Lebensstürme. Characteristisches Allegro.'

948. ' **Hymnus an den heiligen Geist**,' called ' **Hymne** ' (' Komm, heil'ger Geist,' A. Schmidl), **Quartet with Chorus, T.T.B.B.**, second version (XVI 42). May 1828.

MS. Preussische Staatsbibliothek, Berlin.
1ST ED. 1891, Gesamtausgabe.
This is the second version, with the final draft setting of the chorus. See 941 and 964. For an error in the G.A. see Johannes Wolf in *Schubertforschung*, Augsburg 1929, p. 151.

949. ' **Widerschein** ' (Schlechta), **Song**, second version (XX 553). May 1828.

MS. Unknown; former owner—Karl von Enderes, Vienna (*c.* 1860).
1ST ED. 4th January 1832, A. Diabelli & Co., Vienna (no. 4015), as no. 1 of *Nachlass*, book 15.

Diabelli's version of the poem (' Tom lehnt harrend auf der Brucke '), in the first edition, is not identical with that published in Schlechta's collected poems, Vienna, 1824 and 1828, used in the G.A., but is similar to that printed in his *Ephemeren*, Vienna, 1876. For the first version of the song, see 639.

950. Mass in E flat for Quartet, S.A.T.B., mixed Chorus and Orchestra (XIII 6). Begun June 1828.

MS. Sketches — Stadtbibliothek, Vienna; score — Preussische Staatsbibliothek, Berlin (some erasures made with a pocket knife).
1ST PF. 4th October 1829, Dreifaltigkeits-Kirche, Alsergrund, Vienna (conductor Ferdinand Schubert).

1ST ED. December 1865, J. Rieter-Biedermann, Winterthur (score, no. 424; parts, nos. 426–7).

The Mass was written for the above-mentioned Minorite church (cf. 954), where it was performed to celebrate three events: the birthday of the Emperor Franz I, the Festival of the Minorites, and the first anniversary of the church's music society. Michael Leitermayer, the founder of this society, rehearsed the Mass. Brahms arranged the vocal score, anonymously, for the publisher (no. 425).

951. Rondo in A for Piano Duet (Op. 107, IX 13). June 1828.
MS. Preussische Staatsbibliothek, Berlin.

1ST ED. 11th December 1828, Artaria & Co., Vienna (no. 2969) as Op. 107, under the title 'Grand Rondeau' (price—1 fl. 20 kr.).

Written for and at the request of Domenico Artaria.

952. Fugue in E minor for Organ or Piano Duet (Op. posth. 152, IX 28). 3rd June 1828 (Baden, near Vienna).

MS. Sketches—unknown; former owner—Heyer Museum, Cologne (1926); score (instrument not indicated)—Conservatoire, Paris (Ph.).
1ST PF. 4th June 1828, Cistercian Abbey Heiligenkreuz, near Baden (Schubert and Franz Lachner).
1ST ED. c. 1844, A. Diabelli & Co., Vienna (no. 7977), as Op. 152.

Schubert was at Baden with Lachner and (Johann?) Schickh on the 3rd, and visited Heiligenkreuz on the 4th, of June 1828. The fugue was written in competition with Lachner, and played with him on the organ of the abbey church.

953. 'Der 92. Psalm, Lied für den Sabbath' (in Hebrew) **for Baritone Solo and Chorus, S.A.T.B.** (XVII 19). July 1828.

MS. Unknown; former owner—Israelitische Kultusgemeinde, Vienna.

1ST PF. Summer 1828, Juden-Tempel, Vienna.

1ST ED. 1841, Vienna, as no. 6 in Salomon Sulzer's collection of Hebrew religious songs, *Schir Zion* (part 1); 1870, J. P. Gotthard, Vienna (no. 47), published separately, with German words by Moses Mendelssohn.

Written for Sulzer, the cantor of the Juden-Tempel, in the City of Vienna. Another German version was written by Franz Flatz, but never printed.

954. 'Glaube, Hoffnung und Liebe' ('Gott, lass die Glocke glücklich steigen,' Friedrich Reil), **Chorus, S.A.T.B., with Wind Instruments** (XVII 5). August 1828.

MS. Philipp, Graf Gudenus, Waidhofen an der Thaya (Lower Austria).

1ST PF. 2nd September 1828, Dreifaltigkeits-Kirche, Alsergrund, Vienna (cf. 950).

1ST ED. 30th December 1828, Tranquillo Mollo, Vienna (as agent only), under the title '... Zur Weihe der neuen Glocke ...,' score of the wind instruments and vocal score.

The poem was written, and set to music, for the solemn dedication of the recast bell at the restored Minorite church in the Alsergrund suburb, where Beethoven's body had been blessed in March 1827. The text was published on 27th September 1828 in the *Allgemeine Theaterzeitung*, Vienna. The pf. acc. (*ad lib.*) is dubious. The first edition was sold for charitable purposes. Cf. Schubert's song with the same title, but with different words, composed the same month (955).

955. 'Glaube, Hoffnung und Liebe' ('Glaube, hoffe, liebe!' Kuffner), **Song** (Op. 97, XX 462). August 1828.

[Musical notation: Langsam, 3/4, with text "Glau - be, hof - fe, lie - - be!"]

MS. Nationalbibliothek, Vienna.

1ST ED. 6th October 1828, A. Diabelli & Co., Vienna (no. 2905), as no. 240 of the pf. collection *Philomele*.

The MS. is a rough copy, and the tempo was originally indicated ' Nicht zu langsam.' The mordent in the last bar but one of the voice-part was inserted by Schubert. Cf. Schubert's choral work with the same title, but with different words, written the same month (954).

956. **Quintet in C for two Violins, Viola, and two Violoncellos** (Op. posth. 163, IV). (?) August–September 1828.

[Musical notation: Allegro ma non troppo]

[Musical notation: Adagio, 12/8, pp espressivo]

[Musical notation: SCHERZO Presto, 3/4, ff]

[Musical notation: TRIO Andante sostenuto, Va., mf]

[Musical notation: Allegretto, fz]

MS. Unknown; former owner—A. Diabelli & Co., Vienna (*c.* 1850).

1ST PF. Rehearsal—October 1828; first public performance—

17th November 1850, Musikverein, Vienna (Josef Hellmesberger's Quartet and Josef Stransky).
1ST ED. 1853, C. A. Spina, Vienna (no. 9101, plate mark of his predecessors, A. Diabelli & Co.), in parts.

957. '**Schwanengesang**' (Rellstab, Heine, Seidl), **Song Cycle** (XX 554–67). Finished August (October) 1828.

BOOK I.
1. LIEBESBOTSCHAFT
Ziemlich langsam

Rau-schen-des Bäch-lein, so sil - bern und hell,

2. KRIEGERS AHNUNG
Nicht zu langsam

In tie - fer Ruh liegt um mich her

3. FRÜHLINGSSEHNSUCHT
Geschwind

Säu - seln - de Lüf - te we - hend so mild,

4. STÄNDCHEN
Mässig

Lei - se fle - hen mei - ne Lie - der

5. AUFENTHALT
Nicht zu geschwind, doch kräftig

Rau - schen - der Strom, brau - sen - der Wald,

6. IN DER FERNE
Ziemlich langsam

We - he dem Flie - hen-den, Welt hin - aus Zie - hen-den!

BOOK II.
7. ABSCHIED
Mässig geschwind

A - de! du mun-tre, du fröh - li - che Stadt.

8. DER ATLAS
Etwas geschwind

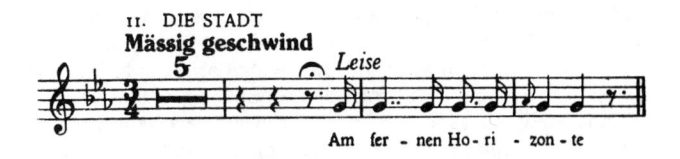

Ich un-glück-sel'-ger At-las,

9. IHR BILD
Langsam

Ich stand in dun-klen Träu-men und starrt' ihr Bild-nis an,

10. DAS FISCHERMÄDCHEN
Etwas geschwind

Du schö-nes Fi-scher-mäd-chen,

11. DIE STADT
Mässig geschwind
Leise

Am fer-nen Ho-ri-zon-te

12. AM MEER
Sehr langsam

Das Meer er-glänz-te weit hin-aus

13. DER DOPPELGÄNGER
Sehr langsam

Still ist die Nacht, es ru-hen die Gas-sen.

14. DIE TAUBENPOST
Ziemlich langsam

Ich hab' ei-ne Brief-taub' in mei-nem Sold,

MS. Sketches to nos. 1 and 3—Gesellschaft der Musikfreunde, Vienna (together with 937); sketch to no. 14—Stadtbibliothek,

Vienna; no. 4—unknown; former owner—Herr Oppenheim, Budapest (*c.* 1865); complete MS. (fair copy)—Musikbibliothek Peters, Leipzig (only no. 1 and no. 14 are dated, August and October 1828 respectively).

1ST ED. Easter 1829, Tobias Haslinger, Vienna (no. 5370 on the title-page, nos. 5371–84 on the plates), in two books, on subscription (with vignette, the list of contents on a separate leaf).

The cycle was sketched, possibly as early as the summer of 1827, in a larger form, beginning with the Rellstab song ' Lebensmut ' (937), followed by ' Liebesbotschaft ' (no. 1), ' Frühlingssehnsucht ' (no. 3), the sketch of which is printed in the *Revisionsbericht*, and, later, probably by ' Herbst' (945). The Heine songs (nos. 8–13) may have been sketched in January and February 1828. In October 1828 Schubert planned to publish the Heine songs, selected and their order altered, separately (each of which was given a title by Schubert himself). According to Josef von Spaun the cycle, then without a general title, was to be dedicated to Schubert's friends. Ferdinand Schubert, on 17th December 1828, offered to Haslinger the seven Rellstab and the six Heine songs. These were to have been published in four books, the Rellstab songs in two and the Heine songs in two. When Haslinger received the MSS. on 13th January 1829 he decided to include the Seidl song (no. 14), which appears to have been Schubert's last song. It was then arranged to publish the fourteen songs in two books: the Rellstab songs to occupy the whole of the first book and the first number in the second book, leaving the remaining numbers for the Heine songs with the Seidl song at the end.

Literature. Max Kalbeck (on the Heine poems), *Neues Wiener Tagblatt*, Vienna, 19th November 1914. Alfred Orel (on the sketch of no. 14), *Die Musik*, Berlin, August 1937.

958. Sonata in C minor for Pianoforte (X 13). September 1828.

MS. Sketch—Stadtbibliothek, Vienna (see *Revisionsbericht*); final version—Frau Marie Floersheim, Wildegg in Aargau (Switzerland).

IST ED. 1838, A. Diabelli & Co., Vienna (no. 3847), as the first sonata in the book called *Franz Schubert's Allerletzte Composition. Drei grosse Sonaten*, dedicated by the publishers to Robert Schumann.

Schubert intended to dedicate the three sonatas to Johann Nepomuk Hummel. The publisher's numbers of the sonatas indicate that the music was engraved as early as 1831. Hummel died in 1837, so the dedication was changed. The MS. of the final version is entitled ' Sonate I.'

959. Sonata in A for Pianoforte (X 14). September 1828.

MS. Sketches—Stadtbibliothek, Vienna (see *Revisionsbericht*); final version—Frau Marie Floersheim, Wildegg in Aargau (Switzerland).

1ST ED. See 958.

See 958. The MS. of the final version is entitled ' Sonate II.' A sketch of the first movement of 960 is to be found on the MS. of one of the sketches.

960. **Sonata in B flat for Pianoforte** (X 15). Finished 26th September 1828.

MS. Sketch—Stadtbibliothek, Vienna (see *Revisionsbericht*); final version—Frau Marie Floersheim, Wildegg in Aargau (Switzerland).

1ST ED. See 958.

See 958. The MS. of the final version is entitled ' Sonate III,' and is dated at the end, ' Wien, den 26. Sept. 1828.' The sketch of the first movement is written on a leaf of the sketches to 959.

961. Second Benedictus of the Mass in C, for Quartet, S.A.T.B., Mixed Chorus, Orchestra, and Organ (XIII 4 (*b*)). October 1828.

[musical incipit: Moderato — "Be - ne - di - ctus qui ve - nit in no - mi - ne Do - mi - ne,"]

MS. Unknown; former owner—Anton Diabelli, Vienna.

1ST ED. (in parts) 1829, A. Diabelli & Co., Vienna (no. 2386).

This version of the Benedictus was advertised by Diabelli as written for performances lacking a good soprano. Cf. 452.

962. Tantum ergo in E flat for Quartet, S.A.T.B., Mixed Chorus, and Orchestra (XIV 22 and XXI 32). October 1828.

[musical incipit: Andante sostenuto — "Tan - tum er - go sa - cra - men - tum"]

MS. Sketch—Stadtbibliothek, Vienna; final version—Nationalbibliothek, Vienna (together with 963 and 964).

1ST PF. 19th June 1890, Stadttheater, Eisenach (see 963).

1ST ED. Sketch—1888, Gesamtausgabe; final version—1890, C. F. Peters, Leipzig (no. 7380/1), pf. score ed. by Max Friedlaender from Ferdinand Schubert's copy of the parts (together with 963).

The final version, first published before the MS. was found, is written in the MS. containing 963 and 964.

963. Offertorium ('Intende voci'), **in B flat for Tenor Solo, Chorus, S.A.T.B., and Orchestra** (XXI 33). October 1828.

[musical incipit: Andante con moto — "In - ten - de vo - ci o - ra - ti - o - nis me - ae,"]

MS. Preussische Staatsbibliothek, Berlin (entitled 'Aria con Coro'); another MS. (together with 962 and 964)—Nationalbibliothek, Vienna (entitled 'Tenor-Aria mit Chor').

1ST PF. 19th June 1890, Stadttheater, Eisenach (see 962).

1ST ED. 1890, C. F. Peters, Leipzig (no. 7384/5), pf. score ed. by

Max Friedlaender from Ferdinand Schubert's copy of the parts (together with 962).

The text is from Psalm v, verse 2. The Vienna MS. also contains 962 and 964. The first edition was published before the MSS. were found.

964. ' **Hymnus an den heiligen Geist** ' (' Herr, unser Gott! ' A. Schmidl), **for eight Male Voices, Soli and Chorus, with accompaniment for Wind Instruments** (two oboes, two clarinets, two bassoons, two horns, two trumpets, and three trombones), third version (Op. posth. 154, XVI 2). October 1828.

[musical notation: Adagio — p Herr, un-ser Gott! - er - hö - re un-ser Fle - hen,]

MS. Nationalbibliothek, Vienna (together with 962 and 963).

1ST PF. 5th March 1829, Landhaussaal, Vienna (Concert spirituel, for which this, the final, version of the hymn was written).

1ST ED. *c.* 1847, A. Diabelli & Co., Vienna (no. 8778), as Op. 154, under the title ' Hymne,' with a pf. acc. (written by Ferdinand Schubert on 31st January 1843, MS.—Gesellschaft der Musikfreunde, Vienna) added as an alternative.

The MS. gives the dates of the second version and of the instrumentation as follows: ' Mai 1828. Oct. instrumentirt.' For the earlier versions, see 941 and 948.

—— ' **Die Taubenpost** ' (XX 567). See 957. October 1828.

965. ' **Der Hirt auf dem Felsen** ' (Wilhelm Müller and Helmina von Chézy), **Song, with accompaniment for Pianoforte and Clarinet or Violoncello** (Op. posth. 129, XX 569). October 1828.

[musical notation: Andantino 37 — Wenn auf dem höch - - sten Fels ich̲ steh',]

MS. Sketch—Stadtbibliothek, Vienna; final version—Gesellschaft der Musikfreunde, Vienna.

1ST PF. March 1830, Riga (Frau Anna Milder-Hauptmann).

1ST ED. 1st June 1830, Tobias Haslinger, Vienna (no. 5570), as Op. 129.

The text of the song was compiled from two sources, possibly at the suggestion of Frau Milder, as follows: the beginning and the end from Müller's ' Der Berghirt,' and the intervening verses from Chézy's ' Liebesgedanken.' The song was written for Frau Milder; she did not receive it, however, until after Schubert's death. On 4th September 1829 a copy made by Ferdinand Schubert was sent to her in Berlin through Johann Michael Vogl. The date, 1827, given in the G.A., is corrected in the *Revisionsbericht*, Series XX, Supplement, p. 2.

UNDATED WORKS

(Works to which no dates can be assigned)

966. Fragment of an Orchestral Score in D. Not printed.
MS. Dr. Franz Roehn, Los Angeles.

966A. Fragment of an Orchestral Score in D. Not printed.

MS. Stadtbibliothek, Vienna.

967. Fugue in Four Parts for Pianoforte. Sketch. Not printed.

MS. Stadtbibliothek, Vienna.

On the first three of the eight pages of the MS. Schubert wrote the fragmentary Allegro moderato in C for pf. of (?) 1816; see 347. Josef Hüttenbrenner, in a letter dated 7th March 1868, mentions that he had in his possession a fragment of a fugue written by Schubert as early as 1813.

968. Allegro moderato in C and Andante in A minor, called 'Sonatine,' for Piano Duet (IX 29).

MS. Stadtbibliothek, Vienna.
1ST ED. 1888, Gesamtausgabe.

Another hand has added fingering and written the words of the Credo and of the Incarnatus under the music on the MS.

—— **Fantasia in C minor for Pianoforte.** See 993.

—— **Four Deutsche Tänze for Pianoforte** (Op. 33, XII 3, no. 16; Op. 127, XII 8, no. 2; XII 10, nos. 13 and 6).
MS. Gesellschaft der Musikfreunde (former owner, J. Brahms).
1ST ED. See 146, 366, 783.

The first of these dances begins an octave lower than in the first edition.

—— **Two Écossaises for Pianoforte** (Op. 18; XII 2, Écossaises nos. 2 and 3).
MS. Gesellschaft der Musikfreunde, Vienna.
1ST ED. See 145.

For a variant of the Écossaise no. 1, see 299, no. 1.

—— **Seventeen Ländler for Pianoforte** (Op. 18; XII 2, Ländler nos. 1–17).
MS. Gesellschaft der Musikfreunde, Vienna (former owner, J. Brahms): (*a*) nos. 4, 6–9, and 12 (together with 680); (*b*) the remainder (together with 970 and XII 10, 366, nos. 1, 9, and 10).
1ST ED. See 145.

For the MS. (*a*), see note to 680.

969. Twelve 'Valses nobles' for Pianoforte (Op. 77, XII 6).

MS. Lost.
1ST ED. 22nd January 1827, Tobias Haslinger, Vienna (no. 4920), as Op. 77.
The title was probably given by the publisher.

970. Six Deutsche Tänze for Pianoforte (XII 13).

MS. (together with eleven dances from the last entry before 969 and three from 366)—Gesellschaft der Musikfreunde, Vienna (former owner, J. Brahms).
1ST ED. 1889, Gesamtausgabe.

971. **Three Deutsche Tänze for Pianoforte (XII 14).**

MS. Lost.
1ST ED. 10th January 1823, in the collection *Carneval 1823,* vol. ii, Sauer & Leidesdorf, Vienna (no. 241).

972. **Three Deutsche Tänze for Pianoforte (XII 15).**

MS. Stadtbibliothek, Vienna.
1ST ED. 1889, Gesamtausgabe.

973. Three Deutsche Tänze for Pianoforte (XII 16).

No. 1.

No. 2.

No. 3.

MS. (together with six 'Valses sentimentales,' 779)—Stadtbibliothek, Vienna.

1ST ED. 1889, Gesamtausgabe.

These three dances are nos. 5, 6, and 9 in the MS., and were probably written in 1823 or 1824.

974. Two Deutsche Tänze for Pianoforte (XII 17).

No. 1.

No. 2.

MS. (together with XII 10, 366, nos. 7, 14, and 15)—Gesellschaft der Musikfreunde, Vienna.

1ST ED. 1889, Gesamtausgabe.

975. Deutscher Tanz in D for Pianoforte (XII 20).

[music]

MS. (entitled 'Deutscher,' together with Op. 127, XII 8, **146,** no. 15; XII 10, **366,** no. 4; Op. 33, XII 3, **783,** nos. 2, 6, and 9)—Gesellschaft der Musikfreunde, Vienna (former owner, J. Brahms).

1ST ED. 1889, Gesamtausgabe.

976. Cotillon in E flat for Pianoforte (XII 22).

[music]

MS. Lost.

1ST ED. 29th December 1825, as no. 5 of various dances in the collection *Ernst und Tändeley*, Sauer & Leidesdorf, Vienna (without publisher's number), printed for the editor, K. F. Müller.

977. Eight Écossaises for Pianoforte (XII 26).

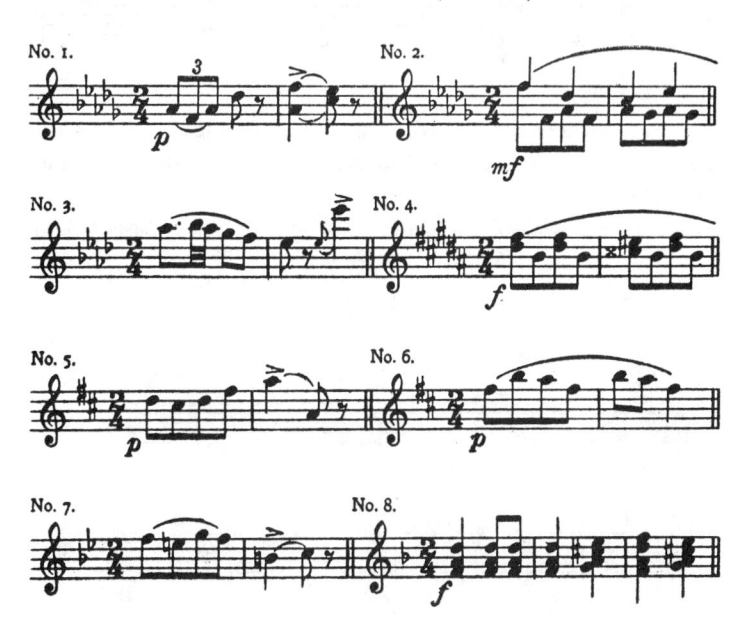

[music: Nos. 1–8]

MS. (together with Op. 18, XII 2, 145, Ecossaises nos. 2 and 3)
—Gesellschaft der Musikfreunde, Vienna.
1ST ED. 1889, Gesamtausgabe.

978. **Walzer in A flat for Pianoforte.**

MS. Lost.
1ST ED. 29th December 1825, as no. 37 of fifty waltzes in the collection *Seid uns zum zweiten Male willkommen!*, Sauer & Leidesdorf, Vienna (without publisher's number), printed for the editor, K. F. Müller.

The title of the collection is taken from Mozart's *Magic Flute*; the theme of the genii trio is used in the introduction to the dances. This waltz was reprinted in *Moderne Welt*, Vienna, 1st December 1925, music supplement, p. 2 (ed. by O. E. D.). Erroneously published again as a first reprint in *Der neue Pflug*, Vienna, July 1928, opposite p. 17 (ed. by Robert Haas).

979. **Walzer for Pianoforte.**

MS. Lost.
1ST ED. 23rd December 1826, as no. 1 of eight dances in the collection *Moderne Liebes-Walzer*, Sauer & Leidesdorf, Vienna (no. 397).

Reprinted in *Zeitschrift der Internationalen Musikgesellschaft*, Leipzig, 1901–2, vol. iii, p. 319 (ed. by William Barclay Squire).

980. **Two Walzer for Pianoforte.**

No. 1.

No. 2.

MS. Lost.

1ST ED. 23rd December 1826, as nos. 1 and 2 of twelve dances in the collection *Neue Krähwinkler Tänze*, Sauer & Leidesdorf, Vienna (no. 398).

Reprinted in *Zeitschrift der Internationalen Musikgesellschaft*, Leipzig, 1901–2, vol. iii, pp. 319–20 (ed. by William Barclay Squire).

—— **Two Minuets for Pianoforte.** See 994.

981. ' **Der Minnesänger,**' Singspiel (author unknown). **Fragment.** Lost.

MS. Lost.

A play called *Die Minnesänger auf der Wartburg*, by Christoph Kuffner, was produced on 15th March 1817 in the Theater an der Wien, Vienna.

982. **Sketches of an Opera.** (Title and author unknown.) Not printed.

MS. Stadtbibliothek, Vienna.

These incomplete sketches comprise a vocal quartet for the characters Sofie, Luise (sopranos), Bretone and Belville (tenor and bass), in score; an arietta no. 1 for Sofie (' Philomele, deine Kehle lockte mich hieher . . .'); and a vocal trio for Sofie, Luise, and Belville. Two fragments of an opera, written in 1814 (see *Schubertforschung*, Augsburg, 1929, p. 165), are in the possession of Robert H. Weir, Boston (Mass.). Two other operas, *Die Salzbergwerke von**, libretto by Johann, Graf Mayláth, and *Der Graf von Glenallan* (author unknown), received Schubert's consideration; only a sketch of Mayláth's libretto was preserved about 1865 (Kreissle, *Schubert*, p. 558).

983. **Four Quartets, T.T.B.B.**: ' **Jünglingswonne** ' (Matthisson), ' **Liebe** ' (Schiller), ' **Zum Rundetanz** ' (Salis), ' **Die Nacht** ' ((?) Friedrich Wilhelm Krummacher), (Op. 17, XVI 20–3).

No. 2. LIEBE
Andantino

pp Lie - be rauscht der Sil - ber-bach,

No. 3. ZUM RUNDETANZ
Vivace

f Auf! es dun - kelt, sil - bern fun - kelt

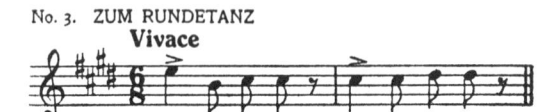

No. 4. DIE NACHT
Langsam

p Wie schön bist du, *pp* freund - li - che Stil - le,

MS. Lost.

1ST PF. (?) No. 1—20th July 1867, Sperl-Garten, Vienna; no. 4—7th October 1868, in front of Schubert's birthplace, Vienna.

1ST ED. 9th October 1823, Cappi & Diabelli, Vienna (no. 1176), as Op. 17.

No. 2 is from Schiller's 'Triumph der Liebe.' No. 3, also called 'Lied beim Rundetanz,' was set by Schubert as a trio (132).

984. '**Der Wintertag**,' called '**Geburtstagslied**' (author unknown), **Quartet, T.T.B.B.**, with (lost) **Pianoforte accompaniment** (Op. posth. 169).

Etwas langsam

pp In schö - ner hel - ler Win - ter-zeit

MS. Voice parts—Stadtbibliothek, Vienna.

1ST PF. 1863, Vienna (Kaufmännischer Gesangverein).

1ST ED. *c.* 1865, C. A. Spina, Vienna (no. 17933), as Op. 169 (ed. Johann Herbeck).

The original pf. acc. is lost. The pf. acc. of the first edition is by J. P. Gotthard. Schubert entitled each voice part 'Der Wintertag.' The editors of the G.A. regarded this Quartet as doubtful, and did not include it in the Collected Edition.

985. '**Gott im Ungewitter**' (Uz), **Quartet, S.A.T.B., with Pianoforte** accompaniment (Op. posth. 112, no. 1; XVII 6).

MS. Lost.

1ST PF. 29th November 1829, Redoutensaal, Vienna (orchestrated by Leopold von Sonnleithner).

1ST ED. 11th March 1829, Josef Czerny, Vienna (no. 336 on the plates, 339 on the title-page), as no. 1 of Op. 112, also published separately.

Sonnleithner's arrangement in MS. is preserved in the Gesellschaft der Musikfreunde, Vienna.

986. '**Gott der Weltschöpfer**' (Uz), **Quartet, S.A.T.B., with Pianoforte** accompaniment (Op. posth. 112, no. 2; XVII 7).

MS. Lost.

1ST ED. 11th March 1829, Josef Czerny, Vienna (no. 337 on the plates, 339 on the title-page), as no. 2 of Op. 112, also published separately.

987. '**Osterlied**' (Klopstock), **Quartet, S.A.T.B., with Pianoforte** accompaniment (XVII 17).

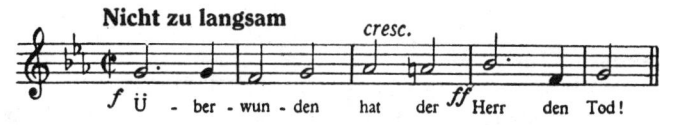

MS. Lost.

1ST ED. 1872, J. P. Gotthard, Vienna (no. 324), as no. 9 of nine partsongs.

The text is based on the hymn 'Jesus Christus, unser Heiland, der den Tod überwand.'

988. '**Liebe säuseln die Blätter**' (words from Hölty's '*Maigesang*'), Canon for Three Voices (XIX 26).

MS. Lost.
1ST PF. (?) 4th May 1927, Musikvereinssaal, Vienna.
1ST ED. 1873, J. Guttentag, Berlin, in Reissmann's *Schubert*, Appendix no. 3, p. 4.

989. '**Die Erde**' ('Wenn sanft entzückt mein Auge sieht,' author unknown), **Song**. **Lost**.

Recorded by Kreissle, p. 602, and Nottebohm, p. 261; otherwise there is no trace. Kreissle entitles the song 'Die Erde, Vollendung,' Nottebohm mentions it by the first line of the text only.

990. '**Der Graf von Habsburg**' (Schiller), **Song**. **Fragment**. **Not printed**.

MS. Stadtbibliothek, Vienna.
Only the setting of the first stanza of the poem is preserved. On the back of the MS. is a pf. piece, B flat major, 2/4, inscribed: 'Kaiser Maximilian auf der Martinswand in Tyrol. 1490 [or rather 1493].'

991. '**O lasst euch froh begrüssen, Kinder der vergnügten Au**' (author unknown), **Song**. **Fragment**. **Not printed**.

MS. Unknown; former owner—Johannes Brahms, Vienna (*c*. 1865).
Recorded by Kreissle, p. 605.

992. '**Wer wird sich nicht innig freuen**' (author unknown), **Part-song**. **Fragment**. **Not printed**.

MS. Leo Liepmannssohn, Berlin (sale, 6th May 1889).
The MS. consists of the last page only of the partsong, on the back of which is the beginning of a sketch of an Adagio, in C minor, 4/4. The words of the partsong continue: 'dass der Gottversöhner ihnen, Himmel, deinen Vorschmack gab.'

—— **Beethoven's Fourth Symphony** (in B flat, Op. 60). Copy of the first four bars only. See Appendix II, no. 8.

— Michael Haydn's 'Deutsches Hochamt.' Copy of an organ score. See Appendix II, no. 9.

ADDENDA

993. Fantasia in C minor for Pianoforte. Unpublished.

MS. (together with 995)—Otto Taussig, Malmö.

The second section, Andantino, is reminiscent of the corresponding section in Mozart's Fantasia in C minor for Pianoforte (K. 475). The MS., probably written about 1813, was formerly in the possession of A. Diabelli (later Spina, then Cranz), and was found after the compilation of this catalogue.

994. Allegro in E minor for Pianoforte. Fragment. Not printed.

MS. Stadtbibliothek, Vienna.

The thirty-eight bars of the MS., written (?) after 1817, are the beginning of a sonata.

995. Two Minuets for Pianoforte. Unpublished.

MS. (together with 993)—Otto Taussig, Malmö.

The note at the beginning of the second minuet indicates that Schubert thought of an orchestral version. Written probably about 1813.

996. Overture in D for Orchestra. Unpublished.

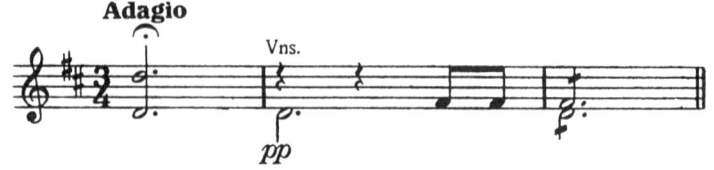

MS. (together with 997 and 998)—Otto Taussig, Malmö.

The MS., probably written about 1812, was formerly in the possession of A. Diabelli & Co. (later Spina, then Cranz), and became available shortly before the conclusion of this catalogue. Cf. 14 and 997.

997. Fragment of a Symphony in D. Not printed.

MS. (together with 996 and 998)—Otto Taussig, Malmö.

The work, probably written about 1812, is based on 996. The MS. has Adagio (complete), followed by nineteen bars of an Allegro con moto.

998. Fragment of a String Quartet in (?) F. Not printed.

MS. (together with 996 and 997)—Otto Taussig, Malmö.

The beginning of this (first ?) movement is missing from the MS., which contains thirty-five bars and is a first draft, probably written about 1812. Cf. 19A. The order of the three works in the MS. (folio) is 996, 997, 998.

N.B. For undated works, see also 582 and 683.

APPENDIX I

SPURIOUS AND DOUBTFUL WORKS

'**Adieu !**'—'**Lebe wohl!**' ('Voici l'instant suprême'—'Schon naht, um uns zu scheiden,' Bélanger), **Song.**

[musical notation: Andante — Voi - ci l'in - stant su - prê - me.]

1ST ED. *c.* 1835—Richault, Paris (in French); *c.* 1840—C. Lonsdale, London (in Italian and Spanish); 1843—Schlesinger, Berlin (in German, transcribed for pf. solo by Th. Döhler).

The song was, in fact, composed by August Heinrich von Weyrauch, with words by Karl Friedrich Gottlob Wetzel, and was published by the composer in 1824, under the title '' Nach Osten!' ('Nach Osten geht, nach Osten der Erde Flug'), together with other of his songs. It was republished, this time separately, in 1846 by C. A. Challier & Co., Berlin.

Literature. Berliner musikalische Zeitung, 25th April 1846; Gerhard Murger, *Allgemeine Kunstchronik*, Vienna, March 1890, and *Montags-Revue*, Vienna, 18th December 1893; Anton Rubinstein, *Die Musik und ihre Meister*, Leipzig, 1891, p. 47; Max Friedlaender, *Vierteljahrsschrift für Musikwissenschaft*, Leipzig, 1893, p. 182.

★

N.B. For spurious works, see also 37 ('Die Advokaten'), 96 (Guitar Quartet), and Appendix II, no. 4.

For doubtful works, see 93, 603, 858, and 984.

APPENDIX II

COPIES OF WORKS OF OTHER COMPOSERS

1. **Franz de Paula Roser's Song ' Die Teilung der Erde '** (Schiller). *c.* 1812.

MS. Unknown; former owner—Max Friedlaender, Berlin.

The song was attributed, even by Schubert, to Josef Haydn; it was reprinted in 1932, as a spurious work, in the Collected Edition of Haydn's works, Series XX, vol. i, no. 50 (ed. by Max Friedlaender). The MS. of Ferdinand Schubert's arrangement of this song for four part male chorus and orchestra (1838) is at the Gesellschaft der Musikfreunde, Vienna.

2. **Mozart's Jupiter Symphony in C** (Köchel no. 551), the first seven bars of the Minuet. *c.* 29th March 1813.

MS. (together with the unpublished chorus ' Dithyrambe,' 47) —Dr. Otto Kallir, New York.

3. **Johann Rudolf Zumsteeg's ' Chor der Derwische,' for S.T.B.** Spring 1813.

MS. Unknown; former owner—Rudolf Weis-Ostborn, Graz.

The copy is written on a MS. of three oblong folios between a canon of 19th April 1813 (54) and a trio of May 1813 (58). The song was published in 1802, in Zumsteeg's *Kleine Balladen und Lieder*, vol. iv, pp. 40 f., by Breitkopf & Härtel, Leipzig. The poet is unknown.

Literature. Max Friedlaender, *Beiträge zur Biographie Franz Schuberts*, Berlin, 1887, p. 20 (on the influence of this chorus on Schubert's early partsongs).

4. **Johann Friedrich Reichardt's ' Monolog aus Goethe's Iphigenia als eine Probe musikalischer Behandlung jenes Meisterwerks.'** 1815.

MS. Fitzwilliam Museum, Cambridge.

According to the wording of the title in Schubert's MS., it is a copy of the first edition of an aria in Reichardt's *Lieder der Liebe und der Einsamkeit*, second part, pp. 62 ff., published by Gerhard Fleischer the younger at Leipzig in 1804. The copy made by Schubert was recopied by another hand, and this time the music was attributed to Schubert. This later copy is to be found in the MS. song book of Frau Franziska Tremier (Stadtbibliothek, Vienna), which also contains the following autograph pages by Schubert: the title-page of his song ' Todesmusik ' (758), and his copy of Beethoven's ' Abendlied unterm gestirnten Himmel ' (Appendix II, no. 7). The index of the Witteczek Collection lists this aria, too, as a work by Schubert

APPENDIX II

written in 1815. This date appears also on the title-page of Schubert's MS. copy (the date written in pencil, ? by Schubert). Curiously enough, Anton Schindler mentions that Beethoven, on his deathbed in February 1827, saw 'Iphigenien's Monolog' among sixty Schubert songs (*Allgemeine Theaterzeitung*, Vienna, 3rd May 1831). Cf. Schubert's setting of Mayrhofer's poem 'Iphigenia' (573).

5. Johann Josef Fux's 'Singfundament,' duets nos. 1–7 and 44 for Sopranos, arranged, and slightly altered in length, as duets for Violins, copied in parts. Not printed. *c.* 1813.

MS. Preussische Staatsbibliothek, Berlin (together with 577).

The original duets were identified by Andreas Liess in Fux's autograph (Gesellschaft der Musikfreunde, Vienna). It is not known who arranged those duets. Cf. 25.

6. Maximilian Stadler's Sacred Aria 'Unendlicher Gott, unser Herr.' Summer 1819 (Steyr).

MS. Dr. Franz Roehn, Los Angeles.

Attached to the MS. is Johann Michael Vogl's copy of the beginning of the voice part. It seems that Schubert wrote his copy of the score for a performance, with the singer Vogl, in the parish church of Steyr. Albert Stadler's letters of 1858 to Ferdinand Luib (Stadtbibliothek, Vienna) are contradictory on this point.

7. Beethoven's Song 'Abendlied unterm gestirnten Himmel' (Heinrich Goebel). *c.* 1821.

MS. Stadtbibliothek, Vienna.

This incomplete copy, transposed from E to D, is to be found in the Tremier song book (see Appendix II, no. 4). Beethoven's song was composed and published in 1820.

8. Beethoven's Fourth Symphony in B flat, Op. 60, the first four bars only. No date known.

MS. Stadtbibliothek, Vienna (Ph.).

9. Michael Haydn's 'Deutsches Hochamt.' No date known.

MS. Moritz von Caesar, Baden, near Vienna.

The version of Michael Haydn's German Mass, of which this is an organ score, is that preserved in the Jakobs-Kirche at Straubing (Bavaria), but with the original words, 'Hier liegt vor Deiner Majestät.' (Cf. 621 and 872.) It seems that Schubert and his friends sang some of Michael Haydn's canons about 1815. Two pages of the second tenor part of nine canons, probably written by Anton Holzapfel, are in the possession of the Krasser family, Vienna, some of which are certainly by Michael Haydn, while another is dedicated to him by F. J. Otter of Salzburg.

APPENDIX III

CONCORDANCE TABLES

1. OPUS NUMBERS

The numbers on the left are the opus numbers, those on the right the numbers of the present catalogue.

1	328	32	550
2	118	33	783
3	121, 216, 257, 368	34	675
4	493, 685, 224	35	813
5	138, 162, 225, 226, 367	36	707, 672
6	541, 542, 504	37	794, 588
7	514, 515, 531	38	209
8	702, 516, 586, 539	39	636
9	365	40	819
10	624	41	800
11	641, 724, 747	42	845
12	478, 480, 479	43	828, 827
13	517, 711, 524	44	457
14	720, 719	45	739
15	760	46	136
16	740, 422	47	223
17	983	48	45_ (961)
18	145	49	735
19	369, 161, 544	50	779
20	741, 686, 552	51	733
21	553, 536, 525	52	837, 838, 835, 836, 846, 839, 843
22	771, 772	53	850
23	751, 743, 744, 761	54	818
24	583, 527	55	859
25	795	56	767, 737, 738
26	797	57	633, 634, 193
27	602	58	312, 113, 191
28	809	59	756, 775, 776, 777
29	804	60	778, 801
30	617	61	824
31	717	62	877

APPENDIX III

63 823
64 825
65 360, 649, 753
66 885
67 734
68 742
69 773
70 895
71 770
72 774
73 745
74 37
75 599
76 796
77 969
78 894
79 851, 852
80 870, 871, 880
81 904, 905, 903
82 908 (603)
83 902
84 823
85 830, 831
86 907
87 713, 637, 638
88 856, 595, 862, 547
89 911
90 899
91 924
92 764, 543, 142
93 834, 853
94 780
95 866
96 930, 909, 768, 881
97 955
98 497, 498, 573
99 898
100 929
101 833
102 875
103 940
104 930
105 865, 867, 878, 879
106 922, 926, 927, 891

Posthumous [1]

107 951
108 884, 758, 229
109 361, 143, 530
110 594
111 189, 395, 391
112 985, 986, 232
113 696
114 667
115 917, 260, 410
116 159
117 149
118 233, 221, 234, 135, 270, 247
119 943
120 664
121 886
122 568
123 786
124 857
125 87, 353
126 134
127 146
128 472
129 965
130 868
131 141, 148, 23
132 706
133 757
134 892
135 921
136 942
137 384, 385, 408
138 608
139 815 (913)

[1] Although the numbers of Opp. 98–9 and 101–5 were assigned by Schubert himself, these works were not published before his death.

140	812	157	748
141	324	158	666
142	935	159	934
143	784	160	802
144	947	161	887
145	505, 506	162	574
146	763	163	956
147	575	164	537
148	897	165	673, 670, 155, 230, 923
149	811	166	803
150	184	167	714
151	912	168	112
152	952	169	984
153	676	170	591
154	964	171	790
155	847	172	213, 214, 196, 231, 283, 691
156	848	173	195, 793, 177, 731, 519, 627

2. POSTHUMOUS SONGS

The numbers on the left are those of the *Lieferungen* (books) of the *Nachgelassene musikalische Dichtungen für Gesang und Pianoforte* (Posthumous Songs with Pianoforte Accompaniment) published between 1830 and 1850 by Anton Diabelli & Co., Vienna; the numbers on the right are the corresponding ones of the present catalogue.

1	534 (521)	16	708
2	282, 217	17	883, 906, 518, 59
3	150	18	789, 614, 526
4	293, 278, 281	19	474, 397
5	375	20	799, 126, 321
6	584	21	622, 792
7	832, 890, 690, 889	22	805, 585, 669, 806
8	246	23	762, 473
9	785, 746, 650	24	910, 842
10	291, 444, 623, 632, 343, 551, 171, 651	25	854, 882, 120
		26	938
11	548, 699, 540, 700	27	931, 932, 933
12	111	28	322, 286, 280, 445, 290
13	860, 861	29	412, 788, 564, 578
14	716, 450	30	876, 210, 616
15	949, 698, 869	31	102, 116, 115

32	620	42	677, 219, 263, 218, 95
33	694, 712	43	710
34	807, 626	44	671, 358, 492, 269
35	182, 822	45	520, 75, 140, 264
36	300, 301, 736	46	749
37	754, 123	47	674, 261, 255, 119, 259
38	393, 508, 715	48	684, 434, 436, 888, 727, 560, 274
39	153, 174, 403		
40	652, 653, 654	49	611, 151
41	352, 442	50	197, 432, 297

3. WORKS WITHOUT NUMBERS IN NOTTEBOHM'S CATALOGUE (1874)

The figures on the left refer to the pages in Gustav Nottebohm's *Thematisches Verzeichnis der im Druck erschienenen Werke von Franz Schubert*; *a, b*, etc., indicate the order of more than one item on a page; the figures on the right refer to the present catalogue.

203	944	214c	366, 814
204a	759	216	420, 529
204b	417	217a	576
205	810	217b	718
206a	173	217c	105
206b	94	218	167
207a	703	219	950
207b	487	220	678
207c	821	221	689
208	417	223	787
209a	485	225	647
209b	592	226	379
209c	928	227–8	872
210	958, 959, 960	229a	953
211	840	229b	440
212a	459	229c	791
212b	946	230a	918
213a	612	230b	356
213b	593	230c	656
213c	915	231	796, 267, 572, 268, 377, 439, 609, 168, 987
214a	606		
214b	925	232a	893, 901

232b	331		359, 295, 476, 579, 937, 545,
233a	337		528, 752, 371, 692, 251, 502,
233b	494		458, 409, 693, 250, 179, 176,
233c	657		466, 509, 264, 210, 165, 402,
234	957		659, 660, 661, 662
242a	882, 833, 546, 768	250	688, 76
242b	52, 73, 296, 765, 114, 495	253a	603
243	726	253b	48
244	855, 808, 766, 768, 561, 454,	259, no. [18]	954
	449, 309, 272, 237, 206, 122,	259, no. [20]	126

4. COLLECTED EDITION (1884–97)

The figures on the left refer to the *Kritisch durchgesehene Gesamtausgabe* of Schubert's works, roman figures indicating the series, arabic figures the number within the series; the figures on the right are the corresponding numbers in the present catalogue.

I. SINFONIEN (1884–5)

1	82	5	485
2	125	6	589
3	200	7	944
4	417	8	759

II. OUVERTÜREN UND ANDERE ORCHESTERWERKE (1886)

1	4	6	591
2	26	7	648
3	470	8	89
4	556	9	90
5	590	10	86

III. OKTETTE USW. (1889)

1	803
2	72
3	79

IV. STREICHQUINTETT (1890)

956

APPENDIX III

V. STREICHQUARTETTE (1890)

1	18	9	173
2	32	10	87
3	36	11	353
4	46	12	703
5	68	13	804
6	74	14	810
7	94	15	887
8	112		

VI. STREICHTRIO (1890)
471

VII. PIANOFORTE-QUINTETT, -QUARTETT UND -TRIOS (1886)

1	667	4	929
2	487	5	897
3	898		

VIII. FÜR PIANOFORTE UND EIN INSTRUMENT (1886)

1	895	5	934
2	384	6	574
3	385	7	802
4	408	8	821

IX. FÜR PIANOFORTE ZU VIER HÄNDEN (1888)

A. MÄRSCHE

1	602	5	885
2	819	6	886
3	733	7	928
4	859		

B. ANDERE WERKE

I. OUVERTÜREN, SONATEN, RONDOS, VARIATIONEN

8	675	14	608
9	597	15	624
10	592	16	813
11	617	17	908
12	812	18	603
13	951		

2. DIVERTISSEMENTS, POLONAISEN, FANTASIEN, USW.

19	818	27	814
20–2	823	28	952
23	947	29	968
24	940	30	1
25	824	31	9
26	599	32	48

X. SONATEN FÜR PIANOFORTE (1888)

1	157	9	845
2	279	10	664
3	557	11	850
4	566	12	894
5	575	13	958
6	537	14	959
7	568	15	960
8	784		

XI. FANTASIE, IMPROMPTUS UND ANDERE STÜCKE FÜR PIANOFORTE (1888)

1	760	9	29
2	899	10	604
3	935	11	612
4	780	12	915
5	505, 506	13	946
6	156	14	459
7	576	15	593
8	718	16	606

XII. TÄNZE FÜR PIANOFORTE (1889)

1	365	10	366
2	145	11	420 (529)
3	783	12	378
4	779	13	970
5	734	14	971
6	969	15	972
7	924	16	973
8	146 (135)	17	974
9	790	18	769

APPENDIX III

19	722	26	977
20	975	27	421
21	643	28	697
22	976	29	158
23	735	30	41
24	925	31	610
25	781		

ANHANG
URSPRÜNGLICHE FASSUNG EINIGER DEUTSCHER TÄNZE

[Eleven dances from Opp. 33, 50, and 127—783, 779, 146]

XIII. MESSEN (1887)

1	105 (185)	5	678
2	167	6	950
3	324	7	872
4	452 (961)		

XIV. KLEINERE KIRCHENMUSIK-WERKE (1888)
A. MIT BEGLEITUNG

1	136	10	488
2	223	11	486
3	676	12	175
4	181	13	383
5	184	14	31
6	739	15	49
7	460	16	66
8	750	17	379
9	106		

B. OHNE BEGLEITUNG

18	696	21	45
19	811	22	962
20	386		

XV. DRAMATISCHE MUSIK (1886–93)

1	84	6	787
2	190	7	644
3	220	8	797 (732)
4	326	9	732
5	647	10	796

11 239	14 137
12 11	15 723
13 435	

XVI. FÜR MÄNNERCHOR (1891)
A. MIT BEGLEITUNG VON STREICH- ODER BLASINSTRUMENTEN

1 913	3 714
2 964	

B. MIT PIANOFORTEBEGLEITUNG

4 641	12 865
5 724	13 892
6 747	14 920
7 740	15 710
8 422	16 75
9 809	17 267
10 835	18 268
11 903	19 513

C. OHNE BEGLEITUNG

20–3 983	34 572
24–6 825	35 656
27 875	36 657
28 912	37 901
29 847	38 331
30 848	39 337
31 709	40 338
32 494	41 893
33 538	42 948

D. ANHANG I
43 110

E. ANHANG II
44 407

F. ANHANG III
45 704

G. ANHANG IV
46 598

XVII. FÜR GEMISCHTEN CHOR (1892)
A. MIT ORCHESTERBEGLEITUNG

1 689	4 294
2 472	5 954
3 748	

APPENDIX III

B. MIT PIANOFORTEBEGLEITUNG

6 985	12 439
7 986	13 609
8 232	14 826
9 942	15 936
10 815	16 168
11 763	17 987

C. OHNE BEGLEITUNG

18 440	19 953

XVIII. FÜR FRAUENCHOR (1891)

(MIT PIANOFORTEBEGLEITUNG)

1 836	4 921
2 706	5 269
3 757	6 140

XIX. KLEINERE DREI- UND ZWEISTIMMIGE GESANGWERKE (1892)

(TERZETTE UND DUETTE)

A. MIT BEGLEITUNG

1 37	5 441
2 930	6 236
3 666	7 277
4 80	8 148

B. OHNE BEGLEITUNG

9 53	22 54
10 58	23 69
11 60	24 357
12 55	25 130
13 63	26 988
14 71	27 244
15 147	28 131
16 129	29 56
17 427	30 199
18 242	31 202
19 243	32 203
20 38	33 204
21 88	34 205

ANHANG

35 65	36 619

XX. LIEDER UND GESÄNGE (1894-5)
Für eine Singstimme mit Pianofortebegleitung

1	5	39	151	75	206
2	6	40	152	76	207
3	7	41	153	77	208, 212
4	10	42	155	78	210
5	30	43	141	79	211
6	23	44	150	80	213
7	44	45	149	81	214
8	50	46	159	82	216
9	52	47	160	83	217
10	59	48	161	84	218
11	73	49	162	85	219
12	77, 111	50	163	86	222
13-15	93	51	165	87	224
16	99	52	166	88	225
17	100	53	169	89	226
18	101	54	170	90	227
19	97	55	171	91	228
20	102	56	174	92	229
21	107	57	176	93	230
22	108	58	177	94	231
23	109	59	179	95	221
24	98	60	180	96	233
25	95	61	182	97	234
26	113	62	183	98	209
27	114	63	187	99	134
28	115	64	188	100	235
29	116	65	186	101	237
30	117	66	189	102	238
31	118	67	191	103	240
32	119	68	192	104	241
33	120	69	193	105	250
34	121	70	194	106	251
35	123	71	195	107	254, 587
36	124	72	196	108	252
37	126	73	197	109	246
38	122	74	198	110	253

APPENDIX III

111	254	152	304	193	388
112	255	153	305	194	389
113	256	154	306	195	390
114	257	155	307	196	391
115	258	156	308	197	392
116	259	157	309	198	393
117	260	158	310	199	394
118	261	159	312	200	404
119	247	160	313	201	403
120	558	161	314	202	405
121	559	162	315	203	350
122	560	163	316	204	351
123	263	164	317	205	395
124	264	165	318	206	409
125	265	166	319	207	410
126	266	167	320	208	406
127	270	168	321	209	411
128	271	169	322	210	412
129	272	170	298	211	413
130	273	171	297	212	414
131	274	172	323	213	415
132	275	173	325	214	418
133	276	174	142	215	419
134	262	175	295	216	436
135	248	176	296	217	398
136	283	177	138	218	399
137	284	178	328	219	400
138	285	179	633	220	401
139	280	180	634	221	429
140	286	181	143	222	430
141	287	182	330	223	431
142	288	183	372	224	432
143	289	184	373	225	433
144	290	185	292, 371	226	434
145	291	186	377	227	442
146	293	187	375	228	443
147	278	188	282	229	444
148	281	189	381	230	445
149	301	190	382	231	446
150	302	191	397	232	447
151	303	192	402	233	448

234 449	277 498	318 536
235 358	278 499	319 554
236 450	279 500	320 561
237 457	280 362	321 562
238 342	281 501	322 563
239 454	282 502	323 569
240 455	283 507	324 565
241 456	284 508	325 573
242 458	285 509	326 518
243 468	286 352	327 550
244 462	287 904	328 583
245 463	288 905	329 584
246 464	289 520	330 585
247 465	290 521	331 586
248 466	291 522	332 588
249 473	292 523	333 594
250 474	293 517	334 595
251 475	294 711	335 579
252 476	295 524	336 611
253 477	296 525	337 614
254 478	297 526	338 616
255 479	298 527	339 620
256–8 480	299 519	340 622
259 481	300 514	341 623
260 359	301 515	342 343
261 367	302 531	343 626
262 368	303 532	344 627
263 369	304 533	345 628
264 482	305 534	346 629
265 483	306 539	347 630
266 489, 493	307 540	348 631
267 490	308 541	349 632
268 360	309 542	350 646
269 491	310 543	351 649
270 492	311 544	352 650
271 495	312 545	353 651
272 361	313 546	354 652
273 530	314 547	355 653
274 496	315 551	356 654
275 504	316 552	357 636
276 497	317 553	358 637

APPENDIX III

359 638	400 741	460 807
360 659	401 742	461 808
361 660	402 736	462 955
362 661	403 752	463 799
363 662	404 753	464 822
364 658	405 754	465 800
365 669	406 743	466 832
366 670	407 744	467 842
367 671	408 745	468 833
368 672	409 756	469 828
369 673	410 751	470 827
370 674	411 758	471 837
371 677	412 761	472 838
372 687	413 762	473 846
373 691	414 737	474 839
374 692	415 738	475 843
375 693	416 764	476 834
376 690	417 765	477 853
377 694	418 766	478 851
378 684	419 767	479 852
379 685	420 768	480 854
380 686	421 785	481 855
381 698	422 746	482 856
382 548	423 786	483-4 857
383 699	424 770	485 860
384 700	425 771	486 861
385 702	426 772	487 876
386 516	427 788	488-91 877
387 707	428 774	492 878
388 708	429 789	493 879
389 712	430 792	494 880
390 713	431 793	495 881
391 715	432 794	496 869
392 719	433-52 795	497 882
393 716	453 775	498 883
394 726	454 776	499 862
395 469, 727	455 777	500 884
396 720	456 778	501 907
397 717	457 801	502 888
398 300	458 805	503 889
399 731	459 806	504 890

APPENDIX III

505 891	516 910	547 927
506 870	517–40 911	548 931
507 871	541 830	549 932
508–11 866	542 831	550 933
512 867	543 917	551 938
513 868	544 922	552 939
514 906	545 923	553 949
515 909	546 926	554–67 957

ANHANG

1. MIT BEGLEITUNG VON ZWEI INSTRUMENTEN
    568 943
    569 965

2. IN ITALIENISCHER SPRACHE
    570 42
    571 76
    572 78
    573 510
    574 528
    575–8 688
    579–81 902

3. GELEGENHEITSSTÜCKE
    582 83

583 81
584 104
585 535
586 578
587 695
588 749
589 945

4. FRAGMENTE
    590 15
    591 329
    592 376
    593 467
    594 484

595 549
596 564
597 577
598 596
599 682
600 721
601 728
602 937

5. MELODRAM
    603 829

REVISIONSBERICHT
    p. 46 144

XXI. SUPPLEMENT (1897)

A. INSTRUMENTALMUSIK

1 11	12 625	22 178
2 12	13 655	23 128
3 345	14 840	24 334
4 438	15 605	25 335
5 581	16 900	26 336
6 668	17 346	27 600
7 798	18 347	28 380
8 154	19 348	29 299
9 567	20 570	30 529
10 571	21 349	31 844
11 613		

B. GESANGMUSIK

32 962	37 51	41 64
33 963	38 57	42 67
34 705	39 61	43 43
35 364	40 62	44 387
36 914, 919		

APPENDIX IV

OTHER COLLATIONS

A. SONG COLLECTIONS
PUBLISHED BETWEEN 1828 AND 1874

The references are to the Concordance Table on pp. 497 f.

Vier Lieder . . . mit Begleitung des Pianoforte. . . . Op. (101). Leipzig, H. A. Probst (no. 431), [1828]. See Nottebohm, p. 242a.

Schwanengesang . . . für eine Singstimme mit Begleitung des Pianoforte. Wien, Tobias Haslinger (nos. 5371–84), [1829]. See Nottebohm, p. 234.

Sechs bisher ungedruckte Lieder . . . herausgegeben [von Franz Espagne], etc. Berlin, Wilhelm Müller (no. 13), 1868. See Nottebohm, p. 242b.

5 Canti per una sola voce con accompagnomento di Pianoforte. Wien, J. P. Gotthard (no. 129), 1871. See Nottebohm, p. 250.

Neueste Folge nachgelassener einstimmiger Gesänge mit und ohne Begleitung. Wien, J. P. Gotthard (nos. 316–24), 1872. See Nottebohm, p. 231.

Neueste Folge nachgelassener Lieder und Gesänge. Wien, J. P. Gotthard (nos. 325–61), 1872. See Nottebohm, p. 244.

B. PUBLICATIONS OF SCHUBERT'S WORKS OTHER THAN THOSE LISTED BY NOTTEBOHM OR FIRST PRINTED IN THE COLLECTED EDITION

The numbers refer to the present catalogue.

1. PUBLICATIONS BEFORE 1874 BUT OMITTED BY NOTTEBOHM

54, 170, 389, 404, 406, 565, 577, 829, 988

2. PUBLICATIONS BETWEEN 1874 AND THE CONCLUSION OF THE COLLECTED EDITION (1897)

124, 142, 156, 183, 188, 192, 199, 202, 222, 227, 239, 245, 252, 253, 254, 256, 258, 285, 303, 314, 342, 350, 398, 411, 429, 431, 446, 448, 455, 456, 465, 467, 475, 489, 491, 496, 499, 523, 533, 558, 559, 563, 615, 631, 646, 729, 803, 962, 963.

All songs published during that period, except 489, are to be found in the following collections of Schubert's works:

APPENDIX IV

Zwölf nachgelassene, zum Teil bisher ungedruckte Lieder, für Pianoforte zu 2 Händen herausgegeben von J. P. Gotthard. Wien, V. Kratochwill (no. 252), 1876. Containing 350, 631, 533, 475.

Sechs nachgelassene, zum Teil bisher ungedruckte Lieder, für Pianoforte zu 4 Händen herausgegeben von J. P. Gotthard. Wien, V. Kratochwill (no. 253), [1876]. Containing 342, 465.

Duette für zwei Singstimmen und Pianofortebegleitung. Herausgegeben von Max Friedlaender. Leipzig, C. F. Peters (no. 6886, Edition no. 2209), [1885]. Containing 199, 202.

Nachgelassene (bisher ungedruckte) Lieder für eine Singstimme mit Pianofortebegleitung. Revidiert und herausgegeben von Max Friedlaender. Leipzig, C. F. Peters (nos. 6895/6, Edition nos. 2208a/b), [1885]. Containing 646, 523, 429, 142, 239, 227, 285, 496, 499, 222, 245, 559, 467, 124.

Schubert-Album. Sammlung der Lieder für eine Singstimme mit Pianofortebegleitung. Herausgegeben von Max Friedlaender, Band VII. Leipzig, C. F. Peters (no. 6896, Edition no. 2270), [1887]. Containing 491, 456, 183, 563, 455, 188, 411, 314, 398, 192, 252, 253, 448, 558, 446, 431, 256, 303.

Bisher unbekannte und unveröffentlichte Compositionen, herausgegeben von H. v. Bocklet. Wien, Josef Weinberger & Hofbauer (nos. 21 and 30), 1887. Containing 156 (instrumental), 254, 258.

Zwei Chöre (bisher ungedruckt), herausgegeben von Max Friedlaender. Leipzig, C. F. Peters (nos. 7380/1, 7384/5), [1890]. Containing 962, 963.

3. PUBLICATIONS BETWEEN 1897 AND 1950

17, 27, 28, 33, 34, 35, 70, 96, 103, 135, 139, 164, 215, 279, 299, 327, 354, 355, 370, 374, 416, 423, 424, 428, 461, 511, 555, 566, 573A, 580, 607, 618, 621, 635, 642, 663, 679, 680, 681, 701, 725, 729, 730, 817, 820, 841, 896, 942.

APPENDIX V

UNPUBLISHED WORKS

1. WORKS LOST

14, 19, 19A, 20, 21, 22, 27, 40, 41, 92, 127, 132, 133, 332, 333, 339, 340, 341, 425, 426, 451, 582, 597, 665, 683, 841 (note), 849, 863, 864, 941, 944A, 981, 989.

2. WORKS NOT PRINTED

2, 3, 8, 13, 16, 24, 25, 39, 47, 85, 91, 172, 201, 239, 249, 311, 344, 363, 396, 409, 437, 453, 503, 512, 598A, 601, 615, 618A, 640, 644, 645, 701, 729, 755, 791, 816, 858, 873, 874, 916, 918, 966, 967, 982, 990, 991, 992, 993, 994, 995, 996, 997, 998.

INDICES

The figures refer to the numbers of the catalogue. No reference is given to the Preface and the Supplements.

GENERAL INDEX

The names of the authors of Schubert's songs, of the *Gesamtausgabe* of Schubert's works, and of Vienna are omitted. Place-names are added to the names of collectors, dealers, publishers, and periodicals.

Abendlied unterm gestirnten Himmel (Beethoven), App. II 4, App. II 7
Abendröte (F. von Schlegel), 633, 634, 646, 649, 652, 684, 690, 691, 692, 693, 694, 745
Abraham, Gerald, 72, 590
Adamberger, Antoine (later married Arneth), 372
Ahnfrau, Die (Grillparzer), 653
Album, Therese Grob's, 343
— *für Gesang*, etc. (Vienna), 872
— *musicale* (Vienna), 229, 769, 780
— *österreichischer Dichter* (Vienna), 864
Alcide al Bivio (Metastasio), 76
Alexander I, Emperor of Russia, 859
Allessandro nell' Indie (Metastasio), 688
Allgemeine Kirchenmusik-Lehre (Kloss), 872
— *Kunstschronik* (Vienna), App. I
— *musikalische Zeitung* (Leipzig), 150, 851
— *musikalische Zeitung mit besonderer Rücksicht auf den österreichischen Kaiserstaat* (Vienna), 518
— *Theaterzeitung* (Vienna), 913, 917, 954, App. II 4
— *Wiener Musikzeitung* (Vienna), 356
Allgemeines Krankenhaus (Vienna), see General Hospital
Almásy, Rosa Gräfin, 592
Alsergrund (Vienna), 954
Als ich einen Freund des nächsten Morgens auf dem Lande zum Besuche erwartete (Baumberg), 270
Alt-Lerchenfelder Kirche (Vienna), 678, 696
Altona (near Hamburg), 788
Anna-Kirche (Vienna), 45, 689, 872
Annual Report of the Library of Congress (Washington), 550
Anschütz, Heinrich, 922
Antcliffe, Herbert, 227
Antony and Cleopatra (Shakespeare), 888
Apollo an der Damen-Toilette (Vienna), entry before 350
Archiv der Gesellschaft der Musikfreunde (Vienna), see Gesellschaft der Musikfreunde
Archiv für Musikwissenschaft (Leipzig), 550, 822

Archiv für Photogramme musikalischer Meisterhandschriften. Widmung A. van Hoboken (Musiksammlung der Nationalbibliothek Wien), see Photogramm-Archiv (Vienna)
Arendt, F. G. (Hildesheim), 199, 201
Arkona (Rügen), 221
Artaria & Co. (Vienna), 96, 298, 606, 896, 951
Artaria, Domenico, 895, 951
Artaria, Matthias (Vienna), 818, 835, 836, 837, 838, 839, 843, 846, 850
Artaserse (Metastasio), 509
Assmayr, Ignaz, entry before 350, 607, entry before 612
Athenaeum (London), 849
Attilio Regolo (Metastasio), 902 (no. 1)
Attis (Catullus), 585
Atzenbrugg (Lower Austria), 145, 365, entries before 729
Auferstehung, Die (Klopstock), 115
Austria, 834, 929

Bacharach, A. L., 803
Baden (near Vienna), 952
Barbedette, Hippolyte, 547
Barnett, John Francis, 729
Barth, Josef, 641, 724, 747, 810
Bass, John (New York), 485, entry before 679
Battle of Lora (Ossian), 327, 376
Bauer, Adolf, 566
Bauer, Hannes, 705
Bauer, Moritz, 630
Bauernfeld, Eduard von, 21, 37, 260, 886, 940; see also Index of Authors
Bauernfeld und Schubert (Nathansky), 819
Bauernschmied, Herr (Ried, Lower Austria), 309
Bayerische Staatsbibliothek (Munich), 686
Becker, Wilhelm Gottlieb, 519 (639)
Beethoven, 189, 216, entry before 350, 568, 718, 742, 954, App. II 4, App. II 7, App. II 8
Beethoven-Haus (Bonn), 566
Beethoven-Jahrbuch (Munich), 718
Beiträge zur Bildung für Jünglinge (Vienna), 536
— *zur Biographie Franz Schuberts* (Friedlaender), App. II 3

515

GENERAL INDEX

Bélanger (? Édouard), App. I
Benedict, Bernhard, 666
Benko, Anton (Vienna), 872
Berchthold, Anton Graf, 813
Berg, Isaak Albert, 887, 929
Berghirt, Der (W. Müller), 965
Berlin, 84, 461, 717, 730, 810
Berliner musikalische Zeitung, App. I
Bernhardt, J., 819
Beromünster, *see* Radio Beromünster
Berra, Marco (Prague), 167
Betulia liberata (Metastasio), 34
Bettelstudent, Der (Weidmann), 4
Black, Frank (New York), 760
Blagrove, Richard Manning, 581
Blätter für Hausmusik (Leipzig), 565
Blätter für Theater, Musik und bildende Kunst (Vienna), 451
Blinden-Institut (Vienna), 863
Blümlein Vergissmein (W. Müller), 795
Bocklet, Heinrich von, 123, 156, 254, 258
Bocklet, Karl Maria von, 760, 850, 895, 934
Bodleian Library (Oxford), 874, 876
Bodmer, Martin (Zürich-Geneva), 159, 530, 659, 660, 661, 662. 817
Bogner, Ferdinand, 802
Böhm & Sohn, Anton (Augsburg), 730
Böhm, Franz Josef (Mürzzuschlag), 616
Bonnet, Charles, 50
Boosey & Hawkes (London), 759
Bosch, Hans, 5, 480
Bösendorfer-Salon (Vienna), 487
Boston Public Library (Boston, Mass.), 116
Brahms, Johannes, 137, 355, 366, 453, 489, 490, 565, 568, 618, 685, 701, 703, 707, entry before 729, 729, 790, 814, 946, 950, entries before 969, 970, 975, 991
Branner's Bibliofile Antikvariat (Copenhagen), 945
Braun-Fernwald, Frau (Vienna), 624
Braunschweig, 124
Breitkopf & Härtel (Leipzig), 5, 159, 328, 397, 536, 729, 944, App. II 3
Breslauer, Martin (Berlin), 725
Bretzner, Christoph Friedrich, 426
Breuner, Sofie Gräfin, *see* Sofie Gräfin Weissenwolff
Breunner, Marie Gräfin (Schloss Grafenegg), *see* Marie Komtesse Esterházy
British and Continental Music Agencies (London), 566
British Museum (London), 224, 225, 227, 324, 636, 639, 787, 894, 902
Britten, Benjamin, 564
Brown, Maurice J. E., 615
Bruchmann, Franz Seraph von, 751; *see also* Index of Authors

Bruchmann, Justine von, 552, 686, 741
Bruchmann, Sybilla von, 762
Bruck, Die (near Göttingen), 853
Brühl, Schloss (near Cologne), 96
Brunswick-Lüneburg, Leopold, Duke of, 124
Buchhändlerbörse (Leipzig), 417
Buchwieser, Katharina, *see* Lászny
Budapest, 735; *see also* Pest
Bürgerspital (Vienna), 675, 829
Burggarten (Vienna), 663, 817
Burgtheater (Vienna), 372

Caesar, Moritz von (Baden, near Vienna), 216, 217, 278, 281, 282, 285, App. II 9
Calderón de la Barca, Don Pedro, 682
Call, Leonhard, 642
Cambridge (England), 564
Campbell, Frank C., 550
Cappi & Co. (Vienna), 588, 672, 675, 783, 794
Cappi & Czerny (Vienna), 360, 649, 753, 778, 801, 824
Cappi & Diabelli (Vienna), 118, 121, 138, 145, 162, 209, 216, 224, 225, 226, 257, 328, 365, 367, 368, 422, 493, 504, 514, 515, 516, 517, 524, 531, 541, 542, 586, 641, 685, 702, 707, 711, 718, 719, 720, 724, 740, 747, 760, 983
Carneval 1823 (Vienna), 971
Carric-Thura (Ossian), 150, 282, 293
Castelli, Ignaz Franz, 908; *see also* Index of Authors
Catullus, 585
Challier & Co., C. A. (Berlin), App. I
Chamber Music (Tovey), 786
Charavey, Étienne (Paris), 686, 773
Charlotte, Queen of England, 147
Chézy, Helmina von, 922; *see also* Index of Authors
Chézy, Wilhelm von, 901
Chodowiecki, Daniel Nikolaus, 689
Chor der Derwische (Zumsteeg), 54, App. II 3
Chronik der Stadt Hof (Wiedemann), 847
Clemenza di Tito, La (Metastasio), 35
Clochette, La (Hérold), 723
Clodi, Therese, 848
Colin Clout's come home again (Spenser), 795
Collections of music by various composers, including Schubert, published during his lifetime (Vienna), 146, 229, entry before 350, 361, 366, 718, 769, 780, 781, 782, 841, 893, 894, 901, 971, 976, 978, 979, 980
Collin, Matthäus von, 771, 772; *see also* Index of Authors
Cologne, 96
Comola (Ossian), 147
Conversationsblatt (Vienna), 698

GENERAL INDEX

Conservatoire (Paris), 11, 12, 39, 58, 119, 126, 135, 136, 138, 139, entry before 146, 146, 149, 150, 156, 174, 181, 197, 198, 254, 255, 259, 285, 310, 312, 321, 407, entry before 435, 450, 456, 458, 465, 466, 481, 537, 542, 547, 558, 559, 560, 578, 579, 595, 609, 612, 644, 670, 671, 681, 740, 750, 798, 821, 832, 952
Conservatoire (Vienna), 706
Copies, in manuscript, of Schubert's works, see Ebner, Stadler (Albert), and Witteczek
Cortot, Alfred (Lausanne), 712, 721
Cranz, Albert (Brussels and New York), 112, 219, 221, 227, 228, 229, 233, 237, 240, 241, 267, 269, 272, 273, 274, 275, 291, 302, 303, 304, 305, 306, 307, 308, 314, 315, 316, 317, 318, 319, 322, 392, 393, (579), 692, 922, 923
Cranz, Alwin (Vienna), 1 (2), 75, 111, 230, 231, 236, 237, 238, 240, 241, 245, 250, 251, 253, 254, 258, 259, 266, 276, 284, 286, 287, 288, 289, 310, 320, 321, 357, 371, 384 (2), 408, 413, 414, 415, 419, 431, 432, 433, 438, 442, 477, 478, 479, 486, 487, 545, 546, 547, 556, 581, 590, 591, 714, 732, 793, 794, 796, 797, 860, 861, 862, 884
Cranz, August (Leipzig), autographs formerly with (present owner unknown), 277, 283, 350, 351, 364, 532, 533; cf. 993, 996
Cronnan (Ossian), 534
Crystal Palace (London), 82, 125, 200, 485, 729
Czernin, Eugen Graf (Neuhaus, Bohemia), 939
Czerny, Josef (Vienna), 23, 87, 134, 141, 148, 149, 189, 221, 232, 233, 234, 247, 248, 270, 353, 391, 395, 594, 664, 667, 810, 865, 867, 878, 879, 985, 986
Czerny, Karl, 356, 796, 798
Cymbeline (Shakespeare), 889

Dacy, Arthur (New York), 162, 163
Daffner, Hugo, 630
Dahms, Walter, 410, 547, 796
Dale, Kathleen, 566
Daly, W., 384
Damian, Franz Valentin, 795
Dankesreither, Johann Nepomuk von, 478, 479, 480
Dante, 630
Darthula (Ossian), 278
Dedications of manuscripts (Schubert's), 145 (waltzes, nos. 5 and 8), 365 (no. 2), 452, 547, 550, 610, 675, 685, 915, 957, 958–60
Dedications of printed works (Schubert's), 118, 121 (216, 257, 368), 136, 138 (162, 225, 226, 367), 142 (543, 764), 159, 161 (369, 544), 209, 224 (493, 685), 328, 452 (961), 478 (479, 480), 504 (541, 542), 514 (515, 531), 516 (539, 586, 702), 517 (524, 711), 525 (536, 553), 552 (686, 741), 588 (794), 617, 624, 641 (724, 747), 672 (707), 717, 719 (720), 737 (738, 767), 760, 768 (881, 909, 939), 771 (772), 773, 795, 804, 813, 818, 819, 835 (836, 837, 838, 839, 843, 846), 845, 850, 851 (852), 866, 870 (871, 880), 877, 891 (922, 926, 927), 894, 902, 908, 940
Deinhardstein, Ludwig, 489, see also Index of Authors
Demofoonte (Metastasio), 42
Deneke, Margaret (Oxford), 812
Der Abend blüht, Arkona glüht (Kosegarten), 221
Dessauer, Josef, 172, 872, 940
Deutsch, Otto Erich, 37, 96, 118, 132, 135, 139, 164, 209, 279, 294, 299, 354, 355, 370, entry before 384, 416, 423, 424, entry before 435, 451, 534, 555, 573A, 580, 621, 624, 639, 660, 663, 679, 680, 681, 759, entry before 769, 782, 797, 817, 820, 826, 841, 847, 849, 872, 978; see also Schubert Documents
Deutsche Blätter für Poesie, etc. (Breslau), 911
— *Lied im 18. Jahrhundert, Das* (Friedlaender), 500
— Öffentliche Wissenschaftliche Bibliothek (Berlin), see Preussische Staatsbibliothek
Deutschen Minnesänger, Die (Wien), 893, 901
Deutscher Liederverlag (Leipzig), 5
Deutsches Hochamt (Michael Haydn), App. II 9
Deux Valentins, Les, 647
Diabelli & Co., A. (Vienna), 37, 59, 75, 95, 102, 111, 115, 116, 119, 120, 123, 126, 136, 140, 143, 146, 150, 151, 153, 155, 161, 171, 174, 182, 184, 197, 210, 217, 218, 219, 223, 246, 255, 259, 261, 263, 264, 269, 274, 280, 281, 282, 286, 290, 291, 293, 297, 300, 301, 321, 322, 343, entry before 350, 352, 353, 358, 361, 365, 369, 375, 384, 385, 393, 397, 403, 408, 412, 432, 434, 436, 442, 444, 445, 450, 452, 457, 473, 474, 478, 479, 480, 492, 497, 498, 505, 508, 518, 520, 526, 534, 537, 540, 544, 548, 550, 551, 560, 564, 573, 574, 575, 578, 584, 585, 599, 608, 611, 614, 616, 620, 621, 622, 623, 626, 632, 650, 651, 652, 653, 654, 666, 669, 671, 674, 676, 677, 684, 689, 690, 694, 696, 698, 699, 700, 706, 708, 710, 712, 715, 716, 718, 727, 732, 733, 734, 735, 736, 739, 742, 745, 746,

GENERAL INDEX

748, 749, 754, 757, 762, 763, 770, 773, 774, 779, 784, 785, 788, 789, 792, 796, 799, 800, 802, 803, 805, 807, 811, 812, 815, 822, 830, 831, 832, 833, 842, 847, 848, 854, 860, 861, 869, 875, 876, 877, 882, 883, 886, 887, 888, 889, 890, 892, 897, 898, 906, 907, 910, 912, 921, 930, 931, 932, 934, 935, 938, 940, 942, 947, 949, 952, 955, 956, 958, 961, 964, 993, 996
Diabelli, Anton, 3, 19, 103, 122, 173, 278, 363, 403, 472, 521, 534, 550, 564, 592, 706, 716, 718, 834, 935, 961
Dichtungen (Seidl), 870
— *für Kunstredner* (ed. by Deinhardstein), 489
Dictionary of Music and Musicians (Grove), 898
Didone abbandonata (Metastasio), 510
Dieter, Christian Ludwig, 84
Dieterle, Wilhelm (Canoga Park, California), 921
Dietrichstein, Moritz Graf, 328
Divertimenti Campestri, Sei (Doblhoff), 513
Doblhoff, Karl Freiherr von, 514
Döbling (Vienna), 921
Documents, *see* Schubert Documents
Döhler, Theodor, App. I
Dohnányi, Ernst von, 566
Doll, Anton (Vienna), 586
Door, Anton, 593
Doppler, Josef, 125, 136
Dornbach (Vienna), 913
Dorotheum (Vienna), 452
Dramatisches Sträusschen auf das Jahr 1823 (Castelli), 787
Dreifaltigkeits-Kirche (Vienna), 950, 954
Drei Masken Verlag (München), 96, 759
Dresden, 190
Drouet, Louis, 624
Dumba, Nikolaus, 251, 466, 550, 692
Dustmann, Louise, 409, 458

Ebenzweier, Schloss (Upper Austria), 848
Ebner, Johann Leopold, 221; *see also* Ebner's copies
Ebner's copies of Schubert's early songs and dances (von Wettstein family, Vienna), 95, 111, 141, 281, 289, 299, 328, 368, 388, 436, 498, 501, 527, 531, 550
Ecclesiazusae (Aristophanes), 787
Eder, Josef (Vienna), 37
Eginhard und Emma (legend), 796
Egmont (Goethe), 210
Einstein, Alfred, 334, 597, 604, 935
Eisenach, 962, 963
Emmental (Switzerland), 851
Emmentaler Lied, 851

Enderes, Karl von, 949
Engelbrecht, Hugo (*sc.* Schwarz), 797
Engelke, Bernhard, 220
Entführung aus dem Serail, Die (Mozart), 426
Entwicklung des Romantischen in Schubert's Liedern, Die (Bosch), 5, 480
Ephemeren (Vienna), 949
Epstein, Julius, 705, 799, 833
Erbschaft, Die (Kotzebue), 372
Erdberggasse (Vienna), 421, 451
Erinnerungen aus meinem Leben (W. von Chézy), 901
Erlafsee (Lower Austria), 475, 586
Ernst und Tändeley (Vienna), 976
Eroe Cinese, L' (Metastasio), 688
Erster Schmerz, letzter Schmerz (W. Müller), 795
Eskeles, Marie von, *see* Gräfin Wimpffen
Espagne, Franz, 52, 73, 114, 296, 328, 495, 765
Essays in Musical Analysis (Tovey), 760
Esterházy von Galánta, Johann Karl Graf, 96, 142, 493, 516, 524, 539, 586, 627, 702, 715
Esterházy von Galánta, Karoline Komtesse, 138, entry before 146, 250, 519, 597, 619, 626, 627, 793, 815, 820, 929, 940
Esterházy von Galánta, Marie Komtesse (later married Breunner), 142, 493, 524, 619, 815
Esterházy von Galánta, Rosine Gräfin, 815
Eumenides (Aeschylus), 450
Eurich, Friedrich (Linz), 770

Falkenhagen (near Göttingen), 834
Fallstich, Johann Georg, 621
Fantasia for Pianoforte in C (Schumann), 646;
— for Pianoforte in C minor (Mozart), 993
Favorite-Walzer (Himmel), 365 (no. 2)
Favoritgalopp (Herrmann), 735
Favorit Galoppe (Vienna), 925
Fellinger, Johann Georg, 305, 308; *see also* Index of Authors
Fellinger, R., 464
Festblätter für das 10. Deutsche Sängerbundesfest, 1928 (Vienna), 354, 355, 423, 424, 428, 663
— *zum 6. Deutschen Sängerbundesfest*, Graz, 374
Festgabe für Julius Wahle, Eine, see Funde und Forschungen
Festival Overture (Rubinstein), 732
Festschrift für Hugo Riemann, 618
— *für Johannes Wolf*, 725
— *Johannes Biehle zum 60. Geburtstag überreicht* (Leipzig), 698

GENERAL INDEX

Festschrift zum 70. Geburtstag Eusebius Mandyczewski's (Vienna), 164
Feuchtersleben, Ernst von, 699, 754
Filosofo di Campagna, Il (Goldoni), 513, 528
Fingal (Ossian), 281
Fischer, Anton, 37
Fischer (engraver), 771
Fitzwilliam Museum (Cambridge), 37, 106, 142, 161, 238, 588, 840, App. II 4
Flatz, Franz, 953
Fleischer, Gerhard (Leipzig), App. II 4
Fleischmann, Friedrich, 96
Floersheim, Marie (Wildegg im Aargau, Switzerland), 366, 381, 382, 550, 591, 731, entry before 796, 911, 931, 932, 933, 940, 958, 959, 960
Flower, Sir Newman (Blandford, Dorset), 938
Forster, G., 701
Förster, Karl Gustav (Breslau), 735
Franck, Josefine von, 142, 543, 764
Frankfurt am Main, 656
Franz I, Emperor of Austria, 104, 678, 748, 950
Franz Josef I, Emperor of Austria, 748
Frey, Martin, 935
Friedlaender, Max, 105, 118, 124, 142, 183, 188, 192, 199, 202, 222, 227, 239, 245, 252, 253, 254, 256, 257, 285, 303, 313, 314, 342, 350, 398, 404, 406, 411, 429, 431, 446, 448, 455, 456, 461, 465, 467, 475, 491, 496, 499, 500, 523, 558, 559, 563, 565, 618, 631, 644, 646, 656, 686, 693, 694, 725, 730, 795, 801, 844, 872, 962, 963, App. I, App. II 1, App. II 2, App. II 3
Fries, Moritz Reichsgraf, 118
Friese, A. R. (Leipzig), 440
Fritzsch, Ernst Wilhelm (Leipzig), 565
Fröhlich, Anna, 706, 757, 763, 887
Fröhlich, Josefine, 920, 942
Frühlingsgedichte (F. von Schlegel), 694
Fuchs, Alois, 731
Fuchs, Johann Nepomuk, 701, 732
Führer, Robert, 167
Funde und Forschungen (Eine Festgabe für Julius Wahle), 844
Fux, Johann Josef, 25, 577, App. II 5

G., J., 27
Gabriele (Johanna Schopenhauer), 890
Gahy, Josef, 169, 170, 608, 642
Gal, Hans, 759
Galuppi, Baldassare, 513
Gänsbacher, Johann Baptist, 551
Gastein, 849, 850, 851, 852
Gatty, Nicholas Comyn, 564
Gedichte (Baumberg), 270
— (Mayrhofer), 527, 586
— (Niemeyer), 689

Gedichte (Rückert), see *Gesammelte Gedichte*
— (Seidl), see *Dichtungen*
— (Senn), 743, 744
— *aus den hinterlassenen Papieren eines reisenden Waldhornisten* (W. Müller), 795, 911
Gegenbauer, Karl, 135
Geigy-Hagenbach, Karl (Basle), 815
Geiringer, Karl, 461, 729, 821
Geistliche Lieder (Novalis), 658
Gemeindehaus,Wieden (Vienna), 17, 239
Gemeinnütziger und erheiternder Hauskalender für den österreichischen Kaiserstaat (Vienna), 931
General Hospital (Vienna), 800
Gerhard, Wilhelm, 701
Gerold, Karl (Vienna), 847
Gesammelte Gedichte (Rückert), 741, 775, 776, 777, 778
Gesänge des jungen Schubert, Die (Schnapper), 5
— *für vier Männerstimmen, Sechs* (Call), 642
Gesangsverein (Iglau), 374
Gesellschaft der Musikfreunde (Vienna), 1, 32, 36, 43, 45, 51, 53, 57, 60, 61, 62, 64, 67, 71, 74, 82, 103, 125, 136, 146, 152, 167, 173, 190, 200, 207, 210, 216, 217, 239, 260, 261, 290, 291, 293, 299, 366, 379, 417, 421, 445, 453, 472, 485, 489, 490, 508, 509, 520, 521, 531, 532, 564, 568, 573A, 575, 589, 609, 643, 644, 647, 652, 653, 654, 672, 674, 676, 678, entry before 679, 680, 685, 687, 696, entry before 697, 697, 702, 703, 707, 708, 714, 723, entries before 729, 732, 739, 747, 748, 759, 780, 781, 787, 790, 795, 797, 805, 806, 829, 872, 906, 911, 918, 928, 929, 937, 942, 944, 957, 964, 965, entries before 969, 970, 974, 975, 977, 985, App. II 1, App. II 5; see also Musikverein and Musikvereinssaal
Gesellschafts-Lieder (Rellstab), 937
Gewandhaus (Leipzig), 944
Geymüller, Barbara Freiin von, 763
Gilhofer & Ranschburg (Vienna), 168, 169, 170, 171, 172, 713, 903, 904, 905, 940
Gioas, Rè di Giuda (Metastasio), 902 (no. 2)
Gladebach, 79
Gleditsch, Johann Friedrich (Leipzig), 736
Glock, William, 803
Glöggl, F. & Sohn (Vienna), 105
Gluck, Christoph Willibald, 287
Gmunden, 847, 848, 849
Goebel, Heinrich, App. II 7
Goedeke, Karl, 284

GENERAL INDEX

Goethe, 124, 217, entries before 384 and 435; see also Index of Authors and Vocal Music, Titles, Classification, Fair Copies of Goethe Songs
Goethe-Museum (Frankfurt am Main), 564
Goldschmidt, Otto (London), 650
Göschen, Georg Joachim (Leipzig), (519), 639
Gosmar, Louise (later married von Sonnleithner), 921
Gottermann, Georg, 787
Gotthard, J. P. (Vienna), 48, 76, 122, 165, 168, 176, 179, 206, 237, 250, 251, 264, 267, 268, 272, 295, 309, 342, 350, 359, 366, 371, 377, 402, 409, 420, 439, 449, 454, 458, 465, 466, 475, 476, 494, 502, 509, 528, 529, 533, 545, 561, 572, 579, 592, 593, 597, 609, 618, 631, 657, 659, 687, 688, 692, 693, 726, 752, 766, 796, 808, 814, 821, 855, 872, 915, 928, 937, 953, 984, 987
Göttingen, 834, 853
Göttinger Musenalmanach, 5, 848
Graben (Vienna), 803
Graf, Robert, 635
Grafenegg, Schloss (Lower Austria), 142, 493, 524
Gräffer, Franz, 847
Graf-Kurz Quartet (Vienna), 103
Graf von Glenallan, Der, 982
Grandjean, M. A., 936
Graun, Karl Heinrich, 115
Graz, 759, 853, 922, 923, 924, 925, 928
Greiner, Johann Lorenz (Graz), 284
Grob family, 487
Grob, Heinrich, 487
Grob, Therese, 118, 187, 223, 343, 437
Grove, Sir George, 849, 850, 898
Gudenus, Philipp Graf (Waidhofen an der Thaya, Lower Austria), 954
Guirlandes (Vienna), 229, 769, 780
Gundelhof (Vienna), 589, 591, 706
Guttentag, J. (Berlin), 54, 126, 170, 389, 577, 829, 988

Haas, Otto (London), 457, 467, 614
Haas, Robert, 121, 978
Hagar's Klage in der Wüste Berseba (Zumsteeg), 5
Hainburg (Lower Austria), 324
Hake, Bruno, 795
Halla & Co. (Prague), 801
Halle, 326
Halt's enk z'samm (Vienna), 146, 366
Hanover, 812
Hardtmuth, Louis von, 698
Harmonie-Verlag (Berlin), 635, 896, 942
Hartmann, Franz von, 734, 907
Haschka, Lorenz Leopold, 748
Haslinger, Karl (Vienna), 45, 379, 899
Haslinger, Tobias (Vienna), 324, 377, 706, 815, 851, 852, 870, 871, 872, 880, 893, 894, 899, 901, 902, 903, 904, 905, 908, 911, 913, 914, 924, 925, 933, 938, 957, 965, 969
Hassak, Heinrich, 930
Hasslinger, Felix (Maria-Enzersdorf), 829
Hatwig, Otto, 485, 589, 591
Haupt, L., 110
Hauptmann, Helene (Leipzig), 366, entry before 796, 814
Haydn, Josef, 748, App. II 1
Haydn, Michael, App. II 9
Haykul, Anton von (Vienna), 872
Heck, V. A. (Vienna), 80, 816
Heidelberg, 858
Heiligenkreuz (Lower Austria), 952
Hein, Carl (New York), 732, 912
Heineman Foundation, The (New York), 164, 174, 328, 792, 895
Heller, Hugo (Vienna), 23
Helling, W. H., 461
Hellmesberger, Josef, 112, 173, 703, 887
Hellmesberger Quartet (Vienna), 112, 173, 703, 887, 956
Hennings, C., 801
Henrici, Karl Ernst (Berlin), 262, 264, 324, entry before 350, 397, 511, 656, 719, 861
Herbeck family (Vienna), 918
Herbeck, Johann, 84, 137, 190, 200, 326, 331, 494, 656, 689, 714, 759, 787, 791, 815, 852, 872, 918, 984
Herbeck, Ludwig, 918
Herder, Johann Gottfried von, 124; see also Index of Authors
Hernals (Vienna), 730
Hérold, Louis Joseph Ferdinand, 723, 908
Herrmann (composer), 735
Hertz, W. M. (Bradford), 46, 68
Hesperus (Vienna), 379
Heuberger, Richard, 1, 118, 191, 607, entry before 612, 635, 714, 794, 896, 942
Heuss, Alfred, 935
Heyer (Wilhelm) Museum (Cologne), 159, 218, 219, 952
Himmel, Friedrich Heinrich, entry before 350
Hinterberger, Heinrich (Vienna), 146, 769, entry before 796
Hirsch (Paul) Library, British Museum, 639
Hirschfeld, Robert, 190
Historische Antiquitäten (Rittgräff), 847
Hoboken, Anthony van (Lausanne), 639, 748; see also Photogramm-Archiv (Vienna)
Hoeckner, Walter (Zwenkau, near Leipzig), 911

GENERAL INDEX 521

Hofer, Alberta von (Constance), 752, 753
Hoffmann's Widow, Josef (Prague), 167
Hofoper (Vienna), 701
Hollabrunn (Lower Austria), 27
Holländer, Hans, 15
Holzapfel, Anton, 132, 133, 339, 340, 341, 425, 427, App. II 9
Holzer, Michael, 452, 460
Hönig, Anna (later married Mayerhofer von Grünbühel), 719, 773, 844
Hortense, Queen of Holland, 618A, 624
Hoven, J. (pseud. of J. Vesque von Püttlingen), 761
Huemer, Georg, 930
Hügel, Fanny, 635
Hummel, Johann Nepomuk, 667, 958
Hüttenbrenner, Anselm, 308, entry before 350, 550, 576, 597, 607, entry before 612, 759, 858
Hüttenbrenner, Josef, 60, 82, 84, 159, 239, 326, 550, 594, 643, 644, 675, 741, 748, 967

Ibach, Rudolf (Vienna), 249
Ich liebe dich (Beethoven), 568
Illustrierte Zeitung (Leipzig), 402
Ireland, 221
Isacco (Metastasio), 17, 33
Isham Memorial Library (Harvard University, Cambridge, Mass.), 599, 618A
Iskian, Anahid (New York), 545
Isoz, K., 735
Israelitische Kultusgemeinde (Vienna), 953
Ivanhoe (Scott), 907

Jaell, Eduard, 590, 591
Jagemann, Karoline, 6
Jäger, Franz, 121, 644
Jägerlied (J. G. Schulz), 909
Jagor'scher Saal (Berlin), 717
Jahrbuch der Grillparzer-Gesellschaft (Vienna), 121
Jahresbericht des K.k. Staatsgymnasiums in Triest (Vienna), 918
Jakobs-Kirche (Straubing), App. II 9
Jansa, Leopold, 556, 796, 944
Jenny (Susanna or Therese) von, 195
Joachim, Josef, 581, 812
Jolles, Heinz, 571
Jones, Sir William, 701
Josephs-Kirche (Vienna), 551
Juden-Tempel (Vienna), 953
Junge Schubert, Der (Orel), 16, 17, 33, 34, 35
Jünger, Herr (Vienna), 526

Kaiser, Josef Franz (Graz), 834, 853
Kalbeck, Max (Vienna), 124, 455, 456, 480, 877, 957

Kallir, Otto (New York), 5, 8, 47, 429, 430, 930, App. II 2
Kandler, Franz Sales, 550
Kanitz, E. (Vienna), 153, 402
Karl & Faber (Munich), 658
Karlsruhe, 796
Kärntnertor-Theater (Vienna), 641, 647, 714, 723, 724, 740, 747
Karolina Augusta, Empress of Austria, 678
Kaufmännischer Gesangverein (Vienna), 984
Kenner, Josef, 654; see also Index of Authors
Kerpen, Karoline Freiin von, see Karoline, Fürstin Kinsky
Kienreich, Josef Andreas (Graz), 834, 853
Kienzl, Wilhelm, 374
Kiesewetter, Irene von, 826, 936
Kind, Friedrich, 639; see also Index of Authors
Kinsky, Georg, 96, 159
Kinsky, Karoline Fürstin, 768, 881, 909, 939
Kirchl, Adolf, 239
Klein, Johann Wilhelm, 863
Kleine Balladen und Lieder (Zumsteeg), 159, 397, App. II 3
Klemm, C. A., 459
Kloss, Josef Ferdinand, 872
Klosterneuburg (Lower Austria), 167
Knaben Wunderhorn, Des, 742
Koller, Josef von, 666, 695
Koller, Josefine von, 299, 664, 685, 695
Köln, see Cologne
Költzsch, Hans, 608
Konzerthaus (Vienna), 461, 642, 689, 730
Körner, Theodor, 79; see also Index of Authors
Kosch, Franz, 27
Kotzebue, August von, 372; see also Index of Authors
Krasser family (Vienna), 84, 132, 133, 199, 201, 326, 339, 340, 341, 388, 425, 427, 507, 555, 556, 567, 651, 701, App. II 9
Kratochwill, V. (Vienna), 342, 350, 465, 475, 533, 631
Kreissle family (Vienna), 332, 333
Kreissle von Hellborn, Heinrich, 17, 21, 48, 93, 134, 207, 250, 331, 421, 453, 625, 636, 665, 701, 763, 771, 800, 829, 852, 913, 929, 982, 989, 991
Kremsmünster (Upper Austria), 67, 297, 756, 930
Křenek, Ernst, 840
Kreutzer, Konradin, 796
Kühnel, Ambros (Leipzig), 642
Kummer, Paul Gotthelf (Leipzig), 84

GENERAL INDEX

Kumpf, Johann Gottfried, 307, 308; see also Index of Authors
Kunstwart, Der (Munich), 894
Kunz, Babette, 597
Kunz, Therese, 597
Kupelwieser, Leopold, 504
Kux, William (Chur, Switzerland), 87, 309, 313, 327, 461, 580, 694, 810, 915

Lablache, Luigi, 902
Lachner, Franz, 37, 799, 940, 942, 952
Lacom, A. (Vienna), 113
Lady of the Lake, The (Scott), 835, 836, 837, 838, 839, 843, 846
La Forge, Mrs. Frank (New York), 77
Lambert, E. G. M. Théaulon de, 723
Landhaus-Saal (Vienna), 220, 239, 470, 472, 591, 825, 907, 934, 964
Landsberg, Ludwig (Rome), 193, 251, 499, 633, 634
Landstrasse (Vienna), 421
Lang, Innocenz, 125
Lang, Josef von, 921
Lang, K., 742
Lanna, Frau von (Prague), 870, 871, 880
Lászny, Katharina von, 672, 707, 818
Laufer, Hans (London), 223, 795
Lebensbilder aus Oesterreich (Schumacher), 855
Legend of Montrose, A (Scott), 830
Leidesdorf, Maximilian Josef (Vienna), 142, 159, 229, 260, 410, 543, 644, 758, 764, 780, 781, 782, 797, 884, 917, 925, 943
Leipzig, 417, 944
Leitermayer, Michael, 950
Lewy, Josef Eduard, 913
Lewy, Josef Rudolf, 943
Leyer und Schwert (Körner), 204, 205
Library of Congress (Washington, D.C.), 48, 263, 265, 295, 385, 398, 399, 400, 401, 550, 595, 620, 676, 869
Library of Congress Quarterly Journal, The, 550
Lichtl, Karl (Pest), 735
Liebenberg de Zsittin, Emanuel von, 760
Liebesgedanken (H. von Chézy), 965
Liebleitner, Karl (Mödling, Lower Austria), 884
Liechtental (Vienna), 452, 487
Liechtentaler Kirche (Vienna), 105, 167, 324, 452
Lieder der Liebe und der Einsamkeit (Reichardt), App. II 4
— *für Blinde und von Blinden* (Vienna), 863
— *von Goethe komponiert von Franz Schubert* (ed. Schünemann), entry before 384

Liepmannssohn, Leo (Berlin), entry before 350, 390, 409, 548, 587, 628, 629, 691, 992
Liess, Andreas, App. II 5
Linke, Josef, 943
Linz, 579, 749
Listener, The (London), 677
Liszt, Franz, 732, 817, 935
Lithographisches Institut (Vienna), 518, 768, 881, 891, 909, 922, 926, 927, 939
Little Orchestra Society (New York), 8
Lives of the Great Composers (Bacharach), 803
London, 581, 929, 944
Lonsdale, C. (London), App. I
Los Angeles (California), 644
Love and Loyalty (MacDonald), 830
Love the Greatest Enchantment (Calderón), 682
Lubi, Michael, 122
Ludwig, August, 759
Luib, Ferdinand, 14, 135, 221, 425, 616, 929, App. II 6
Lunz (Lower Austria), 475
Lysistrata (Aristophanes), 787

Macpherson, James, 375, 534
Magdeburg, 220
Magic Flute, The (Mozart), 978
Magnus, Helene, 359, 502, 509
Mahlerisches Taschenbuch für Freunde interessanter Gegenden, Natur- und Kunst-Merkwürdigkeiten der Österreichischen Monarchie (Vienna), 586
Mandyczewski, Eusebius, 215, 325, 416, 635, 821, 907
Männergesangverein, Wiener, 1, 184, 379, 536
Mannings, W. Westley (London), 822
Manns, August, 82, 125, 200, 485
Mantuani, Josef, 114, 492
Manuscript copies of Schubert's works, see Copies, etc.
Margareten (Vienna), 551
Maria Trost-Kirche (Vienna), 136, 223, 452, 738
Maria-Zell (Styria), 475
Marie (Hérold), 908
Martinswand (near Innsbruck), 990
Marx, Dr. (Bethlen, near Bielefeld), entry before 769
Maschek, Vincenz, 11
Matheson, William (Olten, Switzerland), 96
Matiegka, Wenzel, 37, 96
Maximilian I, Emperor of Germany, 990
May, Sofie, 830
Mayerhofer von Grünbühel, Anna, see Anna Hönig
Mayerhofer von Grünbühel, Xaver (Völkermarkt, Carinthia), 209, 844, 888

GENERAL INDEX

Mayláth, Johann Graf, 833; see also Index of Authors
Mayor encanto amor, El (Calderón), 682
Mayrhofer, Johann, 525, 536, 553; see also Index of Authors
Mayssen, Josef, 730
Meangya family (Mödling, Lower Austria), 99, 107, 343, 344, 372, 392, 403, 405, 432, 437, 445, 448, 465, 501, 503, 504, 512
Mechetti, Pietro (Vienna), 356
Meeresstille und Glückliche Fahrt (Beethoven), 216
Meinert, Karl (Dessau, later Frankfurt am Main), 542, 711
Mendelssohn-Bartholdy, Felix, 729, 784, 944
Mendelssohn, Moses, 663, 706, 953
Merker, Der (Vienna), 451, 794
Merrick, Frank, 759
Messgesänge und Kirchenlieder (Vienna), 872
Metastasio, Pietro, 53, 936; see also Index of Authors
Methfessel, Albert, 110
Meyer, Emilie (Vienna), 2, 428
Meyer, Karl, 812
Meyerstein, E. H. W. (London), 383, 695
Mies, Paul, 677
Milder-Hauptmann, Anna, 717, 965
Minnesänger auf der Wartburg, Die (Kuffner), 981
Mistresse, The (Cowley), 271
Moderne Liebes-Walzer (Vienna), 979
— *Welt* (Vienna), 279, 416, 679, 978
Moller, Meta (Margarethe), 285
Mollo, Tranquillo (Vienna), 954
Monatsberichte der Gesellschaft der Musikfreunde des österreichischen Kaiserstaates (Vienna), 942
Monolog aus Goethe's Iphigenia als eine Probe musikalischer Behandlung jenes Meisterwerks (Reichardt), App. II 4
Montags-Revue (Vienna), App. I
Morley, Charles L. (New York), 117, 614
Mosel, Ignaz von, 121, 216, 257, 368
Moser, Karl, 810
Mottl, Felix, 796
Mozart, 22, 426, 653, 978, 993, App. II 2
Mühlenleben, Das (W. Müller), 795
Muller, Joseph (Closter, N.Y.), 69, 70
Müller, Karl Friedrich, 976, 978
Müller, Sophie, 736, 800, 828, 830, 831
Müller, Wilhelm (the poet), 795, 911, 965
Müller, Wilhelm (Berlin), 52, 73, 114, 142, 296, 328, 495, 765
Müller, Wilhelm (Hake), 795
Müllerlieder (Rissé), 795
Müller'scher Saal (Vienna), 648
Munich, 566
Murger, Gerhard, App. I

Musée musical des Clavecinistes, see *Museum für Claviermusik*
Musenalmanach (Stuttgart), 801
Museum für Claviermusik (Vienna), 894
Museums-Bibliothek (Salzburg), 294
Music & Letters (London), 564, 615
— *Review, The* (Cambridge), 759
Musica Divina (Vienna), 872
Musical Educator, The (London), 384
— *Quarterly, The* (New York), 70, 547, 911
Musik aus aller Welt (Vienna), 164
— *Die* (Berlin), 114, 215, 299, entries before 384 and 435, 492, 566, 573A, 618, 635, 705, 782, 957
— *für Alle* (Berlin), 455
— *und ihre Meister, Die* (Rubinstein), App. I
Musikalisches Angebinde zum neuen Jahre [1825] (Vienna), 366
Musikbibliothek Peters (Leipzig), 255, 256, 257, 935, 957
Musikverein (Tuchlauben), old hall of the Gesellschaft der Musikfreunde (Vienna), 48, 84, 112, 118, 138, 173, 328, 369, 450, 514, 556, 574, 583, 588, 594, 636, 703, 707, 731, 757, 760, 771, 787, 796, 800, 801, 803, 804, 809, 812, 828, 839, 843, 846, 865, 875, 881, 887, 892, 911, 912, 913, 921, 929, 932, 939, 942, 956, 988; see also Musikvereinssaal
Musikvereinssaal (Karlsplatz), new hall of the Gesellschaft der Musikfreunde (Vienna), 26, 75, 84, 110, 137, 267, 326, 357, 364, 416, 513, 657, 729, 759, 820, 835, 847, 903, 914, 936; see also Musikverein

Nach Osten ! (Weyrauch), App. I
Nathansky, Alfred, 918
Nationalbibliothek (Vienna), 114, 121, 137, 208, 492, 536, 608, 647, 689, 715, 718, 719, 720, 723, 732, 752, 754, 797, 848, 850, 887, 897, 940, 955, 962, 963, 964; see also Photogramm-Archiv
National Library of Scotland (Edinburgh), 147
Neitzel, Otto, 796
Neuburger, Hugo (Los Angeles), 746
Neue Freie Presse (Vienna), 849
— *Krähwinkler Tänze* (Vienna), 980
— *Musikzeitung* (Stuttgart), 530, 534, 615, 847
— *Pflug, Der* (Vienna), 978
— *Zeitschrift für Musik* (Leipzig), 440, 701, 732, 796, 812, 840, 944
Neues Beethoven-Jahrbuch (Braunschweig), 573A
— *Wiener Tagblatt* (Vienna), 480, 872, 957

GENERAL INDEX

Neuhaus, Kajetan (Linz), 908
Neumann, Johann Philipp, 701, 872
Newberry Library (Chicago), 384, 396
New York, 8, 459
New York Public Library, 302, 507, 509
Nicolas I, Emperor of Russia, 885
Niemeyer, August Hermann, 689
Normal-Hauptschule zu St. Anna (Vienna), 872
Nottebohm, Gustav, 48, 93, 134, 236, 353, 404, 406, 429, 603, 741, 746, 788, 799, 802, 830, 831, 862, 907, 929, 945, 989
Nouvelles Galoppes favorites et Écossaises (Schubert and Leidesdorf), 781, 782
Nydahl, Rudolf (Stockholm), 73, 611, 690

Ochs, Siegfried (Berlin), 547
Oden (E. C. von Kleist), 757
Öffenliche Wissenschaftliche Bibliothek (Berlin), *see* Preussische Staatsbibliothek
Opera (Vienna), *see* Hofoper, Opern-Archiv, Kärntnertor-Theater
Opern-Archiv (Vienna), 732
Oppenheim, Herr (Budapest), 957
Oppenheim, Paul (Princeton, N.J.), 899
Orel, Alfred, 11, 16, 17, 28, 33, 34, 35, 103, 121, 135, 139, 354, 370, 534, 550, 642, 680, 681, 698, 822, 841, 957
Orkney Islands, 281
Orphanage, *see* Waisenhaus
Orti esperidi, Gli (Metastasio), 78
Ossian, 221; *see also* Index of Authors
Österreichische Gitarre-Zeitschrift (Vienna), 121, 821
Österreichische Musikzeitschrift (Vienna), 1
Östliche Rosen (Rückert), 741, 775, 776, 777, 778
Otter, Franz de Paula Josef, App. II 9

Pachler, Faust, 928
Pachler, Karl, 928
Pachler, Marie Leopoldine, 891, 922, 926, 928
Pálffy von Erdöd, Ferdinand Graf, 617
Pallavicini, (Alfons?) Graf (Vienna), 119, 120, 123
Panofka, Heinrich, 945
Paris, 104, 547, 908, 944
Pastoral-Messe (Ferdinand Schubert), 45
Patzak, Julius, 663
Päumann, Johann von (Vienna), 388, 389, 402
Paumgartner, Sylvester, 667
Pazdirek, Franz, *see* Gotthard, J. P. (pseud.)
Pembaur, Josef, 566

Pennauer, Anton (Vienna), 568, 636, 637, 638, 713, 717, 737, 738, 767, 786, 825, 827, 828, 845, 857, 859, 885
Percy, Thomas, 923
Perlen der heiligen Vorzeit (Pyrker), 852
Pest, 84, 735
Peters, C. F. (Leipzig), 48, 94, 118, 124, 142, 173, 183, 188, 192, 199, 202, 222, 227, 239, 245, 252, 253, 254, 255, 256, 257, 285, 303, 314, 342, 350, 398, 404, 406, 411, 417, 429, 431, 446, 448, 455, 456, 465, 467, 475, 485, 489, 491, 496, 499, 523, 558, 559, 563, 565, 631, 644, 646, 647, 686, 795, 814, 957, 962, 963
Peters-Kirche, Vienna, 461, 730, 750, 839
Peters Library, *see* Musikbibliothek Peters
Pettenkoffer, Anton von, 648
Petter, Gustav (Vienna), 86, 195, 226
Philomele (Vienna), 550, 833, 955
Photogramm-Archiv (Vienna), containing copies of Schubert autographs, 11, 12, 39, 42, 58, 99, 107, 116, 118, 121, 126, 135, 136, 138 (2), 139, 142, 145 (nos. 5, 8, 9), 146, 149, 150, 156, 161, 162, 181, 198, 216, 224, 225, 226, 227, 247, 254, 255, 257, 259, 260, 285, 310, 312, 321, 328, 343, 344, 367, 368, 372, 392, 403, 405, 407, 432, 437, 445, 448, 450, 457, 458, 459, 465 (2), 466, 467, 481, 501, 503, 504, 512, 537, 542, 547, 554, 558, 559, 560, 578, 579, 580, 595, 609, 612, 624, 644, 681, 729, 740, 750, 786, 788, 798, 801, 817, 821, 832, 850, 894, 909, 939, 952, App. II 8
Piatti, Alfredo, 581
Piccolomini, Die (Schiller), 6, 190, 389
Pichler, Karoline, 482, 483, 713
Pinterics, Karl, 737, 738, 767
Pirate, The (Scott), 831
Pirated editions of Schubert's works published during his lifetime, 735, 742
Pirkhert, Eduard, 812
Plagiarisms, 37, 167; *see also* Schubert, Ferdinand, works appropriated by
Platen-Hallermünde, August Graf, 911; *see also* Index of Authors
Poetische Betrachtungen in freien Stunden (Craigher), 828, 842
Poetisches Tagebuch (Schulze), 825, 834, 853, 860, 861, 862, 874, 876, 882, 883, 884
Prager Tagblatt (Prague), 858
Pratobevera, Karl Josef von, 829
Preitz, Gerhard, 899
Preussische Staatsbibliothek (Berlin), 6, 9, 52, 73, 91, 93, 114, 118, 121, 126, 138, 142, 160, 161, 162 (2), 165, 216, 223, 224, 225, 226, 235, 240, 241, 247,

GENERAL INDEX

257, 260, 291, 294, 295, 296, 321, 328, 367, 368, entry before 384, 403, 405, 409, entry before 435, 443, 444, 485, 495, 528, 562, 563, 566, 577, 598A, 619, 669, 670, 686, 704, entry before 722, 722, 728, entry before 729, 732, 743, 744, 754, 764, 765, 766, 767, 808, 811, 851, 854, 855, 870, 871, 873, 875, 893, 901, 908, 948, 950, 951, 963, App. II 5
Prieger, Hella (Bonn), 566
Pritchard, T. C. L., 759
Probst, Heinrich Albert (Leipzig), 546, 768, 833, 882, 929
Pyrker von Felsö-Eör, Johann Ladislaus, 224, 493, 685; see also Index of Authors

Racek, Fritz, 1, 68
Radio Beromünster (Switzerland), 11
Radio Wien (Vienna), 555
Radler-Warhanek, Marie (Graz), 374, 377
Randhartinger, Benedikt, 328
Ratibor, Herzogin von (Schloss Grafenegg), 142, 493, 524
Räuber, Die (Schiller), 195
Redoutensaal (Graz), 641
— (Linz), 724
Redoutensäle (Vienna), 137, 190, 200, 232, 331, 494, 589, 648, 689, 747, 791, 796, 815, 901, 918, 942, 943, 944, 985
Reeves, William (London), 131, 242, 243, 244, 269
Rehberg, Walter, 279, 571, 625, 840
Reichardt, Johann Friedrich, 84, 210, 217, App. II 4
Reinhardt, Werner (Winterthur, Switzerland), 504
Reissmann, August, 8, 54, 126, 142, 170, 300, 389, 577, 829, 988
Reliques of Ancient English Poetry (Percy), 923
Revisionsbericht der Gesamtausgabe (Editors' Report on the Collected Edition), 9, 54, 72, 98, 111, 114, 123, 124, 144, 174, 180, 208, 209, 232, 240, 258, 265, 278, 290, 312, 323, 328, 400, 406, 419, 429, 454, 459, 469, 471, 480, 499, 505, 508, 509, 516, 518, 526, 536, 575, 583, 586, 588, 651, 672, 678, 682, 690, 703, 707, 713, 715, 754, 759, 760, 778, 793, 828, 856, 857, 877, 880, 892, 903, 911, 937, 938, 946, 957, 958, 959, 960, 965
Revue musicale, La (Paris), 624
Riccius, August Ferdinand, 417
Richault, Charles Simon (Paris), App. I
Richter, Edmund, 701
Riemann, Hugo, 618
Ries & Erler (Berlin), 635

Riesenkoppe (Silesia), 611
Rieter-Biedermann, J. (Winterthur, Switzerland), 612, 946, 950
Rietsch, Heinrich, 718
Riga, 965
Rio, Giannatasio del, 787
Rischel, Th. (Copenhagen), 96
Rissé, Julius, 795
Ritter, Herr, 763
Ritterlichen Jägers Liebeslauschen, Des (Schnorr), 698
Ritters Liebeslauschen, Des (Schlechta), 698
Rittgräff (pseud. of Rittig and Gräffer), 847
Rittig von Flammenstein, Andreas, 847
Robitschek, Adolf (Vienna), 16, 17, 33, 34, 35, 103
Rödersche Offizin (Leipzig), 255
Roehn, Franz (Los Angeles), 13, 15, 25, 114, 239, 450, 486, 585, 586, 709, 716, 786, 966, App. II 6
Rolle, Johann Heinrich, 689
Roner, Franziska von (later married von Spaun), 688
Rosenthal, Heinrich (Lucerne), 310
Roser, Franz de Paula, 930, App. II 1
Rossini, Gioacchino, 647
Rothberger, Alfred (Vienna), 769
Rotter, Adalbert, 636
Royal College of Music (London), 729
Rubinstein, Anton, 732, App. I
Rudolf, Archduke of Austria, 845
Rudorff, E. (Berlin), 177
Rügen, 221
Rusticocampius (pseud. of Bauernfeld), 37

Saal zu den 7 Churfürsten (Pest), 735
Sächsische Landesbibliothek (Dresden), 792, 877, 909
St. James's Hall (London), 581
Salieri, Antonio, 17, 25, 34, 35, 53, 70, 74, 76, 84, 138, 162, 220, 225, 226, 367, 441, 513
Salvini, G. R. (Porto), 550
Salzbergwerke von *, *Die* (Maylath), 982
Sankt Pölten, 732
Sartori, Franz, 586
Sauer & Leidesdorf (Vienna), 146, 229, 366, 525, 527, 536, 552, 553, 583, 602, 617, 686, 741, 743, 744, 751, 756, 761, 769, 771, 772, 773, 775, 776, 777, 780, 781, 782, 795, 797, 804, 809, 813, 819, 971, 976, 978, 979, 980
Scaria, Emil, 701
Schaeffer, Erwin, 911
Schatzky, Walter (New York), 228, 229
Schaup, Emma (Vienna), 2, 423, 424
Scheibler, Ludwig, 146, 570
Schellmann, Seraphine, entry before 769

GENERAL INDEX

Schenker, Heinrich, 759, 894
Schickh, Johann, 550, 770, 952
Schimon, Ferdinand, 644
Schindler, Anton, 21, 217, 453, 472, App. II 4
Schir Zion (Vienna), 953
Schlechta, Therese von, 698
Schlegel, August Wilhelm von, 682; see also Index of Authors
Schlesinger, Adolf Martin (Berlin), 732, 911, App. I
Schmidt, Anton, 22
Schmiedel, Johann Baptist, 589
Schnapper, Edith, 5
Schneekoppe (Silesia), 611
Schneider, Eduard (Vienna), 363, 371, 427, 433, 434, 500, 574, 701, 787
Schneller, Julius, 922
Schnerich, Alfred, 730
Schnorr von Carolsfeld, Ludwig Ferdinand, 588, 698, 794
Schober, Franz von, 421, 508, 509, 578, 690, 719, 720, 754, 768, 802, 886; see also Index of Authors
Scholtys, Hans Heinz, 642
Schöne Müllerin, Die (Damian), 795
Schönstein, Karl Freiherr von, 23, 138, 142, 795, 815
Schott's Söhne, B. (Mainz), entry before 350, 875
Schottenhof (Vienna), 485
Schreiber, Friedrich (Vienna), 173, 678, 803, 812
Schubert, Andreas, 1, 531, 644
Schubert, Elisabeth, 79, 500, 611
Schubert family, 472
Schubert, Ferdinand, 1, 8, 20, 21, 22, 24, 26, 27, 31, 45, 68, 74, 86, 89, 90, 105, 106, 111, 128, 136, 167, 184, 199, 201, 220, 223, 294, 324, 328, 345, 379, 388, 452, 470, 472, 485, 486, 507, 509, 555, 556, 572, 580, 588, 590, 591, 597A, 606, 610, 621, 625, 647, 651, 676, 686, 689, 696, 706, 714, 723, 732, 739, 755, 794, 821, 828, 839, 872, 944, 950, 957, 962, 963, 964, 965, App. II 1
— —, works appropriated by, 45, 294, 379, 621
— — —, — arranged by, 86, 105, 111, 167, 294, 324, 328, 379, 556, 647, 676, 706, 714, 723, 732, 828, 839, 872, 964
— —, — written for, 8, 20, 199, 345, 470, 472, 580, 610, 621, 696, 755
SCHUBERT, FRANZ:
Schubert-Album (ed. Friedlaender), 183, 188, 192, 252, 254, 256, 303, 314, 398, 406, 411, 431, 446, 448, 455, 456, 491, 558, 563, 565, 644, 686
Schubert-Album, Supplement (Friedlaender), 118, 257, 489

SCHUBERT, FRANZ—*continued*:
Schubert-Ausstellung 1897 (Vienna), 452
Schubert biographies:
Abraham (editor), 72, 590
Antcliffe, 227
Barbedette, 547
Dahms, 410, 547
Deutsch, see Documents, Dokumente, Sein Leben in Bildern
Einstein, 334, 597, 604, 935
Heuberger, 118, 191, 607, 635, 714, 896, 942
Kreissle, see Kreissle von Hellborn, Heinrich
Reissmann, 8, 54, 126, 170, 389, 577, 829, 988
Vetter, 82
Schubertbund, Wiener, 179, 180, 220, 239, 435, 598, 688, 725, 758, 834, 872
Schubert der Meister des Liedes (Mies), 677
Schubert Documents (Schubert, a Documentary Biography; or: The Schubert Reader) (Deutsch), 72, 324, 511, 802, 886, 944A
Schubert, Die Dokumente seines Lebens und Schaffens (Deutsch), 826
Schubertforschung (Augsburg), 893, 948, 982
Schubert-Gabe der Österreichischen Gitarre-Zeitschrift (Vienna), 121, 821
Schubert-Museum (Vienna), 660
Schubert, Sein Leben in Bildern (Deutsch), 209, 660, entry before 769
Schubert, Thematisches Verzeichnis der im Druck erschienenen Werke von, see Nottebohm
Schubert's fünf erste Lieder (ed. Deutsch), 118, 639
Schubert's publishers, see Artaria & Co., Matthias Artaria, Cappi & Co., Cappi & Czerny, Cappi & Diabelli, A. Diabelli & Co., Josef Czerny, Tobias Haslinger, J. A. Kienreich, Lithographisches Institut, M. J. Leidesdorf, A. Pennauer, H. A. Probst, Sauer & Leidesdorf, *and* T. Weigl; see also Breitkopf & Härtel *and* B. Schott's Söhne
Schubert, Ignaz, 41
Schubert, Marie (Vienna), 279, 412, 416, 663, 797
Schuberth & Co., Julius (Hamburg), 603
Schulhof, Otto, 817
Schulz, J. A. (Leipzig), 158
Schulz, Johann Gottlieb, 909
Schulz, Walter (Stuttgart), 327
Schumacher, Andreas, 855

GENERAL INDEX

Schumann, Robert, 440, 646, 812, 840, 935, 944, 958
Schünemann, Georg, entry before 384
Schuppanzigh, Ignaz, 796, 803, 804
Schuppanzigh Quartet (Vienna), 887, 929
Schuster, Vincenz, 821
Schwarzenberg, Mathilde Fürstin, 877
Schwind, Moritz von, 209, 719, 802, 844, 930
Scitovszky de Nagy-Kér, Johann Baptist, 105
Se solen sjunker (Berg), 929
Sechter, Simon, 833
Sehnsuchts-Walzer (attributed to Beethoven), entry before 350
Seid uns zum zweiten Male willkommen! (Vienna), 978
Seidl, Johann Gabriel, 866; *see also* Index of Authors
Seitenstetten (Lower Austria), 342
Selden-Goth, Gisella (New York), 627
Senff, Bartholf (Leipzig), 703, 942
Seyfried, Ignaz von, 872
Sibley Music Library (University of Rochester, N.Y.), 454, 455, 519, 527, 624
Siebenbürgen, *see* Transylvania
Siedenburg, Mrs. George R. (New York), 28
Siegmund, Anna (Znaim), 1, 215, 216
Siller, Andreas, 83
Simon, Karl (Berlin), 489, 550
Simrock, Nikolaus (Leipzig), 418, 448, 656
Singfundament (Fux), App. II 5
Slawjk, Josef, 895, 934
Slezak, Walter (Hollywood), 749
Society for Poor Gentlefolk (Vienna), *see* Verein für verschämte Arme
Söhne des Tales, Die (Werner), 685
Sollinger, Johann Paul (Vienna), 888
Sommer-Abend, Der (Pichler), 483
Sonnenaufgang auf der Riesenkoppe (Körner), 611
Sonnleithner, Leopold von, 150, 277, 451, 536, 648, 694, 714, 748, 929, 942, 985
Sontag, Henriette, 580
Sotheby & Co. (London), 105, 403, 417, 457, 482, 483, 506, 508, 555, 626, 847
Sowinski, Albert, 547
Spaun, Emma von (Vienna), 74, 631, 632, 736, 745
Spaun, Erwin von (Vienna), 144, 186, 188, 411, 529, 579
Spaun family (Görz), 134, 218, 420
Spaun, Hermann von (Görz), 496
Spaun, Josef von, 5, 22, 297, entry before 384, 420, 421, entry before 435, 496, 517, 524, 579, 594, 688, 711, 749, 771, 778, 800, 819, 894, 957; *see also* Index of Authors
Spaun, Marie von, 299, 420, 421
Spendou, Josef, 324, 470, 472
Spenser, Edmund, 795
Sperl-Garten (Vienna), 983
Spielmann'sches Haus (Vienna), 803
Spina, C. A. (Vienna), 112, 155, 173, 177, 195, 196, 213, 214, 230, 231, 283, 331, 337, 404, 406, 519, 537, 576, 591, 627, 644, 670, 673, 689, 691, 714, 731, 732, 759, 787, 790, 791, 793, 796, 797, 803, 872, 918, 923, 956, 984, 993, 996
Spina's Nachfolger, C. A. (Vienna), 656
Squire, William Barclay, 979, 980
Stadler, Albert, 17, 48, 76, 220, 425, 426, 565, 666, 667, 685, 695, 770, App. II 6; *see also* Stadler's copies
Stadler, Maximilian, App. II 6
Stadler's (Albert) copies of Schubert's early songs (Collection O. Taussig, Malmö), 95, 97, 102, 130, 131, 141, 142, 176, 180, 195, 196, 213, 222, 232, 281, 285, 286, 289, 328, 342, 368, 388, 423, 424, 428, 436, 496, 498, 499, 521, 524, 526, 531, 550, 594
Stadtarchiv (Altona), 788
— (Budapest), 735
Stadtbibliothek (Vienna), 7, 10, 11, 16, 17, 18, 23, 26, 28, 29, 30, 31, 32, 33, 34, 35, 36, 37, 41, 45, 46, 47, 48, 49, 54, 55, 56, 60, 62, 63, 65, 66, 68, 71, 72, 76, 78, 79, 80, 83, 84, 85, 86, 88, 89, 90, 94, 98, 102, 104, 105, 106, 110, 113, 115, 118, 120, 121, 123 (2), 124, 128, 135, 137, 146, 147, 151, 152, 154, 157, 166, 169, 170, 175, 178, 185, 187, 188, 190, 191, 192, 193, 194, 208, 211, 212, 220, 221, 222, 230, 231, 232, 234, 258, 261, 268, 271, 278, 279, 282, 292, 293, 311, 318, 319, 322, 323, 324, 325, 326, 329, 334, 335, 336, 337, 338, 346, 347, 348, 349, 354, 355, 356, 362, 366, 370, 372, 373, 376, 378, 380, 383, 386, 387, 403, 404, 405, 406, 422, 425, entry before 435, 435, 441, 449, 459, 468, 469, 470, 471, 472, 473 (2), 474, 476, 479, 480 (2), 484, 494, 510, 513, 516, 535, 539, 540, 541, 544, 547, 549, 551, 552, 565, 567, 569, 570, 571, 572, 576, 577, 581, 584, 585, 586, 597, 600, 601, 604, 605, 607, 613, 615, 616, 618, 622, 630, 635, 638, 639, 640, 642, 644, 648, 655, 657, 666, 668, 677, 678, 682, 689, 696, 698, 701, 706, 707, 710, 713, 715, 726, 727, 728, 730, 745, 754, 755, 757, 758, 762, 778, 779, 788, 789, 791, 796, 797, 802, 803, 815, 826, 833, 840, 842, 865, 872, 877, 878, 879, 880, 881, 888, 889, 890, 891, 892, 896, 899, 900, 902, 914, 916, 918, 920, 932, 934, 936,

GENERAL INDEX

942, 946, 950, 957, 958, 959, 960, 962, 965, 966A, 967, 968, 972, 973, 982, 984, 990, 994, App. II 4, App. II 6, App. II 7, App. II 8
Stadtkonvikt (Vienna), 5, 26, 79, 82, 125, 137
Stadttheater (Eisenach), 962, 963
Standhardtner, Josef (Vienna), 795
Stanford University (Stanford, California), 917
Stargardt, J. A. (Berlin), 610, 807, 841
Steffan, Josef Anton, 500
Steinacker, Karl, 190
Steinbach, George A. (New York), 820
Steiner & Co., S. A. (Vienna), 576
Steingräber-Verlag (Leipzig), 279, 571, 625, 701, 840
Stephanie, Gottlieb, 426
Steyr, 664, 665, 666, 667, 695, entry before 769, App. II 6
Stockhausen, Julius, 179, 250, 618, 687, 766, 795, 808
Stoneborough, Jerome (Vienna), 24
Strache, Eduard (Vienna), 27, 135, 139, 354, 370, 580, 621, 680, 681, 817, 841
Stransky, Josef, 956
Straubing (Bavaria), App. II 9
Strauss, Anton, selig Witwe (Vienna), 872, 931
Streinsberg, Anna Maria von, 616
Streinsberg, Josef Ludwig von, 616
Stuttgart, 84, 327, 618, 742
Sullivan, Sir Arthur, 729
Sulzbach, Emil (Frankfurt am Main), 439, 557
Sulzer, Salomon, 953
Sweden, 578
Symphonies (Beethoven), no. 4, App. II 8; no. 9, 189
Széchényi von Sárvár-Felsö-Vidék, Louis (Ludwig) Graf, 531; see also Index of Authors

Tagblatt-Bibliothek (Vienna), 797
Taschenbuch für Damen (Tübingen), 284
— — *deutsche Sänger* (Vienna), 913
— — *häusliche Freuden* (Heilbronn), 742
— *zum geselligen Vergnügen* (Leipzig), 519 (Göschen), 639 (Göschen), 736 (Gleditsch)
Tauer & Sohn (Vienna), 855
Taussig, Otto (Malmö), 3, 4, 37, 44, 50, 81, 131, 167, 190, 220, 223, 330, 345, 358, 363, 384, 408, 487, 581, 709, 784, 993, 995, 996, 997, 998
Teilung der Erde, Die (Roser), App. II 1
Temora (Ossian), 221, 375
Terpsichore (Vienna), 841
Teufel, J. C., 580
Teufel ein Hydraulikus, Der (Albrecht), 4
Thalberg, Siegmund, 575

Theater an der Wien (Vienna), 84, 190, 644, 732, 747, 797, 981
Theater in der Josefstadt (Vienna), 796, 930
Theater nächst der Burg (Vienna), see Burgtheater
Theresianum, i.e. Theresianische Ritter-Akademie (Vienna), 748
Tieck, Ludwig, 410, 658
Tietze, Ludwig, 136
Tovey, Donald Francis, 760, 786
Town Hall (New York), 8
Transylvania, 909
Traunsee, 848
Traweger, Ferdinand, 847
Treitschke, Friedrich, 723
Tremier, Franziska, 698, 758, App. II 4, App. II 7
Troschke, A. von, 730
Troyer, Ferdinand Graf, 803
Two Gentlemen of Verona, The (Shakespeare), 891

Udbye, Odd (Oslo), 271, 272, 688
Ulrich, Hugo, 417, 485
Undine (Fouqué), 373
Unendlicher Gott, unser Herr (Maximilian Stadler), App. II 6
Universal Edition (Vienna), 48, 103, 118, 461, 639, 642, 729, 820, 840
Universität (Berlin), 461, 730
— (Vienna), 880
Urania (Leipzig), 911

Vaterländischer Künstlerverein (Vienna), 718
Veilchen, Das (Vienna), 866
Venice, 915
Verein für verschämte Arme (Vienna), 535
Vesque von Püttlingen, Johann, see J. Hoven
Vetter, Walter, 82, 93
Vierteljahrschrift für Musikwissenschaft (Leipzig), App. I
Vierthaler, Franz Michael, 294
Vietinghoff, Karl Baron (Berlin), 645, 646
Vogl, Johann Michael, 297, 328, 372, 504, 541, 542, 636, 666, 732, 795, 965, App. II 6
Volkshymne (J. Haydn), 748
Volkslieder (Herder), 923

Wagner-Schönkirch, Hans, 820
Wahle, Julius, 844
Währing (Vienna), 887, 888, 889, 890, 891
Waisenhaus (Vienna), 199, 202, 203, 204, 205, 294, 470, 472, 535, 580, 621, 696
Walcher, Ferdinand, 915

GENERAL INDEX

Wallishausser, Johann Baptist (Vienna), 787, 872
Walter, Gustav, 206, 237, 272, 295, 402, 579, 937
Walter, Ignaz, 11
Wanda, Königin der Sarmaten (Werner), 521
Watteroth, Heinrich Josef, 421, 451
Weber, Karl Maria von, 170, 911
Weidmann, Paul, 4
Weigl, Thaddäus (Vienna), 113, 191, 193, 312, 547, 595, 633, 634, 823, 856, 862, 866, 868
Weimar, 321, 732
Weinberger (J.) and Hofbauer (Vienna), 123, 156, 254, 258
Weingartner, Felix, 729
Weinwurm, Rudolf, 835
Weir, Robert H. (Boston, Mass.), 982
Weis-Ostborn family (Graz), 679
Weis-Ostborn, Rudolf (Graz), 53, 54, 58, 239, 635, 678, App. II 3
Weiss (Franz?), 84
Weisse, Maximilian, 14
Weissenhofer, Robert (Seitenstetten), 342
Weissenwolff, Sofie Gräfin, 835, 836, 837, 838, 839, 843, 846
Wendling, Fr. (Vienna), 550
Werner, Zacharias, 489, 493, 521, 685
Werther's Leiden (Goethe), 217
Weston, George B. (Cambridge, Mass.), 943
Westrup, Jack Allan, 677
Wettstein, von (family), 111, 299
Wetzel, Karl Friedrich Gottlob, App. I
Weyrauch, August Heinrich von, App. I
Whistling, Karl Friedrich (Leipzig), 840
Whittall (Gertrude Clarke) Foundation Collection in the Library of Congress (Washington), 48, 295, 550, 595, 620, 869
Wieck, Franz, 730
Wieck, Klara, 812
Wieck, L. (Lohnsburg, Upper Austria), 730
Wiede, Alfred (Weissenborn, near Zwickau), 379
Wiedemann, Enoch, 847
Wieden (Vienna), 17, 239
Wiener Allgemeine Musikzeitung (Vienna), 45, 167, 739
— *Allgemeiner musikalischer Anzeiger* (Vienna), 932
— Philharmonischer Verlag (Vienna), 28, 759
— *Zeitschrift für Kunst, Literatur, Theater und Mode* (Vienna), 113, 546, 550, 639, 653, 669, 673, 731, 742, 745, 768, 770, 774, 799, 800, 833, 882, 909, 932, 938

Wiener Zeitung (Vienna), 132, 734, 868
Wildbach (Styria), 374
Wimpffen, Marie Gräfin, 795
Winthem, Johanna Elisabeth von, 287
Wissenschaftlicher Klub (Vienna), 587
Witteczek, Josef Wilhelm, 421, 870, 871, 880; *see also* Witteczek (MSS.) Collection
Witteczek (MSS.) Collection of Schubert's Works (Gesellschaft der Musikfreunde, Vienna), 59, 95, 97, 100, 101, 107, 108, 109, 122, 126, 131, 142, 153, 155, 176, 180, 182, 183, 195, 196, 213, 214, 235, 252, 253, 261, 280, 285, 286, 289, 297, 300, 330, 343, 359, 388, 394, 404, 409, 434, 436, 442, 445, 446, 447, 462, 463, 474, 475, 481, 491, 492, 496, 499, 500, 501, 502, 506, 520, 522, 523, 526, 543, 545, 548, 561, 573, 579, 588, 596, 626, 630, 633, 634, 662, 712, 741, 746, 788, 799, 830, 831, 862, 876, 883, 907, 910, 923, 933, 942, App. II 4
Wittgenstein family (Vienna), 156, 203, 205, 206, 301, entry before 350, 452, 460, 488, 636, 862, 878, 879, 929
Witwen-Institut der Schullehrer Wiens, 472
Witzendorf, Adolf Othmar (Vienna), 487
Wolf, Johannes, 893, 948
Wurzbach, Konstant von, 847

Zauberflöte, Die (Mozart), 978
——, *Zweiter Teil* (Goethe), 261
Zauberring, Der (Fouqué), 93
Zeitschrift der Internationalen Musikgesellschaft (Leipzig), 146, 979, 980
— *für Musik* (Leipzig), 15
— *für Musikwissenschaft* (Leipzig), 11, 28, 37, 96, 294, 630, 935
Zeitung für die elegante Welt (Leipzig), 642
Zellner's (Leopold Alexander) *Blätter für Musik, Theater und Kunst* (Vienna), 230
Zenei Szemle (Budapest), 735
Zeune, Richard (Leipzig), 855
Ziegler, Günther, 326
Zimbalist, Mary Louise (Philadelphia), 105, 204, 404, 406
Zseliz, 366, 493, 524, 617, 618, 618A, 619, 620, 621, 622, 623, 624, 625, 626, 627, entry before 796, 812, 813, 814, 815, 816, 817, 818, 819, 820
Zuckmantel (Silesia), 611
'Zum Römischen Kaiser' (Vienna), 121, 493, 590, 597, 702
Zumsteeg, Johann Rudolf, 5, 54, 159, 217, 397, App. II 3
Zürich, 543
Zweig (Stefan) Collection (London), 42, entry before 350, 547, 607, 912, 942

INDEX OF AUTHORS

Figures in italics refer to part songs, those in round brackets to works for the the stage; single or double figures in square brackets give the number of songs within one catalogue number; triple figures in square brackets refer to a supposed authorship or to a note; (trsl.) = translation.

Aeschylus (Aischylos), 450
Albrecht, Johann Friedrich Ernst, (4)
Anacreon, 737
Anonymous, 39, 75, 81, 83, *88*, *92*, 104, *110*, *131*, 155, 243, 267, *268*, 273, 274, 292, *294*, 311, 329, *333*, *356*, 371, 375, 381, 382, 398, *426*, 432, (435), 498, 512, 520, 523, 534, 535, 596, *609*, 616, *621*, 626, 645, *657*, *665*, *725*, *763*, (791), *822*, *847*, 902, 923, *936*, (981), (982), *984*, 989, 991, *992*; see also Biblical and Liturgical Texts, under Classification
Aristophanes, (787)

Bauernfeld, Eduard von, 864, 888 (trsl.), 891 (trsl.), 906, (918)
Baumberg, Gabriele von, 248, 263, 264, 265 (trsl.), 270
Bernard, Josef Karl, 177
Bertrand, (?) Friedrich Anton Franz, 152, 211
Bruchmann, Franz Seraph von, 737 (trsl.), 738, 746, 762, 785
Bürger, Gottfried August, *598*, *641*

Castelli, Ignaz Franz, *148*, (787), 868
Chézy, Helmina von, (797), 965
Cibber, Colley, 833
Claudius, Matthias, *140*, 344, 362, 496, 497, [498], 499, 500, 501, 504, (527), 530, 531, 532, 533
Collin, Heinrich von, 509 (trsl.), (771)
Collin, Matthäus von, 352, 749, 771, 772, 827
Cowley, Abraham, 271
Craigher de Jachelutta, Jakob Nikolaus, 737 (trsl.), 738 (trsl.), 742 (trsl.), 767 (trsl.), 828, 833 (trsl.), 842

Deinhardstein, Johann Ludwig Ferdinand von, 306, *748*
Dräxler von Carin, Philipp, *451*

Eberhard, August Gottlob, *642*
Ehrlich, (?) Bernhard Ambros, 153
Engelhardt, Karl August, see Richard Roos

Engelhart, Baron, 37
Ermin (pseud. of Johann Gottfried Kumpf), 141, 305

Fellinger, Johann Georg, 176, 182, 307
Fouqué, Friedrich, Freiherr de la Motte, 93 [3],373, 517, *815*

Gleim, Johann Wilhelm Ludwig, [757]
Goldoni, Carlo, *513*, 528
Goethe, Johann Wolfgang von, 118, 119, 120, 121, 123, 126, 138, 142, 149, 160, 161, 162, 210, 215, 216, 224, 225, 226, 234, (239), 247, 254, 255, 256, 257, 258, 259, 260, 261, 295, 296, 310, 321, 325, 328, 359, 367, 368, 369, 440, 469, 478, 479, 480, 481, 484, *538*, 543, 544, 549, 558, 559, 560, 564, *656*, 673, 674, *704*, *705*, *710*, *714*, 715, 716, [717], 719, [720], 721, 726, 727, 728, 764, 765, 766, 767, 768, 877 [4], (App. II 4)
Gotter, Friedrich Wilhelm, 467
Gottwald (pseud. of Johann Georg Seegemund), *916*
Gries, Johann Diederich, 630 (trsl.)
Grillparzer, Franz, (626), 653, *920*, *921*, *942*

Hardenberg, Friedrich Leopold von, see Friedrich Novalis
Harold, Eduard Baron de, *147*, 150, (217), 278, 281, 282, 293, 327, 375, 376, 534 (all trsls.)
Haug, Johann Christoph Friedrich, *901*
Heine, Heinrich, 957 [6]
Hell, Theodor, 456
Herder, Johann Gottfried von, 59, 923 (both trsls.)
Hofmann, Georg Ernst von, (644), (647)
Hoheisel, Johann Baptist, *472*
Hohlfeld, (?) C. C., *863*
Hölty, Ludwig Heinrich Christoph, 38, 44, *127*, *129*, *130*, 193, 194, 196, 197, 198, *199*, 201, *202*, 207, 208, 212, 213, 214, 242, [243], *244*, [292], [398], 399, 400, 401, *427*, 429, 430, 431, [432], 433, 434, 436, 437, 468, 503, [512], *988*

INDEX OF AUTHORS

Hummelauer, Franz von, 217, 282, 293, 375 (all trsls.)
Hüttenbrenner, Heinrich, 702, *825*

Jacobi, Johann Georg, 343, [454], 462, 463, 464, 465, 466, 474

Kalchberg, Johann Nepomuk von, 308
Kalidasa, 701
Kenner, Josef, 134, 209, 218
Kind, Johann Friedrich, 552
Kleist, Ewald Christian von, *757*
Klenke, Karoline Louise von, 922
Klopstock, Friedrich Gottlieb, (115), *168*, 280, 285, 286, 287, 288, 289, 290, 291, 322, *383*, 442, 443, 444, 445, *912*, *987*
Köpken, Friedrich von, 455
Körner, Theodor, 163, 164, *165*, 166, *169*, *170*, 171, 172, 174, 179, 180, (190), *203*, *204*, *205*, 206, 304, 309, 611
Kosegarten, Ludwig Gottfried, 219, 227, 228, 229, 230, 231, 233, 235, *236*, 237, 238, 240, 241, 313, 314, 315, 316, 317, 318, 319, 457
Kotzebue, August von, (11), (84)
Krummacher, Friedrich Wilhelm, *983*
Kuffner, Christoph, 955, (note to 981)
Kumpf, Johann Gottfried, *see* Ermin
Kupelwieser, Josef, (796)

Lappe, Karl, 799, 800, *825*
Leitner, Karl Gottfried von, 770, 896, 926, 927, 931, 932, 933, 938, 939
Leon, Gottlieb von, 522
Lubi, Michael, 122
Luther, Martin, 607 (trsl.)

MacDonald, Andrew, 830
Matthisson, Friedrich von, 15, 50, 95, 97, 98, 99, 100, 101, 102, 107, 108, 109, 114, 115, 116, 186, 187, 188, 275, *339*, *340*, *341*, *357*, 413, 414, 415, 418, 419, *422*, *423*, *424*, *425*, (426), *428*, *494*, 507, 508, *747*, *983*
May, Sofie, 830 (trsl.)
Mayerhofer von Grünbühel, Ferdinand, 888 (trsl.)
Mayláth, Johann Graf, 731, (note to 982)
Mayrhofer, Johann, 124, (137), 297, 298, (326), 360, 450 (trsl.), 473, 475, 476, 477, 490, 491, 492, 495, 516, 524, 525, 526, 527, 536, 539, 540, 541, 542, 548, 553, 554, 561, 573, 585, 586, 620, 654, 669, 670, 671, 672, 682, 699, 700, 707, 752, 753, 754, 805, 806, 807, 808, *809*
Mendelssohn, Moses, 663, *706* (both trsls.)
Metastasio, Pietro, *17*, *33*, *34*, *35*, 42, 76, 78, 509, 510, 688 [2], (742), 902 [2]

Müller, Karl Ludwig Methusalem, 907 (trsl.)
Müller, Wilhelm, 795 [20], 911 [24], 965

Neumann, Johann Philipp, (701), *872*
Nicolaus, *see* Craigher
Niemeyer, August Hermann, *689*
Novalis, Friedrich (pseud. of Friedrich Leopold von Hardenberg), 658, 659, 660, 661, 662, 687

Ossian, *147*, 150, 217, 278, 281, 282, 293, 327, [375], 376, [534]
Ottenwalt, Anton, 579

Petrarch, 628, 629, 630
Pfeffel, 10
Pichler, Karoline, 482, 483, 713
Platen-Hallermünde, August Graf, 751, 756
Plat(t)ner, Eduard, 519
Pollak, Aaron, *914*, 919
Pope, Alexander, 59
Prandstetter, Martin Josef, 262
Pratobevera von Wiesborn, Adolf, 829
Pyrker von Felsö-Eör, Johann Ladislaus, 851, 852

Ratschky, Josef Franz von, 271 (trsl.)
Reil, Friedrich, 888, 889, 917, *954*
Reissig, Christian Ludwig, 320
Rellstab, Ludwig, 937, 943, 945, 957 [7]
Rochlitz, Johann Friedrich, 23, *903*, 904, 905
Roos, Richard (pseud. of Karl August Engelhardt), 736
Rückert, Friedrich, 741, 775, 776, 777, 778
Rustenfeld, *37*

Salis-Seewis, Johann Gaudenz von, *132*, *133*, 300, 330, *331*, *332*, 337, 350, 351, 364, 377, 392, 393, 394, 403, 404, 405, 406, 502, 562, 563, 569, *572*, *983*
Sauter, Samuel Friedrich, 742
Schiller, Friedrich von, 6, 7, 30, *43*, *47*, *51*, 52, *53*, *54*, *55*, *57*, *58*, *60*, *61*, *62*, *63*, *64*, *65*, *67*, *69*, *70*, *71*, *73*, 77, 111, 113, 117, 159, 189, 191, 192, 195, *232*, 245, 246, *249*, 250, 251, 252, 253, 277, 283, 284, 312, 323, *338*, *387*, 388, 389, 390, 391, 396, 397, 402, [435], 577, 583, 584, 587, 588, 594, 595, 636, 637, 638, 677, 793, 794, 801, (827), *983*, 990, App. II 1
Schlechta von Wssehrd, Franz Xaver, 151, 458, 639, 698, 832, 869, 881, 949
Schlegel, August Wilhelm von, 395, 409, 410, 628 (trsl.), 629 (trsl.), 711, 712, 855, 856, 889 (trsl.)
Schlegel, Friedrich von, 631, 632, 633,

INDEX OF AUTHORS

634, 646, 649, 652, 684, 690, 691, 692, 693, 694, 708, 745, 854, (855)
Schmidl, A. (? Adolf), *941*, *948*, *964*
Schmidt ('von Lübeck'), Georg Philipp, 489, 493
Schnitzer von Meerau, Kolumban, *826*
Schober, Franz von, 143, 361, 546, 547, 551, 582, 683, *709*, (732), *740*, 758, 761, 786, 789, 792, *875*, 909, 910, *930*
Schopenhauer, Johanna, 890
Schreiber, Alois, 614, 622, 623, 627
Schubart, Christian Friedrich Daniel, 342, 454, 518, 550
Schubert, Franz, *80*, *407*, *441*, 565, 578, *635*
Schücking (of Münster), 5
Schulze, Ernst, 825, 834, 853, 860, 861, 862, 874, 876, 882, 883, 884
Schütz, Wilhelm von, 857 [2]
Scott, Sir Walter, 830, 831, *835*, *836*, 837, 838, 839, 843, 846, 907
Seckendorf, Karl Siegmund, *848*
Seegemund, Johann Georg, *see* Gottwald
Seidl, Johann Gabriel, *865*, 866 [4], 867, 870, 871, 878, 879, 880, *892*, *893*, *913*, 957
Senn, Johann Chrisostomus, 743, 744
Shakespeare, William, 888, 889, 891
Silbert, Johann Peter, 650, 651
Spaun, Josef von, 545
Spiker, Samuel Heinrich, 831 (trsl.)
Stadler, Albert, (220), 222, [565], *666*, 695
Stolberg, Leopold Graf, 144, 266, 276, 372, 411, 412, 416, 774, 788
Stoll, Josef Ludwig, 301, 302, 303
Storck, P. Adam, *835*, *836*, 837, 838, 839, 843, 846 (all trsls.)
Széchényi von Sárvári - Felsö - Vidék, Louis (Ludwig) Graf, 514, 515

Tiedge, Christoph August, 272
Treitschke, Georg Friedrich, (723 [2])

Uhland, Ludwig, 686
Unger, Johann Karl, *724*
Uz, Johann Peter, 358, 363, *439*, 446, 447, 448, 449, *985*, *986*

Vittorelli, Jacopo Andrea, 688 [2]

Wannovius, J. C., *269*
Werner, Friedrich Ludwig Zacharias, 521, 685
Willemer, Marianne von, [note to 710], 717, 720

Zettler, Alois, 183

CLASSIFICATION

Biblical Texts, see Titles of Vocal Music under Evangelium Johannis (Gospel according to St. John) *and* Psalms
Bilingual Texts, 737, 738, 742, 767, 835, 836, 837, 838, 839, 843, (888), (889), (891)
Hebrew Text, 953
Italian Texts, 17, 33, 34, 35, 42, 76, 78, 510, 513, 528, 688, 902, 936
Latin Texts, 847; *see also* Liturgical Texts
Liturgical Texts, see Titles of Vocal Music under Antiphons, Auguste jam coelestium, Benedictus, Dona nobis, Gradual, Kyrie, Magnificat, Masses, Offertories, Requiem, Salve Regina, Sanctus, Stabat Mater, Tantum ergo
Songs from Novels, 93, 161, 310, 321, 325, 359, 373, 469, 478, 479, 480, 481, 656, 726, 727, 830, 831, 877, 890, 907
Songs from Plays (*Librettos*), 6, (17), (33), (34), (35), (42), (76), (78), 118, 126, 191, 195, 210, 389, 440, 450, (509), (510), 528, 564, 653, 658, 829, 857, 888, 889, 891, (902)
Translations:
from English, 59, 147, 150, 217, 271, 278, 281, 282, 293, 327, 375, 376, 534, 701, 830, 831, 833, 835, 836, 837, 838, 839, 843, 846, 888, 889, 891, 907, 923
from French, 265
from Greek, 450, 607, 737, (787)
from Hebrew, 663, 706
from Italian, 509, 628, 629, 630, 902

INDEX OF SCHUBERT'S WORKS

1. INSTRUMENTAL MUSIC

Adagio and Rondo concertante in F for Pianoforte, Violin, Viola, and Violoncello, 487
— in E flat for Pianoforte, Violin, and Violoncello, 897
Adagios for Pianoforte:
  in G, 178
  in C, 349
  in D flat, 505, (625)
  in E, 612
'Albumblatt,' for Pianoforte, 844
Allegrettos for Pianoforte:
  in C, 346
  in C minor (fragment), 900
  in C minor, 915
Allegro in B flat for Pianoforte Trio, 28
— in C for String Quartet, 103
— moderato in C and Andante in A minor for Piano Duet, 968
Allegros for Piano Duet:
  in A minor, 947
  in C, 968
Allegros for Pianoforte:
  in E, 154
  in C (Allegro moderato), 347
  in F sharp minor, 570
  in F sharp minor, 571
  in C sharp minor, 655
  in C minor, 703
  in E minor, 994
Allemandes, 366 (no. 17), 783 (no. 8)
Allerletzte Composition, 958–60
Andante in A minor for Piano Duet, 968
Andantes for Pianoforte:
  in C, 29
  in A, 604
Andantino in C for Pianoforte, 348
— varié et Rondeau brillant ... sur de motifs originaux Français, 823 (nos. 2 and 3)
Arpeggione Sonata, 821
Atzenbrugger Deutsche (Tänze), 145 (nos. 1–3), 365 (nos. 29–31)

Ballet Music from Rosamunde, 797 (nos. 2 and 9)

'Charakteristisches Allegro,' 947
'Concertos,' 345, 487
Cotillon in E flat for Pianoforte, 976

'Death and the Maiden,' Quartet, 810
Deutsche für Comtesse Caroline (Esterházy), entry before 146
— Tänze for Pianoforte:
  12 Wiener Deutsche, 128
  17 Deutsche Tänze, 366
  12 ,, ,, 420
  1 ,, ,, in C sharp, 643
  1 ,, ,, in G flat, 722
  2 ,, ,, 769
  16 ,, ,, 783
  12 ,, ,, 790
  6 ,, ,, 820
  2 ,, ,, 841
  1 ,, ,, 944A
  6 ,, ,, 970
  3 ,, ,, 971
  3 ,, ,, 972
  3 ,, ,, 973
  2 ,, ,, 974
  1 ,, ,, in D, 975
  See also Ländler and Waltzes
Deutsche Tänze, Ländler und Walzer (ed. by Deutsch and Orel), 135, 139, 354, 370, 680, 681, 841
5 Deutsche Tänze with Coda and 7 Trios for String Quartet, 90
Deutscher Tanz with two Trios and Coda, and two other Deutsche Tänze for Piano Duet, 618
Deutsches Tempo, 790
Divertissement en forme d'une Marche brillante et raisonnée, 823 (no. 1)
Divertissements for Piano Duet:
  à la hongroise, in G minor, 818
  à la française, in E minor, 823
Duet Sonatas, see Sonatas for Piano Duet
Duets for Horns, 199, 202–5
'Duo' for Pianoforte and Violin, 574

Écossaises for Pianoforte:
  9, 145
  1 in F, 158
  12, 299
  6, 421
  1 in E flat, 511
  8, 529
  1 in D flat, 643
  5, 697
  2, 734

534　INDEX OF SCHUBERT'S WORKS

Écossaises for Pianoforte—*continued*:
 8, 735
 12 (11), 781
 1 in D, 782
 2, 783
 3, 816
 8, 977
Entr'actes, 435 (nos. 10 and 15), 797 (nos. 1, 3*a*, and 5)
'Erste Walzer,' 365
Exercises in Counterpoint, 23 (note), 25
—— Imitation, 16
—— Thorough-Bass, 598A

Fantasia in C for Pianoforte and Violin (with Variations on 'Sei mir gegrüsst'), 934
Fantasias for Piano Duet:
 in G, 1
 in G minor, 9
 in C minor, 48
 in F minor, 940
Fantasias for Pianoforte:
 in C (fragment), 605
 in C (the 'Wanderer'), 760
 in C minor, 993
 See also 894
'*Fantasie, Andante, Menuetto und Allegretto*,' 894
Forellen-Quintett, 667
'*Franz Schubert's Begräbnis-Feier*,' 79
Fugues:
 in D minor (for Pianoforte?), 13
 in E minor (for Organ, or Piano Duet), 952
 in four parts (for Pianoforte), 967

Galops for Pianoforte, 735, 925
'Gastein [or rather, Gmunden-Gastein] Symphony' (lost), 849
Grand Duo for Piano Duet, 812
Grande Marche funèbre, 859
—— *héroïque*, 885
'— *Rondeau*,' 951
Grandes Marches, 819
— *Sonates* for Piano Duet, 48, 617, (812)
—— for Pianoforte, 568, 845, 850
Grätzer Galoppe, see Graz Galop
— *Walzer*, see Graz Waltzes
Grave and Allegro in C minor for String Quartet, 103
Graz Galop for Pianoforte, 925
— Waltzes for Pianoforte, 924
Grosse Sinfonie, 589
'*Grosse Sonaten*,' 48, 958–60
'Guitar Quartet' (spurious), 96

Hirtenmelodie (from *Rosamunde*), 797 (no. 6)
Hommage aux belles Viennoises, 734

Impromptus for Pianoforte, 899, 935, 946
Introduction and [7] Variations in E minor on a Theme ['*Trockne Blumen*'] from the Song Cycle, *Die schöne Müllerin*, for Pianoforte and Flute, 802
—— [4] Variations in B flat on an Original Theme, for Piano Duet (doubtful), 603

'Kaiser Maximilian auf der Martinswand in Tyrol, 1490 [or rather, 1493]' (Pianoforte fragment), 990
Kindermarsch, 928
'*Klavier-Konzert*,' 487
Klavier-Stücke, 459, 946; see also Impromptus and Moments musicaux
Kleine Trauermusik für Blasinstrumente, Eine, 79
Komische Ländler, 354
Konzertstück in D for Violin and Orchestra, 345

Ländler for Pianoforte:
 17, 145
 4 (*Komische Ländler*) in D, 354
 8 in F sharp minor, 355
 8 in D, 370
 6 in B flat, 374
 8 in B flat, 378
 2, 640
 2 in E flat, 679
 2 in D flat, 680
 12 (8), 681
 16, 734
 See also *Deutsche Tänze* (366, 790) and Waltzes
'*Lebensstürme*,' 947
'*Leichenphantasie*,' 1
Lessons in Notation, 573A
'*Letzte Sonate*,' 840
'— *Walzer*,' 146

March for two Pianofortes (doubtful), 858
— in E for Pianoforte, 606
Marche brillante et raisonnée, 823 (no. 1)
Marches for Piano Duet:
 3 (*Marches héroïques*), 602
 3 (*Marches militaires*), 733
 6 (*Grandes Marches*), 819
 1 (Alexandre I), 859
 1 (Nicolas I), 885
 2 (*Marches caractéristiques*), 886
 1 (*Kindermarsch*), 928
Minuet and Finale in F of an Octet, 72
Minuets for String Quartet:
 1 in D, 86
 5, with 6 Trios, 89

INSTRUMENTAL MUSIC

Minuets for Pianoforte:
  12, with Trios, 22
  30 (20), with Trios, 41
  2, with 4 Trios, 91
  1 (A), with 1 Trio, 334
  1 (E), with 2 Trios, 335
  1 (D), with 1 Trio, 336
  2, with 2 Trios, 380
  1 (C sharp), 600
  2, 995
Moments musicaux for Pianoforte, 780

Nocturne, 897; *see also* 96
Nonet, 79
'*Notre amitié est invariable*,' 608
Notturno, *see* Nocturne

Octets:
  Minuet and Finale in F for Wind Instruments, 72
  Octet in F for String and Wind Instruments, 803
Orchestral Scores in D (fragments), 966, 966A
Organ Fugue, 952
Originaltänze (Waltzes) for Pianoforte, 365
Overture for String Quartet, 20
— — — Quintet, 8
Overtures for Orchestra:
  Der Teufel als Hydraulicus, 4
  in B flat, 11
  in D, 12
  in D (1812), 26
  in B flat, 470
  in D (1817), 556
  in D (*im italienischen Stile*), 590
  in C (*im italienischen Stile*), 591
  in E minor, 648
  in D, 996
  See also 84, 190, 239, 326, 644 (2), 646, 796, *and* '*Rosamunde* Overtures'
Overtures for Piano Duet:
  Alfonso und Estrella, 773
  Fierabras, 798
  in D (*im italienischen Stile*), 592
  in C (*im italienischen Stile*), 597
  in G minor, 668
  in F, 675
Overtures for Pianoforte, 14, 732

Phantasien, *see* Fantasias
Pianoforte Quartet, 487
— Quintet (the 'Trout'), 667
— Sonatas, *see* Sonatas
— Trios:
  in B flat (1812), 28
  in E flat, Op. 148, 897
  in B flat, Op. 99, 898
  in E flat, Op. 100, 929

Polonaise in B flat for Violin and Orchestra, 580
Polonaises for Piano Duet:
  4, 599
  6, 824
  sketches, 618A
Premier grand Trio, 898
Première grande Sonate, 845

Quartets, *see* String Quartets
Quartett-Satz (Quartet Movement), 703
Quintets, *see* Pianoforte Quintets and String Quintet

'*Reliquie*,' 840
Rondeaux brillants, 823 (no. 3), 895
Rondo concertante in F for Pianoforte Quartet, 487
— for Pianoforte and Violin, 895
— in A for Violin solo and String Orchestra, 438
— — E for Pianoforte, 506
Rondos for Piano Duet:
  in D, 608
  in A, 951
'*Rosamunde* Overtures':
  in C minor, 644
  in D minor, 732

Scherzi for Pianoforte:
  1 in D, 570
  2 in B flat and D flat, 593
'*Schubert's Begräbnis-Feier, Franz*,' 79
Seconde grande Sonate, 850
Singübungen, 619
Sonata in A for Pianoforte and Violin, 574
— — A minor for Pianoforte and Arpeggione, 821
— Movement for Pianoforte Trio, 28
Sonatas for Piano Duet:
  in B flat, 617
  in C, 812
Sonatas for Pianoforte:
  in E (1815), (154), 157
  in C (1815), 279
  in E (1816), 459
  in A minor (1817), (334), 537
  in A flat, 557
  in E minor, 566
  in D flat, 567
  in E flat, 568
  in F sharp minor, 570-1
  in B, 575
  in C (1818), 613
  in F minor, (505), 625
  in C sharp minor, 655
  in A (1819), 664
  in A minor (1823), 784

INDEX OF SCHUBERT'S WORKS

Sonatas for Pianoforte—*continued*:
  in C (1825), 840
  in A minor (1825), 845
  in D, (604), 850
  in G, 894
  in C minor, 958
  in A (1828), 959
  in B flat (1828), 960
Sonaten-Satz for Pianoforte Trio, 28
Sonatina for Piano Duet, 968
Sonatinas for Violin and Pianoforte:
  in D, 384
  in A minor, 385
  in G minor, 408
String Quartets:
  in G (*c.* 1810), 2
  in mixed keys (1811, 1812, lost), 19, 19A
  in (?) F (*c.* 1812), 998
  in mixed keys (1812), 18
  in C (1812), 32, 3
  in B flat (1812–13), 36
  in E flat (1813, lost), 40
  in C (1813), 46
  in B flat (1813), 68
  in D (1813), 74
  in E flat (1813), 87
  in D (1814), 94
  in C minor (Grave and Allegro), 103
  in B flat (1814), 112
  in G minor, 173
  in E, 353
  in B flat (1818?), 601
  in C minor (Allegro), 703
  in A minor, 804
  in D minor, 810
  in G (1826), 887
  See also 20, 86, 89, 90
String Quintets:
  Overture, 8
  Quintet in C, 956
  Rondo in A, 438
String Trios:
  in B flat (1816), 471
  in B flat (1817), 581
Symphonies:
  in D (fragment), 997
  in D (no. 1), 82
  in B flat (no. 2), 125
  in D (no. 3), 200
  in C minor (no. 4), 417
  in B flat (no. 5), 485
  in C, the Little (no. 6), 589
  in D (sketches), 615
  in E (sketch), 729
  in B minor, 759
  in . . . (lost), (812), 849
  in C, the Great (1828), 944
'Symphony without Trumpets and Drums,' 485

'*Tod und das Mädchen, Der*'-*Quartett*, 810
'Tragic Symphony,' 417
'*Trauer-Marsch*,' 819 (no. 5)
'*Trauer-Walzer*,' entry before 350; *see also* 188
Trios for Pianoforte:
  to a lost Minuet, 610
  to a Waltz, 135
Trios, *see* Pianoforte Trios *and* String Trios
Troisième grande Sonate, 568
'Trout Quintet,' 667

'Unfinished Symphony,' 759
Ungarische Melodie for Pianoforte, 817
'*Unvollendete Sinfonie*,' 759

Valses nobles, 969
— *sentimentales*, 779
Variations in A for Violin solo, 597A
— for Pianoforte and Flute, 802
— on '*Sei mir gegrüsst*' for Pianoforte and Violin, 934 (third movement)
— for Piano Duet:
  8 variations in E minor on a French Song, 624
  8 Variations in A flat on an Original Theme, 813
  8 Variations in C on a Theme from Hérold's opera *Marie*, 908
  See also 603, 823 (no. 2)
— for Pianoforte:
  6 in E flat, 21
  7 (5) in F major, 24
  10 in F, 156
  13 in A minor (on a Theme by A. Hüttenbrenner), 576
  1 in C minor (on a Waltz by A. Diabelli), 718
'*Violin-Konzert*,' 345

Waltzes for Pianoforte:
  1 in C sharp, 139
  12 (in Op. 18), 145
  20, 146
  36, 365
  34, 779
  1 in G, 844
  12 (*Grätzer Walzer*), 924
  12 (*Valses nobles*), 969
  1 in A flat, 978
  1 in . . ., 979
  2, 980
  See also Deutsche Tänze and *Ländler*
'Wanderer Fantasia,' 760
Wiener Damen-Ländler, 734
Wiedersehen-Deutscher, 783 (*Deutscher Tanz*, no. 9)
Wiener Deutsche (*Tänze*), 128
'*Wildbacher Ländler*,' 374

INSTRUMENTAL MUSIC

CLASSIFICATION

Album Leaves, entry before 350, 511, entry before 769, 844, 915
Arrangements of other composers' works, 37, 96
Arrangements of Schubert's own works, 366 (no. 17), 592, 597, 732, 773, 798

CHAMBER MUSIC, see Adagio and Rondo, Adagio in E flat, *Deutsche Tänze*, Fantasia, Introductions and Variations, Minuet and Finale, Minuets, Nonet, Octets, Overtures; Pianoforte Quartet, Quintet, *and* Trios; Rondo, Sonata for Arpeggione, Sonatinas; String Quartets, Quintets, *and* Trios

DANCES, see Cotillon, *Deutsche Tänze*, Écossaises, Galops, *Ländler, and* Waltzes; see also Minuets and Polonaises

Fragments and Unfinished Instrumental Works, 2, 28, 32, 68, 72, 103, 157, 279, 346, 347, 348, 349, 471, 570, 571, 601, 605, 613, 625, 655, 703, 759, 900, 966; see also Sketches (below)
French tunes, 624, 823, 908
Funeral Music, 79, 84 (nos. 10 and 16a), 137 (no. 4)

Hungarian tunes, 817, 818

Incidental music, 4, 797

ORCHESTRAL WORKS, see Ballet Music, Concertos, Entr'actes, Orchestral Scores, Overtures, Polonaise, Rondo, and Symphonies

Photostats of autographs, see General Index *under* Photogramm-Archiv (Vienna)
PIANOFORTE DUETS, see Allegros, Andante, *Deutscher Tanz*, Divertissements, Fantasias, Marches, Overtures, Polonaises, Rondos, Sonatas, Sonatina, *and* Variations
PIANOFORTE MUSIC, see Adagios, Allegrettos, Allegros, Andantes, Andantino, Dances (see above), Fantasias, Fugues, Impromptus, March, Minuets, Moments musicaux, Overtures, Rondo, Scherzi, Sonatas, Trios, *Ungarische Melodie*, and Variations

Sketches, 2 (note), 154, 597A, 615, 618A, 655, 729, 759, 967

Variants, 68, 145, 146, 299, 779, 783
Variations on Schubert's own songs, 667, 760, 802, 810, 934 (third movement)
Versions, other, 26, 48, 178, 817, 929

2. VOCAL MUSIC

A. Titles

O = Opera; *P* = Part-song

Abend, 645
—, Der (Matthisson), 108
—, — (Kosegarten), 221
Abendbilder, 650
Abendlandschaft, *P*., 357
Abendlied (Sanft glänzt die Abendsonne), 382
— (Claudius), 499
— (Mayrhofer), *see* Schlaflied
— (Stolberg), 276
— der Fürstin, 495
— für die Entfernte, 856
Abendrot, Das (Kosegarten), *P*., 236
—, — (Schreiber), 627
Abendröte, 690
Abends unter der Linde, 235, 237
Abendständchen. An Lina, 265
Abendstern, 806
Abgeblühte Linde, Die, 514
Abschied (nach einer Wallfahrtsarie), 475
— (Rellstab), 957 (no. 7)
— (von einem Freunde) (Schubert), 578
— von der Erde, 829
— von der Harfe, 406
Adelaide, 95
Adelwold und Emma, 211
Adieu! (spurious), App. I
Adrast, *O*., 137
Advokaten, Die, *P*. (spurious), 37
Agnes, *see* Von Ida
Agnus Dei, *see* Masses
Alcide al Bivio, 76
Alfonso und Estrella, *O*., 732
Alinde, 904
Alleluia, *see* Das grosse Halleluja
Alles um Liebe, 241
Allmacht, Die, 852
Alpenjäger, Der (Mayrhofer), 524
—, — (Schiller), 588
Als ich sie erröten sah, 153
Alte Liebe rostet nie, 477
Altschottische Ballade, Eine, 923
Am Bach im Frühling, 361
— Erlafsee, *see* Erlafsee
— ersten Maimorgen, 344
— Feierabend, 795 (no. 5)
— Fenster, 878
— Flusse, 160, 766
— Geburtstage des Kaisers, *P*., 748
— Grabe Anselmo's, 504
— Meer, 957 (no. 12)

Am Namensfeste des Kaisers, *see* Am Geburtstage des Kaisers
— See (Bruchmann), 746
— See (Mayrhofer), 124
— Strome, 539
— Tage Aller Seelen, 343
Amalia, 195
Ammenlied, 122
Amor's Macht, *P*., 339
— Zauber, *see* Amor's Macht
Amphiaraos, 166
An Chloen (I), 363
— — (II), 462
— Cidli, *see* Furcht der Geliebten
— das Vaterland, *see* Tantum ergo, 461
— den Frühling, 245, 283, 338 *P*, 587
— — Mond (without words), 311
— — — (Goethe), 259, 296
— — — (Hölty):
  Dein Silber schien, *see* Klage an den Mond
  Geuss, lieber Mond, 193
  Was schauest du so hell, 468
An den Mond in einer Herbstnacht, 614
— — Schlaf, 447
— — Tod, 518
— der Bahre, *see* Totengräber-Weise
— die Apfelbäume, wo ich Julien (als ich Laura) erblickte, 197
— — Entfernte, 765
— — Freude, 189
— — Freunde, 654
— — Geliebte, 303
— — Harmonie(n), *see* Gesang an die Harmonie
— — Laute, 905
— — Leier, 737
— — Musik, 547
— — Nachtigall (Claudius), 497
— — — (Hölty), 196
— — Natur, 372
— — Sonne (Baumberg), 270
— — — (Tiedge), 272
— — — (Uz), *P*., 439
— — untergehende Sonne, 457
— eine Quelle, 530
— Elisa, *see* Trost, etc.
— Emma, 113
— Franz, *see* Aus 'Heliopolis' (II)
— Franz Schubert, *see* Geheimnis, etc.
— Gott, 863
— Laura, als sie Klopstock's Auferstehungslied sang, 115

TITLES OF VOCAL MUSIC

An Lina, see Abendständchen
— mein Herz, 860
— — Klavier, see Seraphine an ihr Klavier
— Mignon, 161
— Myrtill, see Heimliches Lieben
— Rosa (I), 315
— — (II), 316
— Schwager Kronos, 369
— Sie (Klopstock), 288
— — (Salis), see Der Herbstabend
— Sylvia, see Gesang, etc.
Andenken, 99, 423
Annot Lyle's song, see Lied der Anne Lyle
Antigone und Oedip, 542
Antiphons, P., 696
Arie (Didone abbandonata), 510
Ariette, see La pastorella
Art, ein Weib zu nehmen, Die, 902 (no. 3)
Artaserse, see Leiden der Trennung
Atlas, Der, 957 (no. 8)
Atys, 585
Auf dem Flusse, 911 (no. 7)
— — See, 543
— — Strom(e), 943
— — Wasser zu singen, 774
— den Sieg der Deutschen, 81, 88, P.
— — Tod einer Nachtigall, 201, 399
— der Bruck, 853
— — Brücke, see Auf der Bruck
— — Donau, 553
— — Riesenkoppe, 611
— einen Kirchhof, 151
Aufenthalt, 957 (no. 5)
Auflösung, 807
Augenblicke im Elysium, 582
Augenlied, 297
Auguste jam coelestium, 488
Aus 'Diego Manazares,' 458
— 'Heliopolis' (I), 753
— — (II), 754
Ave Maria, see Ellen's Gesang (III)

Baches Wiegenlied, Des, 795 (no. 20)
Badelied, P., 340
Ballade (Hölty), see Der Traum
— (Kenner), 134
Bardengesang, P., 147
Befreier Europa's in Paris, Die, 104
Begräbnislied, P., 168
Bei Anselmo's Grabe, see Am Grabe Anselmo's
— dem Grabe Anselmo's, see Am Grabe Anselmo's
— — — meines Vaters, 496
— dir allein! 866 (no. 2)
Beiden Freunde von Salamanka, Die, see Die Freunde von Salamanka
Beim Winde, 669

Beitrag zur fünfzigjährigen Jubelfeier des Herrn Salieri, P., 407, 441
Benedictus, 961; see also Masses
Berge, Die, 634
Bergknappenlied, P., 268
Bertha's Lied in der Nacht, 653
Besuch, Der, see Dithyrambe
Betende, Die, 102
Betulia liberata, La, P., 34
Bild, Das, 155
Blanka, 631
Blind Boy, The, see following entry
Blinde Knabe, Der, 833
Blondel zu Marien, 626
Blumenballade, see Vergismeinnicht and Viola
Blumenbrief, Der, 622
Blumenlied, 431
Blumen Schmerz, Der, 731
Blumensprache, Die, 519
Boat Song, see following entry
Bootgesang, P., 835
Böse Farbe, Die, 795 (no. 17)
Bundeslied, 258
Bürgschaft, Die (Schiller), 246
—, —, O., 435

Cantatas, see Kantaten
5 Canti, 688
Canzonen, see Vier Canzonen
Chor der Engel, P., 440
Cidli, see Das Rosenband
Clärchen's Lied, see Klärchen's Lied
Claudine von Villa Bella, O., 239
Clemenza di Tito, La, P., 35
Clochette, La, see Das Zauberglöckchen
Colma's Klage, 217
Constitutionslied, see Am Geburtstage des Kaisers
Cora an die Sonne, 263
Coronach, P., 836
Credo, see Masses
Cronnan, 282
Crusader's Return, The, see Romanze des Richard Loewenherz

Danksagung an den Bach, 795 (no. 4)
Daphne am Bach, 411
Das war ich, 174
Dass sie hier gewesen, 775
Delphine, 857 (no. 2)
Demofoonte, 42
Deutsche Eiche, Die, see Tantum ergo in B flat
— Messe, see Gesänge zur Feier des heiligen Opfers der Messe
— Trauermesse, 621
Deutsches Requiem, see Deutsche Trauermesse
— Salve Regina, see Salve Regina.
Hymne an die heilige Mutter Gottes

INDEX OF SCHUBERT'S WORKS

Deutsches Stabat Mater, see Stabat Mater (Klopstock)
Didone abbandonata, see Arie
Dithyrambe, 47, 801
'Divan' songs, see West-östlicher Divan
Dom, Aus Goethe's *Faust*, see Szene (im Dom) aus Goethe's *Faust*
Don Gayseros (I), (II), (III), 93
Dona nobis, 185; see also Masses
Doppelgänger, Der, 957 (no. 13)
Dörfchen, Das, P., 598, 641
Drang in die Ferne, 770
Drei Gesänge von Metastasio, 902
— Sänger, Die, 329
Du bist die Ruh', 776
— liebst mich nicht, 756
Dying Christian to his Soul, The, see Verklärung

Echo, Das, 868
Edone, 445
Edward, Edward, see Eine altschottische Ballade
Eifersucht und Stolz, 795 (no. 15)
Einsame, Der, 800; see also 620
Einsamkeit (Mayrhofer), 620
— (Müller), 911 (no. 12)
Einsiedelei, Die, 337 P., 393, 563
Elegie. Bei dem Grabe meines Vaters, P., 127
Elfenkönigin, Die, see Sylphen
Ellen Douglas's Songs, see following entries
Ellen's Gesang (I), 837
— — (II), 838
— — (III), 839
Elysium, 51 P., 53 P., 54 P., 57 P., 58 P., 60 P., 584
Emma, see An Emma
Empfindungsäusserungen des Witwen-Institutes der Schullehrer Wiens, für den Stifter und Vorsteher desselben, see Kantate zu Ehren J. Spendou's
Entfernte Geliebte, Die, see Als ich sie erröten sah
Entfernten, Der, 331 P., 332 P., 350
Entsühnte Orest, Der, 699; see Orest auf Tauris
Entzückung, 413
— an Laura, Die, 390, 577
Epistel an Josef Spaun, see Herrn Josef Spaun
Erde, Die, 989
— und der Frühling, Die, see Kantate zur Feier der Genesung des Fräulein Irene von Kiesewetter
Erinnerung, 101; see also Die Erscheinung
Erinnerungen, 98, 424 P.
Erlafsee, 586
Erlkönig, 328

Erntelied, 434
Erscheinung, Die, 229
Erstarrung, 911 (no. 4)
Erste Liebe, Die, 182
Erster Verlust, 226
Erwartung, Die, 159
Evangelium Johannis vi. 55–8, 607
Ewige Liebe, P., 825 (no. 2)

Fahrt zum Hades, 526
Falke, Der, 829
'Faust' songs, 118, 126, 367, 440, 564
Feier der Auferstehung, Die, see Lazarus
Fernando, O., 220
Feuerwerk, Das, P., 642
Fierabras, O., 796
Fierabras, see preceding entry
Filosofo di Campagna, Il, see La Pastorella
Finden, Das, 219
Fischer, Der, 225
Fischerlied (Schlechta), see Totengräber-Weise
— (Salis), 351, 364 P., 562
Fischermädchen, Das, 957 (no. 10)
Fischers Liebesglück, Des, 933
Fischerweise, 881
Florio, 857 (no. 1)
Flucht, Die, 825 (no. 3)
Flüchtling, Der, 67 P., 402
Flug der Zeit, Der, 515
Fluss, Der, 693
Forelle, Die, 550; see also 667
Fragment aus dem Aeschylus, 450
— — Schiller's Gedicht 'Die Götter Griechenlands,' see Strophe
Fräulein im Turme, Das. Romanze, 114
— vom See, Das, see Sieben Gesänge
Fräuleins Liebeslauschen, Des, 698
Freigeisterei der Leidenschaft, see Der Kampf
Freiwilliges Versinken, 700
Fremdling, Der, see Der Wanderer (Schmidt von Lübeck)
Fremdlings Abendlied, Des, see Der Wanderer (Schmidt von Lübeck)
Freude der Kinderjahre, 455
Freunde von Salamanka, Die, O., 326
Freundschaft und Wein, see Trinklied (Zettler)
Fröhlicher Lebensmut, see Lebensmut (Rellstab)
Fröhliches Scheiden, 896
Fröhlichkeit, Die, 262
Frohsinn, 520
Frühe Liebe, Die, 430
Frühen Gräber, Die, 290
Frühlingsgesang, P., 709, 740
Frühlingsglaube, 686
Frühlingslied (Die Luft ist blau), 243 P., 398

TITLES OF VOCAL MUSIC 541

Frühlingslied (Hölty), see Mailied (Grüner wird die Au)
— (Pollak), 914 P., 919
— (Schober), see Frühlingsgesang
Frühlingsmorgen, Der, see Kantate zum Geburtstag des Sängers J. M. Vogl
Frühlingssehnsucht, 957 (no. 3)
Frühlingstraum, 911 (no. 11)
Fülle der Liebe, 854
Funeral Song, see Coronach
Furcht der Geliebten, 285

Ganymed, 544
Gebet, P., 815
— des Herrn, Das, see Deutsche Messe, Anhang
— während der Schlacht, 171
Geburtshymne, see Hymne zur Genesung des Herrn Ritter
Geburtstags-Hymne, see Am Geburtstage des Kaisers
Geburtstags-Kantate, see Kantate zum Geburtstag des Sängers J. M. Vogl
Geburtstagslied, see Der Wintertag
Gebüsche, Die, 646
Gefangenen Sänger, Die, 712
Gefrorene Thränen, 911 (no. 3)
Geheimes, 719
Geheimnis. An Franz Schubert, 491
— Das, 250, 793
Geist der Liebe (Kosegarten), 233
— — — (Matthisson), 414, 747 P.
Geisternähe, 100
Geistertanz, Der, 15, 116, 494 P.
Geistes-Gruss, 142
Geistliche Lieder für das heilige Messopfer, see Gesänge zur Feier des heiligen Opfers der Messe
Genesungs-Hymne, see Hymne zur Genesung des Herrn Ritter
Genesungs-Kantate, see Kantate zur Feier der Genesung der Irene Kiesewetter
Genügsamkeit, 143
Gesang an die Harmonie, 394
—. An Sylvia, 891
— der Geister über den Wassern, 484, 538 P., 704 P., 705 P., 714 P.
— — Norna, 831
Gesänge aus Walter Scott's 'Fräulein vom See,' see Sieben Gesänge
— — 'Wilhelm Meister,' 877; see also 149, 161, 310, 321, 325, 359, 469, 478–81, 656, 726, 727, 877
— des Harfners aus 'Wilhelm Meister,' 478–80; see also 877
— von Metastasio, see Drei Gesänge
— zur Feier des heiligen Opfers der Messe, (701), 872
Gestirne, Die, 444
Gestörte Glück, Das, 309

Getäuschte Verräter, Der, 902 (no. 2)
Glaube, Hoffnung und Liebe (Kuffner), 955
—, — — — (Reil), P., 954
Gloria, see Masses
Glückliches Geheimnis, see Suleika (I)
Goldschmiedsgesell, Der, 560
Gondelfahrer, Der, 808, 809 P.
Gospel according to St. John, see Evangelium Johannis
Gott, der Weltschöpfer, P., 986
— im Frühlinge, 448
— — Ungewitter, P., 985
— in der Natur, P., 757
— und die Bajadere, Der, 254
Götter Griechenlands, Die, see Strophe von Schiller
Grab, Das, 330, 377, 569
— und Mond, P., 893, (914)
Gräbers Heimweh, see Totengräbers Heimwehe
Grablied, 218
— auf einen Soldaten, 454
— für die Mutter, 616
Gradual, 184
Graf von Gleichen, Der, O., (260), 918
— — Habsburg, Der, 990
Gratulations-Kantate, see Namensfeier für F. M. Vierthaler
Greise Kopf, Der, 911 (no. 14)
Greisengesang, 778
Grenzen der Menschheit, 716
Gretchen, 564
— am Spinnrade, 118
— im Zwinger, see Gretchen
— vor der Mater dolorosa, see Gretchen
Gretchen's Abscheu vor der Liebe, see Die Unterscheidung
— Bitte, see Gretchen
— Gehorsam, see Die Unterscheidung
Grosse Halleluja, Das, 442
Grosses Magnificat, 486
Gruppe aus dem Tartarus, 65 P., 396, 583
Gute Hirte, Der, 449
— Nacht, 911 (no. 1)

Hagar's Klage, 5
Halleluja, see Das grosse Halleluja
Halt!, 795 (no. 3)
Hänflings Liebeswerbung, 552
Harfenspieler, 325
— (I), 478
— (II), 479
— (III), 480
Harper's songs, see Gesänge des Harfners, Harfenspieler, Mignon und der Harfner
Häusliche Krieg, Der, see Die Verschworenen
Heidenröslein, 257

INDEX OF SCHUBERT'S WORKS

Heimliches Lieben, 922
Heimweh, Das (Hell), 456
—, — (Pyrker), 851
Hektor's Abschied, 312
Heliopolis, see Aus 'Heliopolis'
Herbst, 945
Herbstabend, Der, 405
Herbstlied, 502
Herbstnacht, Die, see (Die) Wehmut (Salis)
Hermann und Thusnelda, 322
Herrn Josef Spaun, 749
Himmelsfunken, 651
Hippolit's Lied, 890
Hirt, Der, 490
— auf dem Felsen, Der, 965
Hochzeitsbraten, Der, P., 930
Hochzeitslied, 463
Hoffnung, Die (Schiller), 251, 637
— (Goethe), 295
Huldigung, 240
Hymn to the Virgin, see Ellen's Gesang (III)
Hymne (I), 659
— (II), 660
— (III), 661
— (IV), 662
— (an den heiligen Geist), see Hymnus
— an den Unendlichen, 232, P.
— — die heilige Mutter Gottes, see Salve Regina
— — — Jungfrau, see Ellen's Gesang (III)
— zur Genesung des Herrn Ritter, P., 763,
— — Namens- oder Geburtsfeier, see Hymne zur Genesung des Herrn Ritter
Hymnus an den heiligen Geist, P., 941, 948, 964

Idens (Ida's) Nachtgesang, 227
— Schwanenlied, 317
Ihr Bild, 957 (no. 9)
— Grab, 736
Im Abendrot, 799
— Dorfe, 911 (no. 17)
— Freien, 880
— Frühling, 882
— Gegenwärtigen Vergangenes, P., 710
— Haine, 738
— Hochgebirge, see Aus 'Heliopolis' (II)
— Kirchhof, see Auf einen Kirchhof
— Walde (F. von Schlegel), 708
— Walde (Schulze), 834
In der Ferne, 957 (no. 6)
— — Mitternacht, 464
Incanto degli occhi, L', 902 (no. 1)
Inconstant, The, see Der Weiberfreund
Indische Legende, see Der Gott und die Bajadere
Iphigenia, 573

Irdisches Glück, 866 (no. 4)
Irrlicht, 911 (no. 9)
Isacco, P., 17, 33

Jagdchor, see Jagdlied
Jagdlied, 521
Jäger, Der, 795 (no. 14)
Jägerlied, P., 204
Jägers Abendlied, 215, 368
— Liebeslied, 909
Johanna Sebus, 728
Julius an Theone, 419
Junge Nonne, Die, 828
Jüngling am Bache, Der, 30, 192, 638
— an der Quelle, Der, 300
— auf dem Hügel, Der, 702
— und der Tod, Der, 545
Jünglingswonne, P., 983 (no. 1),

Kampf, Der, 594
Kantate zu Ehren Josef Spendou's, P., 472
— zum Geburtstag des Sängers Johann Michael Vogl, P., 666
— zur Feier der Genesung des Fräulein Irene von Kiesewetter, P., 936
— — — des Prof. Watteroth, see Prometheus-Kantate
— — fünfzigjährigen Jubelfeier Salieri's, see Beitrag, etc.
— — Namensfeier des Vaters, P., 80; see also 294
— — für F. M. Vierthaler, see Namensfeier, etc.
Kehr' ein bei mir, see Du bist die Ruh'
Klage (Nimmer trag' ich länger), see Der Leidende
— (Trauer umfliesst mein Leben), 292, 371
— (Hölty), see Klage an den Mond
— (Matthisson), 415
— an den Mond, 436, 437
— der Ceres, 323
— um Ali Bey, P., 140
Klag(e)lied, 23
Klärchen's Lied, 210
Knabe, Der, 692
— in der Wiege, Der, 579
Knabenzeit, Die, 400
Kolma's Klage, see Colma's Klage
König in Thule, Der, 367
Konstitutionslied, see Am Geburtstage des Kaisers
Krähe, Die, 911 (no. 15)
Kreuzzug, Der, 932
Kriegers Ahnung, 957 (no. 2)
Kyrie, 31, 45, 49, 66; see also Masses

Labetrank der Liebe, 302
Lachen und Weinen, 777

TITLES OF VOCAL MUSIC

Lachens und Weinens Grund, see Lachen und Weinen
Lacrimas, see Zwei Szenen, etc.
Lady of the Lake, The, see Sieben Gesänge
Lambertine, 301
Landende Orest, Der, see Orest auf Tauris
Laube, Die, 214
Laura am Klavier, 388
Lay of the Imprisoned Huntsman, see Lied des gefangenen Jägers
Lazarus, P., 689
Lebe wohl! (spurious), App. I
Leben, Das, P., 269
'Lebensbilder,' see Lebenslied
Lebenslied, 425 P., 508
Lebenslust, P., 609
Lebensmelodien, 395
Lebensmut (Rellstab), 937
— (Schulze), 883
Leichenphantasie, Eine, 7; see also note to 1
Leiden der Trennung, 509
Leidende, Der, 432, 512
Leiermann, Der, 911 (no. 24)
Letzte Hoffnung, 911 (no. 16)
Liane, 298
Licht und Liebe, 352
Lieb Minna, 222
Liebe, P., 983 (no. 2)
Liebe, Die (Goethe), see Klärchen's Lied
Liebe, Die (Leon), 522
Liebe Farbe, Die, 795 (no. 16)
— hat gelogen, Die, 751
Liebende, Der, 207
— schreibt, Die, 673
Liebesbotschaft, 957 (no. 1)
Liebesgötter, Die, 446
— auf dem Markte, Die, see Wer kauft Liebesgötter?
Liebeslauschen, see Des Fräuleins Liebeslauschen
Liebesrausch, 164, 179
Liebeständelei, 206
Liebhaber in allen Gestalten, 558
Liebliche Stern, Der, 861
Lied (Brüder, schrecklich brennt die Thräne), 535
— (Claudius), 362, 501
— (Fouqué), 373
— (Mayrhofer), see Über allen Zauber Liebe
— (Pichler), 483
— (Salis), 403
— (Schiller), 284
— (Stolberg), 788
— an den Tod, see An den Tod
— auf dem Wasser zu singen, für meine Agnes, see Auf dem Wasser zu singen
— aus der Ferne, 107
Lied beim Rundetanz, P., 132, 983 (no. 3)
— der Anne Lyle, 830
— — Liebe, 109
— — Mignon, 359, 481, 877 (nos. 2-4)
— des gefangenen Jägers, 843
— — Orpheus, als er in die Hölle gieng, 474
— eines Kindes, 596
— — Kriegers, 822
— — Liebenden, see Der Liebende
— — Schiffers an die Dioskuren, 360
— für den Sabbath, see Der 92. Psalm
— im Freien, P., 133, 572
— — Grünen, Das, 917
— in der Abwesenheit, 416
— — nach dem Falle Nathos, 278
— ohne Titel und Text, see Song without title or words
— vom Reifen, Das, 532
Lieder nach Ossian, see Ossian Songs
Liedesend, 473
Liedler, Der, 209
Lilla an die Morgenröte, 273
Lindenbaum, Der, 911 (no. 5)
Litanei auf das Fest Aller Seelen, see Am Tage Aller Seelen
Lob der Einsamkeit, see Die Einsiedelei
— — Thränen, 711
— des Tokayers, 248
Loda's Gespenst, 150
Lorma, 327, 376
Luisens Antwort, 319
Lunz, see Abschied (nach einer Wallfahrtsarie)
Lützow's wilde Jagd, P., 205

Macht der Augen, Die, 902 (no. 1)
— — Liebe, Die, 308
Mädchen aus der Fremde, Das, 117, 252
—, Das, 652; see also 631
— von Inistore, Das, 281
Mädchens Klage, Des, 6, 191, 389
Magnificat, 486
Mahomet's Gesang, 549, 721
Maigesang, P., 988
Mailied (Der Schnee zerrinnt), P., 130, 202
— (Grüner wird die Au), 129 P., 199 P., 503
— (Willkommen, lieber schöner Mai), P., 244
Mainacht, Die, 194
Männer sind méchant!, Die, 866 (no. 3)
Marie, 658
Marienbild, Das, 623
Masses:
in F, 105 (185
in G, 167
in B flat, 324
in C, 452 (961)

INDEX OF SCHUBERT'S WORKS

Masses—*continued*:
  in A flat, 678
  in A minor (fragment), 755
  in E flat, 950
  See also Benedictus, Deutsche Trauermesse, Dona nobis, Kyrie, Requiem, *and* 872
Meeres Stille, 216
Mein!, 795 (no. 11)
— Gruss an den Mai, 305
Memnon, 541
Messen, *see* Masses
Mignon, 321
— (I), 726
— (II), 469, 727
—, 1. Weise, 469 (first version)
— und der Harfner, 877 (no. 1)
Minnelied, 429; *see also* 433
Minnesang, *see* Huldigung
Minnesänger, Der (Die?), 981
Minona, 152
Mirjam's Siegesgesang, *P.*, 942
Missa solemnis, 678
Mit dem grünen Lautenbande, 795 (no. 13)
Modo di prender moglie, Il, 902 (no. 3)
Mohrenkönig, Der (Mohrenkrieg?), *see* Don Gayseros (II)
Mondabend, Der, 141
Mondenschein, *P.*, 875
Mondnacht, Die, 238
Morgenfantasie, *see* Der Flüchtling
Morgengesang im Walde, *P.*, 918
Morgengruss, 795 (no. 8)
Morgenkuss (nach einem Ball), Der, 264
Morgenlied (Die frohe neubelebte Flur), 381
— (Stolberg), 266
— (Werner), 685
Morgenstern, Der, 172, 203 *P.*
Müller und der Bach, Der, 795 (no. 19)
Müllerlieder, *see* Die schöne Müllerin
Müllers Blumen, Des, 795 (no. 9)
Musensohn, Der, 764
Mut, 911 (no. 22)
Mutter Erde, Die, *see* Lied (Stolberg)

Nach einem (dem) Gewitter, 561
Nacht, Die (Die Nacht ist dumpfig), 534
—, — (Wie schön bist du), *P.*, 983 (no. 4)
—, — (Uz), 358
— und Träume, 827
Nachtgesang (Collin), *see* Licht und Liebe
— (Goethe), 119
— (Kosegarten), 314
— im Walde, *P.*, 913
Nachthelle, *P.*, 892
Nachthymne, 687
Nachtigall, Die (Hölty), *see* Seufzer
—, — (Unger), *P.*, 724

Nachtmusik, *P.*, 848
Nachtstück, 672
Nachtviolen(lied), 752
Nähe des Geliebten, 162
Namensfeier, *see* Hymne zur Genesung des Herrn Ritter (called Des Tages Weihe, Hymne zur Namens- oder Geburtsfeier); Kantate zur Namensfeier des Vaters; *and* Zur Namensfeier des Herrn Andreas Siller
'— für Schubert's Vater,' 294
— — Franz Michael Vierthaler, *P.*, 294
Namenstagslied (für Josef von Koller), 695
Naturgenuss, 188, 422 *P.*
Nebensonnen, Die, 911 (no. 23)
Neugierige, Der, 795 (no. 6)
Nonne, Die, 208, 212
Norman's Gesang, 846
Norna's Song, *see* Gesang der Norna
Notturno, *see* Ständchen (Grillparzer)

Offertories:
  in C (Clamavi ad te), 85
  in C (Totus in corde), 136
  in A minor (Tres sunt), 181
  in F (Salve Regina), 223
  in A (Salve Regina), 676
  in B flat (Intende voci), 963
Orest auf Tauris, 548; *see also* Der entsühnte Orest
Orpheus, *see* Lied des Orpheus, etc.
Orti esperidi, Gli, 78
Ossian Songs, 147, 150, 217, 278, 281, 282, 293, 327, (375), 376, (534)
Ossian's 'Lied nach dem Falle Nathos,' 278
Osterlied, *P.*, 987
Ostwind, *see* Suleika (I)

Pastorella (al prato), La, 513 *P.*, 528
Pause, 795 (no. 12)
Pax vobiscum, 551
Perle, Die, 466
Pflicht und Liebe, 467
Pflügerlied, 392
Phidile, 500
Philoktet, 540
Pilgerweise, 789
Pilgrim, Der, 794
Post, Die, 911 (no. 13)
Prometheus, 674
— (Cantata), 451
13. Psalm, Der, 663
23. Psalm, Der, *P.*, 706
92. Psalm, Der, *P.*, 953
Punschlied. Im Norden zu singen, 253
— (Vier Elemente), *P.*, 277

Quartett, *see* Geburtstagshymne, etc., *and* Ruhe

TITLES OF VOCAL MUSIC 545

Rast, 911 (no. 10)
Rastlose Liebe, 138
Rattenfänger, Der, 255
Räuberlied, 239 (no. 7), 435 (no. 13)
Refrainlieder, see Vier Refrainlieder
Reiterlied, see Lied eines Kriegers
Requiem (in German), see Deutsche Trauermesse
— (in Latin), 453
Richard Löwenherz, see Romanze, etc.
Ritter Toggenburg, 397
Romanze, 144; see also Das Fräulein im Turme, Des Fräuleins Liebeslauschen, Rosamunde, and Sakuntala
Romanze des Richard Löwenherz, 907
Rosalia von Montanver, see Das Fräulein im Turme
Rosamunde, O., 797
Rose, Die, 745
Rosenband, Das, 280
Rückblick, 911 (no. 8)
Rückweg, 476
Rüdiger, P., 791
Rüdiger's Heimkehr, see Rüdiger
Ruhe, P., 635

Sakuntala, O., 701
Salve Regina (in Latin):
 in F (1812), 27
 in B flat (1814), 106
 in F (1815), 223
 in B flat (1816), 386
 in A, 676
 in C, 811
Salve Regina. Hymne an die heilige Mutter Gottes, 379
Sanctus, 56; see also Masses
Sänger am Felsen, Der, 482
—, Der, 149
Sängers Habe, Des, 832
— Morgenlied, 163, 165
Scene(n), see Szene(n)
Schäfer und Reiter, see following entry
— — der Reiter, Der, 517
Schäfers Klagelied, 121
Schatten, Die, 50
Schatzgräber, Der, 256
Schatzgräbers Begehr, 761
'Schiffende, Die,' see Der Liebende
Schiffer, Der (Mayrhofer), 536
—, — (F. von Schlegel), 694
Schiffers Nachtlied, see Lied eines Schiffers an die Dioskuren
— Scheidelied, 910
Schlacht, Die, 249, 387
Schlachtgesang, 443; see also 912
Schlachtlied, P., 912; see also 443
Schlaflied, 527
Schlummerlied, see Schlaflied
Schmetterling, Der, 633

Schöne Müllerin, Die (song-cycle), 795; see also 802
'Schubert an sein Klavier,' see Seraphine an ihr Klavier
Schwanengesang, 744
— (song-cycle), 957; see also 937 and 945
Schwangesang, 318
Schweizerlied, 559
Schwertlied, 170
Schwestergruss, 762
Sehnen, Das, 231
Sehnsucht (Nur wer die Sehnsucht kennt, Goethe), 310, 481, 656 P.
— (Was zieht mir das Herz so?, Goethe), 123
— (Mayrhofer), 516
— (Metastasio), see Leiden der Trennung
— (Schiller), 52, 636
— (Seidl), 879
— der Liebe, 180
Sei mir gegrüsst!, 741; see also 934 (third movement)
Selige Welt, 743
Seligen Augenblicke, Die, see Die Entzückung an Laura
Seligkeit, 433
Selma und Selmar, 286
Sendschreiben, see Herrn Josef Spaun
Seraphine an ihr Klavier, 342
Seufzer, 198
Shilrik und Vinvela, 293
Sieben Gesänge aus Walter Scott's 'Fräulein vom See,' 835–9, 843, 846
Sieg, Der, 805
Singübungen, see Vocal Exercises
Skolie (Deinhardstein), 306
— (Matthisson), 507
Sommernacht, Die, 289
Sonett I, 628
— II, 629
— III, 630
Song without title or words, 555
— — words, 311
Spiegelritter, Der, O., 11
Spinnerin, Die, 247
Spirit of Loda, see Loda's Gespenst
Sprache der Liebe, 410
Sprüche des Confucius, P., 43, 69, 70
Stabat Mater (in Latin), 175
— — (Klopstock), 383
Stadt, Die, 957 (no. 11)
Ständchen (Grillparzer), P., 920, 921
— (Rellstab), 957 (no. 4)
'—' (? Schubert), see Ruhe
— (Shakespeare), 889
Sterbende, Die, 186
Sterne, Die (Fellinger), 176
— — (Kosegarten), 313
— — (Leitner), 939
— — (F. von Schlegel), 684
Sternennächte, Die, 670

INDEX OF SCHUBERT'S WORKS

Sternenwelten, Die, 307
Stille Land, Das (Gottwald), *P.*, 916
— — — (Salis), *see* Das Grab
Stimme der Liebe (Matthisson), 187, 418
— — — (Stolberg), 412
Strom, Der, 565
Strophe von Schiller, 677
Stürmische Morgen, Der, 911 (no. 18)
Suleika (I), 720
— (II), 717
Sylphen, *P.*, 341
Szene (im Dom) aus Goethe's 'Faust,' 126

Tages Weihe, Des, *see* Hymne zur Genesung des Herrn Ritter
Täglich zu singen, 533
Tantum ergo:
 in C (XIV 7), 460
 in C (1816), 461
 in B flat, 730
 in C (1822), 739
 in D, 750
 in E flat, 962
Tanz, Der, *P.*, 826
Taubenpost, Die, 957 (no. 14)
Taucher, Der, 77, 111
Täuschung, 911 (no. 19)
—, Die, 230
Temora, *see* Der Abend (Kosegarten)
Teufels Lustschloss, Des, *O.*, 84, (787)
Thekla. Eine Geisterstimme, 73, 595
Thränenregen, 795 (no. 10)
Tiefes Leid, 876
Tischlerlied, 274
Tischlied, 234
Tod Oscar's, Der, 375
— und das Mädchen, Der, 531; *see also* 545 *and* 810
'Todeskuss,' *see* Todesmusik
Todesmusik, 758
Totengesang der Frauen und Mädchen, *see* Coronach
Totengräberlied, 38 *P.*, 44
Totengräbers Heimwehe, 842
Totengräber-Weise, 869
Totenhemdchen, Das, 864
Totenkranz für ein Kind, 275
Totenmarsch, *see* Grablied auf einen Soldaten
Totenopfer, *see* Erinnerung
Traditor deluso, Il, 902 (no. 2)
Tränenregen, *see* Thränenregen
Trauer der Liebe, 465
Traum, Der, 213
'Treubruch,' *see* Der Zwerg
Trinklied (Auf! jeder sei nun froh), *P.*, 267
— (Freunde, sammelt euch im Kreise), *P.*, 75
— (Funkelnd im Becher), *P.*, 356

Trinklied (Herr Bacchus ist ein braver Mann), *P.*, 426
— (Castelli), *P.*, 148
— (Shakespeare), 888
— (Zettler), 183
— aus dem XVI. Jahrhundert, *P.*, 847
— im Mai, *P.*, 427
— — Winter, *P.*, 242
— vor der Schlacht, 169
Triumph der Liebe, Der, *P.*, 55, 61, 62, 63, 64, 983 (no. 2)
Trockne Blumen, 795 (no. 18); *see also* 802
Trost (Nimmer lange weil' ich hier), 523
— (Mayrhofer), 671
—. An Elisa, 97
— im Liede, 546
— in Thränen, 120

Über allen Zauber Liebe, 682
— Wildemann, 884
Um Mitternacht, 862
Unendlichen, Dem, 291
Ungeduld, 795 (no. 7)
Unglückliche, Der (Pichler), 713
— — (Schmidt von Lübeck), *see* Der Wanderer
Unterscheidung, Die, 866 (no. 1)
Urania, *see* following entry
Uraniens Flucht, 554

Vater mit dem Kind, Der, 906
Vaterlandslied, 287
Vatermörder, Der, 10
Vedette, Die, *see* Der vierjährige Posten
Verfehlte Stunde, Die, 409
Vergebliche Liebe, 177
Vergissmeinnicht, 792
Verklärung, 59
Verschworenen, Die, *O.*, 787
Versunken, 715
Vier Canzonen, 688
— Gesänge für 4 Männerstimmen, 983
— Refrainlieder, 866
— Weltalter, Die, 391
Vierjährige Posten, Der, *O.*, 190
Viola, 786
Vocal Exercises, 619
Vögel, Die, 691
Volkslied, *see* Am Geburtstage des Kaisers
Vollmondnacht, *see* Mondenschein
Vom künftigen Alter, *see* Greisengesang
— Mitleiden Mariae, 632
Von Ida, 228
Vor meiner Wiege, 927

Wachtelschlag, Der, 742
Waldesnacht, *see* Im Walde (F. von Schlegel)
Wallensteiner Lanzknecht [or rather, Landsknecht] beim Trunk, Der, 931

TITLES OF VOCAL MUSIC 547

Wallfahrtsarie, *see* Abschied (Mayrhofer)
Wanderer an den Mond, Der, 870
——, Der (F. von Schlegel), 649
—— —— (Schmidt von Lübeck), 489, 493; *see also* 760
Wandern, Das, 795 (no. 1)
Wanderschaft, *see* Das Wandern
Wandrers Nachtlied (I), 224
—— —— (II), 768
Wasserflut, 911 (no. 6)
Wegweiser, Der, 911 (no. 20)
Wehmut (M. von Collin), 772
— (H. von Hüttenbrenner), *P.*, 825 (no. 1)
— (Die), (Salis), 404
Weiberfreund, Der, 271
Wein und Liebe, *P.*, 901
Weinen, Das, 926
Wer ist gross?, *P.*, 110
Wer kauft Liebesgötter?, 261
West-östlicher Divan, Songs from, 710, 715, 717, 719, 720
Westwind, *see* Suleika (II)
Wetterfahne, Die, 911 (no. 2)
Widerhall, 428
Widerschein, 639, 949
Widerspruch, *P.*, 865
Wie Ulfru fischt, 525
Wiedersehn, 855
Wiegenlied (Schlafe, schlafe, holder, süsser Knabe), 498
— (Körner), 304
— (Ottenwalt), *see* Der Knabe in der Wiege
— (Seidl), 867
Wilhelm Meister, *see* Gesänge, etc.
Willkommen und Abschied, 767
Winterabend (Der), 938
Winterlied, 401
Winterreise (song-cycle), 911
Wintertag, Der (doubtful), 984
Wirtshaus, Das, 911 (no. 21)
Wohin? 795 (no. 2)
Wolkenbraut, Die, 683
Wonne der Wehmut, 260; *see also* 918

Zauberglöckchen, Das, *O.*, 723
Zauberharfe, Die, *O.*, 644
Zufriedene, Der, 320
Zufriedenheit, *see* Lied (Claudius)
Zügenglöcklein, Das, 871
Zum Punsche, 492
Zum Rundetanz, *see* Lied beim Rundetanz
Zur guten Nacht, *P.*, 903
— Namensfeier des Herrn Andreas Siller, 83
Zürnende Barde, Der, 785
— Diana, Die, *see following entry*
Zürnenden Diana, Der, 707

Zwei Szenen aus 'Lacrimas,' 857
Zwei Tugendwege, Die, 71
Zwerg, Der, 771
Zwillingsbrüder, Die, *O.*, 647; *see also* 701

CLASSIFICATION

Album Leaves, 547, 550, 945

Ballads, 77, 93, 111, 134, 149, 152, 166, 208, 209, 211, 212, 213, 225, 246, 247, 255, 256, 328, 329, 367, 397, 473, 728, 771, 786, 792, 923

Canons, 54, 56, 65, 69, 70, 88, 92, 127, 130, 131, 357, 407, 582, 873, 988
Cantatas, 80, 110, 249, 294, 387, 407, 441, 451, 472, 666, 689, (710), 936, 942
Church Music, *see* Index of Authors, Classification, Liturgical Texts

Dramatic Music, *see* Stage Music
Duets, 92, 126a, 127, 169, 199, 202, 203, 204, 205, 253, 282, 286, 293, 312, 322, 352, 375, 395, 473, 488, 531, 534, 542, 545, 619, 725, 795 (no. 19), 877 (no. 1), 923; *see also* Stage Music

Exercises in Song Composition, 17, 33, 34, 35, 42, 69, 70, 76, 78, 510

Fair copies of Goethe songs (made by Schubert for the poet), 118, 119, 120, 121, 123, 138, 142, 149, 161, 162, 216, 224, 225, 226, 234, 247, 254, 255, 257, 258, 259, 260, 261, 310, 321, 328, 367, 368
Female Part-songs, 140, 269, 706, 757, 836, 921
Folksongs (quoted), 475, 529, 887, 929
Fragments and Unfinished Vocal Works, 11, 85, 132, 133, 137, 172, 239, 311, 327, 329, 332, 333, 339, 340, 341, 363, 425, 435, 453, 467, 484, 549, 564, 577, 596, 682, 689, 721, 725, 728, 755, 937, 981, 990, 991, 992; *see also* Sketches

Goethe songs, *see* Fair copies
Ghazals, 756, 779

Humorous Songs, 37, 271, 558, 749, 826, 866, 868, 902 (no. 3), 930
Hymnen, 55, 61, 64, 184 (note), 232, 659, 660, 661, 662, 687, 763, 839, 941, 948, 964, 983 (no. 2)

Incidental Music, 644, 723, 797; *see also* 458, 521, 829, 857

Kanons, *see* Canons

INDEX OF SCHUBERT'S WORKS

Male Part-songs (mostly Quartets), 75, 110, 267, 268, 330, 331, 337, 338, 356, 364, 407, 422, 494, 513, 538, 572, 598, 635, 641, 656, 657, 704, 705, 709, 710, 714, 724, 740, 747, 791, 809, 825, 835, 847, 848, 865, 875, 892, 893, 901, 903, 912, 913, 914, 916, 918, 941, 948, 964, 983, 984; *see also* Trios (male) *and* Duets

Melodramen, 84 (no. 14*a*), 644, 796 (nos. 15*a*, 16, 17*b*), 829

Mixed Part-songs, 17, 33, 34, 35, 47, 168, 232, 294, 330, 439, 440, 472, 609, 642, 665, 666, 689, 748, 763, 815, 826, 920, 930, 936, 942, 953, 954, 985, 986, 987, 992(?)

Nachgelassene Lieder (ed. by Friedlaender), 124, 142, 222, 227, 239, 245, 285, 342, 350, 404, 429, 465, 467, 475, 496, 499, 523, 559, 631, 646
—— (ed. by Gotthard), 342, 350, 465, 475, 533, 631
— *musikalische Dichtungen für Gesang und Pianoforte*, 59, 75, 95, 102, 111, 115, 116, 119, 120, 123, 126, 140, 150, 151, 153, 171, 174, 182, 197, 210, 217, 218, 219, 246, 255, 259, 261, 263, 264, 269, 274, 278, 280, 281, 282, 286, 290, 291, 293, 297, 300, 301, 321, 322, 343, 352, 358, 375, 393, 397, 403, 412, 432, 434, 436, 442, 444, 445, 450, 473, 474, 492, 508, 518, 520, 526, 534, 540, 548, 551, 560, 564, 578, 584, 585, 611, 614, 616, 620, 622, 623, 626, 632, 650, 651, 652, 653, 654, 669, 671, 674, 677, 684, 690, 694, 698, 699, 700, 708, 710, 712, 715, 716, 727, 736, 746, 749, 754, 762, 785, 788, 789, 792, 799, 805, 806, 807, 822, 832, 842, 854, 860, 861, 869, 876, 882, 883, 888, 889, 890, 906, 910, 931, 932, 933, 938, 949; *see also* pp. 496 f.

Operas, 84, 137, 435, 701, 732, 791, 796, 918, 982
Operettas, *see* Singspiele

Part-song Versions of Poems set as Songs, 38, 51 (53, 54, 57, 58, 60), 65, 67, 88, 129 (199), 203, 243, 331 (332), 337, 338, 364, 422, 424, 425, 494, 513, 538 (704, 705, 714), 656, 747, 809, 914

Part-songs without Titles, 16 (note), 92 (Duet), 131 (Terzet), 333 (Terzet), 657 (Quartet), 665 (Quartet), 725 (Duet), 873 (Sextet), 992 (?)

Photostats of autographs, *see* General Index under Photogramm-Archiv (Vienna)

Romances, 114, 144, 220 (no. 3), 222, 326 (no. 15), 435 (no. 7), 787 (no. 2), 796 (no. 6*a*), 797 (no. 3*b*)

Singspiele (Operetten), 11, 190, 220, 239, 326, 647, 787, 981
Sketches, 15, 39, 144, 201, 249, 269, 292, 387, 510, 598A, 645, 701, 704, 705, 874, 896, 916, 918, 982
Sonnets, 628, 629, 630, 673
Song Cycles, 478–80, 795, 877, 911, 957; *see also* Index of Titles under Sieben Gesänge aus Walter Scott's *Fräulein vom See*
Songs with Chorus, 169, 170, 183, (185A?), 186, 227, 228, (387?), (521?), 569, 822, 903, 920, 921, 942, 948, 953
Songs with Instrumental (other than Pianoforte solo *Accompaniment*, 80, 81, 83, 535, 704, 714, 748, 913, 936, 943, 954, 964, 965
Songs without Titles, 39, 92, 333, 555, 657, 665, 874, 991, 992,
Stage Music, 11, 84, 137, 190, 220, 239, 326, 435, 644, 647, 701, 723, 732, 787, 791, 796, 797, 918, 981, 982

Subjects of Vocal Music:

Apparitions, 15, 73, 116, 126, 150, 328, 494, 531, 545, 595, 957 (no. 13)
Battle, 81, 88, 140, 147, 169, 170, 171, 190 (no. 6), 205, 218, 249, 278, 281, 282, 375, 387, 443, 454, 822, 835, 837, 912, 957 (no. 2)
Biblical, 5, 942
Birds, 196, 201, 399, 497, 552, 691, 724, 742, 911 (no. 15), 957 (no. 14)
Bliss, 234, 262, 362, 433, 455, 501, 520, 743, 764, 795 (no. 11)
Cradle, 304, 498, 527, 579, 867, 927; *see also* 795 (no. 20)
Death, 7, 15, 38, 44, 50, 101, 116, 127, 140, 151, 168, 186, 201, 218, 224, 275, 289, 290, 292, 318, 330, 343, 371, 375, 377, 399, 432, 436, 437, 453, 454, 464, 472, 494, 496, 504, 512, 518, 526, 531, 545, 569, 616, 621, 654, 689, 736, 744, 758, 768, 795 (nos. 18, 20), 825, 836, 842, 864, 869, 871, 893, 911 (nos. 15, 20, 21), 926, 957 (no. 2)
Drinking, 75, 84 (no. 2), 148, 169, 183, 242, 248, 253, 267, 277, 356, 426, 427, 492, 644 (no. 5), 847, 888, 901, 931
Fishing, 225, 351, 364, 525, 550, 562, 639, 881, 933, 949, 957 (no. 10)
Flowers, 257, 431, 519, 622, 731, 745, 752, 786, 792, 795 (nos. 9, 18)
Friendship, 50, 75, 183, 246, 326, 435, 491, 504, 578, 749
Greek Mythology, 47, 51, 53, 54, 57, 58, 60, 61, 62, 63, 64, 65, 166, 312, 323,

TITLES OF VOCAL MUSIC

360, 369, 396, 450, 451, 474, 526, 540, 542, 544, 548, 554, 573, 583, 584, 585, 674, 677, 699, 707, 737, 801, 957 (no. 8), 983 (no. 2)
Hunting, 204, 215, 368, 521, 524, 588, 732 (no. 7), 795 (no. 14), 797 (no. 8), 843, 909, 930
Love, 55, 61, 62, 63, 64, 99, 109, 138, 162, 164, 177, 179, 180, 182, 187, 206, 207, 210, 233, 239 (no. 6), 241, 261, 302, 303, 308, 339, 352, 410, 412, 414, 418, 423, 430, 446, 465, 467, 477, 522, 558, 644 (no. 8a), 673, 682, 698, 747, 776, 795, 854, 909, 933, 957 (nos. 1–7, 14), 983 (no. 2), 988; *see also* Serenades, etc.
Misery, 118, 226, 466, 478, 479, 480, 489, 493, 671, 834, 876, 911, 957 (nos. 8–13)
Moon, 141, 193, 194, 238, 259, 296, 311, 436, 437, 468, 499, 614, 870, 875, 893
Music, 115, 149, 163, 165, 329, 342, 388, 391, 394, 406, 473, 482, 491, 546, 547, 737, 785, 848, 905, 920
Nature, 188, 337, 372, 393, 422, 444, 448, 563, 634, 651, 708, 738, 754, 757, 799, 851, 852, 917, 985, 986; *see also* Birds, Fishing, Flowers, Hunting, Seasons, Times of Day, *and* Water
Occasional, 80, 81, 83, 88, 104, 294, 407, 441, 451, 472, 535, 578, 635, 666, 695, 749, 762, 763, 826, 863, 920, 921, 936, 954
Patriotism, 81, 88, 104, 204, 205, 218, 287, 443, 912
Piety, 126, 168, 171, 232, 291, 379, 383, 440, 442, 443, 444, 448, 551, 623, 632, 650, 651, 658, 689, 757, 763, 815, 839, 852, 912, 941, 948, 954, 955, 964, 985, 986, 987
Professions, 247, 268, 274, 295, 392, 560; *see also* Fishing *and* Hunting
Seasons: Spring, 129, 130, 199. 202, 243, 244, 245, 283, 305, 338, 344, 398, 427, 448, 503, 587, 686, 709, 740, 882, 911 (no. 11), 914, 919, 957 (no. 3), 988; Summer, 289; Autumn, 405, 502, 945; Winter, 401, 911, 938, 984
Serenades (Abend- und Morgen-Ständchen), 119, 265, 635, 644 (no. 9), 698, 795 (no. 8), 848, 889, 891, 905, 921, 957 (no. 4); *see also* note to 96
Solitude, 489, 493, 620, 768, 800, 911 (no. 12), 932, 957 (nos. 8–13)
Stars, 172, 176, 203, 307, 313, 360, 444, 670, 684, 806, 861, 939
Sun, 236, 263, 270, 272, 276, 382, 439, 457, 495, 541, 627, 685, 690, 700, 753, 856, 911 (no. 23)

Times of Day: Morning, 163, 165, 264, 266, 273, 381, 685, 795 (no. 8), 918; Evening, 108, 221, 235, 236, 237, 265, 276, 357, 382, 405, 495, 499, 627, 650, 690, 806, 856, 938; Night, 119, 194, 289, 314, 358, 534, 672, 687, 752, 827, 862, 892, 903, 913, 983 (no. 4); *see also* Serenades
Water, 30, 77, 111, 124, 160, 192, 216, 300, 361, 530, 536, 539, 543, 553, 565, 586, 638, 694, 746, 766, 774, 795 (no. 20), 808, 809, 910, 911 (nos. 6, 7), 943, 957 (no. 12); *see also* Fishing

Terzette, *see* Trios
Transposed Songs, 138, 142, 493, 524, 715, 795 (nos. 7–9), 911 (nos. 6, 10, 12, 22, 24)
Trios (male), 37, 38, 43, 51, 53, 54, 55, 56, 57, 58, 60, 61, 62, 63, 64, 65, 67, 69, 70, 71, 80, 88, 129, 130, 131, 132, 133, 147, 148, 236, 242, 243, 244, 269, 277, 332, 333, 339, 340, 341, 357, 423, 424, 425, 426, 427, 428, 441, (442), 988
— (mixed), 666, 930

Unison Songs (choruses), 169, 569, 822

Versions (two or more settings of songs), 6 (191*a*, *b*, 389), 30 (192, 638*a*, *b*), 52 (636*a*, *b*), 73 (595*a*, *b*), 77 (111), 117 (252), 121*a*, *b*, 126*a*, *b*, 142*a* (*b*, *b*II, B, *c*, *d*), 149*a*, *b*, 160 (766), 161*a*, *b*, 162*a*, *b*, 163 (165), 164 (179), 174(2), 180(2), 187 (418), 208 (212), 215 (368), 223 (2), 235 (237), 245 (283, 587), 250 (793), 251 (637), 259 (296), 278 (2), 285*a*, *b*, 286*a*, *b*, 287*a*, *b*, 289*a*, *b*, 291*a*, *b*, *c*, 292 (371), 295*a*, *b*, 310*a*, *b* (359, 481, 877, nos. 1 and 4), 312*a*, *b*, 316*a*, *b*, 325 (478*a*, *b*), 327 (376), 328*a*, *b*, *c*, *d*, 330 (377, 569), 351 (562), 362 (501), 388*a*, *b*, 390 (577, I, II), 393 (563), 396 (583), 403*a*, *b*, 407 (441), 409 (2), 432*a*, *b* (512), 436 (437), 450*a*, *b*, 469 ([2], 727, 877, no. 3), 473*a*, *b*, 474*a*, *b*, 479*a*, *b*, 480*a*, *b*, *c*, 489 (493), 524*a*, A, *b*, 538 (704, 705, 714), 543*a*, *b*, 545*a*, *b*, 547*a*, *b*, 549 (721), 550*a*, *b*, *c*, *d*, *e*, 579 (2), 598A (641), 588 (2), 639 (949), 677*a*, *b*, 678 (2), 686*a*, *a*¹, *b*, 707*a*, *b*, 709 (740), 713*a*, *b*, 726 (877, no. 2), 745*a*, *b*, 756*a*, *b*, 761*a*, *b*, 764*a*, *b*, 767*a*, *b*, 800*a*, *b*, 833*a*, *a'*,*b*, 851*a*, *b*, 881*a*, *b*, 911, nos. 10 (10*a*), 12 (12*a*), 24 (24*a*), 920 (921), 922*a*, *b*, 923*a*, *b*, 941 (948, 964); *see also* Part-song Versions
Vocal Exercises, 619, 688

INDEX OF SCHUBERT'S WORKS

B. First Lines

Abendgewölke schweben hell. *Stimme der Liebe*, 187, 418
Abendglockenhalle zittern. *Der Herbstabend*, 405
Ach! aus dieses Tales Gründen. *Sehnsucht*, 52, 636
—, der Gebirgssohn hängt mit kindlicher Lieb. *Das Heimweh*, 851
—! es ist schön, fremde Länder zu seh'n. *Der Spiegelritter*, 11 (no. 4a)
— —, Herr, wie lange willst du mein so ganz vergessen? *Der 13. Psalm*, 663
— liebes Herz, ach Theobald. *Der Hochzeitsbraten*, 930
—, mir ist das Herz so schwer. *Lied in der Abwesenheil*, 416
—, mir schallt's dorten. *Der Wachtelschlag*, 742
—, neige, du Schmerzenreiche. *Gretchen*, 564
—, nun ist der Teufel los! *Des Teufels Lustschloss*, 84 (no. 11)
—, um deine feuchten Schwingen. *Suleika II*, 717
—, was soll ich beginnen. *Delphine*, 857 (no. 2)
—, wer bringt die schönen Tage. *Erster Verlust*, 226
Ade! du muntre, du fröhliche Stadt. *Abschied*, 957 (no. 7)
Agnus Dei, *see* Masses
Ahidi, ich liebe. *Hänflings Liebeswerbung*, 552
Aimè, io tremo. *Il traditor deluso*, 902 (no. 2)
Alle Freuden, alle Gaben. *Claudine von Villa Bella*, 239 (no. 4)
All' mein Wirken, all' mein Leben. *Als ich sie erröten sah*, 153
Allein, nachdenklich, wie gelähmt. *Sonett II*, 629
Allgnädiger, heile du. *Lazarus I*, 689
Al par del ruscelletto. *Kantate zur Feier der Genesung der Irene Kiesewetter*, 936
Als bei dem Kreuz Maria stand. *Vom Mitleiden Mariae*, 632
— der Frühling sich vom Herzen. *Vergissmeinnicht*, 792
— — einst schon hinter blauer Berge Rücken. *Fernando*, 220 (no. 3)
— ich still und ruhig spann. *Die Spinnerin*, 247
Alte Liebe rostet nie. *Alte Liebe rostet nie*, 477
Am Bach viel kleine Blumen stehn. *Des Müllers Blumen*, 795 (no. 9)

Am Brunnen vor dem Tore. *Der Lindenbaum*, 911 (no. 5)
— fernen Horizonte. *Die Stadt*, 957 (no. 11)
— hohen, hohen Turm. *Ammenlied*, 122
— Rand der Eb'ne. *Fierabras*, 796 (no. 4c)
— Seegestad'. *Erinnerungen*, 98, 424
An dem jungen Morgenhimmel. *Don Gayseros III*, 93
— der Quelle sass der Knabe. *Der Jüngling am Bache*, 30, 192, 638
— die Türen will ich schleichen. *Harfenspieler II, Gesänge des Harfners III*, 479
Anbetend Deine Macht und Grösse. *Deutsche Messe, Anhang*, 872
Apollo, lebet noch dein hold Verlangen. *Sonett I*, 628
Arbeitsam und wacker. *Pflügerlied*, 392
Arm am Beutel, krank am Herzen. *Der Schatzgräber*, 256
Auf den Blumen flimmern Perlen. *Nach einem Gewitter*, 561
— — Wassern wohnt mein stilles Leben. *Lebensmelodien*, 395
— der Berge freien Höhen. *Punschlied. Im Norden zu singen*, 253
— — Wellen Spiegel. *Auf der Donau*, 553
— dich träufle Taues Regen. *Fernando*, 220 (no. 7)
— einen Totenacker. *Das Wirtshaus*, 911 (no. 21)
—, es dunkelt. *Lied beim Rundetanz*, 132
—, ewig dein. *Widerhall*, 428
— hohem Bergesrücken. *Der Alpenjäger*, 524
—, ihr Freunde. *Trinklied aus dem XVI. Jahrhundert*, 847
—! jeder sei nun froh und sorgenfrei! *Trinklied*, 267
— seinem gold'nen Throne. *Liedesend*, 473
Auguste jam coelestium, 488
Aus Blumen deuten die Damen gern. *Die Freunde von Salamanka*, 326 (no. 10)
Ave Maria! Jungfrau mild! *Ellen's Gesang III (Hymne an die Jungfrau)*, 839
Ave Maria! maiden mild! *see* preceding entry

Bacchus, feister Fürst des Weins. *Trinklied*, 888
Bächlein, lass dein Rauschen sein. *Mein!*, 795 (no. 11)

FIRST LINES

Bald tönet der Reigen. *Fierabras*, 796 (no. 18)
— wird es klar. *Fierabras*, 796 (no. 19)
Bedecke deinen Himmel, Zeus. *Prometheus*, 674
Beglückt, beglückt, wer dich erblickt. *Der Liebende*, 207
Begrabt den Leib in seiner Gruft. *Begräbnislied*, 168
Bei der Liebe reinsten Flammen. *An Chloen II*, 462
— des Entschlaf'nen Trauerbahre. *Deutsche Trauermesse*, 621 (no. 1)
— dir allein empfind' ich. *Bei dir allein!*, 866 (no. 2)
Bekränzet die Tonnen und zapfet mir Wein. *Trinklied im Mai*, 427
Benedictus es, Domine. *Graduale*, 184
Bescheiden verborgen im buschichten Gang. *Die Nachtigall*, 724
Beschlossen ist's, ich löse seine Ketten! *Fierabras*, 796 (no. 8a)
Betrachtend Deine Huld und Güte. *Deutsche Messe*, 872 (no. 6)
Beugt euch aus euren Wolken nieder. *Ossian's 'Lied nach dem Falle Nathos,'* 278
Bist du bereit. *Prometheus* (Cantata), 451
Blüht denn hier an Tauris Strande. *Iphigenia*, 573
Braust des Unglücks Sturm empor. *Trost im Liede*, 546
Brüder, schrecklich brennt die Thräne. *Lied*, 535
—, unser Erdenwallen. *Trinklied*, 148
Bunt sind schon die Wälder. *Herbstlied*, 502

Christ is erstanden. *Chor der Engel*, 440
Cidli, du weinest. *Furcht der Geliebten*, 285
Clamavi ad te. *Offertorium*, 85
Come, thou monarch of the vine, *see* Bacchus, feister Fürst des Weins
Cum angelis et pueris. *Antiphons*, 696 (no. 5)
Cypris, meiner Phyllis gleich. *Die Liebesgötter*, 446

Da droben auf jenem Berge. *Schäfers Klagelied*, 121
— liegt er, starr. *Kantate zu Ehren Josef Spendou's*, 472
— quel sembiante appresi. *Canzone III*, 688
— sitz' ich ohne Bogen. *Philoktet*, 540
— voi, cari lumi. *L'incanto degli occhi*, 902 (no. 1)

Dank dir, Göttin, warmen Dank. *Adrast*, 137 (no. 1)
Darf dich dein Kind umarmen? *Alfonso und Estrella*, 732 (no. 20)
Das also, das ist der enge Schrein. *Vor meiner Wiege*, 927
— Fischergewerbe gibt rüstigen Mut! *Fischerlied*, 351, 364, 562
— Glas gefüllt! *Trinklied im Winter*, 242
— Grab ist tief und stille. *Das Grab*, 330, 377, 569
— hast du wohl bereitet. *Claudine von Villa Bella*, 239 (no. 1)
— Leben ist ein Traum. *Das Leben*, 269
— Meer erglänzte weit hinaus. *Am Meer*, 957 (no. 12)
— Wandern ist des Müllers Lust. *Das Wandern*, 795 (no. 1)
— Wasser rauscht, das Wasser schwoll. *Der Fischer*, 225
Dass der Ostwind Düfte hauchet. *Dass sie hier gewesen*, 775
— ich dich verloren habe. *Am Grabe Anselmo's*, 504
Dein Schwert, wie ist's vom Blut so rot! *Eine altschottische Ballade*, 923
— Silber schien durch Eichengrün. *Klage an den Mond*, 436, 437
— süsses Bild, Edone. *Edone*, 445
Deinem Willen nachzugeben. *Claudine von Villa Bella*, 239 (no. 8)
Dem Erfolg vertrauen wir des Friedens Glück. *Fierabras*, 796 (no. 4e)
— König Heil, dem König Heil! *Adrast*, 137 (no. 3)
— Schnee, dem Regen. *Rastlose Liebe*, 138
— Vater liegt das Kind im Arm. *Der Vater mit dem Kind*, 906
Den Fischer fechten Sorgen. *Fischerweise*, 881
— Tag hindurch nur einmal. *Memnon*, 541
Der Abend blüht, der Westen glüht. *Das Abendrot*, 236
— —, Temora glüht. *Der Abend*, 221
— — rötet nun das Tal. *Abendlied der Fürstin*, 495
— — rückt heran. *Die Bürgschaft*, 435 (no. 16)
— — schleiert Flur und Hain. *Geist der Liebe*, 414, 747
— — sinkt auf stiller Flur. *Fierabras*, 796 (no. 6a)
— bleiche, kalte Mond. *Loda's Gespenst*, 150
— Damm zerreisst. *Johanna Sebus*, 728
— Dämm'rung Schein durchblinkt den Hain. *Geisternähe*, 100
— du so lustig rauschtest. *Auf dem Flusse*, 911 (no. 7)

552 INDEX OF SCHUBERT'S WORKS

Der du von dem Himmel bist. *Wandrers Nachtlied I*, 224
— Eichwald braus(e)t. *Des Mädchens Klage*, 6, 191, 389
— Ernst hat mir bereifet, *see* Der Frost, etc.
— Friede sei mit euch. *Pax Vobiscum*, 551
— Frommen abgeschied'ne Seelen. *Deutsche Trauermesse*, 621 (no. 7)
— Frost hat mir bereifet. *Greisengesang*, 778
— Frühlingssonne holdes Lächeln, *Wiedersehn*, 855
— Hoffnung Strahl, den du gegeben. *Fierabras*, 796 (no. 16)
— Jäger ruhte hingegossen. *Die Wolkenbraut*, 683
— Knabe seufzt. *Atys*, 585
— König sass beim frohen Mahle. *Die drei Sänger*, 329
— Landestöchter fromme Pflichten. *Fierabras*, 796 (no. 4d)
— Lerche wolkennahe Lieder. *Sehnsucht*, 516
— Mond ist aufgegangen. *Abendlied*, 499
— Morgen blüht; der Osten glüht. *Von Ida*, 228
— Nachen dröhnt. *Fahrt zum Hades*, 526
— Odem Gottes weht. *Himmelsfunken*, 651
— Rache Opfer fallen. *Fierabras*, 796 (no. 22)
— Reif hat einen weissen Schein. *Der greise Kopf*, 911 (no. 14)
— runde Silberfaden. *Fierabras*, 796 (no. 1)
— Schnee zerinnt. *Mailied*, 130, 202
— Sieg begleitet meine tapfern Heere. *Fierabras*, 796 (no. 23b)
— Tag entflieht, der Abend glüht. *Das Zauberglöckchen*, 723 (no. 1)
— Tod rückt Seelen vor's Gericht. *Deutsche Trauermesse*, 621 (no. 2)
— Vater mag wohl immer Kind mich nennen. *Die Zwillingsbrüder*, 647 (no. 3)
— Vollmond strahlt auf Bergeshöh'n. *Rosamunde*, 797 (no. 3b)
— Wind spielt mit der Wetterfahne. *Die Wetterfahne*, 911 (no. 2)
Des Jammers herbe Qualen. *Fierabras*, 796 (no. 21)
— Krieges Los hat euch mir übergeben. *Fierabras*, 796 (no. 4b)
— Lebens Tag ist schwer. *Lied*, 788
— Menschen Seele gleicht dem Wasser. *Gesang der Geister über den Wassern*, 484, 538, 704, 705, 714

Des Mondes Zauberblume lacht. *Mondenschein*, 875
— Phöbus Strahlen . . . *Zur Namensfeier des Herrn Andreas Siller*, 83
— stolzen Männerlebens schönste Zeichen. *Lied eines Kriegers*, 822
Dessen Fahne Donnerstürme wallte. *Elysium*, 58
Dich rief ich, Eginhard, den einzig Treuen. *Fierabras*, 796 (no. 6g)
Die Abendglocke läutet. *Wehmut*, 825 (no. 1)
— Angel zuckt, die Rute bebt. *Wie Ulfru fischt*, 525
— Beute lass, o Herr, die Krieger teilen. *Fierabras*, 796 (no. 4a)
— bretterne Kammer der Toten erbebt. *Der Geistertanz*, 15, 116, 494
— Brüder haben sich gefunden. *Die Zwillingsbrüder*, 647 (no. 10)
— Brust, gebeugt von Sorgen. *Fierabras*, 796 (no. 13)
— erste Liebe füllt das Herz. *Die erste Liebe*, 182
— frohe neubelebte Flur. *Morgenlied*, 381
— Liebe hat gelogen. *Die Liebe hat gelogen*, 751
— linden Lüfte sind erwacht. *Frühlingsglaube*, 686
— Luft is blau. *Frühlingslied*, 243, 398
— Munterkeit ist meinen Wangen . . . *An Chloen I*, 363
— Mutter hat mich jüngst gescholten. *Die Unterscheidung*, 866 (no. 1)
— — sucht ihr liebes Kind. *Die Bürgschaft*, 435 (no. 7)
— Nacht bricht an. *Der Unglückliche*, 713
— — — bald herein. *Norman's Gesang*, 846
— Nachtigall singt überall. *Seufzer*, 198
— Nacht ist dumpfig und finster. *Die Nacht*, 534
— — heiter und ist rein. *Nachthelle*, 892
— Prinzessin ist erschienen! *Alfonso und Estrella*, 732 (no. 19)
— Scheibe friert, der Wind ist rauh. *Sehnsucht*, 879
— Schöne, die dich hergesandt. *Des Teufels Lustschloss*, 84 (no. 17)
— Schwerter hoch geschwungen. *Alfonso und Estrella*, 732 (no. 34a)
— Sonne sinkt ins tiefe Meer. *Alinde*, 904
— — —, o könnt' ich mit ihr scheiden. *Der Jüngling und der Tod*, 545
— — steigt, die Sonne sinkt. *Klage*, 415
— — zieht in gold'nen Strahlen. *Die Freunde von Salamanka*, 326 (no. 1)

FIRST LINES

Die Winde sausen am Tannenhang. *Über Wildemann*, 884
— Wogen am Gestade schwellen. *Schiffers Scheidelied*, 910
— Zauberin lasst uns betrügen. *Die Zauberharfe*, 644 (no. 7)
Diese Gnade dank ich dir. *Die Bürgschaft*, 435 (no. 5)
Dioskuren, Zwillingsterne. *Lied eines Schiffers an die Dioskuren*, 360
Dir, Mädchen, schlägt mit leisem Beben. *Liebesrausch*, 164, 179
—, Vater! weihen wir hier Gaben. *Deutsche Trauermesse*, 621 (no. 4)
Doch horch! was regt sich noch in stiller Nacht? *Fierabras*, 796 (no. 6c)
— im Getümmel der Schlacht. *Alfonso und Estrella*, 732 (no. 8b)
— nun werde deinem Retter. *Alfonso und Estrella*, 732 (no. 27)
Don Gayseros, Don Gayseros. *Don Gayseros I*, 93
Dona nobis, 185
Dort blinket durch Weiden. *Des Fischers Liebesglück*, 933
— ist ihr Grab. *Ihr Grab*, 736
— raget ein Berg. *Genügsamkeit*, 143
Draussen in der weiten Nacht. *Im Freien*, 880
Drei Sonnen sah ich am Himmel steh'n. *Die Nebensonnen*, 911 (no. 23)
Dreifach ist der Schritt der Zeit. *Sprüche des Confucius*, 43, 69
Droben nur ist wahres Leben! *Deutsche Trauermesse*, 621 (no. 5)
Drüben hinterm Dorfe. *Der Leiermann*, 911 (no. 24)
Du bist die Ruh'. *Du bist die Ruh'*, 776
— brachst sie nun, die kalte Rinde. *Am Bach im Frühling*, 381
—, der ewig um mich trauert. *Pflicht und Liebe*, 467
— gabst, o Herr, mir Sein und Leben. *Deutsche Messe*, 872 (no. 4)
— gehst in Kerker, du? *Die Bürgschaft*, 435 (no. 9)
— guter Heinrich! Du süsses Kind! *Der vierjährige Posten*, 190 (no. 2)
— heilig, glühend Abendrot! *Das Abendrot*, 627
— holde Kunst. *An die Musik*, 547
— kleine grünumwachs'ne Quelle. *An eine Quelle*, 530
— rührst mich, Teurer, sehr. *Alfonso und Estrella*, 732 (no. 6a)
— sagtest mir es, Mutter. *Die Männer sind méchant!*, 866 (no. 3)
— schönes Fischermädchen. *Das Fischermädchen*, 957 (no. 10)

Du Schrecklicher. *Gott im Ungewitter*, 985
— Schwert an meiner Linken. *Schwertlied*, 170
— staunest, o Mensch. *Die Sterne*, 684
— Turm! zu meinem Leide. *Der Hirt*, 490
— Urquell aller Güte. *Gebet*, 815
— verstörst uns nicht, o Nacht. *Die Nacht*, 358
— wirst mir nicht entrinnen! *Alfonso und Estrella*, 732 (no. 25)
Durch der Ostsee wilde Wogen. *Rüdiger's Heimkehr*, 791
— — Töne Zaubermacht. *Die Zauberharfe*, 644 (no. 13)
— eine ganze Nacht sich nah zu sein. *Der Morgenkuss nach einem Ball*, 264
— Feld und Wald zu schweifen. *Der Musensohn*, 764
— Fichten am Hügel. *Lied der Liebe* 109

Edit Nonna, edit Clerus. *Trinklied aus dem XVI. Jahrhundert*, 847
Eh' die Sonne früh aufersteht. *Morgenlied*, 685
Ehre sei dem Hocherhab'nen. *Das grosse Halleluja*, 442
— — Gott in der Höhe! *Deutsche Messe*, 872 (no. 2)
Ein Blick von deinen Augen ... *Die Liebende schreibt*, 673
— Fräulein klagt' im finstern Turm. *Das Fräulein im Turme. Romanze*, 114
— — schaut vom hohen Turm. *Ballade*, 134
— heilig Säuseln ... *An die Apfelbäume, wo ich Julien erblickte*, 197
— jugendlicher Maienschwung ... *Der Triumph der Liebe*, 61
— Jüngling auf dem Hügel ... *Der Jüngling auf dem Hügel*, 702
— Licht tanzt freundlich vor mir her. *Täuschung*, 911 (no. 19)
— Mädchen ist's, das früh und spät. *Das Bild*, 155
— Münich steht in seiner Zell'. *Der Kreuzzug*, 932
— Schäfer sass im Grünen. *Der Schäfer und der Reiter*, 517
— schlafend Kind! *Adrast*, 137 (no. 7)
— sehnend Streben ... *Fülle der Liebe*, 854
— Sinnbild auf dem blanken Schild. *Der Spiegelritter*, 11 (no. 5)
— Vater starb von des Sohnes Hand. *Der Vatermörder*, 10
— wackres Tier, das müsst Ihr sagen. *Die Freunde von Salamanka*, 326 (no. 11)

Eine Krähe war mit mir. *Die Krähe*, 911 (no. 15)
— Mühle seh' ich blinken. *Halt !*, 795 (no. 3)
Einsam schleich' ich durch die Zimmer. *Die Freunde von Salamanka*, 326 (no. 4)
— wandelt dein Freund. *Adelaide*, 95
Empfange nun aus meiner Hand. *Alfonso und Estrella*, 732 (no. 34)
Endlich steh'n die Pforten offen. *Schwangesang*, 318
Entra l'uomo allor che nasce. *Isacco*, 33
Er fiel den Tod fürs Vaterland. *Grablied*, 218
— ist mein Vater, halte ein! *Fierabras*, 796 (no. 23a)
— — uns geschieden. *Coronach*, 836
— liegt und schläft. *An die Nachtigall*, 497
— schläft so süss. *Der Knabe in der Wiege*, 579
Erhab'ner, verehrter Freund der Jugend. *Namensfeier für F. M. Vierthaler*, 294
Erheit're dich. *Adrast*, 137
Ertöne Leier zur Festesfeier. *Kantate zur Namensfeier des Vaters*, 80
Ertönet, ihr Saiten. *Ewige Liebe*, 825 (no. 2)
Es bellen die Hunde. *Im Dorfe*, 911 (no. 17)
— brennt mir unter beiden Sohlen. *Rückblick*, 911 (no. 8)
— deuten die Blumen. *Die Blumensprache*, 519
— erhebt sich eine Stimme. *Claudine von Villa Bella*, 239 (no. 5)
— floh die Zeit im Wirbelfluge. *Der Flug der Zeit*, 515
— funkelt der Morgen. *Der Graf von Gleichen*, 918
— ging ein Mann zur Frühlingszeit. *Die Perle*, 466
— ist dein streng Gebot. *Alfonso und Estrella* 732 (no. 5a)
— — doch meine Nachbarin. *Der Goldschmiedsgesell*, 560
— — ein halbes Himmelreich. *Blumenlied*, 431
— — so angenehm, so süss. *Lied*, 284
— — so still, so heimlich. *Der Winterabend*, 938
— lebe der meut'rische Tor. *Die Bürgschaft*, 435 (no. 4)
— liebt' in Welschland irgendwo. *Die Nonne*, 208, 212
— lockte schöne Wärme. *Die Rose*, 745
— mahnt der Wald. *Schlaflied*, 527
— murmeln die Quellen. *Die Freunde von Salamanka*, 326 (no. 15)

Es rauschen die Winde so herbstlich. *Herbst*, 945
— reden und träumen die Menschen. *Hoffnung*, 251, 637
— redet und träumet die Jugend so viel. *Der Tanz*, 826
— rieselt, klar und wehend. *Die Einsiedelei*, 337, 393, 563
— schlug mein Herz. *Willkommen und Abschied*, 767
— schmückt die weiten Säle. *Alfonso und Estrella*, 732 (no. 7b)
— tanzen Mond und Sterne. *(Der) Gondelfahrer*, 808, 809
— tönet sein Lob. *Die Gestirne*, 444
— träumen die Wolken. *Beim Winde*, 669
— war ein König in Thule. *Der König in Thule*, 367
— wehet kühl und leise. *Die Gebüsche*, 646
Euch, Blümlein, will ich senden. *Der Blumenbrief*, 622
—, die von uns geschieden. *Deutsche Trauermesse*, 621 (no. 10)
Ewig still steht die Vergangenheit. *Sprüche des Confucius*, 70
Fels auf Felsen hingewälzet. *Aus Heliopolis II*, 754
Ferne von der grossen Stadt. *Lied*, 483
Fliegt der Schnee mir ins Gesicht. *Mut*, 911 (no. 22)
For leagues along the watery way, *see* Mich führt mein Weg
Fort will ich, fort! den Betrug entlarven. *Des Teufels Lustschloss*, 84 (no. 6)
Fremd bin ich eingezogen. *Gute Nacht*, 911 (no. 1)
Freude, die im frühen Lenze. *Freude der Kinderjahre*, 455
—, schöner Götterfunken. *An die Freude*, 189
Freuden sonder Zahl. *Seligkeit*, 433
Freudvoll und leidvoll. *Klärchen's Lied*, 210
Freund, eilet euch zu retten! *Der vierjährige Posten*, 190 (no. 4)
—, wie wird die Sache enden. *Die Freunde von Salamanka*, 326 (no. 6)
Freunde, deren Grüfte sich schon bemoosten. *Die Schatten*, 50
—, sammelt euch im Kreise. *Trinklied*, 75
Freundlich bist du mir erschienen. *Alfonso und Estrella*, 732 (no. 14)
— ist dein Antlitz. *An den Mond in einer Herbstnacht*, 614
Friede sei um diesen Grabstein. *Bei dem Grabe meines Vaters*, 496

FIRST LINES

Friedlich lieg' ich hingegossen. *Der Schiffer*, 694
Frisch atmet des Morgens lebendiger Hauch. *Der Flüchtling*, 67
— auf, ihr Jäger, frei und flink! *Jägerlied*, 204
— trabe sonder Ruh' und Rast. *Auf der Bruck*, 853
Fröhlicher Lebensmut. *Lebensmut*, 937
—, seliger, herrlicher Tag! *Claudine von Villa Bella*, 239 (no. 2)
Füllest wieder Busch und Tal. *An den Mond*, 259, 296
Funkelnd im Becher. *Trinklied*, 356

Ganz verloren, ganz versunken. *Huldigung*, 240
Gar fröhlich kann ich scheiden. *Fröhliches Scheiden*, 896
— tröstlich kommt geronnen. *Das Weinen*, 926
Gefror'ne Tropfen fallen. *Gefror'ne Thränen*, 911 (no. 3)
Gelagert unterm hellen Dach der Bäume. *Die Freunde von Salamanka*, 326 (no. 12)
Geöffnet sind des Winters Riegel. *Frühlingslied*, 914, 919
Geschmückt von Glanz und Siegen. *Alfonso und Estrella*, 732 (no. 4)
Gesetzt, ihr habt wirklich gewagt und gestritten. *Die Verschworenen*, 787 (no. 10)
Gesundheit ist mit Mut verschwistert. *Des Teufels Lustschloss*, 84 (no. 8)
Geuss, lieber Mond. *An den Mond*, 193
— nicht so laut. *An die Nachtigall*, 196
Gib mir die Fülle der Einsamkeit. *Einsamkeit*, 620
—, Schwester, mir die Harf' herab. *Der Liedler*, 209
Glanz des Guten und des Schönen, [Im,] see Dir, Mädchen, *etc.*
Glänzende Waffe den Krieger erfreut. *Alfonso und Estrella*, 732 (no. 10)
Glaube, hoffe, liebe! *Glaube, Hoffnung, und Liebe*, 955
Gnäd'ge Frau, ich hab' die Ehre. *Die Freunde von Salamanka*, 326 (no. 18).
Gold'ner Schein. *Abendlandschaft*, 357
Gott! höre meine Stimme. *Der vierjährige Posten*, 190 (no. 5)
— ist mein Hirt. *Der 23. Psalm*, 706
—, lass die Glocke glücklich steigen. *Glaube, Hoffnung und Liebe*, 954
Gottes Liebe. *Lazarus I*, 689
Grabe, Spaten, grabe! *Totengräberlied*, 38, 44
Gross ist der Herr. *Gott in der Natur*, 757
— — Jehova, der Herr. *Die Allmacht*, 852
Gross und rotentflammet. *Abendlied*, 276
Grosser Taten tat der Ritter. *Romanze des Richard Löwenherz*, 907
Grüner wird die Au. *Mailied*, 129, 199, 503
Guarda, che bianca luna. *Canzone II*, 688
Guerrilla, zieht durch Feld und Wald. *Die Freunde von Salamanka*, 326 (no. 9)
Gute Ruh, gute Ruh. *Des Baches Wiegenlied*, 795 (no. 20)
Guten Morgen, schöne Müllerin. *Morgengruss*, 795 (no. 8)
Gütigster, Bester, Weisester. *Kantate zur fünfzigjährigen Jubelfeier des Herrn Salieri*, 407, 441

Ha! Die Mörder meines Gatten! *Des Teufels Lustschloss*, 84 (no. 20)
Ha, dort kömmt er. *Hermann und Thusnelda*, 322
—, hier waltet ein Verrat! *Fierabras*, 796 (no. 6d)
—! Wie? Emmahier? an des Barbaren Arm? *Fierabras*, 796 (no. 6f)
Hab' ich dich wieder! *Des Teufels Lustschloss*, 84 (no. 21)
Hail to the Chief, see Triumph, er naht
Halte graues Haar in Ehren. *Der Spiegelritter*, 11 (no. 6)
Harfentöne lasst erklingen. *Die Zauberharfe*, 644 (no. 1)
Hark, hark, the lark, see Horch, horch, die Lerch
Harrt ein Fischer auf der Brücke. *Widerschein*, 639; see also Tom lehnt harrend , . .
Hast du Lianen nicht gesehen? *Liane*, 298
— — vergessen, kannst du ermessen. *Des Teufels Lustschloss*, 84 (no. 15a)
Hätt' ich tausend Arme zu rühren. *Am Feierabend*, 795 (no. 5)
Hauche milder, Abendluft. *Grablied für die Mutter*, 616
He is gone on the mountain, see Er ist uns geschieden
He! schenket mir im Helme ein. *Der Wallensteiner Lanzknecht* [or rather, *Landsknecht*] *beim Trunk*, 931
Hebt mich der Stürme Flügel. *Lazarus II*, 689
Heil dem mächt'gen Triebe. *Des Teufels Lustschloss*, 84 (no. 23)
—! dies ist die letzte Zähre. *Die Sterbende*, 186
— Euch, Herr Ritter, in kraftvoller Jugend. *Der Spiegelritter*, 11 (no. 1)
Heil'ge Nacht, du sinkest nieder! *Nacht und Träume*, 827

INDEX OF SCHUBERT'S WORKS

Heilig, heilig, heilig. *Deutsche Messe,* 872 (no. 5)
Heiss mich nicht reden. *Mignon I,* 726; *Lied der Mignon,* 877 (no. 2)
Heiter strahlt der neue Morgen. *Der vierjährige Posten,* 190 (no. 1)
Herr Bacchus ist ein braver Mann. *Trinklied,* 426
—, du hast mein Fleh'n vernommen. *Deutsche Messe,* 827 (no. 8)
— Ritter, zu Hilfe. *Des Teufels Lustschloss,* 84 (no. 9)
—, unser Gott, erhöre unser Flehen. *Hymnus an den heiligen Geist,* 964
Herrlich auf des Berges Höhen. *Alfonso und Estrella,* 732 (no. 21)
— prangt bei Morgenglanze. *Der Frühlingsmorgen,* 666
Herzen, die gen Himmel sich erheben. *An Laura,* etc., 115
Herzliebe, gute Mutter. *Das Echo,* 868
Heute will ich fröhlich sein. *Am ersten Maimorgen,* 344
Hie und da ist an den Bäumen. *Letzte Hoffnung,* 911 (no. 16)
Hier am Hügel heissen Sandes. *Hagar's Klage,* 5
— auf den Fluren, mit rosigen Wangen. *Rosamunde,* 797 (no. 7)
— lasst mich ruh'n die letzte Stunde. *Lazarus I,* 689
— strecket der wallende Pilger. *Elysium,* 57
— umarmen sich getreue Gatten. *Elysium,* 60
— unten steht ein Ritter. *Des Fräuleins Liebeslauschen,* 698
High deeds achieved of knightly fame, see Grosser Taten tat der Ritter
Hilfe, Hilfe! hier ist. *Des Teufels Lustschloss,* 84 (no. 1)
—! Rettung! *Die Bürgschaft,* 435 (no. 1)
—! Welche Stimme! *Alfonso und Estrella,* 732 (no. 26)
Hin und wieder fliegen die Pfeile. *Claudine von Villa Bella,* 239 (no. 3)
Hinab, ihr Brüder, in den Schacht! *Bergknappenlied,* 268
Hinaus mein Blick. *Abendlied für die Entfernte,* 856
Hinter Büschen, hinterm Laub (Räuberlied). *Die Bürgschaft,* 435 (no. 13)
Hinüber wall' ich. *Nachthymne,* 687
Hoch auf dem alten Turme. *Geistes-Gruss,* 142
— — — Gipfel deiner Gebirge. *Auf der Riesenkoppe,* 611
— und ehern schier von Dauer. *Adelwold und Emma,* 211
Holder klingt der Vogelsang. *Minnelied,* 429

Hör' ich das Pförtchen nicht gehen? *Die Erwartung,* 159
Horch die Seufzer uns'rer Mutter. *Die Bürgschaft,* 435 (no. 12)
—, horch, die Lerch' im Aetherblau. *Ständchen,* 889
—, wie Murmeln des empörten Meeres. *Gruppe aus dem Tartarus,* 65, 396, 583
Horcht auf! Es schlägt die Stunde. *Zur guten Nacht,* 903
Hörnerklänge rufen klagend. *Trost,* 367
Hörst du rufen, hörst du lärmen? *Alfonso und Estrella,* 732 (no. 24)
— — von den Nachtigallen. *Die gefangenen Sänger,* 712
Hosanna filio David. *Antiphons,* 696 (no. 1)
Hülfe . . ., see Hilfe . . .
Huntsman, rest, see Jäger, ruhe von der Jagd!

I never yet could see, see Noch fand von Evens Töchterscharen
Ich auf der Erd', am Himmel du. *Der Wanderer an den Mond,* 870
— bin beschämt, das Recht hab' ich verloren. *Die Verschworenen,* 787 (no. 12)
— — der wohlbekannte Sänger. *Der Rattenfänger,* 255
— — ein deutsches Mädchen. *Vaterlandslied,* 287
— — Waller auf der Erde. *Pilgerweise,* 789
— — vergnügt. *Lied,* 362, 501
— — von aller Ruh geschieden. *Tiefes Leid,* 876
— — lockerem Schlage. *Frohsinn,* 520
— danke Gott und freue mich. *Täglich zu singen,* 533
— denke dein, wenn durch den Hain. *Andenken,* 99, 423
— — —, — mir der Sonne Schimmer. *Nähe des Geliebten,* 162
— frage keine Blume. *Der Neugierige,* 795 (no. 6)
— hab' ein Bächlein funden. *Daphne am Bach,* 411
— — — heisses junges Blut. *Das gestörte Glück,* 309
— — — Mädchen funden. *Das Finden,* 219
— — eine Brieftaub' in meinem Sold. *Die Taubenpost,* 957 (no. 14)
— — in mich gesogen, 16 (note)
— hört' ein Bächlein rauschen. *Wohin?,* 795 (no. 2)
— habe gewagt und habe gestritten. *Die Verschworenen,* 787 (no. 9)

FIRST LINES

Ich komme vom Gebirge her. *Der Wanderer,* 489, 493
— lach', ich wein'. *Des Teufels Lustschloss,* 84 (no. 22)
— lag auf grünen Matten. *Die Erscheinung,* 229
— lebe noch und glaub' es kaum. *Des Teufels Lustschloss,* 84 (no. 12a)
— möchte zieh'n in die Welt hinaus. *Die böse Farbe,* 795 (no. 17)
— muss sie finden. *Die Verschworenen,* 787 (no. 8)
— rühme mir mein Dörfchen hier. *Das Dörfchen,* 598, 641
— sag' es jedem, dass er lebt. *Hymne IV,* 662
— sass an einer Tempelhalle, 39
— schiess' den Hirsch. *Jägers Liebeslied,* 909
— schleiche bang' und still herum. *Die Verschworenen,* 787 (no. 2)
— schnitt' es gern in alle Rinden ein. *Ungeduld,* 795 (no. 7)
— sehe dich in tausend Bildern. *Marie,* 658
— sitz' bei der moosigten Quelle. *Cronnan,* 282
— stand in dunklen Träumen. *Ihr Bild,* 957 (no. 9)
— such' im Schnee vergebens. *Erstarrung,* 911 (no. 4)
— träumte von bunten Blumen. *Frühlingstraum,* 911 (no. 11)
— treibe auf des Lebens Meer. *Selige Welt,* 743
— unglücksel'ger Atlas. *Der Atlas,* 957 (no. 8)
— wandre über Berg und Tal. *Im Walde,* 834
— war erst sechzehn Sommer alt. *Phidile,* 500
— will von Atreus' Söhnen. *An die Leyer,* 737
— wollt', ich wär' ein Fisch. *Liebhaber in allen Gestalten,* 558
Ida! gib ein Zeichen. *Die Zauberharfe,* 644 (no. 4)
Ihr Blümlein alle, die sie mir gab. *Trockne Blumen,* 795 (no. 18)
— Freunde und du, gold'ner Wein. *Trinklied,* 183
— habt auf Eure Burg entboten. *Die Verschworenen,* 787 (no. 3)
— hohen Himmlischen. *Antigone und Oedip,* 542
— lieben Mauern hold und traut. *Am Fenster,* 878
— Nymphen herbei. *Prometheus* (Cantata), 451
— Sternlein still in der Höhe. *Der liebliche Stern,* 861

Ihr unsichtbaren Geister. *Des Teufels Lustschloss,* 84 (no. 18)
— wollet mich zum Tode führen. *Des Teufels Lustschloss,* 84 (no. 16b)
Im Abendschimmer wallt der Quell. *Naturgenuss,* 188, 422
— Erlenbusch, im Tannenhain. *Die Täuschung,* 230
— Felde schleich' ich still und wild. *Jägers Abendlied,* 215, 368
— Frühlingsgarten fand ich sie. *Das Rosenband,* 280
— jungen Morgenstrahle den Blick dir zugewandt. *Fierabras,* 796 (no. 7)
— kalten, rauhen Norden. *Aus Heliopolis I,* 753
— Mondenschein wall' ich auf und ab. *Schwestergruss,* 762
— Tode sollt ihr büssen. *Fierabras,* 796 (no. 12)
— traulichen Kreise, 665
— trüben Licht verschwinden schon die Berge. *Der Zwerg,* 771
— Wald, im Wald. *An die Freunde,* 654
— Winde, im Sturme. *Der Schiffer,* 536
In allen guten Stunden. *Bundeslied,* 258
— der Freie will ich leben. *(Die) Flucht,* 825 (no. 3)
— — Tiefe wohnt das Licht. *Rosamunde,* 797 (no. 4)
— — Zeit sprach der Herr Jesus. *Evangelium Johannis,* 607
— des Sees Wogenspiele. *Am See,* 746
— — Todes Feierstunde. *Todesmusik,* 758
— die tiefsten Felsengründe. *Irrlicht,* 911 (no. 9)
— düstrer Nacht. *Blondel zu Marien,* 626
— einem Bächlein helle. *Die Forelle,* 550
— — Tal bei armen Hirten. *Das Mädchen aus der Fremde,* 117, 252
— Grün will ich mich kleiden. *Die liebe Farbe,* 795 (no. 16)
— monderhellten Nächten. *Die Sternennächte,* 670
— monte Oliveti. *Antiphons,* 696 (no. 2)
— schöner heller Winterzeit. *Der Wintertag,* 984
— seinem schimmernden Gewand. *Gott im Frühlinge,* 448
— tiefer Ruh liegt um mich her. *Kriegers Ahnung,* 957 (no. 2)
— tiefster Erde ruht ein alt Gesetz. *Schatzgräbers Begehr,* 761
Ingrediente Domino. *Antiphons,* 696 (no. 6)

INDEX OF SCHUBERT'S WORKS

Ins Grüne, ins Grüne. *Das Lied im Grünen*, 917
— stille Land. *Lied*, 403
Intende voci. *Offertorium*, 963
Ist der holde Lenz erschienen? *Klage der Ceres*, 323
— dies Tauris? *Orest auf Tauris*, 548
— mir's doch, als sei mein Leben. *Am Strome*, 539
Ja, gib, vernimm mein Flehen. *Alfonso und Estrella*, 732 (no. 9)
—, ich bin gerettet. *Alfonso und Estrella*, 732 (no. 28)
—, — weiss es. *Vergebliche Liebe*, 177
—, morgen, wenn die Sonne sinkt. *Des Teufels Lustschloss*, 84 (no. 3)
—, spanne nur den Bogen. *Der zürnenden Diana*, 707
—, wir schwören. *Die Verschworenen*, 787 (no. 4)
Jäger, ruhe von der Jagd! *Ellen's Gesang II*, 838
Jesu! dir leb' ich. *Deutsche Trauermesse*, 621 (no. 6)
Jesus Christus schwebt am Kreuze. *Stabat Mater*, 383
— —, unser Heiland, der den Tod überwand, *see* Überwunden hat der Herr den Tod!
Junger Kraft lebend'ges Walten. *Constitutionslied*, 748
Jüngst träumte mir. *Das war ich*, 174
Kaum hundert Schritt' von dieser Schänke. *Des Teufels Lustschloss*, 84 (no. 5)
Kein Auge hat Dein Angesicht geschaut. *An Gott*, 863
— Geist, ich bin am Leben. *Alfonso und Estrella*, 732 (no. 33)
— Rosenschimmer leuchtet. *Erinnerung*, 101
Keine Blumen blüh'n. *Winterlied*, 401
— Stimme hör' ich schallen. *Um Mitternacht*, 862
Kennst du das Land ...? *Mignon*, 321
Klage, meine Flöte, klage. *Der Sänger am Felsen*, 482
Kling' die Nacht durch, klinge. *Das Zügenglöcklein*, 871
Komm, heil'ger Geist, erhöre unser Flehen. *Hymnus an den heiligen Geist*, 941, 948
—, und senke die umflorten Schwingen. *An den Schlaf*, 447
Kommen und Scheiden. *Lebenslied*, 425
Königliche Morgensonne. *An die Sonne*, 272
Könnt' ich ewig hier verweilen. *Alfonso und Estrella*, 732 (no. 15)
Kyrie eleison, 31, 45, 49, 66

La pastorella al prato ... *La Pastorella*, 513, 528
Lachen und Weinen ... *Lachen und Weinen*, 777
Lacrimoso son io, 131
Lamm Gottes! *Deutsche Trauermesse*, 621 (no. 8)
Lass dein Vertrauen nicht schwinden, 333
— dich mit gelinden Schlägen. *Sprache der Liebe*, 410
— dir als Erinnerungszeichen. *Alfonso und Estrella*, 732 (no. 16)
— immer in der Jugend Glanz, 92
— nur alles leichtfertige Wesen. *Die Freunde von Salamanka*, 326 (no. 8)
— uns mutvoll hoffen. *Fierabras*, 796 (no. 5)
Lasst Friede in die Hallen des Fürstensitzes ziehn. *Fierabras*, 796 (no. 11)
— im Morgenstrahl des Mai'n. *Skolie*, 306
— mich, ich will klagen. *Klage um Ali Bey*, 140
—, ob ich auch still verglüh'. *Hippolit's Lied*, 890
— uns, ihr Himmlischen. *Uraniens Flucht*, 554
Lässt mich mein Verbrechen nicht schlafen? *Fernando*, 220 (no. 2)
Laue Lüfte, Blumendüfte. *Lob der Thränen*, 711
Laura betet. *Die Betende*, 102
—, über diese Welt zu flüchten. *Die Entzückung an Laura*, 390, 577
Lauter Freude fühl' ich. *Lied eines Kindes*, 596
Leb' wohl, du schöne Erde. *Abschied von der Erde*, 829
Lebe wohl, lebe wohl! *Abschied*, 578
Leben lasst den gold'nen Wein. *Die Zauberharfe*, 644 (no. 5)
Lebensfunke, vom Himmel entglüht. *Verklärung*, 59
Lebensmut und frische Kühlung. *Die Freunde von Salamanka*, 326 (no. 5)
Lehnst du deine bleichgehärmte Wange. *Trost an Elisa*, 97
Leise flehen meine Lieder. *Ständchen*, 957 (no. 4)
—, leise lasst uns singen. *Ruhe*, 635
—, rieselnder Quell. *Der Jüngling an der Quelle*, 300
Leiser, leiser, kleine Laute. *An die Laute*, 905
Liebchen und der Saft der Reben. *Wein und Liebe*, 901
Liebe ist ein süsses Licht. *Licht und Liebe*, 352
— rauscht der Silberbach. *Liebe*, 983 (no. 2)

FIRST LINES 559

Liebe säuseln die Blätter. *Maigesang,* 988
— schwärmt auf allen Wegen. *Claudine von Villa Bella,* 239 (no. 6)
— teure Muttererde. *Die Zwillingsbrüder,* 647 (no. 6)
Liebliches Kind. *Claudine von Villa Bella,* 239 (no. 9)
Lieblos verstossen ohne Erbarmen. *Sakuntala,* 701
Linde Lüfte wehen, 725
L'onda dal mare divisa, *see* Vom Meere trennt sich die Welle
Lorma sass in der Halle von Aldo. *Lorma,* 327, 376
Lustig in den Kampf. *Der vierjährige Posten,* 190 (no. 6)
. . . lux perpetua luceat eis. *Requiem,* 453

Mädchen entsiegelten. *Skolie,* 507
— Inistore's. *Das Mädchen von Inistore,* 281
Mag dich die Hoffnung nicht betrügen! *Der vierjährige Posten,* 190 (no. 3)
— es stürmen, donnern, blitzen. *Die Zwillingsbrüder,* 647 (no. 4)
Magnificat anima mea Dominum. *Magnificat,* 486
Mahadöh, der Herr der Erde. *Der Gott und die Bajadere,* 254
Majestät'sche Sonnenrosse. *Der Triumph der Liebe,* 64
Man ist so glücklich und so frei. *Die Freunde von Salamanka,* 326 (no. 2)
Manche Thrän' aus meinen Augen. *Wasserflut,* 911 (no. 6)
Mein Geliebter ist ein Sohn des Hügels. *Shilrik und Vinvela,* 293
— Handwerk geht durch alle Welt. *Tischlerlied,* 274
— Heiland, Herr und Meister. *Deutsche Messe,* 872 (no. 7)
— Herr, ich komm mich anzufragen. *Die Advokaten,* 37
— Herz ist zerissen. *Du liebst mich nicht,* 756
— Leben wälzt sich murrend fort. *Der Strom,* 565
— Ross so müd' in dem Stalle. *Lied des gefangenen Jägers,* 843
Meine Laute hab' ich gehängt an die Wand. *Pause,* 795 (no. 12)
— Ruh' ist dahin. *Klaglied,* 23
— — hin. *Gretchen am Spinnrade,* 118
— Seele, die dich liebt. *Adrast,* 137 (no. 6)
— Selinde. *Stimme der Liebe,* 412
Mich ergreift, ich weiss nicht wie. *Tischlied,* 234

Mich führt mein Weg. *Gesang der Norna,* 831
— umfängt ein banger Schauer. *Claudine von Villa Bella,* 239 (no. 10)
Mild senkt sich der Abend nieder. *Die Freunde von Salamanka,* 326 (no. 7)
Mio ben, ricordati. *Canzone IV,* 688
Mir ist so wohl, so weh'. *Erlafsee,* 586
— träumt', ich war ein Vöglein. *Der Traum,* 213
Misero pargoletto. *Demofoonte,* 42
Mit erstorbnem Scheinen. *Eine Leichenphantasie,* 7
— leisen Harfentönen. *(Die)Wehmut,* 404
— Mädchen sich vertragen. *Claudine von Villa Bella,* 239 (no. 7)
— unserm Arm ist nichts getan. *Schlachtgesang,* 443
Mitten im Schimmer. *Auf dem Wasser zu singen,* 774
Morgen, wenn des Hahnes Ruf erschallt, *Die Freunde von Salamanka,* 326 (no. 3)
Muss ich fühlen in tiefer Brust. *Die Bürgschaft,* 435 (no. 2)
Mutter geht durch ihre Kammern. *Lied,* 373
—! Wo bist du? *Fernando,* 220 (no. 1)
My hawk is tired, *see* Mein Ross so müd'

Nach so vielen trüben Tagen. *Cora an die Sonne,* 263
Nacht umhüllt mit wehendem Flügel. *Bertha's Lied in der Nacht,* 653
Nächtens klang die süsse Laute. *Don Gayseros II,* 93
Nachtviolen, Nachtviolen. *Nachtviolen,* 752
Nein, länger werd' ich diesen Kampf. *Der Kampf,* 594
—, nein, das ist zu viel. *Das Zauberglöckchen,* 723 (no. 2)
Nicht der Erde Schätze lohnen. *Fernando,* 220 (no. 5)
— so düster und so bleich. *Totengräber-Weise,* 869
Nichte, Don Diego da. *Die Freunde von Salamanka,* 326 (no. 16)
Nie bebte vor dem nahen Tode. *Des Teufels Lustschloss,* 84 (no. 13)
Nimm die letzten Abschiedsküsse. *Auf dem Strom(e),* 943
Nimmer, das glaubt mir. *Dithyrambe,* 47, 801
— lange weil' ich hier. *Trost,* 523
—, nimmer darf ich dir gestehen. *Julius an Theone,* 419
— trag' ich länger. *Der Leidende,* 432, 512
— werd' ich, nimmer dein vergessen. *Die Laube,* 214

INDEX OF SCHUBERT'S WORKS

Noch einmal hat das Zauberspiel der Hoffnung. *Des Teufels Lustschloss,* 84 (no. 15b)
— — tön', o Harfe. *Abschied von der Harfe,* 406
— fand von Evens Töchterscharen. *Der Weiberfreund,* 271
— in meines Lebens Lenze. *Der Pilgrim,* 794
— lag die Schöpfung formlos da. *Deutsche Messe,* 872 (no. 3)
Non t'accostar all' urna. *Canzone I,* 688
Nun, da Schatten niedergleiten. *Florio,* 857 (no. 1)
— fasset Mut! *Fierabras,* 796 (no. 6e)
— lasst des langersehnten Glücks uns freuen. *Fierabras,* 796 (no. 23c)
— — uns den Leib begraben, *see* Begrabt den Leib in seiner Gruft
— merk' ich erst, wie müd' ich bin. *Rast,* 911 (no. 10)
Nunmehr, da Himmel, Erde schweigt. *Sonett III,* 630
Nur dir will ich gehören. *Die Zwillingsbrüder,* 647 (no. 7)
— euch, schöne Sterne. *Die Macht der Augen,* 902 (no. 1)
— wer die Sehnsucht kennt. *Lied der Mignon,* 359, 877 (no. 4); *Sehnsucht,* 310, 656, 877 (no. 1)

O, dass ich dir vom stillen Auge. *An die Geliebte,* 303
—, du Entriss'ne mir. *Sei mir gegrüsst!,* 741
— du, wenn deine Lippen mich berühren. *Heimliches Lieben,* 922
—, gib vom weichen Pfühle. *Nachtgesang,* 119
— Götter! O Dank euch! *Die Bürgschaft,* 435 (no. 10)
—, göttliche Ruhe! *Die Bürgschaft,* 435 (no. 14)
— Herz, sei endlich stille. *An mein Herz,* 860
— hohes Glück, vor dir zu steh'n! *Deutsche Trauermesse,* 621 (no. 9)
— könnt' ich, Allgewaltiger. *Lazarus II,* 689
— köstlicher Tokayer. *Lob des Tokayers,* 248
—, lasst euch froh begrüssen, Kinder der vergnügten Au, 991
— Liebe, die mein Herz erfüllet. *Lambertine,* 301
— Menschheit, o Leben. *Totengräbers Heimwehe,* 842
—, mög auf froher Hoffnung Schwingen. *Fierabras,* 796 (no. 2)
— Quell, was strömst du rasch und wild, 874

O sagt, ihr Lieben, mir einmal. *Der blinde Knabe,* 833
—, sing' mir, Vater, noch einmal das schöne Lied. *Alfonso und Estrella,* 732 (no. 11)
— Sonne, Königin der Welt. *An die Sonne,* 439
—, teures Vaterland! *Fierabras,* 796 (no. 14)
— unbewölktes Leben! *Der Sieg,* 805
— wär' ich fern, o wär' ich blind. *Des Teufels Lustschloss,* 84 (no. 19)
— wie dringt das junge Leben. *Lebensmut,* 883
— wie schön ist deine Welt. *Im Abendrot,* 799
Ob er wohl wiederkehrt? *Die Bürgschaft,* 435 (no. 6)
Oben drehen sich die grossen ... *Die Sternenwelten,* 307
Oft in einsam stillen Stunden. *Das Heimweh,* 456
Onda da mare divisa, L', *see* Vom Meere trennt sich die Welle
Or sù, non ci pensiamo. *Il modo di prender moglie,* 902 (no. 3)

Packt ihn, führt ihn vor Gericht. *Die Zwillingsbrüder,* 647 (no. 9)
Pensa, che questo istante. *Alcide al Bivio,* 76
Pueri Hebraeorum. *Antiphons,* 696 (no. 4)
Purpur malt die Tannenhügel. *Der Abend,* 108

Quälend ungestilltes Sehnen. *Die verfehlte Stunde,* 409
Quell' innocente figlio. *Isacco,* 17

Raste, Krieger, Krieg ist aus. *Ellen's Gesang I,* 837
Rauschender Strom, brausender Wald. *Aufenthalt,* 957 (no. 5)
Rauschendes Bächlein, so silbern und hell. *Liebesbotschaft,* 957 (no. 1)
Rein und freundlich lacht der Himmel. *Der Mondabend,* 141
Ritter, treue Schwesterliebe. *Ritter Toggenburg,* 397
Rolle, du strömigter Carun. *Bardengesang,* 147
Ros' und Lilie morgentaulich. *Im Gegenwärtigen Vergangenes,* 710
Rosa, denkst du an mich? *An Rosa II,* 316
Ruhe, schönstes Glück der Erde, 657
Ruh'n in Frieden. *Am Tage Aller Seelen,* 343

FIRST LINES

Rührt die Cymbel. *Mirjam's Siegesgesang*, 942
Rund um mich Nacht. *Colma's Klage*, 217

Sag an, wer lehrt dich Lieder. *Geheimnis. An Franz Schubert*, 491
Sag', wo ist er hingekommen. *Alfonso und Estrella*, 732 (no. 22)
Sah ein Knab' ein Röslein stehn. *Heidenröslein*, 257
Salve Regina, 27, 106, 223, 386, 676
Sanctus Deus Sabaoth! 56
— Dominus Deus Sabaoth! *Antiphons*, 696 (no. 3)
Sanft glänzt die Abendsonne. *Abendlied*, 382
— und still schläft unser Freund. *Lazarus II*, 689
— weh'n, im Hauch der Abendluft. *Totenkranz für ein Kind*, 275
Sanftes Klavier. *Seraphine an ihr Klavier*, 342
Sänger, der von Herzen singet. *Kantate zum Geburtstage des Sängers J. M. Vogl*, 666
Säuselnde Lüfte, wehend so mild. *Frühlingssehnsucht*, 957 (no. 3)
Schad' um das schöne grüne Band. *Mit dem grünen Lautenbande*, 795 (no. 13)
Schaff', das Tagwerk meiner Hände. *Hoffnung*, 295
Schicksalslenker, blicke nieder. *Hymne zur Genesung des Herrn Ritter*, 763
Schlacht, du brichst an. *Trinklied vor der Schlacht*, 169
Schlafe, Liebliche. *Die Zauberharfe*, 644 (no. 9)
—, schlafe, holder, süsser Knabe. *Wiegenlied*, 498
Schlagt mein ganzes Glück in Splitter. *Des Sängers Habe*, 832
Schlumm're sanft. *Wiegenlied*, 304
Schmerz verzerret ihr Gesicht. *Gruppe aus dem Tartarus*, 65
Schmücket die Locken mit duftigen Kränzen. *Frühlingsgesang*, 709, 740
Schneeglöcklein, o Schneeglöcklein. *Viola*, 786
Schon im bunten Knabenkleide. *Die frühe Liebe*, 430
— naht, um uns zu scheiden . . . (spurious), App. I
— schleichen meine Späher. *Alfonso und Estrella*, 732 (no. 6b)
—, wenn es beginnt zu tagen. *Alfonso und Estrella*, 732 (no. 5b)
Schön wie Engel voll Walhalla's Wonne. *Amalia*, 195

Schöne Stunde, die uns blendet. *Der vierjährige Posten*, 190 (no. 8)
— Welt, wo bist du? *Strophe von Schiller*, 677
Schöpferin beseelter Töne. *Gesang an die Harmonie*, 394
Schweige nur. *Das stille Lied*, 916
Schwer und dumpfig, eine Wetterwolke. *Die Schlacht*, 249, 387
Schwüler Hauch weht mir herüber. *Lieb Minna*, 222
Seht den Felsenquell. *Mahomet's Gesang*, 549, 721
—, der Mönch trinkt mit der Nonne. *Trinklied aus dem XVI. Jahrhundert*, 847
— meine lieben Bäume an. *Das Lied vom Reifen*, 532
Sei, gegrüsst, du Frau der Huld. *Das Marienbild*, 623
— —, geweihte Stille. *Auf einen Kirchhof*, 151
— mir gegrüsst, o Mai. *Mein Gruss an den Mai*, 305
— — —, o Sonne. *Alfonso und Estrella*, 732 (no. 2)
— Mutter der Barmherzigkeit. *Salve Regina*, 379
— sanft wie ihre Seele. *Abendständchen. An Lina*, 265
— uns stets gegrüsst, o Nacht! *Nachtgesang im Walde*, 913
Selbst an des Grabes Rande. *Fierabras*, 796 (no. 15b)
Selig alle, die im Herrn entschlafen. *Elegie. Bei dem Grabe meines Vaters*, 127
— durch die Liebe. *Der Triumph der Liebe*, 55
Serbate, o dei custodi. *La Clemenza di Tito*, 35
Sicheln schallen, Ähren fallen. *Erntelied*, 434
Sie haben das Rufen vernommen. *Alfonso und Estrella*, 732 (no. 30)
— hüpfte mit mir auf grünem Plan. *Über allen Zauber Liebe*, 682
— ist dahin. *Auf den Tod einer Nachtigall*, 201, 399
— ist's! Er ist's! *Die Verschworenen*, 787 (no. 1a, b)
— konnte mir kein Wörtchen sagen. *Das Geheimnis*, 250, 793
— sind in Paris. *Die Befreier Europa's in Paris*, 104
Siehe, wie die Mondesstrahlen. *Die Mondnacht*, 238
Sieht uns der Blick gehoben. *Die Berge*, 634
Silberblauer Mondenschein. *Grab und Mond*, 893

INDEX OF SCHUBERT'S WORKS

Sinke, liebe Sonne, sinke. *An die Sonne*, 270
Sitz' ich im Gras. *Am See*, 124
So hab' ich wirklich dich verloren. *An die Entfernte*, 765
— lasst mich scheinen, bis ich werde. *Mignon II*, 469, 727; *Lied der Mignon*, 877 (no. 3)
— legt ihn in die Blumen. *Lazarus II*, 689
— Mancher sieht mit finstrer Miene. *Irdisches Glück*, 866 (no. 4)
— naht nun endlich die kühlende Nacht (new words supplied by Count and Countess Albrecht Wickenburg). *Nachthymne*, 687
— nimm, du junger Held. *Der Spiegelritter*, 11 (no. 7)
— schlummert auf Rosen. *Lazarus I*, 689
— wird der Mann. *Fragment aus dem Aeschylus*, 450
Solang im deutschen Eichentale. *Jünglingswonne*, 983 (no. 1)
Soldier, rest, *see* Raste, Krieger
Son fra l'onde. *Gli orti esperidi*, 78
Sonne, du sinkst. *An die untergehende Sonne*, 457
Sonnenstrahlen durch die Tannen. *Im Haine*, 738
Spute dich, Kronos. *An Schwager Kronos*, 369
Stabat Mater, 175
Starb das Kindlein. *Das Totenhemdchen*, 864
Steh' im letzten Kampf dem Müden. *Lazarus I*, 689
Steig empor, umblüht von Segen. *Am Geburtstage des Kaisers*, 748
Stern der Liebe, Glanzgebilde. *Der Morgenstern*, 172, 203
Still beginnt's im Hain zu tauen. *Abendbilder*, 650
— ist die Nacht. *Der Doppelgänger*, 957 (no. 13)
— noch decket uns die Nacht. *Alfonso und Estrella*, 732 (no. 1)
— sitz' ich an des Hügels Hang. *Im Frühling*, 882
Stille, Freunde, seht euch vor. *Alfonso und Estrella*, 732 (no. 17)
Süsse Augen, klare Bronnen! *Augenlied*, 297
—, heilige Natur. *An die Natur*, 372
Süsses Licht! Aus goldnen Pforten. *Sängers Morgenlied*, 163, 165
— Liebchen! komm zu mir. *Liebeständelei*, 206

Tag voll Himmel. *Entzückung*, 413
Tantum ergo, 460, 461, 730, 739, 750, 962

Te solo adoro. *La Betulia liberata*, 34
The heath this night must be my bed, *see* Die Nacht bricht bald herein
Thronend auf erhab'nem Sitz. *Der Triumph der Liebe*, 62
Tiefe Feier schauert um die Welt. *Nachtgesang*, 314
— Stille herrscht im Wasser. *Meeres Stille*, 216
Tiefer sinket schon die Sonne. *Abendröte*, 690
Tod, du Schrecken der Natur. *An den Tod*, 518
Todesstille deckt das Tal. *In der Mitternacht*, 464
Tom lehnt harrend auf der Brücke. *Widerschein*, 949; *see also* Harrt ein Fischer...
Totus in corde langueo. *Offertorium*, 136
Tôw l'hôdôs ladonoj. *Der 92. Psalm*, 953
Trarah! trarah! *Jagdlied*, 521
Trauer umfliesst mein Leben. *Klage*, 292, 371
Traurig geht der Geliebte von dannen. *Die Freunde von Salamanka*, 326 (no. 17)
Tres sunt. *Offertorium*, 181
Triumph, er naht. *Bootgesang*, 835
Trocknet nicht. *Wonne der Wehmut*, 260
Tronend..., *see* Thronend...

Über allen Gipfeln ist Ruh'. *Wandrers Nachtlied II*, 768
— die Berge zieht ihr fort. *Abschied*, 475
— meines Liebchens Äugeln. *Geheimes*, 719
— Tal und Fluss getragen. *An Mignon*, 161
Überall, wohin mein Aug blicket. *Die Macht der Liebe*, 308
Überwunden hat der Herr den Tod. *Osterlied*, 987
Uf'm Bergli bin i g'sässe. *Schweizerlied*, 559
Um Gottes willen. *Der vierjährige Posten*, 190 (no. 7)
Und frische Nahrung, neues Blut. *Auf dem See*, 543
— nimmer schreibst du. *Herrn Josef Spaun*, 749
Unendliche Freude durchwallet das Herz. *Elysium*, 51, 54
Uns führt der Vorsicht weise Hand. *Fierabras*, 796 (no. 17a)

Vater, du glaubst es nicht. *Drang in die Ferne*, 770
—, ich rufe dich. *Gebet während der Schlacht*, 171

FIRST LINES

Vater, schenk mir diese Stunde. *Namenstagslied*, 695
Vedi, quanto adoro. *Arie (Didone abbandonata)*, 510
Verbirg dich, Sonne. *Auflösung*, 807
Verderben denn und Fluch. *Fierabras*, 796 (no. 10)
Verfliesset, vielgeliebte Lieder. *Am Flusse*, 160, 766
Vergebens schweif' ich durch die öden Hallen! *Des Teufels Lustschloss*, 84 (no. 12b)
Vergessen sei, was uns getrennt. *Fernando*, 220 (no. 6)
Verglühet sind die Sterne. *Die Zwillingsbrüder*, 647 (no. 1)
Vernimm es, Nacht. *Idens Nachtgesang*, 227
Verräterei hab' ich entdeckt. *Die Verschworenen*, 787 (no. 6)
Versammelt euch, Brüder. *Alfonso und Estrella*, 732 (no. 3)
Verschwunden sind die Schmerzen. *Auf den Sieg der Deutschen*, 81, 88
Verweile, o Prinzessin. *Alfonso und Estrella*, 732 (no. 8a)
Viel tausend Sterne prangen. *Das Feuerwerk*, 642
Vier Elemente, innig gesellt. *Punschlied*, 277
Vital spark of heavenly flame, see Lebensfunke, vom Himmel entglüht
Voici l'instant suprême (spurious), App. I
Voll Locken kraus. *Versunken*, 715
Vom Meere trennt sich die Welle. *Leiden der Trennung*, 509
Von allen schönen Waren. *Wer kauft Liebesgötter?*, 261
— der Strasse her ein Posthorn klingt. *Die Post*, 911 (no. 13)
— Fels und Wald umrungen. *Alfonso und Estrella*, 732 (no. 12b)
— tausend Schlangenbissen. *Die Freunde von Salamanka*, 326 (no. 14)
Vor dem Busen möge blühen. *Die Zwillingsbrüder*, 647 (no. 2)
— der in Ehrfurcht all mein Wesen kniet. *Augenblicke im Elysium*, 582
— Thebens siebenfach gähnenden Toren. *Amphiaraos*, 166
Vorüber, ach, vorüber. *Der Tod und das Mädchen*, 531
— die stöhnende Klage! *Elysium*, 53
— ist die Zeit. *Die Verschworenen*, 787 (no. 5)

Wagen Sie, Ihr Wort zu brechen? *Die Zwillingsbrüder*, 647 (no. 8)
Wälze dich hinweg. *Lied des Orpheus, als er in die Hölle ging*, 474

Wann der silberne Mond. *Die Mainacht*, 194
— meine Grillen schwirren. *Der Einsame*, 800
War einer je der Sterblichen beglückt. *Adrast*, 137 (no. 2)
— es also gemeint? *Danksagung an den Bach*, 795 (no. 4)
Wärst du bei mir im Lebenstal. *Lied der Anne Lyle*, 830
— — mir auf immer nicht entrissen. *Fernando*, 220 (no. 4)
Warum bist du nicht hier. *An Rosa I*, 315
— öffnest du wieder...? *Der Tod Oscar's*, 375
Was bedeutet die Bewegung? *Suleika I*, 720
— belebt die schöne Welt? *Die Zauberharfe*, 644 (no. 8a)
— funkelt ihr so mild mich an? *Die Sterne*, 176
— geht hier vor, was wollt Ihr beginnen? *Alfonso und Estrella*, 732 (no. 31)
— glänzt dort vom Walde im Sonnenschein? *Lützow's wilde Jagd*. 205
— hör' ich draussen vor dem Tor? *Der Sänger*, 149
— ist es, das die Seele füllt? *Alles um Liebe*, 241
— — ihm geschehn'n? *Fierabras*, 796 (no. 8b)
— — Sylvia? *Gesang. An Sylvia*, 891
— kümmert mich ein sumpfig Land? *Des Teufels Lustschloss*, 84 (no. 2)
— quälst du mich, o Missgeschick! *Fierabras*, 796 (no. 6b)
— schauest du so hell...? *An den Mond*, 468
— sorgest du? *Der gute Hirte*, 449
— sucht denn der Jäger? *Der Jäger*, 795 (no. 14)
— unterm Monde gleicht uns? *Sylphen*, 341
— vermeid' ich denn die Wege? *Der Wegweiser*, 911 (no. 20)
— weilst du einsam an dem Himmel? *Abendstern*, 806
— zieht mir das Herz so? *Sehnsucht*, 123
Weh' mir, ich bebe. *Der getäuschte Verräter*, 902 (no. 2)
Wehe dem Fliehenden. *In der Ferne*, 957 (no. 6)
—, meines Vaters Scharen. *Alfonso und Estrella*, 732 (no. 29)
Wehmut, die mich hüllt. *Das Sehnen*, 231
Weine du nicht. *Selma und Selmar*, 286
Weit in nebelgrauer Ferne. *An Emma*, 113

Weit über Glanz und Erdenschimmer. *Fierabras*, 796 (no. 9)
Welche Nacht hab' ich erlebt! *Die Bürgschaft*, 435 (no. 11)
Welcher Frevel! So sind die Menschen! *Des Teufels Lustschloss*, 84 (no. 7)
Wenige wissen das Geheimnis. *Hymne I*, 659
Wenn alle untreu werden. *Hymne III*, 661
— andere mit heit'rem Blick. *Adrast*, 137 (no. 5b)
— auf dem höchsten Fels . . . *Der Hirt am Felsen*, 965
— dein Finger durch die Saiten. *Laura am Klavier*, 388
— der Schimmer von dem Monde . . . *Die Sommernacht*, 289
— — uralte heilige Vater . . . *Grenzen der Menschheit*, 716
— hoch im Wolkensitze der Götter Grimm erwacht. *Fierabras*, 796 (no. 20)
— ich dich, Holde, sehe. *Alfonso und Estrella*, 732 (no. 13a)
— — durch Busch und Zweig . . . *Widerspruch*, 865
— — — Wald und Fluren geh'. *Wehmut*, 772
— — ihm nachgerungen habe. *Lazarus I*, 689
— — ihn nur habe. *Hymne II*, 660
— — nur ein Vöglein wäre. *Der Knabe*, 692
— im Spiele leiser Töne . . . *Labetrank der Liebe*, 302
— in des Abends letztem Scheine. *Lied aus der Ferne*, 107
— mich einsam Lüfte fächeln. *Blanka*, 631
— sanft entzückt mein Auge sieht. *Die Erde*, 989
— über Berge sich der Nebel breitet. *Nachtstück*, 672
Wer bist du, Geist der Liebe? *Geist der Liebe*, 233
— — —, holdes Wesen? *Alfonso und Estrella*, 732 (no. 13)
— die steile Sternenbahn. *Der Triumph der Liebe*, 63
— ist wohl gross? *Wer ist gross?* 110
— Lebenslust fühlet. *Lebenslust*, 609
— nie sein Brot mit Thränen ass. *Harfenspieler III, Gesänge des Harfners II*, 480
— reitet so spät durch Nacht und Wind? *Erlkönig*, 328
— sich der Einsamkeit ergibt. *Harfenspieler*, 325; *Harfenspieler I, Gesänge des Harfners I*, 478
— wagt es, Rittersmann oder Knapp'? *Der Taucher*, 77, 111

Wer wagt's, wer wagt's? *Der zürnende Barde*, 785
— wird sich nicht innig freuen? 992
Werde dem geliebten Sohne. *Der Spiegelritter*, 11 (no. 4b)
Wert thou, like me, *see* Wärst du bei mir
Wess' Adern leichtes Blut durchspringt . . . *Die Fröhlichkeit*, 262
Wess' ist der Klage Stimme. *Lazarus II*, 689
Who is Silvia? *see* Was ist Sylvia?
Why does your brand sae drop wi' blude?, *see* Dein Schwert, wie ist's vom Blut so rot!
Wie anders, Gretchen, war dir's. *Szene aus Goethe's 'Faust,'* 126
— blitzen die Sterne. *Die Sterne*, 939
— braust durch die Wipfel . . . *Die junge Nonne*, 828
—, darf ich meinen Augen trau'n? *Die Verschworenen*, 787 (no. 11)
— deutlich des Mondes Licht . . . *Der Wanderer*, 649
— die Nacht mit heil'gem Beben . . . *Sehnsucht der Liebe*, 180
— dürstet der Ätna. *Die Bürgschaft*, 435 (no. 3)
— eine trübe Wolke. *Einsamkeit*, 911 (no. 12)
— erhebt sich das Herz. *Dem Unendlichen*, 291
— glücklich, wem das Knabenkleid. *Die Knabenzeit*, 400
— hat der Sturm zerrissen . . . *Der stürmische Morgen*, 911 (no. 18)
— im Morgenglanze . . . *Ganymed*, 544
— ist es denn. . . . *Abend*, 645
— klag' ich's aus. *Schwanengesang*, 744
— kommt's, dass du so traurig bist? *Trost in Thränen*, 120
— lebt sich's so fröhlich im Grünen! *Rosamunde*, 797 (no. 8)
— lieblich und fröhlich . . . *Die Vögel*, 691
— liegst du starr und bleich, mein Sohn. *Adrast*, 137 (no. 5a)
— rein Gesang sich windet. *Der Fluss*, 693
— rühret mich dein herrlicher Gesang! *Alfonso und Estrella*, 732 (no. 12a)
— sanft entzückt mein Auge sieht. *Die Erde*, 989
— schaust du aus dem Nebelflor. *Idens Schwanenlied*, 317
— schön bist du, güld'ne Morgenröte. *Lilla an die Morgenröte*, 273
— — —, freundliche Stille. *Die Nacht*, 983 (no. 4)
— — ist's im Freien. *Lied im Freien*, 133, 572

FIRST LINES

Wie sich der Äuglein kindlicher Himmel. *Wiegenlied*, 867
— so innig, möcht' ich sagen. *Das Mädchen*, 652
— soll ich nicht tanzen. *Der Schmetterling*, 633
— tönt es mir so schaurig. *Der Blumen Schmerz*, 731
— treiben die Wolken. *Minona*, 152
— tröstlich ist, was Jesus lehrt. *Deutsche Trauermesse*, 621 (no. 3)
— wohl ist mir im Dunkeln! *Die Sterne*, 313
Will sich Hektor ewig von mir wenden? *Hektor's Abschied*, 312
— singen euch im alten Ton. *Hochzeitslied*, 463
Willkommen, lieber schöner Mai. *Mailied*, 244
—, o silberner Mond. *Die frühen Gräber*, 290
—, rotes Morgenlicht. *Morgenlied*, 266
—, schön willkommen. *Die Verschworenen*, 787 (no. 7)
—, schöner Jüngling. *An den Frühling*, 245, 283, 338, 587
Willst du nicht das Lämmlein hüten? *Der Alpenjäger*, 588
Windesrauschen, Gottesflügel. *Im Walde*, 708
Wir bringen dir die Kette hier. *Die Bürgschaft*, 435 (no. 8)
— gratulieren! Dummkopf! *Der Spiegelritter*, 11 (no. 3)
— sassen so traulich beisammen. *Thränenregen*, 795 (no. 10)
— stimmen dir mit Flötensang. *Nachtmusik*, 848
Wirst du halten, was du schwurst? *Die abgeblühte Linde*, 514
Wo Amor's Flügel weben. *Amor's Macht*, 339
— bin ich? *Lazarus II*, 689
— die Taub' in stillen Buchen . . . *Trauer der Liebe*, 465
— ein treues Herze . . . *Der Müller und der Bach*, 795 (no. 19)
— find' ich nur den Ort? *Alfonso und Estrella*, 732 (no. 32)
— ich sei, und wo mich hingewendet. *Thekla. Eine Geisterstimme*, 73, 595
— — weile, wo ich gehe. *Die Freunde von Salamanka*, 326 (no. 13)
— irrst du durch einsame Schatten? *Aus Diego Manazares*, 458
— ist er? *Fierabras*, 796 (no. 15a)

Wo ist sie, was kommt ihr zu künden? *Alfonso und Estrella*, 732 (no. 18)
— weht der Liebe hoher Geist? *Die Liebe*, 522
Woget brausend, Harmonieen. *Zum Punsche*, 492
Woher, o namenloses Sehnen? *Abends unter der Linde*, 235, 237
Wohin? o Helios! *Freiwilliges Versinken*, 700
— so schnell, so kraus? *Eifersucht und Stolz*, 795 (no. 15)
— soll ich mich wenden. *Deutsche Messe*, 872 (no. 1)
— zwei Liebende sich retten. *Des Teufels Lustschloss*, 84 (no. 4)
Wohl denk' ich allenthalben. *Der Entfernten*, 331, 332, 350
— perlet im Glase . . . *Die vier Weltalter*, 391
— weinen Gottes Engel. *Luisens Antwort*, 319
Wohlan! Lasst die rüstigen Gesellen *Der Spiegelritter*, 11 (no. 2)
—, und ohne Zagen. *Die Art, ein Weib zu nehmen*, 902 (no. 3)
Zeit, Verkündigerin der besten Freuden. *An Sie*, 288
Zieh' hin, du braver Krieger, du! *Grablied auf einen Soldaten*, 454
Zögernd leise. *Ständchen*, 920, 921
Zu Aachen in seiner Kaiserpracht. *Der Graf von Habsburg*, 990
— Dionys, dem Tyrannen . . . *Die Bürgschaft*, 246
— Gott flieg auf. *Gott der Weltschöpfer*, 986
— hohen Ruhmespforten. *Fierabras*, 796 (no. 3)
— meinen Füssen brichst du dich. *Der entsühnte Orest*, 699
— rechter Zeit bin ich gekommen. *Die Zwillingsbrüder*, 647 (no. 5)
Zum Donaustrom, zur Kaiserstadt. *Rückweg*, 476
— Saal, der gold'ne Becher blinkt. *Die Zauberharfe*, 644 (no. 2)
Zur Elbe, des Äthers Gewölbe. *Badelied*, 340
— Jagd! *Alfonso und Estrella*, 732 (no. 7a)
Zwar schuf das Glück hienieden. *Der Zufriedene*, 320
Zwei sind der Wege. *Die zwei Tugendwege*, 71
Zwischen Himmel und Erde. *Hymne an den Unendlichen*, 232

A CATALOG OF SELECTED
DOVER BOOKS
IN ALL FIELDS OF INTEREST

A CATALOG OF SELECTED DOVER BOOKS IN ALL FIELDS OF INTEREST

CONCERNING THE SPIRITUAL IN ART, Wassily Kandinsky. Pioneering work by father of abstract art. Thoughts on color theory, nature of art. Analysis of earlier masters. 12 illustrations. 80pp. of text. 5⅜ × 8½. 23411-8 Pa. $3.95

ANIMALS: 1,419 Copyright-Free Illustrations of Mammals, Birds, Fish, Insects, etc., Jim Harter (ed.). Clear wood engravings present, in extremely lifelike poses, over 1,000 species of animals. One of the most extensive pictorial sourcebooks of its kind. Captions. Index. 284pp. 9 × 12. 23766-4 Pa. $11.95

CELTIC ART: The Methods of Construction, George Bain. Simple geometric techniques for making Celtic interlacements, spirals, Kells-type initials, animals, humans, etc. Over 500 illustrations. 160pp. 9 × 12. (USO) 22923-8 Pa. $8.95

AN ATLAS OF ANATOMY FOR ARTISTS, Fritz Schider. Most thorough reference work on art anatomy in the world. Hundreds of illustrations, including selections from works by Vesalius, Leonardo, Goya, Ingres, Michelangelo, others. 593 illustrations. 192pp. 7⅛ × 10¼. 20241-0 Pa. $8.95

CELTIC HAND STROKE-BY-STROKE (Irish Half-Uncial from "The Book of Kells"): An Arthur Baker Calligraphy Manual, Arthur Baker. Complete guide to creating each letter of the alphabet in distinctive Celtic manner. Covers hand position, strokes, pens, inks, paper, more. Illustrated. 48pp. 8¼ × 11.
24336-2 Pa. $3.95

EASY ORIGAMI, John Montroll. Charming collection of 32 projects (hat, cup, pelican, piano, swan, many more) specially designed for the novice origami hobbyist. Clearly illustrated easy-to-follow instructions insure that even beginning papercrafters will achieve successful results. 48pp. 8¼ × 11. 27298-2 Pa. $2.95

THE COMPLETE BOOK OF BIRDHOUSE CONSTRUCTION FOR WOODWORKERS, Scott D. Campbell. Detailed instructions, illustrations, tables. Also data on bird habitat and instinct patterns. Bibliography. 3 tables. 63 illustrations in 15 figures. 48pp. 5¼ × 8½. 24407-5 Pa. $1.95

BLOOMINGDALE'S ILLUSTRATED 1886 CATALOG: Fashions, Dry Goods and Housewares, Bloomingdale Brothers. Famed merchants' extremely rare catalog depicting about 1,700 products: clothing, housewares, firearms, dry goods, jewelry, more. Invaluable for dating, identifying vintage items. Also, copyright-free graphics for artists, designers. Co-published with Henry Ford Museum & Greenfield Village. 160pp. 8¼ × 11. 25780-0 Pa. $9.95

HISTORIC COSTUME IN PICTURES, Braun & Schneider. Over 1,450 costumed figures in clearly detailed engravings—from dawn of civilization to end of 19th century. Captions. Many folk costumes. 256pp. 8⅜ × 11¼. 23150-X Pa. $10.95

CATALOG OF DOVER BOOKS

STICKLEY CRAFTSMAN FURNITURE CATALOGS, Gustav Stickley and L. & J. G. Stickley. Beautiful, functional furniture in two authentic catalogs from 1910. 594 illustrations, including 277 photos, show settles, rockers, armchairs, reclining chairs, bookcases, desks, tables. 183pp. 6½ × 9¼. 23838-5 Pa. $8.95

AMERICAN LOCOMOTIVES IN HISTORIC PHOTOGRAPHS: 1858 to 1949, Ron Ziel (ed.). A rare collection of 126 meticulously detailed official photographs, called "builder portraits," of American locomotives that majestically chronicle the rise of steam locomotive power in America. Introduction. Detailed captions. xi + 129pp. 9 × 12. 27393-8 Pa. $12.95

AMERICA'S LIGHTHOUSES: An Illustrated History, Francis Ross Holland, Jr. Delightfully written, profusely illustrated fact-filled survey of over 200 American lighthouses since 1716. History, anecdotes, technological advances, more. 240pp. 8 × 10¾. 25576-X Pa. $11.95

TOWARDS A NEW ARCHITECTURE, Le Corbusier. Pioneering manifesto by founder of "International School." Technical and aesthetic theories, views of industry, economics, relation of form to function, "mass-production split" and much more. Profusely illustrated. 320pp. 6⅛ × 9¼. (USO) 25023-7 Pa. $8.95

HOW THE OTHER HALF LIVES, Jacob Riis. Famous journalistic record, exposing poverty and degradation of New York slums around 1900, by major social reformer. 100 striking and influential photographs. 233pp. 10 × 7⅞. 22012-5 Pa $10.95

FRUIT KEY AND TWIG KEY TO TREES AND SHRUBS, William M. Harlow. One of the handiest and most widely used identification aids. Fruit key covers 120 deciduous and evergreen species; twig key 160 deciduous species. Easily used. Over 300 photographs. 126pp. 5⅜ × 8½. 20511-8 Pa. $3.95

COMMON BIRD SONGS, Dr. Donald J. Borror. Songs of 60 most common U.S. birds: robins, sparrows, cardinals, bluejays, finches, more—arranged in order of increasing complexity. Up to 9 variations of songs of each species.
Cassette and manual 99911-4 $8.95

ORCHIDS AS HOUSE PLANTS, Rebecca Tyson Northen. Grow cattleyas and many other kinds of orchids—in a window, in a case, or under artificial light. 63 illustrations. 148pp. 5⅜ × 8½. 23261-1 Pa. $3.95

MONSTER MAZES, Dave Phillips. Masterful mazes at four levels of difficulty. Avoid deadly perils and evil creatures to find magical treasures. Solutions for all 32 exciting illustrated puzzles. 48pp. 8¼ × 11. 26005-4 Pa. $2.95

MOZART'S DON GIOVANNI (DOVER OPERA LIBRETTO SERIES), Wolfgang Amadeus Mozart. Introduced and translated by Ellen H. Bleiler. Standard Italian libretto, with complete English translation. Convenient and thoroughly portable—an ideal companion for reading along with a recording or the performance itself. Introduction. List of characters. Plot summary. 121pp. 5¼ × 8½. 24944-1 Pa. $2.95

TECHNICAL MANUAL AND DICTIONARY OF CLASSICAL BALLET, Gail Grant. Defines, explains, comments on steps, movements, poses and concepts. 15-page pictorial section. Basic book for student, viewer. 127pp. 5⅜ × 8½. 21843-0 Pa. $3.95

CATALOG OF DOVER BOOKS

BRASS INSTRUMENTS: Their History and Development, Anthony Baines. Authoritative, updated survey of the evolution of trumpets, trombones, bugles, cornets, French horns, tubas and other brass wind instruments. Over 140 illustrations and 48 music examples. Corrected and updated by author. New preface. Bibliography. 320pp. 5⅜ × 8½. 27574-4 Pa. $9.95

HOLLYWOOD GLAMOR PORTRAITS, John Kobal (ed.). 145 photos from 1926-49. Harlow, Gable, Bogart, Bacall; 94 stars in all. Full background on photographers, technical aspects. 160pp. 8⅜ × 11¼. 23352-9 Pa. $9.95

MAX AND MORITZ, Wilhelm Busch. Great humor classic in both German and English. Also 10 other works: "Cat and Mouse," "Plisch and Plumm," etc. 216pp. 5⅜ × 8½. 20181-3 Pa. $5.95

THE RAVEN AND OTHER FAVORITE POEMS, Edgar Allan Poe. Over 40 of the author's most memorable poems: "The Bells," "Ulalume," "Israfel," "To Helen," "The Conqueror Worm," "Eldorado," "Annabel Lee," many more. Alphabetic lists of titles and first lines. 64pp. 5³/₁₆ × 8¼. 26685-0 Pa. $1.00

SEVEN SCIENCE FICTION NOVELS, H. G. Wells. The standard collection of the great novels. Complete, unabridged. First Men in the Moon, Island of Dr. Moreau, War of the Worlds, Food of the Gods, Invisible Man, Time Machine, In the Days of the Comet. Total of 1,015pp. 5⅜ × 8½. (USO) 20264-X Clothbd. $29.95

AMULETS AND SUPERSTITIONS, E. A. Wallis Budge. Comprehensive discourse on origin, powers of amulets in many ancient cultures: Arab, Persian, Babylonian, Assyrian, Egyptian, Gnostic, Hebrew, Phoenician, Syriac, etc. Covers cross, swastika, crucifix, seals, rings, stones, etc. 584pp. 5⅜ × 8½. 23573-4 Pa. $12.95

RUSSIAN STORIES/PYCCKNE PACCKA3bl: A Dual-Language Book, edited by Gleb Struve. Twelve tales by such masters as Chekhov, Tolstoy, Dostoevsky, Pushkin, others. Excellent word-for-word English translations on facing pages, plus teaching and study aids, Russian/English vocabulary, biographical/critical introductions, more. 416pp. 5⅜ × 8½. 26244-8 Pa. $8.95

PHILADELPHIA THEN AND NOW: 60 Sites Photographed in the Past and Present, Kenneth Finkel and Susan Oyama. Rare photographs of City Hall, Logan Square, Independence Hall, Betsy Ross House, other landmarks juxtaposed with contemporary views. Captures changing face of historic city. Introduction. Captions. 128pp. 8¼ × 11. 25790-8 Pa. $9.95

AIA ARCHITECTURAL GUIDE TO NASSAU AND SUFFOLK COUNTIES, LONG ISLAND, The American Institute of Architects, Long Island Chapter, and the Society for the Preservation of Long Island Antiquities. Comprehensive, well-researched and generously illustrated volume brings to life over three centuries of Long Island's great architectural heritage. More than 240 photographs with authoritative, extensively detailed captions. 176pp. 8¼ × 11. 26946-9 Pa. $14.95

NORTH AMERICAN INDIAN LIFE: Customs and Traditions of 23 Tribes, Elsie Clews Parsons (ed.). 27 fictionalized essays by noted anthropologists examine religion, customs, government, additional facets of life among the Winnebago, Crow, Zuni, Eskimo, other tribes. 480pp. 6⅛ × 9¼. 27377-6 Pa. $10.95

CATALOG OF DOVER BOOKS

FRANK LLOYD WRIGHT'S HOLLYHOCK HOUSE, Donald Hoffmann. Lavishly illustrated, carefully documented study of one of Wright's most controversial residential designs. Over 120 photographs, floor plans, elevations, etc. Detailed perceptive text by noted Wright scholar. Index. 128pp. 9¼ × 10¾.
27133-1 Pa. $11.95

THE MALE AND FEMALE FIGURE IN MOTION: 60 Classic Photographic Sequences, Eadweard Muybridge. 60 true-action photographs of men and women walking, running, climbing, bending, turning, etc., reproduced from rare 19th-century masterpiece. vi + 121pp. 9 × 12.
24745-7 Pa. $10.95

1001 QUESTIONS ANSWERED ABOUT THE SEASHORE, N. J. Berrill and Jacquelyn Berrill. Queries answered about dolphins, sea snails, sponges, starfish, fishes, shore birds, many others. Covers appearance, breeding, growth, feeding, much more. 305pp. 5¼ × 8¼.
23366-9 Pa. $7.95

GUIDE TO OWL WATCHING IN NORTH AMERICA, Donald S. Heintzelman. Superb guide offers complete data and descriptions of 19 species: barn owl, screech owl, snowy owl, many more. Expert coverage of owl-watching equipment, conservation, migrations and invasions, etc. Guide to observing sites. 84 illustrations. xiii + 193pp. 5⅜ × 8½.
27344-X Pa. $7.95

MEDICINAL AND OTHER USES OF NORTH AMERICAN PLANTS: A Historical Survey with Special Reference to the Eastern Indian Tribes, Charlotte Erichsen-Brown. Chronological historical citations document 500 years of usage of plants, trees, shrubs native to eastern Canada, northeastern U.S. Also complete identifying information. 343 illustrations. 544pp. 6½ × 9¼.
25951-X Pa. $12.95

STORYBOOK MAZES, Dave Phillips. 23 stories and mazes on two-page spreads: Wizard of Oz, Treasure Island, Robin Hood, etc. Solutions. 64pp. 8¼ × 11.
23628-5 Pa. $2.95

NEGRO FOLK MUSIC, U.S.A., Harold Courlander. Noted folklorist's scholarly yet readable analysis of rich and varied musical tradition. Includes authentic versions of over 40 folk songs. Valuable bibliography and discography. xi + 324pp. 5⅜ × 8½.
27350-4 Pa. $7.95

MOVIE-STAR PORTRAITS OF THE FORTIES, John Kobal (ed.). 163 glamor, studio photos of 106 stars of the 1940s: Rita Hayworth, Ava Gardner, Marlon Brando, Clark Gable, many more. 176pp. 8⅜ × 11¼.
23546-7 Pa. $10.95

BENCHLEY LOST AND FOUND, Robert Benchley. Finest humor from early 30s, about pet peeves, child psychologists, post office and others. Mostly unavailable elsewhere. 73 illustrations by Peter Arno and others. 183pp. 5⅜ × 8½.
22410-4 Pa. $5.95

YEKL and THE IMPORTED BRIDEGROOM AND OTHER STORIES OF YIDDISH NEW YORK, Abraham Cahan. Film Hester Street based on Yekl (1896). Novel, other stories among first about Jewish immigrants on N.Y.'s East Side. 240pp. 5⅜ × 8½.
22427-9 Pa. $5.95

SELECTED POEMS, Walt Whitman. Generous sampling from *Leaves of Grass*. Twenty-four poems include "I Hear America Singing," "Song of the Open Road," "I Sing the Body Electric," "When Lilacs Last in the Dooryard Bloom'd," "O Captain! My Captain!"—all reprinted from an authoritative edition. Lists of titles and first lines. 128pp. 5³/₁₆ × 8¼.
26878-0 Pa. $1.00

THE BEST TALES OF HOFFMANN, E. T. A. Hoffmann. 10 of Hoffmann's most important stories: "Nutcracker and the King of Mice," "The Golden Flowerpot," etc. 458pp. 5⅜ × 8½. 21793-0 Pa. $8.95

FROM FETISH TO GOD IN ANCIENT EGYPT, E. A. Wallis Budge. Rich detailed survey of Egyptian conception of "God" and gods, magic, cult of animals, Osiris, more. Also, superb English translations of hymns and legends. 240 illustrations. 545pp. 5⅜ × 8½. 25803-3 Pa. $11.95

FRENCH STORIES/CONTES FRANÇAIS: A Dual-Language Book, Wallace Fowlie. Ten stories by French masters, Voltaire to Camus: "Micromegas" by Voltaire; "The Atheist's Mass" by Balzac; "Minuet" by de Maupassant; "The Guest" by Camus, six more. Excellent English translations on facing pages. Also French-English vocabulary list, exercises, more. 352pp. 5⅜ × 8½. 26443-2 Pa. $8.95

CHICAGO AT THE TURN OF THE CENTURY IN PHOTOGRAPHS: 122 Historic Views from the Collections of the Chicago Historical Society, Larry A. Viskochil. Rare large-format prints offer detailed views of City Hall, State Street, the Loop, Hull House, Union Station, many other landmarks, circa 1904-1913. Introduction. Captions. Maps. 144pp. 9⅜ × 12¼. 24656-6 Pa. $12.95

OLD BROOKLYN IN EARLY PHOTOGRAPHS, 1865-1929, William Lee Younger. Luna Park, Gravesend race track, construction of Grand Army Plaza, moving of Hotel Brighton, etc. 157 previously unpublished photographs. 165pp. 8⅞ × 11¾. 23587-4 Pa. $12.95

THE MYTHS OF THE NORTH AMERICAN INDIANS, Lewis Spence. Rich anthology of the myths and legends of the Algonquins, Iroquois, Pawnees and Sioux, prefaced by an extensive historical and ethnological commentary. 36 illustrations. 480pp. 5⅜ × 8½. 25967-6 Pa. $8.95

AN ENCYCLOPEDIA OF BATTLES: Accounts of Over 1,560 Battles from 1479 B.C. to the Present, David Eggenberger. Essential details of every major battle in recorded history from the first battle of Megiddo in 1479 B.C. to Grenada in 1984. List of Battle Maps. New Appendix covering the years 1967-1984. Index. 99 illustrations. 544pp. 6½ × 9¼. 24913-1 Pa. $14.95

SAILING ALONE AROUND THE WORLD, Captain Joshua Slocum. First man to sail around the world, alone, in small boat. One of great feats of seamanship told in delightful manner. 67 illustrations. 294pp. 5⅜ × 8½. 20326-3 Pa. $5.95

ANARCHISM AND OTHER ESSAYS, Emma Goldman. Powerful, penetrating, prophetic essays on direct action, role of minorities, prison reform, puritan hypocrisy, violence, etc. 271pp. 5⅜ × 8½. 22484-8 Pa. $5.95

MYTHS OF THE HINDUS AND BUDDHISTS, Ananda K. Coomaraswamy and Sister Nivedita. Great stories of the epics; deeds of Krishna, Shiva, taken from puranas, Vedas, folk tales; etc. 32 illustrations. 400pp. 5⅜ × 8½. 21759-0 Pa. $9.95

BEYOND PSYCHOLOGY, Otto Rank. Fear of death, desire of immortality, nature of sexuality, social organization, creativity, according to Rankian system. 291pp. 5⅜ × 8½. 20485-5 Pa. $7.95

A THEOLOGICO-POLITICAL TREATISE, Benedict Spinoza. Also contains unfinished Political Treatise. Great classic on religious liberty, theory of government on common consent. R. Elwes translation. Total of 421pp. 5⅜ × 8½. 20249-6 Pa. $7.95

CATALOG OF DOVER BOOKS

MY BONDAGE AND MY FREEDOM, Frederick Douglass. Born a slave, Douglass became outspoken force in antislavery movement. The best of Douglass' autobiographies. Graphic description of slave life. 464pp. 5⅜ × 8½. 22457-0 Pa. $8.95

FOLLOWING THE EQUATOR: A Journey Around the World, Mark Twain. Fascinating humorous account of 1897 voyage to Hawaii, Australia, India, New Zealand, etc. Ironic, bemused reports on peoples, customs, climate, flora and fauna, politics, much more. 197 illustrations. 720pp. 5⅜ × 8½. 26113-1 Pa. $15.95

THE PEOPLE CALLED SHAKERS, Edward D. Andrews. Definitive study of Shakers: origins, beliefs, practices, dances, social organization, furniture and crafts, etc. 33 illustrations. 351pp. 5⅜ × 8½. 21081-2 Pa. $7.95

THE MYTHS OF GREECE AND ROME, H. A. Guerber. A classic of mythology, generously illustrated, long prized for its simple, graphic, accurate retelling of the principal myths of Greece and Rome, and for its commentary on their origins and significance. With 64 illustrations by Michelangelo, Raphael, Titian, Rubens, Canova, Bernini and others. 480pp. 5⅜ × 8½. 27584-1 Pa. $9.95

PSYCHOLOGY OF MUSIC, Carl E. Seashore. Classic work discusses music as a medium from psychological viewpoint. Clear treatment of physical acoustics, auditory apparatus, sound perception, development of musical skills, nature of musical feeling, host of other topics. 88 figures. 408pp. 5⅜ × 8½. 21851-1 Pa. $9.95

THE PHILOSOPHY OF HISTORY, Georg W. Hegel. Great classic of Western thought develops concept that history is not chance but rational process, the evolution of freedom. 457pp. 5⅜ × 8½. 20112-0 Pa. $8.95

THE BOOK OF TEA, Kakuzo Okakura. Minor classic of the Orient: entertaining, charming explanation, interpretation of traditional Japanese culture in terms of tea ceremony. 94pp. 5⅜ × 8½. 20070-1 Pa. $2.95

LIFE IN ANCIENT EGYPT, Adolf Erman. Fullest, most thorough, detailed older account with much not in more recent books, domestic life, religion, magic, medicine, commerce, much more. Many illustrations reproduce tomb paintings, carvings, hieroglyphs, etc. 597pp. 5⅜ × 8½. 22632-8 Pa. $9.95

SUNDIALS, Their Theory and Construction, Albert Waugh. Far and away the best, most thorough coverage of ideas, mathematics concerned, types, construction, adjusting anywhere. Simple, nontechnical treatment allows even children to build several of these dials. Over 100 illustrations. 230pp. 5⅜ × 8½. 22947-5 Pa. $5.95

DYNAMICS OF FLUIDS IN POROUS MEDIA, Jacob Bear. For advanced students of ground water hydrology, soil mechanics and physics, drainage and irrigation engineering, and more. 335 illustrations. Exercises, with answers. 784pp. 6⅛ × 9¼. 65675-6 Pa. $19.95

SONGS OF EXPERIENCE: Facsimile Reproduction with 26 Plates in Full Color, William Blake. 26 full-color plates from a rare 1826 edition. Includes "The Tyger," "London," "Holy Thursday," and other poems. Printed text of poems. 48pp. 5¼ × 7. 24636-1 Pa. $3.95

OLD-TIME VIGNETTES IN FULL COLOR, Carol Belanger Grafton (ed.). Over 390 charming, often sentimental illustrations, selected from archives of Victorian graphics—pretty women posing, children playing, food, flowers, kittens and puppies, smiling cherubs, birds and butterflies, much more. All copyright-free. 48pp. 9¼ × 12¼. 27269-9 Pa. $5.95

CATALOG OF DOVER BOOKS

PERSPECTIVE FOR ARTISTS, Rex Vicat Cole. Depth, perspective of sky and sea, shadows, much more, not usually covered. 391 diagrams, 81 reproductions of drawings and paintings. 279pp. 5⅜ × 8½. 22487-2 Pa. $6.95

DRAWING THE LIVING FIGURE, Joseph Sheppard. Innovative approach to artistic anatomy focuses on specifics of surface anatomy, rather than muscles and bones. Over 170 drawings of live models in front, back and side views, and in widely varying poses. Accompanying diagrams. 177 illustrations. Introduction. Index. 144pp. 8⅜ × 11¼. 26723-7 Pa. $7.95

GOTHIC AND OLD ENGLISH ALPHABETS: 100 Complete Fonts, Dan X. Solo. Add power, elegance to posters, signs, other graphics with 100 stunning copyright-free alphabets: Blackstone, Dolbey, Germania, 97 more—including many lower-case, numerals, punctuation marks. 104pp. 8⅛ × 11. 24695-7 Pa. $7.95

HOW TO DO BEADWORK, Mary White. Fundamental book on craft from simple projects to five-bead chains and woven works. 106 illustrations. 142pp. 5⅜ × 8. 20697-1 Pa. $4.95

THE BOOK OF WOOD CARVING, Charles Marshall Sayers. Finest book for beginners discusses fundamentals and offers 34 designs. "Absolutely first rate . . . well thought out and well executed."—E. J. Tangerman. 118pp. 7¾ × 10⅞. 23654-4 Pa. $5.95

ILLUSTRATED CATALOG OF CIVIL WAR MILITARY GOODS: Union Army Weapons, Insignia, Uniform Accessories, and Other Equipment, Schuyler, Hartley, and Graham. Rare, profusely illustrated 1846 catalog includes Union Army uniform and dress regulations, arms and ammunition, coats, insignia, flags, swords, rifles, etc. 226 illustrations. 160pp. 9 × 12. 24939-5 Pa. $10.95

WOMEN'S FASHIONS OF THE EARLY 1900s: An Unabridged Republication of "New York Fashions, 1909," National Cloak & Suit Co. Rare catalog of mail-order fashions documents women's and children's clothing styles shortly after the turn of the century. Captions offer full descriptions, prices. Invaluable resource for fashion, costume historians. Approximately 725 illustrations. 128pp. 8⅜ × 11¼. 27276-1 Pa. $10.95

THE 1912 AND 1915 GUSTAV STICKLEY FURNITURE CATALOGS, Gustav Stickley. With over 200 detailed illustrations and descriptions, these two catalogs are essential reading and reference materials and identification guides for Stickley furniture. Captions cite materials, dimensions and prices. 112pp. 6½ × 9¼. 26676-1 Pa. $9.95

EARLY AMERICAN LOCOMOTIVES, John H. White, Jr. Finest locomotive engravings from early 19th century: historical (1804-74), main-line (after 1870), special, foreign, etc. 147 plates. 142pp. 11⅜ × 8¼. 22772-3 Pa. $8.95

THE TALL SHIPS OF TODAY IN PHOTOGRAPHS, Frank O. Braynard. Lavishly illustrated tribute to nearly 100 majestic contemporary sailing vessels: Amerigo Vespucci, Clearwater, Constitution, Eagle, Mayflower, Sea Cloud, Victory, many more. Authoritative captions provide statistics, background on each ship. 190 black-and-white photographs and illustrations. Introduction. 128pp. 8⅜ × 11¼. 27163-3 Pa. $12.95

EARLY NINETEENTH-CENTURY CRAFTS AND TRADES, Peter Stockham (ed.). Extremely rare 1807 volume describes to youngsters the crafts and trades of the day: brickmaker, weaver, dressmaker, bookbinder, ropemaker, saddler, many more. Quaint prose, charming illustrations for each craft. 20 black-and-white line illustrations. 192pp. 4⅜ × 6. 27293-1 Pa. $4.95

VICTORIAN FASHIONS AND COSTUMES FROM HARPER'S BAZAR, 1867–1898, Stella Blum (ed.). Day costumes, evening wear, sports clothes, shoes, hats, other accessories in over 1,000 detailed engravings. 320pp. 9⅜ × 12¼. 22990-4 Pa. $13.95

GUSTAV STICKLEY, THE CRAFTSMAN, Mary Ann Smith. Superb study surveys broad scope of Stickley's achievement, especially in architecture. Design philosophy, rise and fall of the Craftsman empire, descriptions and floor plans for many Craftsman houses, more. 86 black-and-white halftones. 31 line illustrations. Introduction. 208pp. 6½ × 9¼. 27210-9 Pa. $9.95

THE LONG ISLAND RAIL ROAD IN EARLY PHOTOGRAPHS, Ron Ziel. Over 220 rare photos, informative text document origin (1844) and development of rail service on Long Island. Vintage views of early trains, locomotives, stations, passengers, crews, much more. Captions. 8⅞ × 11¾. 26301-0 Pa. $13.95

THE BOOK OF OLD SHIPS: From Egyptian Galleys to Clipper Ships, Henry B. Culver. Superb, authoritative history of sailing vessels, with 80 magnificent line illustrations. Galley, bark, caravel, longship, whaler, many more. Detailed, informative text on each vessel by noted naval historian. Introduction. 256pp. 5⅜ × 8½. 27332-6 Pa. $6.95

TEN BOOKS ON ARCHITECTURE, Vitruvius. The most important book ever written on architecture. Early Roman aesthetics, technology, classical orders, site selection, all other aspects. Morgan translation. 331pp. 5⅜ × 8½. 20645-9 Pa. $8.95

THE HUMAN FIGURE IN MOTION, Eadweard Muybridge. More than 4,500 stopped-action photos, in action series, showing undraped men, women, children jumping, lying down, throwing, sitting, wrestling, carrying, etc. 390pp. 7⅞ × 10⅝. 20204-6 Clothbd. $24.95

TREES OF THE EASTERN AND CENTRAL UNITED STATES AND CANADA, William M. Harlow. Best one-volume guide to 140 trees. Full descriptions, woodlore, range, etc. Over 600 illustrations. Handy size. 288pp. 4½ × 6⅜. 20395-6 Pa. $5.95

SONGS OF WESTERN BIRDS, Dr. Donald J. Borror. Complete song and call repertoire of 60 western species, including flycatchers, juncoes, cactus wrens, many more—includes fully illustrated booklet. Cassette and manual 99913-0 $8.95

GROWING AND USING HERBS AND SPICES, Milo Miloradovich. Versatile handbook provides all the information needed for cultivation and use of all the herbs and spices available in North America. 4 illustrations. Index. Glossary. 236pp. 5⅜ × 8½. 25058-X Pa. $5.95

BIG BOOK OF MAZES AND LABYRINTHS, Walter Shepherd. 50 mazes and labyrinths in all—classical, solid, ripple, and more—in one great volume. Perfect inexpensive puzzler for clever youngsters. Full solutions. 112pp. 8⅛ × 11. 22951-3 Pa. $3.95

CATALOG OF DOVER BOOKS

PIANO TUNING, J. Cree Fischer. Clearest, best book for beginner, amateur. Simple repairs, raising dropped notes, tuning by easy method of flattened fifths. No previous skills needed. 4 illustrations. 201pp. 5⅜ × 8½. 23267-0 Pa. $5.95

A SOURCE BOOK IN THEATRICAL HISTORY, A. M. Nagler. Contemporary observers on acting, directing, make-up, costuming, stage props, machinery, scene design, from Ancient Greece to Chekhov. 611pp. 5⅜ × 8½. 20515-0 Pa. $11.95

THE COMPLETE NONSENSE OF EDWARD LEAR, Edward Lear. All nonsense limericks, zany alphabets, Owl and Pussycat, songs, nonsense botany, etc., illustrated by Lear. Total of 320pp. 5⅜ × 8½. (USO) 20167-8 Pa. $5.95

VICTORIAN PARLOUR POETRY: An Annotated Anthology, Michael R. Turner. 117 gems by Longfellow, Tennyson, Browning, many lesser-known poets. "The Village Blacksmith," "Curfew Must Not Ring Tonight," "Only a Baby Small," dozens more, often difficult to find elsewhere. Index of poets, titles, first lines. xxiii + 325pp. 5⅜ × 8¼. 27044-0 Pa. $8.95

DUBLINERS, James Joyce. Fifteen stories offer vivid, tightly focused observations of the lives of Dublin's poorer classes. At least one, "The Dead," is considered a masterpiece. Reprinted complete and unabridged from standard edition. 160pp. 5³⁄₁₆ × 8¼. 26870-5 Pa. $1.00

THE HAUNTED MONASTERY and THE CHINESE MAZE MURDERS, Robert van Gulik. Two full novels by van Gulik, set in 7th-century China, continue adventures of Judge Dee and his companions. An evil Taoist monastery, seemingly supernatural events; overgrown topiary maze hides strange crimes. 27 illustrations. 328pp. 5⅜ × 8½. 23502-5 Pa. $7.95

THE BOOK OF THE SACRED MAGIC OF ABRAMELIN THE MAGE, translated by S. MacGregor Mathers. Medieval manuscript of ceremonial magic. Basic document in Aleister Crowley, Golden Dawn groups. 268pp. 5⅜ × 8½. 23211-5 Pa. $7.95

NEW RUSSIAN-ENGLISH AND ENGLISH-RUSSIAN DICTIONARY, M. A. O'Brien. This is a remarkably handy Russian dictionary, containing a surprising amount of information, including over 70,000 entries. 366pp. 4½ × 6⅛. 20208-9 Pa. $8.95

HISTORIC HOMES OF THE AMERICAN PRESIDENTS, Second, Revised Edition, Irvin Haas. A traveler's guide to American Presidential homes, most open to the public, depicting and describing homes occupied by every American President from George Washington to George Bush. With visiting hours, admission charges, travel routes. 175 photographs. Index. 160pp. 8¼ × 11. 26751-2 Pa. $10.95

NEW YORK IN THE FORTIES, Andreas Feininger. 162 brilliant photographs by the well-known photographer, formerly with *Life* magazine. Commuters, shoppers, Times Square at night, much else from city at its peak. Captions by John von Hartz. 181pp. 9¼ × 10¾. 23585-8 Pa. $12.95

INDIAN SIGN LANGUAGE, William Tomkins. Over 525 signs developed by Sioux and other tribes. Written instructions and diagrams. Also 290 pictographs. 111pp. 6⅛ × 9¼. 22029-X Pa. $3.50

CATALOG OF DOVER BOOKS

ANATOMY: A Complete Guide for Artists, Joseph Sheppard. A master of figure drawing shows artists how to render human anatomy convincingly. Over 460 illustrations. 224pp. 8⅜ × 11¼. 27279-6 Pa. $9.95

MEDIEVAL CALLIGRAPHY: Its History and Technique, Marc Drogin. Spirited history, comprehensive instruction manual covers 13 styles (ca. 4th century thru 15th). Excellent photographs; directions for duplicating medieval techniques with modern tools. 224pp. 8⅜ × 11¼. 26142-5 Pa. $11.95

DRIED FLOWERS: How to Prepare Them, Sarah Whitlock and Martha Rankin. Complete instructions on how to use silica gel, meal and borax, perlite aggregate, sand and borax, glycerine and water to create attractive permanent flower arrangements. 12 illustrations. 32pp. 5⅜ × 8½. 21802-3 Pa. $1.00

EASY-TO-MAKE BIRD FEEDERS FOR WOODWORKERS, Scott D. Campbell. Detailed, simple-to-use guide for designing, constructing, caring for and using feeders. Text, illustrations for 12 classic and contemporary designs. 96pp. 5⅜ × 8½. 25847-5 Pa. $2.95

OLD-TIME CRAFTS AND TRADES, Peter Stockham. An 1807 book created to teach children about crafts and trades open to them as future careers. It describes in detailed, nontechnical terms 24 different occupations, among them coachmaker, gardener, hairdresser, lacemaker, shoemaker, wheelwright, copper-plate printer, milliner, trunkmaker, merchant and brewer. Finely detailed engravings illustrate each occupation. 192pp. 4⅝ × 6. 27398-9 Pa. $4.95

THE HISTORY OF UNDERCLOTHES, C. Willett Cunnington and Phyllis Cunnington. Fascinating, well-documented survey covering six centuries of English undergarments, enhanced with over 100 illustrations: 12th-century laced-up bodice, footed long drawers (1795), 19th-century bustles, 19th-century corsets for men, Victorian "bust improvers," much more. 272pp. 5⅜ × 8¼. 27124-2 Pa. $9.95

ARTS AND CRAFTS FURNITURE: The Complete Brooks Catalog of 1912, Brooks Manufacturing Co. Photos and detailed descriptions of more than 150 now very collectible furniture designs from the Arts and Crafts movement depict davenports, settees, buffets, desks, tables, chairs, bedsteads, dressers and more, all built of solid, quarter-sawed oak. Invaluable for students and enthusiasts of antiques, Americana and the decorative arts. 80pp. 6½ × 9¼. 27471-3 Pa. $7.95

HOW WE INVENTED THE AIRPLANE: An Illustrated History, Orville Wright. Fascinating firsthand account covers early experiments, construction of planes and motors, first flights, much more. Introduction and commentary by Fred C. Kelly. 76 photographs. 96pp. 8¼ × 11. 25662-6 Pa. $7.95

THE ARTS OF THE SAILOR: Knotting, Splicing and Ropework, Hervey Garrett Smith. Indispensable shipboard reference covers tools, basic knots and useful hitches; handsewing and canvas work, more. Over 100 illustrations. Delightful reading for sea lovers. 256pp. 5⅜ × 8½. 26440-8 Pa. $7.95

FRANK LLOYD WRIGHT'S FALLINGWATER: The House and Its History, Second, Revised Edition, Donald Hoffmann. A total revision—both in text and illustrations—of the standard document on Fallingwater, the boldest, most personal architectural statement of Wright's mature years, updated with valuable new material from the recently opened Frank Lloyd Wright Archives. "Fascinating"—*The New York Times*. 116 illustrations. 128pp. 9¼ × 10⅜. 27430-6 Pa. $10.95

CATALOG OF DOVER BOOKS

PHOTOGRAPHIC SKETCHBOOK OF THE CIVIL WAR, Alexander Gardner. 100 photos taken on field during the Civil War. Famous shots of Manassas, Harper's Ferry, Lincoln, Richmond, slave pens, etc. 244pp. 10⅝ × 8¼.
22731-6 Pa. $9.95

FIVE ACRES AND INDEPENDENCE, Maurice G. Kains. Great back-to-the-land classic explains basics of self-sufficient farming. The one book to get. 95 illustrations. 397pp. 5⅜ × 8½.
20974-1 Pa. $6.95

SONGS OF EASTERN BIRDS, Dr. Donald J. Borror. Songs and calls of 60 species most common to eastern U.S.: warblers, woodpeckers, flycatchers, thrushes, larks, many more in high-quality recording. Cassette and manual 99912-2 $8.95

A MODERN HERBAL, Margaret Grieve. Much the fullest, most exact, most useful compilation of herbal material. Gigantic alphabetical encyclopedia, from aconite to zedoary, gives botanical information, medical properties, folklore, economic uses, much else. Indispensable to serious reader. 161 illustrations. 888pp. 6½ × 9¼. 2-vol. set. (USO)
Vol. I: 22798-7 Pa. $9.95
Vol. II: 22799-5 Pa. $9.95

HIDDEN TREASURE MAZE BOOK, Dave Phillips. Solve 34 challenging mazes accompanied by heroic tales of adventure. Evil dragons, people-eating plants, bloodthirsty giants, many more dangerous adversaries lurk at every twist and turn. 34 mazes, stories, solutions. 48pp. 8¼ × 11.
24566-7 Pa. $2.95

LETTERS OF W. A. MOZART, Wolfgang A. Mozart. Remarkable letters show bawdy wit, humor, imagination, musical insights, contemporary musical world; includes some letters from Leopold Mozart. 276pp. 5⅜ × 8½.
22859-2 Pa. $6.95

BASIC PRINCIPLES OF CLASSICAL BALLET, Agrippina Vaganova. Great Russian theoretician, teacher explains methods for teaching classical ballet. 118 illustrations. 175pp. 5⅜ × 8½.
22036-2 Pa. $4.95

THE JUMPING FROG, Mark Twain. Revenge edition. The original story of The Celebrated Jumping Frog of Calaveras County, a hapless French translation, and Twain's hilarious "retranslation" from the French. 12 illustrations. 66pp. 5⅜ × 8½.
22686-7 Pa. $3.50

BEST REMEMBERED POEMS, Martin Gardner (ed.). The 126 poems in this superb collection of 19th- and 20th-century British and American verse range from Shelley's "To a Skylark" to the impassioned "Renascence" of Edna St. Vincent Millay and to Edward Lear's whimsical "The Owl and the Pussycat." 224pp. 5⅜ × 8½.
27165-X Pa. $4.95

COMPLETE SONNETS, William Shakespeare. Over 150 exquisite poems deal with love, friendship, the tyranny of time, beauty's evanescence, death and other themes in language of remarkable power, precision and beauty. Glossary of archaic terms. 80pp. 5³⁄₁₆ × 8¼.
26686-9 Pa. $1.00

BODIES IN A BOOKSHOP, R. T. Campbell. Challenging mystery of blackmail and murder with ingenious plot and superbly drawn characters. In the best tradition of British suspense fiction. 192pp. 5⅜ × 8½.
24720-1 Pa. $5.95

CATALOG OF DOVER BOOKS

THE WIT AND HUMOR OF OSCAR WILDE, Alvin Redman (ed.). More than 1,000 ripostes, paradoxes, wisecracks: Work is the curse of the drinking classes; I can resist everything except temptation; etc. 258pp. 5⅜ × 8½. 20602-5 Pa. $4.95

SHAKESPEARE LEXICON AND QUOTATION DICTIONARY, Alexander Schmidt. Full definitions, locations, shades of meaning in every word in plays and poems. More than 50,000 exact quotations. 1,485pp. 6½ × 9¼. 2-vol. set.
Vol. 1: 22726-X Pa. $15.95
Vol. 2: 22727-8 Pa. $15.95

SELECTED POEMS, Emily Dickinson. Over 100 best-known, best-loved poems by one of America's foremost poets, reprinted from authoritative early editions. No comparable edition at this price. Index of first lines. 64pp. 5³⁄₁₆ × 8¼. 26466-1 Pa. $1.00

CELEBRATED CASES OF JUDGE DEE (DEE GOONG AN), translated by Robert van Gulik. Authentic 18th-century Chinese detective novel; Dee and associates solve three interlocked cases. Led to van Gulik's own stories with same characters. Extensive introduction. 9 illustrations. 237pp. 5⅜ × 8½. 23337-5 Pa. $5.95

THE MALLEUS MALEFICARUM OF KRAMER AND SPRENGER, translated by Montague Summers. Full text of most important witchhunter's "bible," used by both Catholics and Protestants. 278pp. 6⅝ × 10. 22802-9 Pa. $10.95

SPANISH STORIES/CUENTOS ESPAÑOLES: A Dual-Language Book, Angel Flores (ed.). Unique format offers 13 great stories in Spanish by Cervantes, Borges, others. Faithful English translations on facing pages. 352pp. 5⅜ × 8½. 25399-6 Pa. $8.95

THE CHICAGO WORLD'S FAIR OF 1893: A Photographic Record, Stanley Appelbaum (ed.). 128 rare photos show 200 buildings, Beaux-Arts architecture, Midway, original Ferris Wheel, Edison's kinetoscope, more. Architectural emphasis; full text. 116pp. 8¼ × 11. 23990-X Pa. $9.95

OLD QUEENS, N.Y., IN EARLY PHOTOGRAPHS, Vincent F. Seyfried and William Asadorian. Over 160 rare photographs of Maspeth, Jamaica, Jackson Heights, and other areas. Vintage views of DeWitt Clinton mansion, 1939 World's Fair and more. Captions. 192pp. 8⅜ × 11. 26358-4 Pa. $12.95

CAPTURED BY THE INDIANS: 15 Firsthand Accounts, 1750–1870, Frederick Drimmer. Astounding true historical accounts of grisly torture, bloody conflicts, relentless pursuits, miraculous escapes and more, by people who lived to tell the tale. 384pp. 5⅜ × 8½. 24901-8 Pa. $7.95

THE WORLD'S GREAT SPEECHES, Lewis Copeland and Lawrence W. Lamm (eds.). Vast collection of 278 speeches of Greeks to 1970. Powerful and effective models; unique look at history. 842pp. 5⅜ × 8½. 20468-5 Pa. $13.95

THE BOOK OF THE SWORD, Sir Richard F. Burton. Great Victorian scholar/adventurer's eloquent, erudite history of the "queen of weapons"—from prehistory to early Roman Empire. Evolution and development of early swords, variations (sabre, broadsword, cutlass, scimitar, etc.), much more. 336pp. 6⅛ × 9¼. 25434-8 Pa. $8.95

AUTOBIOGRAPHY: The Story of My Experiments with Truth, Mohandas K. Gandhi. Boyhood, legal studies, purification, the growth of the Satyagraha (nonviolent protest) movement. Critical, inspiring work of the man responsible for the freedom of India. 480pp. 5⅜ × 8½. (USO) 24593-4 Pa. $7.95

CELTIC MYTHS AND LEGENDS, T. W. Rolleston. Masterful retelling of Irish and Welsh stories and tales. Cuchulain, King Arthur, Deirdre, the Grail, many more. First paperback edition. 58 full-page illustrations. 512pp. 5⅜ × 8½. 26507-2 Pa. $9.95

THE PRINCIPLES OF PSYCHOLOGY, William James. Famous long course complete, unabridged. Stream of thought, time perception, memory, experimental methods; great work decades ahead of its time. 94 figures. 1,391pp. 5⅜ × 8½. 2-vol. set.
Vol. I: 20381-6 Pa. $12.95
Vol. II: 20382-4 Pa. $12.95

THE WORLD AS WILL AND REPRESENTATION, Arthur Schopenhauer. Definitive English translation of Schopenhauer's life work, correcting more than 1,000 errors, omissions in earlier translations. Translated by E. F. J. Payne. Total of 1,269pp. 5⅜ × 8½. 2-vol. set.
Vol. 1: 21761-2 Pa. $10.95
Vol. 2: 21762-0 Pa. $11.95

MAGIC AND MYSTERY IN TIBET, Madame Alexandra David-Neel. Experiences among lamas, magicians, sages, sorcerers, Bonpa wizards. A true psychic discovery. 32 illustrations. 321pp. 5⅜ × 8½. (USO) 22682-4 Pa. $8.95

THE EGYPTIAN BOOK OF THE DEAD, E. A. Wallis Budge. Complete reproduction of Ani's papyrus, finest ever found. Full hieroglyphic text, interlinear transliteration, word-for-word translation, smooth translation. 533pp. 6½ × 9¼. 21866-X Pa. $9.95

MATHEMATICS FOR THE NONMATHEMATICIAN, Morris Kline. Detailed, college-level treatment of mathematics in cultural and historical context, with numerous exercises. Recommended Reading Lists. Tables. Numerous figures. 641pp. 5⅜ × 8½. 24823-2 Pa. $11.95

THEORY OF WING SECTIONS: Including a Summary of Airfoil Data, Ira H. Abbott and A. E. von Doenhoff. Concise compilation of subsonic aerodynamic characteristics of NACA wing sections, plus description of theory. 350pp. of tables. 693pp. 5⅜ × 8½. 60586-8 Pa. $13.95

THE RIME OF THE ANCIENT MARINER, Gustave Doré, S. T. Coleridge. Doré's finest work; 34 plates capture moods, subtleties of poem. Flawless full-size reproductions printed on facing pages with authoritative text of poem. "Beautiful. Simply beautiful."—*Publisher's Weekly*. 77pp. 9¼ × 12. 22305-1 Pa. $5.95

NORTH AMERICAN INDIAN DESIGNS FOR ARTISTS AND CRAFTSPEOPLE, Eva Wilson. Over 360 authentic copyright-free designs adapted from Navajo blankets, Hopi pottery, Sioux buffalo hides, more. Geometrics, symbolic figures, plant and animal motifs, etc. 128pp. 8⅜ × 11. (EUK) 25341-4 Pa. $7.95

SCULPTURE: Principles and Practice, Louis Slobodkin. Step-by-step approach to clay, plaster, metals, stone; classical and modern. 253 drawings, photos. 255pp. 8⅛ × 11. 22960-2 Pa. $9.95

CATALOG OF DOVER BOOKS

THE INFLUENCE OF SEA POWER UPON HISTORY, 1660–1783, A. T. Mahan. Influential classic of naval history and tactics still used as text in war colleges. First paperback edition. 4 maps. 24 battle plans. 640pp. 5⅜ × 8½.
25509-3 Pa. **$12.95**

THE STORY OF THE TITANIC AS TOLD BY ITS SURVIVORS, Jack Winocour (ed.). What it was really like. Panic, despair, shocking inefficiency, and a little heroism. More thrilling than any fictional account. 26 illustrations. 320pp. 5⅜ × 8½.
20610-6 Pa. **$7.95**

FAIRY AND FOLK TALES OF THE IRISH PEASANTRY, William Butler Yeats (ed.). Treasury of 64 tales from the twilight world of Celtic myth and legend: "The Soul Cages," "The Kildare Pooka," "King O'Toole and his Goose," many more. Introduction and Notes by W. B. Yeats. 352pp. 5⅜ × 8½.
26941-8 Pa. **$7.95**

BUDDHIST MAHAYANA TEXTS, E. B. Cowell and Others (eds.). Superb, accurate translations of basic documents in Mahayana Buddhism, highly important in history of religions. The Buddha-karita of Asvaghosha, Larger Sukhavativyuha, more. 448pp. 5⅜ × 8½.
25552-2 Pa. **$9.95**

ONE TWO THREE . . . INFINITY: Facts and Speculations of Science, George Gamow. Great physicist's fascinating, readable overview of contemporary science: number theory, relativity, fourth dimension, entropy, genes, atomic structure, much more. 128 illustrations. Index. 352pp. 5⅜ × 8½.
25664-2 Pa. **$8.95**

ENGINEERING IN HISTORY, Richard Shelton Kirby, et al. Broad, nontechnical survey of history's major technological advances: birth of Greek science, industrial revolution, electricity and applied science, 20th-century automation, much more. 181 illustrations. ". . . excellent . . ."—Isis. Bibliography. vii + 530pp. 5⅜ × 8¼.
26412-2 Pa. **$14.95**

Prices subject to change without notice.
Available at your book dealer or write for free catalog to Dept. GI, Dover Publications, Inc., 31 East 2nd St., Mineola, N.Y. 11501. Dover publishes more than 500 books each year on science, elementary and advanced mathematics, biology, music, art, literary history, social sciences and other areas.